AFRICA'S DEVELOPMENT IN THE TWENTY-FIRST CENTURY

This book is dedicated to Kwadwo Konadu-Agyemang, my co-editor, for the splendid work he does being the linchpin to our family and academic circle of mutual friendships here in the US, and to my wife, Naana Panford, and to his wife Tina, for their support.

Africa's Development in the Twenty-first Century

Pertinent Socio-Economic and Development Issues

Edited by

KWADWO KONADU-AGYEMANG
University of Akron, USA

and

KWAMINA PANFORD
Northeastern University, USA

ASHGATE

Published by
Ashgate Publishing Limited
Gower House
Croft Road
Aldershot
Hampshire GU11 3HR
England

Ashgate Publishing Company
Suite 420
101 Cherry Street
Burlington, VT 05401-4405
USA

Reprinted 2007

Ashgate website: http://www.ashgate.com

British Library Cataloguing in Publication Data
Africa's development in the twenty-first century:
pertinent socio-economic and development issues. – (Voices in development management)
1. Economic development – Social aspects – Africa 2. Africa – Economic conditions – 21st century 3. Africa – Social conditions – 21st century 4. Africa – Politics and government
I. Konadu-Agyemang, Kwadwo II. Panford, Martin Kwamina
338.9'6'0090511

Library of Congress Control Number: 2006924397

ISBN 10: 0 7546 4478 2
ISBN 13: 978-0-7546-4478-1

Printed and bound in Great Britain by
TJI Digital, Padstow, Cornwall

Contents

Contributors

Olayiwola Abegunrin is Professor of International Relations, Department of Political Science, Howard University, Washington, DC. He was formerly Chair of the Department of International Relations, Obafemi Awolowo University, Ile-Ife, Nigeria. His latest book is *Nigerian Foreign Policy Under Military, 1966-1999* (Greenwood Publishing Group, 2003).

Gerald Acquaah-Gaisie is originally from Ghana but now resides in Australia. Dr. Acquaah-Gaisie was educated at the University of Ghana (BA), Melbourne University (Ph.D. in Criminology), and Monash University (Australia) where he earned his law degrees. He teaches Business Law, Corporate Crime, Information Technology Law and Communications Law in the Faculty of Business and Economics, Monash University. Gerald is a barrister and solicitor in Australia and Ghana. He worked with the Ghana Prisons Service from 1973 and was its national Director when he migrated to the UK in 1982, and subsequently to Australia.

Sesime Adanu is a Ph.D. candidate in Public Administration and Urban Studies at the University of Akron. He obtained his Master's degree in Geography from the same University, and his bachelor's from the University of Ghana, Legon. His research interests include transportation and economic development.

Richard Aidoo is a graduate student at the Department of Geography at York University in Toronto. Richard is interested in Environmental Resource Politics (and current themes in Political Ecology). He is currently writing a dissertation on the conservation and biodiversity discourses in the forest environment of Temagami in Northern Ontario, Canada

Fenda Akiwumi worked as an hydrogeologist for 14 years on the UNDP/FAO Land Resources Survey Project (subsequently Land and Water Development Division, Ministry of Agriculture and Forestry) in Sierra Leone and as an environmental consultant in the Sierra Leone mining industry. Fenda teaches geography and geology at Hill College, Hillsboro, TX, USA. She has written extensively on resource development (particularly water) in Sierra Leone from an interdisciplinary perspective. She holds a Masters of Science degree in hydrogeology from University College London, London University, U.K. and is in the process of completing a Ph.D. in environmental geography at Texas State University – San Marcos.

Abigail Amissah-Arthur is a biophysical Geographer. She received her Ph.D. in Geography in 1997 from the University of Ibadan, Nigeria. She is currently an assistant professor of Geography at Slippery Rock University in Pennsylvania. Dr. Amissah-Arthur has 15 years combined experience as a research scientist and teaching faculty. For several years she was a research fellow and consultant at the International Institute for Tropical Agriculture (IITA) in Nigeria. At IITA her research involved spatial analysis of low input agricultural practices and the development of indicators for recommending sustainable agronomic management decisions. In 1999, Dr. Amissah-Arthur was a postdoctoral research scientist at the International Research Institute for Climate Predictions, Columbia University, NY. Her research at IRI and since then has focused on the application of climate prediction by smallholder agricultural producers in sub-Saharan Africa. Dr. Amissah-Arthur has also researched the influences of El Niño Southern Oscillation phases on major crops in the state of Pennsylvania. Dr. Amissah-Arthur's publications have appeared in leading prestigious international journals such as *Climatic Change, International journal of Climatology,* and *Geojournal.* Dr. Amissah-Arthur is a member of the scientific research society Sigma Xi and is also a member of several leading organizations such as the American Association of Geographers and American Society of Agronomy.

Seth Appiah-Opoku is assistant professor of Geography at the University of Alabama, Tuscaloosa, USA. He teaches planning courses, geography of Africa, and a summer abroad course in Ghana. His research focuses on the impact of ecotourism on indigenous communities in Africa. Dr. Appiah-Opoku serves on the international editorial board of the *Journal of Environmental Impact Assessment Review* and has published several articles on indigenous knowledge and environmental management. He is the author of *Indigenous Knowledge and Environmental Impact Assessment in Developing Countries* (The Edwin Mellen Press, 2005).

Karl Botchway holds a Ph.D. from the Graduate Faculty of Political and Social Science, New School at Kean University, NJ, Sarah Lawrence College, Bronxville, NY, and the State University of New York at Stony Brook. He worked as a Journalist in Ghana and was the recipient of the 1986 Promising Journalist of the Year Award. In 1987, he was awarded the Dag Hammarskjold Fellowship to cover the 46th General Assembly of the United Nations. Currently, he is an Assistant Professor of African-American Studies at the New York City College of Technology, The City University of New York, where he specializes in the political economy of African Development. He has published in the journal *World Development and the Canadian Journal of African Studies.* His manuscript, Understanding Development Interventions in Northern Ghana will be published by the Edwin Mellen Press.

Smile Dube (Ph.D. University of Texas – Austin) is Professor of economics at the California State University – Sacramento. His teaching and research interests focus on African development, international trade and the role of institutions in development. He is currently working on a collaborative book project with Robert Dibie entitled, *Government and the Political Economy of Development in Zimbabwe.*

Richard Grant is Associate Professor of Geography, is a human geographer with teaching and research interests in urbanization and the developing world, West Africa, globalization and international trade. He has conducted fieldwork in Greater Accra, Ghana, for the last seven years; his research has been supported by the National Science Foundation and the National Geographic Society. Dr.Grant recently completed a survey of households in Greater Accra and examined social and spatial polarization in the residential sector. His books include *Globalization and the Margins* (co-edited with John Rennie Short) and *The Global Crisis in Foreign Aid* (co-edited with Jan Nijman). His research articles have appeared in, among other journals, *The Annals of the Association of American Geographers, Political Geography, Environment and Planning A, and Economic Geography.*

Kristin Henrard is senior lecturer at the University of Groningen where she teaches human rights, refugee law and constitutional law. She studied law at the Catholic University of Leuven, Belgium, with special focus on human rights and international law. She graduated magna cum laude in 1994 and obtained an LLM degree at Harvard Law School in 1995 during which she further specialized in human rights and humanitarian law. Between 1995 and 1999 she conducted doctoral research and took her doctorate at the Catholic University of Leuven 17 September 1999. During these years she also worked at the Constitutional Court of South Africa as researcher for Judge Kriegler and monitored the South African constitutional negotiations in 1996 for the Flemish Government. Her main publications pertain to the areas of human rights and minority protection. Dr. Henrard is also managing editor of the Netherlands International Law Review and member of the international advisory board of the Global Review of Ethnopolitics.

Tadesse Kidane-Mariam, (Ph.D, University of Iowa, Iowa City, 2001) is currently assistant professor of Geography at Edinboro University of Pennsylvania. He earned his Master of Arts in Geography/Urban and Regional Development from Kansas State University – Manhattan (1974), and BA from Haile Selassie I University, Addis Ababa, Ethiopia (1969). Between 1976 and 1990, he worked in different capacities in government: as a housing and urban development researcher, national planner (commissioner of physical planning and construction sector and urban manager (Minister of Urban Development and Housing, 1988–1991) in Ethiopia. He served also as a consultant/adviser to the Organization of African Unity (now AU) (1994–1997). Dr. Kidane-Mariam taught a number of courses at the University of Iowa between 1997 and 2001, and at Southern Illinois University at Carbondale (Aug 2001–May 2002), before moving to his current position. He has authored and published a number of articles on environmental and habitat management in Africa, urban management in Ethiopia and the political ecology of land degradation in Ethiopia. He has also presented a number of papers at various international and national workshops and annual conferences of the Association of American Geographers.

Kwadwo Konadu-Agyemang is Associate Professor in the Department of Geography and Planning at The University of Akron, Akron, OH. He earned his bachelor's degree in Land Economy from UST, Kumasi, MUP from the University of Melbourne, and Ph.D. degree from Monash University, Melbourne, Australia. His research interests include housing and urban development in Africa, spatial organization in developing countries, environmental planning and management, and role of NGOs and international organizations in development. Dr. Konadu-Agyemang has published scholarly papers in *The Professional Geographer, Urban Studies, Habitat, The Canadian Geographer and Ghana Studies*. He is the author of *The Political Economy of Housing and Urban Development in Africa: Ghana's experience from colonial times to 1998* (Praeger, 2001), and editor of IMF and World Bank Sponsored Structural Adjustment Programs in Africa: Ghana's Experience, 1983–1999 (Ashgate, 2001).

Peter A. Kwaku Kyem is Associate Professor of Geography at Central Connecticut State University, New Britain, CT, USA. He has a Ph.D. in Geography (1997) from Clark University, Worcester, MA, USA and an M.A. in Geography from Carleton University, Ottawa, Canada. An alumnus of University of Cape Coast, Cape Coast, Ghana, Peter's research interests currently focus on Geographic Information System Applications in Sub-Saharan Africa, Information Communication Technology and Economic Development in Africa and the Caribbean and Conflict Management.

Olivia Kyem is an employee of the Revenue Services Department at Hartford, CT, USA. Olivia holds a Masters Degree in Public Administration from Clark University, Worcester, MA, USA, and an MBA degree from Central Connecticut State University, New Britain, Connecticut, USA. Olivia is an alumnus of University of Cape Coast, Cape Coast, Ghana. Her research interests focus on Information Communication Technology (ICT), International Business and Taxation.

Delphis F. Levia Jr. is Assistant Professor in the Department of Geography and Center for Climatic Research at the University of Delaware. His primary research interests include forest hydrology, ecological climatology, biogeochemistry, and land degradation. His land degradation work has focused on (1) farmland conversion and residential development; and (2) land degradation theory. These studies have been published in internationally peer-reviewed journals such as *Ambio*, *Land Degradation and Development*, and *Environmental Management*.

Calvin O. Masilela (B.A., University of Westminster, UK; M.A. Ph.D., Virginia Tech) is Associate professor of Geography and Regional Planning at Indiana University of Pennsylvania. He also serves as the director of the of the IUP McNair Scholars Program which recruits and mentors first generation, low income, and minority undergraduate students to pursue graduate studies. His teaching and research interests focus on Africa development; land use policy, planning theory; land reform, rural development, and the geography of AIDS.

Joseph Mensah completed his Ph.D. in Geography at the University of Alberta and currently teaches human geography courses at the School of Social Sciences, Atkinson Faculty of Liberal and Professional Studies at York University. He is also cross-appointed to the Graduate Program in Geography at York. His current research interest is in critical development theory; transnational migration; race, space, and employment; and socio-spatial dialectics. He has published in several reputable journals including the *Canadian Geographer, Canadian Journal of Urban Research, Transportation, International Journal of Environmental Studies, International Journal of Canadian Studies, Regional Development Studies, and Tijdschrift voor Economische en Sociale Geografie (TESG)*. He is the author of *Black Canadian: History, Experience and Social Conditions*, and co-editor of *Globalization and the Human Factor: Critical Insights* (Ashgate Publishing, 2004).

Mohameden Ould-Mey Mohameden Ould-Mey is an associate professor of geography in the Department of Geography, Geology and Anthropology at Indiana State University. His major areas of research include development theory and policy, the Arab World and Africa, and the genesis and prospect of Zionism and the State of Israel. His published works include "Currency Devaluation and Resource Transfer from the South to the North," *Annals of the Association of American Geographers* 93(2):463-484, 2003; "The Non-Jewish Origin of Zionism," *The Arab World Geographer* 5(1):34-52, 2002; "The New Global Command Economy," *Environment and Planning D: Society and Space* 17(2):155-180, 1999; and *Global Restructuring and Peripheral States: The Carrot and the Stick in Mauritania* (Lanham, MD: Littlefield Adams Books, 1996).

J. Henry Owusu is Associate Professor of Geography at the University of Northern Iowa, Cedar Falls, IA. He earned his B.A. (Economics and Geography) from University of Science and Technology in Ghana, and an M.S. (Geography and Regional Planning) from Indiana University of Pennsylvania. He studied Public Policy Evaluation and Analysis at the Graduate School of Public and International Affairs, University of Pittsburgh; and Urban Studies at the School of Urban and Public Affairs, Portland State University, OR. He also has an M.A. in Geography (Regional Development) from The University of Iowa, where he obtained his Ph.D. as well. His research focuses on industrialization, international development policies and development in Sub-Saharan Africa. He has published in several scholarly journals including *The Professional Geographer, Journal of African Economies, The Journal of Modern African Studies* and *Review of Human Factor Studies*.

Kwame A. Ninsin is Professor of Political Science, University of Ghana. Has written extensively on Ghanaian politics and contemporary development issues affecting the African continent. Authored and co-edited approximately ten books, including the *Ghana's Transition to Democracy* (CODESRIA, 1998.), *Political Parties And Democracy in Ghana's Fourth Republic* (Woeli, 1993), *The Informal Sector in Ghana's Political Economy* (Freedom Publications, 1991), *The State Development* *and Politics in Ghana* (Codesria, 1987). In addition he has published over 50 articles. Professor Ninsin was Chair, Department of Political Science, University of Ghana for nearly eight years, and until June 2001 Executive Secretary, African Association of Political Science, and editor of the African Journal of Political Science.

Kwamina Panford is Associate Vice Provost and Chair, African-American Studies Department, Northeastern University, Boston. His areas of specialization are comparative economic, social and political development, international labor relations and human rights, public policy and the roles of the new African Union, the International Financial Institutions such as the World Bank, the International Monetary Fund (IMF) and the World Trade Organization (WTO) in Africa and other developing regions. Panford has a Ph.D. degree in Law and Public Policy from Northeastern. He also holds a Masters in Industrial and Labor Relations (MILR), Cornell University; a Masters in Organizations and Comparative Social and Political Development, McMaster University, Canada; Graduate Diploma, Communications and Bachelors in Sociology and Political Science (Honors), University of Ghana, Legon. Professor Panford has published two books (*IMF-World Bank & Labor's Burdens in Africa*, Praeger, 2001 and *African Labor Relations & Workers' Rights: Assessing the Role of the International Labor Organization*, Greenwood, 1994), several articles, essays and reviews on the roles of the IMF and World Bank and more recently the impact of the WTO on developing countries and the impact of the Organization of African Unity (OAU) on Africa. He has also published works on the post Cold war transition to democracy in Africa using Ghana as a case study. These publications have occurred on different continents including Africa, Europe, Asia, Australia and North America. He has additional national and numerous international papers delivered to academic panels and audiences and chaired numerous panels all over the world. He is working toward the completion of a major manuscript on Ghana's labor relations and laws to be published by Kluwer Law and Taxation Publishers, Netherlands.

Judith Shabaya earned her Ph.D. and Master's degrees in Education at the University Akron in Akron, OH. She's currently an assistant professor in the Division of Education at Baldwin-Wallace College, Berea, OH. Prior to her current position, Dr. Shabaya served as Field Service Professor in the College of Applied Science, Center for Access and Transition at the University of Cincinnati, and an assistant professor of education at Park University, Missouri. Dr. Shabaya has been working in the field of education for more than 20 years and has authored several scholarly papers and presented at various national and international conferences. Her research interests include bilingual education, metacognition and learning, gender issues, literacy education, and diversity issues in the learning environment.

Preface and Acknowledgments

Africa presents a paradox that may be difficult to unravel. It is a continent that is so rich in resources, yet it remained the poorest throughout the 20th century. Africa has become synonymous with a litany of ills that includes lack of basic development and political stability, food shortages, environmental degradation, atrophied infrastructure, corruption, low life expectancies, and high levels of illiteracy. What caused such conditions in the last century? What can be done to improve living conditions and enhance Africa's prosperity in the 21st century? While it is not the intention of this volume to bemoan and dwell on Africa's "spilled milk" and lost opportunities in the last century, but rather to explore ways of reinventing Africa for the 21st century, we cannot effectively achieve these objectives without reflecting on the past.

The contributors to this volume have brought together a rich tapestry of experiences from various disciplines, including geography, sociology, political science, economics, law, anthropology and African Studies. The issues covered in the volume range from the theoretical underpinnings of Africa's development crisis, food production, environmental degradation, timber/diamonds conflict, land distribution, the implications of discarding traditional values, gender disparities in education, regional integration, the African Union, urbanization, and information technology. The authors have effectively presented salient and interesting details of these different but interlinked subjects connected to Africa's lack of development and development challenges. The topics covered are, from the authors'informed perspectives, what need to be addressed to improve opportunities and quality of life in the 21st century for Africans.

Although there may be other significant issues pertaining to Africa's development, time and space have made it impossible for us to cover them all, and to address the issues in detail, especially at the individual country level. This volume then should be seen as wide brush strokes and highlights pointing the way to matters to be addressed in later volumes.

Aside from the large number of contributors, this volume is unique as it is a relatively innovative, non-traditional book not only emphasizing a political economy approach but also incorporating historical methodology, and providing a longitudinal view of events in Africa.

This "huge 400-page plus elephant" could not be killed, let alone carried home, through the efforts of the editors alone. On the contrary, its success is owed to a large number of individuals who worked hard and consistently over a three-year period to give birth to this volume. We are especially grateful to the twenty contributors who diligently researched and wrote the chapters found in this volume.

We also wish to express our utmost gratitude to Ms. Linda Bussey of the University of Akron for tirelessly producing the camera-ready version and other aspects of the book. Also to Fred Boateng, Kwame Boate, and Badri Lakkur for their contributions in various ways.

We also wish to thank our families, especially Tina and Naana, for bearing with us as we spent many hours in the office working on the manuscript.

We are also indebted to the staff at Ashgate International, especially Val Rose, the acquisitions editor, for her encouragement, and the editorial, production and marketing staff for their diligence.

Kwadwo Konadu-Agyemang
Akron, Ohio

Kwamina Panford
Boston, Massachusetts

Chapter 1

Introduction and Book Overview

Kwadwo Konadu-Agyemang and Kwamina Panford

Introduction

The 20th century can best be characterized as a century of lost opportunities for Africa. Having been under colonial rule for the first half of that century, many African countries started emerging from colonialism in the 1950s. By 1965, all but a handful had thrown off the colonial yoke and were expected to take off into an era of development with indigenous leaders at the helm of affairs. Many of these new countries were saddled with problems they inherited from the colonial state: absence of basic infrastructure, illiteracy, lack of skilled personnel, over-dependence on a handful of export products, and shaky political institutions. These problems notwithstanding, the new leaders were quite hopeful that with their abundant natural and human resources combined with development planning, the support of the international community, and good luck, they could negotiate the rungs of Rostow's (1962) ladder of development to attain a level of development akin to what pertains in the west.

Africa could not attain appreciable levels of development by the end of the 20th century due to a combination of endogenous and exogenous factors. During the last quarter of the century, the world's second largest continent and the cradle of human kind suffered from the most acute form of underdevelopment, and became associated with a litany of ills. These included extreme poverty, high rates of illiteracy, political instability, economic mismanagement, balance of payment deficits, atrophied infrastructure, housing shortages, civil wars, ethnic conflicts, diseases, low life expectancy, and high levels of infant mortality (Adedeji 1990). A combination of all these and other factors earned African countries the dubious distinction of struggling for bottom positions in all international measurements of well-being. Africa is home to more than half of the world's 44 poorest countries, 33 of the 48 least developed nations of the world, and 30 of the 34 countries with the lowest human development index (UNDP 2000; 2003; 2004). Of the 65 countries with the highest under-five mortality rates, 43 are in Africa (UNICEF 2001; 2004). According to recent World Bank reports there is an expanding human development gap between sub-Saharan Africa and the rest of the world (World Bank 2001; 2003; 2004).

As the 21st century dawned, many questions emerged about Africa's future. What went wrong? What are the prospects for Africa moving beyond its current state of socio-economic and political underdevelopment? Will the 21st century be any different?

What are the opportunities for development? What are the constraints? The primary objective of this book is to explore some of Africa's development opportunities and challenges in the 21st century from multi-disciplinary perspectives. It includes authors from all philosophical and academic/intellectual persuasions. The chapters presented in this volume cover the entire African continent and deal with regional topics, multi-country cases, individual countries and a wide range of issues from agriculture to information technology.

Structure of the Book

The book has four parts and twenty-two chapters. Following the introduction and chapter overview, Panford and Konadu-Agyemang provide a snapshot of Africa's development challenges in the 21st century in Chapter 2. They state that while for many nations the dawn of a new world order began in the early 1990s, for Africa it began in 1884–1885 when, without the presence of a single African, Europeans met in Berlin to balkanize the continent. This period, it is argued is where we should begin to account for Africa's problems. Forty to fifty years have passed since most African countries gained political independence, yet Africa is still steeped in difficult socio-economic and political economic conditions. What has been the role of the international community, especially the International Monetary Fund/World Bank and other Western institutions, donors and governments in Africa's predicament? What has been the role of Africans themselves and their leaders in making and sustaining this mess? Panford and Konadu-Agyemang show that while external forces have contributed to the underdevelopment, African leaders should share some culpability. While it is not the intention of the authors to be pessimistic about Africa's situation, they end up discussing a litany of ills that include ethnic conflict, boundary disputes, acute food shortages and other symptoms of Africa's underdevelopment. These also constitute some of the challenges that Africa must confront if it is to free itself from the current state of underdevelopment, typically lack of: prosperity, secure food sources, personal safety and security.

Considering the role African political leaders have played in Africa's underdevelopment and how ineffective the state has been, Dube and Masilela ask in Chapter 3 if it is not time to rethink the African state. How do we account for the failure of the post-colonial state in Africa to improve the material well being of its citizens 50 years after colonial rule? They argue that such accounting must be broad enough to include political, social, economic factors, and whatever else can be said about the failure of nationalists to deliver equitable material improvements to their societies, as they promised at the time of independence. While most of the colonies became free without violence, some had to be freed by "wars of liberation" of one kind or another. The leaders of these post-colonial societies have, in most instances, stayed too long. For many African leaders who have stayed in power for a long time, the biggest problem has been their failure to understand that holding on to power for too long has not led to increased material prosperity among ordinary citizens. For most countries in Africa, the post-colonial period saw the imposition of either left or right wing "social contracts" that had little to do with the history, culture, and customs of diverse peoples. Equally important has been the failure to recognize that for growth and development purposes, most States in Africa have not been efficient vehicles for growth. This contradicts the claims of socialists in the 1960s and 1970s. The debates on some of the causes of the failure of the post-colonial African State to deliver economic growth and hence improve the standard of living for a majority of Africans have not yielded significant results. This chapter helps to address this problem.

Shifting gears from the endogenous into the exogenous arena, Ninsin in Chapter 4 examines the role of globalization in marginalizing Africa. Globalization has been touted by the west as the most significant factor that has brought the world together, improved trade and delivered unprecedented benefits to the remotest parts of the world. But has the idea of a global village been of benefit to Africa? Ninsin's view is that the global village is structured on unequal relations in which the weaker nations in Africa are mere cogs in the wheels of global accumulation processes. The rich and powerful nations that dominate the world have employed two strategies to secure undisputed hegemony over all others, especially the world's poor nations. First, they have employed economic and ideological tools to undermine the material (economic and ideological) base (capacity/autonomy) of poor nations. Second, the hegemons of the world have used naked military power to destroy the existing state and reconstitute it under their control. This chapter analyzes the negative effects of globalization on Africa by showing that Africa's economies have been reduced to *bantustans* in the global economy while its vital resources are plundered leaving it hopelessly impoverished. A *bantustanized* economy is drained of its material and human resources, leaving it destitute with just enough material means to provide basic subsistence, often-primitive livelihood, to its people. It is further argued that the intensity of control and plunder impoverishes and destroys the institutional and ideological basis of the affected states, and deepens their dependence on the developed world as virtual beggars. The chapter expandss on how the African state has lost the capacity to exercise effective autonomy even in its domestic affairs; and how it has become a captive state employed by foreign interests to pursue their global economic and political domination. Ninsin concludes that Africa could successfully respond to this renewed threat to its identity and development through a political union, driven by its new generation of political and economic elites and the network of Pan African social movements that has emerged since the 1980s.

Is a political union a possible solution to Africa's problems? In Chapter 5, Panford discusses the African Union and its role. This chapter seeks to address one of the basic challenges facing Pan-Africanists in the 21st century: How the new African Union (AU), which replaced the Organization of African Union (OAU), can meet the expectations of Africans and people of African descent in terms of African unity and in a post Cold War and globalization environment, democracy, peace and economic development. This implies real improvements in living and working conditions for the majority of Africans. Thus this entails transforming the new AU into a vehicle for real development and hence social and material progress. These challenges reflect the struggles of pioneer Pan-Africanists whose dreams were only partially met when the OAU was formed in 1963. The chapter also addresses three fundamental issues that impinge on the capacity of the new AU to meet the challenges thrust upon it: The Constitutive Act and proposed new administrative structures, including Pan-African Parliament; New Partnership for

African Development and the prospects for Africa's real economic development, democracy, human rights, rule of law and government accountability and responsiveness to the needs of Africans.

Regional integration has also been suggested as one of the ways to expand the narrow markets in individual African countries that make it impossible for large-scale production to take place. In Chapter 6, Mensah and Aidoo examine the Economic Community of West African States (ECOWAS), its potential contribution and problems. Established in 1975, ECOWAS, *inter alia*, seeks to eliminate custom duties among member states; adopt common external tariff and trade policies towards non-members; remove barriers to the movement of goods, services, and people; harmonize trade, agricultural, energy, and environmental policies among member states. The foundation of ECOWAS is couched in the realization that the domestic markets of the individual members were too small to be competitive in a global economy that is characterized by large trading blocks, such as the European Union (EU) and the North American Free Trade Agreement (NAFTA). With a potential single market of more than 230 million people, ECOWAS expects to promote specialization and large-scale industrialization; enhance job opportunities and wealth creation; and limit the West African sub-region's dependence on foreign markets. This chapter examines the achievements of ECOWAS over the years and highlights the major difficulties facing the organization as it strives to enhance the collective self-sufficiency of West African nations through economic integration and cooperation.

Africa is arguably one of the most endowed continents. Africa's natural resources include a massive expanse of land, mineral resources, forests and a large population. To what extent have these resources been an asset or a curse to Africa? The resources that are supposed to aid Africa's development have in many cases become the basis of warfare. In Chapter 7, Akiwumi discusses the role of timber and diamonds in fuelling new types of conflicts in Sierra Leone. The chapter draws a parallel between the present and past conflicts surrounding timber and diamonds. Through a review of historical literature and analysis of comparative data, Akiwumi demonstrates that many of the factors that helped shape the political ecology of the timber business dictate the diamond-mining environment. The roles of powerful external economic interests and government intervention, tradition-modernity paradoxes in perspectives on land use and ownership, the use of patron-clientele networks and co-optation, intra-ethnic group conflict over resources, illegal trade, the use of mercenary tactics and services, poorly conceived exploitative natural resource policies and legislation influenced by imperialistic mind-sets, and the problem of environmental degradation are addressed. External and internal power and economic relations that evolved with timber exploitation during the colonial period remain largely unchanged in spite of the granting of nation-statehood at independence in 1961. The debate over the question of the post-colonial African nation-state as sovereign and the legacy of patrimonialism is an integral part of this discussion.

In Chapter 8, Amissah-Arthur tackles the crucial issue of food production. Despite the fact that the continent is endowed with diverse agricultural environments and some of the world's major water systems, it experienced food shortages throughout most of the last 40 years. Two major constraints underlie Africa's inability to meet food production targets: rapid population growth and unpredictable climatic conditions.

First, the task of securing food supplies for a rapidly growing population while conserving the natural resource base requires interdisciplinary effort by national and international research groups and agencies. Second, the dependence of crop production on environmental conditions has made the management of climatic risk a critical part of agricultural production. Inter-annual rainfall variability constitutes a major challenge for the region due to its high dependence on rain-fed, low-input production on mostly degraded soils. Through trial and error and centuries of experience, farmers in sub-Saharan Africa have developed coping strategies unique to the environmental conditions confronting them. However, despite the flexible strategies in response to climatic variability and adoption of improved farming technologies, losses due to the vagaries of the weather continue to reduce agricultural productivity and frustrate efforts aimed at feeding the growing population and at poverty reduction on the continent. In the face of continued adverse climatic events, policy makers and producers have to act and develop new and improved strategies to mitigate climatic risk. This chapter is devoted to climatic variability in Africa and the challenges it poses to food production in Africa, emphasizing the case of Nigeria, which lies in several agroecological zones. It also examines the impact of El Niño/Southern Oscillation (ENSO) induced climatic variability on crop production in Kenya. Finally, coping strategies available to farmers and their capability to adopt climate forecasts based on the ENSO phenomenon is examined and a synthesis is carried out on ways this new capability can further the millennium development goals to ensure food security for the people of the region.

Although Africa has abundant arable land much of it has become degraded and unproductive due to many years of mismanagement coupled with unfavorable climatic changes. In Chapter 9, Tadesse Kidane-Mariam and Delphis Levia discuss the case of Ethiopia, which has experienced tremendous droughts and famines in the past 30 years. Land degradation remains the most important environmental problem in Ethiopia. The causes and consequences of land degradation have often been examined from a biased position that emphasizes biophysical dimensions. This chapter argues that a political ecology approach provides a more meaningful explanation of why land degradation has reached alarming proportions. Such a perspective assigns a major role to socio-economic and political institutional arrangements in undemocratic land tenure systems, poverty and marginalization, political instability, inappropriate economic policies, poor governance and maladministration, inappropriate technological choices and poor level of public awareness and environmental perceptions. Current soil conservation, reforestation and other biophysical changes cannot bring about sustainable processes and patterns of land management. Real changes in the political arena and equitable access to wealth and resources are necessary to deal with land degradation problems in a sustainable manner.

Africa's resource management issues cannot be isolated from the international political economy. Since the early 1980s many African countries have been undergoing IMF and World Bank sponsored economic Structural Adjustment Programs (SAPs) that have contributed to overexploitation of Africa's natural resources. Focusing on Ghana's forestry sector, a key component of the economy, Owusu in Chapter 10 uses the country's SAPs, dubbed the Economic Recovery Program (ERP), which began in 1983, to demonstrate that SAPs provided a convenient means for governments and donors to meet mutual economic and political interests. These interests are usually met by sacrificing the physical environment through overexploitation of natural resources. Meeting those interests generates huge environmental costs for the adjusting country. This position is tied to two important perspectives on debt and Third World development. The first is the view that a vital part of the political and economic control mechanisms available to the Western industrialized countries is to keep Third World countries in debt. The second view is that there is a direct relation between the high foreign debts of developing countries and the rapid rate of deforestation, and that the IMF and the World Bank's export-oriented development model (in the form of SAPs), is largely responsible for the deforestation and environmental damage visible in Ghana and the rest of Africa. This chapter contributes to the debate on structural adjustment and environmental consequences in Third World economies, particularly the roles of foreign debt and deforestation. This chapter is rooted in the Brundtland Report, *Our Common Future* (WCED 1987), which emphasized the importance of using resources to meet current needs without compromising the resource needs of future generations.

Africa is, and will continue to be for a long time to come, an agrarian society. Questions relating to land and access to it are therefore crucial. In Chapter 11, Masilela and Dube, applying Hardin's metaphor of the *Tragedy of the Commons,* discuss land reform in Africa, with a focus on Zimbabwe. Because land reforms involve property rights in finite land and few landed resources, they are always a product of the political, economic, and cultural, social and technical history of the society in which they take place. Land reform is an exceptional intervention to solve a specific agrarian question and therefore is part of a general rural development process. This chapter questions the mode of reforms and not its desirability. The promotion of a "no rule-of-law" regime enabled land invasions. The land invasion strategies were extended to extortion of firms in the urban areas. The chapter also provides an extended review of the types of land reforms and offers a brief analysis of the land issue in Zimbabwe. Thus, we shift from the current biased emphasis on free markets for land to interrelationships between the community, the government (including the ruling party elite), and the rule of law. The conflicts between those who favor the status quo (no rule-of-law) and those who prefer the rule of law is captured in two simple models based on game theory. The first is a static model showing the tension between the "no rule-of-law" land and firm invasions (those who strip assets) versus the rule-of-law group (those who prefer upholding CPRM and wish to build value by making irreversible investments on their property). The dynamic version shows that a weak value support for the rule-of-law may actually be worse than that captured in the model. In the absence of the rule-of-law, political insiders can monopolize new sectors, sectors that were not monopolies before invasions.

Could Africa's resource management problems be attributed to the abandoning of indigenous resource management systems in favor of Western ones? Appiah-Opoku in Chapter 12 argues that indeed, this is the case. Indigenous knowledge systems refer to localized knowledge unique to a particular society or ethnic group. Although ignored for many decades through a legacy of colonial neglect, many African governments are now recognizing these systems as a national resource that contributes immensely to environmental stewardship. This chapter links two initiatives. First, it examines the concept of indigenous knowledge and compares it with Western science. Next, based on a field research in Ghana the paper discusses the indigenous beliefs, norms, and practices that contribute to sustainable resource management. Finally, the opportunities and challenges derived from the linking of the two initiatives are discussed. Natural resource management in indigenous societies is often based on a philosophy and environmental ethic that keep exploitative abilities in check and provide ground rules by which the relationship between humans and the environment is regulated. Policy makers and Western scientists must recognize the importance of indigenous knowledge systems in resource management, and take immediate action to honor and protect them in Africa in particular and the world in general.

The final part, consisting of Chapters 13 through to 21, deals with selected developmental issues and challenges. Chapter 13 discusses the problem of corruption, which somc analysts believe is one of the major factors in Africa's underdevelopment, and therefore has to be completely eradicated if the continent is to prosper in the 21st century. In this chapter, Acquaah-Gaisie explores the nature and causes of corruption among African politicians and elites and discusses remedies. Corruption by politicians and officials in Africa hurts the poorest, and also aid donors. Advanced democratic countries in Europe, North America and the Pacific have virile electorates, press and criminal justice systems to combat corruption. But weak African political and civil institutions in effect license pillage with impunity. The countries are heavily in debt, the people are poor, health and education systems are feeble, clean water is scarce, public transport is dilapidated, and in particular, roads are in disrepair. They need their public resources. Acquaah-Gaisie proposes, among others, that serious corruption be classified as a crime against humanity. The Rome Statute of the International Criminal Court 1998 proscribes atrocities to humankind. Corruption by African political leaders and other elites holds a comparable gravity. Large-scale corruption causes the death of infants, devastation by diseases such as AIDS and malaria, denial of a decent education, results as serious as the repercussions of armed conflict.

In Chapter 14, Olayiwola Abegunrin discusses the developmental challenges facing Nigeria, a nation that had all the potential and opportunities to develop into Africa's own world-class economic and political giant, yet it is now regarded as a typical example of squandered opportunities in Africa. Abegunrin contends that in the first 44 years of independence, the political economy of Nigeria has come full-circle, having experienced political change as well as continuity, and economic expansion and contraction. At the end of the 1980s, the fruits of independence had been tasted by only a few and the lessons of freedom learned by even fewer. The high hopes of Nigeria were dashed in her first decade by political coups and counter coups and civil war and in her second decade of independence by economic bust and decay. The erstwhile parliamentary model of the first republic, and presidential system of the second republic were both followed by military dictatorships of the 1980s, and 1990s while the international and industrial ambitions of Nigeria, with much abundant human and natural resources, were squandered by the corrupt and military dictatorship. This chapter examines and critically analyses the problematic of political economy as a struggle between contending parties, and the responses of Nigerians and the Nigerian nation to the dialectic imperative of the survival of the political economy of Nigeria in the global system. The legacy of colonialism has corrupted Nigerian political institutions, including the military, and made the country dependent on Western powers and their multinational corporations that dominate the global economy.

As Nigeria struggles with resurrecting its lost potential, another potential African giant is attempting to deal with its sordid past and to position itself as the new economic power. Will the new indigenous rulers of South Africa learn and benefit from Nigeria's experience? Kristin Henrard in Chapter 15 focuses on South Africa. Henrard contends that the historical importance of the official abolition of Apartheid in South Africa and the first multi-racial elections can scarcely be exaggerated. However, the challenges of South Africa's transformation are not limited to the constitutional negotiation phase and the actual adoption of a constitution for a democratic South Africa. These challenges stretch well beyond that into the actual implementation phase. A successful transformation of a strongly divided society like South Africa necessitates, in addition to redressing past injustices, the creation of a society within which the chances of reccurrence of the kinds of gross violations of human rights that occurred in the past are reduced to a minimum. Consequently, an evaluation is called for the constitutional negotiation process and the way in which the themes of redress of the past, overcoming the legacy of apartheid and its systemic discrimination as well as nation-building and accommodation of population diversity played their role. The ongoing implementation of the relevant constitutional provisions and the related challenges are equally, if not more, important to measure the actual levels of transformation of South African society. Numerous key issues of South Africa's transformation process could be focused on. Here, the cardinal equality principle as well as several issues related to the accommodation of population diversity (minority rights, self-determination, education, language and the position of traditional leaders) will be discussed.

The role of transportation in Africa's development cannot be overemphasized. In many cases, development has been hampered by poor transportation networks. In Chapter 16, Sesime Adanu discusses transportation in Africa focusing on Ghana. Transportation accounts for a major source of sustenance for the Ghanaian economy. Among the major modes of transport in the country, the road sector is the most important, accounting for 94 percent of freight and 97 percent of passenger traffic. Despite its importance, the sector faces several problems, such as deplorable road conditions and poor vehicular maintenance, all of which have contributed to high accident rates in Ghana. The problem is enormous, especially in rural and less economically endowed parts of the country. The key to the problem is the scarcity of financial resource needed to rehabilitate and maintain the road sector of the country. This has led to considerable socio-economic inequities in the development of the country with the resource-poor regions of the country being at a great disadvantage.

The contribution of education to nation building must be emphasized. Education not only impacts significantly labor productivity, and hence economic growth, but is also a vehicle for upward social mobility and even political development. Despite the immense benefits of education, access to education in Africa is unequal and considerable spatial and gender disparities exist throughout the continent. In Chapter 17, Konadu-Agyemang and Shabaya revisit the question of gender disparities in educational access in Africa focusing on Ghana and Zimbabwe. Using cross-country data, this chapter investigates spatial and gender inequalities in education in Africa, and how these inequities affect long-term socio-economic development. Such inequalities are found to have a profound impact on inter-regional, rural-urban and gender differences in the level of human capital, quality of life, incomes, employment, and the like. These have implications for Africa's development in the 21st century, especially in the sphere of global competition.

Many development programs in Africa have been undertaken and/or managed by development agencies, most of which are of Western origin. In Chapter 18, Karl Botchway addresses the politics and apolitics of development emphasizing the case of a development project in northern Ghana. Most development agencies present development projects and strategies as politically unproblematic and as such, see politics as an undesirable element of development interventions. This chapter challenges the apolitical nature of development interventions. With evidence from one of the major and ambitious development interventions in the Northern region of Ghana, Botchway shows that by reducing the promotion of development to an uncompromising technical issue, the development industry misses out on some of the political pre-conditions, which might make for the effective promotion of developmental efforts.

Externally imposed solutions to Africa's problems have, in most cases, ended up in worsening the situation. While IMF and World Bank Economic Restructuring Programs were probably well intended, they ended up impoverishing Africa. Among other things, all adjusting countries are forced to devalue their currencies based on the theory that devaluation makes the tradable items of the country cheaper and therefore leads to an increase in exports while discouraging imports as they become expensive. In Chapter 19, Mohameden Ould-Mey examines the extent to which the systematic devaluation of the Mauritania Ouguiya vis-à-vis the US dollar contributes to poverty in Mauritania. First, the chapter reviews the exchange rate policies advocated by the IMF-backed structural adjustment programs in Mauritania since the 1980s. Second, it assesses the level of currency devaluation and examines the extent to which it contributes to declining Gross National Income (GNI) and export earnings as well as rising external debts. Third, it suggests that any reversal of this trend will likely require a return to protectionism in the form of exchange controls and import restrictions.

Africa is increasingly becoming characterized as urban. One-third of the African population now resides in urban areas, and this share will increase to more than one-half by 2025. Some cities in Africa have achieved their present size in one-fifth to one-tenth the time it took for European cities to reach the same size. The scale of urban development is posing particularly acute challenges for planners and especially for those inhabitants who live in cities with limited opportunities and resources. Focusing on Accra, Ghana, as a case study, Richard Grant in Chapter 20 situates urban development in terms of the city's role in the wider global political economy. He contends that the city can be understood by the ways it is linked to the external economy, which is as much a function of the idiosyncratic features of the city as a place and location, as it is a function of developments in the global economy. Grant employs a political economy-based conceptualization of the city and its spatial organization because (sub)national policies determine to a large degree the exposure of the urban arena to global economic forces. He then outlines the four historical phases in urbanism that led to the emergence of the contemporary city: pre-colonial, colonial, national and global arguing that, during each of these phases, urban geographies have changed in relation to the role of the city in the global political economy.

In Chapter 21, Peter Kyem and Olivia Kyem discuss Africa and the Revolution in Information and Communications Technology. There is little doubt that Information and Communications Technology (ICT) is generating new ways for creating and re-distributing wealth over the globe. What is in dispute is whether or not the ICT revolution is the escalator, which African countries can ride to prosperity. ICT adoption in less-developed countries generates both enthusiasm and skepticism in discussions about cultural implications and socioeconomic consequences. This chapter reviews the debate about ICT adoption in Africa. The authors contend that the embracing of ICTs by Africans reflects the socioeconomic realities of the moment. Consequently, a safeguard for appropriate and less harmful uses of the technology is for the people to train and plan for its adoption. The authors recommend that African countries should participate in the ICT revolution both as consumers and contributors of innovative ideas. It is only by participating fully that the African countries will enjoy a mutually beneficial outcome that can ensure their economic development. The chapter concludes with suggestions for strengthening ICT adoption in Africa.

Panford and Konadu-Agyemang provide a synthesis and conclusions in Chapter 22. They demonstrate that despite Africa's problems, there is still hope. By making appropriate changes in the social, economic and political arenas, Africa could be re-invented and refitted for the 21st century's challenges of development.

References

Adedeji, Adebayo (1990). *The human dimension of Africa'spersistent economic crisis*. London and New York: United Nations Economic Commission for Africa.

Rostow, W.W. (1962). *The Process of Economic Growth*. New York: Norton.

UNDP (2001). *Human Development Report 2001*. New York: Oxford University Press.

UNDP (2003). *Human Development Report 2003*. New York: Oxford University Press.

UNDP (2001). *Human Development Report 2004*. New York: Oxford University Press.

UNICEF (2001). *State of the World's Children 2000*. New York: UNESCO.

UNICEF (2004). *State of the World's Children 2003*. New York: UNESCO.

World Bank (2001). *World Development Report*. New York: Oxford University Press.

World Bank (2004). *World Development Report*. New York: Oxford University Press.

World Bank. (2003). *World Development Report*. New York: Oxford University Press.

Chapter 2

21st Century African Development: Crises and Challenges. An Overview

Kwamina Panford and Kwadwo Konadu Agyemang

Introduction

We use the plural crises in this chapter to draw attention to the many and multifaceted nature of the problems of contemporary Africa. Our intent for writing this chapter is not to disseminate raw gloom and doom. Our overarching concern is to focus more attention on some of the major adverse consequences and new challenges that confront Africa in more stark terms. We want to focus on especially new challenges that have emerged in the last two deca,des significantly impacting the lives of Africans and their future, especially the 48ght states that constitute Sub-Saharan Africa.

Most of the crises we elude to emanate from both the Cold war and, paradoxically, the end of the Cold War. The latter, starting in 1989–1990 led to the emergence of a new international political and economic order. Crucial events occurring in this period include the disappearance of the Soviet Empire in eastern and central Europe. There is in addition, the abandonment of statist economies in different parts of the world and the apparent end of socialism or communism and the so-called triumph of western capitalism. Contrary to the excitement spawned by the collapse of the Soviet Empire, events linked to the end of the Cold War have combined like a tsunami to unleash havoc on Africa, politically and economically. This has culminated in the marginalization of Africa. That means Africa is increasingly deemed to be irrelevant to contemporary world affairs (Keller and Rothchild 1996). Africa, however, continues to be exploited for its raw materials such as agricultural, other forest products, mineral ores and crude oil.

20th Century Africa and the New World Order

Although the rest of the world recognizes 1989–1990 as the start of a new international order, Africans could trace their own uniquely new political and economic order to the Berlin (Germany) Conference of 1884–85. At this conference, Africa was carved and taken over by European colonial powers. Although the US did not share directly in colonizing Africa, it was officially represented at this heinous conference. The partition of Africa resulted in only three independent Black nations in the world: Ethiopia and Liberia in Africa and Haiti in the Caribbean. The origins of the gloom and doom that is often associated with Africa were firmly implanted during this colonial epoch that lasted from the mid-1880s to the official end of apartheid in South Africa when, in 1994, Nelson Mandela was elected president.

Without exception, countries in Africa that were colonized suffered the same fate. As Lofchie (1971) demonstrates, while Africa was colonized, Europe was led by Britain to establish a long-lasting foundation for industrialization and rise as a world power. France, Germany and the US followed the lead of the British and later Japan joined this group of materially advanced countries. Japan's rise was due in part to the Meiji Revolution of the 19th Century. Thus, while other continents were advancing technologically, Africa was cast under the ruinous spell of colonial domination from which it has yet to recover (Rodney 1982)

Like the first new order that was imposed through colonial rule, the post Cold War order of 1989–1990 is also proving catastrophic. Contrary to expectations, the new order has not as yet yielded the anticipated peace and prosperity dividend for most Africans. New, more difficult and previously unimaginable crises have instead emerged with devastating consequences as shown by the real life experiences of Africans.

New Conflicts in Africa

Before 1989, numerous African countries experienced military coups to change governments. Although some of the coups were bloody (due to resistance from loyal government soldiers), the coups tended to last a few days or weeks until new coups and counter coups were executed. In spite of these forceful and unpredictable changes in government and the absence of constitutional rule, there was relative peace in most parts of Africa. Contemporary Africa on the other hand, is replete with many insurgencies and long-drawn attempts by rebel forces to seize territory from governments. The most recent example is Côte d'Ivoire where since September 19, 2002 rebels have controlled approximately a third of the country's territory.

A new dawn of brutal and virtually senseless forms of overt conflicts, especially civil warfare involving the tactical or deliberate use of rape, amputations and child soldiers, started in December 1989. That was when rebels commanded by Charles Taylor and Prince Yameh Johnson assaulted Liberia to unseat Sergeant Samuel K. Doe as Head of State. That led to a brutal civil war that raged on until elections in July 1997 when Taylor was elected the President. Liberians voted for Taylor under severe intimidation. The saying in Liberia during the election campaign was: "You (Taylor) killed my papa and mama, why I no go vote for you!" That meant because Taylor slaughtered Liberians, they were coerced to vote for him.

Additional unending wars can be found in the Great Lakes Region, Central Africa. The war in the Democratic Republic of the Congo has proven virtually unstoppable. It has raged on from 1998 and at one point constituted Africa's first international war involving at least five nations. Even one of the largest United Nations' peacekeeping endeavors has failed to stop it. The result is that an estimated five million people have died in combat and or due to preventable hunger and diseases. All this is taking place while the country's resources, like coltan and diamonds, are exploited for the benefit of a few Congolese and their nefarious partners in Africa and overseas. In both Liberia and the Congo, protracted civil wars led to collapsed states (Young 2004 and Martin 2002).

War broke out in Somalia also in 1989 resulting in the oustering of President Siad Barre. From that year to the present, Somalia has been without a government while all internationally brokered efforts to restore peace and the state have failed. On August 26, 2001, the fighting seemed to have ended when Abdiqassim Salad Hassan was made the new Head of State and he was able to represent the country at the OAU's Summit and United Nations' meetings ("Somalia to Attend First Africa Summit in 10 Years" Africast.com, July 9, 2001, *New York Times* January 30, 2004; *West Africa* December 9–15, 2002: 29). That new government collapsed and there was no government until October 10, 2004, when President Abdullahi Yusuf was elected by the warring factions as new Head of State in Kenya. In spite of pleas by the new president for peace and for 20,000 peacekeeping forces from the AU, the new government failed to gain control of the state to establish stability. This new regime barely settled in Mogadishu before warring factions begun rejecting it by plunging the country right back to civil war and total chaos (*Boston Globe* October 31, 2004).

In addition, a two-year (1998–2000) war in the Horn of Africa between Ethiopia and its new neighbour, Eritrea made this region "the deadliest conflict cluster in the world" (US Institute of Peace June 28, 1999: 1). The war between Eritrea and Ethiopia marked the failure of intra-African diplomacy since the two countries' presidents were friends and supposed to provide models of new intra-African relations with emphasis on good neighborliness. Both were touted as exhibiting one of the most amicable separations of two nations in the world (*Boston Globe* April 28, 1993). The separation of Eritrea from Ethiopia in 1993 was initially so amicable that Ethiopia sponsored Eritrea's application to join the United Nations and the Organization of African Unity (OAU, now African Union) in Cairo, Egypt in 1995. But alas the peaceful coexistence of the two nations was only ephemeral. In less than ten years, both were at each other's throat waging one of the deadliest and costly modern wars. Apparently, the two nations decided to use their military and the arms they acquired during the Cold War (from the Soviets and the US) to fight over disputed territory. It took the intervention of arbiters from the UN and a World Court decision of April 2002 to ensure some modicum of peace in the Horn of Africa (*Boston Globe* November, 4, 2003).

West Africa has also had its share of other destructive civil wars. The more obvious problems of wars are illustrated by the fact that in this sub-region, only a handful of countries (out of the 18 that exist) are not experiencing open hostilities. Thus peace, personal safety, development and prosperity are yet to be experienced by Africans as warfare has become common.

Acute Food Shortages

Even more dramatic is the fact that although African land is fertile, it is the only continent that is not able to feed itself. Even in countries without war, the population has been caught in other equally vicious social and economic catastrophes that have engulfed the entire continent. These food crises, like wars, intensified toward the end of the 20th Century and continue into the 21st Century. We could not have imagined that after the disastrous famine in Ethiopia in the mid-1980s and the devastating famine of the 1990s in Somalia, Africans would confront more acute food shortages. We are referring to the food shortages in Malawi, Zambia and Zimbabwe in 2002. Conditions in Malawi were so desperate that it was reported that some people ate grass, weeds and soil. While this happened, western governments refused to assist on the grounds that the Malawian government was corrupt. One tragic dimension was that the latter was an important breadbasket in Southern Africa.

We wish to acknowledge that this dire food condition preceded the land reforms Zimbabwe has sought to pursue under President Robert Mugabe in the last few years (*Wall Street Journal*, November 5, 1998: A19 and November 12, 1998). Due to the International Monetary Fund's (IMF) advice to sell its maize reserves in the 1980s, Zimbabwe like its neighbours has had to import grain at high cost. Before the intervention of the IMF, Zimbabwe had a stockpile of maize, which it could have used during lean years. Earnings from the sale were used to pay debts to international financial institutions including the IMF. The catastrophic nature of the food shortage was depicted by the fact that the Government of Zimbabwe proclaimed an official national food emergency in April 2002.

One cannot also neglect the fact that in the last few years Zimbabwe has had to grapple with one of the most anomalous effects of colonialism and its twin, racist land tenure, that led to as few as 6,000 white farmers owning a disproportionately large percentage (over 60 percent) of good farm land (*West Africa* December 20, 1999 and January 9, 2000: 18). The experience of one of the co-authors (Panford) attests to the unequal land ownership. In 1997, he drove 45 miles per hour for ten minutes to cross a single white-owned farm about 45 minutes from Harare, the capital. It also took the same time to traverse the farms of six black farmers. The black-owned farms appeared patched and were farther away from sources of water for irrigation. How to alleviate one of the most unusually skewed distributions of land in the world is a dilemma that has to be resolved by Zimbabweans in a hostile international environment.

The Dominance of International Financial Institutions and Deteriorating Living/Working Conditions

In spite of numerous declarations in Africa itself and at various international fora, both economic development and the promise of independence have eluded the average African. Africans entered the 21st Century materially worst off than their counterparts in any other region of the world. Ample evidence points to the fact that Africa remains the poorest continent and solutions are not yet visible. A case in point is Zambia where from 1996 to 1998 poverty rates were 82.8 percent and 83.1 percent for rural areas and 46 percent and 56 percent in urban centers to generate a national poverty rate of over 72 percent (Government of Zambia 2001: 18). In Zambia, conditions have deteriorated to the extent that there is now a unique migration pattern: more people are leaving for rural areas to escape urban poverty and associated problems.

The post-1986 period shows rapid decline in African standards of living. These are also the years when the majority of African countries came under the high-handed influence of international financial institutions (IFIs). For example, both the World Bank and the IMF were joined by the European Union (EU) and the US to require African governments to reform their politics and to ensure that their economies were more market oriented as new conditions for aid. In the political realm, because multiparty democracy was preferred by western donors, the role of the masses of Africans was neglected. Instead, models of democracy imported from overseas were given priority because, as it is in all aspects of life in Africa (reminiscent of the colonial days) the priorities of external donors prevail (Clark 1996).

The failure to build homegrown political institutions contributed immensely to the lack of good, effective and accountable government on two opportune moments: immediately after independence and then after the Cold War. With the passing of each decade, it appears Africans are moving farther from the dream of freedom and democracy that fueled the struggles for independence which cost African lives and blood.

Africa is also the only region where the rate of poverty is rising. While countries in other regions such as Asia, China and India, are emerging from poverty and chronic famine to accelerate the rate at which wealth is acquired to meet social needs and to industrialize, Africa is not only stagnating but is also sliding in the capacity to meet basic human needs. In a few years, China has become the industrial workshop of the world to which the US, Japan, South Korea and Taiwan outsource important manufacturing jobs. India, on the other hand, is becoming a leading global provider of computer programs and other software, largely due to the technical competence of its workforce.

Closely linked with Africa's rising poverty are problems including high incidence of unemployment combined with the massive underutilization of human resources. What exacerbates the resulting social burdens is the fact that most of the unemployed or underemployed have received free or highly subsidized tertiary education up to the masters' degree level. This is a gross waste of public funds that requires urgent public policy remedy. There are several causes of this anomaly.

The major one is the failure of school curricula to meet the economic needs in terms of human capital/resource development. The other cause is the recent decline in the capacity of African economies to employ millions of school graduates. With the formal and public sectors being gutted under the guise of "right sizing" and privatization encouraged by donors, African governments have been misled into believing that the growing informal sector would be the super sponge that would absorb new graduates and those laid off. The situation of Ghana, one of the countries with long experience with the World Bank and IMF is typical. From 1986, when Ghana sought to slash drastically the public sector payroll, several thousands of unemployed workers competed in a shrinking labor market for jobs with over 300,000 new high school graduates each year. Kenya, Tanzania and other countries that also sought to implement IMF and World Bank conditionalities have also had experiences similar to Ghana's with socially devastating effects (*Time* April 24, 2000: 47).

Some of the problems of unemployed university graduates can be attributed to the failure to fundamentally restructure the colonial educational systems into ones that are relevant to Africa's needs. Another constraint is the import substitution industrialization strategy adopted after independence. It failed to fulfill basic needs, did not generate jobs and then made the continent more vulnerable to external economic shocks and debts (Young 2004 and Lofchie 1971). Africa thus continues to grapple with one fundamental problem: over 75 percent of the population is under 30 years old, of which the majority is not employed. Besides, all over Africa, job prospects are not good and not expected to get better soon.

In the early 2000s, the serious joblessness problem was acknowledged officially by the Government of Ghana, which conducted a census of the unemployed. The Ghana Government, however, did not have a plan to put the unemployed it registered to work and the problems of unemployment have kept escalating. At the same time, many governments spend millions of dollars each year for the services of expatriate experts. Although this aspect of contemporary Africa is often neglected, the huge outlays are contributing to the high international debts amassed by countries such as Ghana (with a debt of over US$6 billion in the early 2000s) and two other debtor nations such as Tanzania (*Time* April 24, 2000: 47) and Uganda.

Ironically while some African countries are lauded as the most successfully adjusted, they are receiving debt forgiveness because in the words of the donor community they are "Highly Indebted Poor Countries" (HIPCs). The question that arises is what did the policy prescriptions of the World Bank and the IMF do to these countries' economies and societies? The next question is, if they are economic successes why are they being classified as poor and deserve debt forgiveness? There are some adverse effects linked to the HIPC status granted to Ghana, Tanzania, Mozambique, Benin and Uganda. These countries have become so aid-dependent that, as is happening in Ghana, Uganda and Zambia; external donors have become the *de facto* managers and financiers of national budgets. These donors are also dictating critical domestic policies.

An unanticipated consequence of the cancellation of debts linked to HIPC is that it could erode the meager credit worthiness of these countries because international lenders may treat them as high credit risks. The debtor nations of Africa could be susceptible to higher interest rates and other worsening terms for future borrowing. This could aggravate the financial crises that have already gripped these nations including the ones most favored by bilateral and multilateral lenders.

Demographic factors have also had a role in Africa's crises. While at least 75 percent (that is, three out of four) Africans are under thirty years old, in the last decade and half, fewer children are enrolled in school. An even smaller minority enters tertiary educational institutions like colleges or universities (see Chapter 17, this volume). In Ghana, owing to limited resources, poor planning, lack of national priority and pride coupled with the selfish interests of the elites, only one in five secondary school graduates enrolls in universities. Each year, the number of students who are not able to enroll in college rises steeply as competition for admission to the five national universities heats up. The political leaders and other elites are concerned about sending their children to expensive foreign universities using their newly acquired fortunes—foreign currencies such as the US dollar, the euro and the British pound sterling. Therefore, even in Ghana, which was well known for providing good public education, national interest in maintaining good educational institutions is waning fast. Why should the elites invest in local schools if they can afford to send their children out of the country? Also why should policy-makers invest in good local health care, if as has been the practice in Ghana in the last two decades, the leaders of the nation and their allies can easily fly for medical treatment abroad and at public expense?

Gender in Africa Today

Contemporary Africa reveals adverse trends with respect to gender. For women and girls, available evidence confirms that some of the gains made from the late 1950s to the early 1980s are being rapidly lost. In countries like Ghana and Tanzania, which tremendously boosted the enrollment of girls and young women in schools in the 1960s through the 1980s, fewer girls and women are graduating now. Even Zimbabwe which as recently as the 1980 to 1985 period was experiencing rapid progress in closing the gender gap in educational attainment, is experiencing an accelerated reversal of this trend (Konadu-Agyemang and Shabaya, see Chapter 17 in this volume).

In addition, since women are mostly responsible for providing social services such as water and health care, under IMF/World Bank-imposed higher user fees, more women (especially, the working poor and rural ones) are under severe financial pressure. This is at a time when women face poor job prospects because of the shrinking public sector. Private industries are not able to generate and sustain jobs for women because they are not able to withstand globalization and the massive importation of all imaginable items into Africa under new and unmitigated free trade (Panford 2001).

New High Levels of Social Inequality

Other features of Africa reveal that it is now more susceptible to increasingly deep-seated social cleavages that exist in Latin America and Asia. For instance, although gated communities are not yet as common as in the US, we are seeing more houses in African cities surrounded by security devices such as high walls with barbed wire, big iron gates and security guards or "watchmen." These are meant to deter robbers who could be armed, dangerous and may kill. The new and high incidence of armed robbery in Nigeria, which is spreading to the rest of West Africa, could be the product of socio-economic deprivation and values that are changing rapidly to support inappropriate social behaviors, such as getting wealth at all cost, including murder.

Also linked to the grave economic conditions is the steadily increasing numbers of street children. This started in the 1980s when deteriorating rural conditions, pushed massive numbers of people not excluding children to urban areas where living conditions were not as good as the new arrivals had expected. This results in part from the abandonment of sustainable development for the benefit of the majority as the governments in Ghana under President Kwame Nkrumah, Tanzania during the rule of President Julius Nyerere and Zimbabwe (from 1980–1985) sought to do. Although these attempts were not completely successful, it could be said correctly that prior to the mid-1980s, some African governments, were concerned about local and national needs. In contrast, the policies of the IMF and World Bank duo are contributing to worsening conditions.

We might add that demographic trends are also accentuating the poor conditions in Africa today. Two such factors are that Africa is experiencing one of the fastest rates of urbanization in the world. Owing to rapidly deteriorating urban conditions, Zambia seems to be an exception to this African trend. In the past few years more Zambians have abandoned the city to return to rural areas. In addition, a large percentage of the African population is of school-going age. Governments in Africa without exception are not addressing the challenges such growth presents. They are instead preoccupied with meeting the demands of western donors. This has been the case in Ghana, Uganda, Zambia, Nigeria and Tanzania where presidents and ministers of finance/economic planning commit tremendous national resources to donor relations and go on junkets in search of loans, international aid and foreign investments that often do not yield the desired outcomes of more economic growth, jobs and better conditions of life.

Besides the phenomena of street children and growing unemployment, there is a steeply rising sense of hopelessness fueled by the large number of both uneducated and educated youth who roam major cities playing soccer, drafts/checkers and other board games and watch videos (preferably foreign ones) while scheming to travel overseas by any means. This swells the numbers of Africans leading distressed lives in Europe, North America and other parts of the world. Because hopes of Africa getting out of its present slump are dwindling, most African immigrants endure intolerable, unsafe, exploitative and humiliating living and working conditions overseas. They suffer in interacting with racist immigration officials, police and other security agents in Europe, Asia and North America. To foreign security personnel, Africans could be maltreated because their countries are "in shambles" and because they are deemed to be economic refugees, they do not deserve humane treatment and human rights protections.

Overseas-based African magazines (including the now defunct *West Africa* and *New African*) and newspapers often depict the racist treatment and even the murder of Africans in Europe. Because of racism, and to some extent, the illegal status of some migrants, most murders are not investigated and culprits are not penalized according to law if they are arrested. A Ghanaian informed one of the co-authors that "since conditions at home (Ghana) are not good, I have endured painful experiences abroad." This individual suffered dog bites on two separate occasions in Italy for which he did not receive medical treatment or any compensation. He could not report any incident to the police and the dog owners were not sanctioned. These and other indignities suffered by Africans abroad result partly from failed African politics and economies and the crises that they have engendered.

There are more troublesome aspects of the current African crises. By most indicators, even by developing country standards, Africans are dead absolutely in terms of living conditions. Most of the gains made in the early post-independence years (the late 1950s to the mid-1970s) have dissipated to make Africa to lag behind other Third World nations. *Per capita* income, that is, roughly how much each African earned, in the 1990s was at best US$500, while it was US$620 in Asia and almost US$3,000 in Latin America. The average Gross National Income per capita measured by Purchasing Power Parity (GNI/PPP) for Africa in 2002 was $2100 and $1670 for Sub-Saharan Africa. The situation in some the countries appears to be more pathetic. In 2002, *per capita* GNI/PPP in Sierra Leone was $490, Niger $800, Ethiopia $780, Mozambique $990, and Tanzania $590. By contrast, the *per capita* GNI/PPP for the more developed countries (MDCs) was $23690; $3860 for the less developed countries (LDCs), $6820 for Latin America/Caribbean, and $4680 for Asia (see PRB 2004). No African country has made any significant progress in improving its GNI in the past two decades, not even Ghana which which became "one of the best IMF-World Bank pupils," in the 1980s. After undergoing two decades of massive economic restructuring under the World Bank and IMF, Ghana had a meager *per capita* income of US$320 in 2003 and the goal of reaching $1000 by 2015 seems unrealistic if current conditions remain. All these add up to generate the hard lives of non-elite Africans.

In addition, Africa is home to more than half of the worlds 44 poorest countries, 33 of the forty-eight least-developed poorest nations of the world, 30of the 34 countries with the lowest human development index (UNDP 2000). Over 30 percent of Africans live on less than US$1 per day. Of the 65 countries with the highest under-five mortality rates, 43 are in Africa (UNICEF 2000).

Africans have some of the shortest life spans. The average African lives to be only 52 years while his/her counterparts in Asia and Latin America, live to be 65 years and seventy-two years respectively. This is why Sierra Leone and other African countries are at the bottom rungs of human development indices compiled by United Nations agencies. A recent report by two UN Agencies, The World Health Organization and The United Nations' Children Fund, showed that many African countries including Ethiopia, Somalia, Chad, Mozambique, Equatorial Guinea, Madagascar, Congo, Eritrea, Burkina Faso, Niger, Guinea and the Comoros could least provide basic social services such as clean drinking water and sanitation (*Boston Globe* August 26, 2004: A13). Three out of four African countries are classified as the poorest nations on earth. The short lives of Africans and the unusually high rates of death and the short lifespan of African infants, children and adults are depicted by the following data: In Zimbabwe, Zambia, and Angola, the average life expectancy ranges from 37.9 to 39.9 years compared to 75–80.6 years in the UK, France, Sweden and Switzerland (BBC News December 19, 2003)

The problems we have enumerated are caused by factors internal to and outside Africa. At the top of our list are the poor sanitary conditions and the growing ineffectiveness of health and nutrition policies and practices, such as low technology and low output food production. Since the mid-1980s, more Africans have been sick and not able to afford the high cost of health care.

The spread of diseases, which were controlled in the early years of independence due to concerted efforts, are making a comeback with deadly vengeance. This is due partly to poor sanitation and inadequate social services coupled with high prices, which have placed them beyond the reach of the majority. The skyrocketing costs of public utilities are engendered by structural adjustment and cost recovery measures enforced by the IMF, the World Bank and other western donors since 1986 (Panford 2001). These donors push hard for socially crushing cost recovery policies to ensure that countries such as Ghana, Uganda, Nigeria, Senegal, the Gambia, Tanzania and Zambia pay their foreign debts (*Time* April 24, 2000: 47). Declining access to clean water and unsanitary conditions boost the spread of waterborne and other diseases, in particular, malaria and tuberculosis. These diseases are combining with AIDS to ravage African populations and economies to rob current and future generations of any decent standard of living. Some of the adverse consequences are fairly visible in Africa today.

In some towns and villages, one sees only the very young and aged. Those in their prime of economic activity have died from AIDS or left for abroad in search of "better economic prospects." This has had devastating social and economic effects. AIDS has compounded Africa's health problems by putting more pressure on already weak economic and health care systems. We have many situations where some very young and old ones have to fend for themselves: Grandparents taking care of AIDS orphans in Uganda, Botswana and South Africa. Even the productivity of industries is being affected negatively. Recently, Anglo-Gold, the giant South African Gold mining company, found itself facing stiff foreign competition because AIDS was costing it an extra four to six dollars for every Troy ounce of gold it sells. The decline in revenues and profits could be attributed to extra health care and training costs plus working hours lost due to AIDS and opportunistic infections like tuberculosis and pneumonia.

As we stated already, the policies of the IMF/World Bank and the political catastrophes we associate with Africa have also been part of the crises. For example, massive disruption caused by civil wars in Liberia, Sierra Leone, the Horn of Africa, Angola and the Great Lakes area have made it extremely difficult to eradicate diseases such as polio for which vaccines exist. As shown in the roster of poor African nations, most of the countries that are performing so poorly in meeting basic needs tend to be the ones afflicted by war and other catastrophes. Also, due to IMF/World Bank prescriptions, excessive charges for basic services in particular, and declining incomes, we are now observing - the increased - use of water with bacteria leading to the high incidence of illnesses including typhoid fever and bilharzia.

Kenya's free primary education, which was introduced in January 2003, reveals how poverty, AIDS and the high cost of living are combining to make it difficult to improve living conditions and human capital development in contemporary Africa. The new Kibaki Administration is contending with new challenges besides the hefty direct cost of free education. Some classes grew in size from 54 pupils to over 70 pupils and one school had over 400 orphans, most of whom had lost parents to AIDS. These orphans and other poor students cannot utilize free education because they have to pay for books and uniforms (Public Broadcast News, Boston and November 29, 2003).

Books, uniforms and other living expenses are still burdens to the poor and the relatives of orphans who are unemployed or make meager incomes from informal sector jobs and peasant farming.

In Ghana and Botswana, the brain drain, especially the exodus of doctors, nurses and other health professionals has sapped the capacities of public health authorities to bring AIDS and other diseases under control (*New York Times* November 13, 2003). The rapid loss of Ghanaian doctors and nurses to British and US hospitals is highly instructive because it shows how a poor country like Ghana dissipates its meager resources to train personnel who go overseas and do not benefit the nation. It is estimated that two out of three Ghana-trained doctors hive migrated out of Ghana. These and other professionals are trained at high direct financial and other indirect costs to Ghana and other African countries. European and American hospitals benefit from the prohibitively high cost of training incurred by Africans who ironically do not get treatment when ill. As it is, Africans are supplementing American and European health care systems while their own suffer abject neglect and steadily collapse.

The Cost of Wars and Other Civil Strives

Large numbers of ordinary Africans are trapped in dangerous conflicts and thus feel the pains of war and bear the full cost. This is especially the case in the Horn of Africa (Ethiopia, Somalia and Eritrea, mainly) where warfare worsens the effects of natural disasters like droughts. Droughts wreak more havoc because wars and other human-made calamities, including genocide in Burundi and Rwanda and close to eight years of war in the Democratic Republic of Congo, accentuate their impact. The latter has not only cost millions of lives, but has also led to conditions almost impossible to reverse to create political stability, personal safety, security and economic development in the future. Even Côte d'Ivoire, that was thought to be a haven for peace and a model for development is experiencing highly unsettling political crises. The Ivorian crises were precipitated by Africa's last 20th Century military coup on December 31, 1999. Following this coup, in one instance alone, 50 dead bodies were discovered in a shallow grave. These individuals were murdered for opposing the military.

The military and political stalemate in Côte d'Ivoire (since the failed insurrection of September 19, 2002 and the existence of rebel-controlled territories) reveals the difficulties inherent in the intercine wars that have been proliferating in West Africa, the Great Lakes and the Horn of Africa since the end of the Cold War.[1] These wars are facilitated by the easy procurement of weapons and ammunition from American, European and Chinese arms dealers, whom their governments have failed to regulate for economic reasons. During the Cold War, the US and Soviet Governments placed tight reins over the supply of arms to protect their geo-political and strategic interests (Keller and Rothchild 1996).

The 1975 to 2002 civil war in Angola is a typical example of where not only personal safety was made rare but also tremendous resources—oil and diamonds— were devoted to utter destruction. By some accounts, it may take as much as a decade to rid Angola of land mines. Meanwhile, even after hostilities ceased with the death of Jonas

Savimbi in 2002, children, women and farmers are still the victims of exploding mines that were planted during a civil war that started in 1975. The Russians and Americans and their allies who supplied these weapons have abandoned Angolans to grapple with the on-going deadly consequences of war.

We also need to factor into the outcomes of war, its destructive impact on social infrastructure—roads, bridges, schools and other public amenities such as water, health and electricity. There is besides, the massive social dislocation it creates. Not only are efforts to end war itself and wage peace time-consuming and requireing a great deal of diligence, but also the required nation-building can be a more demanding and difficult process. Liberia's post-war situation illustrates these problems and challenges. That country's meager stock of social infrastructure including the first university, Monrovia University, was virtually wiped out while over half the population of 2.5 million fled internally or went overseas. This is one reason why Africa has emerged as a major source of the world's refugees. Liberians and Africans in other war-afflicted countries need to undertake massive re-settlement of displaced people and infrastructural rehabilitation at high financial cost. This is occurring at a time when the international community is not willing to assist and the affected countries are quickly losing the capacity for nation-building. Politically and financially, the African states affected by wars may not be able to meet the challenges thrust on them by war and post-war conditions.

Due to the brutality of the new conflicts (including the amputation of limbs, as happened in Sierra Leone) the lasting psychological and other related trauma are rising to alarming levels. We also have to contend with rebel groups specializing in the use of boy soldiers and girls to advance their narrow interests. The rehabilitation of these young fighters will come at high social cost to countries like Liberia and Sierra Leone where the use of child soldiers has become common. In other cases, women and girls have been raped, causing deep psychological and physical trauma for which recovery may be painfully slow, if possible. These are the new and dire consequences of new conflicts Africans have to deal with. Because these countries have few, if any, social workers and psychological counselors, the situation could be grave.

The Causes of Africa's Crises

Most of the conflicts and crises we have cited result from new forces unleashed by the end of the Cold War. We have an unprecedented proliferation of inexpensive small arms in West Africa, the Great Lakes area and the Horn of Africa, especially in Somalia. Other conflicts emanate from how these new forces are accentuating old problems.[2] The demise of the Soviet Union has led to new global political and economic realities in which Africans are more marginalized. We also stress the culpability of African leaders. Our broader definition of leadership includes all Africans in responsible positions without exception. There has been the tendency to blame only the military and a few "civilian" politicians. We need to add to the list of failed leaders our traditional leaders, academics, businessmen and women, lawyers/judges, managers and even religious leaders such as priests and pastors, bishops and imams and sheiks. Their actions and lack of creativity have combined with the ineptitude and corruption of both civilian and military rulers to generate the deplorable state of Africa.[3] One example is the collective failure to create appropriate strategies to overcome what Kwame Nkrumah of Ghana called neo-colonialism. This has been the bane of Africa since independence (Nzongola Ntalaja 1989).

Paradoxically, in the last 20 years, some African leaders and their technical and professional counterparts have been working diligently to keep intact Africa's subservient role in the global political economy. This is the role forced on Africa by colonial powers to produce cheap commodities for the world market. Hence the structural weaknesses inherent in economies that depend on the export of low value cocoa beans, tea leaves, latex (raw rubber) and other agriculture produce; unprocessed mineral ores, crude oil and timber logs are being reinforced under the guise of economic reforms supported by the two Bretton Woods institutions with the support of the World Trade Organization (Stiglitz 2003 and Panford 2001). While Africans toil to export agricultural items they cannot eat and often do not need, their leaders travel the globe seeking loans/aid for imported beef, chicken, long-grain rice and other processed food from the US, Europe and Asia (Panford 2001). Most African leaders and their global partners seem to be oblivious to the fact that the export of low value agricultural produce and other cheap raw materials alone will doom any people anywhere in the world!

Getting rid of Africa's role in an unfair/unequal global trade, which benefits Europe and North America mainly, should be the most rational starting point for tackling Africa's failure to develop. Precarious dependence on the sale of inexpensive exports is at the heart of Africa's crises, including protracted wars. Most post-Cold War conflicts in Africa are fueled by rapidly falling economic growth, which exacerbates political tensions (Martin 2002). Even the genocide in Rwanda in 1994 is to a large extent, a manifestation of failed economies and the failure to tackle the resulting political differences (Watson 1994 and Prunier 1998).

Both low and declining revenues from exports and population growth rates of two to three percent have put severe pressure on African economies. With anemic growth rates of less than three percent, Africa cannot sustain large populations. Indeed some countries have experienced negative growth and others have become dependent on the donor community for budgetary support and even for food. Literally, with declining food production, there are more hungry mouths to feed and with less infrastructure, we see growing tensions over its distribution, that is, who gets what and who benefits? Donor support has come at a steep price such as giving up control over financial and other domestic policies. In fact, the sovereignty of most African states is disappearing at a fast pace. This is especially true in countries such as Senegal, Ghana, Uganda and Tanzania that have been singled out by the European Union, the US and Japan as the "successfully adjusted." These are countries that have met donor conditions mostly at huge costs to their citizens. Paradoxically, these have also emerged as the leading HIPCs in Africa.

Why Crises Continue in Africa

Africa's current crises have numerous causes. We therefore, wish to stress that the new policies favored by donors may not *per se* be the sole factors wreaking havoc. With this acknowledgment we may still be correct in asserting that even in the nations most favored by the west, orthodox indicators of economic growth and real conditions on the ground show the absence of substantial and long-term gains. According to T.A. (Trevor) Manuel, South Africa's Minister for Finance, "Ghana remains very poor in spite of many years of adjustment" (BBC Interview, "Poverty in Africa" February 6, 2005). We are curious as to why after two decades of donor support, a country like Ghana is now discovering "the need to alleviate poverty." Both the IMF and World Bank also have a new mantra of "Poverty reduction" in Ghana and other African nations. Current trends reveal that we cannot be optimistic about the future of any African country if existing conditions, including those we refer to, are not changed fundamentally.

Since the 1970s, but more especially in the last decade and half, material conditions in Africa have deteriorated quickly. While in the 1980s, *per capita* was over US$700, by the end of the 1990s it had fallen by almost half, to $400. This has led to 28 of 48 countries south of the Sahara being in the class of the world's least developed nations. Our skepticism stems in part from the fact that even the small economic recovery of 1992 in some countries, was temporal. Thus, since the mid-1990s, Africa has had the infamous record of being the only continent that is not able to feed itself. Also, the rate of poverty is climbing as most people live on a paltry sum of two dollars or less a day. Paradoxically, the SAPs and other economic reforms that donors have forced on Africa have not benefited the majority of Africans who face harsher conditions of life and work (Panford 2001). Visits to, especially, rural and poor urban areas show that almost 20 years of so-called adjustment under the IMF and World Bank have rather worsened living standards.

The news on the political front, to use an African phrase, "has not been palatable." The enthusiasm with which Africans received "the externally assisted" movement for multi-party democracy in the immediate post-Cold War era has waned rapidly. Africans now feel misled by the exaggerated promises of political liberalization and the expected renaissance. Hence as some Africans cast envious glances at the rising economic fortunes of Koreans, Taiwanese, Malaysians and now Indians and the Chinese, they are asking which one they should be getting right first: Economic fundamentals or insuring effective, democratic and responsive government - or both? Besides, Africans seem to be confounded by what has gone wrong in a period that some designated as the era of the African renewal. Meanwhile, the UN is anchoring hopes to revive Africa on the "Millennium Challenge Program" while Prime Minister Tony Blair of Great Britain pushes his Blair Africa Commission as the newly-found panacea to Africa's poverty. One's assessment of the impact of such new initiatives will depend to a large extent on one's optimism or pessimism about the efficacy of external intervention and its track record in Africa. Forty years of Africa's experience raises some serious doubts about being optimistic about the role of external agents and assistance.

Thus we might note that Africa requires governments that are beholding to the majority of the population, not a local minority or foreign interests. The new governments have to be genuine republics in the true sense of the concept: governments that are accountable to the people that elected them. This is the long and difficult road Africans and their leaders must travel if they are to attain meaningful and durable economic growth and political development. This should be the standard for judging current African governments, leaders and economic plans and programs including the ones that the west is now so found of. The new African Union which African governments launched in South Africa on July 9, 2002 has to confront these same challenges to assist Africans to realize their long-lost dreams of independence and modern statehood by creating long-lasting peace, security, and safety followed by real prosperity for most Africans and not a few as it is currently.

Notes

1 It was so unsafe that the Liberian national soccer team relocated to Ghana to avoid players being killed. This and other civil wars have made Africa the source of the largest numbers of both internally and externally displaced persons in the world.

2 An often-neglected fact of African political economy is that the first African leaders who assumed rule from the colonial authorities inherited structurally weak economies. These economies were and continue to be dependent on the vagaries of the climate and the export of cheap single commodities. Equally significant, the new African states had low institutional capacities to withstand the demands of modern statehood. For instance, the former Democratic Republic of Congo, during Prime Minister Patrice Lumumba's rule, lacked human resources to the extent that an inexperienced 27-year old held dual challenging positions—the Permanent Representative to the UN and simultaneously the Ambassador to the US.

3 By 1995, Africa produced the largest number of refugees, over four million out of a total of 30 world-wide (US Department of State, Refugee Admissions 1995). The deplorable conditions are marked by the large numbers of both political and economic refugees who flee Africa to hostile European, North American and other cities searching for jobs and other economic opportunities. Most of these especially, women are exploited through prostitution, low pay, dangerous and menial jobs while contending with racist immigration and police (*Boston Globe* January 25, 2004: A7). The latter's racism is premised on the belief that Africans deserve to be treated badly.

References

Clark, J. (1996). "Reform or Democratization for Africa? Troubling Constraints and Partial Solutions," *TransAfrica Forum*, (Spring): 3–19.

Government of Zambia. (2001). *Selected Socio-Economic Indicators 2000*. Lusaka: Central Statistical Office.

Keller, Edmond J. and Rothchild, D. (eds.) (1996) *Africa in the New International Order: Rethinking State Sovereignty and Regional Security*. Boulder, Colo.: Lynne Rienner Publishers

Lofchie, M.F. (1971). *The State of the Nations: Constraints on Development in Independent Africa*. Berkeley: University of California Press.

Nzongola-Ntalaja, G. (1989). "The African Crisis: The Way Out," *African Studies Review* Vol. 32 (1): 115–128.

Martin, G. (2002). *Africa in World Politics: A Pan-African Perspective*. Trenton, NJ/ Asmara, Eritrea: Africa World Press, Inc.

Panford, K. (2001). *IMF-World Bank and Labor's Burdens in Africa*. Westport, CT: Praeger

Prunier, G. (1998). *The Rwanda Crisis: History of a Genocide*. New York: Columbia University Press.

Population Reference Bureau (PRB). (2004). *Population Data Sheet*. Washington, DC: PRB.

Stiglitz, J. (2003). *Globalization and its Discontents*. New York: Norton.

UNDP (2000). *Human Development Report*. New York: Oxford University Press.

UNICEF (2000). *1999 State of the World's Children Report*. UNICEF.

United States Institute of Peace (1999). *Building for Peace in the Horn of Africa Diplomacy and Beyond*, Washington DC: United States Institute of Peace.

Watson, P. (1994). "Purging the Evil," *Africa Report*. (Nov-Dec): 13–21.

Young, C. (2004). "The End of the Post-Colonial State in Africa? Reflections on Changing African Political Dynamics." *African Affairs*, 103: 23–49.

Chapter 3

Rethinking the African State: A New Conceptualization on Sub-Saharan Africa

Smile Dube and Calvin O. Masilela

Introduction

In assessing the state of growth and development in Sub-Saharan Africa, one might as well begin with the following quote from Thompson (1999: 183):

> It has been almost fifty years since Africa began shedding colonial rule. Fifty years is sufficiently long a time period for those concerned with economic development to begin the process of accounting for the failure of post-colonial governments to improve the material well being of their citizens.

Such accounting must be broad enough to include political, social, economic, and whatever else can be said about the failure of nationalists to deliver equitable material improvements to their societies. While most of the colonies became free without violence, some had to be freed by "wars of liberation." Some leaders of these post-colonial societies have, in most instances, stayed too long.

In Sub Saharan Africa (SSA), few can be said to have succeeded in leaving office in dignity and with their people in prosperity. Few have either died in office or have been forcibly removed after imposing intolerable suffering on their people. Whatever the nationalist slogans employed during and after "independence," what is clear is that the promises made then - the transition to independence and promises of a better life via sustained economic growth - have been anything but a series of catastrophic events, especially to SSA. For many African leaders who have stayed in power for a long, the biggest problem has been the failure to understand that to maintain power they must increase material prosperity for ordinary citizens through economic growth and not confiscatory redistributive policies. For most countries in SSA, the post-colonial period saw the imposition of either left or right wing "social contracts" that had very little to do with the history, culture, and customs of diverse peoples. Equally important has been the failure to recognize that for growth and development purposes, the State has never been an efficient mechanism for generating growth, notwithstanding the claims of socialists during the heyday of revolutions in the 1960s and 1970s. Some Asian nationalists who have kept power for long periods did so because they recognized this.

The debate on some of the causes of the failure of the post-colonial African State to deliver economic growth and hence improve the standard of living for a majority of Africans has not yielded any significant fruits.

There is a tendency among Africanists and those who claim to be students of African development to examine these failures within a framework that categorizes some factors that may have led to this state of affairs as either *external* or *internal* constraints. Almost without exception, politicians, policymakers, and even some academics tend to focus exclusively on identifying external factors that undermine development. Depending on the time period under study, these factors include the IMF and World Bank programs, colonialism and its residual effects, and a host of conspiracies by developed countries against developing countries. The effect of this singular focus on external factors is that it diverts attention from internal factors, which may also account for the disastrous economic performance of almost all African countries.

Briefly, such factors are the failure of post-colonial African governments to integrate and complement traditional customs and rules in the design of national social contracts. In addition, there is a singular focus on national consensus under the "nation-building" concept with no concern for ethnic diversity, despite the fact that most societies are composed essentially of overlapping sub-societies. Similarly, there is a failure to devise political, economic, and social arrangements that are based on reciprocity, self-interest and are self-policing in nature. An important oversight, particularly by the donor community including the World Bank is the failure to include coercive political power in their economic programs that are premised on neo-liberalism formulations. If they did, they would inevitably recognize a fundamental fact: that a theory of Coasian bargaining plus transaction costs often limits their ability to explain political power that is required to enforce contracts. The reality is that coercive political power is often used in attempts to make markets work better, and those possessing such power often take some goods that are traded in the market as incentives.

In Hobbes, the social contract is viewed as an alternative to the existence in a "state of nature." Indeed, during his time his "state of nature" was very unpleasant, since he envisaged it as being a "war of all against all." Some have suggested a parallel of this state of nature and the scenario under which most citizens currently live under dictatorships in some parts of the world. As an alternative, Hobbes saw only the voluntary surrender by all of their rights and liberties into the hands of an absolute sovereign (dictator or military leader). Both his view of human nature then and his preferred alternative are unlikely to find wide voluntary acceptance today, although some versions of the alternative may indeed exist in Sub-Saharan Africa. For economists who work strictly within their discipline, the failure of post-colonial governments is usually attributed to lack of appreciation for the markets and prices rather than the prevalence of "social contracts" imposed on citizens by coercive political power.

The exception to conventional analyses is Englebert's (2000) persuasive argument, which attributes the failure of post-colonial states in SSA to deliver developmental progress to their lack of legitimacy. State legitimacy as Englebert puts it "addresses both the legitimacy of the right to (i.e., the foundations of political authority) and the agreement as to what constitutes the political society, the polity, the community of participants in the social contract" (p.175). States that lack these foundations of social and power relations have sought to legitimize themselves by resorting to "neopatrimonial policies" premised on clientalism, regionalism, nepotism, factionalism, and corruption. Furthermore when it comes to governance, leaders of states lacking legitimacy have demonstrated an inability "to make credible commitments to other economic agents and to safeguard property rights (p.175)." As Englebert eloquently puts it:

> Their use of the state apparatus and its resources to finance and support networks of patronage leads to a weakening of the rule of law, which discourages private economic agents. Their need for access to economic resources makes them more likely to expropriate investors and renege on their contractual engagements, which further discourages domestic and foreign investors, leads to a shortage of investments and a tendency to avoid the formal financial system, and results in an underprovision of public goods by the state. (p.175)

Englebert's analysis is useful in many important respects: it identifies both the causes and dysfunctions of the post-colonial state in SSA as well as the importance of incorporating traditional sources of authority in forging a social contract that has produced positive outcomes in selected SSA countries. We, however, take issue with Englebert's prescription, which on the one hand argues for a redefinition of the post-colonial state (to foster horizontal legitimacy), and on the other, the embrace of "mafia-like protostates" of warlords as an essential element of institutional rebirth and a new social contract. Though not inconceivable for SSA to "re-colonize" itself, this is not a viable solution at this time, given current conditions related to economic stagnation, lack of moral and visionary leadership, and other social pathologies in African states. On the other hand, rewarding the brutal anarchy of warlords that lack legitimate authority other than that conferred by the barrel of the gun is a recipe for disaster, and certainly not an option for SSA as the case of Somalia since 1991 shows.

In articulating a new national social contract for SSA, we adopt a different approach that draws from history, political science and sociology to make the following main points. Economic development requires sustained peaceful coexistence among people, especially in SSA where societies reflect a wide range of diversity in language and customs that have survived for hundreds of years. The post-colonial period saw a sustained effort to rid these societies of traditional institutional structures without an adequate evaluation of their relevance and role in the new emerging social order including the centralization of power by African rulers. This process was unnecessary since self-sustaining and self-policing social contracts could have been grafted onto these traditional structures.

In this chapter, we employ concepts relating to traditional rule, customs, reciprocity, and other norms as foundations upon which institutions can be built to provide national social contracts from many sub-social contracts. Within these norms, core concepts common in Black Africa are useful in negotiating a national social contract. These include *ubuntu* (humaneness) in Zulu, South Africa, and its equivalent, *obuntubulamu* in Luganda, Uganda, and *mOgOya* in Mandenkan, Mali. Their universality allows one to provide a readily recognizable and acceptable basis for institutions. Unfortunately the conventions embodied in these concepts all but disappeared during the construction and the ascendancy of the colonial and post-colonial state.

These concepts by themselves are clearly not sufficient to design and maintain institutions capable of safeguarding some of the countries of Sub-Saharan Africa. To appreciate the difficulties faced by citizens of SSA, an economic model of political power—the "stationary bandit" versus the "roving bandit" (Olson 1993: 567–576)—supplements these concepts with specific reference to Zimbabwe. The Zimbabwe experience is particularly instructive for several reasons. Unlike any other country in SSA (other than South Africa), Zimbabwe emerged on the world stage advantaged with a relatively developed, robust and capitalized economy; infrastructure capacity that was complemented by formidable human resource capital; and 20 years experience of failed development experiments in SSA. Sadly the country has been on a fast track underdeveloping itself, and the long-term prospects are not good. The combined attempts by Robert Mugabe and the ruling party (ZANU-PF) to perpetuate their rule has set in motion forces that have institutionalized corruption; undermined the rule of law; abused and eroded basic rights; and contributed to the implosion of the country's economy. The country is experiencing a 70 percent unemployment rate, 200 percent inflation, a poverty rate of 75 percent, GDP shrinking at the rate of two to five percent, and wages that have declined by seventy percent in the past ten years. In short, Zimbabwe today is much poorer and violently unstable than when Mugabe found it in 1980.

Olson's model provides an alternative explanation of the failure of SSA to achieve growth and development like the rest of other developing regions. In fact, one possible way to reduce its applicability to SSA is to devise a self-policing social contract that can be a basis for institutions that would serve to reduce information asymmetries within the principal-agent framework. Properly constituted institutions provide growth-enhancing and thus welfare-enhancing incentives to individuals, groups and firms. The importance of incentives is crucial to economic development, especially in cases where it is done in a transparent fashion.

Institutional Foundations of a Social Contract

For illustrative purposes we draw on the Zulu language formulations to make our point about the imperatives of concepts that are socially legitimated to arrive at a social contract among the people of SSA. As noted previously, the concept of *ubuntu* (humaneness), and its derivatives *ubukhosi* (the institution of traditional authority), and *isintu* (accepted behavior or behavioral norms), have evolved over time as means of reaching and maintaining mutual agreements. The salience of *ubuntu* is best discerned metaphorically in the statement, "*umuntu ngumuntu ngabantu*" (a person is a person through other people). It emphasizes the respect for human dignity (and yet allows for orderly reciprocal changes to human relations) and clear observation of customs and rules as represented by the practice of the traditional leaders.

Often times during violent conflicts, for example, the murder of white farmers, members of the opposition, teachers, and ordinary rural villagers characteristic of present day Zimbabwe, and at times when violent crimes against both persons and property are rife, distraught members of society decry the loss of *ubuntu*. Thus, heinous crimes can be seen as the antithesis of *ubuntu* to most Africans. According to this view, the treatment of citizens (regardless of color) that is cruel, inhuman or derogatory is bereft of *ubuntu*. The concept of *isintu* (behavioral norms), among other things, embodies the notion of *ubuntu*. In fact, it captures the common understandings of people (such as conventions, customs, habits, moral principles, rules of thumb, traditions and the like) that are important in regulating or coordinating interactions among people who are driven by enlightened self-interest to consent to a social contract. The concept promotes conciliation at the expense of confrontation at all levels within that society.

The third pillar of social foundations is the concept of *ubukhosi* (the institution of traditional authority), which is founded on the principle of *ubuntu* (humaneness). It has not changed for hundreds of years although the particulars have had to change since customary practices have always been flexible to reflect currently accepted modes of behavior that currently function to the benefit of society as a whole. The system of traditional authority derives its legitimacy from the people, which is best illustrated by the expression "*inkosi yinkosi ngabantu(a chief is a chief by the will of the people)*. Thus, power relations between the wielder of authority (the chief, for example) and the polity, encourages a mode of dispensation that stresses consultation and consensus. With roles and rules clearly understood, social contracts are easily enforceable and honored. Perhaps the core lesson to be drawn from *ubuntu* and its derivatives is that the survival of people depends on voluntary cooperation with each other—reciprocal arrangements and self-policing structures. However, the formation of such contracts has continued to be undermined by coercive political power in much of SSA.

Information Asymmetries in the Principal-Agent Model

Information pervades decision-making in households, firms, and in government over society's concern with economic growth, access to productive resources including land, health, the environment, and all aggregates that focus on society's goals related to equity, efficiency and poverty reduction. The political economy of information refers to the role of information in political processes and collective decision-making under various types of regimes, ranging from democracies to dictatorships. Asymmetry of information simply means that different people know different things. For example, top government officials of a collapsing economy know more about the perilous state of affairs than ordinary people. The central idea behind information economics is that *regardless of economic structure (centralized, decentralized), different people (groups) know different things*.

In political economy, there are asymmetries of information between those governing (or ruling) and those governed (or ruled). Such asymmetries exist at every level of government. In situations where political structures are unstable, asymmetries of information between coalitions and between government departments tends to produce a bureaucratic nightmare as groups jostle to provide less and less information as a means of retaining political power. Early work in the economics of information dealt with how markets overcame problems of information asymmetries (Akerlof 1970). Recent work has focused on how actors in markets (economic, social or political) create information problems for purposes of power under conditions where actors are often made of unstable coalitions. We discuss information asymmetries by borrowing from the literature on three elements of the modern theory of the firm: corporate finance, corporate governance, and organizational design. In fact, we focus on issues related to governance because of the similarities with political governance. The discussion here toggles between the theory of the firm and theories of political processes. The strand that unifies these two areas is information asymmetries. Under the New Partnership for African Development (NEPAD), a comprehensive reform program sponsored by African governments and the Monterrey Consensus (UN), there is clear focus on this issue. According to Joseph (2002: 96),

> Good governance is essential for sustainable development. Sound economic policies, solid democratic institutions responsive to the needs of people and improved infrastructure are the basis for sustained economic growth, poverty eradication and employment creation. Freedom, peace and security, domestic stability, respect for human rights, including the right to development, and the rule of law, gender equality, market-oriented policies, an overall commitment to just and democratic societies are also essential and mutually enforcing.

With the exception of dictators such as Mugabe, Ghadafi, and the like, many African leaders have lined up behind these lofty goals and principles. According to Joseph (2002) there are different Africas, and so it is difficult to outline a broad plan for all when each of the states is bound to face different information asymmetries. Political processes entail asymmetries of information. Presidents, dictators or elected leaders are supposed to know more about the state of the economy, the effects of their redistributive policies, economic growth, and the state of public health more than ordinary citizens. This delegation of responsibility for-day-to-day management to elected officials resembles the standard principal-agent problem that is popular in the modern theory of the firm. It is widely used to study corporate finance, governance and organizational design. As is the case for the firm, the problem is providing *incentives* for those entrusted to act on behalf of those they are sworn to serve. Olson (1996) and Stiglitz (2002) show that democracy (contestability in political processes) provides a check on the abuses of the powers that come from delegation. Just as the takeover mechanism in corporations is an imperfect check on management, so is the electoral process on political behavior and outcomes.

In the past, whenever economists discussed informational efficiencies of a market economy, they focused on one subset of information problems, namely, those related to *scarcity*. For competitive models built on these narrow sets of information problems, there was also an implicit understanding that markets do not matter. Laws of demand and supply, regardless of whether institutions existed, largely drove market outcomes or not. The only exceptions were cases of market failure and the provision of public goods that allowed for the government to exist, partly protecting property rights as well. According to Coase (1960), issues related to the distribution of wealth were deemed unimportant as long as property rights were well-defined. Similarly, history, culture, conventions or common understandings matter little since knowledge of preferences, technology and initial endowments was all that was required to account for a growth path of an economy. The development of information economics has been associated with questioning each of these assumptions in order to examine markets with imperfect information. One fundamental result is that with incomplete information, market actions or choices convey information, and outcomes are never Pareto efficient.

In the theory of the firm, existing managers usually take actions that reduce the effectiveness of competition. That is, the threat of a takeover (often hostile) is reduced by management via increasing information asymmetries (increasing non-transparency). As in the theory of the firm where the current management has an incentive to *increase* asymmetries of information in order to retain market power, so too do politicians of whatever stripe. The success of the latter to increase asymmetries and therefore retain power depends crucially on self-policing provisions of the social contract or the political structure that permits such checks on power. Cousins (2002: 46) suggests that despots may retain power by appealing to "authoritarian nationalism combined with a phony attack on imperialism, as elsewhere in Africa, to provide additional ideological cover." He was referring to Zimbabwe's model of radical reform where powerful interest groups aligned with a venal government have taken advantage of the unresolved land question to provide cover for their accumulation of both moveable and immoveable assets by extra-legal means.

Within the theory of the firm, relating corporate governance, increasing disclosure requirements on corporations in fact does affect the effectiveness of takeover mechanisms and the overall structure of governance. Similarly, the requirements of more disclosure (or increase in transparency) of political processes can affect both political contestability and the quality of governance. In cases where "exit" options are few or blocked in political processes, there has to be concern with abuses of power under that regime. The following quote from Hume (1739) indicates the extent to which despots may go to violate self-policing agreements or defy exit opportunities:

> Two men, who pull the oars of a boat, do it by an agreement or convention, tho' they have never given promises to another. Nor is the rule concerning the stability of possession the less derived from human conventions, that it arises gradually, and acquires force by a slow progression. In like manner are languages gradually established by human conventions without any promise. In like manner do gold and silver become the measures of exchange (Hume 1739: 490).

But one may question the idea that despots are sensitive to punishment in cases where they violate the social contract. The New Partnership for Africa's Development (NEPAD) recognized this fact when they saw a need to have some credible enforcement authority external to a particular state. In fact, one may argue that such an act was to reduce the intrusive role of western countries in promoting both economic and political reforms. African governments have promised to establish their own monitoring (policing authority) mechanism to devise acceptable ways of ensuring compliance with international norms (good governance, conflict resolution, the rule of law, curbing of corruption). Joseph (2002) reports that at a NEPAD meeting in Abuja (March 26, 2002), they created a "peer review mechanism" which proposed eight codes of behavior coupled with an agreement that a "credible African institute" would administer these codes "separate from the political process and structures." Rather than rely on third-party authority for enforcement, we argue that in a properly designed social contract, there exists sufficient self-policing conventions.

As stated earlier, with political processes where exit options are limited, there has to be a greater degree of concern for the abuse of citizens by their own leaders. If a firm is not well-managed (such as when managers try and enrich themselves at the expense of shareholders and customers, and prevent a takeover bid), the damage is specific to shareholders and customers. In any case, both shareholders and customers can "exit" the firm by selling their shares (albeit at a loss) and customers can buy from competitors. However, such abuse-reducing options are not available within the political process where switching is not simple. In other words, when citizens attempt to change their condition by supporting an alternative political structure, further abuses can be visited on them. Cousins (2002) points out that the fast-track land redistribution program in Zimbabwe has been accompanied by authoritarian assault by ZANU-PF on the opposition (including sitting MPs), white farmers, and ordinary villagers.

All governments prefer to reveal less rather than more information about their activities. The difference between autocratic and democratic governments lies in the fact that the latter have incentives to reveal some information when institutions are strong. Increased information (more transparency) tends to reduce the ability of those in power to shape policy that ensures that they always retain power. Lack of transparency can be a very powerful tool in limiting both corruption and mistakes by the government. Often times, governments present many arguments for continued secrecy that may not be justified. Drawing from information economics, one can view secrecy as an artificially created scarcity of information, giving rise to rents that are sometimes appropriated by corruption (selling information). With so much secrecy or asymmetries information, checks on the behavior of politicians by ordinary people must necessarily be very limited even in a democracy. The extent of these information asymmetries is more severe under dictatorships, liberalized autocracies or monarchies. In these societies, contestability of the political process (if any) is heavily circumscribed and tends to produce what Joseph (2002: 5) calls "*democracy as presentability*" (looks like the real thing but is not). An understanding of information economics in political processes means that reforms of any kind have to address the construction of a social contract where information availability is made possible by laws and institutions.

The role of the state in situations without asymmetries of information has been related to pursuing issues related to distribution. Redistribution issues naturally focus on income streams that accrue to owners of land, capital, labor, and other identifiable resource inputs. When scarcity is the only informational problem, then fundamental theorems of welfare economies lead us to believe that there will be a Pareto-efficient resource allocation of resources through competitive behavior, provided there exists appropriate lump-sum redistributions. The two fundamental theorems provide support for the reliance on the competitive market (first theorem) and the belief that redistribution (equity) can be separated from matters related to efficiency (second theorem). Such a convenient separation allows the economist to focus exclusively on efficiency regardless of their impact on redistribution.

In cases when society has found distributional consequences of a policy unacceptable, economists would simply advise a redistribution of income (via taxes for example) rather than a redistribution of resources. Admittedly, even economists at the World Bank and elsewhere found this separation unworkable. For example, economists have found support for a one-time distribution of assets (land in this case) in imperfect markets to be associated with higher levels of economic growth (Aghion et al. 1999). In some cases, economists have found that inequality in the distribution of land ownership is associated with lower subsequent growth (World Bank Development Report 2001; Deininger and Squire 1998; Deininger et al. 2000). This view is closely associated with the World Bank that has had to shift its focus towards support for land reform since the mid-1970s. In general, there exists a large body of empirical evidence that points to redistributive land reform as partly responsible for reductions in poverty, increases in efficiency, and being a basis for sustained growth.

It is just as well that economists have often adopted policy prescriptions that run counter to neoclassical welfare economics because it turns out that none of these theorems are particularly relevant to real economies, more so in developing economies characterized by huge informational asymmetries. Information economics recognizes that issues of efficiency and equity cannot be separated. With imperfect or incomplete information, the major source of market failure is *agency problems*, which depend on the distribution of wealth (economics) or the distribution of political power (political processes). Thus, the second welfare theorem that allows for separation of equity and efficiency cannot be true.

A Self policing Social Contract based on Mutual Consent

Given the perilous state of SSA economies, what alternative approaches can be brought to bear on necessary social, economic, and political reforms? Problems related to this question are essentially an invitation to discuss problems of justice, inequality, poverty and the very issue of life itself. Borrowing from English history, the call for reform, especially the type of reforms supported by Whigs, underpins calls for economic and political freedom, thrift, self-help, and equality of opportunity. The enemies of reforms are found both on the left and on the right of the political spectrum. The left supports a larger government, which has a tendency to create a too dependent citizenry, while the right tends to back arbitrary governments and dictators plus the plum of ancient privilege.

John Rawls' *Theory of Justice* is referred to by economists within welfare economics or social choice theory but hardly in a broad study of growth and development. Perhaps, such neglect is due to the fact that most economists concern themselves with efficiency and less about justice and inequality. However, in SSA, the lack of progress in all fronts requires an interdisciplinary approach if we are to contribute to the discussions on economic, social, and political reforms that are now being deemed necessary to promote growth, transparency, poverty alleviation, and so forth. In most developing countries, market failures are more widespread than in developed countries. Market failures are often associated with informational problems. For instance, one of the determinants of growth is the acquisition of knowledge—a particular *form* of information.

It is particularly important to examine Rawls' original contribution rather than his revised views on justice. He traces his philosophical influence through Locke, Rousseau, and Kant. Rawls tried to establish ideal principles of justice to be used as standards for comparison in evaluating society. These standards are determined by abstract contemplation, *independently* of how society is currently constituted and its historical experience. In other words, his approach assumed that any society could arrive at the ideal condition by neglecting their history, culture and whatever means that society achieved its current state. The social contract tradition goes way before Hobbes but it was in Hobbes's *Leviathan* that the notion of a social contract acquired its modern form. He conceived of a state of nature as being very unpleasant indeed: "the war of all against all" in which life is "solitary, poor, nasty, brutish, and short." As a viable alternative, he saw the voluntary surrender by all of their rights and liberties into the hands of an absolute sovereign.

Rawlsian theory dispenses with the state of nature by use of the *original position* as a substitute. The metaphor of the original position is used by Rawls to make judgments about how a just society would be organized. Members of society are asked to think in abstract about the social contract to which they would agree to if their current roles in society were concealed from behind a *veil of ignorance*. Those with such limited information, the distribution of advantage in the planned society would be determined as if by lottery. The idea being that a social contract agreed to in such an original position would be "fair" since any individual could as well end up with the lottery ticket that puts them at the rear in that future society. While Rawls' original position has a metaphysical ring to it, we can discard that portion and put in its place, the *current status quo* of that society.

There are three advantages with such an approach. First we can integrate common understandings, conventions, culture and whatever else embodies a society. In other words, we can use these common understandings to define a social contract that is self-policing. It is conventions plus such concepts as *ubuntu, ubukhosi, isintu* and the like, rather than some central authority charged with enforcement. Second a stable social contract (*equilibrium* as defined below) is supported by common conventions which are part of the current status quo and these have the effect of reducing asymmetries in information in the economic and political processes. Third, any reforms aimed at getting a better social contract are likely to resist attempts by either Left or Right to hijack the process. A rather useful approach is to have the current status quo as the state of nature that includes a society's history, culture, conventions, and other common understandings.

The truth about society is much more complex than either the Left or Right are willing to admit. Society is bound together by common understandings. The Right recognizes conventional arrangements, especially those related to private morality, the preservation and transfer of property rights. The central idea is that given a society's currently dominant but slippery system of conventions, the enjoyment of such property rights is simply due to the fact nobody with the power to do so has sufficient incentive to take away such comforts. For progress to be made, it is necessary for the affluent to appreciate that their freedom to enjoy what their "property rights" supposedly secure is actually contingent on the willingness of the less affluent to recognize such "rights." The common understandings that govern current behavior are *constructs* which can be *reconstructed.* Invoking some game theory, all individuals in any society are players in the game of life, with divergent aims and aspirations that make conflict inevitable. In a healthy society, the balance between different aims and aspirations is struck so that benefits of cooperation are not lost in civil conflicts, tribal wars, or in the worst case, genocide. Borrowing from game theorists, such an outcome is termed equilibrium. Whether we are discussing *homo sapiens* or *homo economicus*, the concept is similar.

The maintenance of such equilibrium requires the existence of commonly understood conventions about how behavior is to be coordinated. It is such a system of coordinating conventions that is identified by a *social contract.* The task is for society to examine a whole class of social contracts that are feasible for a society, and to consider whether one of these may not be an improvement on the current social contract. The Left support reforms but do not understand that there is a feasibility constraint. Thus, they argue for social contracts that are not feasible because such utopian contracts are not in equilibrium. They are unstable social contracts that require propping by force including political coercion or military force. The Right often understands the need for stability but without the need for necessary reforms—thus, their social contracts prevent society from choosing a better one via *mutual consent.* Any society can fruitfully use markets whenever these are appropriate, but a society that relies *only on markets* as a basis for social contracts leaves much of its potential unfulfilled. Olson (1996, 2000) also makes this point in reference to the limits of economic growth.

If one takes the state of nature to be society's current status quo, then one must abandon Hobbes' very conservative estimate of what is available or what is not a social contract. Instead of having only one feasible viable social contract alternative to a Hobbesian state of nature, we argue that there exists a wide class of social contracts among which a choice can be made. The task for a reformist is that of seeking a new social contract to which society can be shifted to by *mutual consent* and maintained by conventions. A natural question arises as to how to arrive at mutual consent? As in neoclassical economics, we assume that individuals, communities, or citizens consent to reforms only if it is in their *enlightened self-interest.* For those who don't consent, one might use the convenient device of an original position and have them imagine themselves as behind the veil of ignorance. Individuals will not be asked to assume they have forgotten how society is organized at present, that is, the current state of nature. They will only be asked to imagine that their fellow citizens don't know their current roles in society and to envision what new social contracts would be commonly agreed to under such an equalizing assumption. It is this social contract that forms the basis of reform.

Game theory usually assumes that *homo economicus*/player or an economic agent is defined by his preferences and subjective beliefs (Hobbes calls these passion and experience). With these in place, an economist is usually ready to predict *homo economicus*' behavior in the economic sphere. But Hobbes' list of characteristics of individuals is a little longer and this part also turns out to be very controversial: the strength of body and the manner of reasoning. Hobbes' strength of body reflects what an individual can or cannot do, that is, game theory is equivalent to the rule of the game and also speaks to what should not be included in those rules. The characteristic of reason refers to the assumption often made in economics that all players are rational. In explanations related to methods by which cooperative outcomes may be sustained as *equilibria in repeated games*, the quote from Hume is in order:

> I learn to do service to another, without bearing him any real kindness: because I foresee, that he will return my service, in expectation of another of the same kind, and in order to maintain the same correspondence of good offices with me or others. And accordingly, after I have serv'd him and he is in possession of the advantage arising from my action, he induc'd to perform his part, as foreseeing the consequences of his refusal.

As far back as the 18th century, Hume seemed to understand that the consequences of refusal to carry out one's side of the arrangement would result in punishment of that party (conventions as means of self-policing). The punishment could range from refusal to deal with that party in the future to disapproval by those whose respect is necessary to maintain one's status in that community. In fact, nothing excludes punishment by the judiciary in cases of a legal contract. There is no contradiction with the basic requirements here that all social contracts arrived at by mutual consent should be self-policing.

Legal contracts and the institution of the judiciary are simply well-codified conventions of that society that reflect the concepts of *ubuntu, ubukhosi, isintu* and similar notions. The police and judiciary are charged with the duty of enforcing laws that a society formally enacts. Officials who believe themselves to be above the law may be persuaded to recognize the fact that society would cease to work in the long run if the duties assigned to them were not compatible with their own individual incentives. This case represents the inevitable process by means of which bureaucracies gradually cease to operate in the interests of those they were designed to serve, and instead end up serving the interests of bureaucrats only. In both economic and political processes, asymmetries of information are the rule rather than the exception. In the case of African countries (applicable to similar countries), politicians continue to neglect the welfare of those they represent to get into office. Often times, corrupt officials deny the charge of corruption. Instead, they may argue that they are merely following customary practices of their professions—now made acceptable by time and tradition. It is the corruption of institutions that perhaps is the greatest danger to African society and leads to failure on identifiable aggregates of interest such as economic growth, poverty alleviation, equity, sustainable development and health provision.

For any viable society bound by a social contract, it is necessary for it to be always in equilibrium including all institutions that mediate power relations. In other words, the system as a whole must be self-enforcing. The glue that holds society is the requirement that we guard each other so that self-enforcement of the contract is evidenced. The discussion of everyone guarding each other invokes familiar images of authoritarian states with oppressive secret agents in dark-glasses. This might well be the case, because nothing about being in equilibrium says that such equilibrium reflects adherence to democracy, human rights and other properties that enhance life. Even dictatorships and whatever form of government exists, need to be in equilibrium if they are to survive. Hobbes states that "the power of the mighty hath no foundation but in the opinion and belief of the people." His clarity on such political realities has been obscured only by his insistence that, without a sovereign to coordinate things, equilibrium would necessarily fall apart. The fact that he saw only one alternative form of a social contract as opposed to a wide range of possibilities, undermines his contribution to institutional reforms. However, given the times in which he lived, the sovereign as a viable coordinator of society is understandable.

The authority of presidents, kings, judges, police, and the army is just a matter of convention and habit. The fact that modern states with elaborate constitutions, judges, moral codes, pomp, and extra-legal forces, including renegades exist in SSA should not blind us to this simple fact. Laws, directives, decrees and whatever else are simply devices that help to coordinate an equilibrium which may or may not be stable. Although coordination under these circumstances may require that our social contract assigns leading roles to certain individuals, the power we lend to them remains in our collective hands, and often times in SSA, corrupt institutions including presidents usurp our power by continuously resorting to illegal means. Alternative theories espoused by both socialists and conservatives tend to obscure the dangers from authoritarian political systems by pretending that we can rely on some metaphysical concepts to protect us. What is needed is that all citizens guard against power accumulation by politicians or any other group. On the importance of social contracts with effective provisions against abuse of power by the ruler, Hume (1758) pointed out that in constraining any system of government and fixing the several checks and controls of the constitution, every man ought to be supposed a knave and to have no other end in all his actions than private interest.

Hume seems to suggest that unless society is careful in guarding against certain groups in society, such groups will necessarily gravitate towards positions of power (socialists, conservatives, ideologues, and any other undesirables). For example, Marx's labor theory of value states that labor provides a stop-gap measure of worthiness. In socialist utopia (after the state has withered away), the rule of their social contract was to be: from—*each according to his ability*—to—*each according to need*. The implications from attempts to implement such utopia have been a disaster in most African countries that implemented some version of the Marxist "social contract" at independence. Human nature being what it is, this social contract converted an incentive scheme designed to encourage ability in society into a needy dependent society in almost every African country that turned to this utopia at independence. For Marx, matters such as social standing, effort, ability, history and common conventions were feudal remnants to be replaced by a social contract that had no bearing to people's history or culture. Had followers of Marx simply recognized that the power structures of today evolved from power structures of the past, SSA could have put together social contracts by mutual consent and these contracts would have provided a stable foundation for institutions that today have been corrupted beyond the pale. Similarly, neo-feudal social contracts existing in developed countries have modern day versions of robber barons. Unlike their cousins from the past, the modern robber barons don't have to plunder to get tribute. Instead, capitalists contrive to pay no taxes at all, while simultaneously enjoying the public goods provided from taxes subtracted directly from the pay checks of the poor. Worse still, there are cases where the public tends to admire the robber baron's display of *noblese oblige*—cases of contributions to charity, and other contributions to development projects in rural areas (*harambee* in Kenya).

Coase (1991) was right to emphasize the importance of assigning property rights when the market mechanism was applied to new context, but the bigger issue is to recognize that setting markets is one of many ways of allocating scarce resources. Societies need not choose between the command control economy advocated by socialists and capitalist economies modeled on competitive markets that are advanced by conservatives. In pressing for reforms based on self-policing social contracts that take the current status quo as the original position, we can choose the middle path, between the Left and Right. The Left cannot deny that a stable society needs to allocate resources efficiently, and hence decisions have to be decentralized to the level where information resides. Nor can the Right pretend not to notice that a stable society needs to plan to allocate resources fairly otherwise those left out may seek a violent redress. The difficulty turns out to be that of designing such a system in countries that have many diverse groups and coalitions.

Whatever vision of society one does have, a reformist agenda will reflect the role of the market where decisions are made on spot but yet their behavior is likely to be constrained by rules that provide incentives for policy makers to choose according to an agreed plan—the social contract. Earlier, we alluded to game theory and its use by economists to predict economic behavior once preferences and subjective beliefs are known. We divide time into short, medium and long run with reference to preferences. We need to find a way of making utility comparisons. A person can sympathize with another (caring directly about that person's well-being) but they can also empathize (feel for one person but remaining indifferent to their plight). The triumph of the market simply records the effects of changing personal preferences over time and the use of the device of the original position as a fairness norm. In the short-run, both personal and empathetic preferences are fixed. In the medium run, personal preferences remain fixed while empathetic preferences adjust to negotiations necessary to arrive at any equilibrium (or bargaining).

In the long-run, all preferences are subject to change and so is technology. The importance of this lies in the fact that the market shapes personal preferences and thus completely leaches out both the culture and independence of the individuals. Put differently, those who are completely immersed in the market culture may have lost both their freedom and culture. This conclusion differs significantly from conservative claims that the market symbolizes the embodiment of true freedom. For middle of the road reformists, the market mechanism is viewed positively in that it reduces the corruption of institutions. Fairness norms of a society provide short-run resolutions to the equilibrium selection problem. For example, a despot that withholds food aid from those who support the opposition may generate so much envy from the downtrodden that they force a temporary disequilibrium—an overthrow of the despot.

Authoritarian governments or liberalized dictatorships impose severe social contracts and punish those who express the need for change harshly. In Zimbabwe, for example, food aid given by donors is used as a weapon to suppress any political processes that would result in the exit of ZANU-PF. Dictators cause so much stress on a society equilibrium that may tear that social fabric and replace it with another social contract. The tragedy is that it often takes a long time to reach a long-run equilibrium. In fact, there may be forces or coalitions of groups that may prefer a state of corruption, which enables more venality. Such is the precarious condition of both the ruled and ruler in the absence of self-policing contracts.

Olson's Model of Political Power: The Stationary Versus the Roving Bandit

Olson grappled with an important question, yet often neglected by economists—why do some economies prosper while other fail? Economists accustomed to working with rigid technical discourse of theoretical economics often find the question uninteresting. However, for economists working in development, the answers to this question are fundamental to whether Sub-Saharan Africa develops or lags behind as it has for decades. The recent emphasis by the World Bank and the IMF on "good governance" after many years of emphasizing only financial variables comes as a relief to those analysts who have argued without much success that acceptable, accountable institutions and by extension the rule of law must precede any program of economic development if SSA and other developing regions are to alleviate poverty through economic growth.

A central feature of the bandit model addresses the nature of political power, and how different types of political power promote different kinds of economic behavior. Various theorists have long thought that the rule of law must protect property rights before markets can operate fairly and efficiently. According to Olson, "if a society is to achieve its highest possible income, the incentives must not only be clear but must induce firms and individuals in the economy to interact in a socially efficient way" (Olson 2000: 1). In contrast, under Hobbesian view of anarchy under dictatorship or autocracy, where there is no restraint on those in power, rulers can and often seize individual or firm's assets for personal gain, and thus discourage trade, production and any form of incentives.

Unfortunately, most economists tend to view the relationship between growth and development, and political power through a lens, which almost invariably extends the market model through voluntary transactions. In voluntary transactions, any transaction costs that would ordinarily limit trade, development, and production are assumed away under the Coarse Theorem, which states that unless transaction costs are exorbitantly high, individuals, firms, and governments will always have an incentive to bargain and hence arrive at a socially efficient outcome. Such a view cannot explain political power by voluntary transactions since it lacks tools to bring about compulsory compliance—the idea of the capacity to coerce (Clague et al. 1999a, 1999b). In order to account for political power and at the same time provide an understanding of events in SSA and Zimbabwe in particular, it is vital that we focus on the incentives and inducements to rational and self-interested action that confronts those with political power.

Olson (1993) has identified institutional structures and incentives that appeal not only to producers and consumers but also to political power as well. His model begins with a metaphor, presenting the example of a stationary bandit whose goal is to maximize the proceeds of theft from the area she/he controls. This type of bandit has an interest in the continued prosperity of his targets, which could be citizens in the country, or commercial farmers and industry, if only to extract more wealth from them. The stationary bandit has an *encompassing interest* similar to that of a drug kingpin that has monopoly in a particular neighborhood. In the limit, the stationary bandit might become the "government" and thus impose taxes on his victims. However, the bandit has an incentive to reduce his "tax rate" as an incentive to production and trade. Furthermore, the bandit has an incentive to supply public goods to those he steals from up to a point where the marginal gains, for example tax revenue equals the marginal cost of providing such public goods (Olson 1993, 1996).

The other type of bandit is the roving bandit. This bandit has no reason *not* to steal 100 percent of whatever is targeted because he/she can always move to fresh targets without concern for the wealth status of their victims. The roving bandit's self-interest is borne by his own cost-benefit analysis based on self-interest. Unlike the stationary bandit, the roving bandit has no stack in the prosperity of society but incurs higher costs if he does not steal everything from both firms and individuals. If political power carries with it coercive capabilities of a roving bandit, then we can infer that such a bandit is likely to have a very *narrow interest*. A roving bandit's territory ensures that any gain or loss to society due to his banditry is not a factor in his calculus since there is always some other group that he can rob.

The criminal metaphor underlines political power in that governments of a large group of people arise because of the rational self-interest of those who have the greatest skill for organizing violence. Thus, the stationary bandit can usually claim that their people would want them to rule, which is usually a false assumption that their power is derived from voluntary choice. To be clear, citizens might prefer a stationary bandit to a roving bandit who might usher in some form of Hobbesian anarchy that undermines order, production, and tax rates. Although the rule of a stationary bandit might seem better than that of the roving bandit, it does not arise out of a voluntary contract or social contract that is any way related to the traditions and customs of the citizens. The improvement (economic growth, trade, public goods, and predictable taxes) over Hobbes's "war of all against all" due to the stationary bandit's autocratic rule is no evidence of the bandit's benevolence but rather an outcome of chance.

To be sure, no citizens of any country like either bandit but there is always preference of the stationary over the roving bandit in the absence of voluntary choice—the better the devil you know syndrome. All considered, citizens might choose to live under political tyranny of the stationary bandit than to be subject to the roving bandit(s). If we assume that the thieves and bandits are alike, in that they are only concerned with what they can extract from their subjects, then how could one form of predacious behavior be preferred over the other? As already indicated, the stationary bandit will have preference for economic growth because such a policy allows him to generate more tax revenues later. In fact, it is likely that the stationary bandit will transform himself into the provision of public goods, and promote the social welfare of his subjects and the good order of society for the purposes of maximizing tax revenues. So far the argument simply states that *autocracy is better than anarchy* (Olson 1982, 2000).

We have not considered the importance of time in banditry. Just as the roving bandit can over time settle down into a stationary bandit with all the trappings of political power, the reverse is true. A stationary bandit who perceives a short time frame in power can become a roving bandit with all the attendant consequences. Such reversals in the stature of a bandit have serious consequences for both individuals and firms in that society. In the case of stationary to roving bandit, investment, savings, economic growth, capital, loan contracts and property rights that seemed secure are seriously undermined. Economic performance under the bandit model can never be secure unless we can guarantee that the bandit has a very long time frame. In other words, autocratic governments tend to produce incentives for other roving bandits to appear because there exists no institutions that can limit their political power.

Suppose a democratic government rules solely in the interests of the majority that perpetually keeps them in power. In other words, the majority exploits the minority just like the tyrant has in exploiting all subjects. Under this scenario, *democracy is preferred to autocracy, which in turn is preferred to anarchy*. The reasoning here being that even a predatory democracy has a government that is more encompassing than a tyranny. The logic of this result comes from the fact that the majority in whose interests the government rules must pay a share of taxes that finance redistribution in its direction. This is because the majority benefits directly from rising incomes and indirectly through redistribution of wealth, and finally through the provision of public goods. Thus, the incentives that guide a tyrant work more powerfully the bigger the majority in whose interests the government rules. The economic performance of democracies tends to be better, in part, because they offer the most reliable long-term security for contract and property rights once a voluntary social contract (in Sub-Saharan Africa's case) is constructed from a series of sub-social contracts of diverse ethnic groups that are negotiated using the concepts of *ubuntu*, *ubukhosi*, and *isintu*.

Constitutions with checks and balances requiring super majorities for certain actions leads to less suppression of minority interests and greater supply of public goods. All these beneficial outcomes depend crucially on the assumption that voters act not out of concern for the greater good but out of pure self-interest. In terms of the language used earlier, social contracts based on reciprocity tend to be more stable than those based on coercion or fear. If this argument is correct, then democracy based on voluntary social contracts makes sense even in poor countries. In other words, it removes the standard response by despots that democracy is a luxury only rich countries can afford (Olson 2000, 1996).

Evidence shows that socialist economies tend to fall victim to stagnation and corruption as managers of large parastatals (nationalized firms) begin to collude in order to skim off part of the bandit's take (stationary or roving), diverting state property to their own. Zimbabwe's parastatals have suffered this fate in recent years as large-scale corruption has proceeded unchecked because the social contract has become unenforceable. In Zimbabwe as elsewhere, the survival of economically useless but powerful parastatals poses the greatest danger to the economy. The stationary bandit/roving bandit model points to the need for self-policing social contracts as necessary foundations to promote good governance, minimize corruption, and promote economic growth. However, the existence of autocrats like Mugabe, Moseveni and Ghadafi, or their vanquished counterparts (Mobutu, Moi and Banda) cannot be fully understood in economic terms. Ideology in addition to maximizing wealth may be required to understand the world of politics. What is not an issue here is that the failure to safeguard contractual and property rights might spring from a ruler's lack of sufficiently encompassing interest and the absence of democracy—all these shortcomings serve to narrow the ruler's interest to simply the need to survive in office.

Democracy can emerge from this bandit model of criminal behavior under certain conditions. Clearly, the conditions that lead to more bandits (autocrats) have to be absent. However, since banditry is very lucrative, the emergence of democracy in this setting would require that those who stage coups would have to be concentrated in entities such as the army or party officials (Dahl 1989). However, there are additional conditions that are necessary for the emergence of democracy besides the plural dispersion of power. In the case of groups that might contend for power, it is important that these groups be dispersed across a wide area or activities so as to reduce the probability of small autocracies forming possible coup leaders. The emergence of democracy essentially requires power sharing but does not guarantee mutually advantageous trades or voluntary exchange as implied by those who believe that market failure can be remedied by an appeal to the Coarse Theorem (Coase 1937, 1960).

Thus, for society to rid itself of banditry and usher in a democracy requires third-party enforcement of contracts. Such enforcement of contracts is in the common interest of citizens including bandits or autocrats. The mechanism for defining and protecting property rights, enforcing contracts, and resolving conflicts requires the establishment of a court system staffed by personnel that have no personal stake or interest in the dispute at hand (Olson 2000: 35). However, if the existing social contract (defined by the autocrat) is such that the autocrat has control of the courts and the judiciary, those judges and other parts of the government can only adjudicate in favor of the autocrat (McGuire and Olson 1996). In such circumstances, it does not matter what the autocrat calls the government of the day (democratic, socialist, communist), it is clear that there is no third-party enforcement of contracts (Kroll 1988). Under this structure, there can be no meaningful attempts at economic growth, sustainable development or land reform. The reform approach we have suggested here relies on recognition of informational asymmetries in political-economic processes.

Conclusion

The reasons why the reconstruction of the social contract in SSA is a necessary condition for economic development is the recognition that individuals, groups of individuals, and firms within a society have two ways of enriching themselves. First, they can perform an economic activity such as producing goods and services that consumers are willing to pay for. The second alternative is simply to acquire wealth from others, usually by extra-judicial means. To encourage the former and discourage the latter requires institutions that channel human activities towards productive activities. Institutions are laws, social norms, traditions, religious beliefs, and other rules of behavior that provide incentives that guide behavior. Economic failures such as hunger, poverty, wars, and unemployment are a result of "institutions" based on either alien or utopian social contracts that give people incentives to behave in a destructive rather than a constructive manner. This chapter points to an alternative basis for social contracts in SSA that is more likely to result in institutions that enhance economic growth and welfare.

The reform approach we have suggested relies on recognition of informational asymmetries in political-economic processes. These asymmetries can be reduced by designing a self-policing contract that is arrived at by mutual consent and policed by an appeal to common understandings, conventions that reflect concepts such as *isintu*, *ubuntu*, and *ubukhosi*. Since independence from colonial powers, many countries in Africa have experimented with a variety of "social contracts" defined and imposed by nationalists of one stripe or the other. In fact, most of these "social contracts" deliberately undermined all institutions that previously acted as checks on agents (the government) by the principal (the people). This was partly carried through limiting information about most activities. The centralization of power by the Left and the suppression of freedom of speech by both the Right and Left meant that issues related to growth and development took a back seat to the need to retain power by the elite. Often ideologies, have defined the existing "social contracts" that have provided the political-economic context under which various economic programs have been conducted.

The Left supports reforms but does not understand that there is a feasibility constraint. Thus, it argues for social contracts that are not feasible because such utopian contracts are not in equilibrium. They are unstable social contracts that require propping by force or political coercion or military force. The Right often understands the need for stability but without the need for necessary reforms—thus, their social contracts prevent society from choosing a better one via *mutual consent*. Any society can fruitfully use markets whenever these are appropriate, but a society that relies *only on markets* as social contracts leaves much of its potential unfulfilled. Olson (1996, 2000) also makes this point in reference to the limits of economic theory.

Olson's model of the stationary versus roving bandit is suitable for the analysis of Zimbabwe. Since the bandits can either be a roving bandit (with a narrow interest) or stationary bandit (with encompassing interest), policies towards land reform point to a roving bandit (an autocrat) who perceives a short time planning horizon. Thus, one would expect the party elites and the well connected to "privatize" state land through sponsored "war veterans" occupations. At a stroke, they can destroy for personal gain, the livelihoods of thousands of farm laborers and their families dependent on commercial farms.

The truth about society is much more complex than either the Left or Right are willing to admit. Society is bound together by common understandings. The Right recognizes conventional arrangements, especially those related to private morality, the preservation and transfer of property rights. The central idea is that given a society's currently dominant but slippery system of conventions, the enjoyment of such property rights is simply due to the fact that nobody with the power to do so has sufficient incentive to take away such comforts. For progress to be made, it is necessary for the affluent to appreciate that their freedom to enjoy what their "property rights" supposedly secure is actually contingent on the willingness of the less affluent to recognize such "rights." The common understandings that govern current behavior are constructs, which can be reconstructed. Invoking some game theory, all individuals in any society are players in the game of life, with divergent aims and aspirations that make conflict inevitable. In a healthy society, the balance between different aims and aspirations is struck so that benefits of cooperation are not lost in civil conflicts, tribal wars, or in the worst case, genocide. Borrowing from game theorists, such an outcome is termed equilibrium. The citizens of Sub-Saharan Africa deserve no less.

References

Aghion, P., Caroli, E., and Garcia-Penalosa, C. (1999). 'Inequality and Economic Growth: The Perspective of the New Growth Theories.' *Journal of Economic Literature* 37: 1615–1660.

Akerlof, George A. (1970). "The Market for "Lemons:" Quality Uncertainty and the Market Mechanism." *Quarterly Journal of Economics* 84 (03): 488–500.

Clague, C., Keefer, P., Knack, S. and Olson, M. (1999). Property and Contract Rights in Autocracies and Democracies. *Journal of Economic Growth* 1(2): 243–276.

Clague, C., Keefer, P., Knack, S. and Olson, M. (1999). *Contract Intensive Money*: Contra Enforcement, Property Rights and Economic Performance. *Journal of Economic Growth* 4: 185–211.

Coase, Ronald (1937). The Nature of the Firm. *Economica*: 386–405.

Coase, Ronald (1960). *The Problem of Social Cost. Journal of Law and Economics* 3:1–44.

Coase, Ronald (1991). *Essays on Economics and Economists*. Chicago: University of Chicago Press.

Cousins, B. (2002). "*Comments*" on Land Reform Policy in Sub-Saharan Africa: Consensus and Controversy, World Bank.

Dahl, A.R. (1989). "The Level of Democratization Related to Socioeconomic Variables in 147 States in 1980–85." *Scandinavian Political Studies* 12(2): 95–127.

Deininger, K. and May, J. (2001). *Is there scope for growth with equity? The case of Land Reform in South Africa.* The World Bank, Washington DC

Deininger, K. and Squire, L. (1998). "New ways of looking at Old Issues: Inequality and Growth." *Journal of Development Studies*, 57(2): 257–285.

Deininger, K., van den Brink, R., Hoogoveen, H. and Moyo, S (2000). "How land reform can contribute to economic growth and poverty reduction: empirical evidence from international and Zimbabwean experience." *SARIPS*. April 2000.

Englebert, Pierre (2000). *State Legitimacy and Development in Africa*. Reinner, Boulder, London.

Hoogeveen, J.G.M. and Kinsey, B.H. (2001). Land Reform, Growth and Equity: Emerging Evidence from Zimbabwe's Resettlement Programme: A Sequel. *Journal of Southern African Studies* 27(1): 127–136.

Hume, David (1739). *A Treatise of Human Nature*. Reprinted in 1978 by Clarendon Press, Oxford

Hume, David (1748) An Enquiry Concerning Human Understanding. Reprinted in Warburton, N. ed. (1998) *Philosophy: The Classics*. London: Routledge.

Hume, David (1985). "Of the first principles of government." In E. Miller, ed., *Essays Moral, Political and Literary*, Part 1. Indianapolis IN: Liberty Classics.

ICG (2002). "Zimbabwe: The Politics of National Liberation and International Division." *Africa Report*, Number 52, Harare/Brussels, October 17, 2002.

Joseph, R. (2002). Smart Partnerships for African Development: A New Strategic Framework: A Special Report. Washington DC: United States Institute of Peace.

Kroll, Heidi (1988). "The Role of Contracts in the Soviet Economy". *Soviet Studies* 40: 349–366.

McGuire, M. and Olson, M. (1996). "The Economics of Autocracy and Majority Rule: The Invisible Hand and the Use of Force". *Journal of Economic Literature*: 72–96.

Olson, Mancur (2000). *Power and Prosperity: Outgrowing Communist and Capitalist Dictatorships*. New York: Basic Books.

Olson, Mancur (1982). *The Rise and Decline of Nations: Economic Growth, Stagflation and Social Rigidities*. New Haven: Yale University Press.

Olson, Mancur (1993). "Dictatorship, Democracy, Democracy and Development". *American Political Science Review* 87(3): 567–576.

Olson, Mancur (1996). *Big Bills Left on the Sidewalk: Why Some Nations are Rich, and Others Poor* 10(2): 3–24.

Rawls, J. (1972). *A Theory of Justice*. Oxford: Oxford University Press

Rawls, J. (1958). "Justice as fairness," *Philosophical Review*, 57: 185–187.

Sandbrook, R. (2000). *Closing the Circle: Democratization and Development in Africa*. Toronto: Zed Books Ltd.

Stiglitz, Joseph E. (2002.) "Information and the Change in the Paradigm in Economics." *American Economic Review*, June: 460–501.

Thompson, W. S. (1999). *A Review* of *The Singapore Story: Memoirs of Lee Kuan Yew*, by Lee Kuan Yew 1998. Englewood, N.J.: Prentice Hall College Division.

World Bank (2002). *Financing for Sustainable Development*. http://www.worldbank.org/deforum/forum_financing.html.

World Bank (1997). *World Bank Report: The State in a Changing World*. New York: Oxford University Press.

Chapter 4

Left in the Ditch: Africa and the Dialectics of Globalization

Kwame A. Ninsin

Introduction

During the last several decades, the revolution in information and communications technology has enabled global capital to intensify its worldwide expansion at an unprecedented rate, and with much greater force. In particular, nations of the developing world have been forcefully brought under the undisputed hegemony of global capital. This new worldwide movement is generally described as "globalization" (Ohmae 1995; Guehenno 1997; Hirst 1997, and Rosenau 1997). As economic and political processes, globalization is generally perceived as a movement toward a universal rational order—capitalism and democracy. The development crisis facing poor nations is explained in terms of this dominant development paradigm, and the prescribed remedy is couched in this ideology of universal rationality—namely, the pursuit of liberalism, which would allegedly enable the weak economies of the world to establish free-market economies within a democratic environment. Globalization is multi-dimensional and has several distinguishing features, including unprecedented global financial flows; deterritorialization and privatization of production; increasing integration of the discrete economies of the rest of the world into the global capitalist economy in accordance with the logic of the new international division of labour; revolutionary changes in communication and information systems, and the triumphal spread of liberal democracy worldwide. The upshot is the so-called "global village" in which the entire world will be governed by a common rationality.

In this chapter, I argue that the global village is structured on unequal power relations in which the weaker nations are mere cogs in the global accumulation processes. In particular, the nations of Africa have been reduced to appendages with no capacity to function even as compradors in global transactions. The rich and powerful nations that rule the world have employed two strategies to secure undisputed hegemony. First, they have employed economic and ideological tools to undermine the material (economic and ideological) base (capacity/autonomy) of their nation-states. Second, the hegemons of the world have used naked military power to destroy the existing state and reconstitute it under their control. In the first instance, they have acted indirectly through the International Financial Institutions (IFIs). In the second instance, they have exploited the exigencies of threats posed by states such as those under the Taliban regime of Afghanistan, al-Qaeda terrorist forces, and Saddam Hussein's regime in Iraq to unleash military attacks to destroy the existing state and replace it with one whose ideological orientation is consistent with that of capitalism and liberal democracy. In either case, the aim is to produce a state that lacks the autonomy and the material means to defend its citizens against threats to their security, which contradicts the prevailing global consensus that affirms the sovereign responsibility of the state to guarantee its citizens protection "against threats to life, health, livelihood, personal safety and human dignity" (The International Commission on Intervention and Sovereignty 2000). The first strategy has been employed against Africa to (i) weaken the already fragile economies of the continent, and (ii) transform the existing state into an agent of global capital, rather than the instrument for sustainable national development and the guarantor of the well-being and security of its citizens. Even though globalization is being touted as a blessing, bringing unprecedented economic growth and opulence to the world, in Africa its effect has not been entirely salutary.

I first analyze the negative effect of globalization on Africa's economies. I argue that Africa's economies have been reduced to *bantustans* in the global economy while its vital resources are plundered leaving it hopelessly impoverished. A *bantustanized* economy is drained of its material and human resources, leaving it almost destitute, and with just enough material means to provide basic subsistence, often primitive livelihoods, to its people. This section is followed by an outline and analysis of the effect of global policies on the African state. I argue that the intensity of control and plunder impoverishes and destroys the institutional and ideological basis of the affected nation-states, and deepens their dependence on the developed world as virtual beggars. The section further dilates on how the African state has lost the capacity to exercise effective autonomy even in its domestic affairs; and how it has become a *captured state* employed by foreign interests to pursue their global projects of economic and political domination. I conclude that Africa could successfully respond to this renewed threat to its identity and development through political union, driven by its new generation of political and economic elites and the network of Pan African social movements that has emerged since the 1980s.

Africa's *Bantustanized* Economies

Throughout its history, capitalism has expanded worldwide in its bid to control the accumulation process in other nations and subordinate their social goals to its own purposes (Polyani 1944, cited in Leys 1996: 94–95; 194–95). Colonization and under development was a phase in this global logic of capitalism. Since colonial times, Africa's relations with the capitalist nations of the world have been defined by capital's incessant attempts to control its internal accumulation processes and social purposes on the one hand, and the continent's counter-attempts to reverse such global expansion and control, and re-subject the capitalist market to its own social purposes. With the rapid expansion of the capitalist market since the 1970s this dialectical relationship between global capital and Africa has intensified with devastating effects. And so have attempts to reign in capital. This period coincided with the sharp deterioration in Africa's position in the world economy. For example, while global financial flows—especially foreign direct investments (FDI), and trade have grown at a phenomenal rate since the beginning of the 1980s (Castells 2000: 102–106; 116–120), Africa's share in these massive global financial and trade transactions has been infinitesimal; in fact, it has declined (United Nations Conference on Trade and Development, UNCTAD 1998:183; Alia El Mahdi et al. 2002: 4–5).

In two crucial segments of Africa's external economic transactions —foreign direct investment and trade—the continent has fared abysmally. An UNCTAD study in 2000 of foreign direct investment practices in Africa found that Multi-National Corporations (MNCs) are reluctant to invest in Africa's smaller economies and in her globally integrated industries such as textiles, mechanical and electrical industries. And even though the success of privatization has become a determinant of FDI in Africa, a handful of countries have actually benefited from the vigorous pursuit of privatization during the last decade. Between 1990 and 1998 the main recipients of FDIs were South Africa [US$1.38 billion]; Ghana [US$778.0 million]; Nigeria [US$500.0 million]; Zambia [US$420.0 million]; and Côte d'Ivoire [US$373.0 million]. These FDI were concentrated mainly in the mining (including oil) and communications sectors. In 2000, for example, net external flows to the continent fell from US$27.3 billion in 1999 to US$26.3 billion. Again, very few countries benefited. In 1999, Angola, Nigeria, South Africa, Morocco, Mozambique and Tunisia—countries that are mostly oil exporters—were the beneficiaries; which is to say that FDIs in Africa were attracted mainly into the mining sector. In general, capital inflows have continued to decline despite accession to the enhanced Highly Indebted Poor Countries (HIPC) initiative by a number of African countries. It is true that under the HIPC initiative 26 countries of this group have enjoyed enhanced financial relief that has enabled investment in such key sectors as health and education. At the same time capital inflows to the 53 very poor and highly indebted African countries as a whole has declined from $6.2 billion in 1998 to $4.3 billion in 2000—a drop of about 40 percent (http://www.jubileeresearch.org/analysis/reports/G8final.pdf.). To compound the problem of capital shortage, capital transfers from Africa during the same period (1999 and 2000) increased from US$5.4 billion to US$8.3 billion—a massive increase of 53 percent—resulting in dire consequences for African governments, which depend precariously on external borrowing for development. Meanwhile, the "loan pushers"—the World Bank and IMF—have continued to push them to contract more loans. For example, the Bank alone granted Uganda a $2 billion loan in 2000 and $1.1 billion to the Democratic Republic of Congo in 2001 despite the fact that these countries and many more in Africa carry a debt burden that is not sustainable and threatens any attempt at social development (see http://www.jubileeresearch.org/analysis/reports/G8final.pdf).

For some time now, the greatest threat to Africa's development comes from the debt overhang. To underscore the devastating social impact of Africa's external debt, the All Africa Conference of Churches, in 1999, described Africa's debt burden as "a new form of slavery as vicious as the (trans-Atlantic) slave trade" (Africa Policy Information Center, 1999). In the 1980–1990 decade the continent's external debt grew at 7.6

percent per annum. The rate of growth per annum abated considerably in 1991–1999 to 1.7 percent. Overall, the continent's total external debt stood at US$350 billion in 1998. Currently debt service per annum is about US$13 billion. Compared to the rest of the developing world, Africa's external debt, estimated at 16.0 per cent of the total debt of all developing countries, appears less problematic. But it is the heaviest in per capita terms and in terms of their capacity to service that debt. When indicators such as debt/GDP, debt/goods and services exports, and debt service/goods and services exports ratios, are taken into account, Africa's debt burden becomes unbearable and immoral. For example, Ethiopia's debt of $10.6 billion at the end of 1996 was 13 times its earnings, compelling a country that is already poor to spend 45 percent of its export earnings to service its debt. When debt repayment to Northern financial institutions and governments takes precedence over the social responsibility of *sovereign governments* towards their people, the result is a social crisis of criminal proportions. The danger is that this debt situation will continue to worsen; it will place the continent in permanent bondage to the North—northern governments and IFIs. This will destroy the capacity of governments to pursue their nation-building agendas. Hence, according to a report by the United Nations Secretary General on the Millennium Development Goals,[1] Africa has made little or no progress in eradicating poverty. Between 1990 and 1999 the number of poor people increased by over six million. At current trends Africa is the only continent in the world where the number of poor people in 2015 will be higher than in 1990. At a recent conference of African Ministers of Finance, Planning and Economic Development, a similar concern was expressed about the development crisis that has plunged the continent into a severe social crisis. They stated that, with the rate of economic growth in Africa slowing from 4.3 percent in 2001 to 3.2 percent in 2002, the number of people living with HIV/AIDS at a staggering 29.4 million, the number of people living in absolute poverty at 380 million, and armed conflict in several countries depressing growth and reversing positive trends in human development, they are very concerned at the poor state of economic and social conditions in Africa.

The continent's development crisis is also the result of its weak position in global trade. Two aspects of this weakness may be highlighted. First, while global trade has exploded since the 1980s, Africa's share has been infinitesimal. Exports from Sub-Saharan Africa, especially, grew at an annual average of five percent during 1985–1990, but fell sharply to zero growth rate during the 1990–1995 period. The decline amounted to as much as 50 percent between 1985 and 1995 (from approximately four percent in 1985 to about two percent in 1995) of the whole of Africa's share of world merchandise exports (El Mahdi et al. 2002: 4–5). Because of the continent's external dependence, the contribution of external trade to the GDP is substantial compared with other regions of the world. In 1990 the ratio of extra regional trade to GDP was for Africa 45.6 percent while it was only 12.8 percent for Europe; 13.2 percent for North America; 23.7 percent for Latin America and 15.2 percent for Asia (Amin forthcoming). A decline in external trade therefore impacts negatively on the level of national accumulation and the well-being of the people as happened in the 1980s and 1990s when the "GDP average annual growth rate declined from 3.3 percent during 1975–1984, to 2.4 percent in 1990s" (El

Mahdi et al. 2002). Already the continent is the poorest in terms of GDP per capita. The dramatic drop in its share of world trade during 1980–1990 was therefore bound to plunge the continent into a severe social crisis.

The second issue related to the continent's weakness in global trade is the cycle of deteriorating terms of external trade. Between 1980 and 2000 the continent's terms of external trade continued to be precarious. With 1995 as the base year, the terms of trade was 141.3 in 1980; it fell to 107.9 in 1990, declined further in 1996 to 104, and collapsed to 101.6 in 1999; then it improved in 2000 to 117.5. The average annual growth in the terms of external trade was 2.4 percent in 1980–1990, and 1.1 percent in 1991–1999. The slight improvement in the terms of trade in 2000 was due largely to favorable world market prices for oil exports, which gave Africa's oil exporting countries a reasonable trade growth and a surplus in their terms of trade. Those without the benefit of oil experienced negative or slow growth in trade. On the whole, 32 African countries experienced a severe trade deficit of more than ten percent of GDP in 2000. Between 1955 and 1990 Sub-Saharan Africa lost $65 billion (at current prices) annually in export due to negative terms of trade. An invisible source of capital leakage is the payment for transport, banking and insurance cost which amounts to a considerable loss to the continent (Yeats et al. 2002). According to these researchers, net transport and insurance payments to foreign suppliers absorbed more than 25 percent of the value of exports for one-third of the sub-Saharan African countries, and exceeded 70 percent for Somalia and Uganda. They estimate the net outflows for shipment and other costs at about US$6446 million in 1985, rising to US$7331 million in 1992. For countries that are so heavily dependent on external financial inflows and foreign trade, the decline in financial inflows and adverse terms of trade have been a major set back to development efforts, especially efforts to reduce poverty. No wonder that as many as 32 African countries have declared themselves Highly Indebted Poor Countries (HIPC) in order to qualify for debt relief and reduced debt servicing (Yeats et al. 2002).

Brain Drain

A major index of a *bantustan* is the institutionalization of migration by its labour force to the major economic centres of the world or within the region. This exodus emanates from the economic reform policies that have resulted in the privatization of basic social services such as education, health, housing, water and sanitation. These policies and the reduction in public expenditure on areas such as the social wages have cumulatively reduced the capacity of the state to provide social security for citizens, and to generally sustain the reproduction of labour through investment in social services that it has been forced to privatize. In the past, such investments and provisions benefited the managerial class more than other workers. This failure in the state's social responsibilities has led to the loss of morale among, especially, the professional classes who have resorted to migration to the developed countries. Africa is losing a sizeable proportion its labour force—trained and untrained, skilled and unskilled, professional and non-professional—to Europe, North America, and Asia as well as Australia and New

Zealand. This constitutes a major loss in human capital to regions that are already developed. Various bodies have made a number of rough estimates of the magnitude and implications of the brain drain interested in this phenomenon.

According to Natal University's Pollution Research Group, about 250,000 of Africa's professional and skilled personnel live and work outside the continent, leaving about 20,000 scientists and engineers to service Africa's population of about 800 million. For South Africa alone the cost of the trained human resource lost to the West in 1994–1997 was estimated at about US$8.9 billion. The Government of Ghana recently released staggering figures on the number of medical personnel the country has lost to the developed world. Between 1993 and 2002, Ghana lost 630 medical doctors, 410 pharmacists, 87 laboratory technicians, and 11,325 nurses. In 2002 alone as many as 70 doctors, 77 pharmacists and 214 nurses migrated to the developed countries, mainly Great Britain (*Daily Graphic*, December 5, 2003). According to the International Organization for Migration, the exodus to the West continues at the rate of between 200,000 and 230,000 per annum (*Africa Insight* 2000). Undoubtedly, this is a huge loss to the continent in terms of past as well as future investments. To grapple with such massive deficit in human capital, African governments spend about US$4.0 billion annually to recruit and pay about 100,000 foreign experts to manage their respective development sectors. The implications of the brain drain for policy formulation and management capacity are enormous. The most immediate impact of the brain drain on the state is the erosion of administrative and management capacity leading to institutional atrophy. Of course, institutional atrophy is not new; it has its origins in what Apter and Rosberg (1994: 14) call "institutional indigestion," and was embedded in the colonial state formation. In the immediate post-colonial period, institutional indigestion produced national development strategies that resulted in the "compradorization" of the new nations and in failed development by the 1970s, some of whose symptoms are the agricultural and food crisis, unsustainable debt, excessive technological dependence; poverty, health and environmental crisis, political instability and civil wars; and the importation of "capitalist models of conspicuous waste" with its negative effect on national ideology and culture (Amin 1990: 47).

The globalizing forces of the post-1970 period have worsened the development crisis, because "the process of the worldwide expansion of capitalism (entails not just a process of underdevelopment) but likewise a process of destruction" of the institutions of state and society (Amin 1990: 52). This has occurred in the wake of the worsening economic and social crisis, and the imposition of a regime of austere economic reforms. In particular, the imposition of capitalist principles of economic management has obliged state institutions to comply with stricter norms of efficiency and work, as well as punctuality. They also have to apply new terminologies, and technologies in consonance with the capitalist economic environment, and accelerate the flow of economic information and related market transactions in the prevailing post-industrial economy, which is driven by a post-Fordist management model of production—flexible in the use of labour and in the labour process—and by the new information technology, which has accelerated the speed with which products and information move from one locality to another (Castells 1996). The rise of the network economy and society has exposed the embedded weakness of existing state institutions, which are still locked in old routines, principles, and norms that have been acquired through respective colonial histories, and from different economic and political environments and contexts since independence.

The brain drain has accelerated this process of institutional atrophy; so that African states lack the human resource or capacity to engage global capital in highly sophisticated negotiations regarding economic transactions. State functionaries lack even the basic rudiments of the new vocabulary necessary for successfully negotiating new agreements in the new global economy, especially at bilateral negotiations with donor government and international lenders, at negotiations with the World Trade Organization (WTO), the European Union (EU), and UNCTAD where rules governing world trade, investment and related issues would be settled. At all these levels, Africa's representatives have been inadequate in numbers; they have exhibited inadequate knowledge; they have been poorly prepared and poorly skilled. It is partly because of such limitations that bilateral and multilateral global economic transactions have been highly unfavorable to Africa. Africa has been forced into the global economy on terms dictated by global capital and implemented under its close supervision. In a nutshell, the African state has become subservient to the interests of global capital and its political partners from the west.

Three related developments in the global economy have compounded Africa's fragile position as a *bantustan* in the world economy. The first is the growing share of knowledge-based goods and services in world trade following the revolution in information technology. Being a primary commodity exporter, this shift in the science and technology of production, which entails the evolution of a new international division of labour, has thrown Africa into its worst crisis having its role as the producer of raw agricultural and mineral products become anachronistic. According to Amin, Africa has been "delinked by default" into the category of the "fourth world" (Amin 1990: 52). Besides trade in high technology, knowledge-based merchandise is concentrated in the OECD countries or in branches of the respective MNCs, which are concentrated in the same OECD countries (Castells 2000: 109–110).

The second development is that these MNCs have become the main forces driving the internationalization of production, distribution, and management of goods and services through FDI. Though FDI worldwide has increased during the last two decades, the bulk of it is intra-MNC which, as noted above, is concentrated in the OECD countries. Furthermore, there has been a strategic shift in the structure of investment, which reinforces Africa's new position as the "fourth world" in the new international division of labour. "Until the 1950s, most FDI was concentrated in the primary sector. But by 1970 FDI in the primary sector accounted for only 22.7 percent of total FDI in contrast to 45.2 percent in the secondary sector, and 31percent in the tertiary sector. In 1994, a new structure of investment emerged, as services accounted for the majority of FDI (53.6 percent), while the primary sector was down to 8.7 percent, and manufacturing's share had shrunk to 37.4 percent" (Castells 2000: 120). By then Africa as a primary commodity producer had already become a less attractive investment destination for FDI.

The third factor is the restructuring of the world economy into three dominant economies—comprising the European Union, US/NAFTA and Japan to which the rest are connected in various asymmetrical trade relationships. There are, for example, the South America Common Market (MERCOSUR) and the Asia Pacific Economic Council (APEC), which are basically loose trading associations; and China and India, which are rapidly emerging (especially China) as independent actors in the global economy. But this triad remains the most powerful economies, accounting for the bulk of total global economic transactions. "Between 1980 and 1993, this triad accounted for seventy-five percent of the world's FDI. If ten of the most favoured additional nations are included, this expanded group accounted for ninety percent of the world's FDI flows over the same period" (Thompson 1999: 145). The reality of the present world economic order is that it is constituted by a well-structured international division of labour in which, for example, the Middle East functions as the producer of oil and North Africa is retained as the satellite of the EU to deter uncontrollable migration from there. Africa, with the notable exception of South Africa, is at the bottom of this global economic apartheid.

The Captured State

Although Africa has become a *bantustan* of the global economy, the state is still needed to mediate between its discrete national economies and the global, and to ensure the implementation of market-based policies that would guarantee its stability and growth as part of the overall prerequisite of a vibrant world economy. The market-based policies as set out in the Washington Consensus demand the assurance of the following economic principles: fiscal discipline leading to a reduction in the budget deficit, tax reform, financial liberalizationa single exchange rate, trade liberalization, privatization of public enterprises, encouragement of foreign direct investment, deregulation—that is, abolition of barriers to competition and secure property rights (Comeliau 2000: 457).

From the 1980s, when direct pressure from Western governments, the IMF and World Bank forced African governments (already burdened with heavy external debt) to reform their economies, the role of the state in ensuring compliance with these economic principles has become crucial, necessitating a redefinition of its role. The redefinition of the role of the state occurred within two main critical spheres: in the economy and politics. The policies of privatization and liberalization of trade, finance and investment gradually forced the state to relinquish its role as an economic agent; it also dismantled the intricate controls it had instituted over various facets of economic activity as a means for safeguarding the national economic interest and promoting growth.

Economic liberalization opened national economies to the overriding rules and regulations determined and enforced by the IMF/World Bank and the WTO; and the state has since assumed responsibility for ensuring a liberalized environment conducive to trade, investment and related economic and social activities by especially multinational capital but also by national capital. For example, even though it is not in the interest of their people and the long-term development of their economies, African governments are obliged to enact laws privatizing the provision of strategic social services such as water, electricity, transport, telephone and electronic services, banking and insurance, and a number of industries. They implement these policies to promote foreign investment despite the fact that foreign investors are showing scant interest in their economies, and those that invest usually do so to rape their economies—in a neo-colonial fashion. But as the tragic case of Mugabe's Zimbabwe clearly shows, failure to implement free market rules on trade, investment, and ensure macroeconomic stability would attract punitive and devasatating sanctions.

The most significant development in the post-1970 political economy of Africa is the dramatic loss of autonomy of the African state in dealing with foreign economic and political agents. This has occurred especially since the accession to power of the neoliberal faction of the continent's political and economic elites following the successful transition from one-party and military authoritarian regimes of the 1960s and 1970s to constitutional democracies. These elites are so infatuated with economic and political liberalism that, for them the interest of global capital is synonymous with the interest of Africa, and therefore they enter into genuine partnerships with them for the development of the continent. They believe that the pursuit of unbridled liberalization is in the best interest of the continent. Consequently, they have diligently divested the state of the most strategic material assets that enabled it to exercise a measure of autonomy in relation to both domestic and foreign political and economic forces. Privatation of state assets, and other forms of liberalization—including reconfiguring the state, have had this effect of 'downsizing' the state as an autonomous agent.

The reconfiguration of the state constitutes a significant reversal of the hegemonic state ideology and practice of the first two decades or so after independence. During that period, the state acted as a dominant economic agent competing aggressively with private capital to accumulate wealth in the public sphere, and distribute it for the benefit of the majority of its citizens. The state represented emergent social forces of the anti-colonial struggle; and for these forces it was obliged to guarantee access to a wide range of citizenship entitlements that global capital did not provide under the colonial state. As the state divested itself of its hegemonic trappings, private interests, domestic as well as foreign, have filled the vacuum to form a new development partnership. In the 1960s and 70s, when the state was the dominant economic, political and social agent, the development ideology extolled partnership with the state in the framework of joint foreign private-state enterprise. In this age of globalization, the development ideology repudiates the state as a hegemon; the new partnership is therefore between foreign and indigenous private capitals with the state acting as a *referee*.

The resurrection of the private sector since the 1980s has proceeded in tandem with a drastic reduction in the responsibility of the sovereign state towards its citizens. This has been the import of privatization and liberalization of the economy. The neoliberal economic and political elite, in collaboration with the IFIs, have stripped the state of its egalitarian trappings; the state no longer pursues those egalitarian policies in education, health, incomes and employment, housing and in respect of other social provisions which were intended to grow citizens of the new nations of Africa, and were the trademark of almost all nationalist governments of the first 10 years or so of Africa's independence.

Today the state lacks the capacity to provide basic security for its citizens, leaving them to contend with appalling levels of poverty, disease, illiteracy, destitution, and abuse against women and children. As a mark of its profound weakness the Africa state now has to seek approval from the Fund and Bank and the development partners of the OECD before it could formulate poverty alleviation policies to relieve its citizens of the scourge of underdevelopment. Also, the state has become so weak that it cannot maintain law and order in the face of pervasive criminality and violence, which have engendered a profound sense of fear and insecurity among the citizenry. Other states have lost control over part of their territories which have been taken over by bandits, economic and military mercenaries (both nationals and expatriates), and warlords. In a nutshell, the state has forfeited a large portion of its legitimacy, which was embedded in its role as the guarantor of rights—economic, social, cultural as well as civil and political. The brain drain, which I have discussed above, and other forms of "exit" from the state (Osaghae 1999), as well as civil wars are related directly to the failure of the state to ensure human security.

What State, Whose State?

The question posed by the reconfiguration of the African state is whether it still represents the sovereign will of the people. As argued above, liberalization of the economy has stripped the state of its role as an agent in the national economy and society. It is now preoccupied with formulating law and enforcing regulations dictated by the IMF/World Bank and WTO for enhancing the private sector in general and foreign capital in particular. In discharging its new functions, the African state is accountable to these multi-lateral bodies whose strict conditional policies it is obliged to implement. If an African state fails to comply, it is denied access to loans and grants from both bilateral and multi-lateral sources. Multi-layers of governance structures have evolved within the international system to closely monitor and regulate the actions of the state. These governance structures operate at both international and national levels.

International

Liberalization policies oblige the state to enact laws in compliance with the best practice principles set out in the Washington Consensus and/or clarified by multilateral institutions like the IMF, WB and the WTO. For example, compliance with normative (e.g., best trade and investment practices) and scientific standards is required for participation in international trade and investment. Under the *African Growth and Opportunity Act*, for example, African governments have to meet certain requirements before the US Government would grant them "a visa" authorizing them to export to the American market. Furthermore, they should comply with good governance practices, open up the public goods and services sector to private participation, enact laws to protect intellectual and property rights, reduce corporate taxes, accord foreign companies equal treatment and privatize state enterprises.

For example, to meet the scientific/technical standards of the US textile and clothing market, the Ghanaian government has established a special school to train workers of textile and clothing companies in correct sewing techniques. In short, African Governments are required to implement correct economic policies that are in consonance with the free market or liberal economy.

The IMF, WB and WTO and their affiliates are leading players in the existing global governance system. There are others that set standards of good practice in the world economy, for example, those that determine the credit rating of countries/governments; countries that are safe investment and export destinations. The African state has no option but to strive to meet all of such standards in order to gain recognition and access to international finance and markets. These bodies operate in either formal or informal networks that constitute a new governance system within the world economy. Their decisions are binding on the African sate, compelling governments to act in specific ways to further the growth of the capitalist economy. The African state has very little autonomy in negotiating with them, very limited room to maneuver, and has no room for alternative action.

With the globalization of political liberalism and human rights ideology, other actors in the global governance system have emerged to monitor and regulate the decisions and actions of the African state. Among such actors is a network of INGOs, especially those engaged in the governance and human rights industries. Global developments regarding international human rights law and human rights institutions underpin the emergence of this segment of the global governance institutions to ensure effective monitoring and compliance with democracy and human rights norms. The appointment of a United Nations Commissioner on Human Rights in 1993, and the establishment of the International Criminal Court (ICC) recently at The Hague, under The Rome Statute 1998, are significant signposts in the rapidly evolving global consensus and commitment to ensure democracy, respect for human rights, and punishment for human rights abuses. As part of this worldwide development, there has also been a surge in human rights consciousness, which accounts for the rapid growth in global concerns about poverty, unemployment, illiteracy, civil conflicts and the rights of the child; the rights of women, including reproductive health issues; homelessness, the rights of the youth, and the aged; sustainable livelihoods and the environment; the rights of indigenous peoples; and many others. It accounts also for the rapid growth in the network of civil society organizations—cutting across national, racial and cultural boundaries—that are pursuing human rights issues. On the whole there has been a global movement to impose monitoring and regulatory mechanisms to ensure global peace and stability. In the case of Africa, the political crisis, which led to state collapse, failed states, weak states and, in general, state incapacity to govern and provide basic security functions for its citizens has facilitated this growing external movement to impose rules and norms of proper economic and political behavior from outside (Deng et al. 1996).

"All these institutional bodies form a complex configuration of overlapping levels of public and private powers; they form a 'governance system'" (Thompson 1999: 142). They are engaged at one level or the other, directly or indirectly, in a carefully coordinated global diplomacy to shape political, trade and investment policy for the African state. In negotiating public policies with these hegemons, the African state is virtually impotent. Hence programmes and policy instruments are literally written for their bureaucrats as governments prepare programme documents with approval and technical support from them.

The weakness of the African state is also an ideological weakness as it is unable to formulate an independent development strategy. Global capitalist interests have been exploiting this to the full. This has taken the form of direct ideological intervention in the internal affairs of African states. Since the failure of the first wave of economic reform policies, political, economic and intellectual elites representing bilateral and multilateral interests have been touring various African countries to lecture the continent's political and economic elites about the virtues of the free market and good governance, and issue veiled threats to adhere strictly to the principles of liberal markets and politics or forfeit promised economic aid. In 2001 and 2002 it was British Prime Minister Tony Blair or International Development Secretary Clare Short; Canadian Prime Minister Jean Chretien; Horst Kohler, Managing Director of the IMF and James Wolfensohn, President of the World Bank; or US Treasury Secretary Paul O'Neill. For the African state, therefore, globalization is more than the localization of the global whereby the international becomes part of the local political economy: the global has captured Africa's sovereign nation-states making the interaction between the global and the nation-state intrinsically unequal. Surely, unequal partners cannot "mutually condition and constrain one another": the global has taken over the national to advance its hegemonic project (see Thompson 1999).

The past 20 years of economic reforms when African governments could easily relapse into bad economic management practices that once more destabilized their economies, has stressed the need for closer external supervision and control. To ensure greater discipline in pursuing further economic reforms, the World Bank has started implementing a policy of decentralizing or localizing its operations. Country directors are being moved from Washington to the capitals of African countries. In addition, the annual Consultative Group Meetings (CGM), which used to be held in Paris or London, have also been localized. A typical CGM comprises representatives of the donor community—bilateral and multilateral, as well as representatives of multi-national corporations. For example, Ghana's eleventh CGM held in Accra from April 8 to 10, 2002 attracted about 300 people, representing 14 bilateral development partners, 18 multilateral development partner organizations and MNCs, as well as representatives of the Government of Ghana, civil society and the private sector. "Equally significant is the creation of the 'Mini-CG' (in the case of Ghana), which provides a more regular framework for the Government to meet formally on a quarterly basis with its development partners under the co-chairmanship of the Minister of Finance and the Bank's Country Director" (World Bank Office, Accra 2000: 6).

Internal

In the liberalized political and economic environment of the moment the state does not, and cannot, act alone. Liberalization and privatization have enhanced the growth of a wide range of private economic and social interests, which have constituted themselves into a vibrant civil society and a pro-active internal governance system. On the one hand, the state must contend with them—at the very least, consult them to arrive at a consensus on appropriate policies and involve them in policy implementation. On the other hand, the civil society institutions directly or indirectly bring pressure on the state to comply with established norms and standards, which are usually derived from the international norms on liberal markets and politics. The growing system of internal governance systems are linked into a complex global network for which they act as agents in enforcing compliance within the national environment. Like their global counterparts, their activities cover a broad range of spheres—the economic, political and social. In the economic sphere, for example, the Government of Ghana recently inaugurated a 24 member Investment Advisory Council (IAC) (see *Daily Graphic,* May 1 and 4, 2002; and *Ghanaian Times* April 29, May 1 and 4, 2002) with the Head of State as Chairman. The IAC's membership includes corporate executives of both foreign and local companies. Its mandate is to advise and help the government on how best to create an environment conducive to private investment. It meets at least once annually. It is significant that Horst Kohler, Managing Director of the IMF and James Wolfensohn, President of the World Bank, mooted the idea of an IAC. According to them, Ghana is the first country in Africa to establish an IAC; and the Fund and Bank would provide financial and technical support for the IAC's secretariat. The establishment of the IAC follows the formation in 1994 of the Private Enterprise Foundation (PEF), representing key business interests in commerce, mining, trade, manufacturing and banking. The PEF regards itself as a national body for advocacy and the promotion of the private sector.

Civil societies are becoming increasingly influential in ensuring good governance practices despite the fact these associations represent private, sectional or special interests. In particular, some civil society associations are undemocratic; and so even where they act in good faith they cannot claim to represent a democratic tendency in national affairs; nor could their positions be deemed to reflect or subsume the national interest. But in the liberal politics and markets of the moment even the most democratically elected government has to contend and interact with civil society in compliance with the prevailing liberal norms of the global political economy. Clearly, the norms of the free market seem to supercede the norms of democracy by which the state is accountable to the people through constitutionally established national institutions.

Conclusion: A Note on Political Integration

Africa entered the 21st Century without fulfilling the hopes of the millions of its citizens. Its peoples are currently caught in the vortex of a morbid culture of poverty, leading to an increase in violence alongside a creeping sense of physical insecurity. Violence of varying magnitude, fed by violent films imported onto the domestic markets, pervades the entire social fabric. Violence against children, including infanticide;

rape, including incest; abuse of women, including murder; murder of neighbours, friends or spouses for very petty disagreements; and armed robbery are among the array of social disorders that currently pervade life in African societies. Suicide and serial killing have also become a common occurrence. These new forms of poverty have produced severe anxieties about life, leading to accusations of witch-hunting; a growing tendency to seek solution and/or salvation through *juju*, black magic, or resort to pentecostal and messianic religious movements.[3] Social dismay, hopelessness, lawlessness and criminality are combining into an explosive cocktail for disaster in Africa's *free market* societies. Today social behavior is governed by an invisible anomic hand; the laws of Social Darwinism are exerting a heavy toll on millions of lives daily; and social experience has become a traumatic script in coping with fear and the unknown. Development ideology is no longer about improving the quality of life of these millions of Africa's people: it is about GDP growth rates, and achieving macro-economic stability. It is development without a human face; even as a short-term project, the IMF/World Bank sponsored development paradigm is without vision and is unsustainable as a socially responsible project. For the majority of Africa's people the state no longer embodies their aspiration for a future that fulfills their humanity; that future is rapidly vanishing if it has not already vanished. It is a dream in a profound crisis of realization!

The on-going social crisis is the result of the yawning gap in power and knowledge that has characterized Africa's relations with the capitalist world since the dawn of modern history. The African state manifests this asymmetry. It is unable to embody and represent the sovereign will and interest of its people and vigorously pursue them. It is powerless against the dictates of the multilateral and bilateral forces that regulate the global economy; neither can it protect even its own capitalist class from the ravages of these global forces. It cannot negotiate equally with counterpart states of the capitalist societies; nor can it negotiate on equal bases with MNCs. Its laws are no longer supreme before multinational capital. It is a state in total paralysis.

In 1951, the leaders of France, West Germany, Italy, Holland, Belgium and Luxembourg signed the Treaty of Paris to lay the foundation for what has become the EU. At that historic moment those European leaders acknowledged the common destiny that bound them together as Europeans and asserted their collective capacity and resolve to lay the foundation for a better future for the whole of Europe. The preamble to this treaty signifies the capacity of Europe's leaders to take resolute action to shape their common future.

> Resolved to substitute for historic rivalries a fusion of their *essential interests*, to establish, by creating an economic community, the foundations of a broader and deeper community among people long divided by bloody conflicts and to lay the bases of institutions capable of guiding their common destiny. (Appiah 1990: 365)

This Treaty affirms the political will of Europe's political leaders to act as the collective agent for constructing a new world in alliance with their *national capitals*. This state-capital alliance in restructuring Europe and then the rest of the world, dates back to the mercantilist era when European governments granted trading and other licenses to corporations as a way of protecting the global commercial and political activities of their respective national capitalist classes against competitors and encroachers. Today, the histories of the EU and of NAFTA illustrate the enormous power of such alliances in reconstructing the politico-economic spaces of the world as a whole. When the US President George W. Bush announced, during his tour of Japan in 2002, that "The 21st century is going to be a Pacific century" he was merely articulating the resolve of the US government, in conjunction with key governments of that region, to bring about the economic integration of the Pacific Rim in conjunction with global capital.

In contrast, Africa has been integrated into the global economy on terms dictated by these powerful external forces. The restructuring policies being pushed by the Fund and the Bank constitute the new stage of what Kwame Nkrumah called *neo-colonialism* in Africa's relations with the developed world, which render the continent increasingly weaker and dependent. Africa can respond to the threat of institutionalized underdevelopment only when its leaders unite to assert the collective political capacity of the continent, and resolve thereupon to shape the common future of the continent together and under a central political authority. There are contending views regarding the most efficient strategy toward Africa's political unification. One of such views is held by some African scholars who consider African unity as a popular national/cultural movement that is being driven by the people across the continent. Kwesi Prah is a leading exponent of this view. He points to the tapestry of ethno-linguistic groups that straddle and unite the colonially constructed nation-states. For him, the way forward towards continental unity is to use these ethno-linguistic groups, rather than the fragile regional economic arrangements, as the building blocs.

> Since most, or almost all, of African ethno-cultural groupings straddle or cross several borders, regional cooperation should be directed towards creating democratic institutional forms which allow the expression of interest across borders without negating the realities of existing states. In other words, we would need to allow the development of Pan-African institutions and understandings which allow the people of Africa to relate more freely and democratically across existing borders without necessarily denying the realities of the present map of Africa. As Pan-African institutions strengthen so also will the dominance of the existing states gradually recede. (Prah 2002: 17)

Nabudere (2000) is equally emphatic on the role of the masses and popular culture in achieving Africa's development and unity; because neither the "new proletariat" nor the "emerging middle class" is capable under conditions of globalization to function as agents in bringing about such transformations. Any strategy to bring about Africa's development and unity must "address and motivate the very people it is supposed to re-awaken and re-energize and the agenda it is supposed to address must be clearly laid out for the real actors in this struggle to comprehend..." The actors in this struggle are "the masses of the African people." It is "the people themselves who can deconstruct the post-colonial and post-apartheid state and reconstitute new states, institutions and agencies that reflect their needs and capabilities." The elite have lost the self-confidence to accomplish this historic task. A "cultural and political reunification of the African people is the key to any African Renaissance and recovery from oppression."

The weak link in such powerful arguments is *political power*, which is the collective social power organized at the level of the nation-state and has the legitimate and autonomous capabilities to drive any social project into fruition. The masses do not control state power: they have been denied the autonomous capacity to translate their numerical majority into political agency for the unification and transformation of the continent. The elites on the other hand have controlled state power since independence when they seized the initiative from the masses at the height of the anti-colonial struggle and inherited the post-colonial state. Since then they have employed it as a platform for exercising their hegemony politically, economically and culturally. As argued above, the state-capital alliance has been the primary catalysts toward restructuring political and economic spaces worldwide. If the masses do not control either the state or capital, they cannot succeed particularly in this age of globalization when Western states and capital are ruling the world.

Significantly, however, there have been two complimentary tendencies in the current African political economy; namely, the emergence of a *counter-elite* that bears a Pan African outlook politically and economically, and social movements sharing similar tendencies. Africa's new social movements are busy networking at the continental level; they are raising common issues, developing identical programmes of action, and developing a common identity. Concurrently, a new generation of African business elites is actively exploring investment opportunities across the continent and actually spreading its business activities into other countries and other regions of Africa. At the same time a new breed of political elites are demanding the establishment of Pan African political institutions that would have a popular mandate to take binding executive, judicial and legislative decisions. These are tendencies that should be maximized to achieve Africa's political and economic integration.

Admittedly, the post-colonial African state is too fragile, too weak, to be rehabilitated; but it remains the only viable starting point in any unity project and, in particular, for establishing a central political authority that would consummate the union of Africa. As the example of the EU affirms, the Westphalian state system as the primary agent in international relations is not dead (Ninsin 2003); it is simply being reconstructed into mega systems. For Africa also, the state remains the only central political organ that can mobilize overwhelming political capacity to strategically position the new African nation in the global political economy, and successfully engage in prudent bargaining with various economic and political actors in the international arena; it is a key agent in internal socio-economic development—providing the quantum of executive and legislative leadership, coordination, implementation and monitoring necessary for accelerating the development of the continent. All other political and economic actors revolve around its super-ordinate leadership.

The creation of a single political authority for the African nation has to be done in a democratic way; that is, "through the creation of inter-state institutions, on a people to people basis" (Prah 1998). Already, agitations for Pan African organs of state power are emerging from a new crop of politicians and business executives. Almost all the existing regional economic groupings are pursuing a project leading to the establishment of a common parliament, and related state organs such as the judiciary. The protocol establishing the AU also provides for a Pan-African parliament and associated state organs. It is equally significant that sections of this crop of politicians are actually agitating for regional parliaments that would be constituted on the basis of popular consent, and vested with legislative powers. An example is the representatives of ECOWAS parliament who declared in a communiqué, following a conference held in 2002 in Accra, that the Community Parliament should be endowed with legislative and supervisory powers instead of its current consultative and advisory powers; it should be constituted through popular elections; and that national parliaments should collaborate with the Community Parliament to implement existing Community protocols. Earlier on, the conference had deliberated on a broad range of concerns including the need for a common tariff and currency for the sub-region, as well as the need for member countries to exercise fiscal and monetary discipline to facilitate the adoption of a common currency and economic policy. They, in addition, called on the leaders of community member-states to subordinate their narrow national sovereignties to a regional sovereign power.

The call for an elective parliament with legislative and supervisory powers has echoed at other fora following the Accra conference. This emerging tendency to bring about political changes that would usher in democratic political institutions at the Pan African level should be supported and sustained. The potential for success is great because the new social movements, in particular, do not owe allegiance to the existing states, and can agitate for such changes without any political constraints. Compared to their counterparts in the anti-colonial struggle, the new social movements have not been absorbed by the political parties that won state power in recent multi-party elections. They have remained outside the ambit of the state, and continue to function as protest movements demanding qualitative changes in certain areas of national life.

We may extend Mazrui's theory of protest (Mazrui 1970) to contemporary African politics by suggesting that the strength of the new social movements lies in the fact that they are agents of political change. Undoubtedly, their emergence is an expression of collective anger. The issues they have been raising also have Pan African relevance; and so are their solutions. As they challenge the state and imperialism over issues ranging from water, education, environment, health women and children's rights to privatization, they should Pan-Africanize this collective anger, and cultivate in the people of Africa the consciousness of a common indignation against the post-colonial state, the ruling class, and imperialism. As in the anti-colonial struggle, the necessary popular Pan African political movement against the nation-state system and its collaborators will eventually crystallize to compel the creation of a democratic Pan African executive and legislative organs and related organs of state power. Political and economic integration of Africa is the ultimate solution to the negation of Africa's underdevelopment, which is being institutionalized during the current global conjuncture. The success of this project depends on an alliance between the popular forces organized as Pan African social movements and the new generation of political and economic elites who see a Pan African nation-state as the only viable theatre for domination and accumulation.

Notes

1 Statement by The Experts Committee Meeting in Dakar, Senegal on November 17–18, 2003 http://allafrica.com/stories/printable/200311210822.html
2 Thirty-Sixth Session of The Commission/Conference of African Ministers of Finance, Planning and Economic Development. Ministerial Statement, Addis Ababa, Ethiopia. 1 June 2003. http://www.uneca.org/conferenceofministers/
3 I am grateful to Patrick Twumasi, a medical sociologist, for bringing this phenomenon to my attention in one of our unscheduled reflections on the African predicament.

References

African Development Bank (2001) *African Development Report 2001*. New York: Oxford University Press.
Africa Policy Information Centre (1999) *Newsbrief*. Washington DC. March
Appiah, Joseph (1990). *Joe Appiah, The Autobiography of An African Patriot*. Accra: Asempa Publishers.
Amin, Samir (1990). *Maldevelopment – Anatomy of Global Failure*. Tokyo/London: UNU/ZED.
Amin, Samir "The political economy of Africa in the world system" in Kwame A. Ninsin, *Globalized Africa: The Political and Economic Implications*. New Jersey: Third World Press (forthcoming).
Apter, D. and Rosberg,Carl G. (1994)."Changing African Perspectives" in David E. Apter and Carl G. Rosberg (eds.) *Political Development and The New Realism in Sub-Saharan Africa*. Charlottesville and London: University Press of Virginia.
Castells, Manual. (1996). *The Rise of The Network Society*. Oxford: Blackwell Publishers.
Castells, Manuel (2000). *The Rise of The Network Society (Second Edition) Volume 1*. Oxford: Blackwell Publishers.
Comeliau, Christian (2000). "The limitless growth assumption", *International Social Science Journal*, 166: 457.
Daily Graphic (2002). May 1 and 4.
Deng Francis M., et al. (1996). *Sovereignty as Responsibility*. Washington DC: The Brookings Institution.
El Mahdi, Alia, Helmy Omneia and Mona El Garf (2002). *African Investment and Trade Opportunities in a Global Context: Possibilities and Constraints*. Research Paper Prepared for the African Association of Political Science.
Ghanaian Times (2002). April 29, May 1 and 4.
Guehenno, J.M. (1997). *The End of The Nation State*. Minneapolis: University of Minnesota Press.
Hirst, P. (1997). "The global economy: Myths and realities" *International Affairs* 73: 12–25.
http://www.jubileeresearch.org/analysis/reports/G8final.pdf .Last accessed May 21, 2003.
International Commission on Intervention and Sovereignty, The (2000). *The Responsibility To Protect*. Ottawa, Canada ICIS)
Leys, Colin (1996). *The Rise and Fall of Development Theory*. Oxford: James Currey.
Mazrui, Ali A. (1970) "Postlude: Toward a Theory of Protest" in R. I. Rotberg and A. A. Mazrui, (eds.) *Protest and Power in Black Africa*. New York: Oxford University Press. 1185–1196.

Nabudere, Dani (2000). "*The African Renaissance in The Age of Globalization: New Perspectives on African Unity and Integration.*" Paper presented at the 2000 Colloquium of the Southern African Regional Institute for Policy Studies (SARIPS) Harare, Zimbabwe; 24–27 September.

Ninsin, K.A. (2003) "*Africa in Search of Unity: The Missing Link.*" Paper presented to the 14th Biennial Congress of the African Association of Political Science (AAPS), Durban, South Africa. June 26–28.

Ohmae, K. (1995). *The End of The Nation State.* New York: Free Press.

Osaghae, Eghosa E. (1999). "Exiting from The State in Nigeria." *African Journal of Political Science* New Series Volume 4 Number 1 June 83–98.

Plahe Jagjit Kaur and Wanyeki Forsyth, J. (1999). *Multilateral Agreement on Investment: National Sovereignty for Sale.* Nairobi: EcoNewsAfrica.

Polyani, Karl (1944). *The Great Transformation* .Boston: Beacon Press.

Prah, Kwesi Kwaa. (2002). Looking Backwards, and then Forwards: Africans and the 21st Century" *Tinabantu* Volume 1 No. 1, 59 May.

Prah, K. K. (1998). *Beyond the Colour Line: Pan-Africanist Disputations Selected Sketches, Letters, Papers, and Reviews.* Trenton, NJ: Africa World Press.

Rosenau, J. (1997). *Along The Domestic-Foreign Frontier.* Cambridge: Cambridge University Press.

Thompson, Grahme (1999). "Introduction: Situating Globalization." *International Social Science Journal.* June No. 160.

UNCTAD (1998). *Trade and Development Report* New York/Geneva: UNO. 1998.

World Bank (2000). *Ghana and The World Bank: A Partnership for Progress.* Accra: World Bank Office

Yeats, Alexander J. et al. (2000) "What caused Sub-Saharan Africa's Marginalization in World Trade." http://www.worldbank.org/fandd/english/1296/articles/061296.htm

Chapter 5

The Transition from the Organization of African Unity to the African Union*

Kwamina Panford

Introduction

This chapter is a study of how and why the old Organization of African Unity (OAU), the Organization, was converted to the new African Union (AU), the Union, as it will be called in this study. This conversion occurred at a public park on July 9, 2002 in Durban, South Africa. Our main objective is to describe how the OAU became the AU and why—as one observer succinctly put it—the OAU is "donning new clothes."[1] In Durban, I also observed some African officials in informal discussions alluding to Africans merely dropping the "O" from OAU to create the AU. Thus we will address key issues including how different the AU is from its predecessor, whether African leaders are conducting African affairs in conformity with the expectations of Pan-Africanists and the types of changes in behavior that most Africans desire and need urgently.

My own first personal encounter with the OAU occurred in Ghana in 1965. I can still vividly recall television scenes from the Second Ordinary Summit of African Heads of State/Government hosted by President Kwame Nkrumah. Like most youth in Ghana or elsewhere in Africa, I also had the expectation that both political independence and the OAU would result in a new era for African affairs. We felt the OAU would change Africa's role in the global community. We expected that the OAU—in Nkrumah's words—would not only ensure the total liberation of Africa but also at the speed of a jet-propelled plane assist the continent in catching up with the developed world in terms of economic development (Nkrumah 1957 and 1972).

The failure of the OAU, with the exception of the achievement of formal political independence for Africa, contributed substantially to the birth of the AU, which is aimed at accelerating the continent's socio-political and economic development.[2] Hence the theme for the premier AU Assembly of Heads of State/Government in South Africa, 2002, being "Peace, Development and Prosperity: The African Century."[3]

The following are the key sections of this chapter:

1. An abbreviated background/history of the OAU and some of its achievements;
2. Post-Apartheid/Post-Cold War External events and conditions in Africa that catalyzed the rapid formation of the AU;

3. The birth and assessment of activities of the AU and its New Partnership for Africa's Development (NEPAD) and
4. The prospects for genuine African unity/integration and what needs to be accomplished by the AU and Africa's leaders.

From the 1884–1885 Berlin Conference to Durban, 2002: 117 Years in the Making of the AU[4]

The OAU, the first continental organization that embodied the aspirations of Pan-Africanists from all over the world and the radical founding fathers and mothers of post-independence Africa, was officially launched in May 1963 in Addis Ababa, the Ethiopian capital. At that time it was heralded as the one organization that would champion African causes globally (AU 2002). In spite of the huge expectations placed on the OAU at its birth, its very nature compromised its efficiency in terms of meeting the myriad challenges of post-independence Africa. Its organizational structure was a compromise between radical African leaders led by Nkrumah, Sekou Toure (Guinea), and Modibo Keita (Mali) who preferred immediate and complete political unity even with a single military called the "African High Command." This radical group was called the "Casablanca Group." These radicals had to contend with the conservatives, the "Monrovia/Brazaville Group" with leaders such as Tafawa Balewa (Nigeria), Houighet Boigney (Côte d'Ivoire), and William V.S. Tubman (Liberia). This latter group wanted a gradual form of economic integration (Amate 1986). The existence of these two groups, which evolved into blocs, was fully exploited by Cold War opportunists, especially the US, Britain, Germany, France, and the Soviet Union to the detriment of Africa (Keller and Rothchild 1996; and Nzongola-Ntalaja 1989).

Even though the OAU did not meet most of the aspirations of the radical founding fathers and mothers, the consensus is that it represented one significant achievement. It was largely responsible for the achievement of nominal independence in Africa. It accelerated the pace at which independence was acquired. Starting in 1963, when several African countries remained under colonial rule, by 1994, through the African Liberation Committee located in Tanzania, all the 54 countries became independent.[5] It was through the OAU that Africa mobilized global efforts to defeat the last vestiges of colonialism in South Africa under the white, racist regime. The hazardous nature of this task was visible in the form of civilian/military casualties suffered by the frontline states.

Factors within and outside Africa contributed to the popular perception that the OAU failed to fulfill its mandate, especially in respect to peace, security, and economic development. Some of the internal causes of the OAU's problems include but are not limited to what Nzongola-Ntalaja (1989) describes as failed African leadership. This leadership was typically parochial in outlook—too ethnic/tribal conscious and short-sighted by not being able to conceive events beyond their own countries' borders. Some of these leaders who also dominated the Casablanca/Monrovia group in the OAU were tightly linked with the west during the Cold War (Nzongola-Ntalaja 1989; Keller and Rothchild 1996; and Harbeson and Rothchild 2000). An example of how such leadership compromised the effectiveness of the OAU and African unity in general is how discussions between Nkrumah and other African leaders were leaked to the Central Intelligence Agency (CIA), the US external security agency.[6]

Some African leaders took positions on crucial African affairs based on briefings the French, in particular, gave to them on their way to African Heads of State/Government Summits convened by the OAU. These and other shortcomings of African leaders undermined the capacity of the OAU to engender peace and security for Africans. These leaders became enmeshed in the machinations of neo-colonists to render African independence meaningless (Nzongola Ntalaja 1989). At the height of the Cold War, tensions between the superpowers (the US and the former Soviet Union) were imported into Africa through the schism between the Brazaville/Monrovia versus Casablanca groups. This rivalry remained with the OAU until the end of the Cold War in 1989–1990.

On the external front, as we have already indicated, Cold War rivalry between the US-led North Atlantic Treaty Organization and the Soviet-led Warsaw Pact countries exacerbated the border problems Africa inherited from the colonial powers (Keller and Rothchild 1996). The Cold War generated conditions that were antithetical to Africa's interests. There were many, but a few will be cited. Even prior to founding the OAU (in 1963) African leaders were sternly dissuaded from being totally committed to using Africa's resources for the benefit of their nationals. The collaborations of CIA and Belgian security operatives to murder the Congolese Prime Minister, Patrice Lumumba clearly sent a chilling signal to all leaders who sought to use Africa's resources for Africans' interests. Four years later, Nkrumah, one of the leading advocates of total African unity was overthrown in a coup in 1966 in which the CIA was implicated (*New African* February, 2002: 18–25 and Stockwell 1975).

Through coups, assassinations and similar nefarious means, the US, Britain, Germany, France and Belgium undercut African unity and prevented genuine and sustained peace and development in post-colonial Africa. Both the economic and military aid given to Africa rendered the continent's independence meaningless. External economic aid was not only meager but also severely mitigated against self-help. In addition, it imported into countries like Angola, Mozambique, Ethiopia, and Somalia large quantities of armaments which in over a decade after the end of the Cold War continue to wreak havoc.

Under circumstances in which Africans were deprived of peace, they could not pursue African unity and attain substantial material development to improve living and working conditions. As we have illustrated with the Congolese and Ghanaian cases, in most situations, Africans could not determine who governed them. Some leaders were imposed and others kept in power by pledging allegiance to foreign powers. Right-wing civilian and military dictators were imposed by the US in Somalia and Kenya. The Soviets—not to be outdone—also had their puppets in Ethiopia and other countries (Keller and Rothchild 1996). Thus the Cold War contributed to conditions in which the OAU and dynamic African leadership could not thrive.

The OAU itself contained the seeds for its own weaknesses. The constitution it adopted in 1963 (OAU 1963) hindered a pro-active approach to managing conflicts, which severely limited economic development. Article III states (OAU Constitution):

The member states, in pursuit of the purposes stated in Article II, solemnly affirm and declare their adherence to the following principles:

1. the sovereign equality of all Member States;
2. non-interference in the internal affairs of States;
3. respect for the sovereignty and territorial integrity of each State and for its inalienable right to independent existence.

Whatever were the intentions of the signatories to the OAU Constitution, Article III and other provisions were used to establish an inflexible definition and practice of sovereignty that stifled collective attempts to protect Africans from reckless, corrupt, and repressive regimes. Territorial integrity was enforced to guarantee regime security in opposition to the welfare of Africans in the post-independence period. The OAU practice hinged on the notion that territorial integrity could not be violated under any circumstances. The view that each country's sovereignty was inviolable was reflected by the fact that until recently there were two instances in which one African country intervened militarily in another. President Julius Nyevere ordered his army into Uganda to topple Ida Amin's government in 1979. The second was in 1981 when Nigerian forces entered Chad.

Three factors explain African leaders' zeal for guarding their sovereignty so keenly. It is important to note that the result of this tendency was that the OAU was made weak vis-à-vis military intervention to protect Africans' real and long-term interests. The first generation of African leaders guarded their sovereignty in part due to its newness. They considered it precious and were therefore unwilling to yield important aspects of it to the OAU to make it strong. Second, some of the leaders feared that if the OAU were authorized to intervene militarily, some leaders might exploit such a provision.

Other leaders were concerned that some governments might use such provisions to dominate the entire continent. We might add that until the last decades of the 20th Century, the notion of military intervention across international borders was not a norm generally accepted under international law. Such interventions began to occur at the end of the Cold War against genocide and on humanitarian grounds. Thus as it was in the case of the international community, it was not until the end of the 1980s that the OAU began to seriously consider the option of military intervention as the Cairo Declaration of 1993 shows. The OAU formed a new mechanism to resolve inter- and intra-state conflicts. This body was the Mechanism for Conflict Prevention, Management and Resolution (MCPMR) (OAU 1990, 1992, and 1993a).

We may therefore observe that the ravages of the Cold War included the failure of the OAU to ensure African unity, the protection of human rights, and peace and security with economic development. The birth of the OAU itself was severely affected by Cold War tensions, which lingered on until it was replaced by the AU in 2002. The majority of member states did not only lack the political will to push for genuine African agenda, but also failed to provide the organization with sorely needed resources. While some African states paid their UN assessments (dues) they neglected the OAU, which was increasingly saddled with debt. For example, in fiscal year 1993–94 (the first year of the new MCPMR), the Cairo Summit of 1993 recommended a paltry sum of one million

US dollars for the Peace Fund (United Press International, December 7, 1993). At the end of the 59th Ordinary Session of the OAU's Council of Ministers Meeting, President Meles Zenawi of Ethiopia expressed his dissatisfaction with the inadequate finances of the Organization. This was due to arrears in dues reaching at least US$69 million by December 1993. For 1993–94, out of the expected dues of US$24.76 million, only US$3.93 million had been paid (*West Africa*, February 14–20, 1994 and *Africa Confidential*, Vol. 43, No. 14, July 12, 2002: 7).

The limited finances of the OAU confined it to a few bureaucratic functions that could not fundamentally change living and working conditions on the continent. This may account for the relative insignificance of the OAU in the eyes of most Africans. That is, beyond liberation from colonial rule, they did not discern tangible benefits from the OAU and other Pan-Africanist activities. Besides, even where some Africans were interested in the OAU, they did not have pro-OAU associations to join. Meanwhile the youth of Africa, along with the faculties of most educational institutions, especially secondary schools, polytechnics, and universities were exuberant about joining United Nations Associations and participated enthusiastically in their events.[7]

Finally, due to both the Cold War and their own parochial/personal interests, several African leaders' loyalty lay outside their borders, as is often the case with Third World countries with the exception of China. Under such conditions, the OAU lacked the necessary ingredients for creating successful programs to benefit most African citizens. All this culminated in efforts to first reform and then dissolve the OAU and replace it with the new African Union.

The Birth of the AU (1999–2002)

As is often the case with any complex international phenomenon, many events led to the launching of the AU in 2002 in Durban, South Africa 33 years after the OAU was founded in Addis Ababa, Ethiopia. For ease of analysis we use two categories—factors internal to Africa and conditions outside the continent. We tackle first the latter causes.

A host of external events prompted the rapid formation of the AU at record pace—barely three years, from the Algiers Summit of 1999 to the launch in South Africa on July 9, 2002. The end of the Cold War spurred the efforts to found a new continental organization. First, the end of Cold War rivalry coupled with the break-up of the Soviet Empire in Eastern and Central Europe led to what President Olesegun Obasanjo of Nigeria and other observers referred to as the marginalization of Africa (Keller and Rothchild 1996). President Obasanjo was alluding to the fact that even though during the Cold War Africa was not extremely important to the two competing blocs, the disintegration of the Soviet Union and the emergence of the US as the world's sole super-power contributed to a steeper decline in the relevance of Africa to global affairs. As soon as the Soviet Union imploded, it was no longer necessary for the US and other western nations to maintain any serious geo-strategic interests in Africa. A good example is that of Liberia. At the peak of the Cold War, it was used by the US for the rapid deployment of forces, and as a CIA spy satellite used to eavesdrop on the Soviets and others. With the Soviet threat subsiding, Liberia was no longer useful militarily and the US could conveniently afford to be aloof while the carnage occurred from 1989 to 1997.

The West, without any competition from the Eastern bloc nations, began withholding the limited aid it had previously provided to African countries. France in 1994 did not only reduce budget subsidies to allies but also engaged in both political and economic disengagement leading to rapidly dwindling official development assistance to its former allies in Africa. Therefore, a situation developed in the 1990s when even the paltry development aid flowing to Africa was curtailed substantially (*Africa Recovery*, July 2003: 13 and 21). While aid was diminishing, worsening terms of trade contributed to the phenomenon of failed and collapsed states as governments increasingly faced stiff internal political and military opposition as the cases of the following countries show: Liberia, 1989–1997; Sierra Leone's ten-year war; Somalia from 1991 to present; Burundi and Rwanda 1994 genocide; Democratic Republic of Congo from 1998 to the present and Côte d'Ivoire from September 2002 to the present. As it is in all the cases we have cited, challenges to existing regimes started with military incursions that turned into deadly and protracted civil wars.

A paradox of post-Cold War Africa is that the end of hostilities between the superpowers has not led to peace and security. A Cold War legacy has been the bloody and massive devastation seen in the countries we have alluded to. As Harbeson and Rothchild (2000) demonstrate, because the Soviet threat diminished, the US and France were no longer keen to intervene militarily even in countries with which they used to have close ties. Because of the end of the Cold War, the US and its allies can conveniently "wait out" deadly conflicts including the 1994 Rwanda genocide that led to the murder of 800,000 Rwandese. These wars have displaced individuals who have become refugees making Africa the continent with the largest number of displaced people in the world. Even though the Organization of African Unity (OAU) was not able to resolve these conflicts that raged throughout Africa, it understood their impact when it emphasized in the Cairo Declaration of 1993 (OAU 1993a: 5) that:

> No single internal factor has contributed more to the present socio-economic problems on the Continent than the scourge of conflicts within and between our countries. They have brought about death and human suffering, engendered hate and divided nations and families. Conflicts have forced millions of our people into a drifting life as refugees and internally displaced persons, deprived of their means of livelihood, human dignity and hope. Conflicts have gobbled-up scarce resources and undermined the ability of our countries to address the many compelling needs of our people.

The "scourge of conflicts" would emerge as one of the toughest challenges that confronted the OAU due in part to the fact that in addition to Article III (which sternly discouraged inter-African military interventions) Article XIX made the OAU even more ineffective in managing the new types of conflicts (OAU 1963): "Member States pledge to settle all disputes among themselves by peaceful means and, to this end decide to establish a Commission of Mediation, Conciliation and Arbitration, the composition of which and conditions of service shall be defined by a separate Protocol to be approved by the Assembly of Heads of State and Government. Said Protocol shall be regarded as forming an integral part of the present Charter." Contrary to expectations, even the Cairo Declaration of 1993 did not equip the newly formed MCPMR. The OAU did not only acknowledge the territorial integrity of African States but went further by strengthening the sacrosanct nature of borders given to Africa through the Conference of Berlin, 1884–85 (OAU 1993b: 7):

> The Mechanism will be guided by the objectives and principles of the OAU Charter; in particular, the sovereign equality of Member States, non-interference in the internal affairs of States, the respect of the sovereignty ad territorial integrity of Member States, their inalienable right to independent existence, the peaceful settlement of disputes as well as the inviolability of borders inherited from colonialism. It will also function on the basis of the consent and the cooperation of the parties to a conflict.

As if the problems caused by civil wars were not difficult enough, globalization aided by the information and communications technology (ICT) revolution made it imperative for African leaders to act to slow down Africa's slide into backwardness. With globalization intensifying with the aid of ICT that sped as if it were on steroids and other regions of the world responding with newly formed and/or revamped regional economic groups, the OAU realized the need for a new continental organization. We refer to the new North American Free Trade Act (NAFTA) and its possibly new twin Free Trade Area of the Americas (FAATA); the Association of East Asian Nations (ASEAN) and the European Union (EU).[8] The EU and in particular the adoption of the euro as a single currency in 2002, and the rapid growth of other regional groupings may have motivated African leaders to speed up the founding of the AU. NAFTA, the EU, and the activities of ASEAN countries demonstrated the crucial need for Africa to accelerate its own economic integration and the adoption of a mild form of political union.

We may thus state that the marginalization of Africa that occurred at the end of the Cold War; the acceleration of globalization aided by revolutionary types of ICT plus attempts by other continents to buffer themselves with regional trade blocs and the new wars that occurred in Africa exposed Africans to the hazards inherent in US/UN/European military intervention/peace-keeping. Africans apparently learned well the lessons of Rwanda and sought to responded by forming a new continental union:

> In particular, we have noted the changing East-West relations from confrontation to cooperation, the socio-economic and political changes in Eastern Europe, the steady move towards political and monetary union of Western Europe, the increasing global tendency towards regional integration and the establishment of trading and economic blocs as well as the advances in science and technology. These we found, constitute major factors which should guide Africa's collective thinking about the challenges and options before her in the 1990s and beyond in view of the real threat of the marginalization of our Continent. (OAU 1990: 1)

Events in Africa Prompting the Birth of the AU

African leaders' appreciation of the profound impact of the end of the Cold War and the intensification of globalization combined with the ambitions and interests of a number of African leaders to collaborate to launch the AU. Four of these leaders who became the leading spokespersons for the new AU and its associated NEPAD will be discussed.

President Abdoulaye Wade of Senegal developed what became the "Omega Plan"[9] which was merged with President Thabo Mbeki of South Africa's "Renaissance Plan" as a new blueprint for rebuilding Africa's political economy. After succeeding to transform Senegalese politics by unseating Abdou Diouf through the ballot box, Wade sought to extend such "democratic" practices to the rest of Africa. President Mbeki, seeing himself as representing a new breed of African leadership, joined the quest for building a new Africa. He referred to this phenomenon as the "Renaissance of Africa," the re-birth of the continent. The third leader was President Olusegun Obasanjo of Nigeria who, on becoming president in May 1999, planned to use his position to continue efforts to create leaders in Africa who practiced good governance, accountability, and economic transparency. These three were all champions of developing a new image for Africa. They believed firmly that a new Africa would attract direct foreign investment (Tieku 2004).

The three Heads of State we have named, together with other leaders, believed in the free market and the role of foreign capital in Africa's economic revival. It is also interesting to point out that these three and others such as J.J. Rawlings of Ghana, Yoweri Musevini of Uganda, Abdelaziz Bouteflika of Algeria, and Paul Kagame of Rwandan Patriotic Front fame were also the ones preferred by the West, especially the US and Britain in the post Cold War era. They were anointed, supported and deemed to be the new "saviours" of Africa. President Bouteflika's role was important in so far as he hosted the 1999 OAU Summit at which President Obasanjo, Mbeki, and Wade mooted the agenda for reforming the OAU. This new push for reforms was one of the important factors that precipitated the birth of the new AU. Besides, these four leaders: Mbeki, Bouteflika, Obasanjo, and Wade emerged as the leading exponents of a new African organization and especially the NEPAD which grew out of their plans to reform African politics and economies.[10]

The strong roles assumed by Wade, Obasanjo, and Mbeki are depicted in the following. These leaders became the cheerleaders for especially NEPAD. They were and still are the leading NEPAD/AU spokespersons, especially at international forae including UN and G-8 Summits.[11] Mbeki and South Africa's important role in NEPAD is evident in the fact that the NEPAD secretariat is located in South Africa. Obasanjo chaired the initial NEPAD Heads of State Summits including the one for 20 African Heads of State during the 2002 Durban Summit.[12]

Even though the roles of the above-cited leaders were crucial, one leader's actions catalyzed the founding of the AU in record fashion. We are referring to Colonel Moumar Ghadaffy of Libya. Colonel Ghadaffy caused the rapid formation of the AU for several reasons, including an attempt to rehabilitate his image as an international statesman. After the Algeria Summit of 1999, he issued the clarion call for a new continental political union that he called the United States of Africa because he perceived a window of opportunity to reclaim his image as an international statesman while championing a brand new continental union. In seeking to emerge from mostly US-imposed sanctions and after being disappointed with the failure of the Arab League to protect Arab interests, he turned his attention to the OAU.[13]

Colonel Ghadaffy convened a special Heads of State Summit at Sirte, Libya from September 6–9, 1999. How this turned into a landmark event is demonstrated as follows:

> ...it was at Sirté, Libya in September 1999 that African leaders took the boldest step to date. At this fourth Extraordinary Assembly of Heads of State and Government, the Sirté Declaration was proclaimed to establish the AU. In addition, leaders decided to accelerate the process of implementing the treaty establishing the AEC, through shortening the implementation periods and establishing all of the institutions provided by the Abuja Treaty, including the creation of a Pan-African Parliament. (OAU, Directory 2002: 44)

Ghadaffy went farther by offering to host the Pan-African Parliament, which was proposed as a key organ of the new AU.[14] Not to be outdone by Ghadaffy, who advocated a complete African political union, the supporters of NEPAD requested that it should be part of the newly proposed union.

The decision to form the AU in Sirté was followed by the regular Summit of OAU leaders in Lome, Togo, where the Constitutive Act of the African Union was adopted on July 11, 2000. It was at the Lome Summit that the 53 Member States signed the Constitutive Act, the name for the new AU's charter (OAU Directory 2002: 44). The next major step toward founding the AU took place in Lusaka, Zambia, in 2001 where the Constitutive Act came into force.[15] Amara Essy (Côte d'Ivoire) was appointed the OAU's transitional Secretary General replacing Salim Salim of Tanzania (*African Business*, September 2001: 11). This led to the last OAU Council of Ministers' Meeting and Heads of State Summit followed by South Africa hosting the premier AU Summit at which the AU was publicly launched on July 9, 2002. The expectation in Durban (where the AU was formally "outdoored") was that if Africans mobilized adequate political will, a strong continental organization would emerge to assume a leadership role to resolve Africa's problems (OAU Directory 2002: 44).

An Assessment of the Structure and Activities of the New American Union: NEPAD

The New Partnership for Africa's Development (NEPAD October, 2001) is the first AU organ to be reviewed because at the onset, it garnered much attention, if not equal attention as the newly formed AU itself.[16] Supporters of NEPAD including the UN, G8, and The World Bank [17]consider it to be an important mechanism to rid Africa of one of its main problems: corrupt and inefficient governments that are unresponsive to the plight of their citizens. NEPAD is also premised on the belief that if Africans "got it right" and managed Africa better, the continent would become the magnet to attract substantial foreign finance capital. Proponents of NEPAD insist that it is different from the World Bank and International Monetary Fund's economic prescriptions collectively known as Structural Adjustment (SAP)[18]. However, several provisions of NEPAD are similar to those advocated by the two Bretton Woods institutions. Key tenets of NEPAD that meet classic western donors' demands include enhanced access to African markets for foreign producers/businesses; trade liberation and reduction of public debts. These seem to support or complement structural adjustment features which are generally viewed as devastating the African economy and society (Panford 2001). African leaders who back NEPAD are still convinced that it is the panacea for the continent's political and economic ills because it is:

> ...a holistic, integrated sustainable development initiative for the economic and social revival of Africa. It is a pledge by African leaders, based on a common vision... and shared conviction that they have a pressing duty to the African people to eradicate poverty and to place their countries ... on a path of sustainable growth and development and ... to participate actively in the world economy and body politic. The initiative is anchored on the determination of Africans to extricate themselves and the continent from the malaise of underdevelopment and exclusion in a globalizing world. It is a call for a new relationship of constructive partnership between Africa and the international community... (NEPAD July 2002: 2)

The advocates of NEPAD respond to criticisms of the program by asserting that it is:

> ...premised on African states making commitments to good governance, democracy and human rights, while endeavouring to prevent and resolve situations of conflict and instability on the continent. Coupled to these efforts to create conditions conducive for investment, growth and development are initiatives to raise the necessary resources to address the development chasm in critical sectors ... Resources will be mobilized by way of increasing domestic savings and investment, by improving our management of public revenue and expenditure, and by increasing capital inflows, via further debt relief, increased targeted Official Development Assistance (ODA) flows, Foreign Direct Investment (FDI) and private capital (NEPAD July 2002: 2).

In order to burnish Africa's image to attract the huge doses of investment that NEPAD's supporters expect, its key feature is a "Peer Review" process. A panel of experts has been constituted to serve on the African Peer Review Mechanism (APRM). The APRM is for certifying that countries are conducting their financial and political affairs judiciously. Countries that are successfully peer reviewed would benefit from foreign investment, official aid and other financial and political support from western donors as stated by NEPAD (July 2002). The advocates are especially concerned with speeding up democratic and other forms of good governance in Africa. It is thus not coincidental that at the crucial Algiers OAU Summit of 1999, the OAU resolved that military regimes were to convert to civilian/constitutional governments by the next summit in 2000[19]. Ghana is the first nation to be peer reviewed (Ghanawebsite, *General News*, May 27, 2004). The reviews will be used by NEPAD/AU to determine which countries will receive aid and other preferential treatment from the West and which ones shall be excluded (*Africa Recovery*, July 2003: 24).

Although proponents of NEPAD take the position that it is homegrown for and by Africans, its creation and launch have raised a number of legitimate concerns and some controversy. President Yahya Jammeh of Gambia is one outspoken critic of NEPAD[20]. One problem is that before it was made known in Africa, NEPAD was unveiled to two G-8 Summits and the President of the World Bank prior to being presented at an African forum, the OAU at Lusaka, 2001 (*OAU Directory*, 2002, *Africa Recovery*, October 2003: 23). Second, as we have alluded to, until 2003, NEPAD and its related bodies remained outside the AU. It remained separate and was only tenuously connected to the AU (*Africa Recovery*, October 2003: 23). Full integration with the AU will be attained by July 2006. Ironically while both the OAU and AU grappled with inadequate finances, NEPAD was better endowed financially because it was bankrolled by two of the richest African nations—South Africa and Nigeria. Thus the doubts surrounding the African origins of NEPAD and, until recently, its autonomy from the AU, may have caused some of the controversy it has had to contend with.

In contrast to a truly homespun African/OAU blueprint for development—the Lagos Plan of Action (OAU, 1981) which apparently could have been a *bona fide* solution to Africa's economic problems— NEPAD seems to complement aspects of the IMF and World Bank's SAPs. The latter are deemed to be seriously undermining Africa's development (Panford, 2001). The Lagos Plan of Action, on the other hand, was viewed as providing indigenous solutions to Africa's underdevelopment (OAU/International Institute for Labor Studies 1979; Ngau 1986 and OAU 1979). NEPAD appears to be a "top-down" neo-liberal plan. Besides, the original plan lacked a focus on women's initiatives. In addition, it did not seek to tap into the huge human capital and financial resources of the African diaspora. The latter defect was rectified at the AU's Heads of State/Government Extraordinary Meeting in Addis Ababa, Ethiopia in February 2003 (*Africa Recovery*, July 2003: 19). At this Assembly, the diaspora, that is, all people who trace their ancestry to Africa, became the sixth African region. The AU, like the OAU, had five regions for operational purposes. Now there are six including the diaspora.

There is also the problem of unrealistic expectations connected with NEPAD. While a leading proponent of NEPAD, President Obasanjo believes that "However much Africa shouts about injustice, nothing will probably change. It is a predator's world" (*New African*, September 2002: 14),[21] he and other leaders still seek over US $60 billion in FDI support for NEPAD (NEPAD, October, 2001). As if African leaders have not learned from past experiences, they have made the success of NEPAD dependent on massive infusions of foreign capital. Global FDI inflows into Africa in the last decade show that this expectation may not be realized. This is also one of the basic causes of Africa's current economic malaise—precarious reliance on FDI.

Some aspects of NEPAD are reminiscent of what African finance and other ministers did at the UN's Special Session on Africa in July of 1986 ("UN Special Session: African Economic Situation," *Gist*, July 1986). At this session in New York, African ministers erroneously accepted full responsibility for all of Africa's economic ills. NEPAD appears to adopt a similar posture in assuming that there are none or few external dimensions to Africa's economic problems. NEPAD either ignores or assumes that unequal/unfair trade and declining rates of exchange of goods and services at the global level are unproblematic. An impact is that the important adverse effects of subsidies to western farmers and manufacturers are not factored into NEPAD's strategy for tackling the continent's economic difficulties. They also seem to discount the havoc wreaked on African economies by both slavery and colonial domination. Thus they do not delve into the underlying causes of Africa's abject poverty.[22]

Rather than working to tackle the causes of Africa's problems, as a condition for donor support, through NEPAD African leaders pledge more allegiance to a global system that has not favored the continent. Because of NEPAD, Africa will remove trade tariffs and open up for more foreign companies; cut public expenditure and quickly privatize the economy to be more in line with neo-liberal economic prescriptions (NEPAD October, 2001). All the above contribute to the perception that the G-8 is NEPAD's progenitor and that it is undermining African's own efforts at development. NEPAD could be viewed as assisting the global economic system to siphon off more resources out of Africa. It may also be seen as reinforcing the roles of Africans in a system that will accelerate widespread poverty and contribute to worsening living and working conditions.

A last point is that NEPAD may engender a narrow focus on economic matters to the exclusion of political unification. Apparently, NEPAD may be ignoring the fact that political unity can enhance Africa's position globally by providing a single voice, currency and policy stance on issues ranging from human resource development, trade, immigration and terrorism to human rights as Europe is showing it can be done through the revamped EU.

The African Union in Action

In barely three short years after its birth, the new African Union is making some important strides toward achieving its objectives. First, in 2003 it pre-empted the potential problems that a separately existing NEPAD may pose (*Africa Recovery*, October 2003: 23). Second, as required by the AU Constitutive Act (2000), a Pan-African Parliament has been established. On March 18, 2004, the founding session with 180 members from 36 states' national parliaments met at the Ethiopian capital, Addis Ababa (*New African*, May 2004: 14 and 17). Each country has five members, one of whom is required to be a woman and should include opposition party members where feasible. At its first sitting, the Pan-African Parliament made history by making a woman, Tanzania's Gertrude Ibengwe Mongella, the President.

Although it may be premature to evaluate the effectiveness of the new African Parliament, it has sent a strong message that in some respects, Africa will not lag in gender/women's issues. The AU also seems to be on the right path with respect to other gender matters. It has ensured that there is gender parity with respect to its important Commissioners. Out of a total of ten, five are women (*New African*, September 2002: 21).[23]

Another important landmark is the effort to use NEPAD's APRM to promote good governance. In May 2004, Ghana signed the first legal document to permit an APRM assessment of the country's economic and political policies and practices (*Ghana Web News*, May 27, 2004 and *Africa Recovery*, July 2003: 24). The results of the review are not yet available but we might observe that the emphasis placed on good governance by both NEPAD and the AU could become an important stimulus for both democracy and efficient economic policies. Together with some of the political conditions imposed by the Bretton Woods institutions, the G-8 and other donors, NEPAD and the AU's preference for good governance, financial probity and accountability may be yielding some of the following positive outcomes.

Admittedly, although the demise of both the old Soviet Union and the Cold War could be significant factors, apparently the AU's thrust starting in the late 1990s toward good governance and constitutional/civilian government could be accelerating the current pace of political change in Africa (OAU, 2002, *Africa Recovery*, July 1997: 5, and OAU, Algiers Declaration 1999). Even if multipartism is not as yet entrenched, fair and transparent elections are leading to relatively competitive elections. Due to term limits, we are also witnessing a decent turnover in who heads African states. Cases in point include Ghana, Madagascar, Senegal, South Africa, Mali, Kenya, Zambia, and Tanzania. This has led to the increasing number of heads of state who are now retired. Despite these important achievements, we need to caution that two or even three successful turnovers in government via the ballot box and internationally sanctioned transparent elections *per se* do not constitute democracy. Africa may be breaking the coup jinx but there are still more challenges ahead in the areas of substantive democracy, human rights, and the use of public policy to create better working and living conditions.

From a constitutional standpoint, the new AU seems to have had a good start. Whereas Article III of the OAU Charter of 1963, explicitly barred military intervention in member states' internal affairs, Article 4 (h) of the AU's Constitutive Act, 2000 states that "...the Union will intervene to fulfill...a decision of the Assembly in respect of grave circumstances, namely war crimes, genocide, and crimes against humanity" (Appiagyei-Atua 2003: 45). It appears that in principle, the AU will no longer treat territorial integrity as inviolable. That was the case in Madagascar when it was suspended from the AU from 2002 to 2003.

At the last OAU Summit and the first AU Assembly in 2002 in Durban, Madagascar was conspicuously absent due to a suspension for what the OAU deemed was the failure of the new government to allow the course of rule of law to run fully. Because of an election dispute in Madagascar in 2001, the OAU and AU did not allow Madagascar to participate until it was returned to the AU fold in Maputo, Mozambique in 2003.[24] Even though the ban on Madagascar was relatively minor and did not last long, it may be indicative of how the AU is slowly but steadily jettisoning the notion and practice of the sanctity of national sovereignty.

The AU seems to be turning the corner in some crucial areas such as conflict management and demonstrating that it may be different from the OAU. In contrast with its predecessor, the AU seeks to put in place an effective conflict management body. It has created the new Peace and Security Council to combat one of Africa's perennial problems—civil wars that lead to insecurity and lack of safety (*African Business*, June 2002; *Africa Recovery*, October 2003: front page and 14; *Boston Globe*, February 29, 2004: A13). The AU has not as yet attained self-sustained peacekeeping but it appears to be changing its mode of operation and shows signs of some improvements. It has been more active in peacekeeping in Darfur, Sudan. It has also not only agreed to send troops from member countries such as Rwanda and Nigeria but has indicated that it will pay for half of the entire cost of peace-keeping. Meanwhile the AU states strongly that the 40,000–50,000 deaths in Darfur cannot be attributed to genocide (AU Assembly, "Decision on Darfur." July 6–8, 2004). The insistence on "no genocide" in contrast to efforts by the US to mobilize world opinion for sanctions against Sudan could indicate attempts by the AU to assert some autonomy in representing Africa in the global arena. We might thus observe that although the AU has not fully funded peace-keeping operations in Africa, it seems to be making some progress in this most challenging area and substantial threat to Africa's "peace, security and prosperity" which it adopted as the theme of its first Assembly in Durban in 2002.[25]

Concluding Observations

Based on our assessments of the transition from the OAU to the AU and what the latter has accomplished in the last three years, we take the position that the AU's prospects seem good. It still has to contend with numerous organizational constraints, some of which are severe, but we are mildly optimistic about its role in Africa.

We present a few of the external bottlenecks that the AU, African leadership and indeed all Pan-Africanists have to overcome if the AU is to succeed. Pusch Commey (*New Africa*, July 2004: 15) succinctly summarized these when he noted that "Africa cannot be blind to the fact that we are also in competition with other forces—predatory forces that feed on our underdevelopment and our rich resources, whose interests have always been to see a fragmented, confused Africa." Commey's pessimism about external aid is supported by developments in the area of international peacekeeping in Africa. It is interesting to note that in the mid-1990s when the OAU realized it needed to revamp its peace-keeping and conflict management body and activities and created the MCPMR (OAU Cairo Declaration, 1993) the US response may have undermined the new OAU mechanism. President Bill Clinton launched the African Crisis Response Initiative (ACRI) and engaged in bi-lateral military exercises with several African countries. When President Clinton left office, President George W. Bush created a sequel to ACRI, African Contingency Operations Training and Assistance (ACOTA) (Ohaegbulam 2004: 245–248). We observe that irrespective of the intent of these and other US initiatives, they have tended to thwart the effectiveness of Africans' own plans. As happened with President Clinton's bilateral military exercises, Nigeria, for example, was excluded. Such practices could split a wedge between African nations that collaborate with the US and those who do not and hence sharpen divisions between them.

More recently, as the AU seeks to chart a new era in peacekeeping, British Prime Minister Tony Blair, is also coming out with his own plan for Africa's development. This is the Tony Blair Commission for Africa (BCA) (http://www.bcstimes.com, November 8, 2004). Both the AU and African representatives on the BCA such as the Economic Commission of Africa's K.Y. Amoako and President Benjamin Mkapa of Tanzania should take measures to ensure that it does not dissipate Africans' own efforts to rid Africa of civil wars and economic ills.

As Africans ought to have learned in stark terms from the important lessons of Rwandan genocide (800,000 plus citizens killed) the AU and other leaders of Africa need to forge ahead with the self-reliant efforts they are making in Darfur, Sudan. According to IRINnews.org (October 27, 2004) the AU is planning to pay half of the US $221 million its expanded Darfur peacekeeping operations will cost. This is a good start the AU must build on rapidly.

The Darfur situation in the Sudan could be seen as a real test of the AU's resolve to be successful in the realm of peacekeeping. We commend the AU for committing to pay half of the cost but it still needs to quickly overcome problems of "bureaucratic shuffling." Delays in sending Rwandan and Nigerian troops to Darfur in early November, 2004, are reminiscent of the bureaucratic wrangling that the EU, US, OAU, and the UN used to watch the carnage in Rwanda in 1994. Apparently, the AU has been indecisive in putting troops on the ground in Darfur due to accommodation and other logistical bottlenecks such as lack of tents (BBC News, October 17, 2004 and *Boston Globe*, October 24, 2004). Darfur presents opportunities for the AU to earn credibility by asserting itself as an organization that can achieve the peace and security necessary for prosperity in Africa as it promised to do during its formal inauguration in Durban in 2002.

Another problem the AU should attempt to resolve soon is the lingering tension surrounding its mission and main objectives. On the one hand, is the thrust toward complete political and economic union. This is the type exhibited by the EU and is supported by Colonel Moumar Ghadaffy (*Africa Confidential*, Vol. 43, No. 14, July 12, 2002: 7). The other preference is fairly akin to the position of the Brazaville/Monrovia group. This is the model that currently prevails within the AU with its emphasis on gradual economic integration using regional economic groups as building "blocs." This group is led by Presidents Obasanjo and Mbeki, and other advocates of NEPAD whose main concerns tend to be economic. The latter group appears to dominate the current AU while macro political matters such as unification *per se* are not dealt with directly. The AU should be able to resolve this latent conflict if it is to attain its ambitious goals.

The AU must also contend with two organizational problems that the OAU grappled with. These are issues of political will and grossly inadequate finances, which are often expressed diplomatically as "lack of financial resources" or "logistical problems." First, the AU will only succeed if member states develop enough political will to succeed (*Daily Graphic*, Accra, Ghana, May 25, 2001: 16). The new union will achieve its objectives if members are willing to back resolutions through timely and effective action. As is in the case of the UN, the AU's usefulness will depend on the cooperation of members. Arrears in dues owed to the OAU in 2002 were US $35 million and US $54 million in 2000 (*Africa Confidential*, July 12, 2004). Second, if members continue the old debilitating practice of not paying their dues, the AU will not be effective. For the 2004–2007 periods, the AU's budget is US $1.7 billion while it has raised only 10 percent of that (AU, The 2004–2007 Strategic Framework of the African Union Commission). This is the kind of financial constraint that causes precarious dependence on western donors, which the AU should strive to wean itself from immediately. As Rwanda (1994), Somalia (1991-present) and recent events in Côte d'Ivoire (from 2002 to 2004) show, depending on foreign aid and peacekeeping may not be in the long-term interests of Africans. We refer, for instance, to the 1962 Franco-Ivorian military pact which is contributing to the imbroglio with which Africans have to untangle because of the civil war in Côte d'Ivoire.

With respect to enforcing NEPAD and other provisions relating to good governance/democracy, the Union could potentially face a dilemma. This is the old practice of declaring life presidency as happened in Togo in 2002 when the Parliament made President Eyadema a "life President" (*West Africa*, June 23–29, 2003: 18).[26] This is the kind of complex political challenges the AU may find difficult to resolve in light of its declarations and resolutions emphasizing democracy, fair, competitive, and transparent elections as key to a new Africa.

In conclusion, we may state that while the AU is facing important organizational constraints, it could still be an important means to fulfill Pan-African aspirations. Firstly, it remains the most important governmental Pan-African organization to date. Second, the AU appears to be making some significant strides toward achieving important Pan-African economic goals. For example, NEPAD's peer review mechanism, if utilized appropriately and aided effectively by new ICTs could be harnessed to improve the state of governance in Africa. This could especially be the case with respect to financial probity and fair/transparent elections. Unlike the case of the Lagos Plan of Action of 1980, which was not appropriately and widely disseminated, with NEPAD the Internet affords Africans tremendous opportunities for widespread distribution. Also through the Internet and other new media, Pan-Africanists could use the AU's Constitutive Act and other pronouncements to make governments more accountable. By working in concert with the new Pan-African Parliament, new processes for ensuring government responsibility may be found and enhanced. This Parliament itself needs to be made accountable to the citizens of Africa if it is to succeed as a genuine voice of all the peoples of Africa and of the diaspora.

Notes

* I express my gratitude to His Excellency, Amara Essy, the interim OAU-AU Secretary General and his senior staff for inviting me to observe the last OAU Council of Ministers Meeting, Summit of Heads of State/Government and the launching of the AU at Durban, South Africa, June-July 2002. I also thank the Office of the Provost, Northeastern University for sponsoring my travel.

1 Observation by this author in Durban, June–July 2002.

2 It is generally agreed that in spite of repeated failure to ensure peace and security the OAU's Arusha-(Tanzania) based Liberation Committee was vital in achieving independence in post-colonial Africa (Amate 1986).

3 A paradox here is that South Africa which was the last to attain independence was the first host nation of the AU.

4 See Rodney (1982) for details of 1884–85 Berlin Conference for the partitioning of Africa by Europe.

5 Although there are 54 countries, both the OAU and the AU and 53 members due to Morroco's withdrawal in 1984. Repeated efforts to get Morocco to join the OAU and AU have failed. Morroco withdrew due to disagreement over the OAU's handling of the disputed territory of Western Sahara.

6 Information from interview by the author with Ebenezer Ako Adjei, Nkrumah's Minister for Foreign Affairs, Ako Adjei Park (Accra), Ghana, August/September, 1991.

7 This was the experience of this author in Ghana in the 1960s and 1970s. Even though there are no or few OAU/AU Associations, there is a proliferation of national/local UN associations all over Africa.

8 "China, ASEAN Plan to End Merchadise Tariffs," *Wall Street Journal*, October 27, 2004; "India, Pakistan Consider Energy Cooperation," *Wall Street Journal*, October 7, 2004; and "East Asia's Financial Activities Grow Closer," *Wall Street Journal*, May 17, 2004.

9 The Omega Plan was presented to the Franco-Africa Summit, Yaounde, January, 2001 (see www.nepad.org.ng).

10 NEPAD was created in 2001 and it was officially adopted as an OAU organ at the Lusaka Summit, 2001 and it was integrated with the AU in Addis Ababa in 2003 *(Africa Recovery* October 2003: 23).

11 See, for example, G-Eight Summits of : Kananaskis, Canada, June 2002; Evian, France, June,2003 and Genoa, Italy, July, 2001 (*Africa Recovery*, July, 2003: 3 and October 2001: 21).

12 NEPAD Private Meeting of 20 African Heads of State/Government, Holiday Inn Elangeni, Durban, South Africa. Nigeria and South Africa contributed half a million dollars each to the fund for the AU's new peace and security body (Amara Essy, OAU Secretary General, Speech at Opening of the 76th Ordinary Session of the OAU's Council of Ministers, Durban, July 4, 2004).

13 "Libya-UK: 20-Year Taboo Broken," *Africa Research Bulletin* (August 1–31, 2002: 14983) and "Libya: Retirement Tent," *Africa Confidential* Vol. 43, No. 19, September 27, 2002: 8).

14 The Pan-African Parliament is now in Addis Ababa.

15 NEPAD was adopted as an OAU organ in Lusaka, in 2001 (*Africa Recovery*, October 2001: 21). and became officially integrated with the AU in 2003.

16 This author observed that at the 2002 AU Summit in Durban. NEPAD was at the center of a flurry of activities including the Special NEPAD Private Meeting of 20 Heads of State at the Holiday Inn at Langeni, Durban, July 7, 2002. Perceptions that NEPAD was a separate entity lingered on until it was fused with the AU Secretariat in 2003 (*Africa Recovery*, October 2003).

17 NEPAD's origins may also be traced to the UN's Special Initiatives on Africa (*Africa Recovery*, October, 2001:21 and 22 and Appiagyei-Atua, 2003: 25–26).

18 This author observed that some of the supporters of NEPAD strongly protested at the Special Private NEPAD Summit that it was completely different. They emphasized that NEPAD was for and by Africans therefore it was a better guarantor of Africa's economic success.

19 The real test of the OAU's resolve to rid Africa of military governments was avoided when, in May 1999, Nigeria reverted to civilian rule by electing General Obasanjo as the Head of State. It would have been interesting to observe how the OAU would have dealt with Nigeria.

20 "Jammeh: NEPAD Will Never Work," *New African*, September, 2002: 18; "NEPAD and its Hidden Dangers," *West Africa*, June 30–July 6, 2003: 6; and Appiahagyei-Attua (2003: 39–44).

21 At the Special Private Meeting of the 20 Heads of State and Government, NEPAD Implementation Committee at the Holiday Inn, Elangeni, Durban, July 7, 2002, President Obasanjo remarked that he has been having problems with SAPs promoted by the World Bank (Observation by the author).

22 On how such subsidies are the source of Third World difficulties associated with world trade see World Trade Organization: Ministerial Conference, Doha, Qatar, November 9–13, 2001, famously called the "Doha Conference."

23 Similarly, three of the six NEPAD APRM panel of experts are women (*Africa Recovery*, July 2003: 24) and *West Africa*, September 9–15, 2002: 5).

24 Because of this two-year sanction, Madagascar's Ambassador to the US would not allow the author's school, Northeastern University, to receive a briefing at the embassy for the Model AU in Washington, D.C., March, 2003. The Ambassador cited the sanction in correspondence with this author.

25 The full theme was "Peace, Security and Prosperity: The African Century."

26 President Eyadema died in February 2005.

References

African Union, The (2002). *African Union Directory 2002.* Port Louis: Mauritius.

———— (2004a)."*Vision of the African Union and Mission of the African Union Commission.*" http://www.africa-union.org (11/15/2004).

———— (2004b). "*The 2004-2007 Strategic Framework of the African Union Commission*".http://www.africa-union.org (11/15/04).

———— (2004c). "*The Action Plans of the Various Departments of the Commission.*" http://www.africa-union.org (11/15/04).

Amate, C.O.C. (1986). *Inside the OAU: Pan-Africanism in Practice.* New York: St. Martin Press

Appiagyei-Atua, K. (2003). "From the OAU to AU, From NIEO to NEPAD: A Rights-Centred Critique of Poverty-Eradication Strategies in Africa." Unpublished Monograph.

Bajusz, W. and O'Prey, K. (1996). "An All-African Peace force: An Immediate Option or Long-Term Goal for the Region," *Strategic Forum*, 86 : 1–4.

Cilliers, J. and Sturman, K. (2002) "Commitments by African Heads of State to Peace, Democracy, Human Rights and Associated Issues," *Institute for Security Studies*, 58: 1–19.

Harbeson, J. and D. Rothchild (ed). (2000). *Africa in World Politics.* Boulder, CO: Westview Press.

Keller, E. and D. Rothchild (ed.). (1996). *Africa in the New International Order: Rethinking State Sovereignty and Regional Security.* Boulder, CO: Lynne Rienner Publishers.

New Partnership for Africa's Development, The (2002a). *NEPAD Progress Report. A*buja, Nigeria.

———— (2002b). "Report of the Secretary General on Strengthening the Role of the OAU/AU in Elections, Observations and Monitoring and the Advancement of the Democratization Process in Africa." Addis Ababa, Ethiopia.

Ngau, P. (1986). Rev. of "The Lagos Plan of Action VS. The Berg Report," *Monographs in African Studies*, Vol. 15 (1 and 2):219–223.

Nkrumah, K. (1972). *Africa Must Unite.* New York: International Publishers.

———— (1957). *Ghana: An Autobiography.* New York: W. W Norton.

Nzongola-Ntalaja, G. (1989). "The African Crisis: The Way Out" *African Studies Review* 32 (1): 115–128

Organization of African Unity (1963) *OAU Charter. Addis Ababa*: Ethiopia, 25 May

———— (1979) Regional Research and Documentation Center 1979

———— (1981) *Lagos Plan of Action.* International Institute for Labor Studies. Geneva, Switzerland.

———— (1990). "*Declaration of the Assembly of Heads of State and Government of the Organization of African Unity on the Political and Socio-Economic Situation in Africa and the Fundamental Changes Taking Place in the World.*" Addis Ababa, Ethiopia.

———— (1992). *Resolving Conflicts in Africa Proposals for Action.* Addis Ababa, Ethiopia.

———— (1993a). *Resolving Conflicts in Africa: Implementation* Options. Addis Ababa, Ethiopia.

———— (1993b). "Declaration of the OAU 29th Summit on Mechanism for Conflict Management." Cairo, Egypt.

———— (2001). *The New Partnership for Africa's Development*, Abuja, Nigeria.

OAU/International Institute for Labor Studies (1979). *What Kind of Africa by the Year 2000.* International Institute for Labor Studies. Geneva, Switzerland: ILO.

Ohaegbulam, F. (2004). *US Policy in Postcolonial Africa.* New York: Peter Lang Publishers.

Panford, K. (1996) "Pan-Africanism, Africans in the Diaspora and the OAU," *The Western Journal of Black Studies*, 20 (3): 140–150.

Panford, K. (2001). *IMF-World Bank and Labor's Burdens in Africa.* Westport, CT and London: Praeger.

Rodney, W. (1982). *How Europe Underdeveloped Africa.* Washington DC: Howard University.

Stockwell, J. (1979). *In Search of Enemies.* New York: WW Norton.

Tieku, T. (2004) "Explaining the Clash and Accommodation of Interests of Major Actors in the Creation of the African Union," *African Affairs*, 103: 249–267.

———— Africa Towards the Year 2000," Special Issue of *Labor and Development*, Regional Economic Research and Documentation Centre, Lome, Togo (179): 1–4.

———— (1996)."The OAU's New Mechanism for Conflict Prevention, Management and Resolution" *CODESRIA Bulletin*, 4:15–27.

Chapter 6

The Economic Community of West African States (ECOWAS): Achievements, Problems, and Prospects for Africa's Development in the 21st Century

Joseph Mensah and Richard Aidoo

Introduction

Many nations have consolidated their power by reinforcing intra-national similarities, while asserting inter-national differences through a systematic process of "othering" and, sometimes, radical alterity. To ascertain the necessary sense of national unity and identity, nation states have had to propagate and diffuse assertions of their internal homogeneity and distinctiveness. Since about the early 1980s, however, globalization—and the attendant time-space compression and proliferation of information technology, international trade, and cross-border migration—has compelled nation states to rethink the basic tenets of their existence, as they strategize to protect their economic base, become more competitive, and explore new visages of comparative advantage (Knox and Agnew 1998; Berry et al., 1998). Ironically, the corollary of this globalization-induced competition has been a growing trend towards international economic co-operation, with many countries resorting to various forms of institutionalized economic integration to eschew undue isolation, and, ultimately, help position themselves in the new "borderless" global economy. The creation of the North American Free Trade Agreement (NAFTA) in 1992; the joining of the ASEAN countries with the United States, Canada, New Zealand, South Korea, Taiwan, Australia, China, and Japan into the new Asia Pacific Economic Co-operation (APEC) group in 1989; the formation of the Andean Common Market among the Andean Pact nations in 1996; and the strengthening of ECOWAS and its institutions in recent years are examples of the worldwide shift toward regional economic integration.

Quite expectedly, while the advanced nations generally use such regional integration bodies to consolidate their advantages in the world-system, developing countries use them to enhance their own participation in the world market, and to curtail their long-standing dependence on the advanced countries. Notwithstanding the potential advantages of regional integration arrangements—including gains from economies of scale, enlarged market, reduction of the cost of trade, and the improvement of intra-regional security—making them work in Africa has been a daunting task.

This chapter examines the main features of the Economic Community of West African States (ECOWAS), its achievements, challenges, and prospects for Africa's development in the 21st century.

Foundation, Objectives, and Institutions

Regional integration has a long history in West Africa. Indeed, many of the African leaders who opposed Ghana's Kwame Nkrumah's ambitious attempt to create a union of African states, at the peak of the Pan-African movement in the late 1950s, opted for various forms of sub-regional groupings. President Tubman of Liberia, for instance, forged a free trade agreement between Liberia, Côte d'Ivoire, Guinea, and Sierra Leone in 1965. However, the scheme, like many others in West Africa at the time, failed because of power struggles among members. Furthermore, with the support of France, many francophone nations in West Africa established a variety of economic unions in the early post-independent period. Notable examples included the West African Custom Union or Union Douaniere de l'Afrique de l'Ouest (UDAO)—which was formed in 1959 and replaced in 1966 by the West African Economic Union or Union Douaniere et Economique de l'Africa de l'Ouest (UDEAO)—and the West African Economic Community or Communaute Economique de l'Afrique de l'Ouest (CEAO) formed in 1973.

Unlike their francophone counterparts, anglophone West African countries did not pursue much economic integration in the immediate post-independent era, as the British administrative structure accorded little sense of economic unity among its colonies. While most of the exclusively francophone unions were successful, the few attempts made to bring francophone and anglophone nations together, including the Burkina Faso (Upper Volta)-Ghana Union and the Ghana-Guinea-Mali experiment failed, mainly because of the inability of most West African nations to break their colonial ties in the immediate post-independence period (Asante 1986).

The first major attempt towards the formation of an economic union embracing all West African nations was made by the Economic Commission for Africa (ECA) through two main resolutions, 142 (VIII) and 145 (VII), passed at its seventh session in Nairobi in February 1965 (Ezenwe 1983). Notwithstanding the enormous institutional and financial support given by the ECA, it took a decade for West African nations to finally come together to form ECOWAS in 1975. The indecisiveness that thwarted the ECA efforts stemmed from several factors, not the least of which were attempts by France, Britain, and Portugal to preserve their economic ties with their respective former colonies through various preferential arrangements. The existence of competing economic unions in the sub-region as well as the uncertainties created by the 1967–1970 Biafra war (in Nigeria) also undermined the ECA initiatives.

A 1972 meeting in Lomé between General Yakubu Gowon of Nigeria and President Gnassingbé Eyadéma of Togo culminated in a communiqué which many analysts (Asante 1986; Onyemelukwe and Filani 1983; Ezenwe 1983) consider as the "embryo" of

ECOWAS. A series of bilateral and multilateral meetings on the viability of an economic union, spearheaded by these two leaders, led to the signing of the ECOWAS treaty on May 28, 1975, in Lagos. The original signatories were fifteen West African nations: Benin, Burkina Faso, Côte d'Ivoire, Gambia, Ghana, Guinea, Guinea-Bissau, Liberia, Mali, Mauritania, Niger, Nigeria, Senegal, Sierra Leone, and Togo. Cape Verde joined in 1977, bringing the total membership to the current 16.

The ECOWAS treaty has as its prime objective to:

	Type of Integration free trade among members	Common barrier to trade w/non-members	Free factor movement among members	Coordination of economic policy	Supranational organizational structure
Free Trade Association	△				
Custom Union	△	△			
Common Market	△	△	△		
Economic Union	△	△	△	△	
Supranational Union	△	△	△	△	△

Figure 6.1 Levels of Regional Integration
Source: Crafted from Bela Balassa (1961) and Berry, et al. (1988, 417).

> Promote co-operation and integration, leading to the establishment of an economic union in West Africa in order to raise the living standards of its people, and to maintain and enhance economic stability, foster relations among Members States and contribute to the progress and development of the African Continent. (ECOWAS, 2000)

Clearly, the main goal of ECOWAS is to enhance the collective self-sufficiency and living standard of its members through economic integration. The organization was founded on the premise that the domestic markets of the individual members were too small to be competitive in a global economy, characterized by large trading blocs, such as the European Union (EU), the North American Free Trade Agreement (NAFTA), and the Asia Pacific Economic Co-operation (APEC). With a potential single market of over 230 million people (about 25 percent of Africa's population), ECOWAS expects to promote specialization and large-scale industrialization, enhance job opportunities and wealth creation, and to limit the region's dependence on foreign markets.

To accomplish its objectives, ECOWAS, *inter alia*, hopes to eliminate all custom duties among member states; adopt common external tariff and trade policies towards non-members; remove barriers to the movement of goods, services, and people; and, ultimately, harmonize trade, agricultural, energy, and environmental and other policies of members. The ECOWAS treaty makes provisions for the synchronization of investment codes and standards, and the establishment of special fund for sub-regional cooperation and development, paying attention to the special needs of the 'poor,' landlocked, and small member states such as the Gambia, Burkina Faso, and Mali. The underlying values of ECOWAS, according to Article 4 of the treaty, include adherence to the principles of equality, solidarity, accountability, non-aggression, maintenance of peace, and the promotion of a democratic system of government in each member state. The treaty permits ECOWAS members to join other regional and sub-regional associations, as long as such concurrent memberships do not conflict with the spirit and purpose of ECOWAS.

The official duties of ECOWAS are undertaken through its many institutions, the most powerful of which is the Authority of Heads of State and Government, made up of all the leaders of the member states; this body meets at least once a year under a rotated chairpersonship. Next in importance is the Council of Ministers, which is responsible for monitoring the activities of ECOWAS and for making recommendations to the Authority of Heads of State and Government for the attainment of ECOWAS goals. This council, made up of two ministers from each member state, meets at least twice a year. Another important institution is the Executive Secretariat, headed by the Executive Secretary, who performs the main administrative and executive duties of ECOWAS and coordinates the activities of all other institutions. The Executive Secretary is appointed by the Authority of Heads of States and Governments for a four-year term, renewable only once for another four years. Other notable ECOWAS institutions are the Community Parliament; the Economic and Social Council; the Community Court of Justice; and the Fund for Cooperation, Compensation and Development. Additionally, ECOWAS has five main Specialized and Technical Commissions, including those of Trade, Customs, Immigration, Monetary and Payments; Transport, Telecommunication, and Energy; Agriculture and Natural Resources; Administration and Finance; and Social and Cultural Affairs. ECOWAS is headquartered in Abuja, Nigeria, where it has its own buildings and administrative staff. In what follows, we shed some light on the structure and strength of ECOWAS economies.

ECOWAS Economies: Basic Characteristics

ECOWAS brings together 16 countries with a total population of 236 million (2000 estimate). The region covers 6,057 square km of land, from Mauritania in the northwest to Nigeria in the southeast. The ECOWAS region is arguably the most fragmented and heterogeneous in Africa, with regards to political boundaries, size of countries, language, religion, and the level of economic development. As Asante (1986: 35) rightly points out, "...if Africa as a whole is badly fragmented, West Africa is even more affected than elsewhere on the continent." Of the 16 member states, nine are officially francophone, five are anglophone, and the remaining two are lusophone (Table 6.1). Also, the region has a number of mini-states, including Cape Verde, Togo, and the Gambia—the latter is an anglophone nation virtually enclosed by Senegal which is francophone. At the other extreme, in terms of physical size, are 'mega' nations such as Mali, Mauritania, and Nigeria, all of which have land masses exceeding 900,000 sq. km.

The population sizes among ECOWAS nations are equally diverse, ranging from lows of 0.4 million in Cape Verde, 1.3 million in the Gambia, and 4.2 million in Togo, to 10.8 million in Mali to as high as 126.9 million (or 54 percent of the entire ECOWAS population) in Nigeria (Table 6.1). Furthermore, the artificiality of many of the national boundaries in the region, as in other parts of Africa, is astounding. There are instances where national boundaries cut across cultural, tribal, and linguistics lines—classic examples are the splitting of the Ewes between Ghana and Togo, and the Yorubas between Benin and Nigeria. No wonder Adebayo Adedeji noted decades ago that "a study of integration efforts in West Africa is inevitably a study in frustration" (Asante 1986: 35).

The ECOWAS region has a vast arable land with varying agricultural capabilities, ranging from rich rain forest belt in the south to poor and dry semi-arid lands bordering the Sahara Desert in the north. The region produces more than half of the world's output of cocoa, coffee, palm oil, and groundnut. Other notable crops include maize, millet, cassava, yams, and sorghum. As Figure 6.2 shows, many ECOWAS nations produce similar crops, with maize, sorghum, millet, groundnut, and cassava being among the top in at least eight of the 16 member states. A notable outlier or exception in this context is rubber, which is produced mainly by Liberia. The mineral resource endowment of the ECOWAS region is also impressive: The region is among the world's leading producers of gold, manganese, diamond, phosphate, and iron. And with Nigeria's extensive coal and petroleum endowment, ECOWAS is well positioned to be a major player in the global oil trade.

Even though the majority of the ECOWAS population is engaged in farming, as in many parts of the developing world, the share of agriculture in the total GDP of many ECOWAS countries is surpassed by the value added in the service sector, due primarily to low agricultural commodity prices in the world market. Still, it is worth noting that agriculture, including forestry and fishing, constitutes more than a third of the GDP of most ECOWAS nations, as seen from Table 6.1. Another striking feature of the ECOWAS economy is the relative weakness of its manufacturing sector. As of 2000, with the exceptions of Senegal, Côte d'Ivoire, and Sierra Leone, the contributions of the manufacturing sector to the GDPs of ECOWAS nations were generally below 15 percent (Table 6.1).

Moreover, as in many developing regions, the vast majority of ECOWAS citizens live in rural areas, under conditions of severe economic deprivation. The World Bank estimates that as high as 72.8 percent of the people in Mali, 70.2 percent in Nigeria, 61.4 percent in Niger, and 59.3 percent in the Gambia live on less than US$1 a day.[1] The per capita incomes among ECOWAS nations are generally low. For instance, while the average GNI per capita for all African countries stood at US$671 in 2000, the corresponding figure for ECOWAS was a mere US$385. Sierra Leone ($130), Guinea Bissau ($180), Niger ($180), and Burkina Faso (210) recorded the lowest GNI per capita in 2000. At the high end are countries such as Cape Verde, Côte d'Ivoire, and Senegal. Despite Nigeria's rich natural resource base—with an estimated GDP of US$32 billion—its income per capita remains unimpressive, due primarily to its massive population coupled with economic and political mismanagement.

The economic structure of ECOWAS nations both reflects and reinforces their long-standing dependence on Western European nations in a core-periphery framework. A corollary of this (neo)colonial relationship is the high level of foreign control over the national economies of ECOWAS states and the diversity of currency regimes in the region (Shaw and Okolo 1994). Most of the former French colonies, with the notable exception of Guinea, are tied to the French CFA franc, just as the former British colonies are closely tied to the sterling bloc and more recently to the US dollar (Masson and Pattillo 2001; Gambari 1991). Not surprisingly, the direction of trade in many ECOWAS nations follows the same pattern, with the bulk to and from Western Europe, the United States, and Japan, than among each other in the region (Okolo and Wright 1990; Onyemelukwe and Filani 1983).

While the available international trade data for ECOWAS nations are sketchy, it is intuitively appealing to expect variations in the level of imports and exports among member nations, just as their natural and human resources, and, consequently, their economic base vary. The leading exporters and importers of ECOWAS include Nigeria, Côte d'Ivoire, Senegal, and Ghana, with countries such as Cape Verde, Guinea Bissau, and Niger accounting for only a small portion of international trade in the region. In 2000, for instance, only Nigeria, Côte d'Ivoire, and Ghana exported more than US$1 billion worth of merchandize; also, only these three countries imported more than US$2 billion worth of merchandize in the same year (Tables 6.2 and 6.3). Both Tables 6.2 and 6.3 suggest that while the exports of many ECOWAS nations are made up of few agricultural commodities, the imports, on the other hand, are quite diverse, with many countries importing food, nonfood, fuel, and capital goods.

Intra-ECOWAS trade is generally low, even though it has been increasing in absolute terms since the 1970s. According to Table 6.4, the value of exports within ECOWAS jumped from a mere $US86 million in 1970 to US$1.5 billion in 1990 and rose again to 3.3 billion by 2000. However, it is important to note that the value of intra-ECOWAS exports, as a percentage of total ECOWAS exports, remained lower than 11 percent (Table 6.4). As noted earlier, the orientation of ECOWAS trade has been toward Western Europe, United States and Japan, with most of the anglophone, francophone, and lusophone states still maintaining strong trading links with their respective ex-colonial metropolises. Ezenwe (1983, 26) observed decades ago that ECOWAS members are "principally not each other's customer"—this is still true. While the value of intra-ECOWAS exports, as a percentage total bloc exports, is higher than that of the Association of Caribbean States (ACS), it is still behind those of other economic blocs in the developing world, including those of the South African Development Community (SADC) and the Association of South-East Asian Nations (ASEAN) (Table 6.4).

The meagerness of intra-ECOWAS trade is further dramatized by the massive amount of zeros in Table 6.5, which shows the trade matrix within ECOWAS for 2000. Only Benin, Côte d'Ivoire, Ghana, Nigeria, Senegal, and Togo recorded sizeable trade (valuing US$1 million or more) with at least six of the 16 ECOWAS states. In fact, only Côte d'Ivoire and Nigeria had trade values of more than US$100 million with three or more ECOWAS states in 2000. A closer examination of the matrix suggests that while linguistic (and currency) affiliations seem to have some influence on intra-ECOWAS trade, the main factor is proximity and the level of economic development. We thus find the relatively well-off nations, such as Nigeria and Côte d'Ivoire, trading across official language lines. While the scantiness of intra-ECOWAS trade remains indisputable, at least compared with those of major trading blocs such as the EU or NAFTA, it is only fair to acknowledge that intra-ECOWAS trade is invariably underestimated due to the informal nature of most cross-border economic transactions in the region. Indeed, informal cross-border trading and migration in West Africa even predate the existence of ECOWAS.

Accomplishments and Challenges

It is important to acknowledge from the outset that the concrete economic achievements of ECOWAS to date are modest. Yet, given the acute poverty, cultural diversity, and the prevalence of ethnic and geopolitical conflicts in West Africa, the mere fact that these nations continue to work together is an epic feat. ECOWAS has spent quite a substantial amount of time on conflict resolution in such countries as Sierra Leone, Liberia, Guinea-Bissau, and, more recently, Côte d'Ivoire, leaving much more to be accomplished in the economic front. Concerns for peace and security have long been on ECOWAS's agenda. The organization adopted its non-aggression protocol only three years after its inception, and followed it up with a defence assistance protocol in 1981, and the creation of the ECOWAS Cease-Fire Monitoring Group (ECOMOG) in 1990. Also, in 1991 ECOWAS members signed a declaration that condemned *coup d'etats* and compels members to adhere to democratic principles. Perhaps, the most important accomplishment of ECOWAS, regarding regional peace and security, is the peacekeeping role it played, through ECOMOG, in Liberia. At the very least, one can commend ECOWAS for alleviating some of the tensions in West Africa. The coalitions and alliances forged between ECOWAS and other international organizations such as the Organization of African Unity (OAU, now African Union), the Economic Commission on Africa (ECA), and the World Bank to promote peace and security across the continent are equally commendable.

On the economic front, ECOWAS has facilitated the free movement of people within the region and improved transportation and telecommunication links between member states. ECOWAS citizens can now enter and reside in any member state for 90 days without visas or entry permits, as long as they have valid passports, or travel certificates, and the necessary international vaccinations. In fact, ECOWAS has introduced its own travel certificate, which is currently in circulation in Burkina Faso, Ghana, Gambia, Guinea, Niger, Nigeria, and Sierra Leone (ECOWAS 2000 and 1999). With this document, ECOWAS travelers are in theory exempted from filling out any immigration papers in member states. However, in practice many member states still have road checkpoints at which police and immigration agents routinely subject ECOWAS travelers and traders to harassment and extortion. Clearly the organization is still a long way from becoming a full-blown common market, given these travel irregularities.

Through its Trade Liberalization Scheme, ECOWAS seeks to establish a custom union and eliminate tariffs among members. The original timeframe was to remove tariffs on unprocessed goods by 1990 and on industrial goods by 2000. While many members

Table 6.1 Basic Indicators of ECOWAS

ECOWAS Members	Population (millions) 2000	Land area (thousands of sq. km)	Infant Mortality Rate 2000	Population growth rate (%) 1990-2000	Real GDP (millions of US$) 1995 price 2000	GNI per capita $US 2000
Benin (F)[1]	6.3	111	87	2.9	2,598	370
Burkina (F)	11.3	274	104	2.4	2.842	210
Cape Verde (P)	0.4	4	---	2.6	670	1,300
Cote d'Ivoire (F)	16.0	318	111	3.1	11,980	600
Gambia (E)	1.3	10	73	3.5	483	340
Ghana (E)	19.2	228	58	2.6	7,978	340
Guinea (F)	7.4	246	95	2.6	4,474	450
Guinea-B (P)	1.2	28	126	2.2	251	180
Liberia (E)	3.1	96	111	2.5	---	---
Mali (F)	10.8	1,220	120	2.5	3,119	240
Mauritania (F)	2.7	1,025	101	2.8	1,321	370
Niger (F)	10.8	1,267	114	3.5	2,197	180
Nigeria (E)	126.9	911	84	2.9	32,184	260
Senegal (F)	9.5	193	60	2.7	5,806	490
Sierra Leone (E)	5.0	72	154	2.4	792	130
Togo (F)	4.2	54	75	2.9	1,479	290
ECOWAS	236.1	6,057	98	2.7	78,174	385
All Africa	797.8	29,367	91[2]	2.6	588,385	671

[1]Letters in parentheses represent official languages: (F) = French; (E) = English; (P) = Portuguese
[2]Figure refers to Sub-Saharan Africa.

Source: The World Bank (2002a & 2002b); Colombo (1994).

(e.g. Côte d'Ivoire, Burkina Faso, Gambia, Ghana, Niger, Nigeria, and Benin) have eliminated their tariffs on unprocessed goods, only Benin has so far lifted tariffs on industrial goods. Tariffs and other trade restrictions continue to undermine intra-ECOWAS trade, which now accounts for a mere 11 percent of members' total trade, valued at US$3.3 billion in the year 2000 (World Bank 2002).

Economic integration invariably entails easy access to each member's market, which, in turn, requires the development of adequate transportation and telecommunication infrastructure. However, such systems are scanty, patchy, and poorly developed across West Africa. Furthermore, while the bulk of the goods traded among ECOWAS members is transported by sea, most of the shipping companies in the sub-region are non-African (or non-ECOWAS). Likewise, most of the sub-regional air travel and telecom-

	Coffee	Cocoa	Seed Cotton	Maize	Sorghum	Cassava	Yam	Oil Palm	Millet	Rice	Ground-nut	Rubber
Benin			△	△	△	△	△					
Burkina Faso			△	△	△				△		△	
Cape Verde												
Côte d'Ivoire	△	△		△		△	△			△		
Gambia												
Ghana		△		△		△			△		△	
Guinea	△			△		△		△		△	△	
Guinea-B				△	△				△	△	△	
Liberia	△	△				△				△		△
Mali			△	△	△				△	△	△	
Mauritania				△	△				△	△		
Niger					△				△		△	
Nigeria		△	△	△	△	△	△	△	△	△	△	
Senegal			△	△	△				△	△	△	
Sierra Leone	△	△					△		△			
Togo	△	△	△	△	△	△	△		△			
Column totals	**5**	**6**	**6**	**11**	**9**	**8**	**4**	**4**	**9**	**9**	**8**	**1**

Figure 6.2 ECOWAS Nations by Major Crops
Source: The World Bank.

munication transactions are done through non-ECOWAS companies. It is against this background that ECOWAS is currently building inter-state highways from Lagos, Nigeria to Nouakchott, Mauritania (i.e., the Trans-Coastal Highway), and from Dakar, Senegal, to N'djamena, Chad (the Trans-Sahelian Highway) to facilitate movement of goods and people in the region. Also, ECOWAS has proposals underway to establish an airline, ECOAIR, and to strengthen the railway networks in the sub-region with a major connection between Lagos and Accra. Moreover, ECOWAS is improving telecommunication facilities in the region with its INTELCOM I and INTELCOM II projects, initiated in 1979 and 1992, respectively, to connect ECOWAS capitals with automatic telefax links (ECOWAS 2000 and 1999; Ajibewa 2002).

With regards to regional energy supply, ECOWAS has a master plan to develop hydroelectric power in several countries including Ghana, Guinea, Sierra Leone, Mali, and Togo. Plans are also underway to develop about 5,600 km of electricity lines connecting various segments of national grids and to establish a "power pool" to facilitate the exchange of electricity between members. Moreover there are initiatives to diversify the energy capabilities of ECOWAS members into biomass, solar, and other renewable energy sources. In a similar vein, the organization has several programs to improve the

Table 6.2 Structure of Output in ECOWAS Nations, 2000

ECOWAS Members	GDP average annual % growth 1990-2000	Agriculture* value added	Industry** value added	Manufacturing*** value added	Services**** value added
Benin	4.7	38	14	13	63
Burkina Faso	4.9	35	17	12	48
Cape Verde	0	0	0	0	0
Côte d'Ivoire	3.5	29	22	19	48
Gambia	3.1	38	13	5	49
Ghana	4.3	35	25	9	339
Guinea	4.3	24	37	4	39
Guinea-B	1.2	59	12	10	29
Liberia	0	0	0	0	0
Mali	3.8	46	17	4	37
Mauritania	4.2	22	31	9	47
Niger	2.4	39	18	7	44
Nigeria	2.4	2	43	0	55
Senegal	3.6	18	27	18	55
Sierra Leone	-4.3	0	34	26	66
Togo	2.3	2	34	8	55

*Agriculture includes forestry and fishing; *value added* represents the net output of an industry after adding up all outputs and subtracting intermediate inputs. The industrial origin of value added in (added is determined by the International Standard Industrial Classification (ISIC); Agriculture correspondes to ISIC divisions 1-5.

**Industry comprises mining, manufacturing, construction, electricity, water and gas; ISIC division 1-5. Percentages do not add up to 100, as manufacturing is also reported as a separate category.

***Manufacturing refers to industries belonging to ISIC divisions 15-37.

****Services correspond to ISIC divisions 50-99.

Source: The World Bank (2002a).

region's agriculture. In 1982, for instance, an Agricultural Development Strategy, which included plans for the selection of high-yielding seeds and cattle species, and called for solidarity among members in international commodity negotiations, was adopted.

Ironically, the organization still faces the same development challenges it encountered at the time of its creation decades ago. Punishing poverty, weak infrastructural base, ethnic and geopolitical conflicts, wide diversity in the levels of development, intrinsically exploitative terms of trade, heavy foreign debt, excessive foreign domination, and, since the early 1980s, socio-economic burdens of IMF and World Bank-sponsored structural adjustment programs continue to plague all ECOWAS states.

The limited financial resources of member states undermines ECOWAS' effectiveness, perhaps more than anything else. As we saw in Table 6.1, the average GNI per capita among ECOWAS states is small, amounting to a mere US$385 in 2000, compared to even the African average of US$671. Not surprisingly, several member states are incapable of meeting their financial commitments, forcing the organization to depend more and more on the financial support of foreign donors. The extreme dearth of financial wherewithal undermines attempts to eliminate custom duties among member states; thus, even the bare- or near-minimum level of integration is difficult to achieve in the region. This is hardly surprising as custom duties account for a large proportion of total government revenue in this part of the world.

Making matters worse is the high level of indebtedness among ECOWAS nations as shown in Table 6.7. The recent Heavily Indebted Poor Countries (HIPCs) initiative, which seeks to reduce the external debt of poor nations may be praiseworthy. However, as long as most ECOWAS nations continue to devote the bulk of their resources to the production of agricultural commodities whose prices are sliding drastically in the world market, their respective balance of payment would forever suffer, culminating in yet another round of indebtedness, subjugation, and dependence on foreign donors.

Table 6.3 Selected Commodity Exports from ECOWAS Nations

ECOWAS Members	Manufactured goods (millions of US $)	Petroleum (thousands of metric tons)	Cocoa (thousands of metric tons)	Coffee (thousands of metric tons)	Forest Products (thousands of cubic meters)	Merchandise exports (f.o.b.*) (millions of US $)
Benin	0	45	0	0	0	186
Burkina Fasa	0	0	0	0	0	206
Cape Verde	0	0	0	0	0	24
Côte d'Ivoire	1,299	472	1,277	132	0	3,672
Gambia	0	0	0	0	0	133
Ghana	0	0	321	6	1,018	1,898
Guinea	0	0	4	7	43	693
Guinea-B	0	0	0	0	8	63
Liberia	0	0	2	0	225	0
Mali	0	0	0	0	0	624
Mauritania	0	0	0	0	0	345
Niger	0	0	0	0	0	253
Nigeria	30	90,672	208	1	248	204,441
Senegal	241	0	0	0	0	959
Sierra Leone	0	0	3	1	0	75
Togo	73	0	8	19	0	363

*Merchandise exports are valued free on board (f.o.b.) and comprise all export transcations involving the change of ownership of goods, including non-monetary gold, between residents of a countray and the rest of the world.

Source: The World Bank (2002b).

Table 6.4 Selected Import into ECOWAS Nations, Millions of US Dollars, 2000

ECOWAS Members	Manufactured goods (imports)	Food (imports)	Nonfood consumer goods (imports)	Fuel (imports)	Capital goods (imports)	Merchandise imports (f.o.b.)*
Benin	0	135	145	80	247	438
Burkina Fasa	0	0	0	0	0	519
Cape Verde	14	55	49	20	106	218
Côte d'Ivoire	0	503	730	562	762	2,525
Gambia	84	9	0	11	14	202
Ghana	0	0	0	533	0	2,759
Guinea	227	87	436	99	0	555
Guinea-B	8	34	10	10	12	88
Liberia	0	0	0	0	0	0
Mali	209	111	165	166	214	714
Mauritania	54	120	12	100	85	329
Niger	0	0	0	0	0	298
Nigeria	0	1,758	0	178	0	12,372
Senegal	0	305	198	280	137	1,342
Sierra Leone	9	66	19	29	54	137
Togo	0	0	0	0	51	491

*Merchandise exports are valued free on board (f.o.b.)and comprise all export transactions involving the change of ownership of goods, including non-monetary gold, between residents of a country and the rest of the world.

Source: The World Bank (2002b).

Many of the companies operating in ECOWAS countries are owned by Multinational Corporations (MNCs) such as Bata, Nestle, and Coca-Cola, which are headquartered in developed nations. And it is not uncommon to find some of these MNCs undermining ECOWAS efforts with the proverbial divide-and-rule tactics to foster their corporate interests in the region. These divide-and-rule tactics are practised not only by MNCs. The fact that many national governments and trading blocs in the North engage in similar covert, underhanded, and hypocritical strategies in their dealings with the South is now well known (Chomsky 2001 and 2002; Stiglitz 2003; de Rivero 2001; Knox and Agnew 1998). For instance, with the Younde Convention of (1963) and Lome Conventions of 1975 and 1979, the European Union came up with a special trading "privilege" for some African, Caribbean and Pacific (ACP) countries, by which the

Table 6.5 Merchandise Export within Selected Regional Trade Blocs, Millions of US$					
Trade Bloc	**1970**	**1980**	**1990**	**1995**	**2002**
ECOWAS	862.91%	69210.1%	1,5337.8%	2,0889.8%	3,33110.8%
ACS	7,589.6%	4,8928.7%	5,4018.4%	10,4498.1%	137,805.5%
SACD	4,838.0%	6,172.0%	16,304.8%	39,638.7%	441,912.2%
ASEAN	14,5622.9%	1,335,018.7%	2,864,819%	8,191,125.4%	10,081,823.9%
EU	7,645,159.5%	45,685,760.8%	98,126,065.9	125,969,962.4%	141,682,562.1%

[1]Intra-bloc merchandise exports, as a percentage of toal bloc exports.

Source: World Bank (2002a).

selected nations can sell their agriculture products to the EU in a reciprocal privilege to the EU or without abandoning their agreements with other nations of the South. While such an arrangement appears benevolent on the surface, it is increasingly becoming clear that this "privilege" is essentially designed to foster the economic interest of the EU, rather than to benefit countries of the South. For one thing, products that compete directly with those produced by EU members, the so-called sensitive products, are either exempted from this 'privilege' entirely, or subjected to restrictions. Furthermore, as Knox and Agnew (1998) point out, this arrangement has compelled many ACP countries to increase their dependence on a handful of export commodities to the EU, thereby making them more vulnerable to price fluctuations in the world market.

The growing poverty in the region is exacerbating the schism between the relatively well-off nations such as Nigeria, Ghana, Senegal, and, until recently, Côte d'Ivoire, and the rest (Ajibewa 2002; Obiozo et al. 1994). The "rich" nations feel they could be better served if they pursue economic links with developed countries rather than with developing nations, such as the very poor ECOWAS nations. Poor and landlocked nations such as Mali, Burkina Faso and Niger are understandably frustrated by their characteristic lack of economic and political clout in the organization (Ajibewa 2002). Given the wide disparity in economic resources and levels of development among the member states, there are bound to be losers and gainers, as ECOWAS tries to establish and locate new infrastructure and productive ventures. Invariably, factors of production would move from relatively poor and less efficient countries to the more efficient and well-off ones. Unless ECOWAS redoubles its development efforts, through its Fund for Co-operation, Compensation, and Development, to safeguard the interest of the economically weak nations, the organization stands to reinforce the spatial and economic polarization in the region. The strict application of economic principles, couched in industrial location theories and the infamous comparative advantage theory, in the distribution of ECOWAS industries and infrastructure is bound to exacerbate tensions and mistrust in the organization. For the sake of stability, one can even argue for special concessions for the poor members with sub-optimal industrial location characteristics. In fact, members need to agree on the specific roles of individual states

Table 6.6 Intra-ECOWAS Trade Matrix, Millions of Current US$, 2000

Importers/ Exporters	1	2	3	4	5	6	7
1. Benin	0	1	0	0	0	0	0
2. Burkina Fasa	0	0	0	0	0	0	0
3. Cape Verde	0	0	0	0	0	0	0
4. Côte d'Ivoire	43	129	1	0	12	134	53
5. Gambia	0	0	0	0	0	0	0
6. Ghana	24	6	0	2	1	0	0
7. Guinea	0	0	0	9	0	0	0
8. Guinea-B.	0	0	0	0	0	*	0
9. Liberia	0	0	0	2	0	0	0
10. Mali	0	2	0	3	0	0	0
11. Mauritania	0	0	0	18	0	2	0
12. Niger	4	1	0	3	0	3	0
13. Nigeria	10	17	0	601	0	545	4
14. Senegal	6	3	2	17	29	2	11
15. Sierra Leone	0	0	0	0	0	0	0
16. Togo	49	10	0	2	0	17	0

*means data not available.

Source: The World Bank (2002b).

through fair negotiations, but there is no denying that such agreement is hard to conclude, given the long-standing mistrust and competing national interests among the members.

Despite improvements, most ECOWAS countries exhibit acute shortfalls in their infrastructure—water supply, sanitation, power supply, and transport and communication facilities—are woefully inadequate. One finds a situation where the bulk of the road, railway, shipping, and air travel networks in ECOWAS countries are still geared toward the export of primary products to European centers, rather than toward intra-West African trade. This is mainly because of the limited trade potential (or, more rightly, the low-level of trade) between ECOWAS members. Since they are all primary producers, with agriculture accounting for a large proportion of their respective GDPs

Table 6.7 ECOWAS Nations by External Debts				
ECOWAS Members	**Total external debt ($million) 1990-2000**	**Present value of debt (percentage of GNI)**	**Total debt services (percentage of GNI)**	**Indebtedness classification***
Benin	1,292	45	12.6	S
Burkina Fasa	834	31	17.3	M
Cape Verde	0	0	0	0
Côte d'Ivoire	17,251	134	22.4	S
Gambia	369	64	7	M
Guinea	3,881	78	19.3	M
Guinea-B	692	345	8.6	S
Liberia	1,849	0	0	S
Mali	2,467	59	4.3	M
Mauritania	2,096	124	11	S
Niger	1,726	58	1.6	S
Nigeria	33,493	74	2.7	S
Senegal	3,736	56	5.9	M
Sierra Leone	1,151	128	2.7	S
Togo	1,281	85	5.4	M

*S = Severely indebted; M = moderately indebted; L= Less indebted

Data (and classification) are from debt sustainability analyses done as part of Heavily Indebted Poor Countries (HIPCs) Initiative.

Source: The World Bank (2002a).

and exports, the demand for their exports and the supply of their imports invariably emanate from elsewhere, notably from the advanced nations, and recently, from the Newly Industrializing Countries (NICs) of the Far East.

ECOWAS and Africa's Development in the 21st Century

In this section we explore the extent to which ECOWAS could be a vehicle for Africa's development in the 21st century, bearing in mind our conception of development as a societal move to enhance the provision of basic needs, couched in self-sufficiency and a respect for traditional knowledge and local practices. Given that ECOWAS is a bloc within Africa, it is not unreasonable to argue that its challenges and accomplishments would have some indirect ramifications for the development of Africa as a whole, especially in this era of globalization. Even beyond this, ECOWAS can directly impact Africa's development in several ways, as we shall soon show.

With ingenuity, backed by strong political will and cooperation from the genuine regional blocs in Africa, including SADC and ECCAS, ECOWAS (see Table 6.8) can spearhead a movement to reduce the number of trading blocs in the continent, by limiting the multiplicity of membership in regional integration arrangements. Minor blocs, such as the Mano River Union (MRU), the West African Economic and Monetary Union (UEMOA), and the Economic Community of the Countries of the Great Lakes (CEPGL), could be persuaded to join forces with the major or truly regional blocs to help reduce duplication, overlap, and competition. Obviously, competition is not bad *per se*. However, in a continent like Africa, where human resources and state capacity are severely constrained, competition could overburden many countries, especially the impoverished ones, such as Mali, Burkina Faso, and Rwanda. In fact, with so many blocs criss-crossing the continent, sorting out the maze of regional agreements alone would require resources that could otherwise be used to improve the human condition and self-sufficiency of Africans.

Unfortunately, even though all the regional blocs in the continent share similar objectives, regarding trade, peace and security, and development, there is very little co-ordination, if any, amongst them, as of now. And, as Isaksen (2003: 213) suggests, the same can said of the various continent-wide initiatives or organizations, such as the African Union (AU) and the New Partnership for African Development (NEPAD), which have the explicit tenet to build alliances with regional blocs across the continent. We contend that without conscious efforts to build bridges and to reduce unnecessary competition and duplication, the continent would remain vulnerable to divide-and-rule tactics from outsiders.

Additionally, to boost their self-sufficiency, we suggest that ECOWAS and the other regional blocs in Africa *limit* their dependence on external financial assistance. Member states of these African organizations should endeavor to, at least, foot the operational cost of their respective blocs. We are not in any way advocating a total avoidance of foreign financial assistance—that, in our view, would be counter-productive and irresponsible, if not outright suicidal, at this stage of Africa's development. Our basic argument is that these African blocs should not be excessively dependent on foreign aid and become so donor-driven, with regards to their initiatives and operations.

In a similar vein, we urge ECOWAS to help mobilize the leading African blocs to strengthen their collective alliance with other blocs in the South, such as the Andean Common Market and the Association of Caribbean States, to fight for fairness in international trade between Northern and Southern countries. The United Nations Conference on Trade and Development (UNCTAD) would perhaps be the most amenable and progressive global platform for such a struggle. Among other things, these Southern blocs should unite to negotiate for reasonable prices and production agreements with the nations of North. It would even be worthwhile to establish a common fund to create buffer stocks of agricultural and other commodities from the South, to help influence

Table 6.8 Regional Blocs in Africa		
ACRONYM	**Full Name**	**Membership**
CEMAC	Economic and Monetary Community of Central Africa	Cameroom, the Central African Replubic, Chad, the Republic of Congo, Equatorial Guinea, Gabon, Sao Tome and Principle (7) [1]
CEPGL	Economic Community of the Countries of the Great Lakes	Burundi, the Democratic Republic of Congo, and Rwanda (4)
COMESA*[2]	Common Market for Eastern and Southern Africa	Angola, Burundi, Comoros, the Democratic Republic of Congo, Djibouti, Egypt, Eritrea, Ehtiopia, Kenya, Madagascar, Malawi, Mauritius, Namibia, Rwanda, Seychelles, Sudan, Swaziland, Uganda, Tanzania, Zambia, and Zimbabwe (21)
CBI*	Cross-Border Initiative	Burundi, Comoros, Kenya, Madagascar, Malawi, Mauritius, Namibia, Rwanda, Seychelles, Swaziland, Tanzania, Uganda, Zambia, and Zimbabwe (14)
ECCAS	Economic Community of Central African States	Angola, Burundi, Cameroon, the Central African Republic, Chad, the Democratic Republic of Congo, the Republic of Congo, Equatorial Guinea, Gabon, Rwanda, Sao Tome and Principe (11)
ECOWAS	Economic Community of West African States	Benin, Burkina Faso, Cape Verde, Cote d'Ivoire, Gambia, Ghana, Guinea, Guinea-Bissau, Liberia, Mali, Mauritius, Niger, Nigeria, Senegal, Sierra Leone, and Togo (16)
IOC*	Indian Ocean Commission	Comoros, Madagascar, Mauritius, Reunion, and Seychelles (5)
MRU*	Mano River Union	Guinea, Liberia, and Sierra Leone (3)
SADC*	Southern African Development Community	Angola, Botswana, the Democratic Republic of Congo, Lesotho, Malawi, Mauritius, Mozambique, Namibia, Seychelles, South Africa, Swaziland, Tanzania, Zambia, and Zimbabwe (14)
UDEAC	Central African Custom and Economic Union	Cameroon, the Central African Republic, Chad, the Republic of Congo, Equatorial Guinea, and Gabon (6)
UEMOA*	West African Economic and Monetary Union	Benin, Burkina Faso, Cote d'Ivoire, Guinea-Bissau, Mali, Niger, Senegal, and Togo (8)

Notes:
[1] The total number of members is in parenthesis.
[2] Blocs to which at least one ECOWAS nation is a member are marked by asterisk(*).

Source: World Bank (2002a: 346.)

the supply, and, consequently, the prices, of these items in the world market. In addition, efforts should be made to secure long-term supply contracts and fair prices, perhaps by indexing primary commodities prices against the prices of goods and services from the North—as suggested by Knox and Agnew (1998) and Knox and Marston (2001)—to help alleviate some of the inequalities and unfairness in the prevailing global economic system.

So far ECOWAS has given only scant attention to the region's manufacturing sector. However, the potential for this sector is enormous, as any analysis of the import structure of the member states would quickly reveal. The region has a considerable potential for import-substitution industrialization, especially in consumer goods such as shoes, household plastics, building materials, agricultural implements, and even in transport equipment. Again, there is a compelling case for an increased coordination and co-operation between ECOWAS and the leading African blocs, notably the SADC, in this area to enhance intra-African trade, and help reduce the continent's dependence on foreign markets. Given the high level of unemployment across the continent, due cognizance should be given to labour intensity in manufacturing. Investment in human capital, education, and the provision of region- and continent-wide public goods and infrastructure (e.g., roads, railways, and telecommunication lines), as well as initiatives towards disease control and environmental sustainability should be taken more seriously now than ever before, if Africa is to move ahead in the 21st century.

Finally, drawing from the works of Chomsky (2001, 2002), Joe Stiglitz (2003), and Oswaldo de Rivero (2001), it is reasoned that for African economies to improve in the 21st century, the major policy makers should treat such western concepts such as "comparative advantage" and "free trade," with immense skepticism. We suggest that ECOWAS and the other African trading blocs concentrate more on strengthening their intra-regional trade for now, with member states focusing on the production of food and other goods and services that are actually needed or used within Africa. We seriously question the rationale of, for instance, devoting the best agricultural land of the continent for the production of such crops as cocoa and coffee for foreign markets, while many Africans are hungry, just because some alien and problematic principle—i.e., comparative advantage—dictates so. In consonance with the operational definition of development adopted earlier on, we urge African nations to undertake purposeful ranking of the goods and service they actually need and try, if possible, to produce them internally, using appropriate, culturally sensitive technology to enhance their self-sufficiency. Chomsky (2001: 361) was correct in observing that "...one reason for the sharp divide between today's first and third worlds is that much of the latter was subjected to 'experiments' that rammed free market doctrine down their throats, whereas today's developed countries were able to resist such measures." We contend, as did the UN Development Report of 1992, that the increasing gap between the rich and poor countries is attributable, at least in part, to the protectionist measures of the rich countries vis-à-vis their dealings with the developing world; yet the World Bank, IMF and now the World Trade Organization (WTO) are constantly pushing the notion of unbridled free trade across the developing world—a notion that is, in the words of Oswaldo de Rivero (2001: 50), "meant to find clients and not to help countries develop."

Concluding Remarks

Clearly, even though ECOWAS has made some headway toward the integrating West African countries into a trading bloc, it still faces some serious challenges, much of which is tied to the extreme poverty and the prevalence of geopolitical conflicts in the region. Notwithstanding these daunting challenges, recent trends in the sub-region point to a promising future for ECOWAS. Among these are the increasing tilt toward providing regional public goods and infrastructure, such as roads and telecommunication networks; flexibility in cross-border migration; and a growing desire to help neighboring countries stabilize and prosper both for altruistic reasons and to avoid spillover of unrest and refugee movements. Still, for ECOWAS to thrive in the 21st century, the need for a clearer focus, better prioritization, and unflinching support of political leaders and citizens of West Africa for ECOWAS programs, as well as improved co-ordination and cooperation with other African blocs are crucial.

Acknowledgments

This research was funded by the Atkinson Faculty of Liberal and Professional Studies' Junior Faculty Grant and SSHRC's Institutional Grant Program through York University.

Note

1 This is the international poverty line, measured in 1985 international prices and adjusted to local currencies using purchasing power parities (PPPs).

References

Ajibewa, Aderemi (2002). *From Regional Security to Regional Integration in West Africa: Lessons from the ASEAN Experience* www.cdd.org.uk

Asante, S.K.B. (1986). *The Political Economy of Regionalism in Africa: A Decade of the Economic Community of West African States (ECOWAS)*. New York: Praeger Publishers.

Balassa, Bela (1961). *The Theory of Economic Integration*. Homewood, IL: Richard D.Irwin.

Berry, Brian J.L.; Conkling, Edgar, C.; Ray, D. Michael (1998) *The Global Economy in Transition*.
Upper Saddle River, New Jersey: Prentice Hall.

Chomsky, Noam (2001). "Free Trade and Free Market: Pretense and Practice" in Fredric Jameson and Masao Miyoshi (eds.), *The Cultures of Globalization*. Durham and London: Duke University Press. p. 356–370.

———— 2002. *Understanding Power*. New York: The New Press.

Colombo, John Robert (1994).*The Canadian Global Almanac* .Toronto: Macmillan Canada.

De Rivero, Oswaldo (2001). *The Myth of Development*. London: Zed Books.

ECOWAS (2000). *Silver Jubilee Anniversary (1975–2000): Achievements and Prospects*. Abuja, Nigeria: ECOWAS.

——————— (1999). *An ECOWAS Compendium on Free Movement, Right of Residence and Establishment.* Abuja, Nigeria: ECOWAS.

Ezenwe, Uka (1983). *ECOWAS and the Economic Integration of West Africa.* London: C. Hurst and Company.

Gambari, Ibrahim A. (1991). *Political and Comparative Dimensions of Regional Integration: The Case of ECOWAS.* New Jersey and London: Humanities Press International, Inc.

Isaksen, Jan (2003). "SADC Restructuring and the Future" In Dirk Hansohm, Willie Breytenbach, and Trudi Hartzenberg (eds.), *Monitoring Regional Integration in Southern Africa.* Windhoek, Namibia: Gamsberg Macmillan. pp. 201–219.

Knox, Paul and Agnew, John (1998). *The Geography of the World Economy.* London: Arnold.

Knox, Paul and Marston, Sallie A. (2001). *Human Geography: Places and Regions in Global Context.* Upper Saddle River, NJ: Prentice Hall.

Masson, Paul and Pattillo, Catherine (2001) *Monetary Union in West Africa (ECOWAS): Is it Desirable and How could it be Achieved?* Washington DC: International Monetary Union; Occasional Paper #204

Obiozo, G.A., Olukoshi, A.O., and Obi, C.I. (eds) (1994). *West African Regional Economic Integration: Nigerian Perspectives for the 1990s.* Lagos, Nigeria: Nigerian Institute of International Affairs.

Okolo, Julius Emeka and Wright, Stephen (eds) (1990). *West African Regional Cooperation and Development.* San Francisco: Westview Press.

Onyemelukwe, J.O.C. and Filani, M.O. (1983). *Economic Geography of West Africa.* London: Longman.

Shaw, Timothy M. and Okolo, Julius Emeka (eds.) (1994). *The Political Economy of Foreign Policy in ECOWAS.* London: The Macmillan Press Ltd.

Stiglitz, Joseph, E. (2003). *Globalization and its Discontents.* New York and London: W.W. Norton and Company.

World Bank (2002a). *World Development Indicators—2002* (Washington D.C.: The World Bank.

World Bank (2002b). *African Development Indicators—2002* (Washington D.C.: The World Bank.

Chapter 7

Conflict Timber, Conflict Diamonds: Parallels in the Political Ecology of 19th and 20th Century Resource Exploitation in Sierra Leone

Fenda A. Akiwumi

...a bitter war began between the two branches of the family, for the possession of the whole chiefdom whose timber-bearing mainland was now as valuable as the slave-exporting coast and islands. They fought with a ferocity unusual in a country where wars were chiefly a means to get slaves.

– Christopher Fyfe, 1968 (on events between 1842 and 1948)

Diamonds are forever' it is said. But lives are not. We must spare people the ordeal of war, mutilations and death for the sake of conflict diamonds.

– Martin Chungong Ayafor, 2000 (on events in the 1990s)

Introduction

The concept of "conflict diamonds" has developed from the consequences of recent devastating rebel wars in African countries like Sierra Leone and the Democratic Republic of Congo (DRC). Conflict diamonds are "diamonds that originate from areas controlled by forces or factions opposed to legitimate and internationally recognized governments, and are used to fund military action in opposition to those governments, or in contravention of the decisions of the Security Council" (www.un.org/peace/africa/Diamond.html). A brutal insurrection led by the Revolutionary United Front of Sierra Leone (RUF/SL) caused the death of thousands, maimed many others and displaced a significant percentage of a population, estimated at around five million. Terrorist activity such as in the United States on September 11, 2001, is believed to have been partly financed by the illicit purchase of gems from this country (Farah 2001b). That there is a direct relationship between low level conflicts in Africa and strategic minerals has been widely documented. Ferme (2001: 5) succinctly states that interests in diamond extraction "cut across local and national domains, and there is a linkage between the extraction of precious resources and violence as a global business".

In the 19th century , many wars were instigated and fought over timber that, like diamonds, was a 'hot' commodity destined for global markets. Notable among the wars was that between branches of the Caulker family of Bumpe who fought ferociously from 1842 to 1848. Other major fighting took place in Masimera from the mid-1850 to 1860s and in Koya in 1861. The government formed militia groups of several hundred men in the Crown Colony (current Western Area), and used naval gunboats to protect timber areas and quell local dissent. The mercenary services of skilled Mende war-chiefs capable of rounding up several hundred men were employed by both the colonial government and indigenous rulers. Towns were burned and sawmills routinely plundered. Casualties of war included rulers and their clans, missionaries and colony traders.

Paul Richards (1996; 2002) has investigated the relationship between resource exploitation and conflict here, particularly in regard to the recent rebel war. He postulates that the problem lies in the fact that true statehood has never been attained. There have, therefore, never been appropriate institutions to manage resources sustainably. The war was a response to this reality by disgruntled and displaced youth, already accustomed to a culture of violence in the diamond areas. By definition, "*a state claims exclusive sovereignty over a demarcated space and all the people and resources within it*" (Bergman and Renwick 2002: 416). By this definition, the very nature of colonial imposition with its demarcation of superimposed boundaries, defeats the notion of nations that have achieved statehood, and has made the legitimacy of the state in Africa an ongoing problem (Englebert, 1997, see Chapter 3).

Roots of Conflict

Sierra Leone has a long history on the matter of statehood by virtue of its history as a haven for freed slaves sponsored by British philanthropists. Following abolition of the transatlantic slave trade, the Black Poor, Maroons, Nova Scotians and Recaptives (collectively the Creoles or Krio) were resettled in a small area on the west coast of the country between the late 18th and mid-19th century. This took place in a region that had diverse ethnic groups; many with a long, rich cultural heritage. Here, traditional governance had long been carried out by religio-political and administrative organizations like 'Poro' headed by a chief. This body, still active today, instills discipline and maintains law and order often through the use of sanctions. Nevertheless, pioneers of the anti-slavery movement like abolitionist such as Granville Sharpe and Henry Venn of the Church Missionary Society (CMS), envisaged the settlement as a model in European style governance. The latter saw "the Christianized, westernized Creole as being best qualified by training, background and physical resistance to disease, to play the major role in West African regeneration" (July 1980: 321). It was believed that a western style self-governing community of black people would evolve into nation-statehood.

This proposition, however, was short-lived. Powerful business interests saw the economic potential of this relocation exercise in a land with abundant natural resources. The Sierra Leone Company (hereafter SLC) was incorporated under Act (31 Geo. III cap. 55), in 1791 to govern. Lands originally granted to settlers were ceded to it and it had the right to "make its own laws for those concerned in its affairs" (Fyfe 1962: 27). Such powers were normally attributed to the Secretary of State for the Colonies. It thus, represented both government and commerce. Conflict quickly ensued over the right to self-determination denied because of 'resources.'

In 1808, the settlement was declared a Crown Colony (hereafter, the Colony) administered from Great Britain. By 1896, the British government had acquired jurisdiction over the entire country through cession of territory, peace, boundary fixing or friendship. Between 1788 and 1895, a total of 156 treaties were made with local chiefs (Goddard 1969). This was, also achieved in an atmosphere of discord over loss of sovereignty by indigenous rulers. Resources like timber created new avenues of status and wealth, and competition for resources added another dimension to existing conflicts.

Sierra Leone attained Independence from Britain in 1961. This granted 'nation-statehood' to the country. People somewhat united by similar value systems and cultural norms would rule themselves and have complete control over the 71,740 square kilometer territory. However, the stranglehold on the country by economic interests and tremendous power vested in leadership has persisted since the days of the SLC with a gray area between the private and public sectors. The Wilsonian Principle of national self-determination, therefore, has never been a reality. The continuing exploitation of resources precludes the formation of appropriate institutions to manage both human and natural resources sustainably and for the benefit of Sierra Leonians

Hence, resource extraction created a complex political ecology that prevails with conflict as an inherent part. Socio-political change has led to modification of traditional perceptions of land use and ownership, and the customary patronage-clientelism political culture. New sources of wealth facilitate co-optation of local rulers to support and perpetuate introduced policies and cause intra-ethnic group rivalry over resource bearing areas. Other aspects of the environment include illicit trade in commodities and the use of mercenary tactics and services to acquire and/or protect economic interests. Moreover, poorly conceived resource policies and legislation have and continue to cause degradation of the natural environment.

Factors that show parallels in the 19th century timber and current diamond trade settings will be presented. Furthermore, the historical foundations of the problem of achieving true sovereignty and hence the existence of effective institutions will be addressed. I go back to the founding of Freetown (now the capital of Sierra Leone) in 1787 as a haven for freed slaves. For the past 41 years, the country has been variously governed under multi-party democracy, one party rule and military dictatorship. Currently, a United Nations peacekeeping force and military technical assistance from Great Britain are supporting a democratically elected government's efforts at rehabilitation following the 10-year war. Administratively, the country is divided into the Northern, Southern and Eastern Provinces, and the Western Area where the capital is located. The regions are further subdivided into twelve districts. Traditional authority is divided into smaller units called chiefdoms with the Paramount Chief as local ruler supported by a Tribal Authority. He holds the land in trust primarily, but not solely for the benefit of the landholding lineages who practice subsistence agriculture. Approximately 70 percent of the population lives in rural areas.

The Natural Resource Base: Timber and Diamonds

Sierra Leone is bordered by Guinea to the northwest and northeast and Liberia to the south. The country lies in the Upper Guinean Forest Zone of the tropical rainforest belt of West Africa. Up to 60 percent of the land area may have been covered in primeval forest. Today the figure is estimated at around four percent. Rainfall averages 3000 mm/ annum. The extensive drainage network traversing the country has eroded underlying ore bearing rocks, redepositing alluvial and lateritic deposits of valuable minerals, including diamonds. These secondary formations are sometimes located in densely forested terrain.

In the 19th century, timber was a major income generator for The Colony that was expected to be self-sustaining. The trade began in 1816, when an Irishman, John McCormack, began exporting logs from the west coast of the country. Fifty ships a year carrying cargo worth 40,000 pounds sterling from factories in the Port Loko Creek sailed to England within the first ten years of the trade (Fyfe 1962). In 1820, 1822 and 1825, 6078, 1433 and 21,650 logs respectively were exported from Sierra Leone (Unwin 1920). From 1827 to 1835, the number exported totaled 82,911 (Moloney 1887). With the advent of iron ships in the mid-19th century the flourishing trade began to dwindle. Beyond 1896, however, lumber was still carried by sailing ship to Boston and New York in the United States. British, French, Belgian, Dutch and German steamers participated profitably in the transport of forest products.

Minerals, particularly diamonds, became an important revenue earner in the 1930s. Gems were first discovered on the Gboboro river in Kono District, Eastern Sierra Leone in 1929 by the Government Geological Survey. The Consolidated African Selection Trust Limited (CAST) obtained an exclusive license from the colonial government in 1931 to prospect for diamonds. Eventually, the Sierra Leone Selection Trust (SLST) was created as a subsidiary. This company negotiated an exclusive prospecting license for the entire country for 99 years. Mining operations began in 1932 and SLST was given the sole right to produce and market diamonds. This was however revised in 1955, the lease being reduced to 15 years and the monopoly area to a 310 square mile zone that contained proven or developed reserves. In 1971, the National Diamond Mining Company (DIMINCO) was formed with the now independent Sierra Leone government holding 51 percent shares in the industry. Since the demise of DIMINCO, numerous small-scale concerns have exploited the diamonds. Illicit mining has been operating concurrently. The industry, at the height of its operations in the 1950s and 1960s, contributed approximately 65 percent of national revenue by producing two to three million carats per annum (Conciliation Resources 1997). A World Bank study estimated that less than one percent of the $183 million worth of diamonds that were recently exported from the country was legal.

The Political Ecology of Resource Exploitation

Resource exploitation has always been instigated by external market forces. The English Navy Board, for example, utilized much of Sierra Leonean timber for dockyards in the 19th century and the Admiralty Contractor had a virtual monopoly. The heavy duty levied, therefore, was reduced. Today, diamonds are exported or smuggled to major trading and polishing centers in Belgium, Great Britain, Israel, the US, Switzerland and India. Both colonial and post-Independence governments have depended heavily on revenue from royalties, taxes, custom duties and rent generated from these two commodities. As such, business has been strongly supported and the government demonstrates double standards in operating as public servants. The legacy of unmitigated power of government and ambiguity between the public and private sectors from the days of the SLC was carried over to the Colony. As Fyfe (1962: 159) observes in regard to the timber trade "policy became a mere continuation of trade by other means". Zachary Macaulay, for example, who served as governor from 1793 to 1799 and SLC company secretary from 1799 to 1807 continued to influence events in the country politically, and economically well into the 19th century.

Well known for his high-handed, ruthless approach to governance, he promoted divide and rule policies, favoritism and nepotism. In spite of the mistrust and disillusionment that he created in Sierra Leone, his opinions were valued in London. He was instrumental in the establishment of the Crown Colony that served as headquarters from which Britain controlled its other West African colonies. In a memorandum to Lord Castlereagh, Secretary of State for War and the Colonies, Macaulay wrongly described Sierra Leone as "a mild but firm and well-ordered Government, of rational liberty, and of secure and productive industry" (Metcalfe 1964: 6). He also discouraged British government support of the Company of Merchants Trading to Africa (long associated with slave marketing) as a participant in a new legitimate trade policy with the region.

On the approval of his recommendations and with major competition removed, he became actively involved in commerce. From 1807 to 1827, he traded in timber, gold and other commodities, initially alone, and later in partnership with his nephew as Macaulay and Babington. This firm was the largest in the country and was backed by substantial outside capital. Managed by his second cousin Kenneth Macaulay from 1815, the business dominated the import-export trade, government supply contracts and money transactions to England. Any competition was ruthlessly crushed. Dala Modu, a local ruler served as agent and received huge commissions. Modu exploited slave labor in a feudal context (Ndole) and used his power base to help his partners acquire more forested terrain.

Other examples of government partiality to business have been documented. Governor MacDonald, for example, in 1843, in response to Chief Momodu Bundu of Foredugu "putting Poro" (sanctions) on felled timber sent a European merchant John Dawson, with a detachment of troops on the steamer HMS Soudan to force him to release the load. Hanson, Government Consul in Sherbro in the early 1850s unequivocally protected the interests of timber traders, frequently requesting armed intervention from Freetown on their behalf. An Afro-West Indian timber trader, Dupigny, even acted as Consul while Hanson was on leave. Representing both government and commerce at this time, he informed the Foreign Office in London of additional timber sources in

Bagru. Another Afro-West Indian trader in this commodity, Jolly, was used as an emissary by Governor Hill in 1861 to enlist the help of Mende war-chiefs at Moyamba. The goal was to coerce Bagru and Sherbro chiefs to cede their land to the British.

Lawlessness, which was widespread, was difficult to contain especially where source areas were outside the Colony's jurisdiction. Even accomplices like Dala Modu, in spite of benefiting from transactions, nevertheless complained that traditional power was being usurped. An 1831 treaty giving chiefs the right to discipline British subjects was ratified. Commonly, "British law served to protect evildoers and not their victims" (Fyfe 1962: 208). Eventually, the Imperial Act of 1861 allowed British subjects who committed offences to be punished under British, not traditional law. Government brought productive adjacent territory into the Colony's jurisdiction by cession or annexation. This was achieved through the coercion of chiefs seeking protection from competitors in the trade. Traders were disgruntled over these new arrangements.

In the diamond mining regions, likewise, rulers saw their power gradually eroded away. The Laws of Sierra Leone (1960: 2023) section 3(1), for instance, state that:

> The entire property in the control of all minerals, and mineral oils in under or upon any lands in Sierra Leone, is hereby declared to reside in the Crown, save in so far as such control may in any case have been limited by an express grant made by the Crown before the commencement of this ordinance. (Conteh 1979: 34)

Petitions were frequently made to government, albeit, a collaborator, about business practices in chiefdoms. Protests in colonial times included Foa Matturie's 1934 demand that commensurate monetary compensation be paid for the profanation and desecration of sacred ground. Fourteen paramount chiefs and tribal leaders from Kono District led by Paramount Chief Tamba Songo Mbriwa, representative for Kono in the Sierra Leone Legislature, and Edward W. Blyden III, president of the Sierra Leone Independence Movement (SLIM) presented a petition to the Colonial Office in London in 1957. It requested a Royal Commission inquiry into exploitation and underdevelopment in diamond mining areas. The dominance and oppression of the SLST, described as 'the government' in Kono District were brought to light. Subsequent complaints to post colonial governments covered matters like forced relocation, desecration of sacred bush sites, pollution of drinking water sources and destruction of farmland. In the dispute over Lake Mondeima, a historically sacred site, the indigenous people in desperation resorted to physical obstruction to prevent mining (Conteh 1979).

The National Reformation Council (NRC) Decree No. 49 of 1967 passed by the ruling military junta took the responsibility of issuing mining licenses away from chiefs and assigned it to the Ministry of Mines (Zack-Williams 1995). This interfered with the historical bureaucratic system of land tenure and deprived rulers of additional revenue through rent and taxation. The strong arm of government was, however, most evident in President Siaka Steven's relationship with industry during his 18-year rule. Through the Ministry of Mines, he controlled the organization of illicit diamond mining by preferentially distributing privatized plots.

Opposition to this policy by chiefs and influential Konos was quelled when they were bypassed in favor of foreigners (mostly Lebanese) in the preferential disbursement of mining plots. Chiefs eventually succumbed to pressure and, by 1981, ten out of twelve were in management positions with DIMINCO. A major conflict of interest was also seen in the industry from 1979 to 1985. The largest private exporter of diamonds known to be in business with the President was made Acting Manager of the company. Together, they co-directed the official government marketing Gold and Diamond Office (GDO).

Conflicting Views on Land Use and Ownership

Differing preferences for land use and ownership have historically caused clashes between indigenous people and business interests supported by government. The traditional Sierra Leonean viewpoint is that land is not a marketable commodity. It is the property of the clan, providing a sense of security to all members. 'Strangers' (those with no kinship ties to the original land-owning lineages) can be granted permission to use land. They, however, require a landlord to be responsible for their actions within the community and are expected to pay customary gifts to the Chief, periodically. European timber traders, as strangers were perplexed at having to renegotiate land deals every time a new ruler came into power. Re-captives also opened factories and became increasingly drawn into, or interfered with local politics to the dismay of Chiefs who had no authority to contain them (Fyfe 1962).

In the diamond fields likewise, the SLST was constantly clashing with the Kono people who considered that the land, and therefore the diamonds the land contained, their birthright (Conteh 1979). Parallel problems with strangers who have "*little knowledge or respect for the spiritual sanctions on which village political institutions still depend for their effectiveness*" (Richards 2002: 132) occur. Typical strangers are foreigners. Business and government have attempted to address this problem on several occasions. The SLST offered chiefs in diamond-rich areas stipends for signing agreements to oust strangers (non-Konos) from their chiefdoms (Zack-Williams 1988). A mass deportation of strangers took place in 1955 after a revolt in the diamond fields by local miners (Lynch 1973; Hirsch 2001). As recently as 1996 there was a major expulsion drive from the area. Mining licenses of foreign-owned businesses were temporarily revoked in 1998 ahead of a the announcement of a new national policy on mining. The president was quoted as saying that ".....the government cannot sit idly by while its citizens are deprived of their own resources and so henceforth, indigenous citizens will be given priority in the mining sector" (Fofana 1998: 3).

Dealing with conflict over land in the face of powerful forces has been a long-term dilemma for indigenous people. One means by which rulers have dealt with the paradoxes of new value systems is by resorting to the use of Poro. Sanctions were frequently used to restrict trade by, for example, declaring a moratorium on the movement or processing of felled timber by local people. Other customary belief systems employed in the diamond mining environment have included sacrifices of appeasement to genies to guarantee good finds (*The Eagle* 1992). These practices according to Ferme (2001: 39) are a means of interpreting the new situations created by non-traditional resources like diamonds in ways that can be easily understood. Thus, "the real basis of economic prosperity for them was founded on the interpretation of occult phenomena and on finding mineral substances that were linked cosmologically to the concealed domains of ancestors and spirits located under the surface of local soils and waters" (39).

Patron-Clientistic Networks and Co-optation

The need for patron-clientistic networks evolved out of conditions of instability in pre-colonial times caused by wars over trade routes and natural resources. Warrior (patron) protection was necessary for personal and collective security and individual and group economic survival. Patrimonialism is considered an adaptation of the traditional form of patronage to suit politics at the national level (Richards 2002). The socio-political environment of the timber trade was rife for patronage. The self-styled "Sherbro Monarch", a wealthy, powerful and ruthless Creole merchant, Solomon Benjamin Augustus Macfoy, was a classic example. Usurping the authority of local chiefs through their financial indebtedness to him, he commandeered lands for his own personal use. Even authorities in Freetown were unnerved by his direct access to the Colonial Office in London through his business associates, the Manchester firm of Callender, Sykes and Mather.

In the diamond fields, patron-client relations still serve as a means of protection for henchmen and tributors. Patrons include chiefs, financiers, diamond dealers, influential Konos and politicians. Traditional rulers, custodians of the land are still used as agents for external business interests. Arrangements like the Contract Cooperative Mining Scheme (CCMS) and the Alluvial Diamond Mining Scheme (ADMS) devised by the SLST to allegedly encourage indigenous participation in the industry have in reality, only benefited collaborating traditional and national authorities (Zack-Williams 1995).

Intra-Ethnic Group Conflict Over Resources

Conflict motivated by greed was and continues to be an integral part of resource extraction. Competition for timber rights and monopoly led to many wars often instigated by European traders who then supplied firearms to opposing factions. At Foredugu, in 1839, a quarrel between a Maroon timber trader and his Re-captive clerk led to the former being killed. The local chief resolved the matter by handing over the murderer to Maroons who burnt him to death. This led to friction between the two Creole sub-groups in the Colony. The timely intervention of soldiers and Marines prevented full-scale war. Ferocious fighting also took place between two arms of the Caulker family of Bumpe and the Plantain Islands for the possession of timber-bearing chiefdoms between 1842 and 1948. Surrounding chiefdoms supported one side or the other and the government took a high-handed attitude to maintain order (Fyfe 1962).

Although intra-ethnic disputes in the diamond areas have not escalated into full-scale war, compensation for desecration of sacred sites has brought ill will among the Kono. Conteh (1979) has described in depth how influential individuals from the region use their positions to monopolize and benefit the most from compensation agreements. Chiefs, whose jurisdictions were directly affected, opposed funds being paid into a general Administration Treasury for development of the District as a whole. Government concurred in this matter. This led to additional discord between rulers and their subjects in cases where authority was seen as benefiting the most from the remuneration.

Illicit Trade, State Security and Mercenary Intervention

Illicit trade is commonly carried out in an atmosphere of state insecurity. This situation has been dealt with by official and unofficial measures to protect their economic interests. These include the use of private security forces and mercenary services. Notwithstanding, would be entrepreneurs flock to productive areas even in the midst of war. In the timber era, traders along the rivers would ship produce directly to Europe without entering their cargoes at the Freetown Customs. The Temne-Loko war that ended in 1836 did not prevent an influx of traders. When war threatened again between the Caulkers in 1857, Heddle, who had succeeded Macaulay as the largest Colony merchant sent a gunboat to Bumpe chiefdom to force Dala Modu to lift sanctions on his logs there. Mercenary services of war-chiefs were frequently employed in counter attacks during the six year war between branches of the Caulker family and in other struggles (Fyfe 1962). As regards diamonds, Sierra Leone has been referred to as "the heartland of IDM" where "illicit diamond mining is a way of life" (Green 1981: 113). Widespread lawlessness involves profit repatriation by foreigners, smuggling, banditry and sometimes murder. Throughout the recent rebel war, illicit mining was on going both in the official lease areas and in the Gola forest reserve. Regular army units of the Republic of Sierra Leone Military Force (RSLMF) and the Kamajo militia group responsible for protecting government interests against the RUF/SL fought over diamond pits (Richards, 2002). Allegations of participation in diamond exploitation have also been made against soldiers of the peace keeping forces from the United Nations and the Economic Community of West African States Cease-Fire Monitoring Group (ECOMOG) brought in to maintain law and order (Farah 2001a; Hirsch 2001).

The SLST, frustrated with the government's inability to help it protect its lease from unauthorized miners in spite of a commitment in a revised agreement, took the law into its own hands with a well armed security force of 35 men (Hirsch 2001). Likewise, Rex Diamond Mining Corporation employed its own security team in 1996 (Conciliation Resources 2001). Even the government endorsed the services of Executive Outcomes, a South African mercenary firm, brought in by the British company Branch Energy who had obtained prospecting rights for kimberlite in 1995. Receiving part payment in mining concessions, they protected the diamond fields (Ferme 2001; Francis 1999; Inter Press 1996). Methods of deterring illegal mining, reportedly, included burying land mines and carrying out atrocities sometimes against innocent civilians. Thus, the government sold 31,929.37 carats valued at over US$3 million in May 1996 while the country was in a state of war (Reuters 1996).

Degradation of the Environment

Primitive accumulation of resources for close to two centuries has led to problems of environmental degradation in the country. Between 1816 and 1860, forests on the Bullom Shores; banks of the Rivers Rokel, Port Loko, Melakori; Yawry Bay, Tasso Island and all through the areas of Waterloo, Mabang and Bumpe chiefdoms, were denuded. A licensing system for cutting down trees in the Crown Colony was set up, belatedly, circa 1858 to put some control on the hitherto uncontrolled deforestation. This policy was, however, overturned in 1872 by a new governor, Hennessy. Moloney (1887) could foresee the long-term consequences of rampant forest exploitation in calling for 'legislative restraints.' Efforts were needed to "put a stop to this unlimited practice of shaving the forest of timber which at one time formed a valuable export" (Moloney 1887: 241). He proposed that a decrease in water supplies was already occurring, basing his premise on fluctuations in rainfall data from 1878 to 1885. The introduction of reforestation programs was vital. Unwin (1918), likewise, concerning the forests of Sierra Leone wrote that:

> ....it does indeed make one pause to think what immense forests must have existed in the days of 1827, when so many loads of timber were exported...money will have to be put into forestry work before adequate returns can be made, owing to the reckless mismanagement of the forest in the early part of the nineteenth century. (Unwin 1918: 40).

A number of Ordinances were subsequently passed starting with the First Forest Ordinance of Forest Reserves and Restricted Areas in 1912.

Environmental deterioration caused by alluvial diamond mining, has led to water pollution from siltation and water-borne diseases like bilharzia and schistosomiasis, flooding and land degradation (Zack-Williams 1995; Gbakima and White 1985; Green 1981). A degree of environmental management and water pollution control are stipulated in the Minerals Ordinance. Cutting down trees by miners in Forest Reserves without the approval of the Forestry Officer is forbidden to aid in pollution control of water sources and regulate tailings disposal. Some legislation is contradictory. A case in point is the stipulation that traditional water supply sources like swamps, rivers and aquifers should be protected when they are coincident with alluvial mine sites.

Limitations to the Creation of a Nation-State

Holding the Reigns on Self-Governance

Following the demise of the SLC, guidelines to the first governor under the Crown Colony were issued in 1811 as "Royal Instructions" from the British government. The first constitution of 1863, officially gave the governor sole power to make unilateral decisions. He was to carry out orders from the Secretary of State for the colonies through the Colonial Office. This was in spite of the creation of Legislative (law making) and Executive (policymaking) Councils who were 'in theory' responsible for devising development policy and legislation. These councils were composed of 'official members' who were the District Commissioner (DC) and Assistant DC; heads of technical departments; and 'unofficial members', citizens of good standing in the community whom the governor deemed fit to serve. However, only the governor could propose questions, or submit bills for debate or consideration in council. A desire to deliberate on any topic by other members could, however, be included in the minutes.

Thus, as Blyden (1959: 40) notes "the prophetic design for Sierra Leone as 'a haven' or 'asylum' for freed slaves where the black man could gradually work out his own salvation and eventually evolve into nationhood, had failed even before it started".

Revisions to the constitution in 1924 and 1951 progressively increased Creole and indigenous membership but still in an 'unofficial' capacity. This meant the continued absence of a local voice on policy. Requests for constitutional reform to improve on this system were made at various times. Governor, Sir Alexander Ransford Slater was approached on the subject in 1922. Lawyer Otto During a vocal 'unofficial' member of the Legislative Council tabled a motion on the matter, first in 1944 and again in 1948 (Wright 2000). A radical member of the 1951 legislature, Wallace Johnson, called for dissolution of the body because it was not a true representation of the people. The President of the SLIM gave a public lecture on November 26, 1956 entitled 'Constitutional Reform-Now or Never' (*The Daily Mail*, November 26, 1956).

The dilemma of establishing a nation state along western lines was still apparent at the granting of Independence in 1961. Pakenham (1991: 675), points out how:

> ... Britain launched a crash program in nation building. Constitutions were borrowed from elsewhere or hammered out overnight, parliaments thrown up like theatre props....There were doubts about the viability of Sierra Leone isolated between French Guinea and Liberia. Like the Gold Coast it was an incongruous marriage between a coastal strip and a wild interior.

This set the stage for future political failure and administrative mal-integration and continuation of existing patterns of leadership by Africans. Reno (1995: 78) documents that more than any other leader, Siaka Steven's "patrimonial strategies were firmly rooted in the social foundations of colonial rule". The parallels between his leadership style and that of Zachary Macaulay are striking. The exercise of arrant power-ruthlessness to quell dissent, co-optation and the use of indigenous rulers as intermediaries, institutional corruption, favoritism and nepotism, likewise, defined the political ecology of his time.

A resistant theme in the nation's constitution is the tremendous power vested in the Head of State. In 1992, the Sierra Leone Bar Association expressed concern over the 1991 Constitution to then military junta leader Valentine Strasser. This document, produced by a Constitutional Review Commission and which "contained the relevant checks and balances was bastardized by an oligarchic clique of corrupt politicians thereby setting the stage for a constitutional crisis" (*The Eagle*, June 4–9, 1992, 6).

Another limitation in the struggle for nation-statehood has been the high turnover of leaders. The resignation with which the early settlers to the Colony accepted the notion of "new governor, new law" (Fyfe 1962: 112), and the 19th century writer Mary Kingsley's commentary on the lack of continuity in policy for the same reason, illustrate the longevity of the problem. A total of 47 governors ruled in the 136 years between 1792 and 1924. Another four covered the period from 1944 to 1961. Since Independence at least ten different leaders have been in control.

Resource Exploitation and the Myth of Sovereignty

The 'official' division of government and company has not diminished the upper hand of the private sector evident since the days of the SLC. In recent times it has been illustrated by events in the mining sector. The Colonial Development and Welfare Act of 1929, for example, was to make low interest loans available to commercial enterprises interested in mineral resource development in colonies like Sierra Leone. This would provide revenue from royalties and taxation. Strategic minerals like industrial diamonds and iron ore could be supplied to the British armament industry. Scientific institutions in Britain were encouraged to research and evaluate the country's resources. The Governor in Sierra Leone at the time the Act was being formulated, expressed some misgivings about government giving financial assistance to private commercial ventures.

Notwithstanding his concern, the upper hand of external business interests in dictating mining policy and legislation was apparent. The Northern Mercantile and Investment Corporation (NMIC), United Africa Company (a subsidiary of Lever Brothers, now Unilever) and the African and Eastern Trading Corporation (AETC) had collectively acquired a concession on the iron ore lease at Marampa in 1929. Before the CDW Act was passed, an application for a loan of 500,000 pounds sterling on their behalf to develop the deposits had already been processed by the Crown Agents for the colonies with no input from the Sierra Leone government. It was approved immediately following passage of the Act and before its full details was officially made public (Segkoma 1986). A customized agreement was drawn up for the Sierra Leone Development Company (DELCO) that emerged from final corporate negotiations. It granted them the "exclusive and preferential right to the use of the Rokel River waters by special agreement" for a period of 89 years (FAO/UN 1979: 168). Disputes frequently occurred between Sierra Leonean members of the Legislative Council over the support of Imperial policy on resource exploitation that was detrimental to the country. The Diamond Supplementary Agreement (1954) Ratification Ordinance, 1954 was described as "*inimical to the best interest* of the people & an iniquitous law that was rushed through council in a most unconstitutional manner" (*The African Standard*, June 11-18, 1954).

An analysis of post-colonial mineral industries by Cleeve (1997) and Segkoma (1986) reveals that government negotiating power remains weak. The mining sector continues to be run by foreign companies that by and large operate as isolated entities within the local economy. Input is in the form of minimal employment, mineral taxation and expenditure on local services. Raw materials extracted are for industries abroad, primarily in Europe and America (as was timber). Government has little control over production decisions and price determinations that are made in foreign corporate headquarters. Companies are rarely required to provide government with records of their operations nor is there adequate Sierra Leonean representation at decision-making levels.

A revised mineral policy in 1969 addressed the problem of local input and control in the management of the mineral industry and increased taxation rates. In the early 1990s, a new mining policy was drawn up, an important aspect of which was the formulation of a National Policy on the Environment. Prospective mining companies are to prepare Environmental Impact Statements and make a commitment to rehabilitation and reclamation (Keili 1993). Matters of the environment are currently the responsibility of the Ministry of Housing and Country Planning, Forestry and the Environment.

Policy initiated by nationals has sometimes been as exploitative and controversial as in colonial times. For example, under Article VII of the Lome Peace Agreement signed between the Government of Sierra Leone and the RUF/SL on May 18, 1999 to end the rebel war, a Commission for the Management of Strategic Resources, National Reconstruction and Development was established (CMRRD). It was chaired by the rebel leader, Corporal Foday Sankoh. All existing mining concessions at the time were made null and void and the commission took over authorization of licensing and responsibility for security in mining areas. A section under the article states that:

> The functions of the Ministry of Mines shall continue to be carried out by the current authorized ministry. However, in respect of the strategic mineral resources, the CMRRD shall be an autonomous body in carrying out its duties concerning the regulation of Sierra Leone's strategic natural resources (Hirsch 2000: 141)

Following his downfall, Sankoh was found to have been carrying out illicit diamond mining in violation of the agreement.

The social and environmental consequences of such shortsighted inequitable policies have long been a matter of concern. In regard to the timber trade, Moloney (1887) recognized the importance of locals knowing the value of the products of their country. He criticized Britain for having an indifferent attitude towards forest preservation compared to France and Germany, noting that "*the annals of almost every English colony would repeat the tale of willful wanton waste and improvidence*" (Moloney 1887: 252). If any doubt existed about the validity of his premise it was made clear by the sentiments expressed by Edward, Prince of Wales whom in a speech while on tour in Africa in 1928 said:

> It may be that in North America, the forests were too recklessly hewn down. In Africa, the forests have had it too much their own way. (Wilson 1928: 35)

This, over a hundred years on from the start of the devastating timber trade in Sierra Leone.

Much legislation on resource extraction was passed in total disregard for the traditional land tenure system and has not been reformed. Waldock et al. (1951) commented on the double standards in legislation especially where the Tribal Authority could easily be overruled by the colonial government. They recommended a more just approach in compensating traditional landholders if forest conservation was to succeed. The Bush-fire Ordinances, for example, drawn up for forest protection clashed with the commonly practiced shifting cultivation method of agriculture. Other Forest Ordinances gave Government the right to constitute a reserve without agreement of the tribal authority. There were no provisions made for settlement of rights or allocation of alternative land for customary needs (Waldock et al. 1951). Tribal authorities however, under the law, were responsible for requesting protected forests and chiefdoms for which they received fees and royalties. Furthermore, the Tribal Authorities Ordinance gave government the right to demand that chiefdoms comply or face prosecution. That all this has remained a historically sore point was exemplified as recently as the 1990s. A handful of farmers in southeastern Sierra Leone encroached on the Gola Forest Reserve, in defiance of a 1936 ordinance to make the point that the land still belongs to their lineage (Richards 2002).

Based on early signs of degradation from gold mining in northern Sierra Leone, land reclamation in the form of leveling of overburden and tailings, and in-filling of excavations was recommended. It was proposed that "where mining operations cannot pay for reasonable rehabilitation of the land, mining should be regarded as uneconomic and not permitted" (Waldock et al. 1951: 79). This has proved to be a tall order in a country where almost half of the surface area has been in mine leases since the 1930s and where illicit alluvial mining is rampant.

Another obstacle limiting sovereignty on decisions about resource exploitation is the recent close business partnership between multinational corporations involved in strategic mineral exploitation and private security (mercenary) firms. Such arrangements sanctioned by weak governments like Sierra Leone, seek to protect economic interests. This can be seen as a modern day equivalent of the hired protection by war-chiefs and compromised cession of territory to the British Crown practiced by chiefs in the volatile, insecure 19th century timber extraction environment. Fyfe (1962: 309), documents a chief's resigned request for annexation in 1861 when, "it was clear to Thomas Stephen that the days of African sovereignty in the Sherbro were over". It has been suggested that since present day security firms thrive on the existence of conflict, it is in their best interest to prolong instability. Further, under such conditions of dependency the country's sovereignty is in reality in the hands of foreign shareholders (Francis 1999).

Following the atrocities of the rebel war, resolutions were put forward by the United Nations Security Council and other organizations including the World Diamond Congress, Partnership Africa Canada and The Campaign to eliminate Conflict Diamonds, to address the problem of illicit trade in the commodity. Measures to be adopted include a uniform worldwide system of 'certification of origin'; the development of standard international legislation to halt the trade; stringent control measures in diamond trading centers; corporate responsibility in diamond-related investment in areas of unrest;

application of sanctions against hostile regimes or controlling factions; policy options for the effective management of the diamond business, and capacity building of African civil society in the areas of research and advocacy.

Conclusion

Exploitation of resources like timber and diamonds has always been externally motivated and national policy predominantly favors business interests. A gray area exists between the private and public sector and government frequently exhibits double standards in rule determination. The powerful influence of multinationals in this natural resource dependent economy is evident. Without a full knowledge of mineral wealth, availability of capital and sufficient technical expertise to exploit its own resources or the means to protect its territorial interests, negotiating power continues to be weak.

Different perceptions of land use and ownership between indigenous people and business interests supported by government have caused major discord. Conflict is a fundamental part of resource exploitation sometimes escalating into full-scale war. New sources of wealth have led to intra-ethnic group strife over resource-bearing areas. Decisions made beyond the country's borders affect the lives of indigenous people who have for generations lived in or owned forested lands or mine lease areas. The problem of an influx of 'strangers' (largely foreigners) into resource rich areas to seek their fortunes at the expense of local populations is an age old and continuing problem. Complaints to government have by and large yielded minimal results for those affected. Paul Richards (2002) has proposed that disregard by government the voice of local protest by the RUF/SL partly caused and aggravated the ten-year war. Insecurities created by changing value systems have been dealt with by the continued use of patron-client relations as a necessary survival mechanism.

The achievement of stable, fair and accountable government remains a challenge. The tremendous power vested in the leadership since the founding of Freetown remains an inherent part of the constitution. This continues to facilitate a patrimonial culture characterized by favoritism and politicization of the administrative bureaucracy. It has also precluded a long-term view to policy and planning, and institutional continuity. Mineral policy, in particular, is poorly conceived and subject to frequent revision and necessary legislative reform has not been carried out. Even where adequate laws exist, they are rarely enforced. Resource areas are often poorly accessible and beyond the logistic control of the central government.

The added dimension of corporate mercenarism becoming a standard means of stabilizing the state in order to encourage foreign investment is also cause for pessimism. Perhaps of even greater concern is the legitimacy of the country's nation-statehood. Efforts at self-determination are continually thwarted and under prevailing conditions new polities like Sierra Leone may never complete the process of building a true nation state, one that is viable and protects the interests of the majority of its citizens

References

Bergman, Edward F. and Renwick, William H. (2002). *Introduction to Geography: People, Places and Environment.* United States: Prentice Hall Inc.

Blyden III, Edward W. (1959). Sierra Leone: The Pattern of Constitutional Change. Ph.D. dissertation. Harvard University.

Cleeve, Emmanuel E. (1997). *Multinational Enterprises in Development:The Mining Industry of Sierra Leone.*

Conciliation Resources United Kingdom (2001). "Resources, Primary Industry and Conflict in Sierra Leone." *West Africa Review.* May 2001. http://www.westafricareview.com/war/vol2.2/2.2war.htm

Conteh, Sorie J. (1979). "Diamond Mining and Kono Religious Institutions: A Study in Social Change." Ph.D. dissertation. Indiana University.

D'Souza, Radha (2001). "How the Genie of the Law Banks the Currents of the Krishna: Sharing Krishna Waters or Metamorphoses of a Colonial Problem into a Development Problem?" *IWHA Conference on the Role of Water in History and Development.* Bergen, Norway, August 10–12, 2001.

Englebert, Pierre (1997). "The Contemporary African State: Neither African nor State." *Third World Quarterly.* 18 (4): 767–775. September

Farah, Douglas (2001a). "Rebels in Sierra Leone Mine Diamonds in Defiance of U.N.: Captured Children and Conscripts Used as Laborers." *Washington Post Foreign Service.* Sunday August 19, 2001.

Farah, Douglas (2001b). "Al Qaeda Cash Tied to Diamond Trade: Gems from Sierra Leone Rebels Raised Millions Sources Say." *Washington Post Foreign Service.* Friday, November 2, 2001.

Ferme, Marianne C. (2001). *The Underneath of Things: Violence, History, and the Everyday in Sierra Leone.* Berkeley and Los Angeles, CA: University of California Press, Ltd.

FAO/UN (1979). Sierra Leone. In: *Water Law in Selected African Countries (Benin, Burundi, Ethiopia, Gabon, Kenya, Mauritius, Sierra Leone, Swaziland, Upper Volta. Zambia.* ed. Dante A. Caponera pp.165–205. Legislative Study No.17. Rome: Food and Agricultural Organization of the United Nations.

Fofana, Lansana (1998). Sierra Leone Stops Foreign Mining. *Electronic Mail and Guardian.* Johannesburg, South Africa, March 31, 1998.

www.mg.co.za/mg/news/98mar2/31mar-slmining

Francis, David J. (1999). Mercenary Intervention in Sierra Leone: Providing National Security or International Exploitation? *Third World Quarterly.* Vol. 20, No. 2:319–338.

Fyfe, Christopher (1962). *A History of Sierra Leone.* London: Oxford University Press.

Gbakima, A.A., and White, P.T. (1985). Mining Health Survey for WHO, NDMC (SL) Ltd. and Ministry of Mines. Njala University College, Sierra Leone.

Goddard, T.N. (1969). *The Handbook of Sierra Leone.* New York: Negro Universities Press.

Green, Timothy (1981). *The World of Diamonds.* New York: William Morrow and Co. Inc.

Hirsch, John L. (2001). *Sierra Leone Diamonds and the Struggle for Democracy.* International Peace Academy Occasional Paper Series. London: Lynne Rienner Publishers.

Inter Press Third World News Agency (1996). "Curse of Riches." May 11, 1996.

July, Robert William (1980) *A history of the African people* New York : Scribner.

Kouassi, Edmond Kwami (1993). "Africa and the United Nations Since 1945." In *General History of Africa, vol. VIII: Africa since 1935.* ed. Ali Mazrui, 871–904. California: James Curry: UNESCO.

Lynch, Hollis (1993). *Black Africa the Great Contemporary Issues.* Advisory Editor New York: Arnos Press.

Metcalfe, G.E. (1964). *Great Britain and Ghana: Documents of Ghana History 1807–1957.* London: Thomas Nelson and Sons Ltd.

Millington, A.C. (1988). "Environmental Degradation, Soil Conservation and Agricultural Policies in Sierra Leone, 1895–1984" *International Journal of Sierra Leone Studies*, Vol. 1. ed. William Okrafo-Smart. London: Biddles Ltd.

Moloney, Alfred (1887). *Sketch of the Forestry of West Africa: With Particular Refer ence to Its Present Principal Commercial Products*. Lon-
don: Sampson Low, Marston, Searle & Rivington.

Pakenham, Thomas (1991). *The Scramble for Africa: White Man's Conquest of the Dark Continent from 1876 to 1912.* New York: Avon Books, Random House Inc.

Reno, William (1995). *Corruption and State Politics in Sierra Leone*. Cam
bridge, England: Cambridge University Press.

Reuters Financial Report (1996). Sierra Leone Diamond Exports Up in May. 12 June. Reuters Ltd.

Richards, Paul (2002). *Fighting for the Rainforest: War, Youth and Resources in Sierra Leone.* London: The International African Institute, in association with James Currey and Heinemann.

Richards, Paul (1995). Rebellion in Sierra Leone and Liberia: A Crisis of youth? In: *Conflict in Africa*, ed. Oliver Furley, pp. 134–165. London: I.B. Taurus & Co. Ltd.

Segkoma, Gilbert A. (1986). The History of Mining and Agriculture in Sierra
Leone: A Study of the Impact of Some Aspects of Colonial and Post

The Eagle (1992). Bar Association Lambast APC Government: Corruption and Bribery. Vol. No. 6 June 4-9 1992.

The London Times (1957). Call for Sierra Leone Inquiry, Petition by Chiefs. November 2 1957, pp 6, column 3.

The Daily Mail (1956). Classified Advertisements. No. 201,594. Freetown, Monday, November 26, 1956. The Proprietors, Sierra Leone "Daily Mail" Ltd.

The African Standard (1954). A Disgraceful Procedure. June 11 & 18 1954, pp 4.

Unwin, A.H. (1920). *West African Forests and Forestry.* London: Waterlow.

United Nations (2001). *Conflict Diamonds: Sanctions and War.* United Nations Department of Public Information in cooperation with the Sanctions Branch, Security Council Affairs Division, Department of Political Affairs. *www.un.org/peace/africa/Diamond.html.*

USAID (2000). *Diamonds and Armed Conflict in Sierra Leone: Proposals for Implementation of a New Diamond Policy and Operations. Office of Transition Initiatives.* Working Paper 05-08-00. *www.usaid.gov/hum_response/oti/country/sleone/diamonds.html.*

Waldock, E.A., Capstick, E.S., Browning, A.J. (1951). Soil Conservation and Land Use in Sierra Leone. *Sessional Paper No. 1 of 1951*. Sierra Leone: Government Printer.

Wilson P.W. (1928). Huge Africa Awakens to a New Destiny: The Prince of Wales Goes to do Royal Advertising for Britains Colonial Empire, As Quickening Development of a Continent Holding One Fifth World's Area has Great Commercial Significance, Sept 16 1928. In: *Black Africa the Great Contemporary Issues,* ed. Hollis Lynch, Hollis, pp 34-35. New York: The New York Times/ Arnos Press, 1973.

Wright, S.V. (2000). *Foundations of Parliamentary Democracy in Sierra Leone: My Memories of Parliament*. Great Britain: REDI Publications.

http://www.partnershipafricacanada.org/hsdp/

http://www.phrusa.org/campaigns/sierra_leone/conflict_diamonds.html

Zack-Williams, Alfred (1995). *Tributors, Supporters and Merchant Capital.* Vermont, USA: Ashgate Publishing Co.

Zack-Williams, A.B. (1989). Sierra Leone 1968-85: The Decline of Politics and the Politics of Decline. In: *International Journal of Sierra Leone Studies*, vol 1, ed. William Okrafo Smart, 122-30. London: Biddles Ltd.

Chapter 8

Ensuring Food Security in Sub-Saharan Africa in the 21st Century: A Potential Role for Climate Forecasts

Abigail Amissah-Arthur

Introduction

One of the greatest problems facing the world today is that of chronic hunger, particularly in the developing countries. In many of these countries, population growth far outstrips food production, resulting in rampant food shortages. Nowhere is this problem as acute as in Africa, which is currently experiencing an annual population growth of 2.4 percent (compared to the global rate of 1.33 percent) with the total population projected to increase from 861 million persons in 2003 to 1.88 billion in 2050 (PRB 2004; UNEP 1999). According to Kueneman (1995), Africa's population has increased by 30 percent since 1970 while the total food production increased by less than 30 percent. Given current population trends and projections in sub-Saharan Africa (SSA), it is anticipated that substantial intensification of agricultural cropland is certain within the next decades.

In order to meet the demands of the growing population, tremendous pressure is being put on finite natural resources to provide for a substantial increase in production of food crops, water, energy, living space and other necessities of life. In the past when land availability per capita was higher the common agricultural practices, slash and burn cultivation and nomadic livestock rearing, were feasible and sustainable. However, due to the present population growth, land is scarcer and opportunities to expand the productive land base are fewer. As a result farmers are moving into newer, less fertile areas more prone to environmental degradation. Evidence of the negative environmental effects of population growth is therefore mounting.

The task of securing food supplies for a rapidly growing population while conserving the natural resource base requires interdisciplinary effort by national and international research groups and agencies. The challenges of meeting the rapidly growing food needs of sub-Saharan Africa cannot be successfully overcome without due consideration of the capacity and limitations of the natural environment (Jagtap 1995a). The agro-ecological conditions of any region largely determine the production potential and population supporting capacity of that region.

In order to improve food production, several international agricultural research institutions collectively known as the Consultative Group on International Agricultural Research (CGIAR) operate in various parts of the world. The mission of the CGIAR is to contribute, through research, to promoting sustainable agriculture for food security in the developing countries. Four of these centers are located in sub-Saharan Africa [1] and work in collaboration with the national agricultural research institutions within Africa to address the agricultural and livestock issues of the different agro-ecological zones of the region. These international institutions in collaboration with their national counterparts have made significant contributions to research and development efforts in germplasm, soil fertility, socioeconomic and policy issues relevant to food security in sub-Saharan Africa. It has however been observed that the impact of climate variability and extreme events on agriculture is adding significantly to the development challenges of food security and reducing poverty in the region.

Africa's high dependence on rain-fed low-input agricultural production on mostly degraded soils increases farmers' vulnerability to the vagaries of weather. For the resource-poor farmer in sub-Saharan Africa, the implications of outstandingly good or bad years can be profound. Thus, for these farmers, the impact of extreme weather conditions far outweigh their apparent probability of occurrence. A common notion is that if farmers could have advance information on the probable outcome of the weather scenario during a growing season, then some of the adverse effects associated with extreme climatic events could be alleviated or minimized. At the close of the 20th century and the start of the 21st century, climate change has become increasingly the focus for research and policy in Africa. With recent advances in the understanding of climate variability and the increasing capability to forecast El Niño Southern Oscillation (ENSO) events with a lead time of months (Mason 1998; Philander 1999) has emerged a growing conviction and interest in using climate information in decision-making processes related to crop production.

International agencies with mandates for managing food security problems in Africa have come to realize the potential value of climate forecasts (Glantz 1994). This may have prompted current independent projects by several research groups sponsored by donor and multilateral agencies (USAID, NOAA, UNDP) in Kenya, Burkina Fasso, Mali, Senegal, Uganda, Zimbabwe aimed at promoting the availability and use of climate forecasts by small-scale farmers in semi-arid areas (Blench 1999). The establishment of the International Research Institute for Climate Prediction (Palisades, NY) further emphasizes the importance placed by the world community on the potential uses of climate forecasts. This institute has the mandate for end-to-end production and application of climate forecasts in developing countries. The development and application of management systems incorporating among others, timely and accurate prediction of rainfall, with consideration of other production factors has the potential to positively impact food production and security in sub-Saharan Africa (Amissah-Arthur 2003).

This chapter examines climatic variability and the challenges it poses with a case study of Nigeria, which encompasses several agro-ecological zones predominant in sub-Saharan Africa. The paper examines the impact of ENSO-induced climatic variability on crop production using Kenya as a study. Finally, coping strategies available to farmers and their capability to adopt climate forecasts based on ENSO phenomenon is examined. An analysis is done on ways this new capability can further the millennium development goals to ensure food security for the people of the region.

Systems Description: Climate Forecasts

Large-scale rainfall anomalies over many parts of Africa have been linked to periods of strong warm and cold El Niño Southern Oscillation (ENSO) phases. Although a number of factors control the inter-annual rainfall variability over Africa, the ENSO is the most dominant factor over eastern and southern Africa. During the ENSO phase, eastern Africa tends to receive abundant rainfall for the short rainy season of October through December (Nicholson and Kim 1997). This rainfall anomaly patterns tends to reverse during La Niña conditions. The development of the 1997/98 El Niño event provided the opportunity to make El Niño forecast and seasonal atmospheric climate anomalies information available to a public audience for the first time. Most meteorological services in sub-Saharan Africa now issue climate forecasts on an operational basis. These forecasts are based on empirical diagnostic analyses with global SST anomaly patterns, the state of ENSO, North Atlantic Oscillation (NAO) and upper level winds (Unganai 2000). Climate forecasts are currently issued for a three-month period for relatively large homogeneous rainfall zones. These forecasts are issued in terciles as probability of rainfall being below normal, normal and above normal. The teleconnections that have been found between ENSO and rainfall in several parts of sub-Saharan Africa affect crops within growing seasons and therefore offer potential understanding and foreknowledge of year-to-year variability (Rosenzweig 2000).

Systems Description: Climatic Variability and Crop Production

Year to year variability in food production in sub-Saharan Africa is a result of climatic variability since agricultural production is entirely dependent on a rain-fed subsistence system. Rainfall, producing available soil moisture and thus, controlling the availability of water to crops is by far the most important climatic factor influencing the pattern and productivity of rain-fed agriculture in sub-Saharan Africa (Amissah-Arthur and Jagtap 1999; Jagtap 1995b). In a general context, climatic variability is virtually synonymous with rainfall variability. Nigeria ,a country of about 110 million people, is the most populous country in sub-Saharan Africa and contains all the climatic zones that characterize sub-Saharan Africa. A look at the climatic trend in Nigeria therefore will provide an indication of the general trend across the sub-region. There is some evidence of changes in pattern and decreasing trends in the annual (Jagtap 1995a) and seasonal (Amissah-Arthur and Jagtap 1999; Amissah-Arthur 1997; Jagtap 1995a) rainfall in Nigeria over both time and space. Amissah-Arthur and Jagtap (1999) examined the trends in seasonal rainfall and its distribution within the growing season for three decades (1960–1990) corresponding to revolutionary changes observed in agricultural systems in West Africa. The study examined short and medium term trends over the 30-year period. Well-defined trends in seasonal rainfall and marked geographical differences in the extent and timing of the trends were found to have occurred during the 1960–1990 period. The most marked trend was the decline in the seasonal rainfall at stations in the Guinea Savanna that lie between latitudes 7.2° and 12.93° N and stations in the arid/semi-arid savannas in northern Nigeria. On the other hand, increasing non-significant trends in seasonal rainfall were found for only four stations, all in the southern high rainfall part of the country. The study however found that mean onset of the growing season in Nigeria is getting delayed and that the growing season across the country is getting shorter by at least a month. Both crops and livestock depend on the timely and adequate occurrence of rainfall without which there would be severe crop failure. This study clearly emphasizes the fact that semi-arid and arid zones exhibit greater rainfall variability than wet zones.

Rainfall variation during the growing season has been directly related to the variation in national average maize yields in Africa (FAO, 1994). This is because the amount, distribution and variability of rainfall from year to year have a large influence on the reliability of cropping (Meinke and Hammer 1995). In recent years, recurrent climatic extremes such as drought and floods have resulted in increases in inter-seasonal variability in food production especially grain production on which a large proportion of Africa's population depends. The induced yield instability that is being experienced is having a great deal of impact on the economic, sociological, and political activities of the entire populace of the region. With increasing capability to forecast ENSO events with a lead time of months (Mason 1998; Philander 1999) has emerged a growing conviction and interest in using climate information in decision-making processes especially regarding crop production. In eastern Africa El Niño is usually associated with wetter than normal conditions and La Niña with drier than normal conditions (Ropelewski and Halpert 1987; Nicholson and Kim 1997). This has implications for the climatic expectations in such years and the use of climate information in decision-making. Using Kenya as a case study the following section examines the characteristics that determine the vulnerability of the agricultural systems to climatic variability and the need for climate forecasts.

Kenya is mainly a semi-arid to arid country. Previous studies in the region and other similar regions around the world suggest that farmers in semi-arid to arid zones experience a higher vulnerability to the vagaries of climate. The majority of Kenyan farmers produce crops mainly for their own needs on about 20 percent of the country's land area, which is all that is suitable for cultivation. Rainfall amounts are greatest in the highlands of Kenya, which are located in the west. The arid lowland of the north receives the least amount of rain. A high degree of inter-annual variability is associated with the rainfall in the country including frequent droughts. Because of the uneven distribution of rainfall and the variation in land elevation, ecological conditions differ throughout the country. Crop production is therefore a highly vulnerable enterprise in this region. El Niño events have been shown to enhance eastern and southern African rainfall and affect the variability in the rainfall in the region (Amissah-Arthur et al. 2002; Mutai and Ward 2000).

Kenya has two cropping seasons: March-June, with planting starting in March or April, and October to January with planting in October or November. The growing seasons are related to the rainy seasons, which extend from March to May and from November to January. Amissah-Arthur et. al. (2002) examined the period between 1979 and 1998 to determine if El Niño related rainfall variability could be used to explain the variability observed in national level maize yields in Kenya. At the national level the study found the year-to-year variability in the rainfall was reflected in the maize yields, which have followed the rainfall trend. It was observed also that the negative change from mean neutral (none-El Niño or La Niña) years seasonal rainfall that occur during El Niño years for the May-June-July season (when 65 percent of maize is produced) may explain the lower national-level yields observed during most El Niño event years. The study noted clear signals between the October-November-December-January (OJ) seasonal rainfall and El Niño in Kenya, particularly in the highlands, where significant positive increases were observed. Significant variability was observed in the El Niño event years' OJ seasonal rainfall for most of the sites used in the study. The study concluded that farmers' might be encouraged to take more advantage of the October-November season during El Niño years, either to increase the area devoted to maize or to adopt the planting of the crop during this season. Zimbabwe in southern Africa is another region where year-to-year variability in rainfall has been linked to variability in crop yields. Cane et al. (1994) observed strong correlations between crop yields and the ENSO cycle.

Clearly, agricultural systems in many parts of sub-Saharan Africa are highly vulnerable to climatic variability. It has often been suggested that in sub-Saharan Africa, availability of climate forecast information would enable farmers to adjust their risk management options in crop production. According to Washington and Downing (1999), the use of climate predictions is related to vulnerability, both in terms of the direct effects and on the ease of accessibility of a given group to climate predictions and to respond to them.

Potential Adopters of Climate Forecasts

Farmers in Kenya and many parts of the world operate in an environment where climatic conditions vary from place to place and from season to season. Thus, they are already alerted to the need to re-examine land use and management practices and farm infrastructure in response to the vagaries of climate. Increasingly the tools and ability to model and predict seasonal climate has been improving over the years; however, the capability to integrate these forecasts with farmers' agricultural strategies and their decision making processes is still very weak. To overcome this hurdle it is important to be able to address the question posed by Blench (1999): "Are there aspects of farmers' existing strategies that can be melded with the new type of data becoming available?" To address this question, Amissah-Arthur (2003) characterized the key production strategies employed by farmers in Kenya and how these strategies may indicate the usability of climate forecasts. According to Stern and Easterling (1999) it is important to match the information provided in forecasts as much as possible to the coping strategies used by the forecasts recipients. The usability of forecasts is strongly dependent on the characteristics of the users and their place in the user-space (Blench 1999) while their ability to modify agricultural production practices and to respond appropriately to forecast information depends on gaining access to the needed resources (Nicholls 1991; Stern and Easterling 1999).

Many smallholder farmers in the tropics utilize the diversity of their environments, and employ a wealth of techniques and means to get around the constraints imposed by climate. In most cases, farmers have developed a wide portfolio of income-earning non-cropping activities that offer some level of income stability in the face of looming crop failures. Walker (1991) concluded that studies conducted in the semi-arid tropics and elsewhere support the notion that the value of climate forecasts and production flexibility are positively correlated. Thus, the greatest benefits will go to those who have the means and resources to take the most advantage of the technology (Stern and Easterling 1999).

Regions with well-integrated markets may derive the most benefits from a new technology because search time for inputs, labor and related transactions costs are low and thus would facilitate the use of weather and climatic information by farmers. According to Amissah-Arthur (2003), for the subsistence farmers in sub-Saharan Africa, the ones who may adopt climate forecasts would be those who already have access to and use productivity enhancing technologies such as improved seeds, fertilizer and labor. By contrast, poor market development limits the demand for farmer-oriented climatic information since the options available to farmers are limited. Figure 8.1 shows the potential adoption zones of climate forecasts as delineated by Amissah-Arthur (2003). This takes into account the degree of orientation of the agricultural production systems toward the market, hence the cash available to the farmers while the second consideration is the land use intensity, which indicates the pressure of population on the land. Zones delineated as highly probable zones are characterized by a production system where surplus from sales of farm produce constitute the major source of income. This surplus increases the capacity to adopt a larger range of technical options for increasing productivity such as purchased inputs and hired labor. In the highly probable zone with high orientation to markets and moderate to high land use intensity, farmers are more likely to adopt and benefit in terms of increasing profitability of their agricultural production by the use of climate forecasts. This is because these farmers are already well integrated into commercial markets, and the financial security that they have affords them the freedom to use forecasts to their advantage.

The regions delineated as Probable zones have agricultural production oriented towards the market with a commercialization index greater than 50 percent, a low (zero to 33 percent) land-use intensity and use of purchased inputs at a moderate level. Since returns from cropping are high these may be used to adopt new improved technologies or finance increased use of inputs. Strasberg et al. (1999) observed that in Kenya, crop commercialization provides cash that allows households to overcome credit-related constraints on the purchase of fertilizer and to facilitate the purchase of draft oxen and traction equipment. The zone characterized as Less Probable is more of a population driven agricultural subsistence system characterized by low to moderate land-use intensity and a low commercialization with little or no utilization of purchased inputs.

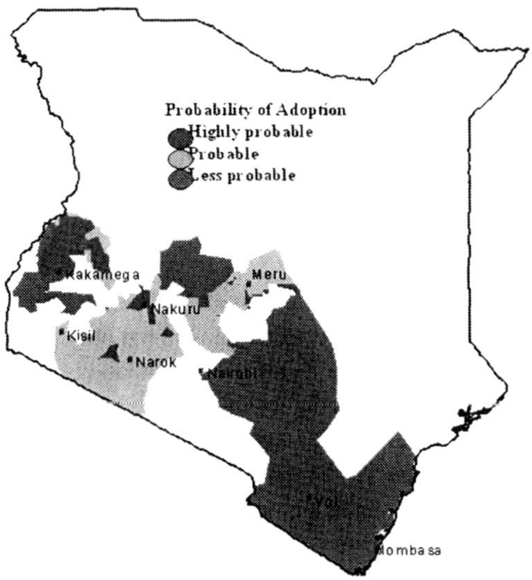

Figure 8.1 Potential Climate Forecast Adopters for Kenya

Source: Adapted from Amissah-Arthur, 2003.

Low productivity results in lack of cash to purchase inputs or other resources to alleviate constraints in which case agricultural production is mainly to meet household food consumption.

Climate forecast is likely to be useful to farmers in sub-Saharan Africa, however the benefits derived from its use may not be equitable because of the inequalities in the options available to individuals or groups of farmers. This may result in one group benefiting more than others. For farmers in the less probable zones where climatic variability is frequent and livelihood vulnerability is a major issue, these farmers can change to more drought- and disease-tolerant crops and the use of livestock breeds adaptable to drought while basing their decisions on climate forecasts. Farmers can achieve greater flexibility in adapting to climatic variability if they or the government can secure the capital needed for additional water reservoirs or boreholes that would provide irrigation for farming activities. However, due to the large costs involved in such infrastructural changes only small incremental adjustments may occur without changes in government policy (Parry and Duinker 1990).

Limitations and Prospects for Climate Forecasts Use

Current seasonal climate forecasts provide general predictions which farmers believe make it difficult to use in formulating farm-specific management decisions. Results from most of the on-going survey projects in sub-Saharan Africa on the farmer usage of climate forecasts indicate that farmers require the following specific climate information:

a. Seasonal rainfall amount;
b. Date of onset of the rains;
c. Date of end of the rains;
d. Possibility, frequency and timing of adverse weather events (e.g., dry spells) within the season;
e. Interpretation of all of the above with respect to farm decisions especially what crops and varieties to plant in addition to when to plant, and
f. More accurate and user friendly forecasts.

Current climate forecasts do not offer farmers all these elements of specificity that they require, rather present capability provides information on the type of event to expect (El Niño, La Niña), the intensity of the events as determined by the Southern Oscillation Index (SOI) and the probability of normal, above normal or below normal rainfall over very broad regions. There is a need to improve and enhance the capability of climate forecasts before its benefits can be realized at the farm level. Several climate outlook forums organized in various parts of sub-Saharan Africa have suggested actions that need to be taken to improve climate forecasts use. These include:

a. Improving the spatial and temporal resolution of climate forecasts. Currently available climate forecasts are produced at too large a scale to be useful for farmers' site level operations. Therefore, spatial and temporal scales of climate forecasts need to be refined for farm-level management operations;
b. Improving information delivery pathways. The average farmer owns a radio. It has been suggested that this could be a good medium to get climate forecasts to farming communities. Climate forecasts need to be issued and presented in the indigenous languages for easier understanding by farmers, although interpretation of probabilities in the local language is often difficult because the local languages are often limited in the expression of abstract concepts;
c. Investment in extension services. For years farmers have worked with extension agents on various issues related to production and farm management issues. Extension agents need to be increasingly involved in advising the farmers on the correct interpretation of climate information and possible outcome of changes to crop and farm management based on the information. Extension agents need to receive proper training in order to adequately advise farmers on the risks and economic benefits of changing decisions based on climate forecasts, and
d. Communicating skill of climate forecasts and timely issuance of climate forecasts. The largest questions remain regarding forecast quality and degree of risk involved in using forecast information versus "business as usual." The skills and level of confidence inherent in the climate forecasts need to be communicated to the end users who are likely to make income-changing decisions based on the forecasts. It must however be emphasized that climate forecast will only be one more piece of information for resource-poor farmers to incorporate into their overall risk-management strategies. The current perspective of many Meteorological Services in sub-Saharan Africa is that of caution in giving advice regarding agricultural management. Furthermore, they emphasize monitoring as the season progresses.

Although potential benefits of climate forecasts to improve farm management have been documented, the issues raised in this section need to be addressed to enhance the benefits of climate forecasts to smallholder farmers who constitute the bulk of agricultural producers in sub-Saharan Africa and are responsible for food security. Although seasonal climate forecasts can play a role in mitigating issues relating to food security in the 21st century, the uncertainty associated with current forecasts makes its use difficult. As improvements in forecasting products continue to be made, progress in utilizing climate information for improving food security can be made.

Notes

1 The International Institute of Tropical Agriculture (IITA) is headquartered in Ibadan, Nigeria. The IITA's mission is to enhance the food security, income, and well-being of resource-poor people in sub-Saharan Africa by conducting research and related activities to increase agricultural production, improve food systems, and sustainably manage natural resources, in partnership with national and international stakeholders.
The International Livestock Research Institute (ILRI) has its headquarters in Nairobi, Kenya. The ILRI works to improve the well being of people in developing countries by enhancing the diverse and essential contributions livestock make to smallholder farming.
The International Center for Research in Agro-forestry (ICRAF) is headquartered in Nairobi, Kenya. The ICRAF's mission is to improve human welfare by reducing poverty, improving food and nutritional security, and enhancing environmental resilience in the tropics through research in agro-forestry systems.
The West African Rice Development Association (WARDA) is headquartered in Bouake, Cote d'Ivoire. The WARDA's mission is to contribute to food security and poverty alleviation in sub-Saharan Africa, through research, partnerships, capacity strengthening, and policy support on rice-based systems, and in ways that promote sustainable agricultural development based on environmentally sound management of natural resources.

References

Amissah-Arthur, A. (2003). "Targeting climate forecasts for agricultural applications in sub-Saharan Africa: Situating farmers in user-space." *Climatic Change* ,58: 1–20.

Amissah-Arthur, A., Jagtap S., and Rosenzweig, C. (2002). "Spatio-Temporal Effects of El Niño events on rainfall and Maize Yield in Kenya." *International Journal of Climatology* , 22: 1849–1860.

Amissah-Arthur, A. and Jagtap, S. (1999). "Geographic Variation in Growing Season Rainfall in Nigeria during Three Decades using Principal Component and Cluster Analyses." *Theoretical and Applied Climatology*, 63(1–2): 107–116.

Amissah-Arthur, A. (1997). "Assessment of the Production Potential of Maize in Rotation with Soybean across Agro-ecological Zones of Nigeria." Ph.D. Thesis. University of Ibadan, Ibadan, Nigeria.

Anyadike, R.N.C. (1992). Regional variations in fluctuations of seasonal rainfall over Nigeria *Theoretical and Applied Climatology*, 45: 285–292.

Blench, R. (1999). "Seasonal Climate Forecasting: Who Can Use it and How Should it be Disseminated?" *Natural Resource Perspectives*, No. 47. November 1999.

Cane, M.A., Eshel, G and Buckland, R.W. (1994). "Forecasting Zimbabwean Maize Yield using Eastern Equatorial Pacific Sea Surface Temperature." *Nature*, 370:204–205.

FAO (1994). *Agrostat PC*. Rome: FAO.

Glantz, M.H. (1994). "Forecasting El Niño: Science's Gift to the 21st Century." *Ecodecision*. 78–81.

Gommes, R. and Petress, F. (1994). "Rainfall variability and drought in sub-Saharan Africa." *FAO Agromet Series* No. 9. Rome: UNFAO.

Jagtap, S.S. (1995a). "Changes in annual, seasonal and monthly rainfall in Nigeria during 1961–1990 and consequences for agriculture." *Discovery and Innovations*, 7 (4): 311–426.

Jagtap, S.S. (1995b). "Environmental characteristics of the moist lowland savanna of Africa." pp. 9–30. In *Moist Savannas of Africa: Potentials and Constraints for Crop Production*. (Kang, B.T., et. al, eds.) Proceedings of an International Workshop. IITA, Ibadan.

Kueneman, E.A. (1995). "Sustainable Cropping Systems for Savanna Ecologies of Africa: Definition of Workshop Gaols." In *Moist Savannas of Africa: Potentials and Constraints for Crop Production*. (Kang, B.T., et al. eds.) Proceedings of an International Workshop. IITA, Ibadan.

Mason, S.J. (1998). "Seasonal forecasting of South African rainfall using a non-linear discriminant analysis model." *International Journal of Climatology* 18: 147–164.

Meinke, H. and Hammer, G.L. (1995). "Climatic risk to peanut production: a simulation study for Northern Australia." *Australian J. Expl. Agric*. 35: 777–80.

Mutai, C.C. and Ward, M.N. (2000). "East African rainfall and the tropical circulation/convection on intraseasonal to interannual timescales." *Journal of Climate* 13: 3915–3939.

Nicholls, N. (1991). "Advances in Long-term Weather Forecasting." In R.C. Muchow and J.A. Bellamy (eds.). *Climatic Risk in Crop Production: Models and Management for the Semi-arid Tropics and Subtropics*. CAB International, Wallingford. 427–444.

Nicholson, S.E. and Kim, J. (1997). "The relationship of the El Niño-Southern Oscillation to African rainfall." *International Journal of Climatology*, 17: 117–135.

Parry, M. L. and Duinker, P.N. (1990). "Agriculture and Forestry." In W. J. McG. Tergart, G. W. Sheldon and D.C. Griffiths. *Climate Change: The IPCC Impacts Assessment*. WMO/UNEP Intergovernmental Panel on Climate Change. Australian Government Publishing Service. Canberra. 45.

Philander, S.G.H. (1999). El Niño and La Niña predictable climate fluctuations. *Rep. Prog. Physics*, 62: 123–142.

PRB (2004). *Population Data Sheet 2004*. Washington D.C.: Population Reference Bureau.

Ropelewski C.F and Halpert, M.S. (1987). "Global and regional scale precipitation patterns associated with El Niño/Southern Oscillation." *Monthly Weather Review*, 115: 1606–1626.

Rosenzweig, C. (2000). "Climate Variability, Seasonal Prediction, and Agriculture." 14–23. Proceedings of the International Forum on Climate Prediction, Agriculture and Development. Palisades, NY. April 26–28, 2000. IRI, NY, Publication No. IRI-CW/00/1.

Stern, P.C. and Easterling, W.E. (eds.) 1999. *Making Climate Forecasts Matter*. Washington, DC: National Academy Press.

Strasberg, P.J., Jayne, T.S.,Yamano, Y., Nyoro, J., Karanja, D and Strauss, J. (1999). "Effects of Agricultural Commercialization on Food Crop Input Use and Productivity in Kenya." MSU International Development Working papers. No. 71.

UNEP (1999). Singh, A., A. Diaye, M. Finco, M.S. Chenoweth, E.A. Fosnight, and A. Allotey, "Early Warning of Selected Emerging Environmental Issues in Africa: Change and Correlation from a Geographic Perspective." UNEP/DEIAEW/TR.99–2. Nairobi, Kenya: UNEP.

Unganai, L. (2000). "Application of Long-Range Rainfall Forecasts in agriculture Management: A reviw of Africa's Experiences." pp. 45–51. Proceedings of the International Forum on Climate Prediction, Agriculture and Development. Palisades, NY April 26–28, 2000. IRI, NY, Publication No. IRI-CW/00/1.

Walker, T.S. (1991). "Improved Technology in Relation to Other Options for Dealing with Climatic Risk to Crop Production in the Semiarid Tropics." In R.C. Muchow and J.A. Bellamy (eds.) *Climatic Risk in Crop Production: Models and Management for the Semiarid Tropics and Subtropics.* CAB International, Wallingford. pp. 511–525.

Washington, R., and Downing, T.E. (1999). "Seasonal Forecasting of African Rainfall: Prediction, Responses and Household Food Security." *The Geographical Journal*, 165(3): 255–274.

Chapter 9

The Political Ecology of Land Degradation in Ethiopia

Tadesse Kidane Mariam and Delphis F. Levia Jr.

Introduction

Land degradation can be broadly defined as the 'loss of utility or potential utility or the reduction, loss or change of features or organisms which cannot be replaced ... it implies a reduction in rank or status' (Barrow 1994: 1). Degradation is widely viewed as the result of a complex relationship between society and nature at various geographical scales — local, regional, national and global (Levia 1999). Hence, the problem is often addressed from the perspective of the stability and resilience of a particular area. This view has been consistently projected in earlier works such as that of Timmerman (1981) who defined land degradation in terms of vulnerability — 'the degree to which a system may react adversely to the occurrence of a hazardous event' and resilience — 'the measure of a system's capacity to absorb and recover from the occurrence of a hazardous event' (Timmerman 1981). An important concept in the definition of land degradation is the temporal dimension. Johnson and Lewis (1995) categorized land degradation as short-term or reversible and long term or irreversible. Based on this categorization, Levia (1999) argued that greater concern should be made on understanding and combating the irreversible type of land degradation (Levia 1999: 200).

There are many competing social definitions of land degradation and prudence dictates that we refrain from accepting or adopting a single scientific definition (Blaikie and Brookfield 1987). Likewise, there are many explanations about the underlying causes of land degradation. Levia (1999) argued that we must acknowledge the concepts of intentional and unintentional land degradation in our attempt to understand the structural causes of the problem. He defined intentional land degradation as one that takes place when 'one purposely degrades one area of land (sacrifice zone) to increase the productivity of another' while the unintentional one occurs when a certain area is degraded without increasing the productivity of the critical zone. He further contended that the intentional land degradation is mostly benign while the unintentional one poses a serious threat to the viability of the biosphere (Levia 1999).

Such definitions and conceptualizations invariably lead to the question of the structural or underlying causes of land degradation. Again, we are faced with multiple perspectives and explanations. Biophysical and political ecology determinants of land degradation are widely invoked in both academic and policy circles. Underlying causes are defined as those that are necessary conditions for land degradation to occur. While such factors as population growth, poverty and urbanization can cause land degradation, they are not necessary conditions (Levia 1999: 200). The underlying causes of land degradation in any society primarily lie in political economy, the structure of science, conflict between human and physical temporal scales and lack of true cost environmental accounting procedures (Levia 1999: 200–201). The political economy of land degradation inevitably deals with the understanding of the continuously shifting inter-relationship between classes and groups within society and between society and natural resources (Blaikie and Brookfield 1987). In this chapter, we contend that the problem of land degradation in Ethiopia should be understood in the context of identifying the sufficient and necessary conditions for the occurrence of the problem by adequately incorporating political economy considerations.

Land degradation has been and remains one of the most important issues in Ethiopia. Ethiopia's economy is inextricably linked with agriculture, which provides the livelihood for almost 85 percent of the country's 60 million inhabitants (2000 estimate) (Girma 2001: 815). Centuries of sedentary agriculture and nomadic herding have brought about serious, and in some areas, irreversible damage to the environment. In the mid 1980s, a Food and Agricultural Organization (FAO) study of the highlands of Ethiopia indicated that an average of 35 to 40 tons ha — per year — was eroded from Ethiopia's highland farms (FAO 1986). The study further noted that about 25 percent of former and current farmland has experienced such high levels of degradation that it is virtually impossible to rehabilitate them (FAO 1986). Given the fact that the Ethiopian highland system constitutes approximately 45 percent of the country's land area, covers 95 percent of its cropped land and provides livelihood to almost 88 percent of the country's population, land degradation is indeed a critical problem that needs to be addressed soon. It is no wonder that land degradation and the resulting loss of biodiversity were singled out as the most important environmental problems by the head of the Ethiopian Environmental Protection Authority (Walta Information Center (WIC), November 1/ 2000).

Numerous studies inform the public about the growing imbalance between Ethiopia's growing population and the vulnerability and resilience of the country's biophysical and social systems. In particular, the relationship between land degradation and famines and other demographic dimensions has been a recurring theme of discourses, narratives, policies, practices and research activities. The highlands reclamation study conducted by the FAO in the mid 1980s has provided benchmark information on the nature and scale of land degradation and its implications for meeting food and energy needs of the population (FAO 1986). Hurni (1988) has indicated that the Ethiopian highlands were losing about 4 mm of soil depth /annum and that such loss had a one to two percent reduction in soil productivity. More recent works continue to emphasize the bio-geophysical and demographic aspects of land degradation. Grepperud (1996), for example, in his study of the impact of population pressure on land degradation, asserted that a rapid degradation of land takes place as the pressure from people and livestock exceeded a certain threshold rather than natural variables (Grepperud 1996: 30). Eweg et al. (1998), in their analysis of degradation and rehabilitation of land in the highlands of Ethiopia have noted that geomorphological factors and the absence of vegetation cover negatively impacted potential and actual erosion risk in the Adwa region of highland Ethiopia. Land degradation has also been attributed to agricultural production on steep slopes, low vegetation cover, harmful agricultural production techniques such as burning dung and crop residues, limited access of farmers to production, increasing technologies, population pressure and land tenure conditions (Girma 2001: 822). Oba and Kotile (2001), in their assessment of landscape level degradation in the pastoralist region of southern Ethiopia suggested that contrary to prevailing assumptions about the destructive practices of pastoralists, indigenous ecological knowledge was effectively used by the *Booran* pastoralists to determine landscape suitability and potential grazing capacity of individual landscapes (Oba and Kotile 2001: 472). The problem with many of these studies is that the physical dimension of the problem has received the bulk of research attention while the social dimensions of land degradation have not been explicitly and adequately discussed.

While the substantive contributions of these studies to the understanding of the bio-geophysical and population dimensions and implications of land degradation in Ethiopia are useful, there is a need to understand more explicitly the contributions of political and economic conditions to the problem. Current explanations of the problems of land degradation in Ethiopia seem to emphasize biophysical dimensions and de-emphasize the role of political and economic processes and regimes. Political economy perspectives provide us with important explanations about the role of the state and different groups within the system in managing the resources of the environment. It is often argued that the state commonly tends to lend its power to dominant groups and classes thus reinforcing the tendency for accumulation and exploitation by these dominant groups and marginalization of the losers through such actions as taxation, food policy, land tenure policy and the allocation of resources (Blaikie and Brookfield 1987: 18; Levia 1999: 200). Such political economy explanations have been reflected in the works of Mesfin (1986; 1991) who has consistently argued that the vulnerability of Ethiopian peasants to famine is associated with their marginal position in the country's political power and decision making structure. Likewise, Alemneh (1990) has associated the problem of land degradation in Ethiopia with population pressure leading to excessive exploitation of the land by overgrazing, over cultivation and deforestation. He further suggested that poor governance and wrong government policies contributed to the downward spiral in the environmental crisis (Alemneh 1990: 114).

In recent years political ecology approaches have linked land degradation problems in developing countries not only to biophysical processes but more importantly to social institutions (Blaikie and Brookfield 1987; Watts 1993). The prescriptions of such approaches have often indicated the need for reforming social institutions. Such perspectives see the manipulation of land through such measures as soil conservation or reforestation as incapable of producing the kind of reform that can establish sustainability in land use (O'Riordian 1989: 95).

In light of the critical role of social institutions in resource management, it is therefore important to pose questions concerning the political, economic and social structures and processes of Ethiopian society to understand the roots of the problem of land degradation. In this regard it is necessary to explore the contributions of land tenure, poverty and marginalization, political instability and maladministration, economic and social development policies; technology and institutional discourses and arrangements as important determinants of land degradation. In particular, the growing influence of external actors such as international development institutions, non-governmental organizations (NGOs) and other humanitarian agencies in dictating environmental management discourses, policies and programs at national, sub-national and local levels needs to be appreciated and objectively evaluated.

The aim of this chapter is thus to identify and discuss the social dimensions of land degradation in Ethiopia more fully. Only when the social and physical aspects of land degradation are dealt with in tandem, will progress be made in combating land degradation in Ethiopia effectively and in a sustainable manner. We believe that the distribution of blame for the current state of land degradation and the vulnerability of millions of people to all kinds of hazards should not be inordinately attributed to bio-geophysical processes and determinants. Political ecology perspectives incorporating both ecological and political economy issues should be addressed to understand the continuously shifting interrelationships between Ethiopian society and its land resources. Since political decision-making has physical environmental consequences, it is important to address the role of different land managers in causing land degradation and seeking ways to minimize or mitigate environmental, socioeconomic and political uncertainties. Hence, the roles of successive governments, farmers, pastoralists, the church, other civic institutions, international organizations, non-governmental organizations (NGOs) and other relevant actors have to be examined. Such perspectives have been reflected in the works of many researchers (e.g. Mesfin 1986; 1991; Alemneh 1990; Fantu 1992; Stahl 1993; Kebrom 1999).

The Physical Environment of Ethiopia

Ethiopia covers a land area of 1.27 million sq. km (435,184 sq. miles), making it the seventh largest country in Africa. According to the 1988 estimates of the Ethiopian Mapping Authority, 10.3 percent of the land was intensely and 12.5 percent moderately cultivated. Land cover estimates indicated that 30.5 percent of the land was under grasslands, 21.4 percent under bush land and scrubland and only 4.4 percent of the land under forests (Transitional Government of Ethiopia (TGE) 1992: 40). Almost two-thirds of the land is a highland system with a general elevation of 1500 to 3000 meters above sea level while the remaining one-third is lowland area surrounding the highland system. The Ethiopian highlands are interspersed by deep gorges, steep valleys and many rivers and streams. Two broad soil types are recognized over the highlands of the country, namely: the well-drained reddish-brown clay loam which is generally well supplied with minerals except phosphorous and the brownish to grey and black soils with high clay content covering the poorly drained parts of flat plateaus and valley bottoms. In the lowlands, sandy desert soils with limited plant nutrients dominate (United Nations Development Program (UNDP) 1995: 1).

In terms of agricultural land use classes, about 51 percent of the country's land is considered to be potentially arable of which 13 percent is marginal with significant moisture limitations and the remaining 49 percent is believed to be non-arable (TGE

1992: 41). The wide diversity of agro-cological conditions in the country as a result of the wide range of altitudes, soils, climatic factors and vegetation cover give the country considerable potential for agricultural and other development activities. Unfortunately, traditional and modern land management practices and political economy conditions have prevented the creation of a sustainable pattern of economic production and a more ecologically stable environment Even a cursory examination of Ethiopia's physical environment clearly shows a growing imbalance between population, natural resources and development. Nowhere is this mismatch more clearly demonstrated than in the area of land degradation.

The mismanagement of land in Ethiopia is neither new nor recent. A German missionary traveler, Krapf, who is reputed to be the first white man to traverse the upper 'Gerado' area of Southern 'Wollo' in north central Ethiopia, had made perceptive remarks about the asymmetrical relationship between land and people in 1832. In his narrative, he was struck by the contradiction between the great potential of the land and the poor state of development and management. After favorably comparing the beauty and fertility of the locality to the valleys of Switzerland, he lamentably concluded that it was a pity that the fertile valley 'was not in the hands of a better people and a better government' (Isenberg and Krapf 1968). He could not have been more perceptive and correct. The area has been the scene of recurrent droughts and so much degradation and human misery as both the 1974 and 1984 droughts tragically demonstrated. Today, it is one of the most vulnerable areas of the country with 75 percent of the soils having a depth of only about ten cm (Henrickson et al. 1983).

Land Tenure and Land Degradation

The differential access of people to land resources has been and remains a fundamental political and economic reality of both ancient and contemporary Ethiopia. The relationship between land ownership and degradation is both direct and significant. Barrow (1991) has discussed the conceptual and practical implications of different regimes of land ownership and their possible contributions to land degradation. He noted that public ownership of land could institute regulatory and pricing mechanisms as well as public works programs to ensure sustainable usage and counter land degradation. Under private land ownership regimes, land managers may tend to seek short-term profits rather than invest in long-term expectations or future returns (Barrow 1991: 18). The converse could also be argued provided that security to ownership is guaranteed and protected by legal and institutional arrangements. Common property regimes of land ownership – here understood as property owned by government, community, no one, multiple users – are often associated with definite land degradation problems because each user is most likely to extract the maximum from the land without any responsibility for conservation or rehabilitation (Barrow 1991: 1; Hardin 1968; Schlager and Ostrom 1992).

In Ethiopia, the land tenure system prior to 1974 could be broadly categorized into communal (*Rest*) and private holdings. The age-old land holding system was characterized by a regime in which members of the feudal monarchy, including the church, owned the largest share of both rural and urban lands. Hence, the state and its elite were important land managers dictating the political economy of land use. The complex land tenure system was so entrenched into the social fabric of Ethiopian society that no major long-term developmental or conservation measures were possible (Girma 1992; Aberra 1998). How did the state affect land management? Is it possible to relate land degradation to the regime of land ownership that the state instituted in different parts of the country at various times? A synoptic assessment of the various land tenure systems prior to the structural land reform of 1975 may shed some light on these questions.

Analysis of the historical configuration of land tenure in Ethiopia prior to 1975 recognizes five major land holding systems, namely: communal, private, grant land, alien and nomadic grazing land holdings (Aberra 1998: 125). The communal land holding system *(rest),* which dominated life over much of the northern highlands of Ethiopia for centuries, bestowed on the owner of land perpetual right of use but restricts his/her right to dispose the property by sale or other means. It also established the right of use to any person who could establish blood relationship to the common ancestor of the family (Aberra 1998: 124). This system of land holding not only allowed the land manager an economic benefit but also bestowed higher social and political status in the prevailing political economy of the state. While it may have given the owner a sense of perpetuity in the use of the land, it could be argued that it provided little incentive for the individual household to improve land through long-term sustainable environmental action because the communal nature of ownership made land amenable to partition upon the request of someone who could trace his/her blood relation to the community. Land was also subject to periodic rotation of use so that all members had the opportunity to till both fertile and less fertile plots at any one time.

The Private land holding system is a later development and mostly asserted its dominance in central, southern and southwestern parts of the country (Aberra 1998: 128). The system exhibited a wide range of ownership; use and management regimes but shared the common feature of empowerment of the proprietor to exercise rights of disposal and usufruct. Again, it is very difficult to make generalizations or draw definitive conclusions on the nature of the adverse impact of such a land holding regime on land degradation. However, the relegation of millions of peasants in the south to the position of tenants could not be expected to introduce sustainable practices of land management. The highly exploitative and oppressive system could not allow millions of tenants the right to make long-term sustainable environmental decisions and commitments. The serious nature of the contradictions of the system eventually led to the unfolding of the 1974 revolutionary changes in the country. The land reform of 1975 nationalized all land in the country and the state has since become the sole land manager with policy setting, regulatory and enforcement prerogatives.

The Grant land holding system (*Gult*) was the third system of land holdings. It was a land holding system operating in both the communal and private holding regimes but circumscribed by the requisite condition of the owner rendering distinguished service to the state. Aberra (1998: 141) appropriately called it compensation land on this account. As in the case of other holding systems, there were variations in the management regime of land. The fact that it could be exercised in both communal and private land holding systems made it amenable to the bestowment of different kinds of privileges and rewards.

The fourth land holding system was designated as an 'Alien' land holding system on account of the superimposition of non-indigenous land tenure systems on the traditional system by the Egyptians (1875–1885) in *Harerghe* region and the Italians in *Eritrea* region during the period of colonial occupation and domination (Aberra 1998: 140). The system introduced both private and government land holding regimes by successive land reorganization and allocation measures in the process causing serious socio-economic problems for the local population. The Egyptians estimated the tax that each peasant had to pay. In addition they created a complex hierarchy of chiefs, assistant chiefs, paramount chiefs, serfs, sub-serfs, tenants and herders as a way of institutionalizing a local system of control and compliance. One of the most oppressive systems of taxation imposed on the peasantry was known as *Zeka* or grain tax. Aberra (1998) noted that many of the peasants were subjected to such an unfair treatment by the tax estimators and collectors to such an extent that they often left the land for good. Only farmers with family obligations continued to be abused (Aberra 1998: 144).

The fifth major land holding system was related to nomadic grazing, a common property regime in which a tribe or a clan of a tribe exercised the right of usage on account of grazing its herd of animals. Claims over water wells and grazing land by clans took the forms of communal holdings, by community leaders and individuals (Aberra 1998: 146). Land under this type of management has often been described as highly abused both by the practices of the herders and the decisions of the state to develop modern agro-industrial projects (Fantu 1992). There are conflicting perspectives about the outcome of common property regimes of resource management. Runge (1981) noted that the breakdown of common property institutions in the Sahel region of Africa has led to serious levels of overgrazing (Runge 1981: 597). McCabe (1990), in his study of Turkana pastoralists in Kenya came to the conclusion that ' practices of East African pastoralists did not degrade the environment, that livestock numbers did not exceed the carrying capacity of the land, and that social institutions successfully functioned to cope with environmental problems' (McCabe 1990: 81). Oba and Kotile (2001), in their assessment of landscape level degradation in the pastoralist region of southern Ethiopia, concluded that 'indigenous ecological knowledge was effectively used to determine landscape suitability and potential grazing capacity of individual landscapes and at regional levels' (Oba and Kotile 2001: 461). In fact they contended that the *Booran* pastoralists of southern Ethiopia not only categorized landscapes in terms of seasons of use but also in terms of grazing capacity and hence had a superior approach to the ones used by ecologists (Oba and Kotile 2001: 472).

Such findings and arguments may be sound in areas of little conflict with other environmental managers and during times of high level of climatic predictability. In Ethiopia, climatic variability and political instability have been important features of development and environmental management. In some parts of Ethiopia, the state has been alienating land from the traditional grazing grounds of nomadic pastoralists. The 1960s saw a significant expansion of commercial farms in the middle and lower courses of the *Awash* valley in central Ethiopia. Since then, there have been ongoing frictions and struggles between the state and the pastoralists for access to various sections of this valley with significant negative repercussions for sound land management. The struggle had expressed itself in various forms ranging from sporadic shootings by pastoralists at commercial farm employees to outright destruction of portions of the commercial farms by tampering with infrastructures and driving camels through farms.

State policy on land tenure under successive governments has empowered and rewarded certain segments of Ethiopian society while disempowering and marginalizing others. The state gave elites not only preferential access to land but also facilitated the mobilization of financial and manpower resources in the form of taxes, feudal dues and labor. Land was used by the state as a major means of social control of peoples and resources by governing elites (Aberra 1998: 147). The privileging of a minority of feudal lords and their supporting groups over a vast peasant and pastoralist population had a major impact on the way land resources were perceived and managed.

As environmental managers, Ethiopian peasants have operated under great social and environmental uncertainty at national, regional and local levels. Preoccupied predominantly with subsistence-oriented agricultural activities, both sedentary farmers and nomadic pastoralists have been adversely affected by unequal power relations in their dealings with other major environmental managers, primarily the state and the few commercial farms (private and state owned) that came into existence with incipient modernization. The Ethiopian state has historically evolved a social system in which an elite group of royal family members, nobles, high clergy and high military officials exercised absolute control over all aspects of national life, most importantly, the access to and utilization regimes of land (Girma 1992). The vast majority of farmers and pastoralists have been so marginalized that they have been unable to cope with even the slightest environmental uncertainty like droughts and flooding. The deadly famine of 1888 to 1889, following the drought of 1888 is reputed to have claimed the lives of one-third of the nation's population and 90 percent of the animal population (Webb and Braun 1994: 20). The 1972 to 1973 drought precipitated the famous 'Wollo' famine in which over 200,000 people perished (Kaplan 1988: 24). Ten years later, the 1983 to 1984 drought claimed more than one million lives (Tsegaye 2002: 3). This was in spite of the fact that a revolutionary land reform had been instituted in 1975 and a socialist government, allegedly committed to the promotion of equity and justice, governed the country. The redistribution of land to peasants was definitely a popular and widely supported move because it removed an anachronistic and deeply entrenched socio-economic and political system that hampered development and the rational management of the natural resources of the country (Aberra 1998: 147). However, it did not lead to a better management of land, forest and water resources.

There are conflicting views on the opinion of Ethiopian farmers on the existing system of landholding. A recent Ethiopian Economic Association and the Ethiopian Economic Policy research Institute survey of 8,540 farmers in 70 'Woredas' of the country indicated that 61 percent of the farmers supported the existing system while 38 percent opposed it. The study also showed that 46 percent of the farmers favored public ownership of land while 32 percent preferred private ownership (WIC November 6, 2002). This result was strongly contested by professional researchers who noted that 80 percent of the opinion providers had expressed that the current land holding system was the most pressing problem facing farmers in Ethiopia (WIC November 6, 2002). Dissatisfaction with the current land holding system was attributed to four major reasons, namely: inability to get additional land (44 percent); inability to buy or sell land (13 percent), fear of losing land (12 percent) and injustice in land administration (11 percent) (WIC November 6,2002). Given the highly politicized nature of the subject, it is difficult to give credence to the findings of the government-sponsored survey. The government's justification for continuing the policy of public ownership of land has often been associated with the fear that farmers would sell their land and flock to the ill-equipped cities and towns of the country thus creating a difficult political and socio-economic problem. This fear was found groundless as 90 percent of the interviewed farmers indicated that they would not sell their land if they had the right to own it privately (WIC November 2, 2002).

Poverty and Marginalization

Political economy perspectives of poverty often see it as a component of the interactive linkage between political and economic change and alterations in the social order. Poverty has often been seen as an important determinant of land degradation (Barrow 1991: 18). In 1994, a World Bank study on poverty in the developing countries noted that 69 percent of Ethiopia's population was living on the equivalent of less than US$1 per day (Chen et al 1994). The number of poor people in Ethiopia has been and is staggering. A 1995 United States Agency for International Development (USAID) report noted that half of the country's estimated population of 60 million lived in abject poverty and that 80 percent was constantly affected by widespread chronic hunger, high unemployment, poor health conditions, minimal infrastructure, wretched housing and an absence of basic services (Bonner 1995: 1). Given the fact that the average land holding of the Ethiopian farmer was found to be 1.02 ha per household, it is not difficult to see the asymmetrical relationship between farm income and household size. The size of land holding has a direct impact on the size of farm income. In particular, the low level of productivity of subsistence farming in Ethiopia has been a characteristic feature and problem of food insecurity. The Disaster Prevention and Preparedness Commission (DPPC) in its January 2002 release noted that 5.2 million Ethiopians were in need of relief assistance for 2002 (WIC January 24, 2002). The warning was made at a time when the country's agricultural harvest was cited to have been good. The interim poverty reduction strategy paper of the country, which is under discussion and further elaboration, estimated that 45.5 percent all Ethiopians live under conditions of "absolute poverty"––a term which refers to some absolute standard of minimum requirement (Addis Tribune December 3, 2001).

Since most of the poor people live in rural areas as farmers and pastoralists, they have no choice but to exploit the land to meet their basic needs thereby inducing land degradation. Kebrom (1999), citing the study of Hurni (1988: 88) noted that the agricultural costs of degradation in the highlands of Ethiopia would amount to about $2,500 million over the 1990 to 2014 period, thus negatively affecting the per capita income of a farmer by about 30 percent. He further indicated that land degradation would result in a high rate of expansion of croplands until it falls to zero by 2040. The cost of maintaining sustainability of all croplands would approximate $200 million per year (Kebrom 1999: 421). While blaming the poor for land degradation is neither new nor recent information, the issue of marginalization is often left unaddressed. State policies under successive governments have marginalized Ethiopian farmers and pastoralists so much that the only major recourse they have is to use more and more marginal lands for crop production and grazing. Their social and economic marginalization is in effect translated into a process that promotes the biophysical deterioration of the Ethiopian environment.

Political Instability, Wars and Conflicts

Land degradation is often cited as the basic cause of Africa's conflicts, wars and political instability. Obi (1998: 44) contended that land degradation has been and is at the heart of the continuous problem of political instability, conflicts and wars in the horn of Africa. Ethiopia's long history of statehood is replete with incessant wars and conflicts of both internal and external causation. In particular, the last 150 years have been marked by incessant conflicts as monarchs and other rulers engaged in wars to establish supremacy over regional contenders for power and control of people and resources. The continuous mobilization and deployment of large number of soldiers from the peasantry not only deprived the rural sector of its most productive manpower but also had serious environmental impact. The demand for fuel wood and construction purposes was such that the conflicts inevitably led to accelerated deforestation and land degradation (Asnake 1983; Mesfin 1991). The social and political ramifications of these conflicts are invariably expressed in the creation of a bifurcated political and socio-cultural environment in which a state enforced separation of urban and rural areas and ethnic groups mediated production and social relations. The civil war raged in the country for almost 30 years (1960–1990) and culminated in the secession of Eritrea from Ethiopia. During these long years of internal strife and instability, hundreds of thousands of peasants and pastoralists were drafted into the armies thus depriving the agricultural sector of the most energetic segment of the labor force.

The impact of such a distortion in the deployment of the labor force on economic production and land degradation has yet to be studied systematically. The civil wars diverted large sums of money into warfare, contributing to stagnation or a decrease in agricultural production, increased food insecurity and the destruction of whatever little rural infrastructure was developed. The looting and destruction of school buildings, health facilities, research institutions and agricultural extension infrastructure in 1990 and 1991 has been the latest demonstration of the negative impact of political instability on development and resource management. The destruction of hillside closures, community forests and soil conservation infrastructures by peasants in the wake of the overthrow of the military government in 1991 was another clear demonstration of the antagonistic attitude and perception of peasants to the top-down, prescriptive and highly coercive resource management strategies employed by the government (Kebrom 2001:424).

The intensified struggle for access and control of resources by organized social groups in Ethiopia has definitely resulted in a new politico-economic and ecological setting that allowed the victors a greater share of the wealth generated from the exploitation of environmental resources. The widespread accusation of the current government's preferential treatment of the 'Tigray' region (home ground of the ruling elite) as a venue for a sustained level of investment in economic production, technical and social infrastructure development stems from such a discursive formation. The degree to which such accusations can be materially substantiated is currently a matter of conjecture.

Technology and Land Degradation

The Ethiopian highlands have been continuously settled for over 5,000 years due to the fertility of the soil and the suitability and diversity of their agro-climatic conditions (Hurni 1988). In spite of the rich biodiversity and genetic resource base of the country, there have been few signs of a technological transformation of Ethiopian society both in its system of production and social relations. The introduction of modern technologies into the country in the later half of the 19th century has not changed the country's production and social organization dramatically. It is particularly disconcerting to see that the attempts to introduce production technologies into the agricultural sector since the end of World War II have registered only patchy and fragmented results. Agricultural extension services and other support systems have generally been very weak in terms of reaching the peasants on a scale that could make them less vulnerable to such critical problems as land degradation and other forms of environmental depredations. Successive governments have been unable to create an enabling environment that supported the generation, adoption and widespread application of technologies that could bring about systemic changes in the country's production, population distribution and resource management systems and practices. The state essentially used top-down blueprints of land management which peasants had to implement. Blaikie and Brookfield (1987) have appropriately called such a conservation strategy as 'fortress conservation' because conservation practices are prescribed by law and people essentially turned into criminals (Stocking 1995: 257). Under such circumstances, resistance to conservation is inevitable as the immediate months of the fall of the military government in 1991 clearly demonstrated (Kebrom 1999; Dessalegn 1999).

The coupling of modern land conservation techniques with its bureaucratic structures and support systems over more sustainable indigenous agricultural technologies has been a concomitant aspect of Ethiopia's land management experience. Kebrom (1999) notes that little attention was given to the attitudes and priorities of local populations in the planning and execution of conservation programs in South 'Wollo' where he conducted research on land degradation (Kebrom 1999: 424). Dessalegn (1999) complemented this view by citing the experience of water resource development and management in the country. The state not only nationalized small-scale irrigation projects but also denied former owners access to water (Dessalegn 1999).

The experiences with hill closures, reforestation and various types of soil conservation schemes have demonstrated that land degradation can be significantly mitigated and ameliorated (FWCD 1989). Yet, much of the work done in this sector over the last 30 years has been based on the introduction of most rudimentary techniques in a highly unstable socio-economic and political rural and urban environment. According to the Office of the National Committee for Central Planning, only 15 percent of the half billion trees planted between 1975 and 1985 over an area of 339,000 hectares survived (FEI 1998).

A Finnish Environmental Report attributed the failure of successive Ethiopian governments to arrest soil erosion, degradation of the environment and decline in agricultural productivity to an emphasis on technocratic approaches that hinged upon the views of professional experts rather than farmers. The report concluded that indigenous land rehabilitation technologies and biological conservation measures have been largely disregarded in past conservation strategies (FEI 1998). The large scale and mostly coercive soil conservation program mounted in Ethiopia between the late 1970s and 1987 constructed 1.5 million km of stone and soil terraces and bunds on 300,000 ha of land and closed off another 80,000 ha from local people. The population participated mainly to receive food and oil from the World Food Program which supported the program or through compulsory peasant association campaigns (Pretty and Shah 1997: 45). The fact that 40 percent of the terraces were broken after one year of their construction clearly indicates that peasants will not maintain technologies that they did not either appreciate or felt the need for (Swedish International Development Agency (SIDA) 1984).

The widespread shortage and absence of even the most rudimentary agricultural implements in rural Ethiopia is another technological reality that remains to be addressed on a system-wide level. One of the authors of this chapter witnessed an interesting discussion that took place at the 'Addis Alem' Institute of Agricultural Research between the former Head of State, Colonel Mengistu Haile Mariam and the Head of the Agricultural Research Institute. After introducing a number of 'technologically improved' models of agricultural implements produced at the research center, the head of the research center enthusiastically proposed that the improved products would revolutionize agricultural production in the country. The Head of State was visibly irritated and sarcastically remarked that the center needed to conduct research on how to get these technological products to the farmers – fully cognizant of the fact that this was the "Achilles heel" of Ethiopian agricultural research.

In spite of the long years of agricultural research operations in the country, there have been few improvements in agricultural implements and other production-increasing technologies at the field level. Agricultural research has been and remains to be largely divorced from the day-to-day lives of the farmer and pastoralist. This does not however mean that the contributions of many devoted and talented agricultural researchers have been insignificant. Many researchers have individually and collectively contributed greatly to the improvement of seeds and breeds and the maintenance of the biodiversity of the Ethiopian ecosystem.

Irrigation and different kinds of water works have been important technological buffers against drought and other forms of water-related stress both in ancient and contemporary societies. Dessalegn (1999) points out that less than six percent of the country's estimated irrigable land of 2.7 million hectares is now under irrigation. He further noted that irrigation in Ethiopia covered less than two percent of the country's cropped land (Dessalegn 1999: 8). State policy in terms of the choice of technology and scale of operations has emphasized large scale projects requiring high management and maintenance costs. In the 1970s and 1980s, peasant perception of irrigation was associated with collectivization and hence their lack of enthusiasm. Dessalegn (1999) contends that both small-scale and large scale irrigation projects were failures because they were poorly planned and designed; based on highly coercive top-down approaches with little or no active participation of stakeholders and beneficiaries and managed by party or government functionaries. Some of the projects are believed to have caused serious damage to the environment (Dessalegn 1999: 10). The salinization of over 1,000 ha of irrigated land in the 'Amibara' irrigation scheme of the central Awash valley through careless irrigation practices is an often-cited example of the adverse impact of poor management of irrigation projects.

Economic Policy and Land Degradation

Inappropriate, misguided and externally driven national development policies and programs contribute to land degradation. Dasgupta (1997) noted that environmental degradation in poor countries is closely associated with 'unreflective public policies, predatory governments and thieving aristocracies (Dasgupta 1997: 14). He cited policies that were discriminatory against agriculture, insecure property rights, disenfranchisement of the poor from economic development as some of the major systematic features of institutional failures that had an adverse effect on land. Likewise, Fantu (1992) noted that much of the poverty and ecological degradation in African countries owed its origin to 'misguided national policies and governments often financed by official external donor agencies' (Fantu 1992: 498). Dessalegn (1999) has complemented this view in his article on water resources development in Ethiopia (Dessalegn 1999: 23).

Economic policy plays a critical role in land degradation because it either increases or decreases uncertainty facing land users such as farmers, herders, private or state managers. The Ethiopian state has been playing a critical role in land degradation in view of its position as a codifier of laws and regulations; establisher of institutions; trainer of manpower and key mobilizer of needed financial and technical resources for the management of environmental resources. The history of economic policy in Ethiopia in the post-war period is replete with frequently changing ideologies structuring the process of production and reproduction of capital and the social relations within which such processes take place. Until 1974, the monarchy thrived on a feudal system of land ownership and social relations in which millions of land managers were tenants with little or no power over land use, production and conservation policies and activities. The insecurity, exploitation and oppression of tenants and other land users led to the neglect of land. The feudal state used land as a remunerative mechanism for services rendered by individuals to the state and as means of paying national debt. The wide range of tenure types and entitlement regimes of the system made them exploitative and backward systems of land management (Aberra 1998: 123–14). The seriousness of the problem was such that it led to the overthrow of the monarchy and the establishment of a military government in 1974.

The new government made a revolutionary change in the land tenure system in the country by nationalizing all rural and urban lands and redistributing land to the tillers. It established a new property rights regime that essentially made the state a landlord and the rest of environmental managers its tenants. While the measure was widely seen as long overdue, the new system of power relations that it instituted engendered an insecure system in which land managers were essentially deprived of the right to make long-term decisions on the management of their lands. The new land management system prohibited land sales, leases, hiring labor and usufruct rights thus alienating the land managers from their land. It launched a massive, highly extravagant and ecologically destructive experiment with the development of state farms in line with its policy of agrarian reform and socialization of agricultural production. Hundreds of thousands of peasants were displaced to accommodate these projects (Fantu 1992: 500). The 'villagization' and resettlement programs launched in the mid 1980s are believed to have displaced close to 13 million farmers from their traditional holdings with serious repercussions for agricultural production, land degradation and management (Fantu 1992).

Since 1991, the Transitional government of Ethiopia has essentially continued the former policy on land management with minor modifications such as allowing land leasing and the hiring of labor. It has also implemented a politically motivated and highly controversial land redistribution program in the 'Amhara regional state.' The social, economic and environmental consequences of such politically motivated land management policies are many and complex. There are few systematic studies that inform the public about the nature and scope of the problem. Benin and Pender (2001) indicated that land redistribution in the 'Amahara' region has had positive impact on land productivity in the short term but could not establish its effect on land improvement (Benin and Pender 2001: 567). While the productivity of land may have increased as a result of new entitlements and the introduction of production increasing inputs such as fertilizer, it is not difficult to imagine the insecurity and uncertainty that it introduces into the long term decision-making process of the land manager. The findings of Marcos and Kassahun (1988) have suggested that uncertainties about land and forest property rights contributed to low performance of community forest development schemes in Ethiopia (Marcos and Kassahun 1988).

Poor Governance and Maladministration

Poor governance and maladministration have a direct influence on land degradation (Barrow 1991). Successive Ethiopian governments have tried to institute a system of governance and public administration aimed at establishing dominant forms of social management of peoples and resources. Both pre- and post-1974 governments have been unrepresentative, highly coercive, and unaccountable to the ruled. The measures taken by the monarchy, the military and the current government in the name of decentralization and democratization have been circumscribed by political exercises aimed at legitimizing the government in power both politically and economically. The current government's balancing act between administering enough repression to weaken any potential opponents and maintain power while introducing some formalities of democratic governance to ingratiate itself before powerful western governments and aid institutions is a clear demonstration of the ambiguity that environmental managers and society have to face in making critical long-term decisions.

The result of such systems of governance and public administration has been the breakdown of law and order and lack of security and social motivation for active and meaningful public participation in public affairs. As Ribot (1999) clearly demonstrated, political decentralization and democratization practices in post colonial African states mimicked the colonial past in that 'central control is administered through locally appointed authorities backed by and advising the state while presenting only a semblance of local representation.' Both the military and the current government of Ethiopia had codified elaborate electoral edicts in their respective constitutions and implemented decentralization and democratization programs (ONCCP 1984; TGE 1992). These administratively driven and control-oriented decentralization and 'democratization' measures have yet to create broad-based, democratic platforms for pluralistic political activity and the evolution of a system of governance that is accountable to the public. The measures taken in the name of democratization and decentralization have contributed little to the promotion of local control of resources, distribution of economic benefits and autonomous decision-making that are so central to democratic governance. The highly contested nature of electoral procedures and practices in Ethiopia has been demonstrated a few times resulting in the major opposition parties boycotting elections. The lack of transparent and accountable system of governance and public administration inevitably increases the uncertainty of land holders including farmers, pastoralists, and private commercial farmers.

Public Perception, Participation and Land Degradation

The lack of active and informed public participation in the planning, design, implementation and follow up on development and resource management projects has been and remains a major factor in land degradation in many developing countries. The centrality of instituting a system of governance that actively promotes and involves Ethiopia's primary land managers, the millions of farmers and herders, has been underscored by many researchers (Mesfin 1986; Eweg et al. 1998; Kebrom 1999; Dessalegn 1999, Benin and Pender 2001). These and other researchers have indicated that successive governments have taken a top-down, technocratic, expert-based approaches to land rehabilitation, environmental management and rural development without the active involvement of peasants and other land managers. The Finnish Environmental Institute (FEI 1998) report on environmental management in Ethiopia had identified disregard of indigenous technologies and poor public participation in the planning and implementation of conservation programs among the major weaknesses of Ethiopia's past conservation strategies.

Dessalegn (1999) attributed the failure of many projects for environmental management and governance to a regime of public participation in which the key land managers–farmers and herders–have been given little attention. He accused Ethiopian planners of emphasizing agronomic, engineering or other technical aspects of water projects and making all important decisions without the participation of the beneficiary population. Peasants have often provided labor and followed instructions in implementing rural development projects either freely or in return for food-for-work remuneration. He suggested that such practices have been unproductive and unsustainable (Dessalegn 1999: 23).

The perceptions of land managers regarding land degradation are equally central to both the understanding of the problem and the successful implementation of land rehabilitation programs. Peoples' perceptions of environmental hazards are structured by existing socioeconomic arrangements (Watts 1993: 231). Obi and Kotile (2001) have found that there are appreciable differences in perceptions between the indigenous environmental knowledge of Ethiopian pastoralists and ecologists regarding landscape changes and areas of management concern in such changes (Oba and Kotile 2001: 473). The findings of Benin and Pender that farmers in the 'Amhara' region of Ethiopia expected the continuation of land redistribution in the future in spite of the regional administration's intentions of ending the policy clearly indicates not only differences in perceptions among important land managers but also the lack of communications and mutual confidence between the state and peasants (Benin and Pender 2001: 567). Such differences in perceptions have important implications for decision-making on medium and long-term investments in land improvements.

Public awareness about the causes and consequences of land degradation is another critical area in environmental management. It not only helps to define the nature and scope of the problem but also to formulate appropriate preventive policies and mitigation strategies and actions at local, regional and national levels. Few studies inform us about the level of environmental awareness among major environmental managers and users in Ethiopia. Aklilu (2001) sheds some light on the level of public awareness among primary school teachers and prospective school administrators. His findings suggested that most of the educators who participated in the study had some level of awareness of the causes and measures against land degradation but had difficulty identifying its consequences. It is particularly noteworthy that 60 percent of teachers failed to identify the areas of the country that were suffering most from land degradation (Aklilu 2001: 77). The assertion made by Oba and Kotile (2001) that *Booran* pastoralists of Ethiopia had a superior categorization of landscapes in terms of seasons of use and grazing capacity suggests the significance of indigenous knowledge systems and public awareness about the dynamics of environmental management (Oba and Kotile 2001: 473.). While it is difficult to make generalizations from a few studies, they nonetheless provide us with some tangential insight into the level of public awareness in Ethiopian society. In particular, it is necessary to be careful about unduly privileging indigenous resource management practices and condemning modern interventions/approaches as many recent discourses and narratives on indigenous environmental knowledge (IEK) seem to suggest.

There are adequate reasons to suggest that the progressive integration of more peasants into the structures of the modern state may have contributed to the weakening of their capability in terms of coping with environmental hazards (Mesfin 1986). The dependency syndrome that has been creeping into the psyche of both policy makers and farmers via food aid and other forms of international assistance since the 1960s has now lodged itself firmly into policy making processes that independent action is virtually impossible. This state of affairs has definitely contributed to changed perceptions about hazards and response mechanisms on a societal level. Both the military government and the current administration have gone on public record warning the international community that they will not be responsible for any famine-related deaths after they made the crisis known to the world. The most interesting part is that the international community has grown accustomed to taking the warnings seriously and acting accordingly to facilitate the flow of food aid. This is definitely understandable in view of the fact that no level-headed representative of international organizations or foreign governments would be willing to take the wrath of his/her headquarters/superiors and the international community for not heeding the warnings of governments.

The mobilization of alms from the international community through the Relief and Rehabilitation Commission (which has now adopted the lesser pejorative name of Disaster Preparedness and Prevention Commission) has become a respectable 'capacity building' strategy. The truth is that it is the ultimate expression of failed governance. No country should be allowed to exercise the rights of sovereignty in decision making over peoples and resources when it conveniently shirks its responsibility in times of hazards that turn millions of peasants into vulnerable and helpless victims. One cannot thus escape from the conclusion that inappropriate resource management and development policies and unrepresentative and unaccountable governments pose serious threats to land degradation and the loss of livelihood for millions of poor and weak land managers.

The attitude of government officials and development agents towards peasants has also been paternalistic and condescending. Dessalegn (1999) explains the reluctance of peasants to become active and concerned participants in development projects largely as a function of this state of affairs (Dessalegn 1999: 24). The disregard that young agricultural extension agents show to indigenous farming techniques and husbandry is definitely a manifestation of a colonially structured mental construct that privileged the modern at the expense of the traditional and indigenous knowledge systems.

Institutional Discourses, Narrative and Arrangements

The ways land degradation problems are defined and represented reflect the patterns of perceiving and experiencing which sources of discourse have been structured to understand social reality (Eder 1996: 166). Stocking (1995) complements this perspective by noting that 'knowledge about erosion and conservation in developing countries is used for particular and subjective ends. In effect, all participants within the debate, or affected by it, become actors: some with central roles, others with little influence that they may as well join the theatre audience' (Stocking 1995: 256). Actors use moral, empirical and aesthetic judgments in the construction of particular perspectives of debate about land degradation. For example, the 1992 state of the world report of the United Nations Fund for Population Activities (UNFPA) claimed that the bottom, very poorest 1 billion of the world's population often imposed greater environmental injury than the three billion of their citizens put together (Hartman 1994). Likewise, the World Bank has been consistently arguing that Africa's developmental and ecological crises stemmed from fast population growth, inappropriate economic policy frameworks and the non-adaptability and non-integration of African agriculture to the ever-changing global market (Cleaver and Schreiber 1996).

In Ethiopia, land degradation has been the subject of concern both discursively and materially for quite a long time. Most often the strategy used by both academic and development agency discourse in constructing the problem of land degradation has been based on a view that placed the state as the most important manager and an institution that had both the capability and willingness to transform the country's economic and resource management dynamics towards a more sustainable direction. The farmers and pastoralists who constitute about 85 percent of the country's population have quite often been cast as the main culprits for the deterioration of the land and other natural resources of the country's environment. Such discursive formations and narratives not only assign blame but also empower certain actors or land managers while disempowering or belittling the contribution of the major stakeholders–the farmers and pastoralists. Likewise, the institutional arrangements to combat land degradation are not only fragmented and weak but also incapacitated by cumbersome bureaucratic arrangements and mandates.

Conclusion

The central argument of this chapter has been that there is a need for a more inclusive understanding of the social and physical determinants of land degradation in Ethiopia and elsewhere in Africa. It has advocated a political ecology perspective in which the role of socio-cultural and political economy determinants is more appreciated and focused upon both in defining the nature and scope of land degradation and evolving appropriate policy, strategy and program interventions at various scales—national, sub-national, and local. Such a perspective should examine the role of the major land managers, namely: the State, the farmers and pastoralists, international development and humanitarian agencies, non-governmental organizations, civic organizations and the public at large. This study suggests that the Ethiopian state has been and remains a critical land manager with both positive and negative consequences for sustainable land management. In spite of the fact that the state has been and remains to be suspended and weak in terms of its symbiotic relationship with the peoples that it rules, its policies of political control and access to the resources of the environment have privileged the few at the cost of the steady marginalization of the many. The experience of past and current approaches and practices to land management suggests that farmers and pastoralists have been perceived and treated by the state not as key environmental managers but as recipients of the advice, expertise, orders and benevolence of the state–the 'real environmental manager.' Past and current discourses and narratives; policies on land tenure; poverty; decentralization and democratic governance; economic development, technology, public participation and institutional development have generally been significant contributors to land degradation and unsustainable processes and patterns of resource management and development in general. The persistent impoverishment of the population and degradation of the land over successive decades cannot be explained by invoking biophysical and bio-geophysical processes. A political ecology approach to land degradation provides a better explanation of the dynamics of the complex nexus because it seeks answers for land degradation in the political, social and economic institutions of society.

References

Aberra, Jembere (1998). *Legal History of Ethiopia 1434–1974: Some Aspects of Substantive and Procedural Laws*. Rotterdam: Erasmus University.

Addis Tribune, December 3/2001. [Online] Available: www.addistribune.com/archives/2001/11/30–11–01/KEEP.html.

Aklilu, Dalelo (2001). Awareness of Educators in Ethiopia about the Problem of Land Degradation. *Zimbabwe Journal of Educational Research* 13 (1): 58–85.

Alemneh, Dejene (1990). *Environment, Famine and Policies in Ethiopia: A View from the Village*. London: Lynne Rienner Publishers.

Asnake, Ali (1983). *Aspects of the Political History of Wollo: 1872–1916*. M.A Thesis, Addis Ababa: Addis Ababa University.

Barrow, C.J. (1991). *Land Degradation: Development and Breakdown of Terrestrial Environments*. Cambridge: Cambridge University Press.

Benin, S. and Pender, J. (2001). "Impacts of Land Redistribution on Land Management and Productivity in the Ethiopian Highlands." *Land Degradation and Development*, 12: 555–568.

Blaikie, P. and Brookfield, H. (1987). *Land Degradation and Society*. London and New York: Methuen.

Bonner. (1995). [Online] Available: http://198.76.84.1/HORN/ethiopia/USAID/budget.95.txt

Brown, L. R. and Wolf, E.C. (1984). "Soil Erosion: Quiet Crisis in the World Economy." *Worldwatch*, Paper 60, Washington DC.

Chen, D. and Ravailllion, M. (1994). *Statistical Addendum to Is Poverty Increasing in the Developing World?* Policy Research Department, Washington DC: World Bank.

Cleaver, K M and Schreiber, G. A. (1996). *Reversing the Spiral: The Population, agricultural and Environmental Nexus in Sub-Saharan Africa*. Washington DC: The World Bank.

Dasgupta, Paratha (1997). *Environmental and Resource Economics in the World of the Poor, Resources for the Future*. Washington DC.

Dessalegn, Rahmato (1999). *Water Resources Development in Ethiopia: Issues of Sustainability and Participation*. [Online] Available: www.ethiopians.com/Main_FSS_Paper1.htm.

Eder, K. (1996). *The Social Construction of Nature*. London: Sage Publishers

Eweg, H P.A et al. (1998). "Analyzing Degradation and Rehabilitation for Sustainable Land Management in the Highlands of Ethiopia." *Land Degradation and Development*, 9: 529–542.

Fantu, Cheru (1992). "Structural Adjustment, Primary Resource Trade and Sustainable Development in Sub-Saharan Africa." *World Development*, 20, (4): 497–512.

FAO. (1986). Ethiopia Highlands Reclamation Study Final Report, Rome: FAO.
Finnish Environmental Institute (1998). *Ethiopia: Mission Report*. Helsinki: Finland.
FWCD. Forestry and Wildlife Conservation Department (1989). *The Last Forests of Ethiopia*. Addis Ababa: FWCD.
Girma, Kebede (1992). *The State and Development in Ethiopia*. New Jersey: Humanities Press.
Girma, Tadesse. (2001). "Land Degradation: A Challenge to Ethiopia." *Environmental Management* 27 (6):815–824.
Grepperud, S. (1996). "Population Pressure and Land Degradation: The Case of Ethiopia." *Journal of Environmental Economics and Management*. 30:18–33.
Hardin, G. (1968). "The Tragedy of the Commons." *Science* 162, (3859):1243–1248.
Hartman, B. (1994). "Population Fictions: the Malthusians are Back in Town." (ed.) Godfarb T. D., 1997, *Taking Sides: Clashing Views on Controversial Issues*, 7th edition. Guilford: Dushkin/McGraw Hill Publishers.
Henricksen, B. S. et al. (1983). *Provisional Soil Depth Map of Ethiopia*. Ministry of Agriculture, Ethiopia.
Hurni, H. (1988). "Degradation and Conservation of Soil Resources in the Ethiopian Highlands." *Mountain Research and Development* 8:123–130.
Isenberg, C.W. and Krapf, J.L. (1968). *The Journals of Isenberg and Krapf*. London: Frank Cass and Sons Ltd.
Johnson, D.L. and Lewis, L.A.(1995). *Land Degradation: Creation and Destruction*. Oxford UK: Blackwell Scientific.
Kaplan, R.D. (1988). "Causes and Characters of Drought in Ethiopia." *Ethiopian Journal Agricultural Sciences*. 10 (1–2): 85–97.
Kebrom, Tekle. (1999). "Land Degradation Problems and Their Implications for Food Shortage in South *Wello*, Ethiopia." *Environmental Management*, 23, (4): 419–427.
Levia, D. F. (1999). "Land Degradation: Why is it Continuing?" *Ambio* 28, (2): 200–201.
McCabe, J.T. (1990). "Turkana Pastoralism: A Case against the Tragedy of the Commons." *Human Ecology*. 18 (1): 81–103.
Mesfin, Woldemariam (1986). *Rural Vulnerability to Famine in Ethiopia: 1958–1977*. Exter: Intermediate Technology Publications.
———— (1991). *Suffering Under God's Environment: A Vertical Study of the Predicament of Peasants in North-Central Ethiopia*. Walsworth, Marceline: USA.
National Villagization Coordination Committee (1989). *Rural Transformation*. Addis Ababa: Ministry of Agriculture.
Nita, Bhalla (January 25,2002). "Flora and Fauna Face total Destruction in Ethiopia." *Addis Tribune*. Online. www.addistribune.com/archives/2002/01/25–01–02/Flora.htm
Oba, G. and Kotile, D.G. (2001). "Assessments of Landscape Level Degradation in Southern Ethiopia: Pastoralists Versus Ecologists." *Land Degradation and Development*.12: 461–475 .
Obi, C. (1998). "Environmental Security in Africa: Some Theoretical Concerns and Emerging Issues." *Africa Insight*. 28, (1/2) 41–47.
ONCCP (1984). *Ten Year Perspective Plan 1984/85–1993/94*. Addis Ababa: Ethiopia.
Pankhurst, A. (1992). *Resettlement and Famine in Ethiopia: The Villager's Experience*. Manchester: Manchester University Press.
Pretty, J. N. and Shah, P. (1997). "Making Soil and Water Conservation Sustainable: From Coercion and Control to Partnerships and Participation." *Land Degradation and Development*, 8: 39–58.
Ribot, J. C. (1999). "Decentralization, Participation and Accountability in Sahelian Forestry: Legal Instruments of Political-Administrative Control." *Africa* 69 (91): 1999.

Runge, C. F. (1981). "Common Property Externalities: Isolation, Assurance, and Resource Depletion in a Traditional Grazing Context." *American Journal of Agricultural Economics*, (63).

Schlager, E. and Ostrom, E. (1992). "Property-Rights Regimes and Natural Resources: A Conceptual Analysis." *Land Economics*. August, 1992 68 (3): 249–62.

Stahl, M. (1993). "Environmental Degradation and Political Constraints in Ethiopia." *Journal of Disaster Studies and Management*. 14: 140–150.

Stocking, M. (1995). "Soil Erosion in Developing Countries: Where Geomorphology Fears to Tread." *Catena*, (25): 253–267.

Swedish International Development Agency (SIDA). (1984). *Soil Conservation in Borkenna Catchment: Evaluation Report*. Swedish International Development Authority, Stockholm.

Timmerman, P. (1981). "Vulnerability, Resilience and the Collapse of Society." *Environmental Monograph*. No.1 Institute of Environmental Studies, University of Toronto.

Transitional Government of Ethiopia (1992). *Proclamation No. 7/1992 A Proclamation to Provide for the Establishment of National/Regional Self-Governments*. Addis Ababa: Berhanena Selam Printing Press.

Tsegaye W.G. (2002). El Nino and Drought Early Warning in Ethiopia. [Online] Available: www.brad.ac.uk/research/ijasno2/giorgis.html

United Nations Development Program (UNDP) Emergencies Unit. (1995). Country Information Brief, Draft. Food and Agricultural Organization (FAO). [Online] Available. www.sas.unpen.edu/African_Studies/eue_web/fao_geo.htm.

Walta Information Center (WIC). (January 23, 2002). Close to 5.2 Million Ethiopians Need Relief Assistance in 2002.

www.telecom.net.et/~walta/profile/articles/article196.hml. Accessed December 10 2004.

Watts, M. (1993). "Natural Hazards Research in Context." Hewitt, K. (ed.) *Interpretations of Calamity*. Boston: Allen and Unwin.

Webb, P. and Braun, J. V. (1994). *Famine and Food Security in Ethiopia: Lessons for Africa*. Chichester: John Wiley and Sons.

Chapter 10

Economic/Political Convenience and Unprecedented Deforestation in Sub-Saharan Africa: Development Lessons from Ghana's Structural Adjustment Program[1]

J. Henry Owusu

Introduction

To foster "accelerated" and "sustainable" development in sub-Saharan Africa (SSA), most countries in the region adopted Structural Adjustment Programs (SAPs) in the last two decades of the twentieth century, under the auspices of The International Monetary Fund (IMF) and the World Bank (World Bank 1981, 1989). SAPs were a package of reforms designed to restore economic health in the ailing economies of the Third World. The package normally included massive devaluation of the local currency to improve the competitiveness of exports, to generate trade surpluses to meet the adjusting nations' debt servicing obligations.

Unlike most adjusting SSA countries, Ghana embraced and implemented the program as prescribed by the sponsors. The subsequent economic changes were touted by the sponsors and the international financial community as a big success, with Ghana being referred to as the "star pupil of Adjustment" (*The Financial Times, London*, July 20, 1989). This claim has been widely disputed, particularly by critics of the IMF and the World Bank such as George (1988, 1992) and Hayter (1989), who argued that SAPs had a strong tendency to cause, inter alia, widespread environmental destruction, while emptying the adjusting debtor countries of their natural resources. In addition, the program was thought to render adjusting countries less able to service their debt each year, and precluded investing in economic recovery (George 1992).

This chapter is rooted in the Brundtland Report, *Our Common Future* (WCED 1987), which emphasized the importance of using natural resources to meet our current needs without compromising the ability of future generations to meet theirs. In light of this perspective, there has been increasing awareness of global environmental issues, and in fact, it is because of such awareness that a number of non-government organizations, like the Environmental Defense Fund and Friends of the Earth, took the position that growth under SAPs, as promoted by the IMF and the World Bank, involves huge environmental costs. Focusing on a key component of Ghana's economy, the forestry sector, this chapter uses that country's SAPs, dubbed the "Economic Recovery Program" (ERP) which began in 1983, to demonstrate that SAPs provided a convenient means for governments and their sponsors to meet mutual prevailing economic and political interests. These interests are usually met by excessively exploiting the physical environment through desperate actions such as overexploitation of natural resources so that the "immediate convenience" of meeting those interests tends to generate huge environmental costs for the adjusting country.

A major viewpoint on the adjustment-environment connection is that the link between adjustment and environmental destruction is not clear. For example, Lensink (1996) points to how difficult it is to objectively determine the influence of IMF and World Bank adjustment programs on the environment. His position rests on an earlier study (Opschoor 1994), which suggested that it is theoretically impossible to predict the direction of environmental effects of adjustment programs. Similarly, Reed (1992) concludes in his empirical study on Côte d'Ivoire, Mexico, and Thailand that environmental effects of adjustment programs are really not clear. Such empirical studies of adjustment and the environment and associated development lessons, particularly for African countries, are conspicuously lacking. In addition to Reed's work, significant work was done by Hogg (1993) focusing on Ghana, the Philippines, and Guyana. Generally, writers in this area like Hayter (1989) and Owusu (1994) tend to address the broad environmental implications of adjustment. Unlike contributions such as Reed (1992) and Hogg (1993), I discuss two important aspects of the debate. First, this chapter focuses on a single country, Ghana whose adjustment program was touted as a big success by the sponsors, and examines the dynamics of the "export-orientation" of the formal wood processing industry. Second, by directly linking adjustment and environmental (rain forest) destruction, in the form of a desperate process of deforestation in the country since the implementation of the ERP, it counters the major viewpoint expressed by Lensink (1996), Reed (1992) and others.

Deforestation refers to any activity in a closed forest, which could potentially affect species numbers and degrade or disturb stand. Such activities constitute forest loss, even where a complete conversion or loss of contiguous forest space has not occurred (Osei 1997). Our discussion focuses on the first decade of Ghana's ERP (1983–1993), and the adjustment-deforestation link is established by a demonstration of how the dynamics of local currency devaluation combine with debt servicing obligations, to exert tremendous pressure on the government and wood exporting firms to systematically increase or maintain high wood export volumes. The burden to produce more tropical wood for export under adjustment constitutes the adjustment-deforestation link. This is based on the premise that the ERP was essentially adopted by the government to accommodate international capital to conveniently meet its own immediate political and economic interests. Sacrificing Ghana's rain forest to meet those interests, by way of a sustained and dramatic rapid increase in wood exports that necessarily involves a rapid and dramatic process of deforestation, was the government's recourse in accommodating international capital.

This chapter has five-parts. It begins with a brief examination of the nature of SAPs and their relevance to Africa by presenting arguments by the protagonists and critics. The second section focuses on Ghana's economy prior to adjustment, including the political and economic rationale for the adoption of the ERP by the Provisional National Defense Council (PNDC) government; and the economic significance of the forestry sector. Part three focuses on Ghana's external debts, the sector adjustment loans (SECALs) advanced to formal wood processing firms in the forestry sector through the government, and the dynamics of both types of debt with respect to production and exports of wood. Part three demonstrates the ERP's short-term economic and political "convenience" to the sponsors and the Ghanaian government. Part four discusses the "unprecedented deforestation" process, by linking the dramatic increase in wood exports under the program to the accelerated deforestation and destruction of Ghana's forests. This is followed by some conclusions and development lessons from Ghana's experience.

The Nature of Structural Adjustment and African Development

The basic features of Africa's persistent underdevelopment are largely defined by the structure of the region's economies (UN/ECA 1986). For most people concerned with economic stagnation and underdevelopment in SSA, structural problems refer to the economic and social imbalances that obstruct development in the region, such as the pervasive export bias of the region's economies. However, for international sponsors of SAPs like the IMF and the World Bank, the root cause of the structural problems is market distortion, a condition which, to them, resulted from state intervention in the ailing African economies. SAPs were therefore required to "get the prices right" in the distorted economies of SSA (Younger 1989).

SAPs were, thus, a set of economic policies and prescriptions, promoted and sponsored primarily by the IMF and the World Bank, to address the perceived market distortions as a strategy for development. Generally, policy measures under SAPs involved shifting public expenditure to the export sector; liberalizing the economy to allow the free market to determine prices; promoting exports to generate foreign exchange; and promoting foreign private investment through the promulgation of investment codes with extensive concessions to foreign investors (Sawyerr 1990: 20-23). SAPs, thus, combined three main measures: the stabilization, rehabilitation, and liberalization of the adjusting economy, resulting in the retreat of government from active intervention in favor of a free market system and the creation of an enabling environment for investment by local and foreign capital. These measures, according to the external sponsors of the program, were essential to the restoration of conditions for long-run economic growth so that market mechanisms could at last come to equilibrium (Schwarz 1990). To the sponsors, therefore, SAPs constituted the best solution to Africa's development problems (Green 1987; Younger 1989).

Ghana, like other SSA countries, adopted and implemented such an orthodox SAP ostensibly to redress past development policy failures that culminated in serious economic malaise in the country by the beginning of 1983. The environmental implications of adjustment constituted a controversy between the neo-liberal proponents of the program such as the IMF, the World Bank, the sponsoring countries and agencies, and its primarily structuralist critics, including environmentalist groups such as Friends of the Earth, the Transnational Institute and Probe International (Lensink 1996). The proponents' position rested primarily on the premise that economic stagnation in Third World countries such as Ghana's pre-adjustment economic malaise, and environmental problems such as forest destruction, were primarily internal (World Bank 1981; Steel 1988). According to the proponents, such problems resulted primarily from market distortions engendered by government interventions in the economy by interfering with the "invisible hand" of the market.

The solution therefore had to begin from within, using domestically produced resources for which the economically stagnant country has a comparative advantage (as in the production and export of timber), to engage in international trade. Since a stagnant economy lacks the capital to exploit and export resources, international capital would "aid" such countries by providing them with loans like the SECALs. "Growth with debt" should enable borrowers to increase their capacity to expand with the aid of net foreign savings, for such indebtedness provides the necessary capital used to produce more than a return to cover the cost of borrowing (Ewusi, 1987:13). In addition, the efficiency engendering free-play of market forces would, over time, correct the stagnation and the associated environmental problems (see Lensink 1996: 111-112). After all, efficiency and rational management, based on the market mechanism, are the cornerstones of the increased productivity and profitability expected under the program (Ould-Mey 1996: 16). For the SAP proponents, therefore, "the invisible hand of the market is the surest path" (Storper and Walker 1989: 36) to addressing the economic and environmental problems. These arguments were, however, rejected by the critics.

The critics' perspective was rooted in the basic structuralist view that problems of Third World economies are largely the consequence of their incorporation into the global market system (Mabogunje 1981; Sawyerr 1990). For Ghana the structural problems were initiated during the colonial period, when Britain organized the colony as a tributary economy to benefit her own economy. Thus, at the time of independence in 1957, the economy was "warped", characterized by a one-sided external orientation based on the export of inexpensive raw materials such as timber and external dependence (Sawyerr 1990).

Hamilton (1989) also argued that liberalization measures under adjustment constituted a neo-colonial mechanism for opening developing economies and their markets to western businesses. For example, in the case of Ghana, the technological requirements for the rehabilitation of the wood processing industry compelled the nation to purchase production, transportation and telecommunications equipment, as well as spare parts. This reinforced dependence on imported technology and, to some degree, on foreign technicians and other related personnel/consultants. The procurement of such equipment and spare parts and expatriate personnel were tied to bilateral and multilateral loan schemes as the SECALs for the industry. It was the huge foreign debts generated in this way that George (1992) linked directly to deforestation. This is because the high foreign debts:

> together with the condition related to most adjustment programs that the indebted countries must meet their debt service, lead to developing countries being forced to increase their production of exports in the short term so that foreign currencies can be earned. Since many developing countries produce relatively cheap products that require the production factor of nature, trade liberalization stimulates overexploitation of the factor of nature. (Lensink 1996: 111)

This overexploitation was seen as one of the causes of the unprecedented deforestation of Ghana's limited rain forest.

Proponents of adjustment emphasized the efficiency it engenders in the production process. In fact, critics did not dispute this notion of efficiency because the pressure to meet the debt obligations tends to elicit efficient operations in the short run (Owusu 1994, 1995). Yet in operations like the export of forest products in Ghana, the positive effects of efficiency (e.g., waste reduction or increase in wood recovery rates) were still lost through the negative environmental effects of the increase in timber extraction for export. In the same way, critics agreed that prices should properly reflect costs. Yet, the IMF and the World Bank's obsession with "getting prices right" overlooked the domestic environmental costs and the associated negative externalities to the broader global ecosystem. In addition, it involved the devaluation of the local currency that tended to stimulate increased production of timber logs for export because of the depreciated value of such materials on the world market. As George (1992: 2) pointed out, "(w)ith so many jostling for a share of limited world markets, prices plummet, forcing governments to seek ever-higher levels of export in a desperate attempt to keep their hard currency revenues stable." This leads to increased volume of exports that lower prices.

The Ghanaian Economy and the Forestry Sector

The nature of the Ghanaian economy at the beginning of 1983 provided a condition for the forestry sector to be exploited, under the adjustment program, as a matter of mutual immediate convenience for the Ghanaian government and international capital because of its potentially rapid income-generating nature as "a dependable goose" that could quickly lay "golden eggs" for both parties - western donors/businesses and members of the government of Ghana and their allies.

Ghana's economy was one of the most promising in terms of development, in SSA at the time of independence in 1957. It was the most economically advanced British colony in Africa, a "middle-income country and the world's leading producer of cocoa" (Engberg-Pedersen et al. 1996). In the 1970s, however, it took a downturn and reached its lowest point in the early 1980s with serious political repercussions (Ninsin, 1990). Between 1979 and 1982, Ghana registered a negative annual average GDP growth rate, -6.1 percent (World Bank 1984: 3). By the beginning of 1983, the economy was heavily in debt and had sunk into a serious economic malaise described in the September 3, 1989 issue of *The Economist* (p. 40), as "an extreme case even in Africa." At the beginning of the 1983 adjustment year, her outstanding external debt was US$1,120,638,000 (disbursed) and US$1,499,479,000 (undisbursed) with a total interest payment of US$38,705,000, and a total service payment of US$99,746,000 (World Bank 1985: 33). Meeting the debt servicing obligations was in jeopardy.

As noted by Engberg-Pedersen et al. (1996: 11), "two decades of financial laxity and mismanagement had led to macroeconomic chaos. Exchange-rate overvaluation and high export-taxation led to rapidly declining exports (cocoa, timber, gold) from the mid-1970s, while external factors plus a large public spending deficit increased the rate of inflation to an average eighty percent per annum." Consequently, in the early 1980s the Ghanaian government, like many others of the heavily indebted developing world, began to lose the option of doing business with foreign lenders on an exclusively bilateral basis. The promotion of SAPs became a concerted effort on the part of lender countries and institutions to deal with borrower countries on a case-by-case basis rather than as a group. The programs were implemented with a strategy of providing loans to the indebted developing countries and dictating policies. Ghana, like other indebted developing countries, was simultaneously seduced by the foreign loans, frightened by its fiscal crises and balance of payments deficit, and haunted by the possibility of being declared insolvent by the IMF and the World Bank (Ould-Mey 1996).

In relation to the economic crisis, the prospect of insolvency, and the government's political survival, Ninsin (1990) shows that the Ghanaian government's adoption of the ERP was essentially metonymical[2] rather than a genuine measure for fashioning and sustaining development. In the main, the nature of the macro-economic policy measures and the specific policies and actions of the program, as in the case of the formal wood processing industry, rather feathered the nest of the PNDC government and simultaneously met some demands of international capital. According to Ninsin (1990), the program was adopted as a convenient measure to simultaneously address a political and economic problem. More specifically, it was a convenient measure to defuse a domestic political and economic crisis the government itself helped to fashion and to stave off its own imminent collapse as a consequence of its initial failure to "accommodate international capital" (Sawyerr 1990: 28).

It was, therefore, within the context of the metonym, that the World Bank (1984: xx) pointed out to the PNDC government that "the forestry sector offers the greatest immediate potential for growth and foreign exchange earnings" at the beginning of the program. Apart from the fact that forestry was and is a renewable resource-based sector with immense potential for upstream and downstream linkages, and employment, the sector had historically accounted for five to six percent of Ghana's total GDP and 11 percent of total commodity export earnings. Wood from this sector was the third most important item after cocoa and minerals. However, this important sector had declined by 1982 (just before the ERP). In 1977, the sector employed 20,900 people but by 1982 employment had declined to 14,442 people. Figure 10.1 shows the composition of and trend in wood exports prior to 1983. It indicates that before 1980, very little of the wood exported was processed. The exports were mainly logs and therefore did not generate much foreign exchange.

A number of factors led to the sector's decline. By 1983, the basic support infrastructure had largely been neglected. For a long time roads and railways had been poorly maintained and were in very poor condition. The ports had also not been upgraded and had become very inefficient in operations and facilities (e.g., no container-handling facilities). The telecommunications system had also been neglected and was extremely unreliable. All these were largely the result of prior economic mismanagement (Huq 1989). This neglect greatly increased the cost of business operations by the wood processing firms (World Bank, 1989) which translated into extra costs for firms (depending on their geographical location). It must be noted that the tropical hardwood species, which were and continue to be exploited primarily for export, have long gestation periods. An average-size Odum tree takes about 200 years to attain harvestable size. Others like Afromosia take as long as 500 years to attain a radius of three feet (Owusu 1994). Yet, despite the heavy export volumes involving heavy collateral environmental damage, tree replanting was and continues to be insignificant. Also, processing the wood for export involved a lot of waste. Wood recovery rates were very low, averaging 42 percent (Chryssides 1974), hence for every 100 m^3 of processed wood exported, 58 m^3 more was wasted. Even in 1988, five years into the program, the Ghana Forestry Commission (set up by the government to review the forestry sector under adjustment) acknowledged the problem by pointing out that:

> [t]he subsector needs more efficient wood-conversion systems, if it should minimize waste while maximizing on rates of recovery during the processing of log and other raw material base. This should be the only way to justify more domestic processing.... (Forestry Commission 1988: v)

In addition, the problem of waste was linked to the sector's over-dependence on obsolete equipment from diverse sources in the developed world that made production integration difficult (Owusu 1994). To simultaneously meet the needs of both international capital and the PNDC government, the forestry sector needed immediate rehabilitation. At the beginning of the ERP, therefore, the sector was infused with the second highest sector adjustment loan (SECAL) of US$157 million, out of the initial loans advanced by the World Bank to the PNDC government (Ofei-Nkansah 1991: 229).

The rehabilitation of the forestry sector with adjustment loans constituted a convenient means for the Ghanaian government to satisfy the demands of international capital by keeping the country's hard currency revenues stable via wood and other primary exports. By so doing, the government could also keep itself in power, cushioned by the adjustment loans that the country received. For international capital, rehabilitating the forestry sector was a priority because a large proportion of the lumber processed was exported as raw material for international consumption. Between 1963 and 1969 for example, the sector exported a minimum of 50 percent of its total output (CBS 1969), and the years preceding adjustment reflected a similar pattern. Other measures included the removal of existing restrictions on the export of some timber species in log form, imposed in 1979 as conservation and valorization measures, and the replacement of the Ghana Timber Marketing Board with two new agencies, the Timber Export Development Board (for export promotion) and the Forest Products Inspection Bureau (to monitor production) to ensure high export performance (Hutchful 1996).

The Dynamics of Indebtedness: "Economic and Political Convenience"

As a result of the capital infused into the sector, there was a dramatic rise in the volume of wood exports, which provided a convenient means for the PNDC government to clear outstanding external debts, and to meet new and increasing debt servicing obligations. Figure 10.2 shows the upward trend in wood production and export from 1983. However, unlike the pre-adjustment period, the proportions of processed wood were significantly greater. This masks the fact that the annual processed wood components in the figure represent only 42 percent of actual volumes harvested and processed due to the low recovery rates (see Chryssides 1974; Forestry Commission 1988). The figure also shows that a decade into the program (1983 to 1993), increases of 500 percent (223,914.06 m^3) and 806 percent (495,613.09 m^3) were achieved in the volume of lumber and logs exported respectively. Exports initially peaked in 1988 with a total combined wood output of 536,213 m^3 and generated US$98.8m in foreign exchange (FPIB 1991: 15).

In 1989, there was a significant drop in the export performance of the forestry sector. Relative to the export volume of 536,213 m^3 and revenue of US$107 m of the previous year, those figures fell to 375,769 m^3 (FPIB 1991: 15) and US$81 m (World Bank 1991: 75) respectively. The steady rise in exports from 1990 through 1992 and the sudden jump in 1993 indicate a response to debt pressures resulting from the drop in 1989. In 1991, wood exports amounted to 427,863 m^3 and generated US$114.2 m (FPIB 1991: 1), which was US$5 m less than the US$119.2 m required to meet the interest payment on the external debt for that year. The $5m shortfall in interest payment required, thus stimulated increased exports of larger volumes of lumber and other wood

Figure 10.1 Volume of Wood & Wood Products Exported, 1973–1983.

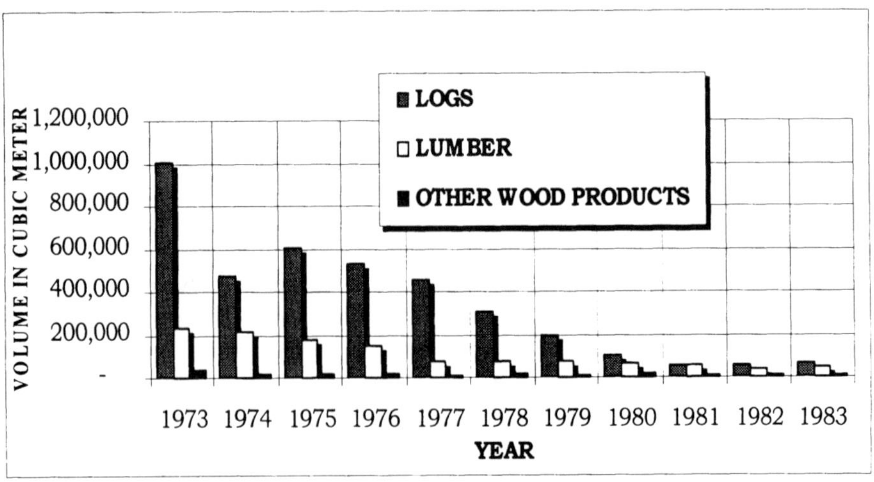

Sources: Central Bureau of Statistics, Ghana (1983, 1984, 1985).

products, which commanded higher values on the international market, for 1992 and 1993. Even though there was an official ban on the export of logs to gain more value from domestic processing, the volume of logs exported in 1993 even exceeded the total export volume of wood for the preceding year, indicating the desperation to meet the external debt obligations.

As a result of increased volumes of export, the international market became inundated with wood from other countries, and buyers developed a tendency to stock up the cheap wood which later depressed prices further because of diminished demand. With respect to Ghana wood, Barker et al. (1991: 5), noted:

> (M)ost of the exports are purchased by only a few buyers in Europe, many of whom resell to other markets in North America and Asia. Although these products are produced in Ghana, they often command prices lower than they would if they were manufactured further or sold to a more diverse market. For example, wood is purchased by companies in Portugal to make doors for sale in the United States. ... lumber is bought by companies in Holland and sold at a profit in the United States.

Also, the recession in Europe at that time, led to a very poor sale of the wood stock (FPIB 1991).

Accommodation of international capital is clearly demonstrated by the steady and dramatic increase in the volume of processed and unprocessed wood exported, with the bulk of the increased exports (a minimum of 81 percent per annum by 1991) going to the donor countries, mostly the then EEC countries. The fact that these raw material exports became so inexpensive that resale often took place on the world market (see Barker et al. 1991: 5) underscores the critics' argument that SAPs *inter alia* provided cheap and reliable sources of raw materials for the sponsoring advanced economies. It should also be noted that lumber and furniture parts that constituted the bulk of the exports are essentially raw materials for firms in the metropolitan or donor countries. Thus exports from Ghana were fueled primarily by indebtedness, particularly from the SECALs and the frequent devaluation, which cheapened the exports and compelled firms to produce and export more processed wood in order to survive.

In terms of foreign exchange generation, in 1983, the export of wood and wood products yielded US$15.77 m (TEDB undated, 15). In 1991, five years after the forestry SECALs had been exhausted, wood exports generated US$114.2 m in foreign exchange (FPIB 1991: 4), an increase of 624 percent over the 1983 figure. The increase in foreign exchange earnings by the sector becomes more significant in relation to Ghana's external debt and servicing each year. At the beginning of 1983, the year in which the ERP was adopted, the total debt including the un-disbursed amount was just below a billion dollars, out of which US$1,120.638 m had been disbursed with a service interest payment of US$38.705 m as interest. By 1987, the disbursed amount had reached US$2.25 billion. Including the un-disbursed amount, the debt had reached well over US$3 billion with interest payments having climbed up to US$53.782 m.

The medium- and long-term outstanding and disbursed external public debt (excluding IMF obligations) at the end of 1990 amounted to US$2.9 billion, or slightly over 50 percent of GDP, i.e., about the same share as in 1987. Bilateral creditors accounted for about 30 percent and multilateral creditors for about 65 percent (World Bank and International Development Association (IDA) loans and credits amounted to about 40 percent of the total); and financial and suppliers credits for the remainder (World Bank 1991). In 1991, the total external debt had reached US$3,769.82 m (55.2 percent of GNP) with service payments as much as US$224.00 m and US$119.20 m for principal and interest respectively (ISSER 1995: 62–64).

Figure 10:2 Volume of Wood & Wood Products Exported, 1983–1993

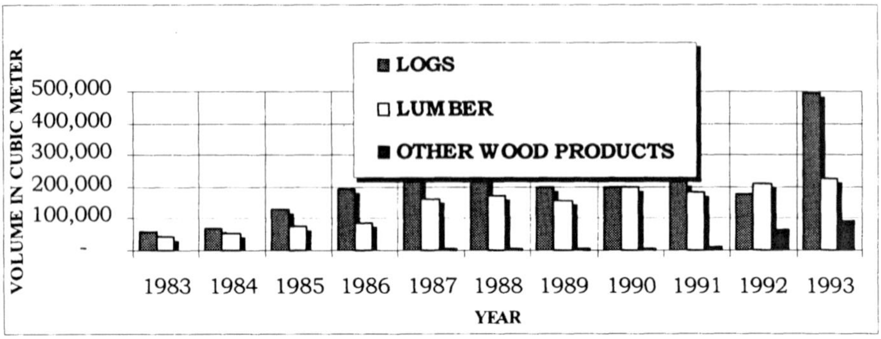

Sources: Timber Exports Development Board, Ghana; Forest Products Inspection Bureau, Ghana; Ministry of Lands and Natural Resources, Ghana.

While the forestry sector's possible contributions to the external debt payments increased sufficiently to absorb the interest payments on the loans, the total burden continued to increase at a much greater rate as shown by the rapid increase in service interest after 1985. In terms of foreign exchange generated by the timber industry, in 1984, a year after adjustment, revenue from timber was US$22 m (3.71 percent) of the total merchandise export (comprising cocoa beans and products, gold, diamonds, manganese, bauxite, timber, and electricity) earnings of US$ 566 m for Ghana. By 1990, the revenue from timber had increased to US$119 m (13.66 percent) of the total merchandise export earnings of US$ 871 m. This was in spite of the worldwide recession (see World Bank 1991: 75; 1995: 75; and FPIB1991: 4).

The contribution made by the timber industry was relatively low prior to the 1985–1986 rehabilitation programs with US$21 m (3.71 percent) in 1984 and grew to US$44 m (5.84 percent) in 1986. Significantly, there was a dramatic change in 1987 reflecting the effects of the capital infusion into the industry for rehabilitation. The sector's contribution jumped for the first time into the double-digit percentages, reaching 10.88 percent from 5.84 percent in 1986, when the infusion program was completed. The significance of the foreign exchange generated by the timber industry becomes more apparent, however, when evaluated as a contribution to service interest payments on the outstanding external public debt over the period 1984 through 1991 as indicated by Table 10.1. The last column in the table, showing the contribution of the timber industry relative to the annual interest payments, indicates the extent to which the timber sector covers the respective annual interest payments. The negative signs prefixing the 1984 and 1985 figures indicate that the contributions to interest defrayal were deficient by US$8.238 m and US$2.458 m respectively. On the other hand, the figures prefixed by the plus signs indicate by how much it was in excess. In 1986, for example, foreign exchange generated by the timber sector was enough to fully absorb the interest payment of US$42.624 m with an excess of US$1.376 m, and reduce that year's principal repayment requirement of US$79.274 m.

For the PNDC government, the need to satisfy international capital by quickly generating foreign exchange to meet its debt servicing obligations was met before long. Foreign exchange generation by the sector increased immediately after the infusion of the SECALs in 1985 and 1986. In 1987, as much as US$36.218 m was generated by processed wood exports that could defray part of the principal of US$102.099 m on the debt service payments, even after the interest payments had absorbed a US$53.782 m contribution made by the industry. In 1990 there was as much as US$51.723 m in excess of interest payments that could be used to address a significant part of that year's principal payment of US$139.466 m (World Bank 1991: 75). It is therefore not surprising that by June, 1990, the PNDC government had been able to pay off all remaining recorded external payments arrears, thereby satisfying international capital in terms of arrears. The debt service ratio (including IMF and arrears) to exports of goods and services also fell from 58 percent in 1989 to 40 percent in 1990. The PNDC government had thus been "successful" in getting back into the "good books" of international capital, and relations were restored with Ghana's creditors, particularly for trade financing in 1990 (World Bank 1991).

The above "successes" in terms of the dramatic increases in exports, in foreign exchange generation, and the recognition of Ghana as a "star pupil of adjustment" in international financial circles are all tied to the pressures unleashed by a combination of indebtedness and the devaluation of the local currency, the *cedi*. In other words, the Ghanaian government was under pressure to meet debt obligations in order to win the "seal of approval" of international capital. At the same time, it had to do so under the pressure of a series of devaluation of the *cedi*, whereby prices plummet, forcing the government to seek ever higher levels of exports in a desperate attempt to keep hard currency revenues stable (George 1992). From a stable rate of 2.75 cedis to US$1.00 in 1980-1982, it jumped to 8.83 cedis in 1983, the year of adjustment with the first devaluation, reaching 1,200.00 cedis in 1995 and had risen to 2,260.00 cedis by the end of 1997. Each devaluation of the *cedi* meant that the timber firms needed ever-higher levels of production/exports in a desperate effort to meet their debt obligations (since interest rates and principal amounts were tied to the depreciating values of the *cedi* to the US dollar). Also, the pressure on the firms was aided by the deregulation of the industry and the free and open market system forced the firms, as a measure for efficient operations, to minimize costs in order to survive. It is, therefore, under this condition of a vicious circle of debt pressure that the Ghanaian rain forest began to be "mined" for tropical wood in a desperate, unprecedented fashion, a process assisted by a lack of a coherent policy of forest management (Hutchful 1996: 178-179). The vicious circle of debt pressure is illustrated in Figure 10.3, showing that the SECALs did play a significant role in the generation of foreign exchange for Ghana over the period.

Since the rapid increase in the generation of foreign exchange by the wood-processing firms under the program was to a great extent driven by the pressure to increase output and exports in order to service the loans they had taken, one could suggest that the government, really, was "squeezing" foreign exchange out of the firms, and the forestry industry to satisfy international capital by paying off loans in the shortest possible time. As noted earlier, the government took the SECALs at interest rates between eight and ten percent, with a ten-year moratorium from the donor countries. The government then turned the SECALs into commercial loans for the firms with the concurrence of the donors, with interest rates of 31 percent to 35 percent and a four-year repayment period. The SECALs were advanced without working capital and therefore created heavy pressure on the firms. Supplementary overdrafts were also hard to secure from local financial institutions because of financial structure reforms under the ERP. Where overdrafts were available, they attracted an interest rate of 27 percent. These were in addition to the fact that the machinery and equipment purchased by the firms for rehabilitation were quite expensive (Forestry Commission 1988). For example, a kiln-drying system of 300 m^3 capacity imported from Europe, cost over US$300,000.00 (Barker et al. 1991: 31) relative to an average of US$1.75 m in SECALs advanced to nine sawmills for plant improvement (Forestry Commission 1988).

To create an enabling environment for investments by local and foreign capital under the program, the wood processing firms were given incentive packages under the investment code (PNDC Law 116 1985) to encourage exports. This also added to the problem since they discouraged sale of lumber on the domestic market. Sawmill operators preferred tax rebates based on volumes exported. Additionally, they could retain at least 35 percent of the export earnings in an external account (for safekeeping), as well as an extra portion of the earnings, ostensibly for the purchase of machinery, equipment, spare parts. The dramatic increase in volumes of wood exported since 1983 and the quick income generated by the forestry sector certainly met the needs of the government and the external sponsors in a convenient way. However, generating such quick income by falling on the forestry sector, as a matter of convenience, led to deforestation as the tremendous pressure on the government and firms to meet their debt obligations translated into rapid deforestation.

The Environmental Cost of Convenience: "Unprecedented Deforestation"

The market-driven extraction of logs to meet export demands is an underlying cause of deforestation in Ghana. The process necessarily involved loss of trees, as well as other flora and fauna through collateral destruction and degradation. The affected areas generally tended to be subsequently utilized for agricultural purposes and other human activities. It is in this vein that the Trade and Environment Database (TED) of American University (TED Case number 193) suggested that Ghana's timber trade had been the main source of deforestation in the country since the beginning of Ghana's adjustment, as evidenced by the dramatic increases in exports.

As noted by Osei (1997), commercial logging encourages the construction of roads in previously inaccessible forest areas. Such roads tend to be widely used by "slash

Table 10.1 Foreign Exchange Generated by the Timber Industry as Contributions to Interest Payments on Ghana's External Public Debt (Outstanding): 1984-1991 (US $ millions)

	Debt Service Payment			
End Year	***Principal***	***Interest***	**Revenue from Timber Exports**	**Contribution Relative to Interest**
1984	64.646	29.238	21.0	-8.238
1985	67.243	30.458	28.0	-2.458
1986	79.274	42.624	44.0	+1.376
1987	102.099	53.782	90.0	+36.218
1988	138.388	69.166	107.0	+37.834
1989	147.444	59.499	81.0	+21.501
1990	139.466	67.277	119.0	+51.723
1991	224.000	119.200	114.2	-5.000

Source: World Bank (1991: 75, 99), FPIB (1991: 4) and ISSER (1995: 63).

and burn" farmers to access new areas of farmland, thus expediting the rate of forest loss. This is particularly the case of farmers who can no longer use the rich lands that have been converted for production of export crops stimulated by adjustment (George 1992). Ghana's case was similar to neighboring Côte d'Ivoire, where Chege (1994) shows that for every 10 km^2 of forest area logged, ten km of road is constructed. In fact based on FAO assessments, the TED suggested that the rate of deforestation in Ghana increased by 50 percent over the ten years of adjustment, thereby driving some of the traditional export species to the point of extinction (see Hutchful 1996: 179).

Fuel wood consumption is often identified as a leading cause of deforestation in Africa (see WRI 1994: 305), but it is really not a significant factor in Ghana, where the annual consumption is 650,000 tons (TEDB, undated). This is because, unlike countries such as Burkina Faso and Chad of the drier region, under the normal, traditional wood collection system in Ghana, deadwood, generated via attrition in areas of various stages of forest succession, are harvested for fuel rather than live trees (Osei 1997). Fuel wood is also generated from abandoned unprocessed trunks, after loggers (and saw millers) have sawn off their contract sizes. The annual charcoal consumption of 120,000 tons in Ghana (TEDB undated) is also generated the same way, thus making the commercial loggers the main source of the deforestation. In fact the fuel wood-processors like the slash and burn farmers also take advantage of logging roads to penetrate the forest (Hutchful 1996). It is not surprising that the percentage increase in the extent of Ghana's cropland, as a reflection of the desperate deforestation, was 23 percent

Figure 10.3 The Vicious Circle of Debt Pressure

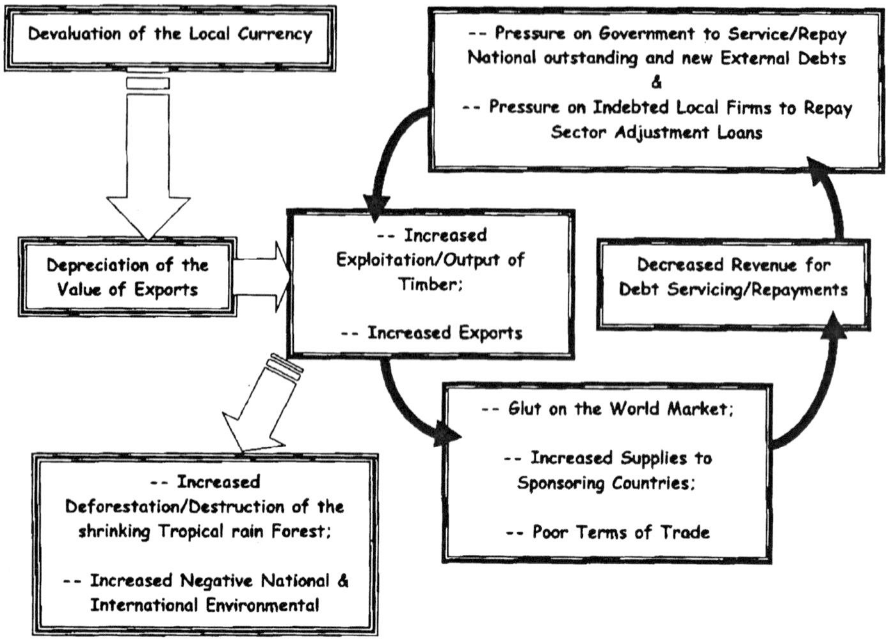

Source: Owusu (1998).

between 1983 and 1993 as compared with 16.7 percent and 6.1 percent of Côte d'Ivoire and Nigeria respectively (see Allen 1997: 90). To put Ghana's deforestation in perspective, the approximate original extent of Ghana's closed tropical moist forest (i.e., all areas that were naturally forested before intensive exploitation set in) was 145,000 km^2 (Table 10.2).

Ghana was one of the countries with the highest extent of closed moist forest in West Africa before the advent of intensive logging beginning in the early 1890s, for export to Western Europe. This was after Britain gained control of much of Southern Ghana. This timber trade coincided with the beginning of cocoa cultivation for export, which also led todeforestation (Dickson 1969). By 1988, the United Nations Food and Agriculture Organization (FAO) noted that the remaining closed tropical moist forest was 17,180 km^2 or 11.8 percent of the original extent. In a booklet, "Ghana: Forests, Wood and People," published in the early 1990s, the government's official timber export promotion agency, the Timber Export Development Board (TEDB), noted that the existing forest comprised 17,000 km^2 of forest reserves and 3,700 km^2 of unreserved forest. Based on those official figures, the Forestry Research Institute of Ghana, noted in 1992, that "Ghana may not have any forest by the year 2030" if the rate of deforestation under the ERP continued (GNA 1992: 1).

As shown in Table 10.3, even though the World Resources Institute (WRI 1994) and the World Bank (1997) indicators show higher figures, with respect to the extent of the forest, they still confirm that the extent of the forest has diminished dramatically since the 1980s and logging has played a major role. The Table also shows that Ghana had the second highest annual rate of natural forest deforestation in West Africa, and registered the highest loss of 13,000 km^2 from 1980 through 1990. This must be seen in the light of the fact that rehabilitation of the forestry sector (using logging equipment purchased with SECALs) began earnestly in 1985, suggesting an extraordinary intensive logging "unprecedented deforestation" from 1985 onwards. As shown in Figure 10.2, 1985 marked the beginning of the dramatic rise in wood exports, in contrast with the two years preceding adjustment in 1983.

Also, logging 110 km^2 annually from 1981 through 1990, as Table 10.3 shows, is significant in terms of deforestation in a fast dwindling forest area, especially in the absence of a coherent forest management system and policy. In 1988, the World Bank itself admitted that "in spite of the importance of Ghana's forest resources ... no up to date and comprehensive policy" existed for the sector (World Bank, 1988, quoted in Hutchful, 1996, 179). Again, in terms of the sustainability of that rate of logging, a World Bank staff appraisal of the sector noted that the actual cuts were far above the allowable cut "by approximately 1.6 to 2.5 times the current allowable cut" 1.8 to 2.7 million m^3 as opposed to 1.1 million m^3 (World Bank 1988, quoted in Hutchful 1996: 179). Despite the long gestation periods of some species (200 to 500 years in some cases), reforestation, natural or tree replanting by the logging companies, is insignificant (Owusu 1994). The haphazard nature of the hunt and extract logging process does not open the canopy sufficiently for many of the important tree species to regenerate naturally (Barker et al. 1991: 26).

According to the World Bank (1997: 246), Ghana's total external debt rose from US$1,398 m in 1980 to US$5,874 m in 1995. Debt service as a percentage of exports of goods and services rose from 13.1 percent in 1980 to 23.1 percent in 1995, and multilateral external debt as a percentage of external debt, also rose from 19.9 percent in 1980 to 50.8 percent in 1995. These figures mean that there is more pressure on the government to meet its debt obligation, and the sacrifice of Ghana's forest as a matter of convenience may well continue until the "special goose", the forest, is unable to deliver the "golden eggs" any longer as a result of depletion or stark environmental damage. Ending the convenience as a result of depletion may, however, be prolonged by a ban on log exports in favor of higher valued processed wood for export. The convenience may also end as a result of pressure from environmentalist groups on the government and international capital, as was the case in the international ivory trade, to save the forests. In the absence of any credible strategy for industrialization, Ghana may then have to fall more on other natural resources, in the name of export orientation and comparative advantage, to meet her debt obligations.

Conclusions and Development Lessons

The foregoing discussion has established a direct link between adjustment and environmental destruction, as illustrated by the vicious circle of debt pressure in Figure

10.2, and the associated desperate deforestation process has been a convenient means for the Ghanaian government and international capital to meet some current mutual needs.

For the government of Ghana, the adjustment program and the contributions of the forestry sector have been convenient means for accessing international loans by actively servicing the country's debts with foreign exchange generated through the export drive. In 1986, the share of official debt (i.e., government and government guaranteed debt) in total long-term debt was 85 percent. In 1992, that had risen to 93 percent (World Bank 1993) indicating increasing indebtedness as result of easier access to international loans. In accommodating international capital, the PNDC government was able to stay in power by defusing the political crisis it faced prior to adjustment. It has even been able to transform itself from a military government into a "democratically elected" one, the National Democratic Congress (NDC) in 1992. It enjoyed "political stability" with support from the West, and became a protégé of the sponsors, making Ghana a "star pupil of adjustment" in the eyes of the World Bank and the IMF.

For the external sponsors or international capital, the adjustment program and the contributions of the forestry sector have been convenient for generating cheap raw materials tropical wood and wood products in abundance, for their home industries. The loans advanced to Ghana by the sponsors, and the interests on them are serviced consistently. The sponsors are also able to control decision-making in the Ghanaian economy. Furthermore, the wood-processing sector has served as a convenient market for products like machinery and equipment from some of the donor countries, and the administration of the SECALs was a convenient way of sustaining, and in fact reinforcing, the market. This was particularly successful with the system of tied-purchases and credit-line system as noted by Hancock (1989). In addition to selling products like sawmilling and other wood processing equipment to firms in the sector, some of which were inappropriate for conditions in Ghana, spare parts had to be subsequently obtained from the same sources for their maintenance. In certain cases, technicians from the seller-companies had to be brought in at the expense of the buyers to either install or repair the machinery or equipment. In quite a number of cases, the equipment purchased broke down quite frequently. The tied-purchase and credit-line systems thus propagated what has been described as an international "junk-yard syndrome," whereby inappropriate and substandard machinery and equipment or technology are dumped in developing countries for profit (Owusu 1994). The sector has thus, become a market of convenience and dumping grounds for products from the donor countries as well.

Before adjustment, the forestry sector was in a state of decline with deteriorated equipment and poor production levels, a situation that dramatically changed with capital infusion, sectoral re-organization and rehabilitation under adjustment. While increased production and exports since 1983 confirm improved efficiency, as asserted by supporters of adjustment, the important question is who benefits from the program's "success" and its underlying "efficiency"? Are the negative environmental consequences domestic and the externalities of the desperate deforestation factored into the "success" of Ghana's program? Clearly, the real (short-term) beneficiaries of the program are the sponsors/international capital, reinforcing the view that "multilateral fi-

Table 10.2 Original Versus Remaining Extent of Closed Canopy Moist Forest in West Africa

Region/Country	Approx. Original	Remaining Extent	Percent Remaining[a]
	Extent (km²)	(km²)[a]	
West Africa[b]	1,251,600	182,180	14.6
Benin	16,800	470	2.8
Côte d'Ivoire	229,400	44,580	19.4
Ghana	145,000	17,180	11.8
Guinea	185,800	20,500	11.0
Liberia	36,100	20,000	20.8
Nigeria	421,000	59,500	14.1
Sierra Leone	71,700	7,400	10.3
Togo	18,000	3,040	16.9

Notes: [a] From FAO (1988). [b] Including Senegal and Gambia.

Source: IUCN (1992); Osei (1997).

nancial institutions, as agents of 'multinational imperialism', work to ensure that the economies of the Third World are conditioned to 'accommodate' international capital, i.e., serve the basic interests of Western industrialized economies" (Sawyerr 1990: 28).

As asserted by adjustment supporters, the right prices may have been restored via the invisible hand of the market; market forces may have fostered efficiency in the forestry sector; and the application of the theory of comparative advantage may have helped to put more of Ghana's wood on the international market. Certainly, however, the overall negative environmental consequences of the desperate deforestation process were not factored into the "success." For critics like George (1992) and environmental groups like Friends of the Earth (1993), and as pointed out in the TED Case number 193, the "success" was achieved at the cost of a squandered environmental capital and economic future with serious national and international implications. To meet the immediate needs of international capital and the Ghanaian government, Ghana's limited tropical rain forest was sacrificed, but this mutual "immediate convenience" for the PNDC and NDC governments and international capital certainly translated into "desperate deforestation," which environmentally, seriously jeopardized our common future.

Table 10.3 Changes in the Extent of West Africa's Natural Forest, 1980-1990

	Extent of Natural Forest (000 km²)			Annual (1981-1990)	
Region/Country	1980	1990	Net Change 1980-1990	Deforestation Rate (%)	Extent of Logging (km²)
West Africa	615	556	-59	1.0	3,120
Benin	56	49	-07	1.2	0
Côte d'Ivoire	121	109	-12	1.0	850
Ghana	109	96	-13	1.3	110
Guinea	76	67	-09	1.1	90
Liberia	49	46	-03	0.5	790
Nigeria	168	156	-12	0.7	1,270
Sierra Leone	20	19	-01	0.6	10
Togo	16	14	-02	1.4	10

Source: World Resources Institute (1994).

Two major lessons for African development, however, must be learned from Ghana's experience for the 21st century. First, African governments should always remember that they are trustees or stewards, hence in formulating or implementing development policies, a prime consideration should be that they have a responsibility to both the living and those yet-to-be-born. Consequently, it is imperative that they safeguard the environment notwithstanding the cost. Second, it is clearly evident that despite the desperate deforestation, adjustment played a major role in the dramatic increase in the production and export of processed wood. This demonstrates that production and export levels in various sectors of other African economies also have the potential for dramatic increases. Such general increases would be largely possible, if African governments could really focus their energies, in the 21st century, on the development of such sectors, operate them with a strong commitment, and provide an enabling environment and support, as was the case in Ghana under the PNDC and NDC governments, which had a vested interest in the success of the wood processing sector. Indeed, African economies, as noted by Adjibolosoo (1993: 142) cannot function effectively without being upheld by a network of committed persons, who strongly believe in and continually affirm the development ideals of their society.

Notes

1 An earlier version of this contribution was published as "Current convenience; desperate deforestation: Ghana's Adjustment program and the Forestry sector" in the *Professional Geographer*, Vol. 50, No. 4, 418–436.

2 Development policies are said to be metonymical when they are used by a government, policy makers or a group of political actors in tandem with their development objectives to achieve hidden policy objectives or to promote a hidden interests or agenda (see Gore 1984: 258).

References

Adjibolosoo, S. (1993). "The Human Factor in Development." *The Scandinavian Journal of Development Alternatives*. 12 (4), 139-149.

Allen, John L. (1997). *Student Atlas of Economic Development*. Guilford, CT: Dushkin/McGraw-Hill.

Barker, Kirtland, Boateng, Peter and Moreno, Amalio (1991). *Timber and Wood Products Section of Export Diversification in Ghana*. Report prepared for the U.S. Agency for International Development, Bethesda, MD: Development Associates Inc.

Central Bureau of Statistics (CBS) (1969). *Statistical Handbook 1969*. 3rd Ed. Accra: CBS.

________ (1983). Industrial Statistics 1977–1979. (July). Accra: CBS.

________ (1984). Industrial Statistics 1980–1982. (December). Accra: CBS.

________ (1985). Industrial Statistics 1981–1983. (November). Accra: CBS.

Chege, N. (1994). "Africa's non-timber forest economy." *World Watch*. 7: 19–23.

Chryssides, John C. (1974). "Economic Problems of the Ghana Timber Industry with Special Reference to the Problem of Wastage." Ph.D. Dissersation. Centre of West African Studies and Faculty of Commerce and Social Science. University of Birmingham, England.

Corbridge, Stuart (1993). *Debt and Development*. Cambridge, MA: Blackwell.

Dickson K. (1969) *A Historical Geography of Ghana*. Cambridge, UK: Cambridge University

Engberg-Pederson, Peter, Gibbon, Poul, Raikes, Phil and Udshot, Lars (eds.). (1996). *Limits of Adjustment in Africa*. Portsmouth, NH: Heinemann.

Ewusi, Kodwo (1987). *Structural Adjustment and Stabilization Policies in Developing Countries: A Case Study of Ghana's Experience in 1983-1986*. Legon, Ghana: ISSER, University of Ghana.

Food and Agriculture Organization (FAO). (1988). *An Interim Report on the State of Forest Resources in Developing Countries*. Rome, Italy: FAO.

Friends of the Earth (1993). *Plunder in Ghana's Rainforest for Illegal Profit*. Vols. 1 and 2, London: Friends of the Earth.

Forestry Commission (1988). "A Review Report on the Economic Recovery Programme: The Forestry Sector, 1982–87." Report prepared by the Forestry Commission for the Ministry of Finance and Economic Planning. (April). Accra: Government of Ghana.

Forest Products Inspection Bureau (FPIB). (1991). Export Permit for the Year 1991. Takoradi, Ghana: FPIB.

George, Susan (1988). *A Fate Worse than Debt*. Hammondsworth: Penguin.

________ (1992). *The Debt Boomerang: How Third World Debt Harms Us All*. Boulder, CO: Westview Press.

Ghana News Agency (GNA) (1992). "Ghana's Forests to be depleted by 2030." *People's Daily Graphic*. (March 10). No. 12842: 1, 8.

Gore, Charles (1984). *Regions in Question: Space, Development Theory and Regional Policy*. London: Methuen.

Green, Reginald H. (1987). "Stabilization and Adjustment Policies and Programmes." *Country Study 1: Ghana*. Annankatu, Finland: WIDER.

________ (1991). "Reduction of Absolute Poverty: A Priority Structural Adjustment." *Institute of Development Studies*. Discussion Paper 287. Sussex: IDS.

Hamilton, Clive (1989). "The irrelevance of economic liberalization in the Third World." *World Development*. 17(10): 1523–1530.

Hancock, Graham (1989). *Lords of Poverty: the Power, Prestige, and Corruption of the International Aid Business*. New York: The Atlantic Monthly Press.

Hayter, Teresa (1989). *Exploited Earth: Britain's Aid and the Environment*. London: Earthscan.

Hogg, D. (1993). *The SAP in the Forest: The Environmental and Social Impacts of Structural Adjustment Programmes in the Philippines, Ghana and Guyana*. London: Friends of the Earth.

Hutchful, Ebo (1996). "Ghana." In *Limits of Adjustment in Africa*. eds. Engeberg-Pederson, P., Peter Gibbon, Phil Raikes and Lars Udshot. 143–214. Portsmouth NH: Heinemann.

Huq, Mozammel M. (1989). *The Economy of Ghana*. London: Macmillan Press.

Institute of Statistical, Social and Economic Research (ISSER). (1994). *The State of the Ghanaian Economy*. Legon, Ghana: ISSER, University of Ghana.

________ (1995). *The State of the Ghanaian Economy*. Legon, Ghana: ISSER, University of Ghana.

Lensink, Robert (1996). *Structural Adjustment in Sub-Saharan Africa*. New York, London: Longman.

Mabogunje, Akin L. (1981). *The Development Process: A Spatial Perspective*. New York: Holmes and Meier.

Ninsin, Kwame A. (1990). "Ghana under the PNDC: Delinking or structural adjustment?" In *Adjustment or Delinking?: The African Experience*. ed. Azzam Mahjoub, 131–156. The UN University. *Third World Forum: Studies in African Political Economy*. Tokyo/ London: UN Univ. Press/Zed.

Ofei-Nkansah, Kingsley (1991). "Ghana's timber boom." *West Africa*. No. 3833 (February 18–24): 229.

Opschoor, Johannes B. (1994). "De Bretton Woods-instellingen en het milieu." In *Preadviezen van de Koninklijke Vereniging voor de Staathuishoudkunde, Vijfit jaar na Bretton Woods*. Utrecht: Lemma, 93–119. Cited in: Lensink, R. 1996. *Structural Adjustment in Sub-Saharan Africa*. New York, London: Longman.

Osei, William Y. (1997). "Human-environmental impacts: Forest degradation and desertification." In *Geography of Sub-Saharan Africa*. ed. Aryeetey-Attoh, S. 35–60. Upper Saddle River, NJ: Prentice Hall.

Ould-Mey, Mohameden (1996) *Global Restructuring and Peripheral States: The Carrot and the Stick in Mauritania*. Lanham, MD: Rowman and Littlefield.

Owusu, J. Henry (1994). "Ghana's Economic Recovery Program and Changes in the Structural and Organizational Patterns of the Formal Wood-Processing Industry (1983–1991)." Ph.D. Dissertation. University of Iowa. Ann Arbor, Michigan: University Microfilms International.

________ (1995). "Structural adjustment and African development: Evidence from Ghana's formal wood-processing industry (1983-1991)." *Review of Human Factor Studies*. 1, (2): 60–79.

_______ (1998). "Current Convenience; Desperate Deforestation: Ghana's Adjustment Program and the Forestry Sector." *The Professional Geographer*. Vol. 50, No. 4, pp. 418–436.

Reed, David (ed.) (1992). *Structural Adjustment and the Environment*. Boulder, CO: Westview Press.

Sawyerr, Akilagpa (1990). *The Political Dimension of Structural Adjustment Programmes in Sub-Saharan Africa*. Accra: Ghana Universities Press.

Schwarz, Gilson (1990). "Stabilization policies under political transition: Reform versus adjustment in Brazil 1985–1989." *The Developing Economies*. 38 (1): 16–41.

Slater, David (1975). "Underdevelopment and Spatial Inequality: Approaches to the Problem of Regional Planning in the Third World." *Progress in Planning*. 4 (2): 97–167.

Steel, William F. (1988). "Recent policy reform and industrial adjustment in Zambia and Ghana." *The Journal of Modern African Studies*. 26: 157–64.

Storper, Michael, and Walker, Richard (1989). *The Capitalist Imperative. Territory, Technology and Industrial Growth*. Cambridge, MA: Blackwell.

Timber Exports Development Board (TEDB). Undated. "The Ghana Timber Industry: Basic Information, Facts and Figures."Mimeo. Takoradi, Ghana: TEDB.

_______. (1991). *Ghana Hardwoods: Trade and Industry Directory*. London: TEDB.

The Economist Magazine (1989). *A change in Africa*. (September 3), 39–42.

United Nations Economic Commission for Africa (UN/ECA) (1986). *African Alternative Framework to Structural Adjustment Programmes for Socio-Economic Recovery and Transformation (AAF-SAP)*. New York: E/ECA/CM.15/6/Rev. 3.

World Bank (1981). *Accelerated Development in Sub-Saharan Africa*. Washington, DC: World Bank.

_______ (1984). *Ghana: Policies and Program for Adjustment*. Washington DC: World Bank.

_______ (1985). *Ghana: Towards Structural Adjustment*. Vol. II: Statistical Appendix. (Oct. 7). Report No. 5854-GH. Washington, DC: World Bank.

_______ (1988). *Staff Appraisal Report: Ghana Forest Resource Management*. (May 2). Washington, DC: Western Africa Department, Agricultural Operations Division, World Bank.

_______ (1989). *Sub-Saharan Africa: From Crisis to Sustainable Growth*. Washington, DC: World Bank.

_______ (1991). *Ghana: Progress on Adjustment*. Report No. 9475-GH. Washington, DC: World Bank.

_______ (1993). *World Debt Tables: External Finance for Developing Countries*, 1 and 2. Washington, DC: World Bank.

_______ (1994). *World Development Report 1994*. Washington, DC: World Bank.

_______ (1995). *World Tables 1995*. Baltimore, MD: Johns Hopkins Univ. Press/World Bank.

_______ (1997). *World Development Report 1997*. New York: Oxford University Press/ The World Bank.

World Commission on Environment and Development (WCED) (1987). *Our Common Future*. Oxford: Oxford University Press.

World Resources Institute (WRI) (1994). *World Resources: 1994–1995*. New York: Oxford University Press.

Younger, Stephen. D. (1989). "Ghana: Economic Recovery Program A Case Study of Stabilization and Structural Adjustment in Sub-Saharan Africa." *Successful Development in Africa A Case Studies of Projects, Programs and Policies*. Economic Development Institute of the World Bank: Analytical Case Studies, #1. Washington, DC: World Bank.

Chapter 11

Land Reforms and Land-Redistribution in Zimbabwe: A 'Tragedy of the Commons'?

Smile Dube and Calvin O. Masilela

Introduction

Land reform and tenure[1] are issues of major importance in many countries in sub-Sahara Africa today. From Eastern (Eritrea, Uganda, Rwanda, Tanzania and Kenya) to Southern Africa (Mozambique, Zambia, Zimbabwe, Namibia, and South Africa), to name a few, important land tenure reforms have recently been promulgated, or land commissions are revisiting the land issue (Adams 1995; Adams et al. 1999). There seems to be a general recognition that the resolution of the land question is vital to the political, economic and environmental well-being of Africa as it confronts challenges of the 21st century. Land issues are back on the growth and development agenda in the region because rural populations have put them there. Indeed, the demand by rural populations for access to land and other rural resources, needed for food self sufficiency, has never stopped. This is especially true in those situations where under-utilized or idle land and grossly unequal land holdings are found in countries with landless and poor rural producers.

Nowhere is the challenge to resolve these land issues more pronounced than in Southern Africa where the conflicts over land are largely a product of a colonial legacy that produced and reinforced unequal landownership and access to agricultural resources. The need to resolve this issue has been further heightened by recent 'land and farm invasions' in Zimbabwe, and the fears that similar invasions could occur in other countries (for example South Africa and Namibia) as a way to reverse the effects of colonization. Specifically, the sanctioning since 2000 of a 'farm and land invasion' strategy by the Mugabe regime as a pretext for redressing the country's land question has unleashed forces that have not only undermined the rule of law, but also turned what was once the continent's breadbasket into a basket case economy. The beneficiaries of land invasions and farm seizures have been, with a few exceptions, ruling party cronies, Mugabe and the army. Marginalized are the landless peasants, in whose name land reform has been rationalized, and displaced farm workers and their dependants that number in the millions. Without access to land and facing a collapsed economy, the victimization of the landless is dangerously climaxing into a zenith of uncertainty and starvation. Consequently, alarm bells have been sounded as to whether a "tragedy of the commons" is underway in Zimbabwe.

This chapter discusses the nature of Zimbabwe's land reform with a view to demonstrating its undesirability as a model for other countries. It questions the mode of reforms and not its desirability. We show, first that the "tragedy of the commons" metaphor is just that: a metaphor. It cannot provide us with any understanding of land reform in Zimbabwe. While it might explain the population pressure and associated problems in communal areas, it cannot account for the land and farm invasions that began in 2000. For that purpose, we examine the impact in the breakdown of the rule of law. The promotion of a "no rule-of-law" regime enabled land invasions. The land invasion strategies were extended to extortion of firms in the urban areas. We also provide an extended review of the types of land reforms that easily are applicable anywhere depending on specific circumstances of the country as a precursor to analyzing the land issue in Zimbabwe. Thus, we move away from the current emphasis on free markets in land to interrelationships between the community, the government (including the ruling party elite), and the rule of law. The tension between those who favor the *status quo* (no rule-of-law) and those who prefer the rule of law is captured in two game-theoretic simple models. The first is a static model showing the tension between the "no rule-of-law" land and farm invasions (those who strip assets) versus the rule-of-law elements (those who prefer upholding common property resources management and wish to build value by making irreversible investments on their property). The dynamic version shows that a weak value support for the rule-of-law may actually be worse than that captured in the model. In the absence of the rule-of-law, political insiders can monopolize new sectors—sectors that were not monopolies before invasions.

The Tragedy of the Commons: An Unhelpful Metaphor

Hardin's famous article (1968) gives a stylized picture of population-induced impoverishment through overexploitation of common-property resources. His reference is to pre-enclosure rural England, describing a situation in which each new person in a rural community supposedly added a further claim to use of common grazing lands. Beyond some limit in livestock numbers the productivity of the commons would decline, perhaps drastically. Implicitly, the community is taken as composed of members with more or less uniform power, unable or unwilling to act concertedly to impose a management regime to resolve the predicament or to countenance its imposition by unilateral action. The situation is modeled by an n-person Prisoner's Dilemma, in which each player has an immediate incentive to pursue autonomously self-interested behavior unless a binding agreement to act in the common interest can be reached. Of course, if such an agreement can be reached, the outcome is superior for all (Herring 1991). Dasgupta et al. (1997) note that there is no necessity that agreement has to entail centralized intervention: decentralized participatory arrangements can be found and would often be preferred. Hardin's aim, like many subsequent writers on the case, is to illuminate processes of ecological degradation in rural poor country situations. The common property resources in question are usually assumed to be open-access forests (as sources of fuel wood and leaf fodder) and local aquifers (for well water). With overuse, the productivity of these resources declines, with immediate and disproportionate impact on the poor.

In Hardin's classic formulation of the "tragedy of the commons," the tragedy was the failure of collective social institutions to prevent the externalities of private maximizing behavior from ruining a common resource to the detriment of all individuals in the social system. In this sense, the "tragedy of the commons" is simply another, though one of the most dramatic, examples of what the French philosopher Sarte calls "counter-finality": the unintended negative consequences at the collective level of the individually 'rational' decisions (cited in Elster 1993). The problem of the commons, if a problem at all, is nothing more than a necessity of coming to terms with a fundamental dilemma of social life: certain collective goods can be achieved only through the interference with a Hobbesian world of individual maximizing behavior. There must be rules. It is in the theoretical elaboration of the sources, nature, and enforcement of those rules that the tragedy paradigm generates the most contentious issues. Those issues will remain important whether or not one shares the values embedded in the original "tragedy of the commons" statement and its extensions. The association of the tragedy of the commons with conservative values lies in (a) the person of Garrett Hardin; (b) the individual maximizing assumption about human nature, which *denies community*; and (c) the two traditional solutions to the 'tragedy': the Leviathan and vigorous creation of exclusive private property rights in land. The logic of the tragedy of the commons depends crucially on conceptualizing the 'commons' as used as resources of nature. That is, the logic of uncoordinated pursuit of interests threatens that which is a common interest.

The challenge to Hardin's tragedy of the commons followed a clear pattern: design institutions to manage resources rather than changing the tenure system. The theories of common property and open access have been proposed (Bromley 1992 and Ostrom 1990). According to Bromley (1992), common property has something in common with private property—the exclusion of non-owners. Given that Bromley considered traditional land tenure to be common property regimes, he argued that exclusivity was inherent in traditional systems of resource management[2]. The question raised by these developments is obvious: are these design principles (exclusivity and open access) common across countries? For Zimbabwe, Mandondo (2001) found that exclusivity and open access tend to differ from community to community across country. He concluded that the term exclusivity could be reconciled with open access. This evidence gives support to those who seek a broad understanding of common and pooled resources in societies where communal tenure is practiced. The term communal land tenure is not legal, but a term developed by colonial administrations, particularly British social scientists to describe *non-western property systems*. Central to the Boserup's (1965) now classic proposition, for example, is the idea that when land scarcities develop because of population pressure, indigenous land tenure arrangements evolve towards more individualized land rights in response to factor price changes. This means the underlying demographic and economic processes that induce agricultural intensification and technical change are those that simultaneously generate a demand for socially sanctioned institutional change in the tenure system. Whereas initially, households are allowed only to continuously cultivate land, they are later able to bequeath and sell it. This not only creates greater security of tenure, thereby providing incentives to make farm investments, but it supposedly facilitates the commercialization of agriculture as allocative efficiencies begin to emerge with a land market. Eventually, this evolutionary process of institutional development produces a unified system of land documentation and registration, backed up by the enforcement of property rights.

We also learn from North (1990) that because rules are based on culture, they change only incrementally and marginally, persisting along a path of institutional change over time. The challenge facing policy makers in Zimbabwe and other Southern African countries is how to modify these deeply ingrained traditional rules and guide them along a path of evolutionary institutional change towards a system of more sustainable natural resource management.

Types of Land Reform

'Land reform' is used to refer to a number of rather distinct processes. We divide the broad spectrum into types. These processes are not at all mutually exclusive. Many countries might have two or more of these types of land reform as part of their rural development programs. These are: land tenure reforms; negotiated land tenure reforms; market-led reforms; land reforms through restitution and imposed redistributive reforms. The latter two types provide a major explanation of land invasions in Zimbabwe. In subsequent sections we model this type of 'land reform' and land re-distribution as a 'no rule-of-law' regime. We briefly discuss each of these to out point differences.

Land Tenure Reform

This type of reform is used in all other categories, but is often used as the main instrument of achieving both more efficient and equitable distribution of land and landed resources (water, for example). The focus is on techniques and institution rebuilding that makes land tenure institutions work in a more efficient, effective and fair way. Thus, the focus is on the social, political, and economic support needed for institutionalized transactions in rights in property (Feder and Feeney 1991). The core of this approach is good legal support and effective land information systems. Repeatedly, it has been observed that where the cadastre and land registry are poorly maintained or non-existent, there are high costs for proper survey, valuation and creation of new land records. The transaction costs for property exchange often exceed the economic value of the property involved. Experience has shown that landowners have many tools available to frustrate the process of creating fair and open economic transactions.

Land tenure reform is usually based on the creation of unambiguous property rights in land through legal reform and land registration. First, the newly established private rights must be clear. Second, 'private' refers largely to control (i.e., legal capacity): private tenure imbues the owner with control over the acquisition, use, enjoyment and disposal of the property. These rights are conditioned by the context-specific statutes and laws that limit the absolute freedom of an individual through restrictions on land use, and so forth. The new institutionalist approach has also brought back an important observation. Property is not the same thing as ownership, nor is ownership equivalent to control. These distinctions are relevant to the theoretical model developed later in the chapter. Property rights (entitlements) establish a relationship between the holder and the resources on the one hand and the legitimizing norms and institutions on the other. Property rights establish relations and makes possible new economic activity through adaptive and culturally recognized procedures. They also make possible confirmation of title in order to verify and secure land titles for those who already have a demonstrable claim to the land and replace doubt and contention with certainty and so inspire confidence and encourage development. The concepts here are also relevant to the discussion of the 'tragedy of the commons.'

Negotiated Land Tenure Reforms

The thrust of this approach is the negotiated transfer of land from large owners to the land needy. The clearest uses of this are the very different processes that are taking place today in Colombia, Brazil and South Africa. In all cases, it is the alliance between landless and near landless farming families and civil society who are directing government where, when, and how to focus their negotiations on their behalf. That is, *the land seekers negotiate what they need, as opposed to a more traditional approach to land reform where the recipients get what is given to them*.

Market-led Reform

This is a type of land reform that combines very naturally with the realization that when they work, property markets are the best arbiter of supply and demand of goods and services. The question is quite naturally raised: why could we not get land markets to function in a way that those who really want to farm and are the best farmers would get land, and inefficient land holders and absentee land owners would be driven out by market forces? This usually involves direct government intervention in the market by making assets available to those too disadvantaged to enter into normal land market transactions. This includes the distribution of public lands; state expenditure on land reclamation and subsequent allotment as private property; mortgage interest tax relief; support to institutions to administer the necessary land acquisition and distribution mechanisms and to advice services to prospective landowners.

A land market always requires some state intervention. A land market by itself will not do much to transfer land to the poor, who want to be independent, land-owning producers. This is because where the former owner has to be compensated at market or near market value by the purchaser, a poor farmer cannot repay out of farm profits alone. Land always contains a premium value over and above the value of its agricultural productivity due to its collateral value in a market economy and preferential access to credit. It has been the unfortunate observation that where the market is not sufficiently monitored after land distribution, it is quickly followed by land return to the former owners. These market-led reforms have been strongly resisted in former colonies where natives think that it is unfair to purchase ancestral lands from descendants of British settlers who obtained the land for free under the questionable legal doctrine of *terri nullis*. It is partly this thinking that underpins most of the farm land invasions in Zimbabwe. It goes without saying that a market-led land reform requires an active land market (Taylor 1988). That is, there have to exist willing sellers and willing buyers (in established market economies, we anticipate that a small percentage of the national privately owned land will change hands annually through the market).

Land Reform through Restitution

Under this type of reform, the focus is on the restoration of rights that some feel have been taken unjustly. This process is technically a legal and judicial process that returns rights to a pre-determined date. In most of Eastern and Central Europe this is 1948, in South Africa it is 1913, in Zimbabwe it is 1890. While land restitution is a form of land reform to address past injustices, in Eastern and Central Europe, Zimbabwe, and in South Africa it is running into a number of practical problems. The principal one is that the entire physical infrastructure has changed dramatically since the rights to individual parcels were unjustly acquired. Citizens, quite understandably, insist on the return of their original property, but this nowadays is usually at odds with access, service provisions or even sound sustainable land use. Where original properties have been restituted, the general experience has been one of disappointment and limited economic utility. This will be expected to change through innovations in the land tenure reform that will allow equitable property rationalization by the restituted owners.

Imposed Redistributive Reforms

No discussion of land reform would be complete without coverage of imposed redistribution of land. This is the kind of land reform that most people would first think of when hearing the term. In a redistributive land reform, the land is taken from large holders and given to landless and poor farmers. From an institutional side this normally includes nationalization; redistribution policies involving expropriation of land on grounds of excessive size, underutilization, and ownership by absentee landlords and/or foreigners. This type of land reform often (but not always, e.g. Chile) grows out of a post-crisis situation such as a war or civil war. The police power of the state is used to redefine the property rights of landholders. Thus, such a land reform requires an exclusive control on political power. It can succeed only where the power of the existing rural, land-based elite is either transferred or eliminated. It is not at all surprising, therefore, that such land reforms have been often directed more by ideological fervor than sound technical planning.

Zimbabwe's Experience

Before 2000, Zimbabwe's land reform was largely based on imposed redistribution, though within a market framework. Under various land re-settlement schemes, the government purchased land from white farmers and absentee landlords under a willing-seller, willing-buyer arrangement. The government would then parcel out plots of land to African families and provide them with seeds and agricultural extension services. The program worked well until the late 1990s when five events set the stage for land and farm invasions.

First, the ruling party elite began to keep the best farms for themselves under a 99-year lease, which cost them about $10 a year. The practice signaled the ascendance of institutionalized corruption. Second, farmers and other owners of large estates raised their offer prices far above the appraised values of farm properties. Third, a combination of drought, high unemployment among the youth, and high inflation eroded the standard of living and increased poverty rates. Fourth was the pressure from 'war veterans' who had been demobilized without adequate income support. This climate led Chenjerai "Hitler" Hunzvi, a self-declared standard bearer of the "war veterans" movement to demand pensions for his followers, which eventually escalated to the demand for land (see Johnson 2000; Bloch 2000). The final straw was the loss of a constitutional referendum in 2000 that would have allowed the government to expropriate white commercial farms without compensation in order to fulfill its short-term political objectives. The referendum was defeated by a coalition of urban and rural voters that Mugabe blamed on white farmers for allegedly bank rolling the anti-vote. This also coincided with the rise of the newly formed Movement for Democratic Change (MDC) opposition, which for the first time further exposed the vulnerability of the ruling party.

The combination of these events led to the unemployed (rural and urban youth) to be reconstituted into a youth militia that teamed up with "war veterans" to directly challenge the ruling party (ZANU-PF) elite for material spoils. The ruling party perceived this challenge to be credible. Thus, with the tacit approval of Mugabe and the ruling party, this paramilitary coalition began to invade farms to 'speed-up' land reform and re-distribution on the eve of the 2000 parliamentary elections. Recognizing the potential opportunity Mugabe stated "If white settlers just took the land from us without paying for it, we can, in a similar way, just take it from them without paying for it." (Power 2003: 3). The mayhem that followed has been direct and effective. For example, of the 4,000 large-scale commercial farmers who controlled 70 percent of Zimbabwe's arable land in 2000, all but 500 have been forced off their land with devastating effects on the national economy, the livelihoods of nearly a million farm laborers and dependants as well as the rural poor, who must now depend on food aid.

Background to the Zimbabwe Land Issue

Zimbabwe was colonized in 1890. From that date, appropriation of land by white settlers ensued to the extent that that by 1898, Native Reserve Orders-in-Council (series of colonial laws passed in England) had been passed to establish 'reserves' for indigenous people in drier and more remote parts of the territory (Rhodesia). By 1914, the policy of giving reasonably good land to 'natives' for them to cultivate, graze and water their livestock was abandoned. Good land found in the 'reserves' was allocated to white settlers. Since independence in 1980, Zimbabwe has been attempting to tackle the problem of environmental degradation, land underutilization, low levels of investment, low productivity and low incomes in the rural sector. Table 11.1 shows land use classification as of 1990. The basic land issue in Zimbabwe emanates from the land invasions by Africans (largely in rural Communal Areas) into large and small-scale commercial farms (largely white-owned and with better rainfall) (Rukuni, 1994).

Large-Scale Commercial Farming (LSCF) Areas

Much of LSCF is in areas of high agricultural potential (Natural Regions II and III). The land there is owned by individuals, private/family companies, parastatals, government and transnational companies (TNCs). Freehold tenure is the title to land. The large-scale farms in this sector employed some 228,000 permanent and casual workers in 1988, with a population of about 1,571,300 in 1992 growing at 3 percent per annum. The majority of the farm owners are white colonial settlers or their descendants. The average farm size in the LSCF areas is about 2,406 ha nationwide, while individual farms average some 1,402 ha. Private individual farms take some 50 percent of the total number of LSCFs, but they hold only 34 percent of that land. Some 38 percent is taken by large companies who account for more than 61 percent of the LSCF sector. The state owns up to two percent of LSCFs that are leased out to white farmers and some blacks (Muir and Blackie 1994). The administrative framework is provided by the Ministry of Agriculture, (AGRITEX); Ministry of Lands and Water Development (Water Development); Ministry of Justice, Legal and Parliamentary Affairs (Deeds Office); and the Ministry of Local Government, Rural and Urban Development (Department of Physical Planning).

Small-Scale Commercial Farming (SSCF) Areas

Much of the land in this category falls in Natural Regions III (35.4 percent) and IV (38.2 percent) comprising some 8,653 allocated farms with an average farm size of 124.2 ha. Some 564,800 ha are allocated under agreements of lease and purchase, and 484,000 ha were deeds of grant and transfers. This left some 37,800 ha of which some 177,400 ha were transferred for resettlement by 1985, leaving about 202,400 ha vacant or not allocated. Thus, the two basic tenure forms in this sub-sector are leasehold and freehold systems (Rukuni, 1998). Under the leasehold, tenure ownership of land is often under a settlement scheme whereby the settler leases a farm with an option to purchase by the lessee. Under the freehold tenure, when a lessee eventually purchases the land, he gains freehold title to the land after a five-year period of lease.

Table 11.1 Land Use Classification by Farming Sector, 1990

Farming Sector	Amount of Land Held
Communal areas	16.35 million hectares
Large-scale commercial farms	11.22 million hectares
Small-scale commercial farms	1.38 million hectares
Resettlement	3.29 million hectares

Source: Land Tenure Commission Report, (1995).

State Land

This is composed of land on lease in small-scale and large-scale commercial sectors and land in the reserved areas (RAs), which is allocated, on a permit basis. State involvement in direct productive farming predates independence. Land under the state occupies some 353,006 ha through 20 estates managed by Agricultural Development Authority (ADA). In addition, the state holds title to some 20 percent of national land managed by the Forestry Commission and the National Parks Authority. The former is a parastatal body while the latter is a government department. These two institutions are land 'lessees' via legislation enabling them to manage and utilize the state lands but with no legal lease contracts. State lands also expand through district councils' control of increasing quantities of woodland areas in the Commercial Areas (CAs). There are growing land-centered conflicts between local government councils and communities over rights to exploit natural resources on these lands and the right to the proceeds from tourism and hunting operations undertaken therein.

Almost all economists recognize the importance of institutions (law) for behavior, but we are just beginning to recognize that institutions, like law, are in fact, *endogenous*. One of the important social changes in Southern Africa is the taking of land by force from those who have farmed it and the encroaching on public lands by the landless. The failure of the state to create a permissive institutional environment based on the 'rule-of-law' finds its open expression in 'land invasions' mostly by many rural Africans in the name of 'land reform.' By 'rule-of-law,' it has meant a legal regime where property rights are secure, since there are rules on which even the ruler cannot easily infringe; access to legal rights is broad; and rules for solving disputes are predictable and have legitimacy. The rule-of-law is the institution that makes possible a competitive market economy as formulated in the neoclassical model.

During colonization, many economists and political scientists argued for the granting of independence and subsequent development plans were premised on upholding the rule-of-law and using a combination of laws and courts to redress inequities in income, employment, education, and land reform. However, the recent breakdown in the rule-of-law forces us to ask the question: What theories could explain this weakness in upholding the institution of the rule-of-law in Zimbabwe? Relating specifically to farms, any theory that purports to explain such a state must take into account asymmetries in political power. Some individuals or organized groups may believe that they can extract for themselves more farms and other physical property on such farms by undermining the rule-of-law than they can obtain through any rule-bound system. Those who abhor the rule-of-law may displace legal owners of property and obtain 'control,' especially when the government condones such behavior.

In the next section, we present a simple game theoretic model to characterize land invasions and extortions under two possible regimes: the initial 'no rule-of-law' and the probability of re-establishing the 'rule-of-law.' We show the difficulties faced by a constituency that supports the rule-of-law against the constituency that supports a 'no rule-of-law' (land invaders and the ruling party elite). Later, we use a simple dynamic model to show how deeply entrenched these land reforms and re-distribution could be and thus pose the question: Could the violators of law end up as winners even in the event that a 'rule-of-law' regime is re-established? The section draws from the work of Hoff and Siglitz (2002a, b)

A Static Model of Land Invasions, Corruption and Entrenchment: The Law of the Jungle

It is useful to consider an economy in which the possible legal structures vary along the dimension of the security of property rights in land (farms, timber estates, wild game reserves). There exist two possible legal regimes, which capture the end of the spectrum: the 'no rule-of-law' and the 'rule-of-law.' We speculate on the conditions that must exist before the rule-of-law is re-established. Furthermore, the 'no rule-of-law' regime is characterized by a government dominated by a party (ZANU-PF) which has intentionally created a tragedy of commons, especially in public or state land. To be sure, land invasions were accompanied by firm invasions. In all cases, the strategies are similar: strip assets or extort money and inventories versus building value or making irreversible investments.

Agents with control rights over private property (through land invasions) or converting public property to private property (squatting on timber estates, wild game reserves) seek to maximize their wealth and choose between two strategies: continuing to develop the growth potential and thus building value, whose payoff depends on the legal regime in place, and stealing and stripping assets, including existing livestock, cash and food crops, which ensures a sure return. The probability of the re-establishment of the rule-of-law depends on the political constituency for it in equilibrium. The legal environment often leads individuals to adopt certain economic strategies and, given the economic choices that they have made, they may not support the rule-of-law. The simple model presented below supports this observation.

Agents

Assume that time consists of two periods. Each agent (land invaders and ruling party elites) exercises some control rights over either private property (part of a farm belonging to a white farmer) or part of public land (timber estates) in the first period, and chooses between two actions:

Actions or Strategies

1. Continue to *develop the property by making irreversible investment* to increase the enterprise's value.
2. *Strip the property* of hosehold iems, crops, equipment, and launder the proceeds in other business ventures in the city or abroad.

We assume that the economy consists of a continuum of agents indexed by $\varnothing$, where $\varnothing$ is uniformly distributed on [0, 1]. The group with higher strip $\varnothing$ assets better (these are closely connected to the ruling party, specifically 'war-veterans' that are closely associated with farm and firm invasions). In fact, the returns are larger if the target farm, firm, or wild game reserve has more liquid assets or assets that can be quickly converted to cash. In addition, it helps if the target has greater equity in the hands of the small minority of white Zimbabweans, overseas British, and white South Africans.

The Political Environment

The initial state is a 'no the rule-of-law' position. Agents who want to build value insist on the maintenance of the rule-of-law because it is the only legal regime that can enforce contracts, criminal law, and protect private property rights. Those who prefer stripping value through control rights prefer 'stripping assets very quickly' and may resort to illegitimate and extra legal means to obtain profit from control rights. The economic strategy of an agent determines the agent's politician position or attitude to the government's stance on the rule-of-law. Let x represent the fraction of agents who support the 'no rule-of-law.' The probability ρ (.) of the establishment of the 'rule-of-law' depends on the size and influence of those who support it, $(1 - x)$. This assumption is captured by the expression,

$$\rho(x) = (1 - x)^2$$

The Payoffs

The technology is constant returns to scale. An agent of type $\varnothing$ who strips firms, invades farms, obtains $\varnothing$ per unit asset. An agent, who builds value, obtains a return of 1 if the rule-of-law is established and ¼ if it is not.

Given x, the threshold below which agents build value and press for the return of the rule-of-law, and above which they do not, is a type Φ^* such that

$$\Phi^* (x) = \rho (x) + \frac{[1 - \rho (x)]}{4} \tag{1}$$

This is the *switching line* between 'rule-of-law' and 'no rule-of-law,' therefore, a population fraction $1 - \Phi^*$ strips/extorts and supports the initial 'no rule-of-law' status.

Equilibrium

An equilibrium is a value of citizen support for the 'no rule-of-law' status that solves the following problem:

$$x = 1 - \Phi^* (x) \tag{2}$$

This states that for a fraction x of the agents, the expected return on stripping assets under the current land reform and land re-distribution exceeds the return on building value and making irreversible investments. If we substitute from (1), (2) implies that $x = 3/4 - 3/4(1-x)^2$. Equilibrium is defined at $x^* = 0$ and $x^{**} = 2/3$ (Figure 11.1).

From this example, we can deduce many points related to the current land reforms and land re-distribution issues in Zimbabwe. Even if building value under the rule-of-law is preferred to stripping by every agent, a small group of citizens (NGOS, human rights groups and ordinary citizens) may be a unique stable equilibium. For example, at $x = 0$, the 'switch line' in (1) is steeper than the linear stripping or 'invasion benefit curve' (defined by the uniform distribution of stripping intensity). Any slight increase in x above zero lowers the switch point by more than it lowers the return of the marginal asset-stripper, which induces movement away from the equilibrium. Thus, the efficient equilibrium, where the transition to the rule-of-law occurs with certainty in the next period is inherently *unstable*. In other words, land invasions/extortions become more frequent and the rule-of-law less probable, the more firm and land invasions there are. This is the situation that characterizes the period 2000 to the present day in Zimbabwe. By similar reasoning, the inefficient equilibrium where only 1/3 of the agents support the rule-of-law is *stable*. In this unique stable equilibrium, the equilibrium of re-establishment of the rule-of-law is just 1/9—a small probability indeed.

Do the implications of this static model extend to a dynamic framework? For example, one may indeed ask if forward-looking behavior of agents affect their political actions (viz, support the ruling party (= no rule-of-law or support the opposition = rule-of-law). If such agents are so affected, even the asset strippers or war-veterans might support the re-establishment of the rule-of-law. In order to extend the framework to a dynamic framework, we add two variables that link an agent's current decisions to his future opportunities. First, a current decision to strip and or/invade reduces the *stake* that an agent has in the future legal regime. Second, such a decision reduces the agent's relative return from the rule-of-law (relative to no rule-of-law) because the establishment of the rule-of-law at the end of a given period constrains his ability to strip. To be sure, the basis for the rule-of-law cannot be only power, the rules have to have legitimacy. In other words, if there are investigations established by law to review the process of land reform and redistribution) after the rule-of-law is established, the agents who might have gained from stripping cannot be protected from legal action to recover property.

Given these links between present future and present, stripping (firm's assets) or theft of cash crops, and other farm property can give agents an interest in prolonging the 'no-rule-of law' state. Thus, the results from the static model carry over with politically sophisticated agents.

In the model, how agents align themselves, influences other agent's actions (*spill-over or externality effect*) and how each agent acts influences his political position (an *intertemporal incentive effect*). This is a two-period model. Each individual, in attempting to influence the choice of the environment, focuses on the impact on himself, not on others. Externalities that affect political outcomes result in externalities that affect economic choices.

When an economy (in this case, the Zimbabwean economy) fails to coordinate on the rule-of-law (upholding private property rights) and instead coordinates on something resembling the law of the jungle, then society as a whole suffers. No one doubts that current price controls, fuel shortages, foreign exchange shortages, rising unemployment and inflation, increasing crime, corruption, and worse of all, loss of human life and human rights reflect the extent and pervasiveness of negative externalities. In such a political arena, each individual or group, in attempting to influence the choice

Figure 11.1: Land Reform: Rule of Law and Farm Invasion

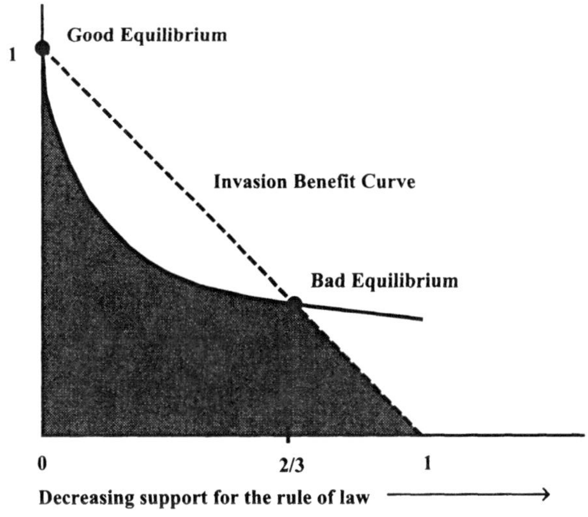

Source:Adapted from Hoff and Stglitz (2000)

environment, focuses on the impact on himself or on the group, not others (in this, farmers are deprived of farms and other property, and the rest of society that must endure the economic hardships alluded above). *Externalities that affect political outcomes give rise to externalities that affect economic choices.* A concrete example of this statement and its relationship to land reforms in Zimbabwe is in order.

Suppose, the process of land reform (for example, imposed redistributive commons) was transparent and observed the rule-of-law, then each farm owner would take actions to maximize the social value of their output because they would have ownership of the produce or goods. Under this scenario, all farmers (white and black) would take out loans from banks, purchase seeds on time, and produce enough food and cash crops to feed the population and have excess for exports. In a way, this was the state of things prior to 2000. There were indeed calls for an orderly land reform that was supported by a majority of Zimbabweans. However, as soon as groups of individuals (the so-called war-veterans) began to invade private farms and public lands, the political group in power, acting strategically to preserve political power, gave tacit support to these land grabs. At that point, negative externalities in the political market spilled into the economic market. The imperfections in the political market cause inefficient behaviors that, in turn, induce rational and yet inefficient economic outcomes. White farmers who were afraid of immediate farm invasions stopped borrowing from banks. At the same time, banks stopped making loans to farmers due to the high probability of default should the farm be invaded. In some cases, farmers moved capital equipment and other movables to cities in order to prevent war-veterans from getting their hands on the stuff. The government has succeeded in creating *systemic* change – undermining the rule-of-law in return for the chance to retain political power. Land invasions in Zimbabwe have had a more adverse impact on institutions and the rule-of-law than the above analysis suggests, for these led to the rise of small groups within ZANU-PF that made huge fortunes from the induced collapse of the rule-of-law.

Entrenchment by Party Functionaries and War-veterans

In practice, land reforms and land-redistribution and, to a lesser extent, control over firms are more adverse to the establishment of the rule-of-law than the preceding analysis suggests, for they led to the creation of a group of people closely associated with the ruling party, and members of the Zimbabwe Defense Forces with vast fortunes and influence over the state-controlled media, parliament, and the judiciary. This aspect of the rise of this group might be related to an 'oligopolistic' model. That world and the world analyzed here have three salient differences. In such a world, it is not true that their actions will have no effect on the behavior of other participants. Second, oligopolists/party functionaries will typically obtain significant rents and will accordingly direct some of their political energies to the preservation of these rents. To the extent that they succeed, the legal framework that emerges will not be the one that promises economic efficiency. Third, in some cases these party functionaries or elite may be actually be against a rule-based system, believing that they can extract for themselves more rents and other proceeds from the arbitrary exercise of their economic influence than they can obtain through any rule-bound system. Such a result is predicated on the existence of plausible constraints on the kinds of rules that they can impose, for example, under the political process, they may be restricted from writing down rules that are clearly discriminatory. Because 'bargaining' goes on behind closed doors, the party elite and their associates may be able to achieve more under such behind-the-scenes bargaining than through any rule-based system. They may be willing to bear the risks associated with the non-rule based system, given the amount that this group as a whole would have to transfer to the rest of society under the alternative.

We next set out a hypothesis about the 'logic of reform,' and then sketch a simple model to shed light on the equilibrium basis for the rule-of-law.

The Logic of Political Constraint Hypothesis

At the outset of the collapse of the rule of law and other institutions in Zimbabwe, most observers thought that it was politically feasible to quickly re-establish the rule-of-law before the 'no rule-of-law' regime undermined a market economy, or before land and farm invasions were in full swing. However, since the ruling paty, its rural supporters, and more critically 'war veterans' gave tacit support to the process of undermining institutions, it was political infeasible to do so. The implications of this statement are explored in this section.

Assume two reforms:

$a = rol$ (rule-of-law) and $b = nrol$ (no rule-of-law) under consideration.

Let P_{ab} denote the power of the coalition in favor of a over b .

The statement that a particular coalition is stronger in a certain circumstances than another coalition means that it is either large, controls credible military power to oppress opposition, or that the coalition is willing or abe to rovide resources to push for or against) a certain set of proposals than another set of proposals. We have assumed that a is not politically feasible, and b is observed to occur. Together, this implies the following coalition power distributon:

$$P_{bs} > P_{as}, P_{bs} > P_{s} \quad \text{and} \quad P_{as} < P_{s}$$

The coalition in favor of b over status quo (P_{bs}) is *stronger* than the coalition in favor of a over the status quo (P_{as}), the coalition in favor of b over the status quo is stronger than the coalition in favor of remaining in the status quo (P_s), and the coalition in favor of a is *weaker* than the coalition in favor of remaining in the status quo; s represents the *status quo*.

Consider one such alternative reform and examine the process from the perspective of supporters of the rule-of-law within the ruling party and government that is divided between land reform/redistribution within the rule-of-law (R and the radicals (the ruling party elites and war-veterans (W). Reformers consider two alternative reforms: *Reform r*: regulations and then reforms on land and re-distribution; and *Reform p*: land reform and land re-distribution without regulations.

Let $P_{ps}(R)$ represent the political power of the reformers in favor of *p* over the status quo, and let denote the political power of $P_{ps}(W)$ the radicals in favor of *p* over the status quo.Assume that poliical power is addictive. The usefulness of the logic of reform can be seen in evaluating the following often-heard assertions:

A. The reform *p* is politically feasible, but *r* is not. Formally, this amounts to the following two equations:

$$P_{ps}(R) + P_{ps}(W) > P_{s}(R) + P_{s}(W) \quad (3).$$

$$P_{rs}(R) + P_{rs}(W) < P_{s}(R) + P_{s}(W) \quad (4).$$

B. The war-veterans, party elite and members of the party in parliament are currently using their control over the public sector, and existing 'rules' for the private sector, and public lands to obtain rents for themselves, impeding any form of efficiency.
C. Land reforms, land re-distribution, and the resulting in invasions of farms and public land, and firms, will result in owners who have an incentive to use those resources efficiently. That is, while *p* is feasible but *r* is not, *p* will result in increased efficiency. That is, those who get 'control rights' under the no rule-of-law will use their new power to lobby for reforms in the legal structure (which by hypothesis were not feasible earlier) that will protect property and contracts and restrict anti-competitive practices. That is, these kinds of reforms that could not be implemented initially can be implemented later.

There are two implications that follow from these statements. First, under the assumption that regulations would be socially efficient, equations (3) and (4) imply that before land and farm invasions actually occurred, bargaining within the government failed to yield the efficient outcome. Second, (4) implies that if reformers have no power under the status quo, and yet farm and firm invasions are feasible, then for the no rule-of-law group, the *status quo* and such invasions are equivalent. That, in turn, implies that if invasions occur, then government officials must prefer these to the rents that they receive under the rule-of-law regime. For Zimbabwe, this makes sense since invasions convert public income streams (under the rule-of-law) to private income streams (under the no rule-of-law regime).

There is a clear, and highly disturbing, implication: *there must be more corruption (in dollar value to the ruling party in power and their associates) associated with land and farm invasions than with the process in which farms, firms, timber estates and so forth remain in private hands*. More critical, however, is the implication that there is more corruption under invasions than under the process where state-owned enterprises remain under government control. What the current wave of farm and firm invasions has done, is to allow those in power to extract the present discounted value of future rents — in effect, to capitalize corruption. Since 2000, this has not been difficult at all in Zimbabwe. A common method is for a member of the ruling party to target a factory or farm, and then employ a group of 'veterans' to physically take over the targeted enterprise, and bar anyone who owns it from removing any assets. Often, these invasions have resulted in loss of human life. Usually, the police do not interfere since under the 'no rule-of-law,' the party is above the law. The point is that logic drives us to at least consider as a serious possibility that land and farm invasions provide an enormously powerful tool for redistribution towards those currently in power.

In the next section, we present a model that questions this implication in societies such as Zimbabwe that now have ill-defined property rights. The premise of the model is that incumbents have the ability to shape economic institutions in their favor after the invasions, and *political outsiders* can reveal their preferences for more public protection of property rights only once they have entered a business activity. In the model, the method of invasions may have implications for *political evolution*, that is, for the power of various coalitions in the future, and thus, for the design of – even the existence of – the rule-of-law.

Dynamic Model of Entrenchment Following Land Reforms and Land-Redistribution

The economy has a continuum of goods. Each good is produced in its own sector. In a proportion γ of these sectors, there is a single farm (firm) that has been invaded. In addition, in each sector there is a competitive fringe of potential entrants. In the case of farms, subdividing farms creates many potential entrants. After the agents in the competitive fringe have moved, the legal framework is established and agents obtain payoffs conditional on the legal framework. The probability of the establishment of the rule-of-law, ρ depends on the size of the citizen groups that supports it. By assumption, only agents who are in the land re-distribution invasions or firm invasions have the information and the 'concentrated' interests (some of these are interested partiesalready in government or belong to the ruling party) lobby government and thereby reveal their preferences.

In each sector, individuals in the competitive fringe are a measure of 1 and are indexed by f. A higher value f corresponds to a higher fixed cost of production and f is uniformly distributed on $[0,1]$. In the monopolized sector, the payoff to a new entry is negative; hence, no individual enters such a sector. In a sector that is not monopolized, the payoff is $\gamma - f$ (γ is income or returns) if the rule-of-law is established and otherwise it is $-f$. Assume that Then there $y \in (0,1)$. is a critical value of f,

$$f^* = \rho y \tag{5}$$

which is the type of the marginal entrant who is just indifferent between entering or not. The fraction of potential entrants in the competitive fringe who choose to enter is: $f^*[1-\gamma]$: this is because a fraction $1-\gamma$ of the sectors is not monopolized, and a f^* fraction of the competitive fringe of each of these sectors enters.

The probability of the establishment of the rule-of-law ρ is a function of the size of the constituency for it. The equilibrium value f^* solves the following problem.

$$D \equiv y\rho(f^*[1-\gamma]) - f^* = 0 \tag{6}$$

This says that the difference between expected return and fixed costs for the marginal entrant is zero. There always exists at least one equilibrium, and it is stable if

$$\frac{\partial D}{\partial f}(f^*) = y\rho'([1-\gamma]) < 1 \tag{7}$$

Restructuring, which reduces γ,gives the constituency for the rule-of-law $(f^*[1-\gamma])$ two positive effects: evaluated in the neighborhood of a stable equilibrium, a fall in γ not only increases the set of sectors into which new entrants flow, but also increases the number of new entrants in each sector by

$$\frac{df^*}{-d\gamma} = \frac{\partial D/\partial\gamma}{\partial D/\partial f} = \frac{y\rho' f^*}{1-y\rho'[1-\gamma]} > 0 \tag{8}$$

The outcome of a high value of γ and weak value support for the rule-of-law may actually be worse than that captured in this simple model. In the absence of the rule-of-law, political insiders can monopolize new sectors – sectors that were not monopolies before invasions.

Conclusion

The presumption under land reform and land re-distribution was that the faster such properties were turned over to Africans and the ruling party elite, the earlier this would eliminate or minimize land restitution pressure, and lead to faster growth, plus the re-establishment of the rule-of-law regime. There was no theoretical analysis of how this process was supposed to work. The 'technologies' developed in this chapter – stripping assets through land and farm invasions and bribery may block the emergence of a constituency for the rule-of-law. This chapter shows that, if *eventually* a rule-of-law is established, asset stripping and bribery/corruption may unleash forces that *delay* the re-establishment of the rule-of-law.

Without land and farm invasions, control of land and state-owned firms would have resided in the hands of the owners and the state respectively. In the latter case, those interests within the government would have stripped assets from state-owned firms anyway. The main point is that the ability to strip assets without fear of going to prison was enhanced when the party elite successfully instituted a no rule-of-law regime. Through this process, the ruling party elite, and others associated with the government, who are less interested in the rule-of-law, created the means and the incentives to use one's wealth and influence to preserve monopoly rents and bar entry of new firms in the sectors that they now control. If, in particular, natural resource-rich sectors or previous state monopolies had not been invaded, then both the ability to strip and the power to capture the state and block entry would not have been so significant. The *manner* of invasions plus the attendant abuses in human rights influences the *constituency* for a beneficial legal regime. If there had been more time to ensure political legitimacy to land reforms and land-redistribution, it would have been easier to provide security for private property and reduce capital flight rather than the collapse of the economy that has been experienced since 2000. Under this scenario, there would have been more political support for the rule-of-law and thus a better political and economic equilibrium might have emerged.

So what lessons standout for other countries looking for models to replicate? Not much, except the following. Zimbabwe's approach is a good example of how not to conduct land reform and land-redistribution. A country that was once the region's breadbasket has been transformed into a food aid beggar, and a basket economy. Meanwhile, millions of hectares of productive land lie idle, or in the hands of unproductive ruling party elites and army. As a result, Zimbabwe's landless rural poor are not fulfilling their aspirations for land. Instead they have progressively become poorer and more violently oppressed than in pre-independence conditions. Decrying the saga of Zimbabwe's ill-conceived approach to land reform, veteran nationalist of the Zimbabwe revolution, Edison Zvobgo has stated "*We have tainted what was a glorious revolution, reducing it to some agrarian racist enterprise*" (Quoted in Chan 2003: 176). This perhaps is the tragedy of Zimbabwe.

Notes

1 Tenure reform describes legal reforms of tenure whether by state or local communities. It is different from land reform. Land reform involves the redistribution of landholdings and changes in the agrarian structures (pattern of distribution of and among owners), while tenure reform leaves people holding the same land, but with different rights

2 *Common property* is a commons from which a community can exclude non-members and over which the community controls. *Commons* is land or another natural resource used simultaneously or serially by the members of a community. *Open Access* is the use of commons without controls.

3 Communal land tenure in Asia and Africa describes tenure that involves a large amount of community control over land use. The community owns the land, but it allocates land to its members for cultivation. The member's rights are use rights (or usufruct). This implies a long-term right for an individual or household to use land and may include inheritance rights, but it does not imply a right to sell the land. In fact, the community may retain the right to

reallocate landholdings among its members. A communal land tenure system usually involves both use rights allocated to households or individuals and also common property in other resources.

4 Subtracting (3) from (4) yields , which

can, be also written as $P_{rp}(R) < -P_{rp}(W)$. In other words, the power of the reformers (rule-of-law group within the government) to impose transparent regulations rather than invasions is less than the power of the war-veterans and their close associates in government to resist regulations.

5 In the case where $P_{ps}(R) = P_s(R) = 0$.

References

Adams, M. (1995). "Land Reform: New seeds on old ground?" *Natural Resources Perspectives*, No.6, October. London: Overseas Development Institute.

Adams, M., Sibanda, S. and Turner, S. (1999). "Land tenure reform and rural livelihood in Southern Africa." *Natural Resources Perspectives*, No. 39, February. London: Overseas Development Institute.

Bloch, Eric (2000) "Impact of land invasions on Zimbabwe's economy". Speech given on May 5 in Bulawayo, Zimbabwe.

Boserup, E. (1965). *The Conditions of Agricultural Growth.* London: George Allen and Unwin.

Bromley, Daniel W. (1992). *Making the Commons Work: Theory, Practice, and Policy*, ICS Press.

Chan, S. (2003). *Robert Mugabe: a life of power and violence.* University of Michigan Press.

Dasgupta, Partha (1993). *An Inquiry into Well-being and Destitution.* Oxford: Clarendon Press.

Dasgupta, P., Maler, K.G., and Vercelli, A. (eds.) (1997) *The Economics of Transnational Commons*. Oxford: Clarendon Press

Diamond, Larry (1994). Rethinking Civil Society: Towards Democratic Consolidation. *Journal of Democracy.* 5: (3): 4–17.

Elster, J. (1993). "Why things don't happen as planned.," In N. Akerman, ed. *The Necessity of Friction*. Heidelberg: Physica Verlag. 248–56.

Feder, G. and Feeney, D. (1991) "Land Tenure and Property Rights: Theory and Applications for Development Policy." *The World Bank Economic Review*, 5:1, 135-154.

Hardin, Garrett. (1968). "The Tragedy of Commons." *Science.* 1243–1248.

Herring, R. (1991). "The Commons and its "tragedy" as an analytical framework: understanding environmental degradation in South Asia." in *Sundarbans Workshop*. Washington DC: Smithsonian Institution. .

Hoff, K and Stiglitz, J.E. (2000a) "After the the Big Ban? Obstacles to the emergence of the rule of law in post-communist societies." Discussion Paper # 0203-03 Columbia University

Hoff, K and Stiglitz, J.E. (2000b) The Political Economy of Property Rights in the Transition Economies: The Role of New Entry. World Bank Manuscript.

Johnson, R.W. (2000). "A Classic Third World Force Operation: 'Hitler' Hunzwi is just the frontman for farm invasion." *Focus* 18, 2-5

Mandondo, A. (2001). "Allocation of Governmental Authority and Responsibility in Tiered Governance Regimes: The Case of the Chivi Rural District Council Land se Planning and Conservation By-Laws." *African Studies Quarterly*, 5{3).

Muir, K .and Blackie, M.J. (1994). "The Commercialization of Agriculture" in: M. Rukuni and C.K. Eicher eds. *Zimbabwe's Agricultural Revolution*. Harare: University of Zimbabwe Press

North, D. (1990). *Institutions, Institutional Change and Economic Performance*. Cambridge: Cambridge University Press.

Ostrom, Elinor. (1990). *Governing the Commons*. Cambridge. Cambridge University Press.

Power, S. (2003). "How To Kill A Country: turning a breadbasket into a basket case in ten easy steps—the Robert Mugabe way." *The Atlantic Monthly*. December 2003, 1–12.

Rukuni, M. (1994). *Report of the Commission of Inquiry into Appropriate Agricultural Land Tenure System*. Harare: Government Printers.

Rukuni, M. (1998). " Why land tenure is central to Africa's future governance." Paper presented at the African Conference on Policy Perspectives and Practice for Sustainable Development. Harare, Zimbabwe: Scandinavian Seminar College.

Taylor, J. (1988). "The Elical Foundations of the Market." In: V. Ostro, D. Feeney and H. Pricht eds. *Rethinking Institutional Development Issue Alternatives and Choices*. San Francisco: Institute for Contemporary Studies Press.

Chapter 12

Indigenous Knowledge and Environmental Management in Africa: Evidence from Ghana

Seth Appiah-Opoku

Introduction

Africa is endowed with abundant natural resources, which provide a potential springboard for economic development in the region. Unfortunately, exploitation of these resources has left a trail of environmental problems including desertification, deforestation, and air and water pollution. In their attempt to solve these problems, African governments and policy makers have shown a preference for strategies and techniques which have worked in developed countries but are not suitable to conditions in Africa. In doing so, they have overlooked a wealth of experiential knowledge, norms, taboos, and a range of cultural practices that have sustained local ecosystems in Africa for centuries (Wamalwa 1991). This is not surprising because in most contemporary societies, western intellectual ideals have become the 'narrow path' to knowledge (Nakashima 1990). Against this background, indigenous knowledge is unjustly viewed as somehow inherently primitive, or naïve; reflective of an earlier and inferior stage of human cultural progress; and beyond this, however poetic or endearing, as completely irrelevant to modern needs and times (Knudston and Suzuki 1992; Appiah-Opoku and Mulamottil 1997). Consequently, the learning mode between western scientists and indigenous societies has been one of 'teach indigenous people how to solve their problems.' Ironically, indigenous societies have their own 'experts' who not only possess valid information about their environment but also have much to teach western scientists. This chapter, therefore, examines the role of indigenous knowledge systems in natural resource management and environmental conservation in Africa in the 21st century.

Indigenous Knowledge

Indigenous knowledge is built up by societies through generations of living in close contact with nature. It includes norms, taboos, a system of classification of natural resources, a set of empirical observations about the local environment, and a system of self-management that governs resource use. It often takes the following forms:

(a) an intimate and detailed knowledge of the environment, including plants, animals and natural phenomena;
(b) development and use of appropriate technologies for resource utilization, including uses of biotic materials and humane environmental conservation practices; and
(c) cultural beliefs, norms, taboos and a holistic world view that parallels the scientific discipline of ecology.

Indigenous knowledge is checked, validated, and revised daily and seasonally through the annual cycle of activities and differs from Western science in a number of ways (Howes 1980). This knowledge is site-specific and rooted to a particular place. Transferring the knowledge to other places runs the risk of dilution, dislocation, or misapplication. Indigenous knowledge is orally transmitted, subjective, and experiential in character. Thus, whereas data gathered by Western science is often selective and based on scientific inquiry, including tested hypothesis, those generated by indigenous knowledge are more inclusive and based on spirituality, including the inexplicable (Wolfe 1992).

There are several examples in the literature on development regarding project and policy failures in Africa due mostly to policy makers failing to incorporate local norms, beliefs, knowledge systems, and value-sets. For instance, in his evaluation of an irrigation project in Sudan, Rondinelli (1983: 84) notes:

> Social acceptance became a problem in irrigation projects where nomads were expected to be available for scheduled work in their fields at time periods which apparently clashed with their livestock herding interests. In nearly all cases, the projects had been designed by central government planners who knew little about local knowledge and conditions, and who made little or no attempts to understand the cultural practices that would be essential to successful implementation.

Similarly, of a failed groundnut scheme in Tanzania, Chambers (1983: 95) writes: "The problems...might have been foreseen more clearly if the local inhabitants had been consulted about why they did not cultivate in the areas proposed for the project".

Again, the Gibbons (cited in Brokensha et al. 1980) suggests that by relying on local informants in Sudan and drawing on their technical knowledge, it is possible to undertake a perfectly satisfactory soil survey and mapping in a few days even though a formal scientific approach could take several months. Also, Richards (1985) who worked in West Africa concluded that the knowledge of local people on the grasshopper *Zonocerus variegates* in relation to feeding habits and breeding habitat equaled that of Western-trained ecologists in sophistication and detail. These knowledge systems are not simply the result of accumulated passive observations. They often include years of analytical and experimental approach to natural resource and environmental management (Appiah-Opoku 1999). Yet western, and in some cases African, scientists are only recently discovering that indigenous knowledge is extremely accurate, even though anthropologists have commented on its strength and rationality for years (Rappaport 1968; Appiah-Opoku 1999).

A systematic study of indigenous knowledge began with a series of studies eliciting and analyzing the terminologies by which indigenous peoples classify objects in their natural environments (Bulmer 1970). A study of classification systems shows that all cultures recognize what they consider to be classes of animals and plants (Berlin 1973, Hunn 1975). These early anthropological studies enhanced the recognition of indigenous knowledge among some members of the scientific community. Emphasis in recent years has been on understanding the ecologically sound practices and belief systems that contribute to sustainable resource use among indigenous peoples, and ways that this knowledge could be successfully integrated with western scientific resource management. It is in this light that the indigenous knowledge potential for natural resource management in the 21st century is explored. The study is based on the Ashanti region of Ghana.

Method

A random sampling technique was used to select six districts in the Ashanti region (Figure 12.1) of Ghana where interviews were conducted. The region was home to the Ashanti Empire, which not only managed to retain its culture, but also had significant cultural influence on other parts of the country. Hence, observations about the region may be applicable to other parts of the country.

Using a purposive sampling technique, a list of 304 potential key informants in 20 randomly selected settlements was compiled. However, it was possible to interview only 180 individuals with the help of three research assistants. The remaining could not be interviewed due to reasons ranging from unavailability and unwillingness to participate in the survey. Those interviewed were: indigenous farmers (50); traditional healers (50); traditional hunters/fishermen (50); government officials and academicians (5), and village elders (10); environmentalists (5); and officials of non-governmental organizations (10). Interviews were preceded by visits to explain the purpose of the survey and to seek permission from opinion leaders. Interview transcripts, field notes and observations were analysed using qualitative techniques. These were supplemented with quantitative secondary data from official government publications and other related data.

Findings and Discussions

Ghana's economy relies largely on her primary and tertiary sectors. A greater majority of the people of Ghana are directly or indirectly employed in agriculture, mining, lumbering or the tourism sector. The high dependence on primary production has had a toll on the environment. The Ashanti region reflects the varied environmental problems in the country. The following observations depict the vulnerability of the region's environment and the need to use endogenous environmental management tools to enhance currently used conservation methods.

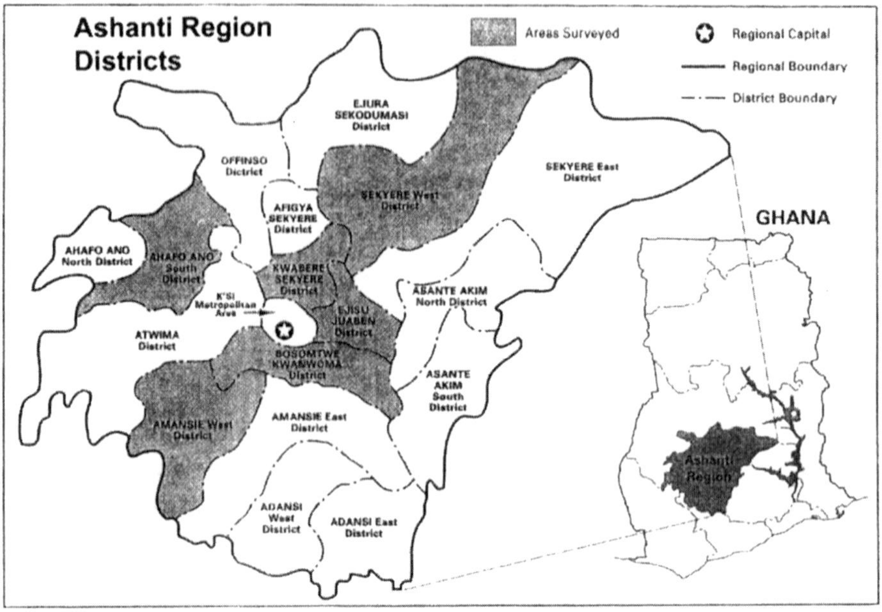

Figure 12.1 The Study Area

Biophysical Profile

The climate of the Ashanti region is basically tropical. The minimum monthly temperature ranges between 26°and 30°C. Maximum temperatures occur between March and April and ranges between 30°C and 34°C. The region experiences two rainy seasons. The peak rainy season occurs between late March and July. A minor rainy season occurs between September and November. The mean total monthly rainfall ranges between 120mm in the northern part of the region and 180mm in the south. The region's rainfall pattern can be described as erratic and unreliable. The dry season lasts from December to February. Fluctuations in rainfall and prolonged dry spells create problems that impede farming activities and crop yields.

The region lies almost entirely in the forest zone. Generally, two main vegetation types are recognized in the zone. The northern part of the region falls within a transitional or dry semi-deciduous vegetation are, while the southern part is a mostly moist semi-deciduous vegetation zone. The dry semi-deciduous zone consists of tall grass interspersed with short, fire-resistant trees. The original forest cover has been degraded into secondary forest as a result of the impact of human activities. In response to the fragile ecosystem, more than 50 official forest reserves have been established in the area since 1925. Ironically, these forest reserves have failed to protect watersheds and endangered species encroached on by human activities such as the felling of trees, the clearing of land for farms, and the grazing of livestock. These activities have caused changes in the structure and composition of the region's vegetation.

The region is drained by big rivers like Anum, Pra, Offin, and Afram, which provide excellent sites for dam construction in the future to generate hydroelectric power. The only natural lake in Ghana, Lake Bosumtwi, is found in the region. Lying just 28 km from the regional capital, Kumasi, the lake occupies approximately 48km^2.

Environmental problems identified in the region include deforestation, soil erosion, land degradation, agrochemical and water and air pollution. Deforestation is the most common form of environmental degradation in the region and is the result of large-scale mining and logging. The most affected areas include the Onuem Beposo Reserve, Dampia Range and Supuma shelterbelt, all in the Bekwai Traditional Area. Soil erosion is also common and pronounced at Bompata, Kwaso, Beposo, and Tetrefu. In fact, at Bompata, gullies up to 11 feet (four meters) were observed.

Agrochemicals used to boost agricultural productivity have had unintended adverse consequences. In vegetable and cereal producing areas such as Ejura, Akomadan, Afrancho, Sekodumase, Sabronum, Akomadan, and Kwanwoma where agrochemicals are increasingly used by farmers, birth defects, sudden deaths and cancer cases have increased. In addition, water pollution is increasing tremendously as a result of a combination of factors including inadequate human and other waste disposal facilities. As a result, most streams have been turned into places of convenience, where people wash clothes, bath, or dump wastes. In urban centers such as Kumasi, Mampong, Kumawu, and Obuasi, untreated industrial and mining wastes are dumped in Subin, Oda, Kwabrafoso and Pompora rivers. Air pollution in the region is localized in the industrial and mining areas such as Atonsu, Kumasi, Obuasi, and Konongo. Air pollution emanates from industrial plants and automobile exhausts. In Obuasi, as a result of a roasting operation of the Ashanti Goldfields Mining Corporation, huge plumes of arsenic oxide and sulfur oxide incessantly pour out of a mine chimney into the surrounding countryside. Consequently, arsenic concentration in cooked food in Obuasi is high.

Social Profile

The population of Ashanti region is fairly diverse in ethnicity but the most dominant group is the Akan. By current estimates, the population of the region is approximately 3,130,394 and the average density is 86 persons per square km. Rural population forms 67.5 percent of the total population in the region. High population growth rate, reduced land productivity and economic prospects in the rural areas have resulted in a high incidence of urbanization in the region.

Indigenous institutions and belief systems are still active in the region. These include economic and socio-political institutions such as an extended kinship system, land tenure, norms or taboos, judicial and chieftaincy systems. The region is divided into 21 traditional councils headed by traditional chiefs. The Asantehene is the overall traditional head. He has his seat in the regional capital, Kumasi, and rules the region through paramount chiefs and sub-chiefs. He occupies a Golden Stool, which is believed to be a medium that contains the souls of all Ashantis. The chieftaincy institution is enshrined in the country's constitution, and chiefs continue to play a key role in the implementation of government programs at the local level.

Economic Profile

Agriculture is the dominant primary economic activity in the region and employs about 90 percent of the rural population. Major agricultural activities in the region include cash cropping, food cropping, and livestock. Cash crops include cocoa, coffee, cola, oil palm, avocado and citrus. The non-traditional cash crops include ginger, fiber and sugarcane. Food crops include maize, cassava, rice, yam, cocoyam and plantain. Livestock include poultry, pigs, cattle, sheep and goats.

Small-scale entrepreneurs and indigenous economic activities dominate the industrial sector of the region. Small-scale industries are scattered all over the region and they include:

(a) brick and tile manufacturing;
(b) pottery and ceramics;
(c) local gin or 'akpeteshie' distilling;
(d) palm oil extraction; and
(e) agricultural processing industries such as soap and beverage manufacturing

The region is also rich in precious and industrial minerals such as gold, bauxite, and manganese. Gold is mined in large quantities at Obuasi and Konongo, sand and stone are mined at Buoho, Ntonso, Asoromaso and Bekwai. High quality clay for beads, brick and pottery is mined in large quantities at Afari and Asaman in the Atwima district. In addition, the region has a great tourism potential and it is famous for its cultural pomp and pageantry. Tourist attractions include the Manhyia Palace (seat of the Asantehene), National Culture and Craft Center, Atiwa Rock Formations, Traditional Fetish Shrines, Lake Bosumtwi, Owabi Wildlife Sanctuary, and the Bomfobiri Waterfalls near Kumawu.

Indigenous Beliefs and Resource Management

Like other countries in sub-Saharan Africa, Ghana's environmental problems are multifarious but the greatest concern is the effects of deforestation and bush fires on rainfall patterns, water resources, soil erosion and desertification. The onslaught of desertification through over-cultivation, forest clearing, and overgrazing has been worsened by extreme changes in the climate of West Africa. Vegetation has become so impoverished that it is difficult for forests to recuperate even with the onset of rains (Dankelmann and Davidson 1987). The degradation of the environment constitutes a serious threat to the region's productive base, food sufficiency and sustainability. Yet all observations seem to indicate that official response and strategies for dealing with these problems have been very ineffective (Nsiah-Gyabaah 1994). What is even more serious is the lack of reliable official environmental information and data for planning purposes. Indigenous knowledge could be useful in this regard. Indigenous peoples in traditional Ghanaian societies have long lived off the land successfully using several time-tested strategies for sustainable utilization of resources. Their strategies are based on traditional beliefs, norms, taboos and knowledge coupled with experience. Some of these strategies are discussed below.

Ancestral Veneration

Belief in the spirits of the dead and in their influence over activities of the living was widely shared among respondents. Ancestors are the departed relatives who not only led exemplary lives on earth but fulfilled other criteria. The criteria include attainment of adulthood, moral uprightness, successful life, died at an old age, and of a natural cause. Family members who departed tragically or through suicide, or 'unclean' diseases such as leprosy or acquired immune deficiency syndrome (AIDS), do not qualify to become ancestors. The general belief among respondents is that such a death is the result of a person's hidden crime against humanity or his/her wanton destruction of natural resources. If a living person is not good, their ghost cannot be good. But it is only a good 'ghost' that can bless the living.

Ancestors receive constant attention and veneration. There is a general belief that, having joined the spiritual world, the ancestors are in a position to influence life on earth for better or for worse. They can punish a person who violates traditionally sanctioned mores, destroys the environment, or indulges in immoral conduct. Thus, ancestral veneration is a powerful source of social control by which the conduct of individuals is regulated. This belief serves as a deterrent against aberrant behaviour among the villagers. Burial and ritual sites are believed to be the abode of ancestors and are kept as sacred groves. Resource exploitation activities such as farming, hunting, and tree cutting are prohibited in these places until certain rituals are performed. It is therefore not surprising that sacred groves harbour economically and socially important ecological species.

Belief in Totem

The term *totem* comes from a North American Indian language, and is widely used to refer to objects of the animal and vegetation kingdoms which are held to be in a special relationship with a particular group of people, or with individuals in a society (Beattie 1964). It comes from the Ojibwa American Indian word *ototeman*, meaning "a relative of mine" (Ember and Ember 1990). The Ashanti society can be divided into eight clans and each is associated with a totem, which has some special significance to the group. The clans include Ekuona, Asona, Asenee, Bretuo, and Asakyiri. The totem of the Asakyiri is the vulture or eagle, each of which signifies strength; the Asona has the fox, elephant and crow as its totems, and they stand for wisdom and cunningness; the Bretuo has the leopard as their totem, and this signifies aggressiveness; the Ekuona has the buffalo which means conscientiousness; and the Asenee clan has the bat, which implies diplomacy.

Members of a clan would generally shudder at the idea of killing, harming, or eating their totem. The respect that a group shows its totemic species is believed to be reciprocal. For instance, the elephant would not hurt members of the Asona clan. If it does, the interpretation is that the member might have offended the totem in some way. Thus, either consciously or unconsciously, totemic beliefs contribute to the conservation of biodiversity in the region.

Divinities and Spirits

Another belief that has contributed significantly to biodiversity conservation in the region is the belief that divinities and spirits or lesser gods were created by the Supreme God to perform special functions on earth. Whereas the Supreme God lives in cosmic space (sky), the lesser gods or divinities have their places of abode on earth and are believed to dwell in such natural resources as rivers, lakes, seas, rocks, trees, hills, and animals. Not surprisingly, the exploitation of these natural resources is regulated by social norms and taboos. The Earth and large bodies of water are regarded as sacred. For instance, the Lake Bosumtwi is considered sacred among inhabitants of the surrounding settlements, and this prevents it from being polluted with waste. The lake contains a variety of endemic cichlid fishes that provide a source of protein for the surrounding villages. Tradition forbids the use of motorized boats on the lake. Instead, the fishermen sit on flat boards, rafts, or pieces of wood when fishing (Figure 12.2). The fishermen propel these wooden planks on the lake by paddling with their hands or with calabashes cupped in their hands. Formed by a meteor, the lake has a diameter of ten kilometers and a maximum depth of 86 m in the center. The lake is surrounded by hills up to 400 m high, which are covered in lush vegetation, including cocoa and cassava plants. About 30 small villages dot the 30 km perimeter of the lake.

Customary Land Tenure System

The fundamental principle of traditional land tenure in the region is based on communal ownership. Under this system, land is held corporately by a social group formed on the basis of kinship or a network of relationship established by blood or marriage. Land is said to belong to a vast family of whom many are dead, a few are living and countless hosts are still unborn (Ollenu 1962). The ultimate land titleholder is a traditional chief who functions as a trustee on behalf of the whole community. The general functions of the chief are to:

- (a) hold land in trust for the whole community and future generations;
- (b) settle land disputes arising in the community;
- (c) pouring of libation and the pacification of the land when sacrilege has been committed;
- (d) making arrangements for annual sacrifices to ensure peace and the prosperity of the community; and
- (e) taking appropriate actions against trespassers and those who abuse the land assigned to them.

The chiefs are helped by a council of elders in the administration of the land. Families and individuals from the landholding groups hold customary freehold interests or common rights in land. A stranger who wishes to acquire land must first seek permission from a chief. If permission is granted, the stranger may contact any landholder or a family head for land as a 'gift' or on contractual basis. The stranger's interest is potentially secure unless he 'abuses' the land, denies or subverts the ultimate authority of the land. With the exception of forest reserves, sacred groves and fallow

Figure 12.2 Lake Bosumtwi, Ghana. Fishermen sit on flat boards, rafts, and pieces of wood when fishing

lands, the following communal rights are exercised on undeveloped and unoccupied lands: (a) livestock grazing on any pasture; (b) fishing in ponds, rivers and springs; (c) hunting; and (d) farming. Among conservation techniques, communities have created sacred groves and reserved headwaters, river courses, and old cemeteries. These areas are said to be the abodes of ancestral spirits and must not be disturbed by the living, and thus rarely polluted or degraded.

Conclusion

The ability to use resources sustainably stems from a combination of two factors (Berkes 1988): (a) the possession of appropriate knowledge and methods or technology to exploit resources; and (b) a philosophy and environmental ethic that keep exploitive abilities in check, and provides ground rules by which the relation among humans and animals are regulated. Thus, no matter how much Western science has to offer, the knowledge in greatest demand in environmental stewardship is that which reconnects human beings to the biosphere and its bioregions, incorporating respect and implicit socio-cultural, moral, and spiritual expressions (Tyler 1993; Appiah-Opoku and Mulamoottil 1997). In this regard, the fundamental attributes of indigenous knowledge and belief systems in Ashanti appear to support the principles of sustainable development and ecological preservation. Yet, as discussed earlier, the region has serious natural resource depletion and environmental problems. This is because the indigenous knowledge and self-regulating systems that existed in the past have been neglected by the current generation. One of the key reasons is the rapid and continuing loss of indigenous knowledge, in part due partly to the spread of Christianity and Islamic principles. In communities where Islam or Christianity has taken a stronghold, the worship of nature is discouraged and traditional beliefs are lost. Anderson (1996: 20) offers a vivid description of this picture:

> in urban centers like Accra, the people have lost their traditional beliefs. They no longer have the same sense of community as those in remote areas, and are often preoccupied with making money

Another reason is the high rate of population growth in the region. With population pressure and a high demand for more land, customary landholding systems have been assaulted with disastrous environmental consequences. This has resulted in frequent land disputes and government intervention in the land market and litigation. Through various statutory and legislative powers such as the Administration of Land Act of 1962 and the Public Conveyance Act of 1965, the government of Ghana has vested in itself vast tracts of land for various purposes. These include plantations, forests and game and wildlife reserves which seek to exclude local communities from enjoying their hitherto communal landholding rights and traditional resource conservation practices. Unfortunately with inadequate, poorly staffed, and weak management, the government is unable to protect these lands (Kasanga 1994). Also, the global consumer culture and commercialization of subsistence economies in rural Ghana have contributed to the breakdown of indigenous knowledge and self-management systems. Incentives to create surplus breaks down the self-limiting principle of indigenous knowledge and belief systems (Berkes 1988).

Notwithstanding these limitations, indigenous knowledge seems to have survived in indigenous communities where it still serves as the foundation of productive initiatives of indigenous people. Although indigenous knowledge systems have suffered and continue to suffer erosion, they are not necessarily outdated (Howes 1980; Adugna 1996; Appiah-Opoku 1997). This is partly because cultures do advance on the basis of new experiences (Banuri and Apffel-Marglin 1993). Thus, far from being an anachronism in today's world, indigenous knowledge systems have much to offer contemporary policy makers searching for a bottom-up approach to sustainable natural resource and environmental management in Africa in the 21st century.

Acknowledgement

The author wishes to acknowledge financial support by the International Development Research Center (IDRC) in Ottawa, Canada, for the field research in Ghana on which this paper is based.

Notes

1 Bourque et al. *A Canadian Led International Program on Traditional Knowledge*, (Unpublished manuscript. UNESCO/Canada Man and Biosphere Program) 1992.

References

Adugna, G. (1996). "Dynamics of knowledge systems versus sustainable development." *Indigenous Knowledge and Development Monitor* 4(2): 31–32.

Anderson, T. (1996). "Ghana: The nightmare lagoons." *International Development Research Center report*, Ottawa, Canada, January.

Appiah-Opoku, S. (1999). "Indigenous economic institutions and ecological knowledge: A Ghanaian case study." *The Environmentalist*. Vol. 19, No. 3, pp. 217–227.

Appiah-Opoku, S. (1997). *Indigenous Institutions: A Resource for Environmental Impact Assessment in Ghana*. Unpublished PhD Thesis, SURP, University of Waterloo, Waterloo, Ontario

Appiah-Opoku, S., and Mulamoottil, G. (1997). "Indigenous institutions and environmental assessment: The case of Ghana." *Environmental Management*. 21(2):159–171.

Banuri, T. and Apffel-Marglin, F. (1993). *Who will Save the Forest? Knowledge, Powerr and Environmental Destruction*. London: Zed Books.

Beattie, J. (1964). *Other Cultures, Aims, Methods of Achievements of Social Anthropology*. London: Oxford Press.

Berkes, F. (1988). "The Intrinsic Difficulty of Predicting Impacts: Lessons from the James Bay Hydro Project," *Environmental Impact Assessment Review* 8:201-250.

Berkes, F. (1993). "Traditional Ecological Knowledge in Perspective." In Inglis, J.T. (ed.) *Traditional ecological Knowledge: Concepts and Cases*. Ottawa, Ontario: IDRC.

Berlin, B. 1973. Folk systematics in relation to biological classification and nomenclature. *Annual Review of Ecology and Systematics*, 4, 259-271.

Brokensha, D.W., Warren, D.M and Warner, C. (1980). *Indigenous Knowledge Systems and Development*. Lanham, MD: University Press of America, Inc.

Bulmer, R. (1970). Which came first, the chicken or the egghead? In Pouillon, J. and Maranda, P. (eds.), Échanges et communications. Vol. II. Mouton and Co., The Hague, Netherlands. pp. 1069-1091.

Bulmer, M. (1977). *Sociological Research Methods*. London: Macmillan Press

Chambers, R. (1983). *Rural development: Putting the Last First*. London, UK: Longman.

Dankelman, I. and Davidson, J. (1987). *Women and Environment in the Third World: Alliance for Future*. London: Earthscan Publications Ltd.

Ember, C. R., and M. Ember. (1990). *Cultural anthropology*. Englewood Cliffs, NJ: Prentice-Hall.

Howes, M. (1980). "The use of indigenous technical knowledge in development." In *Indigenous knowledge systems and development*. eds. D.W. Brokensha, D.M. Warren, and C. Warner, 230–45. Lanham, MD: University Press of America, Inc.

Hunn, E. (1975). *Cognitive processes in folk-ornithology: the identification of gulls. Language-Behaviour* Research Laboratory, University of California, Berkeley, CA, USA. Working Paper No. 42,73 pp

Kasanga, K.R. (1994)."Land Tenure and the Development Dialogue: The Myth Concerning Communal Land Holding in Ghana," Occasional Paper 19, Department of Land Economy, University of Cambridge, UK: Ganta Editions.

Knudston, P. and Suzuki, D. (1992). *Wisdom of the elders*. Toronto, Canada: Stoddart Publishing Company.

Nakashima, D.J. (1990). *Application of Native Knowledge in EIA: Inuit, eiders and Hudson Bay oil*. Hull, Quebec: Canadian Environmental Assessment Research Council.

Nsiah-Gyabaah, K. (1994). *Environmental Degradation and Desertification in Ghana*. Brookfield, VT: Ashgate Publishing Company.

Ollenu, N. A. (1962). *Principles of Customary Land Law in Ghana*. London, UK: Sweetand Maxwell.

Rappaport, R. (1968). *Pigs for the Ancestors*. New Haven, CT: Yale University Press.

Richards, P. (1985). *Indigenous Agricultural Revolution: Ecology and Food Production in Africa*. Boulder, CO: Westview Press.

Rondinelli, D.A. (1983). *Development Projects as Policy Experiments: An Adaptive Approach to development administration*. London: Methuen.

Tyler, M.E. (1993). "Spiritual Stewardship in Aboriginal Resource Management Systems." *Environments*. 22(1): 1–8.

Wamalwa, B.T. (1991). "Indigenous Knowledge and Ecological Knowledge." In Juma, C. and A. Kiriro (eds.) *Gaining Ground: Institutional Innovations in Land Use Management in Kenya*. Nairobi, Kenya: Acts Press, African Center for Technology Studies.

Wolfe, J. (1992). *Indigenous and Western Knowledge and Resource Management System*. A Report Based on Past and Continuing Research of the Faculty and Graduate Students, University School Rural Planning and Development, University of Guelph, Ontario.

Chapter 13

Stealing from the Poor: Securing Integrity in African Public Service in the 21st Century

Gerald Acquaah-Gaisie

Introduction

Among the litany of ills that has been identified as hampering Africa's development and which portend to derail the continent's development in the 21st century is the canker of corruption (Ayitteh 1993; Mbaku 1998; Njoku 1998; Hope and Chikulo 2000). Corruption connotes decay, immorality, or impairment of integrity or virtue. In this chapter, it denotes the abuse of power (e.g., in politics, the corporate sphere and public service) to gain personal advantage, often in the form of financial or other material resources. It may consist of reciprocal favors. The culprits exploit their offices to, and/or, acquire advantages to which they are not entitled (Theobold 1990; Le Vine 1975; Huntington 1989). Given the opportunity and the ease of concealment, many people would be tempted to engage in corrupt activities. One antidote is a criminal law that detects corruption and orders restitution. Other antidotes are a fearless press, a vigilant democracy and savvy electorate.

Ayittey comments that there was colonial exploitation in the past, but today the main exploiters and oppressors of African peasants are African elites. African officials, public and private, extort commissions on foreign loan contracts and deposit them in overseas banks. The people who are supposed to defend and promote the peasants' interests have been responsible for the institutionalized looting and capital flight that have plagued the African economy. An estimated $20 billion, more than Africa receives in foreign aid, is lost annually (Ayitteh 1993; *Africa Insider* 1994).

Corruption in Africa

Corruption by African political elites has permeated the whole continent to the extent that no region is immune, as the examples presented in this session show. In Kenya, East Africa, critics of the Moi government said that many officials had the biggest accounts in foreign banks and that there is more money from Kenyans in foreign banks than the entire Kenyan foreign debt, which is about $8 billion (*The Washington Times* 3

August 1995: A18). Corruption emerged soon after independence and got worse. "The first President of independent Kenya, Jomo Kenyatta, and his family amassed a large fortune in land, precious gems, ivory and casinos during his rule from 1963 to 1978 (*New York Times* 21 October 1991: A9). After Daniel Arap Moi took over, corruption became institutionalized. Koigi wa Wamwere, a former MP, who was detained for three years (1975–1978) and fled to Norway in 1986, said:

> When a former chairman of the National Bank of Kenya took over 300 million shillings from the Bank, that was robbery, not incompetent management. When the Kenya Chemical and Food Corporation in Kisumu cost 1.3 billion shillings instead of 540 million shillings and then hired MPs to defend it in parliament in return for personal rewards that was theft, not incompetent management. (*Weekly Review* 19 February 1982)

> When in March 1982 Joseph Kamere, an attorney general, and Titus Mbathi, a minister for labor, received three million and one million shillings respectively to cover up illegal foreign repatriation by the bank of Baroda, that was corruption. When government ministries engaged in the employment of 85,397 bogus employees that allowed government officers to receive from the government nearly 85,397,000 shillings every month in the form of fake salaries, the creation of such a hole in government coffers was corruption. (*Weekly Review* 26 April 1985)

> Nicholas Biwott, a member of Moi's Kalenjin tribe and considered to be President Moi's closest political confidant, was paid an official salary of Ksh 21,033 but was worth "hundreds of millions of dollars, chiefly in offshore holdings." (*New York Times* 21 October 1991: A9)

In neighboring Tanzania, which was seen as a transparent less corrupt country during the presidency of Julius Nyerere, ordinary citizens say they have been let down by the leadership. Even essential services such as education, hospitals, and police are up to their necks in corrupt practices. People who use government hospitals expect to have to bribe doctors and nurses before they can be treated (*The New African* April 1990: 16).

The situation is no better in North Africa. Egypt has $50 billion in private savings stashed abroad. Customers fight over Mercedes sports cars that sell for $400,000. This country of 58 million people has a foreign debt of $35 billion, nearly equal to its Gross Domestic Product. A typical monthly wage is $50, and rubbish is collected by small dirty children in rickety donkey-carts (*The Economist* 18 January 1992: 42). In Libya mismanagement and corruption have so eroded the country's economic base that the country sometimes fails to pay its foreign bills on time and some government employees go unpaid for months (*Washington Post* 15 February 1992: A23).

A case from Mali also illustrates the extent of corrution in West Africa. The former head of state, Moussa Traore, looted the country to amass a personal fortune worth over $2 billion—an amount equal to the size of Mali's foreign debt (Ziegler 1992, cited in *West Africa* 4–10 May 1992: 746). Even countries whose leaders embarked on massive anti-corruption campaigns have not done better. Declaring corruption as the scourge of Ghanaian society, the military government of Ghana embarked on a crusade against corruption in 1982. After eight years of imposing stiff sentences and executing the guilty by firing squad, the government learned that it could not even clean up its own house. Top government officials fraudulently purchased equipment (*West Africa* 4–10 December 1989: 2036), demanded and collected bribes (*West Africa* 9–15 April 1990: 598) and embezzled government funds (*West Africa* 9–15 April 1990: 598). A number of politicians and officials in the Rawlings regime have been tried or investigated for corruption-related charges: these investigations are exposing some serious corrupt practices that went on during Rawlings' 18-year rule from 1982–2000. In neighboring Togo, Mba Kabassema, Minister of Trade and Transport in Eyadema's government in 1977, alleged that Eyadema pillaged the country's resources with the connivance of a Moroccan adviser, Maurice Assor. Another alleged that Eyadema's personal fortune was 800 billion CFA francs ($2.8 billion) most of which has been put into foreign banks. He said that the Nangbeto dam project which was costed at CFA eight billion, was then increased to CFA 48 billion, so that funds could be "diverted" into the wrong pockets. Eyadema spent CFA 50 billion to build a chateau at Pya, his hometown in northern Togo (*The New African* October 1991: 12).

In the Côte d'Ivoire, Professor Laurent Gbagbo, a critic of the late President Houphouet Boigny who spent seven years in exile, alleged that corruption was rife: "We are the country with the most millionaires, which means we have the most thieves. The more Houphouet ages, the more his collaborators sense an end to the regime, and the more they steal. "The central bank calculates that some CFA 130 billion [or $456 million] are spirited out of the country illegally each year (*Africa Report* May–June, 1990: 14). Houphouet-Boigny was reputed to have held a vast personal fortune amounting to 6 billion Euros (*Guardian Weekly* (London) 17 June 1990: 9). In 1983 he said, "I do have assets abroad. But they are not assets belonging to Côte d'Ivoire. What sensible man does not keep his assets in Switzerland, the whole world's bank? I would be crazy to sacrifice my children's future in this crazy country without thinking of their future (La Croix, Paris, 13 March 1990).

Examples from Nigeria, Africa's most populous and oil rich-country, are quite depressing. Anthony Ebeh described the conception of public office in the country. According to Ebeh, a major cause of the problems in Nigeria is that

> our leaders have a primitive concept of public office. Public office in civilized societies, including some non-Western nations, is seen as a way to provide selfless service to one's nation. It is a way to give back to one's country. Public office is cherished and respected. Public office holders are generally accountable to the people they serve. However, in the Nigerian context, public office is seen as a huge opportunity to enrich self and kindred. This explains why Nigeria is now one of the poorest nations in the world. In Nigeria, public office is seen as a means to acquire wealth and personal aggrandizement. By all standards, this concept of public office is primitive. (*African News Weekly* 27 May 1994: 7)

After the 1975 coup that toppled the regime of General Yakubu Gowon, a commission of inquiry found ten of the twelve state governors guilty of corruption and the misuse of funds totaling over 16 million *naira*. But those amounts were small in comparison with the levels of corruption during Nigeria's oil boom in the 1970s, when political elites grabbed large monies right, left and center and displayed sickening affluence. In the late 1970s favourable market conditions yielded oil revenues at a level of $29 billion a year. From 1979 through 1983, scandals involving billions of dollars dominated the headlines. These included: the illicit auction of much of the $2,500 million annual allocation of import licenses; the arrest of several top officials of the Federal Capital Development Authority in Abuja over an alleged $20 million fraud; and the revelation by a federal minister that Nigeria was losing $50 million a month to ghost workers and other forms of payroll fraud. The Babangida regime did not account for the $10 billion in oil windfall occasioned by the Gulf War in January 1991. When the Lagos correspondent of the *Financial Times*, William Keeling, reported a misuse of this bonanza in August 1991, he was promptly deported from Nigeria with less than 24 hours notice. "For all the promises of probity, the military elite [has been] as corrupt as any regime that preceded it, taking kickbacks on contracts and diverting government funds."

According to *The Washington Post*, "corruption robs Nigeria's economy of an estimated $2 billion to $3 billion each year" (21 July 1992, p. A16). This allegation was confirmed by a report presented by Pius Okigbo, chairman of the panel on The Reform and Reorganization of the Central Bank of Nigeria, to General Sani Abacha on 27 September 1994. It noted:

> Nigeria's military rulers squandered more than $12 billion of oil revenue without proper accounting between 1988 and June 1994. The money had been placed in special accounts set up in 1988 for special projects and to receive a windfall of oil revenue from the Gulf War. But Pius Okigbo called the handling of the accounts "a gross abuse of public trust." He said $21.2 billion—more than a third of the country's total foreign debt—was spent in less than six years on "what could neither be adjudged genuine high priority nor truly regenerative investment. Neither the president nor the governor of the Central Bank of Nigeria account to anyone for these massive extra-budgetary expenditures. (*African News Weekly* 14 October 1994: 3)

The late dictator General Abacha, who promised to clean Nigeria of corruption, turned out to be the most corrupt leader in the country's history. His name and those of his sons and associates have featured prominently in the international press. It is alleged that he stole some $4 billion, much of it directly from the central bank, as well as taking bribes from foreign contractors, some from the UK.

Further examples of corruption on the continent could be cited from Central Africa. In Angola, the bulk of the money bypasses the budget, disappearing straight into the hands of the presidency. Angolans, who have long suspected something of the kind, call the nexus of the presidency, the Central Bank and Sonangol (the state oil company), the Bermuda Triangle: the place where money vanishes without a trace (*The Economist*, 15 January, 2000: p.48). Much of the money is used to finance a war that has devastated the country, and to finance the lifestyles of the super-rich "oiligarchy" with whom the president has surrounded himself. When the cash runs out, the powers-that-be take out short-term, high-interest loans, guaranteed against future oil production. Thus the entire profits from Angola's oil production for the next three years are said to have already been spent (*The Economist* 15 January, 2000: 48).

In Zambia President Kenneth Kaunda dismissed as "a big lie" allegations that he had transferred $6 billion in state funds to personal bank accounts abroad (*New York*

Times 15 August 1990: A6). Civil servants who had retired ten years earlier from Zambia's Ministry of Power, Transport and Communications were found to be drawing their salaries on a regular basis. "A snap survey carried out on various public service departments found that three percent of the names on the government payroll were counterfeit . . . It was estimated that the government was losing 500 million *kwachas* ($12.5 million) a year in fraud of this kind (*New African* December 1991: 33).

Zaire's President Mobutu bragged in a 1984 CBS *60 Minutes* profile that he was the second richest man in the world with more than $8 billion in a numbered personal account at a Swiss bank. Mobutu's fortune had been estimated to be between $3 billion and $10 billion. President Mobutu's fortune approached $5,000 million in a Swiss Bank account, a fortune larger than Zaire's $4,400 million foreign debt. The President's official salary alone amounted to 17 percent of the annual budget, while the country's foreign debt amounted to 70 percent of the GNP (*West Africa* 30 November 1981: 2881). Together with his family and friends, Mobutu owned more than 26 extensive properties in Belgium, France and elsewhere. They included a 15-acre beach resort, a plantation of orchards and a huge vineyard in Portugal, a 32-room Villa les Miguettes in Savigny, east of Lausanne in Switzerland, and a 16th-century castle in Spain. Mobutu also owned property in Brazil, Senegal, Morocco and Ivory Coast. In 1981 Mobutu's budgetary allocation was nearly trebled to 1.48 billion BF. The 1981 budget had a section for the president's personal expenses amounting to another 600 million BF. The entire province of Shaba had a budgetary allocation of 535 million BF for the year. By 1989 Mobutu was receiving almost $100 million to spend as he wished. "This is more than the Government spent on education, health and all other social services combined (*New Internationalist* June 1990: 18).

When US Rep. Mervyn Dymally asked Mobutu about his personal wealth, he responded, "Yes, I have a fair amount of money. However, I would estimate it to total less than $50 million. What is that after twenty-two years as head of state of such a big country?" (*World Development Forum* No. 9, 1988: 3). After visiting Kinshasa in April 1990, a US congressional delegation led by Rep. David R. Obey requested that the US suspend aid to Zaire because President Mobutu Sese Seko was corrupt and did not respect human rights. According to Insight, Obey, a member of the House Appropriations Committee, said, "No bill bearing my name will include any money destined for that idiot (*Insight* 14 May, 1990: 37). Nevertheless the Bush administration allocated $53 million for Zaire in 1991.

It is not only politicians who are guilty of corruption. High-ranking officials in the judiciary, civil service, state and corporate institutions also engage in corruption. A civil servant whose signature is needed to process a document may delay until the client pays a bribe. A businessman seeking a bank loan may have to bribe the manager; an institution manager may demand kickbacks in a tendering process. Often the person who pays most wins the contract, little consideration being given to competence: people who know next to nothing about engineering may win contracts for construction projects and then sell the contracts to professionals for substantial gain; a police officer may extort money from drivers; military people may take bribes from political aspirants to stage a coup d'tat and hand political power to those who paid. The corruption seeps down to very junior personnel: the office messenger may delay until a client needing to see the boss has paid money before the client is let into the boss's office. Ostentation often accompanies corruption by these elites. They throw extravagant parties, own fleets of expensive vehicles, and houses. Many of those enjoying ostentatious lifestyles have access to monies beyond their official incomes. Yet the community, even the law enforcement agencies, turns a blind eye. People engaging in such lifestyles tend to command wide respect; few question the source of their wealth. The practice is widespread and institutionalized and has gone on for decades.

How do they Steal the Wealth?

How can such large sums of money be taken into secret overseas bank accounts? Travelers may often carry most funds that leave Africa. Sometimes cash is carried overseas in suitcases for money laundering. Abacha's sons are said to have carried several suitcases full of cash through Heathrow Airport. "They took out the money in sacks stuffed with millions, then flew the notes in suitcases to London where they passed money from one bank to another and out to Switzerland like rugby players working a spectacular try (*Evening Standard* 20 October 2000: 4). Another principal method of siphoning funds out of Africa is through money laundering. Money laundering is the process whereby proceeds of crime are run through the financial system to disguise their illegal origins and make them appear to be legitimate funds. Even though money laundering is often associated with organized crime, it can be linked to any crime that generates significant proceeds, such as extortion, drug trafficking, arms smuggling, white-collar crime, and for our current purposes, corruption by political and other elites.

There are three basic steps to money laundering: placement, layering and integration. The first is a physical disposal of cash. The cash is deposited in domestic banks or other formal or informal financial institutions, or shipped across borders for deposit in foreign financial institutions, or used to buy high-value goods, such as artwork, airplanes, and precious metals and stones that are then resold for payment by check or bank transfer. Secondly, layering—complex layers of financial transactions to separate the illicit proceeds from their source and disguise the audit trail, e.g., wire transfer of deposited cash, the conversion of deposited cash into monetary instruments such as bonds, stocks, and traveler's checks, resale of high-value goods and monetary instruments, and investment in real estate and legitimate businesses, particularly in the leisure and tourism industries. Offshore havens are a common tool in layering. Shell companies, whose directors often are local attorneys acting as nominees, obscure the beneficial owners through restrictive bank secrecy laws and attorney-client privilege. Thirdly, integrate the wealth to make it appear legitimate, using front companies to "lend" the proceeds back to the owner or using funds on deposit in foreign financial institutions as security for domestic loans; or over-invoicing or producing false invoices for goods sold, or supposedly sold, across borders.

Why do they Steal so Much Money?

Political elites are relatively highly paid (compared with their compatriots), and fare well in social and economic terms. They have at their disposal well-appointed official residences, guards, vehicles, chauffeurs and domestic servants. Political leaders need not incur much personal expenditure. And they usually get handsome retirement packages. So why steal?

(a) Sheer greed and ostentation? Many Third World politicians see office as a means to riches; they put up mansions and acquire luxury cars shortly after gaining office; they throw lavish parties; and they see extravagant lifestyles as their norm. Such insensitive opulence in the midst of poverty cries out for reform.

(b) A little bit extra is always good? Payments from entrepreneurs seeking state favors represent an important source of extra-legal income for civil servants. State regulatory programs can place a significant burden on business enterprises and entrepreneurship and encourage investors to seek ways to minimize these state-imposed costs. Paying bribes to civil servants has emerged as an important method to compete for rents. For profit-maximizing enterprises faced with ruinous government regulations, bureaucratic corruption can be viewed as a survival mechanism (Mbaku 1996).

(c) Family pressures? African political elites feel obliged to share the proceeds of office with kinfolk. The extended family system leads officeholders into corrupt and nepotic practices to meet these expectations (see Apter 1963; Gould and Mukendi 1989; Agbese 1999).

The extended family contribute toward a child's welfare on the understanding that the child will later reciprocate: a Ghanaian proverb states that if others nurture you while you are growing your teeth you must look after them when they lose their teeth.

(d) An African way of life? Some studies suggest that the African way of life breeds corruption. Werlin (1972) cites nepotism as a primary cause. He also mentions poverty, inadequacy of checks and balances within the bureaucracy, and the slowness, costliness, and inflexibility of bureaucracy against which corruption lubricates sluggish processes.

(e) Self-preservation? Public office lacks secure tenure: many middle and top-level manag ers feel anxiety about the future. Politicians lose office in elections or *coup d'état*, and many bureaucrats go along with them. Military regimes are unstable. Other members of the armed forces try to emulate military rulers and stage counter-coups to replace them. In stable political systems a public servant can expect to retain his or her job as long as he or she commits no indiscretion. Consequently politicians and top officials have been eager to line their pockets quickly to maintain their lifestyle.

Of course, these reasons do not justify theft. That simple crime, however, is a symptom of a perhaps deeper malaise: the leaders' want of, care for, and confidence in their people. They do not work reliably and prudently to stabilize and strengthen their local economy. They invest assets abroad rather than showing a vested interest at home; so they preside over crumbling economies.

Another question of interest here is: Why is the stealing done with such impunity? The concept of public office holder as a servant of the people has shallow roots in African countries. This view might have some source in the undue status of the chief in some African communities. While an erring chief can be punished through de-stoolment, by and large Africans respect chiefly office. In certain communities the chief is seen as the link between living members of the community and their ancestors. Among the Asantes of Ghana, for example, the Asantehene (king of the Asantes) presumably commands greater respect than the national political leader.When Westerners came into Africa, even though they were resisted on many fronts, they managed to command great respect possibly because of their greater technological advancement and also because they had the force of arms behind them while they ruled.

With independence, Ghanaians took over this political power and were accorded similar respect. And this attitude continues. Sometimes political officeholders demand deference, even aggressively. Some politicians and officials feel they have a right to lord it over others. Others use their political power and public resources to set up groups of sycophantic diehards to intimidate opponents and harass critics. They appoint family, tribesmen and other ciphers to key posts. A corollary of that is that they see the national treasury as their personal kitty. Thus the sons of Abacha, the late Nigerian Head of State, were untouchable in Nigeria, and brazenly carried suitcases full of American dollars or British pounds to the UK.

Politicians and other officials in more developed countries are not angels. There were travel reports by Australia MPs in 1998; and an Australian government minister was reprimanded by the media and the public for carrying a toy (a Paddington bear) in a diplomatic bag. There is to be a probe into travel allowance payments to 44 Upper House members of the Victoria Parliament. The system works better in politically developed countries because of well-established democratic practices: a vigilant opposition, press and electorate keep politicians on their toes. Offenders are often exposed and penalized or restitution made. Society ensures that the system works! Where governments in more efficient societies fall short they are thrown out of office by fair elections: politicians respect the verdict of the electorate. The checks and balances and other mechanisms of accountability inherent in more mature systems ensure that economic activity thrives and generates wealth that benefits the population as a whole. Third World countries should plan to attain such conditions.

Where do they Hide the Stolen Wealth?

The stolen monies are seldom kept in local banks, for that would defeat part of the purpose for which the monies are stolen. Since many African political and other elites envisage life in foreign countries, especially in Europe and America, when they leave office, they stash their monies normally in Europe, USA and many offshore financial centers like Guernsey, Jersey, Cayman Islands and Nauru. Many know that because of the manner in which they handle their countries' affairs their lives would not be secure in their countries when they no longer have the state apparatus or the trappings of office to protect them. By contrast, past Heads of State from more advanced countries spend their retirement in their own country continuing the good work.

Recent investigations by the Financial Services Authority (FSA) in the UK revealed that 15 British banks have been linked to money laundering accounts belonging to General Sani Abacha, the dictator who was President of Nigeria. A probe into the whereabouts of N34 billion of public money General Abacha is said to have embezzled before his death in 1998, has spread across the world's leading financial centers. The investigation moved from Switzerland to London last year, when it emerged that millions of pounds had been transferred from private Swiss accounts into the UK. The FSA said it had investigated anti-money laundering controls at 23 banks where accounts linked to General Abacha and the family had been identified.

Politicians are elected and officials appointed to advance political stability, prosperity and dignity. But many Third World leaders lay a nest egg in foreign countries in anticipation of their demise from office: Estrada of the Philippines was in office for only 31 months, and amassed millions of dollars. They are not up to the tasks of political office, but seek office just to milk the system.

Consequences of Corruption and Some possible Solutions

Corruption and mismanagement hurt social and economic development by denying schools, hospitals and other public services and by the loss of investor confidence, buoyant economic activity, and public morale. Miscreant officers become enemies of the people. In most countries where democracy and political accountability are not firmly entrenched, economic crime is rife and politics unstable. This has been evident in Africa with countries like Ghana and Nigeria, in South America with Brazil, Chile and Argentina, and in Asia with the Philippines and Indonesia.

According to the UN Human Development Index 2001 the least livable countries in the world in ranking order are: Sierra Leone, Niger, Burundi, Burkina Faso, Ethiopia, Mozambique, Guinea-Bissau, Chad, Central African Republic, Mali, Rwanda, Malawi, Guinea, Eritrea, Benin, Angola, Senegal, Ivory Coast, Zambia, Democratic Republic of Congo, Uganda, Tanzania, Mauritania and Sudan (http://infoplease.lycos.com/ipa/A0778562.html. Accessed 28 September 2001). Among the factors taken into consideration in determining the most and least livable countries in the world are general social and economic standards. All those countries are in Africa. By most socio-economic indicators (e.g. adult literacy rate, combined primary, secondary and tertiary gross enrolment, GDP per capita, life expectancy index, education index, human development index, human poverty index, probability at birth of not surviving to age 40, population not using improved water sources, underweight children under age five, population below income poverty line, undernourished people, children under height for age, infants with low birth weight, people living with HIV/AIDS, malaria cases, tuberculosis cases, life expectancy at birth, infant mortality rate, under-five mortality rate, probability at birth of surviving to age 65, public education expenditure, and per capita GDP), the Third World, in particular African countries, perform worst (UNDP 2001).

> Three times as many people die of preventable, curable diseases as die of AIDS [in Third World countries]. These include malaria, tuberculosis, and acute lower respiratory infections. (Silverstein 1999)

The acts of pillage described above go on in Third World countries where those socio-economic indicators are worst: starvation, preventable diseases, and feeble education. UN Secretary Kofi Annan said, "Billions of dollars of public funds continue to be stashed away by some African leaders, even while roads are crumbling, health systems have failed, school children have neither books nor desks nor teachers, and phones do not work." (Annan 2000) The responsible political and other elites seek medical help or educate their children in overseas countries, sometimes at state expense; they shamelessly rape their constituencies. Something drastic needs to be done.

What is the world community doing when scare resources are stolen by the greedy? What are effective answers to officials who seek donations for their impoverished countries only to see them stolen again? What restitution is feasible from these rich criminals? What remedies are the UN General Assembly, the Economic and Social Council, and the UNDP advancing to do justice to both aid donors and poor peoples?

The world community rallies to help the needy, and the UN human rights instruments enjoin development co-operation and aid. But aid programs driven by altruistic charity rather than by economic justice are a farce. The poor need to be saved from criminal politicians and officials; and donors deserve reliable auditing of the use of their gifts. Those who cry for help must show that their scarce resources are used lawfully and judiciously. Leaders who do not account satisfactorily must not be trusted with more resources. In the Parable of the Talents (Matthew 25:14–30), the trustee who made best use of his money was given more.

International banking institutions should continue to put a freeze on and make public any accounts held with them by Third World political leaders, their family and friends. This is being done to some extent under the "Know Your Customer" rule, which many progressive banks have adopted. This does not imply that such amounts are stolen. But such leaders will need to demonstrate the sources of those monies. Those who fail to do that will be deemed to have acquired them illicitly, and such monies should be confiscated and repatriated to the countries where these people are ruling or used to rule. The idea is not only to recover stolen money but also to bring offenders to justice. It does not help countries from which monies are stolen, or the world community, to wait till the culprits are dead before disclosing information on their dubious bank accounts. Financial institutions failing to do that would demonstrate that they are consorting with the corrupt leaders and are equally responsible for widespread suffering.

Often because stolen monies stashed in foreign banks are deposited under dubious names, when these corrupt leaders die, as they often do dramatically, the monies are lost to the countries from which they were stolen. There are inadequate details on the beneficiaries of the deceased's estate in the banking records. The monies then remain stuck within the banking systems, enriching the banking institutions and their home bases while the plundered country continues in penury.

Efforts are being made on a number of fronts to combat corruption in the Third World. Among these are conferences, domestic initiatives and international co-operative endeavors. In 1999, 11 African countries adopted 25 principles to combat corruption. Later that year, at the Ninth International Anti-Corruption Conference in Durham, South Africa, African countries agreed to incorporate the 25 key principles into their national policy frameworks. In 2002, the African Union proposed a convention that would provide a blueprint for tackling corruption. All public officials would declare their assets when they take office, government would take powers to seize bank documents where necessary, and those convicted would have their assets confiscated. Parties would extradite those charged with corruption (http://news.bbc.co.uk/1/hi/world/africa/2265387.stm. Accessed 16 July 2004).

In 1998, President Kim Dae-Jung of Korea initiated a campaign to detect and prosecute corrupt bureaucrats. In 1996 the Organization of American States adopted the Inter-American Convention against Corruption; in 1997 the General Assembly of the Organization of American States adopted the Comprehensive Plan against Corruption. There are joint efforts by international organizations like the OECD and regional institutions like the Asian Development Bank to combat corruption. There is the annual International Symposium on Economic Crimes held at Jesus College, Cambridge, and the biennial International Anti-Corruption Conference (http://www.transparency.org/iacc/pastiacc.html Accessed 17 July 2004). Other international endeavors include the following:

• *The 1990 Council of Europe Convention*

This established a common criminal policy on money laundering. It set out a common definition of money laundering and common measures for dealing with it. It lays down principles for international cooperation among the contracting parties, which may include states outside the Council of Europe. Its scope is not limited to money from drug trafficking.

• *Basle Committee statement of principles*

In 1988 the G-10s Basle Committee on Banking Supervision issued a statement of principles with which the international banks of member states are expected to comply. These principles cover identifying customers, avoiding suspicious transactions, and cooperating with law enforcement agencies. The committee noted the risk to public confidence in banks, and thus to their stability, that can arise if they inadvertently become associated with money laundering.

• *European Union directive*

In 1991 the Council of the European Communities adopted a directive on the Prevention of the Use of the Financial System for the Purpose of Money Laundering. This was issued in response to the new opportunities for money laundering opened up by the liberalization of capital movements and cross-border financial services in the European Union. Member states must outlaw money laundering; financial institutions must establish and maintain internal systems to prevent laundering, obtain the identification of customers with whom they enter into transactions of more than ECU 15,000, and keep proper records for at least five years. Financial institutions must report suspicious transactions and ensure that such reporting does not result in liability for the institution or its employees.

• *Resolution of the International Organization of Securities Commissions*

In 1992 the IOSCO adopted a report and resolution encouraging its members to take necessary steps to combat money laundering in securities and futures markets. A working group of IOSCO's Consultative Committee was set up to collect information from IOSCO members' self-regulatory organizations and exchanges on their efforts to encourage their own members to fight money laundering.

I propose the following additional measures to combat corruption:

a. The media should name and shame the thieving political and other elites.
b. Courts should punish the criminals more severely, and order full restitution.
c. We should name and ostracize banks, which facilitate these thefts.
d. We need impeachment proceedings in the countries where these crimes occur. The im peachment of Estrada in the Philippines and Wahid in Indonesia are good examples for other Third World countries to emulate.

Law enforcement agencies in more advanced countries say that even where they know of the corrupt practices they cannot do much unless the alleged offenders are convicted in their home country. But where the corrupt politicians wield absolute power, choose the judges, and control criminal justice institutions, the domestic apparatus cannot bring them to book. The intelligence bodies of the advanced countries may have dossiers on the corrupt practices of the politicians and officials. We should use such data to prosecute offenders and repatriate the monies to the victim country. We need to establish universal jurisdiction over such crimes in order to prevent the recourse to arguments of national jurisdiction.

We should confront these thieves and deal with them while they are still in office, before they die or fall in disgrace. Government and bank officials knew that General Abacha of Nigeria was stashing huge sums of money in Swiss and other bank accounts, yet little was done about it. When he died it was said that he had as much as US$8 billion dollars stashed in secret bank accounts overseas. Why did we have to wait till his death before these details were made public?

Financial institutions that hold private accounts of politicians or high-ranking officials in the Third World should periodically publish details of such accounts. This reduces privacy, but the secrecy of accounts helps people hide the stolen wealth. The publication of account details may be made one of the conditions-precedent for opening bank accounts under the "Know Your Customer Rule." Richard Pratt, director-general of the Jersey Financial Services, proposes that banks should have access to databases listing "at least" the identity of ministers and senior bureaucrats in countries with which they do business, and friends and associates of politicians in corrupt regimes (cited in Peel 2001). He stresses that "Know Your Customer" rules should be extended so that banks become familiar with the beneficiaries of company or trust clients. He proposes the vetting of individual clients; he says banks and other institutions must know the nexus of familial, political and business associates around notorious individuals; he envisages that these proposed rules would be an extension of the Wolfsberg Principles (http://www.transparency.org/pressreleases_archive/2000/wolfsberg_principles.html. Accessed 24 July 2004). Mr. Pratt calls for an international fund to which proceeds of alleged corruption are paid pending resolution of legal issues relating to the freezing and seizure of assets. Financial institutions that breach such an arrangement would commit offenses under the "Know Your Customer Rule," the Financial Services Act (UK) and the Financial Action Task Force guidelines. They would be seen as accomplices of corrupt political leaders. Countries and international bodies, which give development aid to poor countries, should make it a condition that the financial affairs of members of government and their families are made public to an international body. This institution would preferably operate under the auspices of the UN Development Program; it would be responsible for promoting transparency in Third World governments. This overrides but does not violate national sovereignty: governments are not compelled to seek financial aid. If they seek such aid from the more developed countries or international agencies like the World Bank and the International Monetary Fund, they would have to take on board that requirement. Countries that fail to meet this condition should receive no outside financial assistance.

Details of bank accounts collected by the financial institutions should be supplied to the international body for transparency in governance. This financial institution would have to check for discrepancies in the accounts.

Where inconsistencies exist, an international police organization for fighting corruption among politicians should be notified. That police force should have the power to prosecute any suspected person in any jurisdiction it deems appropriate, and to seek the help of law enforcement agencies in any part of the global community. An international convention would establish and empower such a body: this could be an extension of the UN principles on the Elimination of Corruption by Public Officials. Governments that fail to ratify such an instrument would risk being seen as corrupt or at least as bedmates of corrupt officials.

Ayittey (1993) proposes a corrective system, which he calls Organization, Incentive, Discipline, Efficiency and Accountability (O-IDEA). For accountability, in particular, freedom of expression and freedom of the press are necessary for citizens to demand an accounting of public monies appropriated by officials and for the press to expose malpractices.

1. Let us adopt principles of UN General Assembly Resolution 51/59. Third World countries can take a cue from the UN International Code of Conduct for Public Officials. Articles state 2-7) state:

2. Public officials shall ensure that they perform their duties and functions efficiently and effectively, in accordance with laws or administrative policies, and with integrity. They shall at all times seek to ensure that public resources for which they are responsible are administered in the most effective and efficient manner.

3. Public Officials shall not use their official authority for improper advancement of their own or their family's personal or financial interest. They shall not engage in any transaction, acquire any position or function, or have any financial, commercial or other comparable interest that is incompatible with their office, functions and duties or the discharge thereof.

4. Public officials, to the extent required by the official's position, shall in accordance with laws or administrative policies, declare business, commercial and financial interests, or activities undertaken for financial gain that may raise a possible conflict of interest. In situations of possible or perceived conflict

of interest between the duties and private interests of public officials, they shall comply with the measures established to reduce or eliminate such conflict of interest.

5. Public officials shall at no time improperly use public monies, property, services or information that is acquired in the performance of, or as a result of, their official duties for activities not related to their official work.

6. Public officials shall, in accord with their position and as permitted or required by law and administrative policies, comply with requirements to declare or to disclose personal assets and liabilities, as well as, if possible, those of their spouses and/or dependants.

7. Public officials shall not solicit or receive directly or indirectly any gift or other favors that may influence the exercise of their functions, performance of their duties or their judgment. (UN General Assembly Resolution 51/59 Action against Corruption and International Code of Conduct for Public Officials, Annex. Adopted on 12 December 1996).

The UN General Assembly urges:

> Member States carefully to consider the problems posed by the international aspects of corrupt practices, especially as regards international economic activities carried out by corporate entities, and to study appropriate legislative and regulatory measures to ensure the transparency and integrity of financial systems and transactions carried out by such corporate entities. (United Nations 1996).

These general principles guide legislative policy and executive operations everywhere. Some Third World countries have passed laws incorporating some of the principles and acted to minimize corrupt and other serious economic crimes. But there is often an undue gap between the law and its implementation. Third World governments may need new mechanisms to realize these basic UN principles: they can request technical assistance [from the UN] designed to improve public management systems and to enhance accountability and transparency (United Nations 1996). Third World countries must also train their bureaucrats in civil service best practices, drawing on models like the UK. They must strengthen supervisory controls in the public service, and shuffle public officers at regular intervals so that they do not stay in one post long enough to establish links that may lead to corruption. Also public officers who are found to be corrupt should be punished severely but in a utilitarian manner. Third World countries can also provide training in corporate best practices for corporate managers.

Third World countries should establish democratic accountability in all sectors, inculcating a culture that nobody is above the law and that all are penalized equally under the law. In more developed countries junior police officers have, without fear of recrimination, pulled up high-ranking officials including their own commanders and even Premiers on roads and issued them with fines for exceeding speed limits. Democratic accountability depends on a vigilant opposition, electorate, press and public to keep politicians and bureaucrats on their toes. The more watchful the people, the more accountable public officials will be. Thus Third World countries should institute measures that strengthen democratic practices.

Efficient administration incorporates social and economic reform. The *raison d'etre* of governments is to seek the welfare of the people who entrust them with running their affairs. Third World countries are rich in resources, and need to manage them well, strengthening their UN and regional links in order to reduce national military spending.

Let us strengthen financial sector supervision: an economy grows with corporate integrity. Third World countries should, among other things, strengthen the regulation of financial institutions, institute more biting sanctions for corruption such as imprisonment in addition to fines, and other heavy penalties.

Let us classify serious corruption as a crime against humanity. The Rome Statute of the International Criminal Court 1998 proscribes atrocities to humankind. Corruption by Third World political leaders and other elites holds a comparable gravity. Large-scale corruption causes the death of infants, devastation by diseases such as AIDS and malaria, denial of a decent education, and results as serious as the repercussions of armed conflict. The Statute of Rome article 7 states:

> For the purpose of this Statute, "crime against humanity" means any of the following acts when committed as part of a widespread or systematic attack directed against any civilian population, with knowledge of the attack.
> (k) Other inhumane acts of a similar character intentionally causing great suffering or serious injury to body or to mental of physical health.

Robertson states:

> It is difficult to see why [the International Criminal Court] should not simply have jurisdiction over crimes against humanity, whether committed in war, in times of internecine struggle, in periods of riot and unrest or at times of utter and seemingly blissful peace. The individuals responsible for any widespread pattern of barbarity, imposed or supported by the state, (through its politicians or police or military) or by armed organizations fighting to attain some (or more) power, should be indictable and the charges against them should not depend on technical legal characterization of the nature of the background conflict. (Robertson 1999)

Conclusion

This chapter has examined the nature of official corruption in Africa. This nefarious practice has serious economic repercussions. It depletes the coffers of communities which are otherwise rich in resources. Many suffer untold hardships including infant mortality, poor healthcare and education. The world community can minimize it. Banks and intelligence agencies usually know who is stealing and hiding monies in secret accounts, yet they seldom blow the whistle until the thieving leader is dead or no longer in power. Agencies aware of such practices should report them so that efforts can be made to recover the stolen monies before too much harm is done. Corruption needs to be tackled with similar urgency as we use to stop terrorists hiding monies in secret accounts. The effects of corruption are as devastating as those of terrorism in terms of the numbers of those who die or suffer needlessly in Third World countries from simple illnesses like malaria, malnutrition and AIDS.

Corruption can be curbed. Singapore provides a lesson worthy of emulation. As the Political and Economic Risk Consultancy notes:

> The fight against corruption began back in 1959, when Lee Kuan Yew and the People's Action Party came to power through elections. From the beginning, PAP set out to have a clean administration, and it used its position in power to progressively tighten up the laws relating to graft and to give added muscle to the official agencies set up to deal with corruption. It has never let up in this campaign and the country's leaders had the wisdom to apply the rules indiscriminately (i.e. to themselves as well as to others) and in a public manner. This government practices what it preaches, and while some have criticized it for being too straight-laced and controlling, even its critics admit it is clean. Our survey grade clearly reflects this perception. (http://www.asiarisk.com/lib10.html Accessed 16 July 2004).

This calls for statesmen and other leaders of vision and commitment who will marshal every little bit of their resources for socio-economic development in the 21st century.

References

Age. *The Melbourne*. 16 July 2004.

Apter, D.E. (1963). *Ghana in Transition*. London: Antheneum.

Agbese, P.O. (1999). "With Fingers on the Trigger: the Military as Custodian of Democracy in Nigeria." *Journal of Third World Studies*. 9 (2), 1999, pp. 220–253

African Business. December 1993:10.

Africa Insider. July 1994: 4.

Africa Report. May–June, 1990: 14.

Annan, Kofi (2000). Speech at the UN. March 14, 2000.

Ayitteh, G. (1993). *Africa Betrayed*. St. Martin's Press (NY), Macmillan (London) 1992, Chapter 10.

Economist, The. 18 January 1992. p.42.

Economist, The. 15 January 2000. p.48.

Economist, The. 15 January 2000. p.48.

Evening Standard. 20 October 2000. p.4.

Financial Times. 22 May 1992. p.6.

Gould, D.J. and Mukendi, T.B. (1989). "Bureaucratic Corruption in Africa: Causes, Consequences and Remedies." *International Journal of Public Administration*.12(3). pp. 427–457.

Guardian Weekly (London). 17 June 1990. p.9.

Hope, R.K. (2000). "Corruption and Development in Africa." In K. R Hope and B. C. Chikulo, eds. *Corruption and Development in Africa*. Houndmills, Hampshire, UK: Palgrave.

Hope, K.R and and Chikulo, B.C. (eds). *Corruption and Development in Africa*. Houndmills, Hampshire, UK: Palgrave.

http://news.bbc.co.uk/1/hi/world/africa/2265387. Accessed 16 July 2004.

http://www.worldbank.org/html/fpd/notes/48/48scott.html. Accessed 1 October 2001
http://infoplease.lycos.com/ipa/A0778562.html Accessed 28 September 2001.
http://news.bbc.co.uk/1/hi/world/africa/2265387.stm. Accessed 16 July 2004.
Huntington, Samuel P. (1989). "Modernization and Corruption." In Heidenheimer, A.J., Johnston, M., and Levine, V. (eds.) *Political Corruption: A Handbook*. New Brunswick, N.J: Transactions Books. pp.377–388.
Insight. 14 May, 1990: 37.
La Croix, Paris. 13 March 1990.
Levine, V.T . (1975). *Political Corruption: The Case Of Ghana*. Stanford, Ca: Hoover Institute)
Mbaku, John M. (ed.) (1998). *Corruption and the Crisis of Institutional Reforms in Africa*. Lewiston, NY: E. Mellen Press.
Mbaku, John M. (1996). "Bureaucratic Corruption in Africa: The Futility of Cleanups." *Cato Journal*. Vol.16. No.1. p. 3. Also http://www.cato.org/pubs/journal/cj161-6.html.
New African. The. April 1990: 16.
New African. The. December 1991: 33.
New African. The. October 1991:12.
New Internationalist. June 1990: 18.
New York Times. 15 August 1990: A6.
New York Times. 21 October 1991: A9.
Njoku, T.N. (1998). "Corruption in Africa". *Finance and Development*. 35(2). 8.
Nye, Joseph S. (1989). "Corruption and Development: A Cost Benefit Analysis." In Heidenheimer, A.J., M. Johnston, and Victor Levine.1989. *Political Corruption: A Handbook*. New Brunswick, N.J: Transactions Books. 963–984.
Peel, Michael (2001). "Call for Anti-Corruption Shake-Up." *Financial Times*. 16 July 2001.
Robertson, Geoffrey (1999). *Crimes against Humanity: The Struggle for Global Justice*. Allen Lane. Penguin Press.
Silverstein, K. (1999). "Millions for Viagra, Pennies for Diseases of the Poor: Research Money goes to Profitable Lifestyle Drugs." *The Nation*. 19 July 1999. 309.
Theobald, R. (1990). *Corruption, Development And Underdevelopment*. London: Macmillan.
United Nations (1996). *UN General Assembly Resolution 51/59 Action against Corruption and International Code of Conduct for Public Officials, Annex*. Adopted on 12 December.
UNDP (2001). *Human Development Report 2001*. New York: Oxford University Press.
The Times of London. 3 September 2001.
Washington Post. 15 February 1992: A23.
Washington Post. 21 July 1992: A16.
Washington Times, The. 3 August 1995: A18.
Weekly Review. 19 February 1982.
Weekly Review. 26 April 1985.
Werlin, H.H. (1972). "The Roots of Corruption—the Ghanaian Enquiry." *Journal of Modern African Studies*. 10:2, 251.
West Africa. 4–10 December 1989: 2036.
West Africa. 9–15 April 1990: 598.
West Africa. 4–10. May 1992: 746.
West Africa. 9–15 April 1990: 598.
West Africa. April 3–9, 1989: 536.
West Africa. 30 November 1981: 2881.
World Development Forum. No. 9, 1988: 3.
Ziegler, J. (1992). *Le sang des pauvres*. [The blood of the poor.] *Liberation Newspaper*.

Chapter 14

The Military and Nigerian Political Economy in The Global System

Olayiwola Abegunrin

Introduction

Because this chapter deals with the Nigerian political economy in the global system, I first define what *global economy* or *globalization* is. Globalization is the process by which structures of international political economy have become less strictly associated with the boundaries of nation-states. This has resulted in the free movement of capital, goods, and services across national boundaries. Economic globalization is the expansion of market activity, including especially, finance and production, from national to a global scale. The global economy is a system generated by cross-national production and international finance. Global production is able to make use of the international economy, playing off one territorial jurisdiction against another so as to maximize reduction in costs by using cheap labor, savings in taxes, avoidance of most regulations, control over labor, and guarantees of political stability and other favors. Global finance has achieved virtually unregulated and electronically connected 24/7 networks. The collective decision making of global finance is centered in world industrialized cities: New York, London, Tokyo, Frankfurt, Paris, Rome and extends by modern technologies, such as computers, Internet and fax machines to the rest of the world (Pearson and Payaslian 1999: 51–52; Crane and Abla 1997).

The two components of the global economy are in potential conflict. Global production requires stability in politics and finance. Global finance has the upper hand because its power over credit creation determines the future of production; yet global finance is in a perilously fragile condition. "A calamitous concatenation of accidents would bring it down.... For now, governments, even the combined governments of the G-8, have not been able to devise any effectively secure scheme of regulation for global finance that could counter such a collapse" (Pearson and Payaslian 1999: 62). There is, in effect, no explicit political or authority structure for the global economy, the existence of World Trade Organization (WTO), World Bank, International Monetary Fund (IMF), and the international trade arbitration notwithstanding. There is, nevertheless, something there that remains to be deciphered, something that could be described by the notion of *governance without government.*

The purpose of globalization is to allow capital to freely chase profits around the world. To allow multinational corporations to make more money by manufacturing their goods in dirt-wage, cheap labor, low or no regulation underdeveloped countries instead of in high-wage, high-regulation developed countries. This is globalization's claim for being a vehicle for the spread of democracy and wealth as a byproduct. The issue of globalization has important implications for democracy. Therefore, the ideologues of globalization are quick to identify democracy with the free market economy.

Globalization is Not a New Concept in International Relations/Political Economy

The scramble in the 19th century that culminated in the partition of the African continent at the Berlin Conference of the European Powers of November 1884 to February 1885 was a European scheme for global economic domination (Pakenham 1991). Each European nation was attempting to maximize its global economic interests (and yet they all conceived of their crusade in terms of romantic nationalism). There were journalist-explorers like Henry Stanley, sailor-explorers like Pierre de Brazza, soldier-explorers like Frederick Lugard; pedagogue-explorers like Carl Peters, and gold and diamond tycoons like Cecil Rhodes. All these imperialists were after the global trade of that period (Pakenham 1991). These globalist traders were not out to save Africa but Africa became the savior of their countries' economies and industries. The European attitude to Africa was aptly summed up by King Leopold of Belgium who saw Africa as "a magnificent cake" to be shared among them.

Consequently, the European governments and their multinational corporations had dreams of El Dorado, of diamond mines and gold fields criss-crossing the Sahara. In Europe, these were the years of the great depression and mounting stocks of unsold Manchester cotton, Lyons silk and Hamburg gin. Africa was the answer to the merchants' prayers (Pakenham 1991).

This chapter discusses the problematic of political economy as a struggle between contending parties (the military and the political class as well as military-civilian alliances), and the response of Nigerians and the Nigerian nation to the dialectical imperative of the survival of the political economy of Nigeria in the global system. The interdependence and conflicting relationship of contending forces of political economy and globalization clearly illustrate this dialectic. The legacy of colonialism has made Nigeria dependent on Western powers and their multinational corporations, which dominate the global economy.

The Nigerian Political Economy

Nigeria's major export is crude oil and this resource is highly valued and in demand globally. But have Nigerian leaders made use of this wealth wisely for the benefit of their people? After 44 years of independence, the political economy of Nigeria has come full-circle, having experienced both negative and positive political changes as well as continuity as a nation, economic expansion and contraction. By the end of the 1980s, the fruits of independence had been enjoyed by only a small percentage of the country's population. The high hopes that the giant of Africa would be an example for the rest of the continent were dashed in Nigeria's first decade of independence by military *coup d'état*, counter coups and a civil war; and in the second decade by economic boom, and bust, culminating in economic crises in the 1980s and 1990s.

This combination of political and economic instability resulted in a political economy crisis in the 1980s, which ended both the second democratic experiment and the *oil boom*. The parliamentary model government of the First Republic, and the presidential system of the Second Republic were both replaced by the military dictatorships of the 1980s, and 1990s while the international and industrial ambitions of Africa's aspiring great power (blessed with abundant resources) were squandered by corrupt and dictatorial military regimes, especially of Generals Ibrahim Babangida and Sani Abacha (see Omoruyi 1999; Diamond et al. 1997; Osaghae 1998). These developments constituted the main elements of Nigerian's disastrous political economy.

Nigerian Oil Economy

Since World War I, oil as a source of energy has become more important for industry and war. Transportation, industry and indeed all sectors of the modern economy are driven by oil, and consequently some countries that possess considerable petroleum and other forms of energy resources such as natural gas have acquired an influence in international affairs. The emergence of oil as an important raw material has brought about a relative shift in the power of the politically, militarily and economically leading nations. For example, the United States of America has become a powerful country since it has better access to sources of oil and other strategic minerals around the world.

The economic structure of a nation is an important factor both in its growth and development potential, and in its international and regional competitiveness. Economic measures play a major role in contemporary international relations. "Economic policies (and the quality of human resources in the form of the knowledge economy) may serve economic ends, such as the maximization of profit or the optimum allocation of resources, or they may serve political ends, such as increasing national security or extending control over other countries" (Hass and Whiting 1956: 209). There is a general consensus among many Nigerian leaders, especially the intellectuals, that the first priorities of any government are stability, economic and social development and that, all other policies must be directed to these ends. According to the Federal Military Government's statement in 1974 during the launching of the Second National Development Plan, "the overall objective of Nigeria's foreign policy is linked to our external relations with the development needs of the country" (Government of Nigeria 1978). This central guiding principle of the national interest in external relations continues to be reiterated by successive administrations. Therefore, any attempt to conduct foreign relations devoid of credible economic policies to promote growth and prosperity will not enjoy the support of the Nigerian public and will not be sustained.

Nigeria is a member of the Organization of Petroleum Exporting Countries (OPEC), and the sixth largest oil producer in the world, and the largest in Africa. Nigeria oil production stood at two million barrels per day in 1979 (*Nigerian-American Economics*

1980). At that time the US consumed 58 percent of Nigeria's production, representing 16 percent of the country's petroleum imports. The US still remains the the number one importer. The Netherlands is the second largest importer with 15.8 percent of Nigerian crude oil, followed by Britain with 12 percent. As of July 2004, Nigeria was producing 2.4 million barrels per day. 90-three percent of Nigeria's export trade was and still is from petroleum production. The emergence of Nigeria as a key player in African politics and in the international scene has come about largely through her vast production of oil since the end of the civil war in January 1970, and especially from 1973-1980 when oil revenues increased dramatically (see Table 14.1).

Throughout the 1970s, there were very strong correlations between the domestic health and prosperity of the Nigerian economy and the conduct of foreign policy. The more affluent and self-reliant the Nigeria economy became the greater has been the tendency for an assertive foreign policy based on the major principles and objectives on which all Nigerian governments tend to agree (Abegunrin 1992). During the oil boom, which was linked primarily to increases in the price of crude oil, and given the disposition of individual foreign policy makers, petroleum resources and finance became the principal tool for achieving foreign policy goals that would otherwise have been pursued by traditional diplomacy. Notable examples were found during the Generals Muhammed and Obasanjo military administrations. The celebrated 'Africa has come of Age' speech of General Murtala Muhammed at the OAU Special Summit in Addis Ababa in January 1976 was a direct challenge and defiance of the United States' position on Angola. That speech laid the basis for the Angola policy, which was carried on by General Obasanjo after the assassination of General Muhammed. Then, in July 1979, at the height of the controversy over Britain's handling of the Zimbabwean decolonization process, the Obasanjo regime nationalized British Petroleum and took over all its assets in Nigeria (Adeniji 2000: 35–36).

These two decisions, taken in vigorous pursuit of Nigeria's commitment to the decolonization of Africa, were decisive for Angola and Zimbabwe's independence. Indeed, Generals Muhammed and Obasanjo saw the national economy as an instrument for pursuing the decolonization of Africa, as well as for the economic benefit of Nigeria. Both leaders were willing to risk direct confrontation with the largest importer of Nigerian petroleum and her most important trading partners (Sanu and Onwuka 1997).

The instances mentioned above were the most spectacular examples of the use of the country's economic assets (power) as leverage for achieving foreign policy objectives. They were by no means the only instances nor were they the first. At the beginning of the oil boom after the civil war, the Gowon Administration started using wealth from oil to pursue foreign policy goals by cultivating Africans in the diaspora and pursuing a leadership role in the West African sub-region. This took the form of financial assistance to poor countries in the Caribbean, specially Grenada, and in West Africa, particularly during the drought, which devastated the Sahelian zone. This financial assistance was formalized by the Obasanjo military regime when, in 1978, a Nigeria Trust Fund (NTF) with an initial capital of $80 million was established at the African Development Bank (ADB) for financing development projects in African countries.

Table 14.1 Crude Oil Revenue as Percentage of GDP, Total Export Earnings and Total Revenue 1960-1983*

Year	Oil Revenue (in billion Naira)**	Percentage of GDP	of Export	Percentage Total Revenue
1960	2.4	0.1	2.7	1.0
1965	29.9	3.4	25.4	9.1
1970	176.4	9.4	57.5	26.9
1971	603.0	4.4	73.7	43.6
1972	735.0	15.9	81.6	54.4
1973	1,368.0	17.2	83.1	59.9
1974	4,824.0	29.3	92.6	82.1
1975	4,568.0	21.7	94.0	77.5
1976	4,834.0	23.7	93.6	79.3
1977	6,187.9	22.5	92.8	75.2
1978	5,017.5	16.3	90.0	63.1
1979	9,583.5	25.5	95.2	81.4
1980	12,791.7	28.7	96.1	69.5
1981	10,258.4	22.2	96.9	62.4
1982	8,609.7	21.8	98.5	66.5
1983	7,508.3	19.7	96.4	62.0

**Source:* Olusanya and Akindele, (1986: 2).

***Source:* Figures are expressed in Nigerian Currency *Naira*, because they are not available in dollars.

Nigeria's Leadership in the ADB was marked not only by the establishment of the NTF but also by Nigeria's assistance to the maintenance of the fundamentally African character of the Bank. In the same vein, the 1970s strong economic performance induced by oil revenue encouraged the decision of the Gowon regime to organize and host the World Black and African Festival of Arts and Culture, which was staged by the Obasanjo military regime in February 1977 (Esedebe 1994). This event was staged to project the dynamic Pan-Africanism and Black Cultural Renaissance of Nigeria's foreign policy, and her role in Africa.

Despite the worldwide oil glut of 1978 that kept the price of oil low that year, Nigeria's GDP rose from $31.768 billion in 1977 to $40.637 billion in 1979, an increase of nearly 28 percent. However, in that period, Nigeria's foreign reserves fell from $3.908 billion in 1977 to $1.948 billion in the recession of 1978, but rebounded to $5.295 billion in 1979 (US Department of Commerce 1980). The oil dominant character of Nigeria's economy endows her with a product that American businesses find attractive. Six American oil companies are among the eight major foreign oil companies in which the government holds the majority shares of their Nigerian operations. They are Exxon/ Mobile, Texaco, Chevron, Shell, and Agip. The sale of petroleum accounts for most of the country's revenue and foreign exchange. About 80 percent of the government's revenue and 90 percent of its foreign exchange is derived from this source. However, the US was unable to take advantage of the growing Nigerian trade, and to worsen the situation there was the removal of Iranian oil from the world market because of the domestic problems of that country from 1979 to 1980, which resulted in more dependence on Nigerian oil and increased US trade deficit with Nigeria.

During the Arab oil embargo of 1973–1975, Nigeria was the largest oil supplier to some of the Western countries, especially the United States, but after that embargo Nigeria dropped to third largest oil supplier to the United States, and as of June 2000 was in the fifth place. Nigeria's sulfur-free Bonny light crude oil is one of the best and is in high demand in Western markets because it is easily refined into gasoline. Accordingly, in 1978, the Obsanjo military administration indicated its intention of using oil to influence the Western Powers' policies on Zimbabwe, which led an American to observe that it was "incredible that a superpower should feel these foreign policy constraints from Nigeria" (*Newsweek* Magazine 1979: 37). Nigeria also intended to use oil as leverage against western investors in South Africa the way the Arab governments used it against the west in 1973–1975 over the Palestine question.

As proof of the Government's intention during General Obasanjo's visit to the US in October in 1977, he warned Western countries and their multinational corporations in Nigeria and South Africa that, "All such double-dealers will have to choose between our hospitality and their adventurism by which they prop up the oppressive regime in South Africa" (*West Africa* 1977: 2158).

Through specific actions, the Federal Military Government underscored its intentions. For instance, at the August 1977 World Conference for Action Against Apartheid held in Lagos, General Obasanjo announced the creation of a special Nigerian Economic Intelligence Committee, that would report to him directly (West Africa 1977: 2158). The committee was to formulate policies and strategies for discouraging investment and trade with apartheid South Africa. It would recommend action against collaborators with the South African apartheid regime, "who also availed themselves of the Nigerian hospitality and magnanimity of the Nigerian people and benefits of the Nigerian economy" (Obasanjo 1977).

One of the recommendations of this committee was that all Western corporations with investments in Nigeria and South Africa would have to either do business in Nigeria or in South Africa, but not with both countries. In line with this recommendation, the Federal Military Government required the insertion of clauses in all major contracts certifying that the company concerned did not do business with South Africa. Enforcement of this policy recommendation would have caused two problems for the Government. First, strict application of this rule would have resulted in the immediate cut-off of important imports to Nigeria from the United States; and second, to counter the Arab boycott of Israel after the 1967 Arab-Israeli war, United States law prohibits compliance with boycotts or blacklists. Therefore, American companies that signed these contracts with the anti-apartheid clause could be subject to penalties under US law. However, selected American companies did comply with this clause without penalty from the US government, while some American companies (e.g. Colgate Corporation) left Nigeria. As a result of these setbacks, enforcement of this rule was uneven, although the Federal Military Government took actions consistent with this policy through major initiatives.

Nigeria in the Global Economic Crisis

Beginning with the civilian interregnum of President Shehu Shagari's administration (1979 to 1983), there have been strong domestic and external pressures to pull out of OPEC, which continued to insist on production ceilings from member states. Nigeria consistently exceeded her quota, even as the Federal Military Government continued to reaffirm its commitment to OPEC, and successfully negotiated an increase of 250,000 barrels per day in 1984. However, commitment to OPEC, limited the options open to the Buhari military regime, that overthrew the Shagari Administration on December 31, 1983, and as a result forced it to adopt a counter-trade policy in December 1984. The counter-trade policy was adopted in return for essential goods and machinery at agreed prices with special arrangements. Nigeria shipped oil to the countries that were willing to buy under this policy. In many different deals with a total value estimated at over $2 billion, Nigeria's oil was bartered for goods from Austria, Brazil, Canada, France, Germany, Italy, the Netherlands, Romania and the former Soviet Union. Other countries with considerable balance of trade deficits with Nigeria welcomed counter-trade arrangements (Gambari 1989: 149).

Nigeria joined Algeria, Angola, Benin, Libya, Cameroon, Gabon, and Congo to establish the African Petroleum Producers Association (APPA), which was inaugurated in Lagos in January 1987 (Central Bank of Nigeria 1987). Ivory Coast, Egypt, Democratic Republic of Congo, and Equatorial Guinea joined the association in 1988. This association was formed to strengthen the use of oil as a weapon by the African oil producing countries, following the example of Organization of Arab Petroleum Exporting Countries (OAPEC), and as part of Nigeria's *economic diplomacy*. Another aim of the association was to promote cooperation among member states in hydrocarbon exploration, production, refining, petrochemical, manpower development, acquisition and adoption of technology, harmonization of oil policies and maximization of oil revenues. Most important was to increase economic and technical cooperation on the continent, and to facilitate the "achievement of the objective of collective self-reliance in the field of energy"(Central Bank of Nigeria 1987). APPA never benefited Nigeria strategically because the member-states found it difficult to reconcile their divergent interests. OPEC therefore, remained the country's main collective platform for employing oil as a weapon and vital a instrument of economic policy. General Babangida reaffirmed this policy when he stated that "Nigeria has no intention of leaving OPEC, and committed to the principal objectives which gave rise to the formation of the organization (Central Bank of Nigeria 1987).

The economic downturn that began in the 1980s and persisted till the dawn of this millennium arose not only from the sharp decline in the price of petroleum but also from the mismanagement of the economy during the oil boom. The windfall from oil, which should have provided long-term investment for the transformation of the nation's economy, rather provoked the monumental excesses of the 1980s and early 1990s. This manifested in large-scale corruption, and all kinds of foreign exchange fraud: the most popular one is *419 scam* (*Guardian* 2000) which has enriched a few Nigerians and their foreign collaborators, and also damaged the reputation of the country abroad, and left the country with very little to show for the billion of dollars she earned from oil. The oil boom also led to the total neglect of agriculture that had been the backbone of the country's economy and the installation of a faulty industrial strategy that was constructed essentially on importation of not only machinery but also raw materials. Thus, the industrialization process rather than facilitating the earning of foreign exchange became a major consumer of scarce foreign exchange.

The 1980s has been described as the lost decade for African countries, particularly Nigeria. According to the United Nations Development Program (UNDP), the cumulative result of the bad, and inadequate industrial strategy is that Nigeria, whose level of industrialization compared with those of the East and South-East Asian countries in the 1960s and 1970s, was left far behind these countries by the 1990s (UNDP1996).

Nigeria, The IMF and Structural Adjustment Programs

Nigeria maintained a pro-western position and the colonial legacy that negatively linked her economy, trade and political relations with western powers. However, after Babangida had implemented World Bank and IMF-inspired Structural Adjustment Programs (SAPs) in the initial years of his regime, the situation in Nigeria was glowingly portrayed by some international observers as:

> The years in which the potential economic recovery was very bright and a return to prosperity seemed likely. The country's past glory appeared restorable, with its improved standing in the international community, thanks to final agreement with Western creditors and General Babangida's high international profile. The World Bank and IMF in fact regarded Nigeria as one of the new success story of SAPs, and some commentators even spoke of the possibility of an economic miracle. There was also the democratic transition program, which reinforced the regime's credibility in the international community, as it was in consonance with the world at that time. (Osaghe 1998: 188)

Like all developing countries, Nigeria is no exception when it comes to the legacy of colonialism. The legacy of colonial domination was evident as the regime attempted to address persistent economic hardships by restructuring the ailing economy. Babangida encountered the same difficulties as the Buhari administration, as he attempted to get the country's debt rescheduled. For example, the Central Bank of Nigeria's (CBN) report for the first half of 1992, gave a very gloomy economic picture. The CBN report described the situation as, "disturbing socio-economic conditions, characterized by a slow down of economic activity, a worsening inflation, higher unemployment, greater tension in the private and public sectors" (*West Africa* 1990). Nevertheless, the IMF continued to insist on conditionalities that eventually resulted in increased economic hardship on Nigerians. However, "when Babangida introduced the so-called SAPs in 1986, this was expected to increase the ability of the country to borrow, and enable her to reschedule her debt. Despite SAPs, problems relating to debt rescheduling persisted" (King 1996: 26).

The retired General, now President Olusegun Obasanjo, launched his first attack on SAPs by exclaiming: "Adjustment is part of the process of existence. But it must have a human face, human heart and milk of kindness and must not ignore what I call human survival and dignity-issues of employment, food, shelter, education and health" (*West Africa* 1990: 1841). As usual, debt rescheduling, procurement of more credit and promotion of foreign investment were the main themes of the regime's so-called *economic diplomacy*, which was vigorously pursued under General Ike Nwachuku as the foreign minister. Nevertheless, Nigeria remained a committed member of OPEC, which continued to peg member-states' production quotas in its bid to shore up oil prices in the international market.

The Government introduced the SAPs allegedly to address the underlying malaise and the new challenges posed by the further collapse of oil revenues. The intended objective was to help promote economic efficiency and private sector development as a basis for improving prospects for long-term growth. Nigeria's SAPs combined exchange rate and trade policy reform aimed at revitalizing the non-oil economy, with stabilizing policies designed to restore equilibrium to the balance of payments and so make prices more stable. The program included efforts to downsize the public sector and improve the management of publicly owned assets (World Bank 1994a). Under the SAPs, Nigeria eliminated import licenses and agricultural marketing boards, lifted price controls, launched a program of privatization, and took steps in deregulating the banking system. Although some reforms were sustained during the SAPs period, especially between 1986 and 1992, others were implemented unevenly. Successive cycles of contradictory and expansionary policies with their attendant affect on prices and activity levels rocked the economy. In addition, to their irrational policies, the military regimes built up large fiscal deficits from 1989, and by 1993, the deficit was ten percent of Gross Domestic Product (GDP). Forced by the need to finance the fiscal deficit, monetary policy also vacillated, and became increasingly inflationary as the budget went out of control (World Bank 1994b). For instance, the Nigerian Naira was N1.8 to one US dollar in 1978, and one to one in 1983, but even under the civilian administration, Nigerian currency continued to fall and by August 2004 the Naira was N135 to one US dollar. This is one of the problems and results from the IMF and the World Bank SAPs.

To compound the already complex situation, the self-styled *evil genius*, General Ibrahim Babangida, was alleged to have used outright bribery with full the financial weight of the Federal Military Government to buy the Nigerian political class. According to *Africa Confidential*, "General Ibrahim Babangida doled out contracts to a wide circle of supporters, allowing them to take commissions from oil traders" (*African Confidential* 1998). It has been alleged that General Babangida's regime was tainted with corruption, and that it was the corrupt practices he started that his successor General Sani Abacha continued and perfected. Curbing the excesses of the Buhari regime proved to be the least difficult task facing General Ibrahim Babangida. Besides corruption, a far more difficult job was the task of reviving the economy, which was declining rapidly into a serious depression. According to the 1986 estimate, per capita income had fallen 19 percent from 1970 when the civil war ended and 35 percent since 1977 (The Economic Intelligence Unit 1989). Domestic manufacturing was in its worst state, as factories were operating at less than 30 percent of their capacity. Debt service payments on Nigeria's almost $20 billion foreign debt as of 1987 (it had increased to $30 billion by 1999) amounted to 50 percent of export revenue (*The Washington Post* 1987). There is no single development project from the government to show for these huge debts, which means that this money went to private individual military/government officials' pockets or their bank accounts abroad. According to the Nigerian *Sunday Vanguard* (2004) "Money suspected to have been stolen by some Nigerian government officials and kept in foreign accounts increased from $50 billion in 1999 to $170 billion in 2003".

The major causes of the depression were the corruption in the high places and the continuing drop in the global oil price. Despite the nation's many efforts to diversify exports, oil still continued to account for about 90 percent of Nigeria's export earnings. The sluggish global demand and the world's reduced dependence on OPEC oil combined to drive Nigeria's earnings further down. For instance, in 1981, a barrel of Nigerian oil sold for $40. By January 1986 the price had fallen to $25, and by the end of the same year declined to only $14.15. By 1988, it had plummeted to about $10 per barrel (Hackett and Reynolds 1989). While world oil production fell by four percent from 1970 to 1985, Nigeria's production over the same period fell by 15 percent. From 1979 to 1988, Nigeria's output decreased very rapidly. Consequently, export revenues dropped from $25 billion in 1980 to $12.6 billion in 1985 and to $6.8 billion in 1986 (US Department of Commerce 1980).

Political economy must begin with recognition of the inherently conflicting nature of international relations. One of the reasons for the slump in Nigeria's oil production was the change in relationship between Nigeria and the United States under the Reagan Administration, which was virtually unnoticed. Throughout his eight years in office, President Reagan's interest in Sub-Saharan Africa was limited to Southern Africa, and a few areas where the former Soviet Union and Cuba were involved. Consequently, between 1985 and 1989, the oil trade that had linked the two countries for two decades decreased dramatically as the US increasingly replaced imports of Nigerian oil with non-OPEC oil. Neither interest nor necessity drew the US to Nigeria, and US interest in Nigeria diminished, and did not completely return until democratic civilian rule was established in May 1999. Since 1999, Nigeria has resumed providing about eight percent of America's oil imports, while the country was producing 2.4 million barrels per day as of July 2000 (*New York Times* 2000). In addition, "reassured that the democratic world's enemy General Sani Abacha is dead and buried, President Clinton visited Nigeria in August 2000" (Akintunde 2000). As a result of President Clinton's visit to Nigeria, President Obasanjo became the first Nigerian Head of State to have hosted two American Presidents on state visits. As military Head of State in March 1978, he received President Jimmy Carter in Lagos to cement an American-African relationship. No United States President had paid a state visit to Black Africa prior to 1978.

Boosting Nigerian Economy in the Global Market in the 21st Century

The new civilian administration under President Obasanjo should seek to stabilize the country by promoting sustainable development and strengthening civilian democratic institutions. Besides, the Federal Government should intensify efforts in the nation's liquefied natural gas development, which is another major source of revenue. This $3.8 billion project, the biggest in Africa, will boost the Nigerian economy tremendously (*The News* 2000). When this project is fully developed, Nigeria would have joined the community of nations with diversified foreign exchange earnings, and this will improve Nigeria's balance of trade position. The way forward is to create a conducive environment that encourages industrial production and export. Government must, therefore, focus on the National Electric Power Authority's (NEPA) rehabilitation and regular power supply to make locally manufactured goods competitive with imported goods. For instance, President Clinton's August 2000 visit to Nigeria, besides emphasizing the importance of protecting a functioning democracy from abuse and corruption, was also designed to help integrate the Nigerian economy into the global market and strengthen the climate for investment.

President Clinton tried to sell to the Nigerian Government the US House of Representatives' new bill known as Africa Growth and Opportunity Act (AGOA) (US House of Representatives 1999). This bill was designed, according to its protagonists, to relieve the development crisis in Sub-Saharan Africa by shifting away from a focus on aid toward private enterprise and trade. However, the bill stipulates that before any African country can benefit from the AGOA, it must comply with International Monetary Fund rules requiring reorganization of domestic economic and social policies including cuts in domestic spending and corporate tax rates, and broad privatization through divestiture. In addition, the bill specifically requires African countries to join the World Trade Organization (WTO) and to comply with its trade liberalization rules. However, it paid mere lip service to issues such as debt relief and aid, issues that are indeed very vital and in some cases indispensable to real economic growth and development in Nigeria and most African countries.

Conclusion: Need for a New Approach

It is unfortunate to see the terrible economic situation in Nigeria that after the civilian administration of President Obasanjo has taken over from the military since May 29, 1999, the nation's economy has not improved. It is an irony that President Obasanjo, who in 1992 as a retired military General was strongly opposed to the IMF and World Bank SAPs conditions for the country under the Babangida regime (West Africa 1990), has taken a U-turn to embrace similar IMF and World Bank policies.

Nigeria is the biggest US trading partner in Africa, and the biggest market in the West African Sub-region. It is the fifth largest supplier of oil to the United States market while her sulfur-free Bonny light crude oil is especially prized because it is easily refined into gasoline. In this age of globalization, Nigeria's influence extends well beyond Africa, as her role in the petroleum trade as a member of OPEC, peacekeeping contributions around the world, particularly in Liberia, Sierra Leone, and the Darfur region of western Sudan attest. If Nigeria remains trapped in the quicksand of political malaise, economic decline, religious conflicts, and ethnic rivalry, the world, and particularly Africa will be worse off in this 21st century.

Nigeria and Africa's performance is not improving, judging by what happened in the 1980s and 1990s and still continues in this millennium. Nigeria needs a new direction/approach for the new century. For better growth and economic development in Nigeria in the 21st century there is the need to change her direction and adopt new economic strategies by encouraging inter-state trade within the continent, and increased economic and technical cooperation among the African Union (AU) States to achieve collective self-reliance in the field of agriculture (especially in food production). In addition, Nigeria and South Africa as the two leading economic powers in Africa should and need to encourage the member states of AU to be courageous enough to enforce the New Partnership for Africa's Development (NEPAD) peer review mechanism of member states launched in 2003 ("Abuja Conference " 2004). They should reduce dependency on former colonial countries so as to earn human dignity, fight corruption, economic waste, and mismanagement of their natural resources. There should be a commitment to social justice, and innovation, hard work and merit based on performance; commitment to protecting our African sovereignty and values, democracy and the rule of law. Nigeria and the AU should recommit and rededicate itself under the New Partnership for Africa's Development to eradicate poverty and call for a new partnership between Africa, the industrialized countries and international organizations, including the United Nations. Each of Africa's five sub-regions (East, West, South, North and Central), should identify priority projects in the eight major sectors of the NEPAD programs, namely good and democratic governance, infrastructure, education, health, agriculture, new information/communication technologies, energy and free and open market access. Nigerian masses are suffering and they want and need good, dedicated and committed leadership, not military dictators, corrupt, and self-centered leaders. The civil societies in Nigeria and in the continent should be encouraged to be involved and actively participate in some of the economic decisions in their societies.

It will be rather difficult if not impossible for Nigeria, or any African country for that matter, to achieve the much desired sustainable growth and development without considerable input from the outside world. However, while it is desirable to encourage Nigerians and other Africans to embrace globalization, the rules of current global political economy have nevertheless made it practically impossible for them, at least in most cases, to achieve any meaningful measure of growth or development. Nigeria and Africa's economic and social prospects depend heavily on foreign investment, which in turn depends on the global economy and political stability at home. Nevertheless, the Federal Government should promote and protect emerging Nigerian industries, because this is a common practice in the global economy. Besides, the federal administration must emphasize her economic objective striving for harnessing the resources of the nation and promoting national prosperity, efficient, dynamic and self-reliant economy; and promotion of a just global economic order in the 21st century.

References

Abegunrin, Olayiwola (1992). *Nigeria and the Struggle for the Liberation of Zimbabwe: A Study of Foreign Policy Decision Making of an Emerging Nation.* Stockholm, Sweden: Bethany Books.

Adeniji, Olu (2000). *Essays on Nigerian Foreign Policy, Governance and International Security.* Ibadan: Dokun Publishing House.

Africa Confidential (London), June 1998.

Akintunde, Muyiwa. (2000) "Clinton's Message of Democracy and Unity: The World Needs Nigeria to Succeed." *Africa Today* (London), September: 16.

Crane, George and Abla, Amawi (eds.) (1997). *The Theoretical Evolution of International Political Economy: A Reader,* 2nd edition. New York: Oxford University Press.

Central Bank of Nigeria (1987). *Annual Report* (Lagos). January 21–22.

Diamond, Larry, Greene, Kirk and Oyediran, Oyeleye (eds.) (1997). *Transition Without End: Nigerian Politics and Civil Society Under Babangida.* Boulder, CO: Lynne Rienner Publishers.

Esedebe, Olisanwuche (1994). *Pan-Africanism: The Idea and Movement, 1776–1991.* 2nd edition. Washington, DC: Howard University Press.

Gambari, Ibrahim A. (1989). *Theory and Reality in Foreign Policy Making; Nigeria After the Second Republic.* Atlantic Highlands, NJ: Humanities Press International, Inc.

Government of Nigeria (1978). *Second National Development Plan.* Lagos: GON.

Guardian (Lagos) (2000). "419 Goes Internet." August 10.

Guardian (Lagos) (2001). "Oputa Panel Summons Akhigbe, Ogohi, others." January 19.

Hackett, Paul and Reynolds, Simon (1989). "Nigeria Economy." In *Africa South of the Sahara 1989,* 18th edition. London: Europa Publications.

Hass, Ernest B and Whiting, J. (1956). *Dynamics of International Relations.* New York: McGraw-Hill.

New York Times, The (New York). (2000). "Clinton in Nigeria to Show Support for Civilian Rule." August 27.

Newsweek Magazine (New York) (1979). June 25: 37.

Nigeria, Government of (1978). *The Second National Development Plan, 1970–1974.* Lagos: Government Printer.

Obasanjo, Olusegun (1977). "No Compromise with apartheid," *Speech Delivered at the Opening Ceremony of the World Conference for Action Against Apartheid.* Lagos. Federal Ministry of Information. August.

Omoruyi, Omo (1999). *The Tale of June12: The Betrayal of the Democratic Rights of Nigerians (1993).* London: Press Alliance Network Limited.

Osaghae, Eghosa E. (1998). *Cripple Giant: Nigeria Since Independence* Bloomington and Indianapolis, IN: Indiana University Press.

Pakenham, Thomas (1991). The *Scramble for Africa: White Man's Conquest of the Dark Continent from 1876 to 1912*. New York: Avon Books.
Pearson, Frederic S. and Payaslian, Simon (1999). *International Political Economy: Conflict and Cooperation in the Global System*. New York: McGraw-Hill.
Sanu, Olu and Onwuka, Ralph (1997). *Nigeria-Africa and the European Union: Beyond 2000*. Ibadan: Dokun Publishing House.
Sunday Vanguard (Lagos) (2004). "$170 billion alleged loot alarms Obasanjo" August 29.
United Nations Human Development Program (1996). *Nigeria*. New York: United Nations.
US Department of Commerce. (1980). *Foreign Economic Trends, FET 80–097*. Washington, DC. October 1980: 2.
Washington Post (2002). February 12, 2002.
Washington Post (1987). March 8.
West Africa (1977). October 24.
West Africa (1990). January 15–21.
West Africa (1990). "Rumbles in the Corridors of Power," November 6–12 p.1841.
World Bank (1994a). *Nigeria: Structural Adjustment Program: Policies, Implementation, and Impact*. Washington, DC: World Bank.
World Bank (1994b). *Adjustment in Africa: Reform, Results and the Road Ahead*. Washington, DC: World Bank.

Chapter 15

South Africa's Successful Constitutional Transformation meets the Challenge of Implementation: Equality and the Accommodation of Population Diversity

Kristin Henrard

Introduction

The historical importance of the official abolition of apartheid in South Africa and the first multi-racial elections can scarcely be exaggerated. However, the challenges of South Africa's transformation are not limited to the constitutional negotiation phase and the adoption of a constitution for a democratic South Africa. These challenges stretch well beyond that into the actual implementation phase.

A successful transformation of a highly divided society like South Africa necessitates, in addition to redressing past injustices, the creation of a society within which the chances of reoccurrence of the kinds of gross violations of human rights that occurred in the past are reduced to a minimum. Consequently, an evaluation is called for of the constitutional negotiation process and the way in which the themes of redress of the past by overcoming the legacy of apartheid and its systemic discrimination as well as nation building and accommodation of population diversity played their role. The ongoing implementation of the relevant constitutional provisions and the related challenges are equally if not more important to measure than the actual levels of transformation of South African society.

Numerous key issues of South Africa's transformation process could be focused upon. Here, the cardinal equality principle as well as several issues related to the accommodation of population diversity (minority rights, self-determination, education, language and the position of traditional leaders) will be analyzed. A brief description of the most striking features of the apartheid regime is followed by an explanation of the overall constitutional negotiation process, which is peculiar to South Africa. The subsequent section goes on to analyze the constitutional negotiations with respect to the provisions dealing with controversial issues like equality, language and education, self-determination and minority rights, and the position of traditional leaders within the democratic dispensation.

The picture of the implementation phase is not unequivocal. Indeed, both important progress and continuing refinement (e.g., the Constitutional jurisprudence regarding the equality principle) as significant hurdles, delays, and apparent lack of political commitment can be identified.

The Most Relevant Features of the Apartheid Regime

It is appropriate to give an overview of events, policies and mechanisms related to the apartheid era that explain not only the heightened sensitivity in post-apartheid South Africa of certain concepts and techniques but also certain reactions and attitudes of the Afrikaner, Colored and Indian population groups. Several historical events and regulations of the apartheid system have negatively tainted, amongst others, the concepts of group classification, group rights, ethnicity/race, minority rights, mother tongue education and self-determination on ethnic grounds.

Apartheid is generally said to have started after the 1948 election victory of the National Party (NP), which used that concept and program as the focus of its election campaign (Davenport 1991: 519; Worden 1994: 87). However, segregationist policies and attempts to classify the South African population were already noticeable centuries before, effectively since the early roots of colonialism in South Africa (Brown 1988–1989: 40; Worden 1994: 112). By the end of the 18th century certain racially discriminatory regulations were in place (Worden 1994: 66–67), but it has been argued that 'it was only in the period between the end of the Anglo Boer War in 1902 and the 1930s (Wilkins and Strydom 1978: 141) that a cogent ideology of segregation emerged and was implemented' (Worden 1994: 72). Although apartheid started as an Afrikaner project, which is visible in several of its preferential measures for Afrikaners, it managed to get broader white support, as it also entailed distinct advantages for the white English-speaking population.

Apartheid is characterized by its central policy of 'divide and rule', which was aimed at ensuring white survival and hegemony by dividing the non-white population along racial and even ethnic lines (Kashula and Anthonissen 1995: 98; Bennett 1995: 7; Goldin 1989: 241. See also Cloete 1991: 37). Consequently, the majority was divided into a host of minority groups, which could no longer pose a threat to the white minority (including both the Afrikaners and the English population). In that way apartheid can also be described as a scheme to disempower the non-white population (Soudien 1998: 128; Cross and Mkwanazi-Twala 1998: 28) while giving privileges to the white, and especially the white Afrikaner population. That design of apartheid was *inter alia* demonstrated by the official language policy, which excluded any indigenous language and was limited to English and Afrikaans, by the job reservations for Afrikaners in the public service and by the attempt to promote the Afrikaner people through a highly compartmentalized education system (Wilkins and Strydom 1978: 253). Consequently, apartheid was described as a pervasive system of affirmative action for the white population and especially for Afrikaners (Sachs 1992: 98; Sonn 1993: 6).

Apartheid and its labyrinth of regulations were based on an imposed group membership on the basis primarily of race but, for the black population, also ethnicity

(Manby 1995: 27; Kotze 1997: 2). The entire classification process was legally imposed and ascribed, more specifically on the basis of the 1950 Population Registration Act, and often arbitrarily implemented (Coetzee 1995: 90; Harries 1989:110). The act distinguished four major racial categories, namely white, black/African[1], Colored and Indian/Asian. The apartheid regime indeed did not limit its racial classifications to black and white but also further subdivided the overwhelming non-white majority in three subgroups namely Africans, Coloreds and Indians/Asians. In furtherance of its divide and rule policy and in an attempt to prevent the emergence of a unified resistance movement, the apartheid government deliberately created an intermediate position for the Coloreds and the Indians (Carrim 1996: 47, 50).

The preferential treatment of these two population categories, *inter alia* in respect of the distribution of resources (Manby 1995: 28), contributed to some kind of internalized white racism and a concomitant condescending attitude towards the African population (Carrim 1996: 47; Sonn 1993: 66). This apartheid strategy entailed for the Colored and Indian population group an ambiguous but still marginalized position, which has ongoing implications and effects (Galiguire 1996: 14–15). Furthermore, the African group was subdivided into ethnic categories, such as Zulu, Xhosa and Ndebele. Subsequently, this rigid scheme was implemented and extended to just about every area of human life through legislation, and '(e)very South African was compulsory registered at birth as a member of one race, on which depended all future rights and entitlements' (Manby 1995: 28). The most important acts, revealing the all pervasiveness of the classification and concomitant segregation (Davenport 1991: 328), included the 1950 Group Areas Act (implementing nationwide and obligatory residential segregation), the 1953 Reservation of Separate Amenities Act (instituting obligatory segregation of all public amenities), a host of pass laws and labor control legislation (to support the segregated residential pattern while instituting migrant labor for the black population), the 1953 Bantu Education Act (and the other acts implementing segregation in education) and the 1959 Promotion of Bantu Self-Government Act. The latter Act laid down the basis for the policy of independent homelands or Grand Apartheid (Davenport 1991: 336–341).

Verwoerd and his successors implemented a broad plan of political and social engineering, called 'separate development' or Grand Apartheid, which attempted to concentrate and limit African political rights to the respective, ethnically defined Bantustans (Bennett 1995: 7). Indeed, '(e)thnic homeland loyalty was to replace national political aspirations in a move which the state hoped would defuse calls for the moral necessity of African self-government within South Africa itself' (Worden 1994: 110–111). The above analysis of Grand Apartheid elucidates why ethnicity is such a sensitive concept in post-apartheid South Africa (Bonthuys 1993: 128). Because the Grand Apartheid strategy was justified in terms of self-determination for the distinctive ethnic groups, that concept, as well as a system of federalism on ethnic grounds, is burdened with negative connotations and thus looked upon with suspicion in contemporary South Africa (*Report of the Commission on the Demarcation/Delimitation of SPRs* 1993: 4, 13).

Several issues pertaining to education during apartheid should be mentioned as they represent sensitive issues in the current, post-apartheid phase. A first issue is the racially segregated structure of education in South Africa, which went hand in hand with marked differences in state funding, affecting teacher/pupil ratio, qualifications of the teachers and other quality features. The curriculum was also differentiated on racial lines so that the distinctive groups could be prepared for the jobs they were meant to take up. 'Bantu Education' or the system for the African population can be described as a system that prepared for a subordinated position in the workplace via a focus on practical subjects and an inferior curriculum (Davenport 1991: 535; Dube 1985: 93–97). Even tertiary education was designed to be segregated from 1959 onwards as most of the faculties in the open universities were closed to African, Indian and Colored students and separate ethnic institutions of higher education were set up 'as agencies of academic apartheid' (Davenport 1991: 535).

Language policy regarding education has been and still is very sensitive in South Africa. Under apartheid, the policy regarding the African population, was constructed in such a way as to promote ethnic identity while hampering proficiency in the official languages in order to limit access to employment (Desei and Taylor 1997: 169). Indeed, the principle of mother tongue education was conveniently applied to further the political interests of division amongst all communities (Heugh 1995: 42). The sudden change from mother tongue instruction to the double medium or 50/50 policy (English/Afrikaans) caused a great deal of educational deficiency among African students[2] and caused major upheavals.[3]

The concept of Christian National Education was based on Afrikaner exclusivity and aimed at single medium institutions for Afrikaners. During apartheid, education was the only sector in which a strict distinction was made between Afrikaners and English-speaking people (Dube 1985: 87; Heugh 1995: 42). Christian National Education furthermore required schools to educate their students about and in line with the spirit of Christian values (Malherbe 1977: 147). The official apartheid policy wanted to give a Christian character to state schools and targeted state funding preferentially to private schools with such a character (Beckman 1995: 97). Furthermore, the courses that were part of the public curriculum, namely 'religious studies' or 'biblical studies', had an essentially reformed and very conservative theological perspective in the sense that the focus was on Christian essentials, while hardly anything was said about other world religions.

The latter feature of apartheid education can be related to the broader phenomenon that since the beginning of colonial times an unequal legal status was accorded to the different belief systems (Moosa 1998: 199). Public policy was indeed characterized by Protestant hegemony and a concomitant restrictive attitude towards other religions (Prozesky 1995:14), which manifested itself *inter alia* in the non-recognition of Muslim and Hindu marriages, having various pernicious consequences for the families concerned (Sachs 1992: 83).

Two final sensitive (and closely related) issues, which need to be highlighted, are the status of traditional leaders and of customary law. During the apartheid era, there had been a partially successful attempt to co-opt traditional leaders while interfering with leadership structures. These leaders hence got the reputation to be puppets of the apartheid regime (Bennett 1995: 69) and their legitimacy was questioned (French 1994: 26). Nevertheless, traditional leaders are still a reality that cannot be ignored in the post-apartheid era, as the institution still receives considerable support especially in the rural areas (Bennett 1995: 70). It should also be remarked that several of its features, like its hereditary nature and its male predominance, sit uneasily with the new constitutional, democratic dispensation.

A related point concerns the position of customary law in the South African legal order. The Native Administration Act of 1927 recognized customary law in South Africa subject to the repugnancy provision and only between 'black' persons. In the process codes of customary law were made. However this codification entailed a distortion of customary law (de Koker 1996: 112–120). Consequently, the post-apartheid era does not only have to address the problem of identifying the exact content of 'true' customary law but also the thorny question of the position of this body of law with its inherent gender discriminatory features in the democratic dispensation, which is focused on equality.

The Constitutional Negotiation Process in General

In the 1980s, there were increasingly intense negotiations between the National Party (NP) government, and the African National Congress (ANC) and other parties from the resistance movement. Eventually, they led to president De Klerk's famous speech on 2 February 1990 at the annual opening of parliament, which set in motion the protracted constitutional negotiation process leading up to the first multi-racial elections in April 1994 and the first democratic constitution for South Africa (De Klerk 1994: 4–6; Manby 1995: 35).

An important issue for all sides to the negotiations was the process envisaged for achieving a constitution to govern the post-apartheid, democratic South African state. The need for a transitional period and related mechanisms was obvious to every one but the issue was mainly whether there would be a one- or two-stage process. For the NP government it was important to be able to secure certain issues to limit the 'damage' of giving up power. For the ANC, on the other hand, it was crucial that 'the Constitutional Assembly should be bound as little as possible by the non-elected negotiating forum' (de Villiers 1994: 38). Consequently, the NP was in favor of a one-stage process so that the negotiating parties at the Congress for a Democratic South Africa (CODESA) would draft the Constitution. This would have ensured an important voice for the NP in the formulation of the eventual Constitution. The ANC, however, wanted an elected body to be responsible for the drafting of the so-called 'final' Constitution so that it would have full legitimacy (Coveliers and Veys 1998: 236), while the period before the adoption of the latter constitution would be governed by an interim constitution, drawn up at CODESA (Van Wyk 1994: 143; Corder 1994: 498).

During the course of the negotiations at CODESA a two-stage process was accepted with sufficient consensus and it was a firm point of departure for the Multi Party Negotiation Process (MPNP) negotiation round (Corder 1994: 500). The eventual acceptance of this unique process of constitution making (Erasmus and de Waal 1997: 40–41) reflected a genuine concern for reconciliation and accommodation to include the previously ruling minority and to take its concerns seriously.

In the first stage an interim Constitution would be drafted by the negotiating political parties before any democratic election. That Constitution would govern the country during the period covering the first democratic elections and during the negotiations leading up to the adoption of the so-called final Constitution. 'In order to give greater comfort to all parties, it was agreed that the final Constitution could not erode the fundamental values and principles contained in the interim Constitution. Agreement was reached on a series of 34 Constitutional Principles with which the final Constitution had to comply' (Chaskalson and Davis 1996: 430). These 34 Constitutional Principles undeniably imposed constraints on the subsequent negotiation process as they provided the obligatory foundation for the 'final' constitution.

The Constitutional Negotiations

Equality, including Affirmative Action (in the Public Service)

In view of apartheid's divide and rule policy, its legacy of group-based discrimination (Currie 1994: 154) and the exclusion of the non-white populations from political participation, it is understandable that there was throughout the negotiations extensive emphasis on equality, the need to redress previous disadvantages, democracy and on nation building (Kentridge loose leaf: 14.1; De Waal 1998: 153). There can be no doubt that the equality principle lies at the heart of the constitution and pervades it. Regarding the equality principle, it should be underlined that 'the Constitution is not neutral as between different conceptions of equality. It subscribes to a particular vision of equality, one which is usually called substantive equality' (Kentridge loose leaf: 14.35), which can be contrasted with mere formal equality. Substantive equality demands a contextual approach, which takes into account relevant differences in circumstances (Loenen 1997: 403). In this regard, substantive equality allows and even requires remedial measures 'geared to redressing both individual and group disadvantage created by a history of oppression and apartheid' (Kentridge loose leaf: 14.35). Consequently, the principle of affirmative action to address disadvantages due to past discrimination in itself was easily agreed upon for the 1993 Constitution (Davis 1994: 210; Van Wyk 1994: 158), which sharply contrasts with the controversy surrounding its formulation in the 1996 Constitution and its implementation (Du Plessis 1994).

Understandably, in view of the history of legally instituted and entrenched discrimination under apartheid, the equality sections of both the 1993 and the 1996 Constitution contain a non-discrimination clause (Loenen 1997). Equality before the law and equal protection of the law are also taken up so that the entire section deals with most aspects of the equality principle as distinguished and recognized in international law (L'Heureux-Dube 1997: 340–341; Smith 1995: 94). Regarding the non-discrimination provision, it should be noted that indirect discrimination is expressly included. The prohibition of indirect discrimination not only embraces substantial equality considerations (Loenen 1997: 429), it can also be related to the pervasive impact of apartheid policies and the desire to prevent any re-appearance of these and related policies.

A related issue concerned the horizontal applicability of the equality provision (Section 8 (1), 1993 Constitution). While this was vital for the ANC in order to get to the roots of the legacy of apartheid's pervasive discrimination, it would also have implications for the position of both Muslim personal law and customary law in the new dispensation due to their patriarchal and gender discriminatory features. Some of the other parties, including the Democratic Party (DP) and the NP, cautioned regarding complete horizontal application because of its potential disruptive effects. After intense discussions, the non-discrimination provision was divided in two, one part dealing with discrimination by the state, the other with discrimination by private persons. The latter subsection also included a requirement for national legislation to prohibit unfair discrimination, which could then give further guidelines to the courts on how to deal with claims of unfair discrimination against a private person.

A problematic issue in the negotiations for the 1996 Constitution was the affirmative action clause in general, and the recognition of the need for affirmative action in public administration. Although the principle of affirmative action as a means of addressing disadvantages due to past discrimination was not contentious, the exact formulation of the affirmative action clause was. Eventually the following formulation was agreed to:

> Equality includes the full and equal enjoyment of all rights and freedoms. To promote the achievement of equality, legislative and other measures designed to protect or advance persons, or categories of persons, disadvantaged by unfair discrimination may be taken.' (Constitutional Talk Number 1 9 February 1996, Constitutional Talk Number 2–8 March 1996)

> Arguably, this clause clarifies that affirmative action is an implementation of and not an exception to the equality principle, thus confirming the fact that the constitution embraces a substantive conception of equality. (Loenen 1997: 404)

The debate on affirmative action does become rather contentious the more it is applied to concrete situations or fields of law, as exemplified by the discussions with respect to the chapter on public administration. Whereas the transitional provisions of the 1993 Constitution had secured the positions of the members of the public administration of the old order, the ANC felt very strongly about the need to include a constitutional commitment to affirmative action in that specific chapter, as otherwise the *status quo* would remain (Ellmann 1994: 27). The DP and the NP, however, felt that a general affirmative action clause in the Bill of Rights would be sufficient.

The minister of constitutional development underscored that in view of the fact that during apartheid the public service had excluded non-white people more than in any other area in South African society, the affirmative action principle should be repeated in the provisions on the public service to emphasize its importance. At the beginning of the post-apartheid era, it was indeed the case that '(o)fficials who dominate senior positions in these institutions ... are predominantly white, and many or most still harbor strong sympathies for the apartheid order they served for many years' (Ellmann 1994: 27). However, it is difficult to deny in relation to the civil service that 'the make up ... is an issue with ramifications for the future of *ethnic and racial* politics in South Africa' (Ellmann 1994: 27).

In the end, the following clause was included as one of the basic values and principles governing public administration, which demonstrates that 'affirmative action in public administration has won the day'(Ellmann 1994: 27):

> Public administration must be governed by the democratic values and principles enshrined in the Constitution, including the following principles: ... (i) Public administration must be broadly representative of the South African people, with employment and personnel management practices based on ability, objectivity, fairness, and *the need to redress the imbalances of the past to achieve broad representation*. (Italics added).

Language and Education

Prior to elaborating on the issues raised during the constitutional negotiations pertaining to language and education, some demographic information is appropriate. A review of the constitutional provision on the status of languages reveals the extent of the linguistic diversity present in South Africa. Next to the 11 official languages (Afrikaans, English, Sepedi, Sesotho, Setswana, siSwati, Tshivenda, Xitsonga, isiNdebele, isiXhosa and isiZulu), section 6 also mentions in a non-exhaustive enumeration of languages used in South Africa: Khoi, San, Nama, German, Greek, Gujerati, Hindi, Portuguese, Tamil, Telegu, Urdu, Arabic, Hebrew and Sanskrit.

The results of the official census of 2001 pertaining to the 11 official languages clearly establishes that no single language is overwhelmingly dominant, and that English is only the mother tongue of a mere 8.5 percent of the South African population. The most numerous linguistic group are the Zulu, isiZulu being spoken by 22.7 percent, while isiXhosa by 17.7 percent. Afrikaans is, due to its prevalence among Coloreds, the mother tongue of a large group of South Africans, namely 14.3 percent. The other language groups are, in descending order of demographic importance: Sepedi (9.1 percent), Setswana (8.1 percent), Sesotho (7.6 percent), Xitsonga (4.3 percent), siSwati (2.5 percent), Tshivenda (2.2 percent) and finally the Ndebele (1.4 percent).

The respective status of the languages spoken in South Africa, the regulation of language in education and 'separate' schools for distinctive population groups proved sensitive issues during the negotiation process, which can once more be related to apartheid's legacy. *Several* (white) Afrikaners were and still are very concerned about the status of their language, especially in relation to English, which can be explained by the severe language struggles in the past (Currie loose leaf: 37.1). On the other hand, most parties felt strongly about the fact that measures should be taken about the undervalued and neglected African indigenous languages. An attempt to accommodate all sides resulted in a very extensive and detailed provision.

It was not a problem for the NP (and other 'white' parties) that there would be 11 official languages as long as Afrikaans was among them. They did, however, bargain for a non-diminishment provision, which would ensure that the rights and status of the pre-1994 official languages were maintained (Currie loose leaf: 37.6–37.7), to prevent the erosion of Afrikaans in favor of English. The other parties could accept such a provision to the extent that it was understood that 'it was envisaged that the other nine languages would be developed to the point that all 11 languages enjoyed the same status and rights' (Currie loose leaf: 37.6). Although it was not required that all 11 official languages were treated equally (Sachs 1994: 9–15), it was agreed that efforts should be made to develop and promote the equal use of all official languages. The possibility of provincial legislatures to declare any of the national official languages as official language(s) of the province can furthermore be considered 'an attempt to recognize and accommodate the regional concentration of various linguistic groups' (Brand 1997: 692). Provision was also made for the establishment of an independent Pan South African Language Board, which is meant (*inter alia*) to further the development of the official languages and to promote multi-lingualism in South Africa.

Education was not as much a cause for deadlock in the negotiations during the CODESA and MP/NP rounds as in those preceding the adoption of the 1996 Constitution. Agreement was relatively easily reached on a guarantee for equal access to educational institutions. The equalization of educational opportunities is indeed crucial in view of apartheid's policy of separate but unequal education that resulted in grossly inferior education Africans and the concomitant under-qualification of this population (Dlamini 1994 589–590).

The freedom to choose the medium of instruction was very important to the parties representing the previously disadvantaged groups, in view of the mandatory regulation during apartheid. It also remains very important for an important section of the Afrikaner population, because this would enable them to choose mother tongue instruction, which is felt to be vital to maintain and promote the Afrikaner language and culture. However, it was clear to everyone that there are certain practical constraints to its complete realization and the right to chose the medium of instruction was thus made dependent on a requirement of 'practicability'.

Finally, the urge of certain Afrikaners to have separate educational institutions, conforming to their specific cultural values was also voiced. In so far as there would be no racial discrimination, this was something the ANC could agree to. However, subsequent events during the negotiations leading up the 1996 Constitution demonstrated that there were some attempts to circumvent such a prohibition by relying on arguments of culture and the like. This attempted circumvention incited resentment, and burdened the ongoing negotiations.

Indeed, two of the issues that remained unresolved until the very last moment in the negotiations leading up to the 1996 Constitution concerned the status of languages and the Bill of Rights on education. These matters involved core principles for the two major parties, namely NP and ANC, and the formulation of the respective clauses remained contentious even after the momentous three-dimensional agreement on minority protection issues.

It is appropriate and even necessary to give some information about the general trend as to language use in the public sphere since the adoption of the 1993 Constitution. Despite the 1993 Constitution's insistence that the state was required to promote the equal use and enjoyment of all 11 official languages, there was (and is) an undeniable shift towards mono-lingualism in the public sphere, with the effect that English is increasingly emerging as the *lingua franca*. The establishment of the Language Plan Task Group (LANGTAG) as an advisory body to the minister of Arts, Culture, Science and Technology in December 1995 was *inter alia* meant to counter this trend. LANGTAG's mandate was to advise the minister on a coherent national language plan which would aim at promoting national unity, while at the same time promoting respect and tolerance for linguistic and cultural diversity. Although both the draft and the final report of the language board only came out after the adoption of the (first version of) the 1996 Constitution, both reports criticize the official attitude in the national and also the provincial sphere of government for moving towards an English-only policy.

Both the NP and the Freedom Front (FF) feared that Afrikaans was going to be marginalized and completely swamped by English, and they wanted therefore the retention of the 1993 Constitution's non-diminishment provision. Although the negotiators of the other parties, and especially the ANC, realized that it was vital to find a balanced way to calm this fear, the ANC was adamant about the fact that the non-diminishment provision was not acceptable in the long run. For the ANC it was vital that there should be the constitutional possibility to improve the indigenous languages by reducing the status of Afrikaans so as to reach an equitable overall use of and status for all 11 official languages. In the end, the deadlock was resolved by an *in se* minor, but for the NP symbolically important, addition to one of the other subsections of the language clause. The NP was only prepared to agree that the non-diminishment provision be dropped on condition that the section dealing with 'use of language for purposes of government' at the national and provincial levels would require that this could not be only one language. The party felt that such a provision would at least counter the tendency that only English would be used at these levels.

The proclamation of 11 official languages in the 1996 Constitution, as in the 1993 Constitution (Young 1995: 65), has important symbolic value (Currie loose leaf: 37.2), especially for the speakers of the nine African languages, which used to be deprived of such status. The feeling of inclusiveness that is created by this linguistic policy should not be underestimated. It confirms that accommodation of a state's population diversity tends to have positive implications for the project of nation-building (Currie loose leaf: 37.5). Nevertheless, it is striking that the 1996 constitution no longer has the equal treatment of the 11 official languages as an—albeit distant—objective, but 'merely' the equitable treatment and parity of esteem of these languages. 'Equitable' treatment can be considered to strengthen the internal reference to subsection 2, which expressed the need for positive measures by the state to elevate the status of the official indigenous languages. 'Equitable' would make explicit that there is, in view of the 'history of official denigration and neglect' of these indigenous languages, a need for differential and preferential treatment and not merely formally equal treatment (Currie loose leaf: 37.5). However, 'equitable treatment' may also acknowledge that not all 11 official languages should or can always be used for all purposes. 'Parity of esteem' would then 'insist(s) that considerations of practicality aside, a sincere attempt must be made to ensure that particular languages do not dominate while others are neglected' (Currie loose leaf: 37.6), and would imply a rejection of an over-powering *lingua franca*.

Finally, the right to education, and more specifically the issue of language in education and single medium institutions, proved to be the greatest stumbling block of all and was only resolved on May 7, 1996, the day before the adoption of the (first version of) the 1996 Constitution (Currie loose leaf: 35.7; Loban 1997: 107). Eventually, the discussions turned around the issue of single medium institutions, as pressed by the NP (and the FF), which was (after many rounds of negotiations) integrated, to a certain extent, in the subsection on the medium of instruction. The starting point of the controversy around the education provision had been the NP's proposal for a right 'to educational institutions based on a common culture, language or religion, provided that there shall be no discrimination on the ground of race and, provided further that the state shall not, in granting aid to educational institutions, discriminate against any educational institution on the ground that it has been established on the basis of a common language, culture or religion'. Whereas such a right to state-funded schools with a distinctive linguistic, cultural or religious character was considered to be imperative by the NP to protect and promote the Afrikaner culture and language, while offering the same advantage to other minorities, this was completely unthinkable for the ANC as it would imply a return to Verwoerdian (apartheid) practices (Currie loose leaf: 35.6–35.7).

Furthermore, the judgment of the Constitutional Court in the *Gauteng education case* of April 4,1996, had clarified that the analogous section of the 1993 Constitution (which did not contain the explicit words 'at their own expense'), reflected the appropriate option about state obligations regarding the funding of minority schools. According to the Constitutional Court, the state has, under section 32(c), 1993 Constitution, a mere negative obligation of non-interference regarding private efforts to that effect.

This judgment influenced the eventual formulation of the right to set up independent educational institutions, in the sense that the 1996 Constitution makes explicit that this is 'at their own expense' and that two other provisos are added to the one that prohibited racial discrimination. The Constitutional Court had indeed held that the 1993 Constitution also implied that these independent institutions should be registered with the state and should live up to certain minimum standards. The outcome of this case furthermore 'increased anxiety about the formulation of the education clause on the side of the Afrikaners' (Malherbe 1997: 63). Subsequently, the NP insisted on the need for a right to single medium institutions in the public education sector, which indicated a shift of emphasis in its claim regarding the right to education. However, the ANC was not open to any concessions in this regard and the NP finally agreed to a 'much diluted version' of its original proposal in the provision on the medium of instruction.

> Everyone has the right to receive education in the official language or languages of their choice in public educational institutions where that education is reasonably practicable. In order to ensure the effective access to, and implementation of, this right, *the state must consider all reasonable educational alternatives, including single medium institutions*, tak-

> ing into account (a) equity; (b) practicability and (c) the need to redress the results of past racially discriminatory laws and practices. (Section 29 [3], 1996 Constitution. Italics added)

Although the NP's position with hindsight was that 'they have lost this one', it can be stated that this subsection makes 'express concessions to minority interests' (Kriel loose leaf: 38.15). The factors which the state is to take into account when implementing the right to receive education in the official language or languages of choice apparently have some but not much potential for single medium Afrikaans institutions. Although the third factor does not seem to be conducive to a choice for single medium Afrikaans institutions, this might be balanced out in certain circumstances by the 'equity' factor, for example in areas where the majority of the people speaks Afrikaans. Furthermore, and in view of the collective aspect of an educational institution of this kind, section 31 and its recognition and protection of the collective dimension of the rights of persons belonging to (cultural, religious and) linguistic communities, can arguably also be used to canvass claims of single medium institutions for linguistic communities.

At the same ultimate session where section 29(2) was agreed, the DP also proposed an additional subsection, which would provide for the possibility of state subsidies for independent educational institutions, as catered for in section 29 (3). This proposal was readily accepted by the ANC and welcomed by the NP since it carries the possibility of their 'educational institutions based on a common language, culture or religion' to be private but nevertheless state-funded. In the end, the further implementation of the education clause, its application and eventual adaptation, will demonstrate to what extent this provision effectively caters for minorities and accommodates South Africa's overall population diversity (Brown 1997: 3).

Self-determination, the Volkstaat and Minority Rights

Claims of some Afrikaners for self-determination, and more specifically a Volkstaat, proved controversial during the 1993 constitutional negotiations which remained outstanding until the last moment. In the end, the ANC made several concessions so as to make the constitution as inclusive as possible and to persuade all parties to participate in the elections. Eventually, constitutional amendments were agreed to in the Constitution of the Republic of South Africa Amendment Act 2 of 1994 so as to placate the parties advocating a Volkstaat. The amendment provided *inter alia* for a Volkstaat Council and another Constitutional Principle dealing with the right to self-determination for a community sharing a common 'cultural or language heritage' (Corder 1994: 504–505).

Constitutional Principle XXXIV embodies a qualified recognition of a right to self-determination, not limited to the internal dimension of that right (Currie loose leaf: 35.33), in that it states that would not be precluded: 'constitutional recognition for a notion of the right of self-determination by any community sharing a common cultural and language heritage, whether in a territorial entity within the Republic or in any other recognized way' (Schedule 4, 1993 Constitution).

The Volkstaat Council was meant to 'enable proponents of the idea of a Volkstaat to constitutionally pursue the establishment of such a Volkstaat'. Nevertheless, it should be pointed out that the Council's powers were not far-reaching as it was envisaged to be an advisory body that has powers to gather information and make representations on the Volkstaat issue to the Constitutional Assembly, entrusted to the elaborate 1996 Constitution (Van Wyk 1994: 165, 168).

Indeed, one of the sensitive issues in the 1996 constitutional negotiations was the right to self-determination for an ethnic group ('a community sharing a common cultural and language heritage') and the way in which CP XXXIV would be realized in the 1996 Constitution in view of its merely permissive wording. Self-determination on ethnic grounds tends to have many negative connotations due to apartheid's Grand Apartheid scheme, but the idea of a Volkstaat was furthermore perceived to be an attempt to perpetuate the concept of apartheid and to hold on to privileges gained during that era. Nevertheless, the ANC was aware of the fear felt by *some* Afrikaners that their language and culture would be swamped (or die) if they did not have some form of (preferentially territorial) self-determination.

During the negotiations, virtually no reference was made to the right to self-determination and its shape in the final Constitution (Currie loose leaf: 35.33). In view of the Freedom Front's mandate and its focus on the Volkstaat ideal, that party argued that CP XXXIV legitimized their demand for constitutional recognition of a territorial Volkstaat. The ANC resisted such a recognition and relied *inter alia* on the fact that the first interim report of the Volkstaat Council, as presented to the Constitutional Assembly (CA), had demonstrated that there was a lot of internal division on the future shape of such a Volkstaat (Currie loose leaf: 35.34). Whereas initially these discussions only involved the ANC and the FF (bilateral), eventually, as time-pressure was getting stronger and the need to make 'deals' grew, this issue was settled at a 'marathon of 36 hours of negotiations' from April 18–19, 1997 (Currie loose leaf: 35.5; Strydom 1998: 900–901). During several hours of that marathon there was a trilateral of the ANC, the NP and the FF. Since during the previous bilaterals between the ANC and the FF, the ANC had formulated promises of cultural councils and rights analogous to article 27 ICCPR, the NP joined the discussion to further their goal of including minority rights in the constitution.

Eventually, the result of this trilateral was a three-dimensional agreement on a Commission for the Protection and Promotion of the Rights of Cultural, Religious and Linguistic Communities, cultural rights like article 27 ICCPR (section 31) and a provision on self-determination, the wording of which mimics CP XXXIV. Although the word 'community' is used instead of 'minority', the similarities between article 27 ICCPR and section 31 are striking. The concept 'community' was preferred because 'minority' is related to the apartheid ideology and because the former concept would express ties of affinity and connectedness rather than ties of blood (Currie loose leaf: 35.12). It can nevertheless be argued that 'the most pragmatic way to deal with the difficulties of definition of the term community is to see it as doing more or less the same work as the term it substitutes for article 27's category of a 'minority'' (Strydom 1998: 899–900). Apartheid's abuse of ethnicity furthermore explains the use of 'cultural' instead of 'ethnic' (Currie loose leaf: 35.12).

It was decided that this Commission would be provided for in the chapter on State Institutions Supporting Constitutional Democracy, thus confirming the link between democracy and minority protection. The Commission is to be broadly representative of the several communities in South Africa and is empowered to monitor, investigate, research, educate, advise and report on issues concerning the rights of these communities. Further details are provided by the legislation actually establishing this commission. Section 185 (1) explicitly enumerates the following primary objectives of the Commission, which reveals that it is meant to contribute to the accommodation of South Africa's population diversity (Erasmus and de Waal 1997: 35.34):

(a) to promote respect for the rights of cultural, religious and linguistic communities;
(b) to promote and develop peace, friendship, humanity, tolerance and national unity among cultural, religious and linguistic communities, on the basis of equality, non-discrimination and free association; and
(c) to recommend the establishment or recognition, in accordance with national legislation, of a cultural or other council or councils for a community or communities in South Africa.

Secondly, agreement was reached on the inclusion in the Bill of Rights of a section with additional 'cultural rights', meant to reflect the spirit of article 27 ICCPR. The rights are indeed framed as collective rights, more specifically in terms of 'members belonging to .... communities' and arguably enshrine a right to identity. There was some contention about the exact wording of the clause, namely whether it would be negative like article 27 ICCPR or positive, but eventually the first option was taken up and section 31 (1) (a) of the 1996 Constitution reads as follows:

> Persons belonging to a cultural, religious or linguistic community may not be denied the right, with other members of that community – (a) to enjoy their culture, practice their religion and use their language.

The third and final component of the package agreed to by the ANC, FF and NP was that a provision would be added to the Constitution, to enshrine the content of CP XXXIV. The eventual provision, which was acceptable to the parties, is equally vague in its formulation as the Constitutional Principle and so open-ended that it cannot be said to enshrine a right at all (Currie loose leaf: 35.33–35.34):

> The right of the South African people as a whole to self-determination, as manifested in this Constitution, *does not preclude, within the framework of this right, recognition of the notion of the right of self-determination* of any community sharing a common cultural and language heritage, within a territorial entity in the Republic or in any other way determined by national legislation. (Section 235, 1996 Constitution. Italics added).

The fact that national legislation will determine the acceptable ways of implementing self-determination underscores that section 235 actually does not grant a right to self-determination to communities but leaves this to the discretion of the national legislator. Nevertheless, it was argued section 235 requires that the phrase 'self-determination' should be interpreted so as not to exclude the possibility of vindication of the right of self-determination by 'external or by internal political means' and also that the expression 'community sharing a common cultural and language heritage' refers to an ethnic minority (Currie loose leaf: 35.34). Consequently, section 235 would leave the door ajar to forms of both external and internal (even with a territorial dimension) self-determination for 'minorities', thus securing the possible emergence of a Volkstaat, however tenuous that possibility might seem.

It should be pointed out that section 235 is part of the chapter with General Provisions and thus not of the Bill of Rights (Strydom 1998: 907). Finally, the overall tendency of the 1996 Constitution to move away from a recognition of self-determination that would result in a Volkstaat, is clearly demonstrated by the fact that the Volkstaat Council can be abolished by Parliament at will.

This three-dimensional agreement led to many spontaneous and emotional speeches by several of the party leaders present at the Constitutional Sub-Committee. Roelf Meyer (NP) underscored that in this way the real needs of *all* cultural groups are accommodated and that it consequently amounted to an important step in the creation of a country where *all* peoples feel at home. Valli Moosa (ANC) added that these agreements capture in a democratic manner the aspirations of the country in that it may be a new way of dealing with the 'national question' without contradicting the concept of nation building. The speeches of the other parties also acknowledged the importance of this breakthrough dealing with the stigmas of the past and working towards unity in diversity. Although these provisions came about due to claims and demands put forward by political parties representing (a section of) the Afrikaner population, it is clear that all parties realized and underscored its broader potential, namely for all population groups in South Africa that have a distinct identity and a wish to preserve that.

Without wanting to negate the importance of this kind of agreement so soon after apartheid was formally abolished, it should also be put in perspective. Section 31 and the provision for the Commission imply the introduction of collective rights and the recognition of collective interests (Currie loose leaf: 35.5) and thus amount to the entrenchment of some minority rights (and minority protection). Although at first sight this contradicts the ANC's strong rejection of special treatment for ethnic/cultural groups, it was the 'price' they were willing to pay to placate the Freedom Front by accepting the weak recognition of the right to self-determination, while giving the National Party the minority rights it wanted (Currie loose leaf: 35:5; Sacks 1997: 679).

It seems appropriate to mention at this point that the ANC emphasized the objective of nation building in subsequent talks on the establishment of that Commission (and the rights provided for in section 31). At the same time it also acknowledged the need to accommodate the country's population diversity, thus taking up the theme of unity in diversity. It is not entirely clear to what extent the prime objective of national unity and nation building will leave effective scope for genuine protection and promotion of diversity, as are made possible by sections 31 and 185 of the 1996 Constitution (Sacks 1997: 672). Further implementation as well as application will show whether the ANC, as the dominant political party, senses that the goal of nation building can be furthered, instead of threatened, by accommodating South Africa's population diversity effectively. In the end, the exercise will be about finding the right balance between promoting unity and accommodating diversity, which is not a straightforward matter and requires thorough consideration of all the relevant circumstances.

A related point that can be addressed concerns the possibility in the 1993 and the 1996 Constitution for legislation to recognize marriages and other systems of personal and family law under non-Christian religions, since this reflects a positive predisposition for the protection of religious minorities. However, during the negotiations for the 1996 Constitution, the parties wanted to avoid the impression that 'systems of religious law trumped all provisions of the Bill of Rights' (Smith 1995: 222), with special attention for the equality principle and the prohibition of gender discrimination. In the end, also taking into account concerns of the Muslim minority, the parties included the qualification that the legislation 'must be consistent with this section [on freedom of religion] and the provisions of the Constitution.' While the former assuaged certain fears of the Muslim minority, the latter was felt crucial to safeguard the central position of the equality principle in the Constitution. In view of the crucial place given to equality concerns in the Constitution, there seems little scope for acceptable limitations on the prohibition of gender discrimination to allow religious prescripts to be maintained (Smith 1997: 222–223; Van der Schyff 2003: 522).

Traditional Leaders and Customary Law

During the negotiating process, traditional leaders pressed not only for an entrenchment and recognition of their status and role, but also for some exemptions for customary law from the Bill of Rights (and especially the equality clause) (Sacks 1997: 678). The inherent problems of these submissions are that 'the institution of traditional leadership rests on patriarchal and authoritarian foundations rather than on democratic values while the body of indigenous law recognized and applied by the courts is pervaded by rules and customs that discriminate against women'. This obviously is not easily reconciled with the key objective of the new democratic dispensation which attempts to establish open and democratic governance backed by guarantees of individual freedom and equality (Currie loose leaf: 36.1–2).

Throughout the negotiations in the Constitutional Assembly it was obvious that the negotiating parties were strongly inclined to confirm the supremacy of the Bill of Rights in general. At the same time all the role players realized that it is not possible to simply abolish customary law all together. A similar dilemma was encountered regarding the appropriate status of traditional leaders in a democracy.

The dilemma and ensuing ambivalent attitude toward traditional leaders and customary law resulted in a constitutional provision (section 211, 1996 Constitution) which recognizes traditional leadership according to customary law 'subject to the Constitution', and customary law subject to the Bill of Rights. Furthermore, there is (in contrast to the Interim Constitution) no longer an obligation to establish a National House or Provincial Houses of Traditional Leaders, nor a guarantee of an *ex officio* membership at local government level after the 1999 elections (section 212, 1996 Constitution). Obviously, one has chosen to pass a controversial issue to the implementation process, so that the ensuing legislation and policy development have to make the hard choices and find the appropriate balance between democratic principles and the supremacy of the Bill of Rights on the one hand and the protection of cultural diversity as related to traditional leaders and customary law on the other hand (Strydom 1998: 905–906).

The constitutional negotiation process and the ensuing constitution have clearly demonstrated a balanced approach in line with the multiple objectives of the transformation process. The themes of redress of the past, overcoming the legacy of apartheid and its systemic discrimination as well as the accommodation of South Africa's extensive population diversity all have their role to play. This is clearly visible in the constitutional provisions on the equality principle, the status of languages, education, minority rights, self-determination on ethnic grounds, and the position of traditional leaders and customary law in the new, democratic dispensation.

However, these themes do not always point in the same direction, which comes to the fore in the implementation process. As the following sections will demonstrate, the latter is very slow and often highly deficient, reflecting various challenges that need to be met in the coming years and decades.

The Implementation Phase

Although the agreement on aforementioned constitutional provisions and its contribution to the reconciliation and reconstruction process are crucial, the actual and ongoing implementation is equally, if not more, important.

This overview of ongoing implementation of the constitutional provisions relevant to equality and the accommodation of population diversity is not meant to be comprehensive but sets out to include the most important developments. When possible, references will be made to legislation as well as broader policy, and related documents for detailed information can be found.

An Equality Provision

In regard to the equality provision of the Constitution, both the jurisprudence of the Constitutional Court and three pieces of implementing legislation are analyzed and discussed. While the first act of legislation is mostly important in terms of the prohibition of discrimination, the last two deal predominantly with the highly sensitive area of affirmative action. The equality jurisprudence of the Constitutional Court has so far dealt with the non-discrimination principle. This case law has not only clarified the stages of scrutiny of a discrimination complaint, but also has underlined the importance of substantive equality under the new Constitutional dispensation (De Vos 2000: 66–68; Freedman 2000: 314–319). Nevertheless, only one judgment addresses (to some extent) the problem of redressing the disadvantages from the past in its relation to the prohibition of discrimination (against previously advantaged groups) explicitly. A true affirmative action case pertaining to employment has not yet come before the Constitutional Court.

The South African constitutional provision on non-discrimination is rather peculiar because it adds the term 'unfair' to discrimination, whereas in international law the latter concept is understood to have a pejorative connotation in itself. The Constitutional Court has chosen different criteria to evaluate 'discrimination' and 'unfairness'. While *Prinsloo v. Van der Linde and another* (18 April 1997) clarifies the meaning of 'discrimination,' *President of the Republic of South Africa and another v. Hugo* focuses on the implications of 'unfair' and the criteria to determine unfairness.

In *Prinsloo* the Court distinguishes between enumerated and non-enumerated grounds of differentiation. A differentiation on one of the enumerated grounds would constitute *per se* discrimination (no further proof required), a differentiation on another ground would require proof that the differential treatment infringes the fundamental human dignity of the person concerned (§§ 27 and 31). *Hugo* adds that differentiations on one of the enumerated grounds carry a presumption of unfairness that needs to be rebutted by the respondent. Conversely, if one can prove that a differentiation on another ground amounts to discrimination, one additionally has to proof that it is unfair. The Court also identifies three criteria to evaluate the unfairness of an instance of discrimination, more specifically 'the nature of the group who is disadvantaged, the nature of the power in terms of which the discrimination was effected and also the nature of the interests which have been affected by the discrimination' (§ 33). While the first factor implies an opening towards substantive equality concerns, the last one underscores that certain interests are so fundamental that even socially advantaged groups cannot be expected to tolerate their denial. These two factors are obviously the most important as they go to the core of the dilemma of the entire affirmative action/non-discrimination debate.

In *Harksen v Lane NO and Others* (7 October 1997) the Court slightly reformulates these criteria of unfairness, while indicating that the list is neither static nor closed (§ 51). More importantly, the Court adds a third stage of inquiry by indicating that a finding of unfair discrimination might still be saved under the general limitations clause of the Bill of Rights (§ 52). Arguably, when one takes these three stages of inquiry together the South African approach to non-discrimination cases is quite similar to the approach of the ECHR and other international supervisory bodies.

City Council of Pretoria v Walker (17 February 1998) highlights the pervasive effects of apartheid and its policy of separate development as it deals with the issue of indirect discrimination on the basis of race as related to geographical areas. The case concerns the practice of the Pretoria City Council to charge different tariffs for municipal services in previously white areas (based on actual consumption) and previously black areas (flat rate) and also the practice of differential enforcement regarding failure to pay for the services, as legal steps to recover such arrears were only taken in respect of residents in the previously white areas.

The Court qualifies these differential practices as indirect discrimination on the basis of race (§ 32), which would be presumed to be unfair. The majority of the Court held that the presumption of unfairness also applies to indirect forms of discrimination on one of the enumerated grounds. Hence, the City Council had to rebut the presumption of the unfairness of the discrimination concerned. The Court finds unfair discrimination on the basis of race and it underscores that whereas the equality provision 'recognizes the need to redress past disadvantages, the guarantee that it gives extends to all sections of the community, not only those who have been disadvantaged in the past.'(§ 73). Apparently, the Court is trying to find the right balance in the current transition period between treating the previously advantaged groups appropriately while leaving sufficient scope for redress of the disadvantages the non-white population suffered during apartheid.

Despite the critical comments regarding the use of the presumption of unfairness in the case of indirect discrimination on an enumerated ground, the subsequent case law has followed the non-discrimination principles as outlined in *Harksen*. Later case law dealt more specifically with differential treatment on the basis of sexual orientation and HIV infection, and clearly set out to counter societal prejudice in these respects (Carpenter 2002:181–182), while underlining the vital importance of substantive equality in the new, democratic South Africa.

When evaluating the implementation of the equality clause of the 1996 Constitution, an important piece of legislation that surely needs to be discussed is the *Promotion of Equality and Prevention of Unfair Discrimination Act* of 2000. According to its preamble the Act sets out to 'facilitate the transition to a democratic society, united in its diversity, marked by human relations that are caring and compassionate, and guided by the principles of equality, fairness, equity, social progress, justice, human dignity and freedom'. The Act is mainly focused on the prohibition of discrimination and basically takes up the jurisprudence of the Constitutional Court in this respect. An important point is that the Act binds not only the state but also private persons, thus reaffirming the horizontal applicability of the equality clause. The Act furthermore foresees the establishment of so-called equality courts, with a wide range of possible rulings, and provides for an *actio popularis* allowing standing for any person acting in the public interest. These features are to be welcomed as they are meant to enhance the effective implementation of the Act. Chapter 5 reveals the focus on substantive equality and hence opens the door to the development of affirmative action schemes as it establishes the duty of the State to promote equality in a number of ways, while the general duty to promote equality is also imposed on every person, NGO and traditional institutions.

Notwithstanding the explicit Constitutional basis for affirmative action measures, most affirmative action schemes developed and implemented up until now have been controversial, especially affirmative action in the public service, the Employment Equity Act of 1998 and to some extent also the Broad Based Black Economic Empowerment Act of 2003.

There are strong misgivings among the white, Colored and Indian population in this respect. The last two categories were in an intermediate category under apartheid and feel that they are now not black enough because affirmative action policies are perceived to be completely or mainly geared towards the African population groups. On the side of the white population, most complaints seem to focus on the irrational and rigid way in which affirmative action policies are implemented, overemphasizing numbers and lowering of standards. Typically, debates relating to affirmative action for victims of past discrimination and the use of the dreaded apartheid classifications reigned supreme.

Until now the *Employment Equity Act* (EEA) has undoubtedly been the most controversial affirmative action measure. In addition to a ban on unfair discrimination the Act also obliges employers with 50 or more workers to take steps towards employment equity which would mean a more proportional representation of the various racial groups in the work force (Zalesne 2001: 512–513). The Act tries to strike an appropriate balance in this respect by stressing the need to prevent a lowering of standards and to avoid strict quota (section 15), while at the same time countering that capacity would only be based on formal qualifications (section 20(3)). Furthermore, the Act attempts to calm fears of the white population by explicitly providing that employers are not required to establish an absolute barrier to the prospective or continued employment or advancement of people who are not from designated groups (section 15(4)). While initially the response and implementation was rather disappointing, it seems that by 2004 employment equity legislation is indeed beginning to change the composition of South African companies. Nevertheless, a lot needs to be improved concerning top management positions. In this respect it has been pointed out that it is crucial that organizations implement training and development programs to fast-track previously disadvantaged individuals to correct the racial imbalance and to ensure that they have the necessary skills.

Finally, reference needs to be made to the *Broad Based Black Economic Empowerment Ac*t of 2003. Its preamble indicates that it is enacted in order to 'promote the achievement of the constitutional right to equality' through the promotion of the effective participation of black people in the economy.

Importantly, Article One defines 'black people' broadly to include the Indians and Coloreds. It furthermore indicates that 'broad based black economic empowerment' includes strategies to 'achieving equitable representation in all occupational categories and levels in the workforce', which seems to complement the achievements of the EEA. Article 2 adds to this that one of the objectives of the Act is 'achieving a substantial change in the racial composition of ownership and management structures and in the skilled occupations of existing and new enterprises.' This Act has an obvious affirmative action approach but it is much to soon to evaluate its impact as it is just in the beginning stages of implementation.

Overall, post-apartheid South Africa has chosen to adopt a substantive conception of equality but it is still searching for the exact balance in achieving that, without alienating the population groups that were (more or less) privileged under apartheid (Carpenter 2002: 184–185).

Language and Education

The actual practice regarding language use for purposes of government and other related public functions, like the public broadcaster, are a far cry from the promising constitutional principles of the 1996 Constitution. Consequently, there is a rather uniform complaint about the dominant status of English as *lingua franca* and the concomitant negation of meaningful multi-lingualism, as demanded by the Constitution (Du Plessis, Legal Policy Forum no 6: 4).

Although certain public institutions and national departments are trying to develop language policies, which also set out to incorporate the nine indigenous official languages in its internal and external communication, English ostensibly keeps its predominant position. One of the underlying problems is also that these indigenous languages' vocabulary and grammar needs to be refined and developed so that they can be used in these more technical areas. However, this is not really materializing.

In the end the main issue is the lack of political will to make multi-lingualism a reality on the ground, probably in view of its low stance on the priority list of government. Hence, the overall situation amounts to a *de facto* denial of several constitutional principles with respect to the status of languages and multi-lingualism.

The lack of political will to work towards meaningful and equitable multi-lingualism in the public sphere is *inter alia* revealed by the slow development of the National Language Action Plan and the even more sluggish delivery. The National Language Action Plan was only approved by Cabinet in March 2003, that is, over six years since the coming into force of the 1996 Constitution, while the principle of multi-lingualism and the designation of 11 official languages was already in place in the 1993 Constitution! The South African Languages Bill, which purports to implement certain portions of the Language Plan, was not finalized until more than one year after its publication. The provinces also have certain competencies regarding language use but most of them are awaiting the finalization of the national language legislation. While some of them have at least draft policies in place, others do not have anything at all. Only the Western Cape has devised and implemented a language policy on the basis of the Western Cape Provincial Languages Act of 1998.

The National Language Plan also proposed three structures to implement the policy it contained. However only one of them, the National Language Forum, is actually established and is functioning. The forum meets four times a year and provides a platform for deliberation for provincial and national departments on policy matters pertaining to language use. So far not much harmonization has ensued but this would be hard to expect as the national level of government still has not finalized its own legislation (and hence policy stances in this respect).

The Plan also proposed 12 mechanisms, of which only three are operative. These three, terminology development for the indigenous languages, translation and editing have been on offer in the Department of Arts and Culture since 1994. The remaining mechanisms which have not materialized are language technology, a language code of conduct, a directory of language services, language audits and surveys, language awareness campaigns, the telephone interpreting service for South Africa, an information databank, the development of Sign Language and language learning and budgeting. While the drawn-out policy process has resulted in very promising ideas, strategies etc., the actual delivery rate seems to indicate that the political will to realize multilingualism is simply not present (sufficiently).

Education is, in general, a very sensitive matter in post-apartheid South Africa, which is revealed by numerous teacher strikes and instances of student unrest, because of the lack of financial aid for most students from previously disadvantaged backgrounds, the lack of racial transformation at schools and tertiary institutions, the decisions regarding choice of medium of instruction, especially at tertiary institutions, the religious policy at schools and the overall restructuring of the curriculum (Henrard 2002). The theme of equal access to and integration of educational institutions is very important and should be seen against the background of racially structured education during apartheid. At the level of schools, non-discriminatory access is required and protected, while with respect to tertiary education several attempts are made to facilitate access for students from previously disadvantaged communities by adopting flexible and progressive methods to establish ability for higher education.

A very sensitive aspect of curriculum choices is the policy pertaining to language of instruction. The Constitution determines in section 29(2) that 'everyone has the right to receive instruction in the official language or languages of their choice in public educational institutions where that education is reasonably practicable'. This provision is often understood as enabling mother tongue education, which is considered to be important not only for the transfer of culture and values but also for the optimal cognitive development of the students concerned.

At the level of schools the national minister of education has proclaimed in 1996 National Norms and Standards regarding Language Policy. These can be considered as a genuine attempt to realize the individual student's choice regarding medium of instruction as much as reasonably possible, while taking resource and other practical constraints into account. However, severe problems of effective implementation persist. There might be a change on hand as the new minister has announced in her budget speech recently that she favors mother tongue education in the first three years of study. However, so far no changes have occurred in practice or policy.

There was a big hype in 2003 after the announcement of the then minister of education, Kader Asmal, of the new policy on religion in education. Following that policy all students in government schools, private schools and even those undergoing home schooling would have to be taught about religions from a neutral perspective from material prescribed by the state. Hence, separate classes in the respective religions would be phased out, while in depth education in one's own religion would have to be done outside the school hours, in one's private time. The controversy has not lasted longer then a few months and it seems that most people have accepted this policy as very sensible given the high degree of religious diversity of the population.

Education and the decisions taken in that policy area have obvious important repercussions for the future of South Africa. It will be mandatory for the state to ensure that access to education becomes a reality for all, that the decisions on the medium of instruction will promote optimal levels of cognitive development of the students, while overall tolerance and mutual respect (also on religious issues) are adequately promoted. This amounts to a considerable challenge indeed, which requires in addition to the necessary political will, adequate investments of human and financial resources.

Minority Rights and the Right to Self Determination

Regarding the most obvious minority rights provision of the Bill of Rights, section 31, there is so far not a single case of the Constitutional Court nor implementing legislation clarifying its ambit and implications. Nevertheless, certain statements in case law pertaining to the equality principle can be pointed to as auguring well for a certain openness towards minority claims before the Constitutional Court.

As indicated above, section 185 of the Constitution was meant to complement section 31's recognition of the rights of persons belonging to these communities and indicated that a Commission is to be established 'for the protection and promotion of the rights of cultural, religious and linguistic communities'. The Act actually establishing the Commission only came into effect on 30 November 2002, after a very lengthy elaboration process. Since April 2004 the Commission is finally established but so far its contribution to the protection of minorities in South Africa is hard to gauge.

It seems fair to say that the slow pace of its establishment underscores the *de facto* reluctance of the current government to deal with these issues. Furthermore, a few comments are in order on the wording of the Act. The Act does not clarify in any way the content of the rights in section 31, while it was expected to at least reveal whether these rights had a significant group dimension, as the constitutional title of the Commission seemed to imply. Overall, the formulation of the Act is so careful and open-ended that it does not clarify the potential impact of the Commission. This is particularly evident concerning the functions and powers of the Commission, which are specified in part 5 of the Act. The question of the criteria for the establishment and recognition of a cultural council for a community remains completely untouched, while functions of these councils are left to be decided by further legislation.

It has been noted that section 15(3) of the Constitution empowers the legislator to recognize, within certain parameters, religiously inspired systems of personal law. This has substantial potential towards the protection of the Muslim minority in South Africa. Several cases since 1994 confirmed that the main and most urgent problem is the lack of recognition of marriages celebrated according to Muslim rites and its unjust results, such as the illegitimate children and the unprotected position of the wife in respect of third persons. The South African Law (Reform) Commission (SALC) worked on a report and draft bill pertaining to the (circumscribed) recognition of Muslim marriages since 1986 and only concluded it in July 2003. However, so far no draft bill or bill has emerged and been brought before Parliament by the Department of Justice. A significant problem here is that several sections of the Muslim community do not accept the equality-based approach of the SALC in this respect, notwithstanding that this approach is aimed at ensuring the compatibility with the Bill of Rights (Henrard 2001: 66–67). There is indeed a difficult balance to be struck between the right to equality (between spouses) and the right to cultural identity (as protected by section 31 of the 1996 Constitution), about which not all public authorities might see eye to eye. Nevertheless, similar problems can be identified in relation to the recognition of customary marriages but this has not prevented the Recognition of Customary Marriages Act becoming a reality already in 1998 (see infra). Furthermore, significant breakthroughs were already realized in certain cases, in which courts relying on the new constitutional ethos of tolerance, pluralism and religious freedom had given recognition to certain legal effects flowing from *de facto* monogamous Muslim marriages.

When considering the right to self-determination on ethnic grounds, overall the 1996 Constitution moves away from a recognition of a right of self-determination that might result in a Volkstaat. Since the coming into force of the 1996 Constitution, negotiations between the ANC and the FF are ongoing without, however, any significant break-through. Nevertheless, it is striking that whenever there is a strong reaction by Afrikaners, due to perceived threats to their language and culture by one or another new policy document, which includes stronger claims to retreat and even use of violence and secession, there is a revamp of high-level negotiations.

It needs to be acknowledged that the latest elections have revealed a very poor result for the FF, which seems to indicate that most Afrikaners do not really want a Volkstaat. Nevertheless for a small section of Afrikaners it remains an important goal. This explains how in view of the lack of progress on the official level and the increasing unlikelihood that an official Volkstaat will come about, there are some private initiatives towards the development of a Volkstaat, one of which, Orania, appears to be rather successful (ANC news briefing August 10, 2001). While the population growth of Orania is very slow, there are several noteworthy attempts to empower the community including the development and official recognition of its own bank and its own currency.

Still, it remains to be seen how this town will develop, what reaction it will provoke from both the wider public and the authorities, but it sends a strong signal to the state that certain Afrikaners choose to separate instead of integrate and take this kind of action because they feel that their right to identity is not sufficiently protected.

Traditional Leaders and Customary law

The relevant constitutional provisions already demonstrated an ambiguous attitude towards traditional leaders and their place in terms of the new constitutional, democratic dispensation. This ambivalent picture is confirmed and perpetuated in the implementation phase. On the one hand one can point to an extensive degree of institutional support for traditional leaders, which arguably reveals a genuine attempt to integrate that institution into the democratic state structure. Three national bodies have been established soon after the 1996 Constitution took effect (4 February 1997) more specifically a Chief Directorate on Traditional Leaders in the Department of Constitutional Development, a MINMEC on traditional leaders and a National Council (now House) of Traditional Leaders. On the other hand, this institutional support has been rather weak in its actual 'delivery'. The Chief Directorate needed seven years to finalize its White Paper on Traditional Leadership and Governance (September 2003), which led to the Traditional Leadership and Governance Framework Act of 19 December 2003. The MINMEC's political discussion forum, consisting of national and provincial ministers responsible for traditional leaders has not adopted any meaningful decisions. The National House on Traditional Leaders might have an important symbolic function but does not have more then advisory powers.

A similar ambivalent attitude can be noticed in *the Remuneration of Public Office Bearers Act of 1998*. Traditional leaders are obviously considered part of the state structure as they are explicitly listed among the public office bearers who receive salary from the state. However, this important inclusion is considerably weakened by the fact that the national minister is empowered to identify traditional leaders with apparently full discretion.

Furthermore, the *Local Government: Municipal Structures Act no 117 of 1998* establishes in its part 6 'Participation of traditional leaders in municipal councils' a co-operative model of rural governance in which traditional leaders would work with and be represented in local councils. However, the exact implications of this co-operative model, and more specifically the actual powers of the traditional leaders are not straightforward. Although 'traditional authorities that traditionally observe a system of customary law in the area of a district or local municipality' are allowed to attend and participate in meetings of municipal councils, it is not clear whether the traditional leaders have the right to vote on matters directly affecting the area of traditional authority.

The White Paper on Traditional Leadership and Governance and the ensuing Act have reduced some of the ambivalence, albeit not always to the benefit of the status of traditional leaders. The White Paper emphasizes the importance of the legitimacy of those occupying positions within the institution of traditional leaders. Hence, the State should play only a limited role in the identification and designation of traditional leaders, and be guided by the culture and tradition of the relevant community. The Traditional Leadership and Governance Framework Act of 2003 translate this approach in a procedure concerning the appointment and removal of office bearers (articles 8–15). The procedure entitles the public authorities (premier of province and president) to make the actual decisions but obliges them to do so in conformity with customary law and processes, for which they have to consult the relevant royal family. The actual procedure reflects a conscious attempt to ensure the legitimacy of the office bearers in conformity with customary law, revealing an important acknowledgement of the ongoing relevance of the institution and the body of law.

Regarding the function of the traditional leaders the White Paper clearly takes the position that government will transform and support the institution in accordance with the constitutional principles of democracy and equality. This would mean that traditional leaders should be mainly custodians of tradition and culture, while their role in respect of governance should be advisory, supportive and promotional in nature. In this regard the traditional leaders are expected to work with all three spheres of government. At the same time the White Paper underlines that the advisory role they play should be enhanced by 'among others, ensuring that the National and Provincial Houses play a meaningful role in legislative processes and other matters affecting tradition and culture' (p. 71). Also this approach to the functions of traditional leaders is neatly translated in the Act. While their actual decision making power has in principle been reduced to advisory, supportive and promotional competencies, the Act obliges the various levels of government to ask the advice of the relevant structures of traditional leaders in respect of issues pertaining to customary law or customs of traditional communities (article 18). Furthermore, the Act enables national or provincial government to provide a role for traditional councils or traditional leaders in respect of matters, including not only arts and culture but also land administration, agriculture, health, the administration of justice and safety and security (article 20). The national government and all provincial governments are even obliged to promote partnerships between municipalities and traditional councils (article 5).

Overall, it seems fair to conclude that traditional leaders are accepted as a reality on the ground, whose leadership structures are taken seriously. Nevertheless, their actual powers have been considerably eroded or better sidelined to advisory, supportive and promotional activities in order to be better aligned with the new constitutional dispensation, which is based on democratic principles.

The 1996 Constitution recognizes customary law as part of the South African legal system but subject to the Constitution, including the Bill of Rights (section 211(3)). This obviously brings about an equally difficult tension between the full respect of equality principle and more specifically the prohibition of gender discrimination on the one hand and the protection and promotion of diversity, of a traditional way of life governed by customary law and its inherent patriarchal features on the other hand (Bonthuys, 2002: 42; Himonga and Bosch, 2000: 314–331). The first initiative undertaken in this respect led to the adoption of the *Recognition of Customary Marriages Act of 1998*, which effectively recognizes existing customary marriages, including the polygamous ones, and also future customary marriages as long as they comply with the requirements in the Act. As was to be expected, the Act is quite firm on the equal status of spouses in customary marriages and hence aims at bringing customary law in line with the provisions of the Constitution's Bill of Rights. Nevertheless, this Act demonstrates a certain willingness to recognize and respect some culturally specific features of marriages according to customary law, like polygamy, while holding on to the equality principle within the marital relationship. It remains to be seen whether the indigenous communities will accept it and live accordingly, especially the proclaimed equal status of the wife in a customary marriage (Akkinnusi 2000: 143–154).

The South African Law (Reform) Commission has in the mean time finalized its report on Conflicts of Law, while projects on succession and the administration of estates are still on going. In all these instances the same tension is present as sketched in relation to the recognition of customary marriages. No further acts or bills before parliament have materialized so far. Apparently the appropriate balance between the contending values is not easy to strike.

In the mean time, the case law of the courts (not yet the Constitutional Court), which are confronted with the application of customary law, indicates that courts are convinced that they should apply customary law but only to the extent that the norms comply with the Bill of Rights. Nevertheless, certain judgments 'lean towards a trusting recognition rather than a critical questioning of customary law, lest traditional lifestyles be dismissed in a high-handed, condescending manner' (Du Plessis, Legal Forum no 6: 8). The courts seem indeed inclined to take the complete picture into account regarding customary obligations when judging the compliance of a norm of customary law with the equality principle of the Bill of Rights.

Regarding the rule of primogeniture for succession purposes, the High Court deciding on *Mthembu v. Letsela* took into account that 'the devolution of the deceased's property onto the male heir involves a concomitant duty of support and protection of the woman or women to whom he was married by customary law and of the children procreated under that system and belonging to a particular house' (944-B). Consequently, the court held that 'even if this rule is prima facie discriminatory on the grounds of sex or gender and the presumption of unfair discrimination comes into operation, this presumption has been refuted by the concomitant duty of support.... Should the counterbalance of the right to support fall away, however, the whole matter assumes a different aspect' (945-E/F). However, some academics have criticized this judgment because it would not take the egalitarian promise of the 1996 Constitution sufficiently into account (Mbatha 2002: 277–278).

Obviously, the post-apartheid era wrestles with the desire to fully respect the Bill of Rights and its crucial tenet of (gender) equality, while acknowledging the importance of the right to cultural identity and the ensuing protection of cultural diversity and a traditional way of life in conformity with customary law. Further acts of legislation are being awaited in this respect to guide the decisions of the courts, which so far have been trying to accommodate customary law without transgressing the dictates of the Bill of Rights and its central equality prescript.

Conclusion

The first fully democratic Constitution of South Africa indicated a successful constitutional transformation in view of its basic tenets of redress of the past, the fundamental importance attached to the principle of (substantive) equality and the various openings towards the accommodation of population diversity.

This promising beginning of the transformation process quickly ran into multiple challenges of implementation and realization. These challenges are partially caused by a lack of political will (e.g. language and education, minority rights and self-determination), partially by conflicting values of the new constitutional dispensation (the recognition of Muslim personal law, traditional leaders and customary law) and partially by ingrained and difficult to counter prejudices or a combination of the above (the equality principle).

It is remarkable that a country so deeply scarred and divided by apartheid, has a constitution which not only contains individual human rights, but also 'minority rights' and a reference to self-determination for cultural communities. The constitutional foundations to achieve a system that successfully accommodates a plural society's diversity, while guarding the Bill of Rights and the special position of the equality principle are available, but further implementation in the future will be determinant.

Notes

1 The term 'black' does not have an unambiguous meaning in South Africa. During the 1960s-1980s 'black' referred to non-white and thus applied to and the Africans, the Coloureds and the Indians; whereas from the 1980s onwards 'black' referred to the Africans and currently there exists considerable confusion about the exact coverage of the term.

2 The shift from mother tongue education to the dual medium English/Afrikaans education occurred at a stage when the students did not have the adequate proficiency in these two languages to meet the requirements of the syllabus which was in any event cognitively impoverished.
3 The 1976 Soweto uprisings, rather significant for the entire resistance movement, were mainly caused by the inflexible attempt to implement the 50–50 policy after 1975.
4 Groups were accorded a central position in Christian National Education since the 1870s (see Davenport 1991: 536).

References

Akkinnusi, A. (2000). "The Consequences of Customary Marriages in South Africa: Would he Recognition of Customary Marriages Act, 1998 make any difference?" *Journal for Juridical Science*, 143–154.

Anaya, S.J. (1997). 'On Justifying Special Ethnic Group Rights: Comments on Pogge,' in Shapiro, I. and Kymlicka, W., eds. *Ethnicity and Group Rights*. New York: New York University Press. 222–231.

Beckman, J.L. (1995). 'Religion in the Schools: Some Implications of a New Constitution.' *South African Journal of Education*. 97–100.

Bennett, T.W. (1995). *Human Rights and African Customary Law under the South African Constitution*. Kenwyn: Juta.

Bonthuys, E. (1993). *The Legitimacy of Group Rights in the South African Legal System*. Stellenbosch: Stellenbosch University Press.

Bonthuys, E. (2002). "Accommodation of Gender, Race, Culture and Religion: Outside Legal Subjectivity." *S.A.J.H.R.* 41–58.

Brand, D. (1997). "Constitutional Language Rights in Canada and South Africa." *T.S.A.R.* 689–699.

Brown, D. (1988–1989). "Speaking in Tongues: Apartheid and Language in South Africa." *Perspectives in Education*. 33–46.

Carpenter, G. (2002). "Equality and non-discrimination in the new South African constitutional order: Update." *T.H.R.H.R.* 177–185.

Carrim, Y. (1996). "Minorities Together and Apart." In James, W. et al. eds. *Now that we are Free: Coloured Communities in a Democratic South Africa*. Johannesburg, IDASA. 46–51.

Chaskalson, M. and Davis, D. (1996). "Cases and Comments: Constitutionalism, the Rule of Law, and the First Certification Judgment: Ex Parte Chairperson of the Constitutional Assembly in Re: Certification of the Constitution of the Republic of South Africa. 1996 (4) SA 744 (CC),' *S.A.J.H.R.*, 430–445.

Cloete, F. (1991). "Minority Rights and Interest Groups." *SA Public Law*. 32–41.

Coetzee, T. (1995). *Die Verrekening van die Etnisiteitsfaktor in Grondwetskrywing*. In *Suid-Afrika: 'n politikologische Analyse*, Bloemfontein: University of the Orange Free State.

Corder, H. (1994). "Towards a South African Constitution. *Modern Law Review*. 491–528.

Coveliers, H. and Veys, M. (1998). "De Zuid-Afrikaanse Grondwet van 1996." *Tijdschrift voor Bestuurswetenschappen en Publiek Rech*. 235–244.

Cross, M. and Mkwanazi-Twala, Z. (1998). "The Dialectic of Unity and Diversity in Education: Its implications for a National Curriculum in South Africa." In Cross, M. et. al, eds. *Dealing with Diversity in South African Education: A Debate on the Politics of National Curriculum*. Kenwyn: Juta. 30–34.

Currie, I. Loose leaf (n.d) "Official Languages." In Chaskalson, M., ed., *Constitutional Law of South Africa*. Juta, Kenwyn. 37.1–37.15.

Currie, I. Loose leaf (n.d) 'Minority Rights: Education, Culture and Language,' in Chaskalson, M., ed., *Constitutional Law of South Africa*. Juta, Kenwyn, 35.1–35.35.

Currie, I. (1994). "The Future of the Lobola Debate." *Acta Juridica*. 146–158.

Davenport, T.R.H. (1991). *South Africa: A Modern History*. Toronto: University of Toronto Press.

Davis, D. (1994). "Equality and Equal Protection." In Van Wyk, D. et al. eds. *Rights and Constitutionalism: the New South African Legal Order*. Kenwyn: Juta.196–211.

Deijl, F. (van der). (2001). *More language to the people: language planning and language politics in South Africa*. Leiden University.

De Klerk, W. (1994). "The Process of Political Negotiations: 1990–1993." In De Villiers, B., ed. *Birth of a Constitution*. Kenwyn: Juta. 1–11.

De Koker, J.Y. (1996). "Die Status van die Inheemse Reg in die Suid-Afrikaanse Regssysteem na 27 april 1994." *Tydskrif vir Regswetenskap*. 112–122.

Desei, Z and Taylor, N. (1997). "Language and Education in South Africa," World Yearbook of Education London: Kogan.

De Villiers, B. (1994). "The Constitutional Principles: Content and Significance." In B. de Villiers, ed. *Birth of a Constitution*. Kenwyn: Juta. 37–49.

De Vos, P. (2000). "Equality for All? A Critical Analysis of the Equality Jurisprudence of the Court." *Tydskrif vir die Hedendaagse Romeins-Hollandse Reg* 63, 61–75.

De Waal, J. (1998). "Equality." In De Waal, J. et. al, eds. *The Bill of Rights Handbook 1998*. Kenwyn: Juta. 152–174.

Dlamini, C.D. (1997). "The Relationship between Human Rights and Education." In De Groof, J. and Malherbe, E.F.J. eds. *Human Rights in South African Education*. Leuven: Acco. 39–52.

Dube, E. (1985). "The Relationship between Racism and Education in South Africa." *Harvard Educational Law Review*. 86–100.

Du Plessis, L.M. (1994). "A Background to Drafting the Chapter on Fundamental Rights." In de Villiers, B., ed. *Birth of a Constitution*. Kenwyn: Juta. 89–100.

Du Plessis, L.M. "The Future of South Africa: Perspectives of Integrating Different Cultures – Means of Law." *Legal Policy Forum. No. 6*, 3–17.

Ellmann, S. (1994). "The New South African Constitution and Ethnic Division." *Columbia Human Rights Law Review*. 5–44.

Erasmus, G and de Waal, J. (1997). "Die Finale Grondwet: Legitimiteit en Ontstaan." *Stellenbosch Law Review*. 31–44.

Freedman, W. (2000). "Forma versus Substantive Equality and the Jurisprudence of the Constitutional Court." *Tydskrif vir die Hedendaagse Romains-Hollandse Reg*. 314–320.

French, C. (1994). *Functions and Powers of Traditional Leaders* (Occasional Papers). Johannesburg, Konrad Adenouer Stiftung.

Galiguire, D. (1996). "Voices from the Communities." In James, W. et. al. (eds.) *Now that we are Free: Coloured Communities in a Democratic South Africa,* Johannesburg, IDASA. 9–15.

Goldin, I. (1989). "Coloured Identity and Coloured Politics in the Western Cape Region of South Africa." in Vail, L. ed. *The Creation of Tribalism in Southern Africa*. Berkeley: University of Columbia. 241–251.

Harries, P. (1989). "Exclusion, Classification and Internal Colonization: The Emergence of Ethnicity Among the Tsonga-speakers in South Africa." In Vail, L. ed. *The Creation of Tribalism in Southern Africa*. Berkeley: University of Columbia. 82–110.

Henrard, K. (2001). "The Accommodation of Religious Diversity in South Africa against the background of the centrality of the equality principle in the new constitutional dispensation." *J.A.L.* 51–72.

Henrard, K. (2002). *Post-Apartheid South Africa and the Accommodation of Population Diversity*. Westport, CT: Greenwood Press

Heugh, K. (1995). "From Unequal Education to the Real Thing." In Heugh, K. et al. (eds). *Multilingual Education for South Africa*. Johannesburg, Heinemann. 42–52.

Himonga, C., and Bosch, C. (2000). "The Application of African Customary Law under the Constitution of South Africa: Problems Solved or Just Beginning?" *South African Law Journal*. 314–331.

Jenkins, J. (2000). "After the Dry White Season: The Dilemmas of Reparation and Reconstruction in South Africa." *S.A.J.H.R.* 415–485.

Kashula, R.H. and Anthonissen, C. (1995). *Communication Across Cultures in South Africa: Towards a Critical Language Awareness*. Johannesburg: Hodder and Stoughton.

Kentridge, J., loose leaf, 'Equality', in Chaskalson , M. et al, eds., *Constitutional Law of South Africa,* Kenwyn, Juta, 14.1-14.58

Klaaren, J. and Varney, H. (2000). "A Second Bite at the Amnesty Cherry? Constitutional and Policy Issues Around Legislation for a Second Amnesty." *S.A.L.J.* 572–593.

Kotze, H. (1997). *Culture, Ethnicity and Religion: South African Perceptions of Social Identity*. KAS.

Kriel, R.R., loose leaf, 'Right to Education', in Chaskalson, M. et al. (eds.) *Constitutional Law of South Africa*. Juta, Kenwyn 38.1-38.25

L'Heureux-Dube, C. (1997). "Making a Difference: The Pursuit of Equality and a Compassionate Justice." *S.A.J.H.R.* 335–353.

Loban, M. (1997). "Un Accord Négocié: Le Processus Constitutionnel en Afrique du Sud depuis 1991". *Revue de Droit Public*. 71–109.

Loenen, T. (1997). "The Equality Clause in the South African Constitution. Some Remarks from a Comparative Perspective." *S.A.J.H.R.* 401–429.

Malherbe, E.G. (1977). *Education in South Africa 1923*–1975. Cape Town: Juta.

Malherbe, R. (1997). "The Education Clause in the South African Bill of Rights: Background and Contents." In De Groof, J. and Malherbe, E.F.J., eds. *Human Rights in South African Education*. Leuven: Acco.

Malherbe, E.F.J. (1997). "Reflections on the Background and Contents of the Education Clause in the South African Bill of Rights." *Journal of South African Law.* 85–8.

Manby, B. (1995). "South Africa: Minority Conflict and the Legacy of Minority Rule." *Fletcher Forum of World Affairs*. 27–52.

Mbatha, L. (2002). "Reforming the Customary Law of Succession." *S.A.J.H.R.* 259–286.

Moosa, N. (1998). "The Interim and Final Constitutions and Muslim Personal Law: Implications for South African Muslim Women." *Stellenbosch Law Review*.196–206.

Pieterse, M. (2001). "It's a Black Thing: Upholding Culture and Customary Law in a Society founded on Non-Racialism." *S.A.J.H.R.* 364–403.

Prozesky, M. (1995). "Religious Justice at Last? Believers and the New Constitution in South Africa." *Journal of Theology of South Africa*. 1–19.

Report of the Commission on the Demarcation/ Delimitation of Sprees. (1993). Pretoria.

Sachs, A. (1992). *Advancing Human Rights in South Africa*. Cape Town: Cape Town University Press.

Sachs, A. (1994). *Language Rights in the New Constitution*. Johannesburg: Constitutional Studies Center.

Sacks, V. (1997). "Multiculturalism, Constitutionalism and the South African Constitution." *Public Law*. 672–691.

Sarkin, J. (1996). 'The Trials and Tribulations of South Africa's Truth and Reconciliation Commission,' *S.A.J.H.R.*, 617–640.

Smith, N. 1995. "Affirmative Action under the New Constitution." *S.A.J.H.R.* 84–101.

Smith, N. (1997). "Freedom of Religion under the Final Constitution." *South African Law Journal*. 217–225.

Sonn, F. (1993). "Afrikaner Nationalism and Black Advancement as Two Sides of the Same Coin." In Adams, C. ed. *Affirmative Action in a Democratic South Africa*. Kenwyn: Juta. 1–10.

Soudien, C. (1998). "The Debate on Equality and Equity in South African Education." in Cross, M. et al. (eds.) *Dealing with Diversity in South African Education. A Debate on the Politics of a National Curriculum*. Kenwyn: Juta. 125–134.

South African Embassy. (1998). *Essays on the Truth and Reconciliation Commission*. Pretoria.

Strydom, H. (1998). "Minority Rights Issues in Post-Apartheid South Africa." *Loyola of Los Angeles International and Comparative Law Journal*. 873–914.

Van der Schyff, G. (2003). "Freedom of Religious Autonomy as an Element of the right to Freedom of Religion." *T.S.A.R.* Vol. 3. 512–539.

Van Wyk, D. (1994). "Introduction to the South African Constitution." In Van Wyk, D., et. al, eds. *Rights and Constitutionalism: The New South African Legal Order*. Kenwyn: Juta.

Wilkins, I. and Strydom, H. (1978). *The Broederbond*. New York:Paddington.

Worden, N. (1994). *The Making of Modern South Africa: Conquest, Segregation and Apartheid*. Oxford: Blackwell.

Young, D. (1995). "The Role and Status of the First Language in Education in a Multilingual Country." In Heugh, K. et al. (eds). *Multilingual Education for South Africa*. Johannesburg: Heinemann. 63–69.

Zalesne, D. (2001). "The Effectiveness of the Employment Equity Act and the Code of Good Practice in Reducing Sexual Harassment." *S.A.J.H.R.* 503–530.

Chapter 16

Transportation as a Factor in the Socio-economic Development of Ghana

Sesime Adanu

Introduction

Transportation is considered a key factor in the socio-economic development of any country. Efficient transportation not only facilitates spatial interaction and reduces the friction of distance, but it is also a pre-condition for effective economic, social and political development (Healey and Ilbery, 1990). Gillen (1996), after conducting an extensive survey of the transportation and development literature concluded that there is a very strong relationship between economic development and transportation. Taaffe et al. (1973) noted that in the economic growth of underdeveloped countries, a crucial factor has been the improvement of internal accessibility through the expansion of transportation networks that are important factors for development. They are of the view that many social and political forces influence the process of transportation construction and expansion networks. In spite of its importance, there appears to be considerable setbacks in its development especially in developing countries as a result of the high financial requirements expected in meeting its cost. This has led to the slow pace of development in most countries in Africa, of which Ghana is no exception.

Transportation accounts for approximately nine percent of government's Gross Domestic Product (GDP) and generates a considerable proportion of government's revenue. The country has a reasonably well developed transportation system consisting of two large deep water ports, which handle about seven million tons of imports and export traffic; a 944 km railway system serving the southern part of the country and a 40,000 km road network consisting of 13,433 km of trunk roads, 24,000 km feeder roads, and over 22,000 km of urban roads. The country also has one international airport and eight regional airports and airstrips spread throughout the country (World Bank 2001). However, there exists inequality in the provision of transportation facilities in Ghana, which has led to differential development patterns in the various regions of the country.

The zest of the Government of Ghana to meet the road requirements of the various regions led to the establishment of the Ghana Roads Sector Development Program (GRSDP) which is aimed at achieving sustainable improvement in the supply and performance of roads as well as road transport services in a regionally equitable manner. The issue of equity has to do with the geographic disparity in road networks between the southern and northern parts of the country. The GRSDP is to increase Ghana 's competitiveness in foreign trade and promote linkages in domestic markets, which are crucial factors for rapid and sustained growth. These linkages are to decrease the cost of accessibility of the poor and particularly women, to social services, markets and economic opportunities, thereby contributing to social sustainability. It is also to reduce transport cost through maintenance, rehabilitation and the reconstruction of roads (World Bank 2001).

This chapter discusses transportation inGhana with a specific focus on the road sector since it constitutes the predominant mode of transport accounting for the vast majority of freight and passenger travel. The chapter focuses on the theoretical frameworks to the study, the status of roads in the country, regional disparities in the road transportation sector, the status of roads maintenance and construction, funding sources for roads maintenance and construction, and accident rates on roads. This chapter does not touch extensively on other means of transportation in the country such as the seaports, airports and railroads even though they may be mentioned under certain circumstances.

The Ghana Investment Promotion Center (2000) noted that roads service 94 percent of freight and 97 percent of passenger traffic. Government is, therefore, atempting to ensure that by 2005 the road network is improved to 70 percent good, 20 percent fair and ten percent poor. This justifies the need to consider the road sector in this study.

Problem Statement

Despite the crucial role that road transportation plays in the Ghanaian economy, the sector is faced with numerous problems such as poor road networks, poor maintenance, the lack of funds to maintain and construct roads, and high accident rates among others. The poor road network is mostly seen in the disparity between rural and urban areas, where almost all the regional capitals and most of the district capitals have accessible roads while most rural areas have deplorable road conditions. The irony of this is that the rural areas happen to be the major production sources of food as well as major exportable commodities such as cocoa, mineral resources and timber that help sustain the economy through earned foreign exchange. The poor nature of roads in rural areas has meant that produce such as cocoa and foodstuffs perish because of inaccessible roads. Van Burren (2001), for example, noted that the poor nature of roads made it difficult to transport cocoa from the hinterland to the major ports for export. The result is that farmers end up losing substantial income, which makes it difficult for them to meet their basic needs, let alone properly educate their children. This perpetuates the poverty cycle in these already economically stressed parts of the country. These poor folks are at the same time expected to purchase goods and services from the same market as those who have economic resources, further widening the inequality gap between urban and rural areas.

Not only are markets inaccessible to deprived communities because of poor roads, but also access to modern health care becomes a problem worsoning the mortality statistics of these inaccessible communities.

Owen (1987) sums it all up that large parts of the third world are characterized by the lack of year-round merchandised transport, and movement is by unreliable, high cost, labor-intensive methods. Much of the infrastructure is poorly maintained, is in disrepair and is inadequate for present and future needs. The majority of the population lives in spatially circumscribed local socio-economic systems and a relatively static state in which immobility and poverty are clearly related.

Increasing accident rates are other key problems facing the road sector of Ghana as reflected in the number of lives lost on average every month. The Public Agenda newspaper (2003) revealed that 150 people die in the country every month through road accidents alone. This means a lot for the active labor force of the country in terms of the human resources needed for the economic development of the country.

One of the major sources of the problem facing the road sector of the country has to do with the lack of funds needed to revamp the sector, and to solve this, the government resorted to raising local funds through the Road Fund as well as borrowing from multilateral financial institutions. However, to understand the nature of the problem of road transport in Ghana, there is the need to look at past trends.

Road development in Ghana began in 1874 after the British assumed the role of colonizing the country. In 1894, a roads department was set up, which immediately started a program aimed at building improved roads and maintaining them in the colony. The earliest roads constructed by the department before 1900 all followed a north-south alignment and this trend was the pattern of road development into the 20th century, while east-west road network development remained weak. Most of the roads acted as feeders. Railroads played important roles in the linking process and led toconsiderable growth in internal trade particularly in foodstuffs for the gold and other mines. During the initial construction of railroads, roads changed their roles as primary transportation routes to a subsidiary role, feeding the railways. This helped link inaccessible areas of agricultural production to the railways and world market (Gould 1960).

The emergence of cocoa as a highly valued economic commodity in 1905 brought about a big boost into the development of road networks in the country. A positive correlation exists between the growth in cocoa yields and expansion in the road network. What was lacking at the time was an overall plan, which could offer effective guidance in further development of the network and its expansion (Addo 1975). Most of the road networks during this period were mainly concentrated in the exportable raw-material producing areas and port facilities of Secondi-Tarkoradi, Cape Coast and Accra. The roads during this period were mainly used for the transportation of exportable goods such as gold and cocoa. This view is supported by the World Bank (2001), which noted that roads in the country account for the movement of bulk commodities for export such as timber, cocoa, bauxite, and manganese, which are aided by rail transport from central collection centers and mining areas to the ports. Passenger travel during that time was very limited. The northern sector of the country, for example, had little development of accessible roads during this time period. This was because not much of valuable resources for export could be found in that part of the country during the colonial administration.

The urge to qualitatively and quantitatively develop a social and economic infrastructure after independence in 1957 resulted in quick draw down of the country's foreign exchange reserves. In response, the Convention People's Party (CPP) government began imposing foreign exchange transaction restrictions and import controls in 1961. The 1970s also witnessed considerable economic declines characterized by inflation all of which greatly affected the development of the road sector of the country. The persistence of the problem led to the launch of the Economic Recovery Program (ERP) in the early 1980s (Dordunoo et al., 1997). The road network in the country at that time was in a very deplorable state. Cocoa, the major exportable commodity could not be moved from the hinterland to the ports for export as a result of the poor nature of roads and the lack of spare parts for vehicles (Van Buren 2001).

Problems of this kind led to several efforts aimed at dealing with them. The ERP led to the ingestion of money into the economy from the International Monetary Fund (IMF), the World Bank and their allies for the construction and resurfacing of motorable roads in the country linking the productive sectors of the country. In 1991, the government initiated a major five-year program of road development and rehabilitation at an estimated cost of US$142.3 million. Work commenced in 1996 on eight new roads with a combined length of 466 kilometers (km) at a combined cost of 326,500 million *cedis*. The overwhelming focus of construction in the transport sector in the late 1990s was on roads, with work being completed on four new roads in 1996. In addition, 87 km of roads were graveled in that year and a further 213 km were resurfaced including two roads in the Obuasi area of Ashanti region where gold is mined on a large scale. Government spending on road construction in 1999 was expected to total 603,500 million *cedis* with 832,700 million *cedis* projected in 2000 and 863,900 million *cedis* in 2001. The 2000 annual budget allocated funding for 11 road projects and the construction of 28 bridges (Van Burren 2001).

Economic crisis in the 1970s and 1980s combined with weak institutional capacity led to deterioration in the infrastructure network and its operations. This left transporters and producers without the ability to expand services to a larger segment of the population and unable to compete effectively in regional markets. In 1997, the Government of Ghana reformed its own role and function in the sector by merging its involvement in all transport modes into one ministry, the Ministry of Roads and Transport. However, in 2001, the government again split the roads and transport ministries into two separate ministries namely the Ministry of Roads and Highways (MRH) and the Ministry of Transport and Communication (MTC). However, the envisaged role of government remains the same (World Bank 2001). While some people argue that government's decision to split the ministries was a political strategy aimed at finding jobs for its staunch supporters, there are those who are also of the view that the split is necessary considering the enormous duties confronting the previously combined ministry, thus justifying their separation of roles.

With the population of the major cities growing at an average rate of nearly two percent per annum, most cities now record population sizes that doubled those of 1984 and about tripled based on the 2000 population census. This led to a corresponding growth in the transport industry, where small and medium sized service providers emerged to satisfy the growing demand. Also, the GDP averaged four percent during the late 1990s, with growing sectors like, timber, agriculture, mining, and tourism all compounding the need for the upgrade of roads, maintenance and public transportation (Ghana Investment Promotion Center 2000).

By the time the government began the ERP in 1983, the transport sector had deteriorated considerably at the same time that the sector's institutions were deficient in organizational and incentive structures. Years of maintenance neglect and mismanagement had left the road network in such poor conditions that it became a liability to the national economy and hindered the effectiveness of the recovery program. Forty-six percent of the 14,134 km of trunk roads had either failed moderately or severely and the majority of the 21,000 km of feeder roads could not be used at all during the rainy season. The government and the World Bank agreed to deal with the problem. Between 1978 and 1998 three successive transport projects in the country emerged that took important steps aimed at rehabilitating important roads as well as instituting maintenance programs in order to arrest the situation of deteriorating roads. The first project was approved in 1987 and at the end of the year 58 percent of the roads network remained in poor conditions. The World Bank committed itself to providing support to the government so as to bring the network to 70 percent good condition and 20 percent fair condition by 2005 (World Bank 2000).

The World Bank (2001) has noted that a key problem preventing the effective operation of the maintenance and rehabilitation of roads in Ghana had to do with the substantial sums of money that government owes contractors for road works carried out in the past. It therefore considered the elimination of these arrears as prerequisites to the proper management of the road sector, which is necessary to ensure a sound financial platform for the program of economic recovery.

In its effort to deal with the problems of the road sector of the country, the government in 1996 formulated a road sub-sector strategy with the principal objective of clearing the backlog of maintenance on a sustainable long-term basis. The major donors were Denmark, Germany, Great Britain, Japan, The Netherlands, African Development Bank, European Union, and the World Bank. In 1999, the Government of Ghana and the donors agreed to a joint evaluation of the achievements of the program, finding expression in a shared responsibility for planning and implementing the evaluation. Each donor considers this a break from the individual, often project-based evaluations that are separate and this reflects a tendency towards a joint and integrated approach (Ministry of Foreign Affairs, The Netherlands 2000).

From 1996 to 1999, the Ghanaian government committed a total of US$592 million to roads improvement of which US$458 million was spent. The donors also committed US$621 million out of which only US$380 million was spent. The Netherlands government spent almost US$15 million during the evaluation period, justified by the potential of the road sector for poverty alleviation. The main objectives of the evaluation were to assess achievements, identify the key issues, and to formulate lessons. The core criteria used in the evaluation were efficiency, effectiveness, impact, relevance and sustainability. The Netherlands Economic Institute (Rotterdam) carried out the evaluation (Ministry of Foreign Affairs, The Netherlands 2000).

Theoretical Framework

Hilling (1996) dealt with two models that influence transportation development, namely the demand-led and supply-led models. The school of thought with respect to the supply-led approach to transport development is of the view that at early stages in the development process in many developing countries, the provision of transport facilities led to the widening of markets, increased production, and associated multiplier effects of an economic and social nature. This is considered the traditional view of transport and this approach is said to have worked in the then Gold Coast in 1903 and northern Nigeria in 1912 through the provision of new railway lines, which stimulated the expansion of cultivation for export.

There is, however, also the view that transportation provision is invariably a response to demand, and it is rarely developed except where there is the demand for it. The demand for transport could be seen in different forms such as revealed demand and latent demand. Revealed demand is expressed in the journeys that are actually made or the goods that are transported, and the use that is being made of the existing infrastructure. Latent demand comprises components of the existing demand, which cannot be satisfied perhaps due to inadequacies in the infrastructure or prohibitive cost, and which might also be called delayed demand. This includes completely new demand that may be created by additional or improved infrastructure. Transportation could have its most obvious impact on development where there is some latent demand or prior dynamism. Based on this, it is suggested that the supply-led demand models of transport should be viewed with some caution (Hilling 1996).

Hanson (1995) identified two key concepts that are pertinent to the understanding of transportation. These are accessibility and mobility. Accessibility refers to the number of opportunities available within a certain distance or travel time, while mobility refers to the ability to move between different activity sites such as from home to the shop or market. As distance between activity sites become longer, accessibility becomes dependent more on mobility, particularly privately owned vehicles. Hanson (1995) considers transportation to be crucial to life in the US because it is absolutely a necessary means to an end because it allows people to carry out a diverse range of activities that make up daily life. Hanson further noted that considering the spatially diverse land uses such as food stores, banks, hospitals and schools among others, people need to travel in order to obtain necessary goods and services. The question, which then arises, is which of these scenarios apply to developing countries?.

Taaffe et al. (1963) have noted that transportation constitutes an important component of the development agenda of developing countries by making internal areas accessible, taking into consideration factors such as the physical environment, intermediate location and commercialization. In order to better explain the development of transportation facilities in developing countries Taaffe et al (1963) identified six idealized stages of preliminary transportation development. The first phase consists of scattered small ports and trading posts along the seacoast. These places are barely connected except for small indigenous fishing crafts and irregularly scheduled trading vessels, and each part has an extremely limited hinterland. Taaffe et al. (1963) consider the first phase with scattered ports as matching the development of roads in Ghana and

Nigeria during the early periods when small, scattered ports and a coastal settlement existed or came into being between the end of the 15th century and the end of the 19th century. At the time, indigenous people around European trading stations or forts populated the coastal areas. Many people engaged in trade with Europeans and served as middlemen for trade with the interior. Also, bush trails connected small centers to their restricted hinterlands.

With the second phase, small lines of penetration emerge leading to reduced cost of transport for certain ports. This, in turn, leads to the expansion of both the port and the interior. Feeder routes begin to focus on the major ports and interior centers. Taaffe et al. (1963) consider this stage to be the most important single phase in transportation history since it led to the emergence of major penetration lines from the seacoast into the interior. Later phases typically evolved around the penetration lines and ultimately there is a strong tendency for them to serve as the trunk-line routes to more highly developed transportation networks. The authors attributed three main reasons to the construction of the penetration lines: first, the desire to connect administrative centers along the seacoast with the interior area for political and military control; second, the desire to reach areas of mineral exploitation; third, the desire to reach areas of potential agricultural export production. Mineral exploitation, for example, led to the construction of early railroads in Ghana. The desire to reach Kumasi, capital of the Ashantis formed the essential military-political motive for the first penetration roads, which followed an old bush tract occasionally cleared when the local people were goaded into activity. Two penetration lines forming the sides of the rail triangle were now complete and a considerable amount of subsequent transportation development of the country was based on these two trunk lines.

The great north road is the chief line of penetration north of Kumasi, built with a strong political and administrative motive to Tamale. Early feeder development focusing on Tamale helped fix the position of this trunk line and its existing extension to the northern markets of Bolgatanga, Navrongo and Bawku. The Western trunk road was built with similar motive and grew out of the extensive Kumasi feeder network to link the city with a moderately populated area north of the barren middle zone. The road through the former British Togoland was originally extended from the Hohoe cocoa area and was associated with a political desire to forge a link with British Togoland, and with an economic desire to prevent the diversion of the area 's cocoa traffic to the port of Lome in then French Togoland.

In stage three, feeder roads led to a sort of hinterland piracy that made the major port enlarge its hinterland at the expense of its adjacent smaller ports. This led to the emergence of small nodes along the main lines of penetration. The penetration was later followed by lateral interconnections as the feeder lines begin to move out both from the ports and nodes and from along the penetration lines. The process of concentration among the nodes is analogous to the process of port concentration and this results when the feeder networks of certain centers reach out and tap the hinterlands of their neighborhoods. As feeder networks become stronger at the interior centers, some hinterland nodes sink and, therefore, interconnect the original penetration lines.

Stage four leads to the development of more feeders, which in turn become the focal point of feeder networks of their own. Interior concentration begins and pirates the hinterlands of the smaller nodes on each side. The most recent phase associated with this stage is the dominance of roads over railroads, which previously complemented rail transport. As some of the centers grow more rapidly than others, their feeder networks became intensified and reached the hinterlands of nearby centers.

With stage five, more feeders developed around the ports and interior centers, and main online nodes with some of the layers beginning to link up. Lateral interconnection theoretically continues until all the ports, interior centers and main nodes are linked. In stage six, the concentration is repeated but at a higher level. This is because certain centers will grow at the expense of others leading to high-priority linkages among the largest centers. As old as these theoretical stages are they could still be considered pertinent in explaining the road network of the country.

Pas (1995) identified three major interrelated components of a transportation planning process namely the pre-analysis phase, the technical analysis phase, and the post-analysis phase as shown in Figure 16.1.

The assumption of the theoretical model in Figure 16.1 is that, in order to deal effectively with transportation problems, the pre-analysis phase has to be dealt with first. This includes the need to first identify the problem, come out with goals and objectives of the problem, collect data and generalize on its alternatives. The pre-analysis phase has two components, namely defining the current situation and problems as well as specifying the desired characteristics of improvements; developing the data to be used in the technical analysis and formulating the alternative plans and policies to be tested. The activities in the pre-analysis phase provide necessary inputs to the technical analysis phase.

The technical analysis phase of the transportation planning process concerns predicting the impact of alternative courses of action. This impact includes capital and operating cost, energy usage, land requirements, air quality, noise levels, accident rates, and the quality and quantity of traffic flow on the transportation network. The forecasting techniques used for this purpose are often generally referred to as the Urban Transportation Model System (UTMS). Important inputs to this system are the distribution of employment, housing and other activities and these distributions are predicted by land use models. The post-analysis phase is concerned with assessing the impacts of the alternatives, and monitoring the performance of implemented plans.

The State of Transportation in Ghana

The Government of Ghana continues to invest in the road sector of the country due to the indispensable role it plays. Between 1990 and 1996, for example, government's investment into roads and waterways was 16,088.6 million Ghanaian *cedis* constituting 6.10 percent of capital expenditure. It increased to 69,481 million *cedis* constituting 8.88 percent in 1993. This went further to 273,431 million *cedis* in 1996 representing 11.34 percent (The State of the Ghanaian Economy 1996).

In 1996, there was an estimated 37,800 km of classified roads of which 24.1 percent were paved. Among the problems associated with the road sector are that maintenance was a constant problem from the early 1960s to date. Vehicle spare parts were also

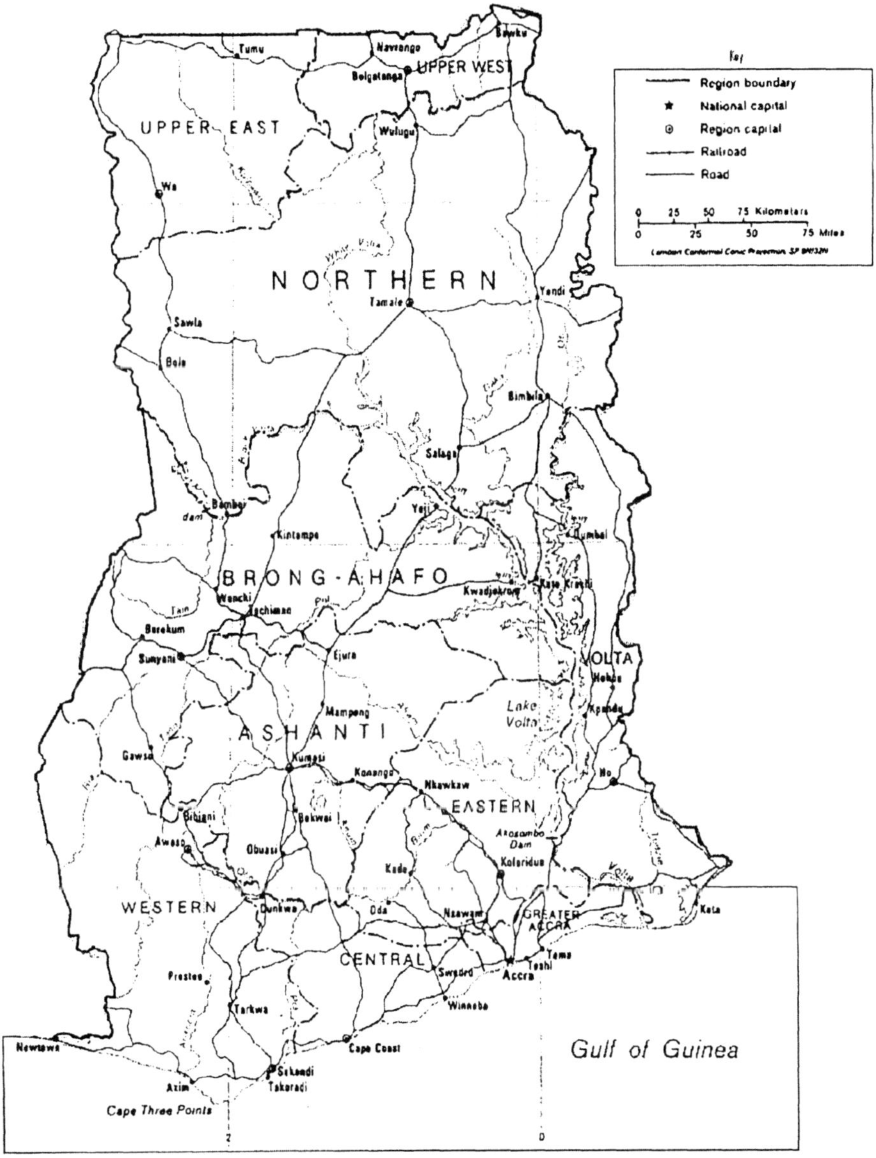

Fig 16.1 Map of Ghana Showing the Regions, Roads and Railways

scarce and the internal distributive system deteriorated physically (Van Buren 2001). Now vehicle parts are available in the market, but the cost of road maintenance is still a problem.

Donor assistance has been made available for road improvement. The International Development Association (IDA), an associate of the World Bank, has provided loans to the tune of $600 million for the country 's highway development programs.

Government also devoted 30 percent of the State 's budget to transportation. A special levy on the sale of fuel is also given to the Ghana Highway Authority (GHA) to use for he maintenance ofroads.

Nyangaga (2001) noted that in the late 1980s, the annual budget of most Sub-Saharan African countries allocated for road maintenance hardly exceeded 20 percent of required funds. Not only are budgetary allocations highly insufficient, but they are also at times cut down without warning or not released on time due to other high priorities. Nyangaga (2001) therefore, attributed the insufficient and uncertain funding for the maintenance of roads as one of the main causes of the large-scale deterioration of roads in Sub-Saharan Africa. Also there is the fact that most governments do not normally like sharing responsibility in managing road resources and instead prefer to manage roads like a social service.

Ghana's transport and communication network has deteriorated since the 1960s. However, in the 1980s after the economic recovery program, the rehabilitation of the road network was embarked upon. The length of tarred roads almost doubled between 1970 and 1990. About one-third of the country's main roads are now tarred. The roads from the port at Tema to Akosombo have been upgraded so as to permit easier shipment of goods to Burkina Faso across Lake Volta (Nyagaga 2001).

The need to deal with poor road networks in the country led to three major phases of road rehabilitation projects in the country. The first phase of the project was designed to help expand exports, farm products, and labor mobility through physical rehabilitation and maintenance of the transport infrastructure. The components of the program included road and railway rehabilitation and road maintenance and pilot programs for road and rural transport. It was implemented in May 1998 and ended in December 1993. The second phase of the project started in June 1991 and closed at the end of December 1997. Its focus was to remove physical barriers to export expansion, farm produce and labor mobility as well as reduce transportation cost. Its design, however, went beyond that of the first project in that rehabilitation and maintenance of road and railway infrastructure had the additional goal of facilitating private sector investment. The second phase involved equipping, civil works, and institutional strengthening of roads as well as institutional development of the public and private transport sectors. Also included was low-cost rural maintenance systems and infrastructural development that emphasized women's employment by providing civil works and institutional support for non-governmental organizations (NGOs). This project, also like the first one, had a railway component, which was designed to strengthen institutions and improve capacity by providing locomotives and wagons, equipment and tools, and civil works (World Bank 1999).

The National Feeder Roads Rehabilitation and Maintenance Project (NFRRMP), which was also implemented in July 1992, ended in June 1997. It was aimed at increased food and cash crop production by improving assess to feeder roads used to move agricultural inputs and produce to and from farms, and nearby markets; improve mobility and economic opportunity for the rural poor and build the institutional capacity of the Department of Feeder Roads so as to ensure the maintenance of rehabilitated road networks as well as sustain feeder roads over time (World Bank 1999).

Currently, Ghana has a total road network of 38,071 km out of which, 11,158 is classified as trunk roads; 2,914 km are considered as urban roads and 23,999 km fall under feeder roads classification. The road network condition survey conducted in 1999–2000 under the Road-Sub-Sector Development Program and Strategic Plan for 2000–2005 established that 30.6 percent of the trunk roads in Ghana are good, 38.4 percent are in fair condition and 31.0 percent are considered as being poor. The urban road network has a mix of 37.6 percent as good, 26.6 percent as fair and 35.8 percent as poor. The mix of the feeder roads is 27.5 percent good, 21.9 percent fair and 50.6 percent poor. However, the overall road network mix in 1999–2000 stood at 29.2 percent good, 27.1 percent fair and 43.7 percent poor as compared to 28.6 percent good, 27.7 percent fair and 42.7 percent poor in 1998–1999. The differences in the figures for 1998–1999 and 1999–2000 could be attributed to the fact that the rate of deterioration was almost the same as the rate of restoration through periodic maintenance and reconstruction works (Building, Construction and Property Services Market in Ghana 2003).

Regional Disparities in the Road Transportation Sector

Even though the entire road network in the country cannot be considered as well developed, there exist disparities in its level of development. Inequalities have led to considerable debate in the country as to what best criteria should be used in determining which roads should be given priority in terms of improvement. While economic resources such as cocoa, gold, timber, bauxite, and manganese are largely considered as the basis in allocating funds for the construction and upgrading of roads in the various regions of the country, there are others who think that not only these resources but also human capital coupled with other economic resources should be considered as factors in the allocation of funds for road construction. Politics can also not be ruled out as an influential factor.

The well-endowed mineral and forest regions such as the Ashanti, Eastern, Western and Central regions have a fairly well-developed road network in the country compared to regions such as the Northern, Upper East, Upper West, and to some extent the Volta regions. Even though the Brong-Ahafo region is fairly endowed with resources it was not until recently that it has had its fair share of the road resources. The Greater Accra region has benefited considerably from roads improvement not because it is excessively endowed with resources, but because it happens to be the national and administrative capital of the country coupled with the harbor in Tema.

It is important to know that even though the Ashanti, Western, Eastern and Central regions are considered to have more improved road networks, the gains are not equitably distributed. The big cities and district capitals gain at the expense of remote rural areas where accessibility to the resources leaves much to be desired.

In its efforts to improve road transportation in the country, the government resorted to borrowing from the World Bank and the IMF. As at June 2003, periodic maintenance on five roads in the Brong Ahafo region were completed while 12 other roads were at various stages of completion. The Berekum-Nkawkaw, Duayaw-Kyeremasu,

Prang-Kintampo, Kintampo-New Longoro and Nkawkaw-Jema roads were among those completed at a total cost of 3.52 billion *cedis*. A number of culverts on the Kwadwokrom-Atebubu road have been completed at a cost of 215.9 million *cedis*. Rehabilitation of the 30-kilometer Wenchi-Sampa road at a cost of ten million *cedis*, was 54 percent completed as at June 2003, while the upgrading of the ten kilometer Sunyani-Odumase-Adentia road was said to be behind schedule and was 85 percent complete. The re-graveling of the 65-kilometer Kwadwokrom-Atebubu road costing 7.3 million *cedis* is about 65 percent complete. The Atronie bridge is to be rehabilitated at the cost of 573.38 million *cedis* and is yet to start. Also, the 51.7 kilometres Wenchi-Bamboi road is to be resurfaced as well as the upgrading of the 47.8 kilometres Sunyani-Ntotroso-Acherensua (Ghanaweb.com June 3 2003).

The 57.6 kilometres Aframso-Sekyedumase-Nkoranza road and the 50.4 kilometres Ejura-Nkoranza are also progressing slowly. The re-gravelling of the 60-kilometer Prang-Kintampo-New Longoro road is 25 percent complete while the 30-kilometer stretch of road is 90 percent complete. The 36-kilometer Berekum-Nsakaw road was expected to be completed by August 2003 (Ghanaweb.com June 3 2003).

The Deputy Minister of Roads and Transport, Mr Emmanuel Boye, noted at a two-day workshop of Ghana Rural Travel and Transport Program in Ho that the Government has allocated eighty billion *cedis* from the Highly Indebted Poor Countries (HIPC) fund to the Department of Feeder Roads (DFR) for the construction and maintenance of feeder roads and transport infrastructure in poverty-stricken areas. It has also released a total of 470 billion *cedis* from the Road Fund to the DFR to carry out its activities.

The fund to the DFR was in recognition of the crucial role that the road infrastructure and transport services play in alleviating poverty and enhancing socio-economic development. The government is of the view that improvement in road networks will help reduce poverty and bridge disparities that exist among regions. It is also to improve upon the quality of life in the rural areas, as well as protect investment in feeder roads (Ghanaweb.com August 15 2003). The rehabilitation is to include re-graveling, culvert construction, shaping, surface dressing and construction of bridges. Available statistics show that out of a total of 3,093 km length of feeder roads in the Volta Region, about 45 percent is unpaved. Yet, the length of feeder roads in the Region represents only nine percent of the total of 32,600 km of feeder roads in the country (Ghanaweb.com August 15 2003).

Road Rehabilitation and Maintenance

Road management in the country falls under three agencies: the Department of Feeder Roads (DFR), the Department of Urban Roads (DUR) and the Ghana Highway Authority (GHA). They all fall under the oversight of the Ministry of Roads and Highways (MRH) (World Bank, 2001). The Ghana Highway Authority was established in 1974 as the organization responsible for the development and management of the entire national road network. However, since the Ghana Highway Authority Act of December

1997, its role got limited to the administration, control, development and maintenance of trunk roads and related facilities. The Department of Feeder Roads was established under a government instrument in July 1981 with the responsibility of planning the development and maintenance of the feeder road network in the country. Prior to its establishment, the responsibility for the maintenance of feeder roads shifted from one agency to the other. Some of the notable agencies that assumed responsibility for feeder roads in the past are the Public Works Department, Department of Social Welfare, Department of Rural Development, Ghana Highway Authority and the Cocoa Marketing Board. The Department of Urban Roads (DUR) was also established in 1989 as an implementing agency within the Ministry of Roads and Transport. It is responsible for the entire network of roads within five cities of the country, namely Accra, Kumasi, Secondi-Takoradi, Tema and Tamale as well as the urban areas of the Ga District. Prior to the establishment of DUR, the responsibility for the planning, development and maintenance of all roads and related infrastructure in the five cities were the responsibilities of the Public Works Department and the Municipal/Metropolitan assemblies of the respective cities (Danida 2000). The major limitation associated with these ministries had to do with the fact that they experienced weak management problems (World Bank 2001).

A measure adopted by the government aimed at road improvement is the implementation of a Road Fund in 1985, which made Ghana one of the first countries in Sub-Saharan Africa to establish such a fund (Overseas Development Administration (ODA) Japan 2002). The Road Fund did not make any significant impact until 1997 when it was restructured to make it more effective and efficient. Key among the reforms included the adoption of the principle that the government's role should be one of regulating, managing and monitoring, and not an executing agent. This in effect brought in considerable private sector participation, which early on was dominated by the government (World Bank 2001).

The ODA (2002) has also noted that restructuring is aimed at achieving a public-private harmonization in fund management and to strengthen its financial base. The main sources of finances to the fund include fuel levies, tolls, vehicle license and inspection fees, international transit fees and other sources approved by parliament. The collection and disbursement of these revenues are under the authority of the Road Fund Board, which has the majority of private sector stakeholders (World Bank 2001).

As part of the Government of Ghana's efforts to address the deplorable road conditions in the country, the government signed a US$7 million agreement with the Organization of Petroleum Exporting countries (OPEC) fund to co-finance the upgrading of the Achimota- Anyinam road, which is an important route linking the national capital, Accra, with Kumasi, the major inland economy city. The Achimota-Anyinam road is considered of particular important since it runs through major agricultural and commercial areas as well as functioning as the main highway connecting Ghana with Burkina Faso and Côte d'Ivoire. About 96 km of the existing road is heavily distressed in most sections and is no longer capable of supporting the high volume of traffic. The rehabilitation is, therefore, to help improve the road, and hence make it faster, cheaper and safer to travel on (OPEC Fund News 2000).

Table 16.1 Road Fund Revenue by Sources

Sources of Funding	1996	1997	1998	1999
Fuel Levy	59.35	98.65	180.60	193.49
Bridge tolls	0.85	1.60	2.36	2.74
Road tolls	0.74	1.83	2.77	3.35
Ferry tolls	0.07	0.06	0.02	0.06
Vehicle registration fees	1.85	2.10	7.81	11.89
Road use fees	0.000	0.00	0.00	0.00
International transit fees	0.00	0.00	0.18	0.53
Grand totals	**62.86**	**104.24**	**193.74**	**220.11**

Source: Overseas Development Administration (2002).

Table 16.1 show the major sources of funds for the Road Fund. It has become evident that fuel levy constitutes more than 90 percent of funding sources followed by vehicle registration fees. The least contributors have been road use fees and international transit fees. Fuel levy no doubt constitutes the major source of revenue because the entire economy depends on fuel for its operation. As a result of this the price set for fuel in the budget statement of the government determines the prices of goods and services in the country. The ODA (2000) noted that out of the Road Fund resources, 45 billion *cedis* were spent on periodic maintenance.

Contributions from the road fund is expected to grow and the total estimated inflow of 1,552 billion *cedis* (US$210.8 million) will cover around 18 percent of total program expenditure. Table 16.2 shows a progressive increase in revenue from the road fund, which suggests that it could be a good source of sustainable local revenue generation for road construction and maintenance in the country. In the 2001 fiscal year, a total of approximately 700 billion *cedis* was estimated to be spent on the road sector. Out of this, the road fund was to contribute 326.4 billion *cedis* whilst the donor community contributes 286 billion *cedis*. The 2001 petroleum levy of 230 *cedis* per liter contributed 88 percent of the Road Fund revenue, but forms less than ten percent of the overall fuel price (World Bank 2001).

The World Bank (1999) has revealed that three successive transport projects in Ghana contributed to the success of the country's Economic Recovery Program. Implemented between 1987 and 1998, the projects rehabilitated Ghana's economically important roads and instituted maintenance programs to arrest road deterioration. By removing physical constraints, the projects reduced transport costs, stimulated exports and

Table 16.2 Past and Projected Trends in Road Fund Revenue

Year	1998	1999	2000	2001	2002	2003
Revenue (billion *cedis*)	189	227	241	326.4	517	679
Growth percentage	---	20%	6%	35%	58%	31%

Source: World Bank (2001).

improved the mobility of passengers and goods. They also made it possible for the rural population to gain access to markets, socio-economic activities, agricultural production and marketing.

Periodic maintenance, minor rehabilitation and minor upgrading of trunk roads and urban roads come in the form of spot improvement, repairing and resurfacing of short sections of roads, repairs of slopes and resealing. A total of 4,060 km of trunk roads, 12,995 km of feeder roads and 1,612 km of urban roads were to receive periodic maintenance and minor rehabilitation in the three-year period.

Table 16.4 shows the cost components of road rehabilitation and maintenance in the country. The table shows that the rehabilitation of roads constitutes the greatest percentage of cost followed by periodic and routine maintenance. The high expenditure on road rehabilitation is a manifestation of the bad nature of roads in the country. Also, in terms of the sources of funds, it has become evident that the majority of the fund comes from foreign sources, which is indicative of the poor nature of roads since government does not have enough resources to construct and maintain roads hence has to resort to borrowing. Considering the fact that the government is faced with competition for its limited resources for other sectors of the economy, the road sector no doubt suffers a great deal.

With Table 16.5, the 'works' category requires more funds compared to the other categories. This could be due to the high capital expenditure associated with this component compared to those such as training and goods, as seen in Table 16.4. It has also become evident from this table that a sizeable proportion of the funding comes from foreign sources compared to local sources.

Road Accidents

The Ghanaian Chronicle news paper (2003) noted that statistics released by the National Road Safety Commission (NRSC) for the first quarter of 2003 revealed a negligible decrease in the number of fatalities associated with road accidents in the country from 332 deaths in the first quarter of 2002 to 331 deaths in 2003, representing a 0.30 percent reduction over last year's figure. However, the number of vehicles involved in accidents increased from 4,078 to 4,278. The regional breakdown of the statistics is shown in Table 16.6.

Table 16.3 Ghana Road Fund Resource Allocation to the Road Sector (in Billion *cedis*)

Department	1996	1997	1998	1999
GHA	24.9	46.9	93.9	77.9
DFR	5.9	11.0	36.4	39.4
DUR	9.9	18.3	49.3	39.3
Sub Total	**40.7**	**76.2**	**179.6**	**156.6**
MRT	0.0	2.7	0.4	1.3
NRSC	0.0	0.0	0.0	0.3
Total	**40.7**	**78.9**	**180.0**	**158.2**

Source: Ghana Road Fund (2000.)

Table 16.4 Cost Components of Roads Rehabilitation and Maintenance in the Country

Project Cost by Component	Local US$ million	Foreign US$ million	Total US$ million
Routine maintenance	86.17	15.20	101.37
Periodic maintenance	176.82	176.99	353.81
Rehabilitation	194.64	293.62	488.26
Traffic management	6.00	5.00	11.00
Institutional strengthening	26.67	21.19	47.86
Program management	48.00	0.00	48.00
Total baseline cost	538.30	512.00	1,050.30
Physical contingencies	60.20	32.40	92.60
Price contingencies	33.10	15.00	48.10
Total project cost	**631.60**	**559.40**	**1,191.00**

Source: World Bank (2001).

Table 16.6 shows that the Greater Accra region leads in terms of accident rates with respect to the number of vehicles involved in accidents, and the number of people injured, but is less than the figure for Ashanti region in terms of the number of deaths through accidents. These high rates could be attributed to the significant role of the region as the seat of government, which meant that administrative, commercial, economic social and other services at the highest level are all located in the region, hence attracting more traffic, which in turn results in high accident rates. Accra, which acts as the national capital also, has a lot of human and vehicular traffic hence this could be a contributory factor to high accident rates compared to regions such as the Brong-Ahafo and Upper West that have less human and vehicular traffic. The Ashanti region follows but leads in terms of the number of deaths through accidents. The high rates in the region could be attributed to its nodal location as the transportation hub of the country, where road networks from the southern, northern, eastern and western parts of the country converge. Coupled with this is its socio-economic significance as an area with a sizable proportion of the country's mineral resources, timber and cocoa, which account for the nation's major export commodities. Also, there is the booming commercial and food trade in the region. These factors could account for more traffic on those roads leading to more accidents. The eastern, central and western regions also have their share of the nation's economic resourses, which also need to be moved for export and to the consuming centers, and hence lead to accidents in the process. The northern region also has a substantial amount of accidents and deaths, which could be attributed to its nodal location for roads from the Brong-Ahafo, Ashanti, Upper East and Upper West regions. Its important role as a food-producing center also means more traffic. The Brong-Ahafo and Upper West regions recorded fewer road accidents as noted in Table 16.6. This could perhaps be due to less use of those roads as compared to those with high accident rates, or to more caution by drivers using the roads. In any case, it is difficult to attribute a reason for this. Data for the Volta and Upper East regions were not available and it is difficult to tell whether accidents did not occur in these regions or the data could simply not be accessed.

Table 16.5 Projected Cost by Category

	Local US$ million	Foreign US$ million	Total US$ million
Goods	2.13	18.72	20.85
Works	533.70	509.30	1,043.00
Services	41.24	30.83	72.07
Training	6.53	0.55	7.08
Program management	48.00	0.00	18.00
Total projected cost	631.60	559.40	1,191.00
Total financing required	631.60	559.40	1,191.00

Source: World Bank (2001).

The patterns shown in Table 16.6 reveal that a strong relationship exists between the socio-economic vibrancy and resourcefulness of regions and their associated high rates of accidents. It could be inferred from this that some regions attract more of the government's investment in road construction and maintenance at the expense of less

Table 16.6 Regional Breakdown of Accident Rates in Ghana, First Quarter 2003

Regions	Number of vehicles involved in accidents	Number of people injured	Number of deaths through accidents
Greater Accra	2,639	760	93
Ashanti	833	551	98
Eastern	262	156	31
Western	263	265	23
Central	168	152	30
Northern	89	107	18
Brong-Ahafo	6	---	---
Upper West	4	---	---

Source: The Ghanaian Chronicle, June 26, 2003.

resourced regions. There, however, exists disparities within regions with respect to quality of roads and a notable example is the northern region where its regional capital, Tamale, has good roads yet the hinterland communities, where the bulk of the food is produced have deplorable road conditions.

The October 20, 2003, issue of the Public Agenda newspaper revealed data from the Ghana Road Safety Commission as stating that 150 people in Ghana die every month through road accidents, thus five deaths everyday, with over 1000 people sustaining injuries. The Kumasi-Accra road accounted for 25 percent of the accidents. Annually, more than 1000 people of all ages die through road accidents and there is an average of over 10,000 injuries such that fatalities through accidents in Ghana is projected to be over 10,000 from 2003 to 2010 with over 70,000 injuries during the period. The vehicle population during this period is also expected to reach 2.5 million.

Buses and heavy duty vehicles account for over 70 percent of the accidents on the roads and contributory factors identified are fatigue, which accounts for 25 percent of accidents, over speeding 50 percent and drunk driving. Over 70 percent of the accidents are said to involve males and 25 percent of the 25- to 35-year old group. The economic implications of these include the loss of valuable labor needed for socio-economic development (Public Agenda October 20, 2003).

Conclusions

It has become evident that the transportation, and for that matter road transport sector, constitutes the hub around which the development of the Ghanaian economy evolves.

Despite its importance, road networks, especially in rural areas of the country have for a long time been in the most deplorable condition. This acts as a setback to the farmers in the hinterland who are unable to transport their produce to consuming centers in the cities. The result is that farm produce rots in the inaccessible areas, and hence acts as a disincentive for farmers to produce. Not only are the roads bad, but there also exist inequalities in motorable and accessible roads in the country, attributed mainly to economic resource availability in the area. The inequality has affected development in inaccessible areas.

In order to ensure equity, a need exists for government to diversify its domestic revenue sources by enhancing the efficiency of the road fund, for example, so as to reduce over reliance on dwindling foreign sources.

References

Addo, S.T. (1975). "Rural-Urban Linkages in Development Planning in Developing Countries." *The Bulletin of the Ghana Geographical Association.*

Boateng, E.A. (1966). *A Geography of Ghana.* Cambridge, MA: Cambridge University Press.

Building, Construction and Property Services Market in Ghana. 2000. Accessed on August 23 from www.tradepartners.gov.uk/building/ghana/profile/overview/shtml.

Chronicle. (June 26, 2003). *No Decline in Road Accident Fatalities.* Accessed on Thursday, June 26, 2003, from www.ghanaian-chronicle.com.

Danish International Development Administration (DANIDA) (2000). *Evaluation: Ghana-Joint Evaluation of the Road Sub-Sector Program, 1996–2000.* DANIDA.

Dordunoo, C.K. and Nyanteng, V.K. (1997). "Overview of Ghanaian Economic Development." In Nyanteng, V.K. (ed.). *Policy and Options for Ghanaian Economic Development.* ISSER.

Gauthier, H.L. (1973). "Transportation and Regional Development." In Hoyle, B.S. (Ed.) *Transport and Development.* New York: Harper and Row Publishers Inc.

Ghana Investment Promotion Center (2000). *Ghana Investment Profile: Roads and Transportation.* GIPC.

Ghanaweb News (2003a). *Five Roads in Brong Ahafo Regions Completed.* www.Ghanaweb.com/GhanahomePage/newsarchive/Kalender.php?Accessed on June 3, 2003

Ghanaweb News (2003b). *Government Allocates 80 Billion from HIPIC Fund for Feeder Roads.* Ghanaweb.com/GhanahomePage/newsarchive/Kalender.php? Accessed on August 15, 2003

Ghana Road Fund Secretariat. (2000). *Annual Report and Accounts 1999.*

Gillen, David W. (1996). Transportation Infrastructure and Economic Development.

Logistics and Transportation Review. Vol. 32:1 39-63.

Gould, P.R. (1960). *The Development of the Transportation Pattern in Ghana.* Northwestern University Press.

Hanson, S. (1995). "Getting There: Urban Transportation in Context." In S. Hanson (Ed). *The Geography of Urban Transportation.* The Guilford Press.

Hilling, D. (1996). *Transport and Developing Countries.* London: Routledge.

Healey M.J. and Brian W.I. (1989) *Location and Change: Perspectives on Economic Geography.* Oxford University Press, Oxford.

Ministry of Foreign Affairs (2000). *Joint Evaluation of the Road Sub-Sector Program in Ghana.* Evaluation Report. *Policy and Operations Evaluation Department.* The Netherlands.

Nyangaga, F.N. (2001). *Africa Transport Technical Note. Road Management Initiative RMI No 32.*

Nyanteng,V.K. (ed). (1997). *Policy and Options for Ghanaian Economic Development.* Legon: ISSER

Organization of Petroleum Exporting Countries (OPEC) Fund (2000). *Ghana to Undertake Road rehabilitation with US$ 7 Million OPEC Fund Loan.* Accessed on August 27, 2003, from www.opecfund.org/news/press/2000/pr0004.html.

Overseas Development Administration (ODA), Japan (2002). *Field Survey of Anwainkwanta-Yamoranza Road Rehabilitation Project.* ODA.

Owen, W. (1987). "Transportation and World Development." *Transportation Engineering.* Chichester; Wiley.

Pas, E.I. (1995). "The Urban Transportation Planning Process." In S. Hanson (ed.). *The Geography of Urban Transportation.* The Guilford Press.

Public Agenda (2003). *One Hundred and Fifty Ghanaians Die from Road Accidents every Month.* Accessed on October 20 from www.Ghanaweb.com/public_agenda/

Rostow, W.W. (1946). *The Stages of Economic Growth.* Cambridge University Press.

Taaffe, E.J., Morril, R. L and Gould, P.R. (1963). "Transport Expansion in Underdeveloped Countries: A Comparative Analysis in Transport and Development." In Hoyle, B.S. (Ed.) *Transport and Development.* Macmillan Press Ltd.

The Institute of Statistical, Social and Economic Research (1996). *The State of the Ghanaian Economy.* ISSER, University of Ghana, Legon.

Van Burren L. (2001). "Ghana Economy." In Middleton, J. (Ed.) *Africa South of the Sahara.* Europa Publications.

World Bank (1999). *Ghana Building a Stronger Transportation System.* Washington, DC: Operations and Evaluations Department.

World Bank (2001). *Ghana Road Sector Development Program.* Transport Group, Africa Regional Office.

World Bank (2000). *Ghana Building a Stronger Transportation System.* World Bank Operations Evaluation Department.

Chapter 17

Gender Disparities in African Education: Some Socio-economic Implications for Africa's Development in the 21st Century

Kwadwo Konadu-Agyemang and Judith Shabaya

Introduction

Quality education, and the resulting literacy, are among the most important factors that propel socio-economic development, which is defined to include but not limited to higher living standards, increases in Gross National Income (GNI), lower mortality rates, access to health services, high literacy levels, and access to good nutrition. Available research demonstrates conclusively that education increases the productivity and earnings of both men and women, and that there is a potential increase in income by 10 to twenty percent for each additional year of schooling (Hartnett and Henevel 1993). Education and literacy also raise creativity, promote entrepreneurship and aid in the understanding and appreciation of socio-economic issues at the local, national and international levels (Tien 1996; World Bank 1996). The education of parents, especially mothers, has been shown to affect the cognitive and physical development of the child. In addition, the expansion of scientific knowledge and technologies that is necessary for development depends on education.

It is also recognized that education is an important ingredient in the development and nurturing of an educated leadership and effective governance. For women, especially, education helps to break down some of the entrenched barriers to advancement and enable them to participate in the workforce, and in community civic activities with male counterparts. Consequently it is not surprising that available evidence suggests that no nation in modern times has been able to develop and improve its standard of living without an educated workforce, and that there is a strong correlation between indicators of development such as GNI per capita and literacy levels (Tien 1996). Hence, access to quality education is not only critical to the economic well being of nations and communities but a *sine qua non* for effective socio-economic development.

Despite the crucial role of education and literacy in development, Africa has not been able to provide enough education. In fact, literacy levels on the continent lag behind the rest of the world (with the possible exception of South-central Asia) in all age categories (see Table 17.1 for 15 to 25-year-olds for instance), and falls below the average for developing regions. Consequently, Africa's socio-economic development suffers from lower literacy levels.

Table 17.1 Comparative Literacy Levels for 15-24 year olds among the world's major regions

World	**1990 (84.2)**	**2000 (86.8)**
Developed regions	99.6	99.7
Developing regions	81.1	84.4
Northern Africa	**66.3**	**76.1**
Sub-Saharan Africa	**66.5**	**76.4**
Latin America	93.4	95.7
Caribbean	86.1	87.1
Eastern Asia	95.4	97.7
South-central Asia	63.0	70.8
Western Asia	81.6	85.9
Oceania	77.3	82.0

Source: United Nations (2003). Millennium Indicators.

While the problem of low educational levels vis-à-vis the rest of the world affects Africa's population as a whole, African women, especially those in the rural areas and the peripheral regions, have traditionally received less education and lag behind their male counterparts. This has not only created a gender gap between African women and men, but also a wide disparity between them and their counterparts in the rest of the world. African women fall behind the rest of the world in school enrollment from primary to tertiary levels, except South-central Asia. In 2000, whereas the average illiteracy rate was 31 percent for males in Sub-Saharan Africa, it was well over 50 percent for women (United Nations Statistical Division, 2003). The gender gap in African education cuts across the continent at all three levels of primary, secondary and tertiary education (see Table 17.2a/b), although in countries such as Botswana and Namibia women have attained higher levels in certain categories in recent years.

According to the United Nations, while female illiteracy continues to be a major problem worldwide, Africans have a disproportionate share of the problem. Sixteen of the 22 countries with 70 percent or more female illiteracy levels are found in Africa, and 90 percent of the women in at least two African countries cannot read or write (UNICEF 2000).

Since education is a *sine qua non* for effective participation in the modern economy, African women by virtue of their lack of education, are confined to the fringes of society in menial jobs, due primarily to poor access to education and training. As a result, the countries of Africa are denied all the benefits that accrue to a nation when the women become as educated as their male counterparts. For African countries to participate effectively in a competitive global market, there is a need to produce a highly literate population of both genders. Therefore making changes in Africa's educational system to ensure both quality and equal access for men and women regardless of their place of residence and socio economic status is the way to guarantee high socio-economic development and the continent's ability to become competitive in the global economy in the 21st century.

Purpose and Data Sources

This chapter seeks to elucidate the factors causing differential gender access to education, and to analyze current national comparative data, and its ramifications for Africa's socio-economic development. What are the causes of gender inequities in access to education in Africa? Are there any spatial and temporal variations among women in different countries, regions in same countries? What factors are responsible for these variations? The study seeks to identify the nature of the gender gap in African education and why it continues to persist at national, regional and local levels. While the chapter's general focus is on Africa as a whole, emphasis will be placed on Ghana and Zimbabwe as case studies. The analysis is primarily based on comparative data from the Ghana Demographic and Health Survey (GDHS) and the Zimbabwe Demographic and Health Survey (ZDHS). The GDHS and ZDHS are nationally representative data collected by US-based Macro International, the respective statistical authorities in all the countries. For instance, the GDHS 1998, surveyed 4,843 women ages 15 to 49 and 1,546 men ages 15 to 59 (GSS and MI, 1999), whilst the Zimbabwe survey, 1999, interviewed 6,208 women ages 15 to 49 and 2,970 men ages 15 to 54 (CSO and MI, 2000). Demographic and Health Surveys (DHS) also provide rural-urban representativeness. In Ghana's sample, 67 percent of the respondents lived in rural areas and the rest in urban areas, and in Zimbabwe the distribution was 69 percent rural and 31 percent urban. The surveys used a similar questionnaire instrument and canvassed the respondents for information for a wide spectrum of socio-economic and demographic information, including place of residence, educational attainment, and employment status. In addition to the DHS, a wide range of reports from UNESCO, World Bank, IMF, United Nations and other international and local sources, such as census data, were consulted.

The chapter is divided into six sections. The introduction is followed by section two which discusses the research methods and data sources. It then proceeds to review the literature on the significant contribution that educated women can make to the betterment of nations in section three. Section four examines the data on the gender gap

Table 17.2a: The Gender Gap in Educational Attainment in African Countries

Country	Primary Education	Secondary Education	Tertiary Education
Seychelles	20.4	29.4	46.0
Botswana	-0.4	-4.6	4.6
Eritrea	9.8	15.8	80.0
Namibia	40.8	-8.4	-22.2
South Africa	1.0	-7.0	4.4
Tanzania	1.0	10.0	75.0
Cape Verde	0	3.8	28.3
Uganda	8.8	25.4	35.4
Lesotho	-5.4	87.8	-10.6
Gambia	13	23.4	27.8
Mozambique	16.6	32.0	55.6
Burkina Faso	21.6	29.6	50.0
Guinea	30.0	48.2	83.4
Zimbabwe	1.6	9.2	40.6
Benin	26.8	39.8	64.8
Rwanda	1.4	13.6	-50.0
Mauritius	0.4	-3.0	2.2
Angola	0	20.4	69.2
Swaziland	2.6	1.2	2.6
Mali	21.8	32.6	75.0
Guinea Bissau	26.8	35.6	59.2
Ghana	8.4	22.2	55.6
Chad	32.0	61.0	69.2
Côte d'Ivoire	15.0	32.6	51.2

Table 17.2b The Gender Gap in Educational Attainment in African Countries			
Country	**Primary Education**	**Secondary Education**	**Tertiary Education**
Gabon	0.2	27.0	40.2
Tunisia	2.8	3.0	10.6
Niger	23.6	21.8	69.2
Sao Tome & Principe	21.4	30.4	46.8
Zambia	3.2	22.6	41.2
Congo	4.8	16.2	63.2
Liberia	18.2	43.2	52.2
Burundi	90.6	24.2	50.0
Ethiopia	27.4	11.8	57.2
Morocco	13.4	14.2	17.6
Senegal	10.0	24.2	50.8
Nigeria	11.6	8.6	45.0
Sierra Leone	18.4	27.2	66.6
Cameroon	5.0	19.0	74.6
Central Africa Republic	21.0	41.4	38.6
Demo. Republic of Congo	18.6	24.4	70.2
Egypt	7.2	8.0	20.4
Mauritania	5.8	32.2	83.1
Equatorial Guinea	25.6	45.0	69.0
Malawi	40.8	28.8	38.2
Kenya	0	8.2	42.0
Algeria	5.4	5.4	17.6
Togo	16.8	47.8	69.2
Sudan	8.6	6.8	18.6
Madagascar	1.6	0.4	9.6
Libya	0	3.4	1.4
Comoros	7.4	10.0	38.4
Djibouti	15.6	16.8	0
Somalia	31.7	30.8	54.2
Averages	**11.2**	**21.8**	**40.2**

in Ghana and Zimbabwe, while section five provides an overview of the factors that lead to the persis10ce of the gender gap in Africa, emphasizing the country cases we selected. Conclusions and implications for development are provided in section six.

Women's education in the African context

The importance of female education, especially in the developing countries need to be highlighted (Hartnett and Heneveld 1993). Indeed, education is considered the strongest factor that enables women to improve their lives and those of their dependants (King and Hill 1993; Summers 1992). Female education generates a wide range of benefits that do not accrue to society from male education (Hartnett and Heneveld 1993). Many studies show a correlation between maternal educational attainment, and child health. As schooling improves knowledge and use of health practices, children born to educated women 10d to suffer less malnutrition and are more likely to receive immunizations at appropriate age levels, and therefore experience lower infant/child mortality than children born to women with little or no education (Schultz 1989; Summers 1992; Weale 1992; World Bank 1992; The New Internationalist 1999). It is estimated that each additional year of schooling for a mother decreases the mortality rate of children under age of five by up to 10 percent (World Bank 1995; Hartnett and Heneveld 1993). In most cases, educated women also 10d to have lower fertility rates than their non-educated counterparts (Dodoo 1992).

Female education influences fertility in a number of ways. Besides deferring marriage, and therefore child birth to a later date as a result of career development, educated women also have a 10dency to opt for fewer children than their non-educated counterparts. Furthermore, according to the DHS conducted in several African countries, there are higher levels of contraceptive knowledge and use among educated women than the non-educated (Ghana Statistical Services and Macro International Inc. 1994; 1999; Central Bureau of Statistics and Macro International Inc.1999; Central Statistical Office and Macro International Inc.1995; 2000). Therefore educated women are likely to have more control over their reproductive behavior. Education also influences fertility by changing perceptions of the costs and benefits of having children, postponing the time of marriage and shaping attitudes to contraception (World Bank 1993; King and Hill 1993).

All things being equal, educated mothers are more likely to send their children to school. Research in many countries indicates that each additional year of formal education completed by a mother translates into her offspring remaining in school for an additional one-third to one-half year (The Partnership on Sustainable Strategies for Girls 2000). The World Bank also has concluded that educating girls may have greater economic benefits than educating boys, and of10 leads to higher levels of economic development. Knowles (1999) has confirmed the validity of the Bank's assertion. In his 1999 study on female education and economic development he concluded that gender gaps between male and female school enrollment rates in developing countries could be a serious drawback on economic development. In another related study, Knowles et.al (2002) using data from a number of countries found evidence to underscore the positive relationship between female education and labor productivity. Klasen (2002) also found that gender inequality in education may lower directly affects economic growth by lowering the level of human capital. Besides, female education is an important catalyst for economic growth and human development (Klasen 2002; Oxfam 2000). Evidence from research suggests also that educated women 10d to play a more active role in civic matters in their communities than their non-educated counterparts, and are of10 an important resource for other women and children in the community (USAID 1999).

Considering all the above, it could be concluded that, girls' education is crucial to sustainable development and that the old adage that educating a woman is tantamount to educating a whole nation is true. Yet according to a report from the Forum of African Women Educationists (FAWE), an NGO that has championed female education in Africa in the last decade, 36 million girls in sub-Saharan Africa were out of school in the early 1990s, and those who gained access were poorly served (FAWE 1995). Even when an equal number of girls and boys enroll in first grade, by fourth grade, 50 percent of the female students have dropped out and 64 percent leave school before they acquire full literacy. By the end of the primary school cycle, the completion rate for girls is only 34 percent. At secondary and tertiary levels, the discrepancies between boys' and girls' education increase radically. Only 10 percent of girls as compared to 36 percent of boys atttend secondary school. Four times as many boys as girls continue to tertiary level. All across the continent, the mean years of schooling among women aged between 15 and 49 tend to be lower than men, and illiteracy levels among women aged between 15 and 60 are significantly higher than males (Bloch and Vavrus 1998).

Following more than a century of colonial rule, Zimbabwe (Southern Rhodesia) emerged as an independent nation in 1980. Due to the racism and discrimination that characterized white rule, access to education was unequal between whites and blacks. As a result, literacy levels, especially among black women, were very low. To ameliorate the high illiteracy levels, the indigenous leaders who took over the administration in 1980, determined to make universal access to education one of the cornerstones of their development programs. Consequently, the educational system was expanded to unprecedented levels, especially during the decade of 1980 to 1990, enhancing access for the population that had been deprived of schooling. As a result of the government's universal education policy and the huge investment, the number of primary schools increased by 42.5 percent from 3,161 to 4,504. Within the same period, the number of secondary schools increased from 197 in 1980 to 1502, an increase of 662 percent. School enrollment also increased dramatically. For instance, primary enrollment increased from 820,000 in 1979 to 1.2 million in 1980, rising to a further to 2.2 million by 1989. In the 1990s, enrollment peaked at nearly 2.5 million in 1996 before falling to 2.4 million in 2000. Expansion in the secondary schools was even more impressive. Enrollment shot from 66,000 in 1979 to 150,000 in 1981, reaching 670,000 in 1989, and peaking at 844,000 by 2000 (CSO 2000).

While the new approach to access education in Zimbabwe was designed to be gender and racially blind in theory, women did not get equal access in practice, especially at higher levels, and therefore, gender gap remains an important issue. In all fairness, Zimbabwe has done much better bridging the gender gap than many African countries, and at some levels women even out number men in enrollment ratios (CSO,

2000). However, the gap between men and women still remains a problem. Across the country, enrollment figures for girls and boys are about equal at grade one. But as the cohorts move up, a gap appears. As a result, only 93 percent of girls in Zimbabwe complete grade five, according to a United Nations Report (UNICEF 2000). Yet, Zimbabwe's gender gap in education appears to be much better than many other African countries (see Table 17.2a).

Net School Enrollment Ratio (NER), which indicates participation in schooling among school age children, also shows that in 1999, at the primary school level (ages 7–12), girls were more likely to be enrolled in school than boys (82 percent versus 80 percent nationally, and 86 percent versus 84 percent in urban areas). These figures are also reflected at the regional levels where female enrollment was higher than males in all but three of the 10 regions. This fact notwithstanding, women still face educational inequities in the country. At the secondary school level, the statistics change in favor of males: 36.7 percent versus 39.9 percent. For the Gross School Enrollment Ratio (GER), which measures the participation of children aged seven to 18 years, female participation is 4.2 points below males, and 2.1 points below the national average of 107.4 (see Table 17.3). Again, in 1999, only 23 percent of eligible women in the 15 to 24 age group were attending school. While several factors may account for this situation, 64 percent had left school because they could not afford it, and five percent due to pregnancy.

Wide disparities in school enrollment also exist among the provinces. Indeed, in Zimbabwe, as it is in the other African countries, an urban bias exists that makes it easier for the urbanized regions to have better access to goods and services including education and healthcare, than in rural areas. Urban children are more likely to enroll and stay in school vis-à-vis their rural counterparts. Therefore it is not surprising that enrollment at both primary and secondary levels for women are significantly higher in the core metropolitan regions of Harare and Bulawayo than they are for the periphery regions such as Manicaland, Midland, Mashonaland Central and Masvingo (see Table 17.3). While the female enrollment figures were much better than the situation in 1994 when the average secondary school enrollment for women was 23 percent (43 percent urban and 16.2 percent rural) and 59.8 percent for primary school (63.6 percent and 49 percent urban-rural respectively) (see CSO and MI 1995), there may still be a lot of room for improvement.

The gender gap widens further from secondary to tertiary level (CSO 2000). Although only a small percentage of Zimbabweans have attained higher education, there is a significant gap between males and females. At independence in 1980, Zimbabwe had only one university. In 1980, only 20 percent of total university students in Zimbabwe were female. Although by 1994, this figure had improved to 26 percent, female representation in higher education leaves much to be desired. To facilitate university education to meet manpower needs, a second institution, the University of Science and Technology was established in 1986, and the Open University which specializes in long distance education was established in 1993. While the creation of additional institutions of higher learning has definitely fostered access to higher education, the institutions are still male dominated. Although the percentage of women in the Open University (see Table 17.4) increased from 23 percent in 1993 to 41 percent in 2002, a much better female-male ration than the two other, imbalances still exist.

Table 17.3 School enrollment rations by sex and place of residence for Zimbabwe, 1999
Net enrollment rations (NER) and gross enrollment rations (GER) for the defacto household population age 7-18 years, by level of schooling, sex, residence, and province, Zimbabwe 1999

	Net Enrollment Ration (NER)[1]				Gross Enrollment Ratio (GER)[2]		
Residence and Province	**Male**	**Female**	**Total**		**Male**	**Female**	**Total**
			PRIMARY SCHOOL				
Residence							
Urban	83.7	86.1	84.9		99.7	100.9	100.3
Rural	79.4	80.9	80.2		112.4	106.6	109.6
Region							
Manicaland Mashonaland	78.6	76.5	77.6		117.0	108.1	112.6
Central Mashonaland	78.5	81.1	79.8		111.8	107.2	109.5
East Mashonaland	78.5	82.9	80.6		107.0	106.0	106.5
West Matabeleland	80.9	79.7	80.4		109.6	105.2	107.6
North Matabeleland	79.7	86.4	83.1		101.7	101.9	101.8
South	82.8	81.1	82.0		108.7	101.4	105.0
Midlands	80.5	83.0	81.8		107.7	101.7	104.6
Masvingo	83.0	81.2	82.1		121.3	111.5	116.5
Harare	81.2	88.8	85.0		94.0	102.6	98.3
Bulawayo	83.5	86.6	85.1		100.0	100.9	100.5
Total	**80.4**	**82.1**	**81.3**		**109.5**	**105.3**	**107.4**
			SECONDARY SCHOOL				
Residence							
Urban	59.9	49.0	53.9		69.4	55.0	61.5
Rural	33.9	31.4	32.8		38.5	33.0	35.9
Province							
Manicaland Mashonaland	43.8	33.1	38.6		47.7	33.5	40.8
Central Mashonaland	28.2	25.8	27.0		36.2	27.5	31.8
East Mashonaland	36.5	35.0	35.8		43.2	38.4	41.1
West Matabeleland	27.6	33.5	30.4		33.1	33.5	33.3
North Matabeleland	31.3	36.8	33.8		32.5	36.8	34.4
South	29.1	37.4	33.0		31.6	41.0	36.0
Midlands	36.3	35.7	36.0		41.4	40.3	40.9
Masvingo	37.4	33.3	33.5		42.0	36.9	39.6
Harare	67.5	49.0	57.2		79.5	54.4	65.5
Bulawayo	59.8	51.4	55.4		68.6	58.3	63.2
Total	39.9	36.7	38.3		45.6	39.5	42.7

[1]The NER for primary school is the percentage of the primary-school-age (7-12 years) population that is enrolled in primary school. The NER for secondary school is the percentage of the secondary-school-age (13-18) population that is enrolled in secondary school. By definition the NER cannot exceed 100%.

[2]The GER for primary school is the total number of primary school students, regardless of age, expressed as the percentage of the official primary-school-age population. The GER for secondary school is the total number of secondary school students, regardless of age, expressed as the percentage of the official secondary-school-age population. If there are significant numbers of coverage and underage students at a given level of schooling, the GER can exceed 100%.

Source: Central Statistical Office [Zimbabwe] and Macro International Inc. (2000).

In an attempt to redress the disparities, the University of Zimbabwe, in the 1990s, embarked on an affirmative action program aimed at doubling the number of female students entering the institution and increasing female enrollment to at least 40 percent. On the whole the gender gap in school enrollment over time across the country has created different levels of literacy in the regions. Whereas only about five percent of women in Harare and Bulawayo are considered illiterate, female illiteracy levels range from 20 percent in Masvingo to 32 percent in Mashonaland Central (see Table 17.5).

As is the case of Zimbabwe, Ghana too has a wide gender gap in educational attainment (see Table 17.6). In Ghana, one in three women has no education (compared to one in five for males). 89 percent of all women 65 and above (compared to 66 percent of men) have no education. The no-school level drops to 76 percent for the 55 to 59 cohort, 49 percent for 45 to 49 and 15 percent for the 15 to 19 age group, a clear indication of long-term improvement (Comparable no school figures for males are 39 percent, 29 percent and nine percent for the age brackets 55 to 59; 45 to 49 and 15 to 19 years old respectively). The median years of education for women are only 2.3 compared to 4.9 for males. While long-term improvement is evident in the much lower no-school rates for the lower cohorts, nevertheless the question still remains that Ghanaian women have less education than men. This is especially true in the rural areas and in the periphery regions, namely, Upper West, Upper East and Northern regions where clearly 67.9 percent, 66.5 percent and 75.9 percent of all women respectively have no education at all. These figures are about double the national average for women (38 percent) and more than three times the average for males (26.6 percent). Although Ghana's female population is slightly higher than males in all the age cohorts, this is not reflected in the school enrollment at all levels. From primary school through secondary to tertiary levels, vast disparities exist (Tables 17.7 and 17.8).

Given Ghana's history of compulsory free education for all genders between 1957 and 1985, it's quite surprising that illiteracy levels among certain segments of the population continue to be high. The smaller number of women enrolled in primary and secondary schools and at the tertiary levels after 1985, however, is not too surprising. The introduction of user-pay into Ghana's educational system under the IMF/World Bank sponsored economic restructuring made it difficult for some parents to pay for their children's education, and if they were constrained to choose between educating a son and a daughter, the former was preferred, as happens elsewhere.

Understanding the Causes of the Gender Gap

While the data depicting unequal access presented in this chapter may be specific to Ghana and Zimbabwe and as such may be attributed in part to factors unique to these countries, most of the discussion in this section will explore the factors that have made the gender gap a continent-wide problem. Indeed, a close examination of the data set for each of the African countries for which DHS data have been collected in the past 10 years reveals disparities between men and women, rural and urban, and between the various regions in each country.

Table 17.4 Male-Female Enrollments at the Zimbabwe Open University, 1993-2002

Year	Male	Male %	Female	Female %	Total
1993	573	77	176	23	749
1994	2,184	71	881	29	3,065
1995	2,166	68	1,009	32	3,176
1996	2,324	74	1,105	26	3,129
1997	3,857	71	1,572	29	5,429
1998	5,007	66	2,613	34	7,620
1999	9,697	68	4,734	32	14,313
2000	10,775	63	6,342	37	17,117
2001	11,432	61	7,392	39	18,824
2002	8,149	59	5,687	41	13,836

Source: Open University, Zimbabwe.

Table 17.5 Adult Literacy Rates by Region and Gender, 2000

	Male	Female	Total
Manicaland	90.16	81.01	85.13
Mashonaland Central	82.21	68.48	74.98
Mashonaland East	89.96	81.66	85.41
Mashonaland West	87.41	76.3	81.7
Matabeleland North	83.65	74.36	78.64
Matabeleland South	86.22	78.49	81.77
Midlands	90.67	81.11	85.56
Masvingo	88.58	79.91	83.7
Harare	96.91	95.08	96.02
Bulawayo	96.06	94.66	95.36
Zimbabwe	90.3	82.11	85.97

Source: CSO Zimbabwe.

Table 17.6 Educational Level of the Male and Female Households Population

	No Education		Primary		Middle/JSS		Secondary/Higher		Median Years	
Residence	Male	Female	Male	Female	Male	Female	Male	Female	Male	Female
Urban	12.2	22.3	31.3	30.3	35.0	34.5	21.4	12.9	7.8	6.1
Rural	32.9	46.8	34.3	30.8	27.0	20.4	5.8	1.9	3.2	1.0
Region										
Western	17.8	34.1	35.6	34.4	35.5	25.8	11.1	5.7	5.7	2.8
Central	18.5	35.6	34.9	33.9	37.8	26.9	8.8	3.6	6.2	2.9
Greater Accra	9.8	19.4	28.1	28.9	34.3	34.0	27.7	17.8	8.9	6.6
Volta	20.8	34.3	36.4	34.5	30.7	27.4	12.1	3.7	5.4	2.9
Eastern	16.9	27.1	34.0	34.2	37.3	33.1	11.7	5.6	6.4	4.6
Ashanti	17.4	33.0	38.4	33.7	37.0	28.8	7.2	4.5	5.6	3.2
Brong-Ahafo	21.7	30.8	36.8	34.8	33.0	30.7	8.5	3.7	4.3	3.8
Northern	62.0	75.9	25.7	16.5	7.5	6.1	4.8	1.6	0.7	0.6
Upper West	56.9	67.9	27.1	22.9	11.5	7.5	4.4	1.7	0.8	0.7
Upper East	50.9	66.5	30.2	21.1	11.5	7.7	7.1	4.6	0.9	0.7
Total	**26.2**	**38.3**	**33.3**	**30.7**	**29.6**	**25.3**	**10.9**	**5.7**	**4.5**	**2.5**

Source: Ghana Statistical Services and Macro International (1999).

The gender gap in African education as is illustrated in the context of Ghana and Zimbabwe may be comparable to what pertains in other male dominated societies. However, it is significant to note that while some of the factors contributing to the gender gap in education in other male-dominated societies may also be applicable to Africa, the relevant literature demonstrates that the variation, complexity and interrelatedness of the factors that constrain female education in Africa and perpetuate the gender gap may be unique to the continent (Odaga and Heneveld 1995). A number of socio-cultural factors, extreme poverty, political factors, the multiplicity of socio-cultural and ethnic groups, the wide range of religious heritage, entrenched perspectives on gender roles, and Africa's colonial past, among others, have worked to contribute to and perpetuate gender inequality, not only in access to education, but also to other benefits. (Logan and Beoku-Beta 1996; Coeyman 2000; Odaga and Heneveld 1995; FAWE 2000; Hyde 1996; Rose and Al-Samarrai 2001; Oxfam 2000). It is important to keep in mind, though, that the relevance of the factors in each milieu may differ to some degree due to differences in micro and macro conditions as well as colonial history.

Socio-cultural and economic factors that constrain girls' education at the household and community levels are closely interwoven (Odaga and Heneveld 1995). In their analysis of the trends in female education in Africa, Logan and Beoku-Betts (1996) also concluded that the disenfranchisement of women in education results from economic factors, cultural and societal norms, as well as stereotypes of gender roles. These factors directly or indirectly impact government policy and initiatives on education as well as career support and advice given to women.

Table 17.7 School enrollment ratios for Ghana, 1998
Net attendance ratios (NAR) and gross attendance ratios (GAR) for the defacto household population by level of schooling, sex and residence, Ghana 1998.

	NAR[1]				GAR[2]	
Residence and region	**Male**	**Female**	**Total**	**Male**	**Female**	**Total**
			Primary School			
Residence						
Urban	86.0	84.8	85.4	118.3	111.4	144.8
Rural	70.8	70.5	70.7	98.2	95.0	96.7
Region						
Western	88.4	84.0	86.2	115.8	107.0	111.4
Central	82.9	84.7	83.7	110.2	114.1	112.0
Greater Accra	87.1	82.0	84.7	126.7	117.4	122.2
Volta	73.6	79.7	76.4	104.3	113.5	108.5
Eastern	85.8	86.8	86.3	115.6	111.8	113.6
Ashanti	80.8	77.2	79.1	104.2	98.4	101.5
Brong Ahafo	67.2	75.3	71.5	103.7	102.6	103.1
Northern	37.6	30.7	34.2	56.1	38.1	47.3
Upper West	44.3	44.9	44.6	71.6	67.6	69.7
Upper East	40.8	37.3	39.2	61.7	49.9	56.2
Total	**75.0**	**74.0**	**75.0**	**104.0**	**100.0**	**102.0**
			Secondary School			
Residence						
Urban	41.2	39.5	40.3	55.9	46.4	51.0
Rural	31.2	28.0	29.7	36.4	30.6	33.7
Region						
Western	36.5	34.5	35.5	41.7	36.9	39.4
Central	39.6	32.1	36.0	44.4	35.2	39.9
Greater Accra	35.7	36.1	35.9	54.6	44.1	49.2
Volta	34.8	26.7	31.0	41.2	29.1	35.5
Eastern	41.7	33.4	37.9	47.1	34.3	42.6
Ashanti	40.0	38.3	39.1	48.4	44.3	46.3
Brong Ahafo	27.6	34.6	31.1	29.1	35.3	32.3
Northern	16.1	11.9	14.4	28.4	13.9	22.6
Upper West	15.6	16.5	16.0	20.5	18.1	19.5
Upper East	22.8	22.8	22.8	34.0	28.0	31.3
Total	**34.0**	**32.0**	**33.0**	**42.0**	**36.0**	**39.0**

[1]The NAR for primary school is the percentage of the population of primary school age (6-11years) that is attending primary school. The NAR for secondary school is the percentage of the population of secondary school age (12-18 years) that is attending secondary school. By definition, the NAR......

[2]The GAR for primary school is the total number of students attending primary school--regardless of age--expressed as a percentage of the official primary school-age population. The GAR for secondary school is the total number of students attending secondary school--regardless of......

Table 17.8 Gender Gap in Enrollment in Ghana's Five Universities, 1993-1998

		Number				
University	**Gender**	**1993/1994**	**1994/1995**	**1995/1996**	**1996/1997**	**1997/1998**
University of Ghana	Male	4,123	5,288	5,288	5,853	6,383
	Female	1,540	1,668	1,668	2,644	2,223
	Total	5,663	6,956	6,956	8,497	8,606
University of Science & Technology	Male	3,389	3,897	3,734	4,791	5,496
	Female	811	993	887	1,288	1,280
	Total	4,200	4,890	4,621	6,079	6,876
University of Cape Coast	Male	2,383	3,197	3,197	3,904	5,341
	Female	807	1,076	1,076	1,438	1,923
	Total	3,190	4,273	4,273	5,342	7,264
University College of Education	Male	1,368	1,246	1,246	2,223	2,597
	Female	472	501	501	732	957
	Total	39	134	134	255	384
University of Development Studies	Male	39	124	124	222	332
	Female	--	10	10	33	52
	Total	39	134	134	255	384
TOTAL	Male	11,302	13,752	13,589	16,993	20,149
	(%)	75.7	76.4	76.6	73.5	75.5
	Female	3,630	4,248	4,142	6,135	6,535
	(%)	24.3	23.6	23.4	26.5	24.5
	Total	14,932	18,000	17,731	23,128	26,684

Source: Ghana Statistical Services, (2000).

A number of studies in several African countries seem to suggest also that the obstacles to female access to education include poverty, which puts price tags on girls, the direct cost of paying for schooling, and the opportunity costs of sending girls to school, both of which may be too high (Coeyman 2000; Odaga and Heneveld 1995; FAWE 2000; Hyde 1996; Rose and Al-Samarrai 2001). Poverty is an important and ever-present obstacle to female education in Africa (Oxfam 2000). In Ghana and Zimbabwe, as it is in many parts of Africa, families whose incomes barely pay for basic necessities may also be responsible for tuition and other fees that may be beyond their means. Indeed, the IMF/World Bank sponsored Structural Adjustment Programs (SAPs) that were implemented in Ghana, Zimbabwe, Kenya and many other African countries, starting from the early 1980s had user pay for education, health and other services as one of their cornerstones (Assie-Lumumba 2000). In her study on the relationship between SAPs and educational policies with regard to gender equity and access, Assie-Lumumba (2000:115) found that the economic restructuring programs have had adetrimental impact on education and access to women by imposing suppression of public support for education without considering the actual needs of the users. Even for countries whose constitutions obliged them to provide free and compulsory primary education, the conditionalities set by the IMF and the harsh economic realities prevented them from providing free education even if they had the political will to do so (Assie-Lumumba 2000). In countries where parents are not required to pay school fees, they may still be responsible for purchasing school uniforms, supplies and even furniture. For instance while rural primary schools in Zimbabwe were fees exempt in 1992, parents still had to pay for books and furniture. The costs of these items could be prohibitive for some families. Consequently, it is not surprising that parents who cannot appreciate the benefits of educating their daughters are the least likely to send them to school (FAWE 2000). Thc opportunity cost of educating women may also be prohibitive, especially from the viewpoint of rural families. Poor families are of10 dependent on their children's labor for survival. In many African societies, girls are conditioned to play the role of mothers and care providers at a very young age. The responsibilities of a girl-child may include but are not limited to selling in the market, cooking, fetching firewood, and taking care of siblings. If their mothers need to work outside the home, it is older girls, rather than their brothers, who 10d to be kept out of school. A 1994 study of poor rural families in northern Ghana found that girls were of10 the sole breadwinners in their ex10ded families, and had to juggle the conflicting demands of work and school. Hence, household poverty combines with cultural and social attitudes to keep girls out of school (FAWE 2000; Oxfam 2000). These factors are reflected in the very high female illiteracy rates and inter-regional and rural-urban disparities depicted in Table 17.2.

Another factor is the priority given to girls' future roles as mothers and wives, which may have a strong negative bearing on their formal education. The idea that girls need a limited education due to their defined societal roles is rooted in both traditional practices and the colonial experience. African societies prior to colonialism practised informal education. This was the type of education that taught survival skills that were necessary for the efficient societal functions. This type of education had a gender bias in that women were accorded with the less dangerous and more submissive roles in society. The African man automatically declared himself the major provider for his family and delegated the duties of mother craft, housewifery and cookery to his female counterpart. The introduction of colonialism and colonial education further enhanced these cultural practices that created superior and inferior roles in society. For the colonizer in Africa, the initial priorities were to develop limited infrastructures such as roads, rails and mines that were to facilitate the exploitation of the continent's resources. All these efforts required some endurance and stamina, and the African male became just the right person for the job. Work places that were established in Ghana, Zimbabwe, Kenya and elsewhere during this period were male dominated and of10 had few or no women.

The newly established colonial schools had more male enrollment than female for a variety of reasons. First and foremost, the colonial administrators carried over to Africa Victorian-era values about girls that were prevalent in Europe at the time. Among other things, girls were not expected participate in certain activities (Burstyn 1980), especially those that would enligh10 them and poise them to challenge male dominance and hegemony. Therefore, girl learning was generally frowned upon except in the case of the elite class when it was tolerated to some ex10t. The Victorian values reinforced the already existing African values that sanctioned gender roles. Culturally, since women were housekeepers, the males got the opportunity for spare time away from home. Since female children were ingrained in the societal values of helping around the home, some parents did not see any reason for sending the female children to school. If the purpose of education was to train the workers in the colonies to communicate with the colonizer at the work place, then it was not necessary for the girls to be involved since they were not working away from home. The type of education offered did not cater for opportunities that were inclusive for both sexes; therefore parents viewed education for girls as a waste of time and resources. Moreover, in patrilineal societies such as Zimbabwe there is that strong belief that investing in girls' education is not worth the family spending their resources because the girl will get married into a different family altogether and her own birth family will not benefit from that education. Some of these antiquated perspectives are, unfortunately, still entrenched in many African societies (Martineau 1997). The effects of these factors on girls' education are far-reaching, and affect the performance and persis10ce of those girls who remain in school. An understanding of how these factors govern household decisions leading to low investment in and ambivalence towards female education is the key to formulating strategies to address the low societal demand for female education (FAWE 2000; OXFAM 2000).

Within the schools and classrooms themselves, the attitude of both teachers and male students, which obviously have their foundation in established cultural norms, 10d to hinder the progress of girl students. The of10 held belief that girls cannot think as boys, as Gordon (1998) found in her study of Zimbabwe but which no doubt may be equally prevalent in Ghana and in most African societies, may make girls spectators in the classroom and discourage them from active class participation. But learning is not a spectator sport. Students who delve into and fully participate in class activities of10 exude more confidence and perform better. While the schools should play a leading role in dismantling traditionally held norms of gender roles, they still play a major role in socializing children into the adult gender roles they will be expected to play, not only in their own families, but also in the political economy in general. Boys are taught to be 'masculine' and girls 'feminine,' according to the norms of their society (Gordon 1998).

Another significant factor that of10 creates a hostile learning environment for girls is sexual abuse. There is a body of evidence that suggests that sexual abuse and harassment do take place across the board in schools throughout Africa (Shumba 2001). In a study of abuse and harassment in Zimbabwean schools, Gordon (1995) found widespread abuse of female students committed by both male students and teachers alike. According to Gordon, harassment takes the form of verbal harassment—teasing, derision—and other behavior aimed at belittling and embarrassing girls. In some cases assault in the form of beating, and rape takes place. An analysis of 246 reported cases of abuse by teachers in secondary schools in Zimbabwe, 1990 to 1997, identified 212 cases of sexual abuse, 33 cases of physical abuse and one case of emotional abuse (Shumba 2001). Investigations in Kenya also reveal that many girls are forced into sexual relationship with teachers but suffer in silence for fear of victimization if they reveal their tormentors (Mathangani 2001). Similar stories could be told from Ghana, Nigeria, Botswana, and indeed other African countries. There is no gainsaying that these acts of violence, that are mostly overlooked by school and law enforcement authorities, create a hostile environment in which women cannot thrive for their best and achieve the education they desire. Outside the schools, the so-called "Sugar Daddies", or adult males who have sexual relations with students, have been responsible for ending the educational careers of female students. Through money, gifts and promises of marriage, they tempt girls into sexual liaisons, impregnate them and thereby end their school careers. While a complex set of factors including adolescent peer group culture may cause this situation, evidence suggests that female students from poor households are, all things being equal, the most likely to become the victims of sugar daddics (Lcach and Machakanja 2001).

Besides the issues raised in the preceding paragraphs, female education in Africa is also affected by other factors that include the parental, especially mother's, educational attainment and occupation, and geographical location of the family. In their recent study in Guinea, focusing on the effects of parental education and income on schooling, Glick and Sahn (2000) found that while an improvement in a father's educational attainment can lead to more investment in the education for both sons and daughters, an improvement in a mother's education of10 leads to a significant impact on daughters' education relative to their sons. The researchers also found a positive relationship between increases in household income and investing in the education of girls. All things being equal, educated parents living and holding good jobs in urban areas are most likely to provide educational opportunities for their daughters than illiterates or less educated people. Evidence from studies in Ethiopia also shows that well-nourished children from wealthier households whose mothers and fathers are literate are more likely to at10d and complete primary school (Rose and Al-Samarrai 2001). The family's place of residence also plays a crucial role in the type of education, quality of education and the longevity of the female student in school. Female students in urban areas 10d to last longer in the school system that those in rural areas. This, again, is a result of the cultural demands on the girls who should be household workers. The rural family depends on subsis10ce farming while the urban family usually has at least one adult family member who is employed in either the formal or informal sector. On rare cases are young women the breadwinners in the urban settings. The younger rural elementary school girl has chores such as fetching firewood and water while the urban girls may be free of such chores. The rural elementary school girl may be pulled out of school to take care of younger siblings should that need arise. The rural secondary school girl may adopt her mother's role of taking care of the younger ones should misfortunes such as illness or death occur.

Once girls are enrolled in school, their persis10ce and success depends upon a number of factors. Studies in a number of African countries demonstrate the critical importance of factors such as the local functions of marriage, mothers' and daughters' workloads, distance from home to school, discrimination against women in the job market as well as political commitment (UNESCO 1998).

Conclusions and the Implications of the Gender Gap for Development

This chapter has sought to shed light on gender and spatial inequities in education in Africa and implications for socio-economic development emphasizing the case of Zimbabwe and Ghana. It has argued that while the benefits of female education for all aspects of socio-economic development are incalculable, many obstacles exist that keep women out of school and therefore perpetuate the gender-gap. As pointed out earlier in this chpater, there is a very significant relationship between education and development. But of even more significance is the strong relationship between female literacy and development. An investment in female education, it has been observed, has the po1 0tial to yield more dividends than most other investment. Educating girls could generate widespread benefits that cut across all aspects of socio-economic and political development. Even the World Bank has acknowledged this fact. As Larry Summers, a one time Vice-President and Chief Economist of the World Bank succinctly put it:

> I have tried to concentrate on the concrete benefits of female education and explicitly contrast it with other proposed investments. Expenditures on increasing the education of girls do not just meet the seemingly easy test of being more socially productive than military outlays. They appear to be far more productive than other social sector outlays." (Summers 1992)

The time has come for a level playing field for both male and female. As African countries attempt to reinvent their economies for the 21st century, the need to make changes in their educational programs to provide more access to all their citizens, but more so for girls cannot be overemphasized. The continuing dominance of men in all aspects of socio-economic life in Africa is primarily the result of traditions, belief systems and policies that have kept the African woman out of the educational system (Gordon 1998). Although countries like Ghana and Zimbabwe are among a the few countries in Africa where the governments have taken consis1 0t steps since independence in 1957 and 1980, respectively, to create a climate of equal opportunity for men and women, men have 10ded to play the more prominent roles in the development process (Mhloyi and Mapfumo 1998). For the African woman to be able to participate fully in economic production, management and higher level decision making, old myths about women and their role need to be broken. Evidence from many African countries suggest that the few women who have been able to shatter the barriers built around education have been able to perform equally, if not better, than their male counterparts as judges, chief executive officers, university professors and the like. Therefore the need for programs and policies that will pave the way for women not only to enroll in school but to complete the schooling cannot be overemphasized. Since very little data from the other African countries were included in this discussion, more research is needed to ascertain the existing conditions in the other countries.

References

Assie-Lumumba, N.T. (2000). Educational and economic reforms, gender equity, and access to schooling in Africa. *International Journal of Comparative Sociology* 41 (1): 89–120 2000.

Bloch, M. and Vavrus, F. (1998). Gender and educational research, policy, and practice in Sub-Saharan Africa: Theoretical and empirical problems and prospects. In Bloch, M., Beoku-Betts, J and Tabachnick, B.R. (eds.) *Women and Education in Sub-Saharan Africa: Power, Opportunities and Constraints* (pp. 1-24). Boulder & London: Lynne Rienner.

Burstyn, Joan N. (1980). *Victorian Education and the Ideal of Womanhood*. London: Croom Helm.

Carr, D.(1994). *Way A Women 's Lives and Experiences: A decade of research findings from the Demographic and Health Surveys Program*. Calverton, MD: Macro International.

Central Statistical Office [Zimbabwe] and Macro International Inc. (1995). *Zimbabwe Demographic and Health Survey, 1994*. Calverton, MD: Central Statistical Office and Macro International.

Central Statistical Office [Zimbabwe] and Macro International Inc (2000). *Zimbabwe Demographic and Health Survey, 1998*. Calverton, MD: Central Statistical Office and Macro International.

Coeyman, Marjorie (2000). Bridging Ethiopia's Educational Gender Gap. *Christian Science Monitor* March 14.

Dodoo F. Nii-Amoo. (1992). Female Education, Age, Parity, and Reproduction Cessation in Ghana. *Social Biology* Spring-Summer; 39(1–2): 102–108.

Evans, K. (1995). *Barriers to Participation of Women in Technical Education and the Role of Long Distance Education*. Commonwealth of Learning Occasional Paper.

Evans, T and King, B. (1991). *Beyond the Text: Contemporary Writing on Distance education*. Victoria, Australia: Deakin University Press.

Forum of African Women Educationist (FAWE) (1993). *Educating Girls and Women in Africa*. Pan-African Conference on the Education of Girls, Ouagadougou, Burkina Faso.

Forum of African Women Educationist (FAWE) (1995). *Girls and African Education*. Nairobi, Kenya: FAWE.

Forum of African Women Educationist (FAWE) (2000). Closing the Gender Gap in Education: Curbing Dropout *FAWE Newsletter* Vol. 8 (3).

Ghana Statistical Services (GSS). (2000). *Quarterly Digest of Statistics*. Accra: GSS.

Ghana Statistical Services (GSS) and Macro International Inc. (1999). *Ghana Demographic and Health Survey, 1998*. Calverton, MD: Ghana Statistical Services and Macro International.

Ghana Statistical Services (GSS) and Macro International Inc. (1994). *Ghana Demographic and Health Survey, 1993*. Calverton, MD: Ghana Statistical Services and Macro International.

Glick, Peter and Sahn, David E. (2000). Schooling of girls and boys in a West African Country: the effects of parental education, income and household structure. *Economics of Education Review* 19: 63–87.

Gordon R. (1998). 'Girls Cannot Think as Boys Do': Socializing Children through the Zimbabwean School System. *Gender and Development* 6: 2, pp. 53–58.

Hartnett, Teresa and Heneveld, Ward (1993). *Statistical Indicators of Female Participation in Education in Sub-Saharan Africa*. AFTHR Technical Note No. 7. Africa Technical Department. Washington, DC: World Bank.

Hyde, Karin A. L. (1996). *Girl's Education in Eastern and Southern Africa: An Overview*. Prepared for the regional Mid-Decade Reviewing Meeting, South Africa, February. Forum for African Women Educationalists.

King, E.M. and Hill, M.A. (1993). *Women's Education in Developing Countries: Barriers, Benefits and Policies*. Baltimore: Johns Hopkins University Press.

Klasen, S. (2002). Low Schooling for Girls, Slower Growth for All? Cross-Country Evidence on the Effect of Gender. Inequality in Education on Economic Development. *The World Bank Economic Review*, 16: 3, pp. 345–373.

Knowles, S. (1999). *Female education and economic development.* http://www.commerce.otago.ac.nz/econ/Research/ Growth/intro.htm Accessed March 20, 2002.

Knowles, S., Lorgelly, P.K and Owen, P.D. (2002). Are Educational Gender Gaps a Brake on Economic Development? Some Cross-country Empirical Evidence. *Oxford Economic Papers* 54 (1): 118–48.

Leach, Fiona and Machakanja, Pamela (2001). The sugar daddy trap. Peer pressure pushes girls into sex. *Insights Gender Violence Special Issue*. August.

Logan B.I. and Beoku-Betts J.A. (1996). Women and education in Africa: An analysis of economic and sociocultural factors influencing observed trends. *Journal of Asian and African Studies* 31 (3–4): 217–239.

Martineau, R. (1997). Women and education in South Africa: Factors influencing women's educational progress and their entry into traditionally male-dominated fields. *Journal of Negro Education* 66 (4): 383–395.

Mathangani, Patrick (2001). Sexual Abuse Rife in Schools. *The Nation Newspaper*, Nairobi.

Mellington, N. and Cameron, L. (1999). *Female Education and Child Mortality in Indonesia.* Department of Economics. University of Melbourne. http://www.ecom.unimelb.edu.au/ecowww/research/693.html. Last Accessed February 10, 2004.

Mhloyi, Marvellous and Mapfumo, Owen (1998). *Zimbabwe: Impact of Family Planning on Women's Participation in the Development Process.* A Report Prepared for The Women's Studies Project Family Health International. Harare: University of Zimbabwe.

Mlama, P and Colclough, C. (1999). Empty desks, empty futures: the curse of classroom gender gaps. Sussex, UK: Institute of Development Studies, University of Sussex.

The New Internationalist (1999). Gender Canyon. Issue 315, August.

Odaga, Adhiambo and Heneveld, Ward. (1995). *Girls and schools in sub-Saharan Africa: From analysis to action.* Technical Paper No. 298. Washington DC: World Bank.

Oxfam (2000). *Education: The Global Gender Gap.* Parliamentary Briefing Oxfam Policy Papers Number 9–4/4/00. Oxford: Oxfam.

Oxfam (1999). *Education Now — Break the Cycle of Poverty.* Oxford: Oxfam.

Partnership on Sustainable Strategies for Girls Education. (2000). *Measuring the Gap: Female Education in Sub-Saharan Africa.* http://www.girlseducation.org/PGE. Last accessed November 11, 2003.

Population Action International. (1998). *Educating Girls: Gender Gaps and Gains. Report on the Progress Towards World Population Stabilization.* Washington DC: PAI.

Population Reference Bureau (PRB) (1999). *Population Data Sheet.* Washington DC: PRB.

Rose, Pauline and Al-Samarrai, Samer (2001). Household Constraints on Schooling by Gender: Empirical Evidence from Ethiopia. *Comparative Education Review* 45:1, February.

Shumba, Almon (2001). Child abuse by teachers in Zimbabwe. *Insights Gender Violence Special Issue,* August

Schultz, T. Paul (1989). *Benefits of Educating Women.* Washington, DC: World Bank, Background Papers Series, Education and Employment Division, Population and Human Resources Department.

Summers, Lawrence H. (1992). *Investing in All the People.* Washington, DC: World Bank, Office of the Vice President, Policy Research Working Papers, Report No. WPS 905.

Tien, F.K. (1996). How Education Drove Taiwan's Economic Development. *Market Solutions to Social Issues* Number 4.

UNESCO (1998). *UN System-Wide Special Initiative on Africa Status.* Report of UNESCO Activities. April.

UNICEF (2000). *Educating Girls, Transforming the Future.*? New York: UNICEF.
United Nations Statistics Division. (2003). *Millennium Indicators*. New York: UN Department of Economic and Social Affairs.
USAID (1999). Girls' Education: Good for Boys, Good for Development .*Gender Matters Information Bulletin* No. 5 October.
Weale, Martin (1992). *Education, Externalities, Fertility, and Economic Growth.* Washington, DC: World Bank, Population and Human Resources Department, Policy Research Working Paper No. WPS 1039.
World Bank (1992). *Poverty and Income Distribution in Latin America: The Story of the 1980s.* Washington, DC: Technical Department, Latin America and the Caribbean Region, Regional Studies Program, Report No. 27.
World Bank (1993). *The benefits of education for women.* HRO Dissemination Notes. Human Resources Development and Operations Policy. Washington, DC: World Bank.
World Bank (1996). *Leveling the Playing Field: Giving Girls an Equal Chance for Basic Education: Three Countries' Efforts.* EDI Learning Resources Series. Washington DC: World Bank.
World Bank (2000) *World Development Report.* New York: Oxford University Press.

Chapter 18

The Politics and Apolitics of Development: The Case of a Development Project in Northern Ghana*

Karl Botchway

Introduction

Development agencies present development projects and strategies as politically unproblematic and as such, see politics as an undesirable element of development interventions. This study challenges the apolitical nature of development interventions. With evidence from one of the ambitious development interventions in the Northern region of Ghana, I show that by reducing development to a technical issue, the development industry misses out on some of the political pre-conditions, which might make for the effective promotion of development effort. What exactly do I mean by the apolitics of development? In the context of this chapter, I am concerned about "development" projects, which purport to ensure a "qualitative" transformation of society, but yet present the process of development as a profoundly apolitical process. The perception is that development projects and strategies are politically unproblematic and that bringing politics to bear on them is undesirable.

Drawing on the work of advocates who are pushing for politics to be at the center of development, I will first make a case for the claim that development is a profoundly political process, hence the need to study and understand the political and institutional pre-conditions for effective development action. I then examine the elements of an ambitious development project in Northern Ghana to explore how the case for development is presented. In the process, I examine how in practice, this project generated conflicts and power struggles, issues which lie at the heart of politics. In conclusion, I take the position that any attempt to engage in a fundamental transformation of any society must at a minimum realize that this process is fundamentally political.

A reading of most development reports will suggest that the process of social development is a profoundly apolitical process. Such reports, for instance, tend to reduce the role of state, politics and power to a secondary and inconsequential aspect of the process of development. In one of the more influential books on development, anthropologist James Ferguson (1994) indicates that in most "development" planning reports, the state is mostly presented as an apolitical machinery. He points out that the state:

> appear[s] as a machine for implementing "development" programs, an apolitical tool for delivering social services and agricultural inputs and engineering economic growth. Military metaphors— successful "operations," well-executed "attacks" and "assaults" on "targets," etc.—abound, and the image is of a single, unitary, righteous army doing battle against a universal enemy. Issues involving the political character of the state and its class basis, the use of official position and state power by the bureaucratic elite, the functions of bureaucratic "inefficiency" and corruption—matters which are central to academic understandings of modern African states—are nowhere found...Where "bureaucracy" is seen as a problem, it is not a political matter... the bureaucratic apparatus, like the economy, responds unambiguously to the directives of planners, and the state machinery has policies, but no politics. (Ferguson 1994)

Politics Matter

Despite the position asserted by the development industry, politics, as Leftwich (1990, 1994, 2000) points out, is primary to the development process. Leftwich (2000) emphasizes that the processes of development, irrespective of how it is defined, at one point or the other involves the mobilization, organization, combination, and the use and distribution of resources which inevitably gives rise to conflicts and disputes among individuals and groups. Invariably, there will be struggles over who wins and loses as a result of the projected changes (Leftwich 2000). More so, it is important to acknowledge that politics is a pervasive feature of social life and occurs in all groups, institutions and organizations, formal or informal, private or public, local, national or international (Leftwich 1990). Development, thus, is inescapably political, for at any point in the promotion of development what is crucially at stake is how material resources made available by the promotion of development will be distributed and the inevitable disputes that arise from calculations as to who wins or loses (Leftwich 1994). Thus, whatever arguments—whether in economics, hydrology, agricultural or health—may be advanced in favor of any policy option or strategy of development, the argument seldom alone determines the results or direction of the processes of development. Politics will be central to the outcome (Leftwich 1990).

This study should be seen as a challenge to how the dominant discourse, generated by the development industry, presents the principle of "government" as a passive entity devoid of politics or interests. Government bureaucracies are presented as responding mechanically in an objective manner to plans and policies. Such an approach "seems to take little or no account of the fact that "government" is always the exercise of power—activity of rulers, not servants" (Ferguson, 1994). In the context of this study the implementation of development projects should also be seen as concerned fundamentally with the mapping, making and the spatial reach of power, with the ability to control and manage other people, environments and places (Crush 1995).

It is in this context that some academics writing on development treat the state as an important actor in the process of development (Samatar 1999). The state, as an important actor in development is seen as the agency with the "political power" and capacity to provide direction. It can cajole, persuade and at times even instruct a wide range of economic agents to facilitate what it perceives as its own development agenda (Leftwich 2000). It is indeed becoming clearer that to understand the pervasive forms of underdevelopment or non-development that has become a constant feature of African states, one needs to focus primarily on the character and capacity of the African state and the forms of politics that have sustained these states. Perhaps it is this concern that prompted the late Claude Ake (1991: 316) to argue:

> We never are going to understand the current developmental crisis in Africa, much less contain it as long as we continue to think of it as an economic crisis. What is before us is primarily a political crisis; its economic consequences are serious, but they are nonetheless incidental. Not only is the crisis essentially political in character, it is also political in origin.

In most African countries, as Ake notes, there is a tendency to depoliticize economic interactions. This has led to the unleashing of powerful social forces and a form of political competition, which makes the task of overcoming underdevelopment virtually impossible. As the premium on political power becomes important and the struggle for it gets intense, politics becomes a zero sum game. In the end "the struggle for power becomes[s] so intense and so absorbing that it ...overshadow[s] everything else, including the pursuit of development" (Ake 1991: 318).

As a result, the state is unable to develop an institutional capacity to effectively induce development and an equitable resource allocation. In his study of the developmental experience in Botswana, Abdi Samatar suggests that at a minimum:

> a disciplined and legitimate political leadership of the dominant class is essential in developing state capacity and insuring that public power and resources are not used for personal gain. Second, a purposive and effective state guidance of the economy can lead to sustained growth and development. The third, and maybe the most important...is that an effective and capable African state can minimize the deleterious effects of the international system while enabling the country to take advantage of whatever opportunities the system offers. (Samatar 1999)

What lessons do we learn from the problems of development in Africa? It is a basic but an important one. Politics do matter. If we are to understand development or the lack of it, as Leftwich (2000) points out, we have to understand the state and the social forces—that is the politics that shape it and in turn are shaped by it. If politics is central to development, as I demonstrate in this chapter, then one must of necessity address the question of why development planners and the entire development industry refuse to see it as central, when almost everyone else agrees that politics matter. Most development projects, it seems, take for granted the existence of a social structure or a developmental coalition that will avail itself of the opportunities created for development by projects.

Development Agencies and Apolitical Development

Until recently, with its nebulous pronouncement on "governance" as an important variable in the process of development, the World Bank treated the process of development as a profoundly apolitical process. The World Bank, we are informed, has long been aware of its apolitical image and takes pride in that. Eugene Black, the Bank President, in 1962 wrote: "we ask a lot of questions and attach a lot of conditions to our loans. We would never get away with this if we did not...render the language of economics morally antiseptic" (Nelson 1995). Indeed proponents for the World Bank affirmed this position in recent times when they argued that: "the Bank's credibility and strength has traditionally depended on its status as a quintessential technocracy concerned with economic efficiency" (Leftwich 2000).

NORRIP: The Ghana Story

In what follows, I present attempts by the Canadian International Development Agency (CIDA) and the Northern Region Rural Integrated Program (NORRIP) to engineer development in the Northern Region of Ghana beginning in 1980. My aim is to critically evaluate the de-politicizing process of development projects as presented in the reports by the consultants to the project, by examining how the political struggles generated at the implementation phase provide insights into the processes of development.

To do this, let me first provide some historical context. The Northern Region of Ghana presents a classic case of regional inequality in development that one finds in the Third World. Some districts within the region are described as "among the world's very poor and ultra-poor" (Jackson and Associates Ltd. and G.A.S. Development Associates Ltd. 1993). This concern has led to several development endeavors in the region since Ghana's independence in 1957. One of the more ambitious projects to promote development in the Northern Region of Ghana was The Northern Region Rural Integrated Project (NORRIP). Ghana and the Canadian International Development Agency (CIDA) initiated this project in 1980. The Technical Unit set up during the initial stages in 1980 produced a three-volume regional development strategy accompanied by several sectoral papers. The first volume of the regional development strategy report presents an overview of the region in terms of its development potentials and constraints, the second volume outlines the strategies for promoting development in the region and the third describes the regional development projects and programs. The NORRIP project managers, after several modifications, decided that the provision of water would be the lead sector for the promotion of development in Northern Ghana. This was referred to as the Integrated Village Water Project (IVWP).

Essentially, the Reports present the NORRIP projects as designed primarily to provide services to the rural poor. As such one of the important program objectives is creating an effective administration for the delivery of rural services. In this regard, the Plan of Operation stresses the need to "improve the delivery capabilities of the GOG [Government of Ghana] . . . departments and other selected agencies in the Northern Region generally, but more specifically in . . . two target areas" (NORRIP 1987: 37-40).

The Report emphasizes the need to secure the best administrative and managerial capacity for the promotion of "development." Few people would deny the significance of an effective, fair and open administrative system as a necessary requirement for the promotion of "development." But to suggest that the process of "development" is that of securing the best managerial and administering environment independent of politics is illusory.

The Plan of Operation, which recorded the understanding between CIDA, representing the government of Canada, and the Ministry of Finance and Economic Planning (MFEP), representing the GOG, spelled out fully the responsibilities of the Ghanaian state. These included ensuring "overall coordination and cooperation of all participating line ministries/parastatals...for the duration of the program; to ensure sufficient numbers of qualified Ghanaian staff at various levels, and to fund all Ghanaian salaries" (NORRIP 1987: 40).

The Plan of Operation focused on four main areas of administration in the management of NORRIP's program by the Ghanaian state. These are project coordination, funding, accountability and information management for the execution of program objectives. The prime responsibility of the Ghanaian state, it seems, is to secure the most conducive operational environment for the successful execution and administration of the planned projects in NORRIP.

However, as Ferguson (1994: 253) cautions, "government services" whether in the form of "development" projects or not, "are never simply 'services;' instead of conceiving this phrase as a reference to simply a 'government' whose purpose is to serve, it may be at least as appropriate to think of 'services' which serve to govern". The Report, by simply seeing the implementation of "development" projects as a government-coordinated service, fails to engage with the history and practice of the Ghanaian state as an agent representing certain social, political and economic interests in the development process (Leftwich 1994). Thus even though the Ghanaian state was assigned a major role in administering the project, the political pre-conditions that make for effective project implementation and administration were either never identified or completely ignored.

Making the plea for placing politics at the center of "development" studies, Leftwich (1994) argues that the study of "development" is more rewarding and revealing if studies and reports on the subject matter do not depoliticize the necessary processes of "development" by emphasizing technical bureaucratic factors to the exclusion of others, since the form and distribution of state power and the manner in which this power is used by the state is crucial to understanding the promotion and delivery of "development" (Adrian Leftwich Ibid: 377).

"Development" Projects and Electoral Politics

In Ghana, one could not escape the manifestation of the politics and power of "development" projects during the presidential and parliamentary election year of 1996. From August to December in 1996, when I conducted fieldwork in Ghana for this study, the local newspapers were full of stories of government officials commissioning "development" projects. These projects were not merely seen as the provision of government services, but rather as Ferguson (1994: 253) emphasizes, are "services which serve to govern" and more importantly help to win elections. The actions of government officials at the commissioning ceremonies served to vividly remind rural people in particular, that the political power of the state and its officials in making available the public good services.

The commissioning of "development" projects in Ghana, which often generates a carnival-like atmosphere, involves colorful ceremonies in which the local traditional elites, bureaucratic elites and political elites compete for public attention. As Claude Ake (1991) reminds us, "development" projects, with the material resources they make easily available, become a viable source of tremendous political power. Thus it is not unusual for socio-political struggles to be generated around the control of "development" projects. After all, it is through the implementation of such "development" projects that governments claim to exhibit concern for the people. As some members of the rural communities of the NORRIP projects in Northern Ghana indicated to me during my fieldwork, the provider of a necessity such as potable water is seen as the "savior" bringing "development."

It is important for the purposes of this study to put into perspective how the resources made available through "development projects" fit into the Ghanaian political landscape the period under consideration such that they became important political instruments in the elections of 1996. Most news report analyses indicated that resources made available by "development" projects played a crucial role in the re-election of President Rawlings. The period preceding the ascendancy of Rawlings in Ghanaian politics was a period of economic decay. It was a textbook example of the crisis facing sub-Saharan Africa. Between 1971 and 1982 output in all sectors of the economy declined. Food production fell by 30 percent against a 2.6 percent annual growth of population. The manufacturing sector's contribution fell from 11 percent to six percent. Export earnings dropped by 52 percent and cocoa production, which provides the bulk of the national revenue, fell from 454,000 tons to 220,000 tons. Mineral production in 1981 attained only half the 1971 level. The volume of food imports in 1982 was more than three times that of 1971. The social consequences were grave.

This adverse socio-economic condition made the availability of "development" projects crucial for Ghanaian politicians during the transition to constitutional rule in the fourth republic. Even, the increasing reliance by foreign donors on local non-governmental organizations (NGOs) to execute "development" projects has not escaped government political manipulation. In most cases, the government has used its leverage with bilateral donors to determine which local NGOs can receive aid to facilitate the execution of development projects.

The instructive case in Ghanaian politics is that of the 31st December Women's Movement led by the wife of the former President, Nana Konadu Agyemang Rawlings. With the transition to constitutional government, the 31st December Women's Movement began to describe itself as "non-governmental organization…[that] the revolution gave birth to" (Amanor et al. 1993: 188). By virtue of its status as an NGO, the Movement has been able to secure resources from foreign donors to support women's "development" programs. During the 1996 presidential elections, First Lady Nana

Konadu Agyemang Rawlings' commissioning of projects on behalf of the Movement was given extensive media coverage. Most observers saw the commissionings as campaign appearances. In his analysis of the elections and democratic transitions in Ghana between 1991–1996, Panford (1998: 22) points to the "overwhelming advantages of incumbency" enjoyed by the Rawlings regime as an important factor in the outcome of the elections. He notes that with the support of western donors, Rawlings initiated development projects such as the linking of all 110 districts capitals to the national electricity grid, the provision of potable water to villages, the construction of new roads and access to telephones. These developments contributed immensely to the success of Rawlings in the 1996 elections.

Political Symbolism of NORRIP Projects

In general, the activities of the NORRIP organized community-based organizations were looked upon favorably by the central government. These community groups were largely seen as responsible for the provision of social welfare at a time when the government was reducing the provision of infrastructural services. More importantly, for the government of President Rawlings, the encouragement of self-help community groups were a continuation of the "progressive" discourse of "power to the people," and the "decentralization" of the central government. It was a continuation of the rhetoric of "popular government" of the "revolutionary" days (Botchway 2001). The lead project of NORRIP (IVWP) even though it provided a source of potable water for some of the rural communities within the two target districts of Northern Ghana, should be seen more in terms of its "political symbolism" rather than a substantive commitment by central government in the fight against the structural causes of rural poverty in Northern Ghana.

More importantly, Canadian involvement in NORRIP made available scarce financial and other material resources from a foreign donor. The symbolism used in the fight against rural poverty involved not only the Ghanaian national elite but also the foreign partners. For the foreign countries involved, Canada in the case of NORRIP, the aid was concrete evidence of of its commitment to international humanitarian assistance. For Ghana, the host national government, besides making available badly needed aid and other material resources, Canadian assistance contributed to political legitimation. It is not unusual to hear African political leaders use the amount of foreign assistance and donations received as indicators of the confidence of the international community in their political and socio-economic policies. The case of President Paul Biya of Cameroon illustrates this point well. Less than two months after being re-elected to office in a seriously flawed election, he was allocated FF 600 million in French economic aid. This signified a vote of confidence by France and French support for President Biya (Martin 1995).

NORRIP: The Political Struggles

Two important developments in 1993 highlight the contentious nature of political struggles surrounding NORRIP. In April of 1993, there was a meeting between the Northern Region Parliamentarians and the NORRIP Program Manager. The meeting was to deal with the reduction in the number of Canadian Technical personnel and the termination of Canadian funding perceived to be due to the Program Manager's actions. On October 2, 1993, NORRIP purchased a full-page advertiser's announcement, signed by all three deputy program managers, in response to press allegations in an article entitled "What is wrong in NORRIP? (The Statesman 27 June 2000). The news article alleged that the Program Manager's managerial style was incompatible with the interests of the region and that his bad management was directly or indirectly contributing to the withdrawal of Canadian personnel and funding. Why was there a confrontation over the actions of NORRIP and, in particular, why did this confrontation not come from the villagers but from members of the urban political elite?[1]

To address this question, it is important to refer to an observation I made among some of those I interviewed in Tamale, the regional capital and home of the Northern region urban elite. Most people—including present and former NORRIP employees—readily associated the birth of NORRIP, the arrangements for funding, and the arrival of the Canadian Team with the activities of the first Ghanaian Program Manager of NORRIP, Mr. Rafik Mahama. The imposing offices of NORRIP along the main Tamale-Bolgatanga road, the bungalows of the beautifully landscaped NORRIP village—residence of the officers of the NORRIP, both Ghanaian and Canadian—and the arrival of the first Canadian consultants to assist the Technical Team with the preparation of NORRIP sectoral reports were all credited to the actions and activities of the first Program Manager, Mr. Mahama. He was a mechanical engineer by profession and a royal from Yendi, home of the paramount chief of the Dagombas. He started as the first Program Manager of NORRIP in 1980 and died of cancer in 1987 when the implementation phase of NORRIP was about to begin.

In an interview with a former Regional Minister for the region, Mr. Mahama was described as a "missionary for NORRIP [who]...[bore] the NORRIP profile to a large extent on his shoulders. The contacts he made in Accra and the high profile he gave NORRIP in Accra seem to have died when he died."[2] Another observer described the performance of the first Program Manager as follows, "[He] did what he felt the people wanted and so everybody saw him as the darling boy. . . . The Canadians also had a similar perception of him, somebody they felt comfortable working with."[3]

The acting Program Manager in 1996, who was the third Program Manager, with a tenure beginning in March 1994, provided some context to this perception:

> when the program started Northern Region was in a terrible socio-economic condition. Even in the capital, Tamale, there was no water, no roads, no power, nothing! It was in the midst of this situation that the program [NORRIP] came into being and so it was hailed. We have now got our saviour. And so the people saw [the first Program Manager] as their saviour...Many people didn't know how he was appointed. In fact, up to the time of his

> death many people thought he was an employee of Canada and not an employee of the Ghana government...he also reinforced [this perception] by his attachment more to the Canadian High Commission than to the Ministry of Finance.[4]

The attachment by the first Program Manager to the Canadians, according to the 1996 acting Program Manager, enabled him to deal directly with CIDA to free himself from the bureaucratic politics of NORRIP's parent organization, the Ministry of Finance and Economic Planning. The appointment to NORRIP of a new and second Program Manager seems to have been a turning point. The second Program Manager's tenure began with the implementation phase in 1989 and ended with his resignation in March 1994. His tenure coincided with important developments in the history of the NORRIP program.

First, the role of NORRIP was changed from that of a purely planning agency for Northern Ghana to that of an implementing agency for potable rural water supply. Second, the scope of NORRIP II was reduced from 15 project proposals to seven because the original 15 projects were seen as too ambitious and insufficiently focused. Also, the second Program Manager's tenure saw the departure of the Canadian technical personnel and the subsequent termination of CIDA funding.

These developments were associated by some elements both within and outside NORRIP with the managerial style of the second Program Manager. In a news report titled "Trouble Brews at NORRIP" the writer indicated that:

> Trouble is brewing in the Northern region's citadel of rural development...Its Programme Manager, [the second] is in the center of it... A cross-section of NORRIP staff also charge that [the second Program Manager] is autocratic, and rarely delegates authority to his sectional heads. He takes unilateral decisions and discountenances those who make initiatives to solving problems by reversing decisions. He convenes meeting without agenda, and his resolutions are irreversible. (Kassim 1993)

To what extent was the managerial style of the second Program Manager so problematic as to lead to charges that his continued stay in office would lead to the withdrawal of Canadian personnel and funding? Some of the NORRIP administrators I interviewed were critical of the second manager. For instance, one of the interviewees noted that the second Program Manager "liked to control professional people the way you will control unskilled labor," and as such, might have stifled the initiatives of professionals within the organization. Some of the reasons suggested for this managerial style, were that the second Program Manager "being someone who came from outside...had his own crisis of confidence, crisis of trust, who can he trust and who will try to undermine him. He did not take to criticism of the way he did things"[5] . Despite these comments, almost all persons I interviewed, including some of the present and former NORRIP administrators, cautioned against attributing the withdrawal of Canadian technical personnel and funding to managerial incompetence or managerial style of the second Program Manager. Instead, they suggested that the reasons for the Canadian departures were much more complex.

For instance on the question of the departure of some Canadian Personnel, the official reason provided by NORRIP was that the departures were due to the outcome of a program review meeting in Canada in October 1992. The meeting concluded that there was the need for a:

> reduction in the cost of Technical Assistance on donor projects in order to divert more funds to beneficiaries [and] . . . reducing the number of the foreign experts is a normal thing to do. After all, the foreign experts are expected to transfer their skills to the Ghanaian counterparts within a given period and when their contracts end they may not be renewed because the Ghanaian staff are then considered capable of handling the sectors all by themselves. Thi[s] . . . is the reason for the reduction in the number of Canadian staff in NORRIP from nine (9) in the past to four (4) by today and definitely not because they are dissatisfied with the performance of [the] Programme manager…[6]

Indeed, in the Quarterly Progress Report for January to March 1993, it was noted that 66 percent of the funds had been expended on technical assistance while only 34 percent had gone to training and procurement. Also around this time, CIDA's developmental policies worldwide were undergoing changes with priority support earmarked for projects relating to environment, basic education, and good governance. As evidence of how this change in CIDA policy affected what was considered a very useful program in Northern Ghana, the NORRIP officials indicated how a successful program—the Canadian Universities Services Organization Women-In-Development (CUSO-WID)—which was designed to assist women through the provision of credit for income-generating projects, was terminated on the instructions of CIDA. The worldwide policy changes by CIDA, NORRIP officials claim, partly influenced the decision to eventually terminate funding of NORRIP's activities in favor of direct project activities relating to environment, basic education and good governance.

In March of 1993, in the NDC-dominated Ghanaian parliament of the Fourth Republic, some members of parliament, notably those from the Northern Region, re-opened a debate on what was described as the "water problem" . The NDC Member of Parliament for the Gukpegu-Sabongida constituency in the Northern Region noted that "water has been a major problem for the people in the North . . . [and] suggested that the GWSC [Ghana Water and Sewerage Corporation] and . . . NORRIP should work together to identify areas where wells could be dug." Another NDC member of parliament, Mr. Moses Bukari Magbena, from Saboba constituency in Northern Ghana, "regretted that NORRIP has limited its activities to only two districts…in the region and called on the house to put pressure on NORRIP to expand its operations."[7]

Thus, when rumors of the withdrawal of Canadian Technical personnel and the termination of Canadian funding for NORRIP became widespread within the region, the Regional Minister, who was also Chairman of the Board of Directors of the Management Committee of NORRIP, invited the Program Manager to meet the Northern Region Parliamentarians at the offices of the regional administration to clarify issues arising out of the rumors about the program. On the day of the meeting, the Program Manager, who had a prior international assignment and was en-route to the Philippines, so sent his deputies to the meetings. This was unacceptable to the parliamentarians and as one commentator puts it, "pressure had to be brought …and the [Program] Manager was removed from the plane to go and meet his bosses. At the meeting he saw a number of pressmen and he stated clearly that he was not volunteering any information before the press. Again pressure had to be brought on the [Program] Manager before he answered questions thrown at him" (The Statesman 27 June, 1993). The Program Manager indicated to me that he requested a closed-door meeting since some of the issues to be discussed were of a sensitive and confidential nature. However, in a twelve-page brief prepared earlier for the meeting, the goals, objectives and principles of NORRIP were delineated. The brief further outlined the program's achievements, constraints and its future directions.

The significance of this meeting should not be seen in terms of the explanations provided by NORRIP, but on the contrary should be seen in light of the political significancc and symbolism of "development" projects in the context of a region that lacks basic amenities. In particular, given the history of neglect in the allocation of resources from the central government to the region, NORRIP, because of its access to international aid resources such as funding, housing, vehicles and personnel, became crucial in making available resources for "development" and, consequently for enhancing the political power and image of the region's parliamentarians with their constituents as providers of "public goods."

Control of NORRIP's Infrastructural Power

The control over the resources of NORRIP was soon to develop into a conflict between the Regional Minister and the second Program Manager. This conflict, according to some of the people I interviewed, may have contributed to the resignation of the second Program Manager. NORRIP was a well-endowed organization within the context of Northern Ghana and a dependable outlet for the delivery of material resources to the region. Through its program of institutional strengthening, NORRIP contributed immensely toward the strengthening of the bureaucratic (infrastructural) capacity of the central government's administrative functions within the region.

For instance, NORRIP provided a total of ten vehicles to the Ghana Water and Sewerage Corporation (GWSC), plus four pick-up trucks, 13 motorcycles, an ambulance, maintenance workshop equipment and a computer to the region's Ministry of Health (MOH). In addition, they provided a 33-seater bus to the region's Community Health Nursing School. The Department of Community Development (DCD) also received two pick-ups, 14 motorcycles and audio-visual and kitchen equipments. The newly created District Planning and Budgeting Units of the Yendi and East Mamprusi District Assemblies in Northern Ghana also received motorcycles and office equipment.

Furthermore, NORRIP sponsored formal overseas training for two staff members of the GWSC, two staff members of the MOH, four staff members of the DCD, two Agricultural Extension Officers and one planner of the Yendi District Assembly. NORRIP seems to have been the envy of most organizations in the region. In an interview with other organizations about their perception of NORRIP, some of these agencies suggested that other government organizations could make better use of NORRIP's resources because of their sectoral expertise. They pointed out that despite NORRIP's abundant funding, NORRIP has not been a cost-effective manager of its resources. In addition they lamented that whenever NORRIP involved other line agencies in implementation activities, it controls them too closely.[8] It is plausible that given the resources at the disposal of NORRIP, the Program Manager possessed tremendous power and leverage within the region. In fact, as the Regional Director of the Department of Community Development indicated to me, when the NORRIP Program Manager called for him, he ran.

The clash between the Regional Minister and the second Program Manager developed around the question of who was to be the ultimate controller of NORRIP. Was it the regional political boss or NORRIP's parent organization, the Ministry of Finance and Economic Planning (MFEP) in Accra, the national capital? Related to this was the question of whether the Program Manager of NORRIP should seek clearance from the regional political boss or its parent organization, the MFEP, before acting on day-to-day organizational matters. This question of line of authority eventually developed into a personality clash between the Regional Minister and the second Program Manager. Many saw this personality clash as one of the factors that led to the latter's resignation from NORRIP. The first Program Manager, Rafik Mahama, as I was informed in an interview, had not had that problem. He was described as a willing partner who unlike his successor did not adhere rigidly to rules and regulations and other legal documents pertaining to lines of authority (Ghana Gazette #38, 1st August, 1980).

The origin of this conflict is in what some observers describe as a structural deficiency in the bureaucratic setup of NORRIP. The Gazette announcing the establishment of NORRIP stated that institutionally, NORRIP was a "unit within the Ministry of Finance and Economic Planning" and its "management committee [was to] be responsible to the Minister of Finance and Economic Planning."[9] This provision effectively made NORRIP a part of the civil service apparatus and as such NORRIP was bound to operate by the rules of the civil service. At the same time the Gazette also appointed the Regional Minister chairman of the NORRIP Board of Directors, officially called the NORRIP Management Committee. The composition of the Board as confirmed in a September 26, 1980 exchange of letters between Canada and Ghana, was as follows:

> Regional Minister, Chairman;
> Regional Administrative Officer;
> Program Manager;
> Canadian Consultant Team Leader, (Counterpart Deputy Program Manager);
> Canadian High Commission (CHC) Representative;
> Representative of the Ghana/German Agricultural Development Program (GGADP);
> Ministry of Finance and Economic Planning (MFEP) Representative;
> Ministry of Agriculture Representative;
> Ministry of Health Representative;
> Ghana Water and Sewerage Corporation (GWSC) Representative

Three additional Representatives from each of the three traditional areas (Dagomba, Mamprusi, Gonja or Nanumba) to be nominated from the traditional areas and appointed following consultations and agreement between the Governments of Ghana and Canada; and Ex-officio members, including representatives of other government organizations may be brought in, as required (when projects related to their specific interests are under discussion).[10]

The Board of Directors, according to the Gazette, among others was to determine the general policy of NORRIP relative to the scope, methods and timing of its programs and projects; approve or modify long or short range capital development programs submitted by the Program Manager; approve or modify the organization and classification of employees of the Program; determine the terms and conditions of services of employees of the Program; and, subject to whatever authority would be delegated to the Program Manager, approve all contracts and agreements between the Program and other persons (Ghana Gazette, Ibid: 245). Overall, as the Plan of Operations puts it: "The NORRIP Board of Directors and its operative arm, the NORRIP Office, shall guide the implementation of the program on behalf of the...Northern Region" (Ghana Gazette #38, 1st August, 1980: 245).

On the other hand the Plan of Operation indicated that "the executive arm of the NORRIP Board will be headed be a Program Manager. The Program Manager will be responsible for the day-to-day management of the program, and will supervise the work of the three NORRIP units comprising Resources and Technical Services, Planning, and Finance and Administration" (Ghana Gazette #38, 1st August, 1980:45).

Collectively however, the NORRIP Board could be said to be impotent in the discharge of some of its important functions. The general policy of NORRIP was never determined by the Board and neither was the Board able to approve or modify NORRIP's capital development program. CIDA and the Ministry of Finance and Economic Planning, which provided the bulk of the funding, in effect directed and determined the general policy and major capital expenditure items of NORRIP. The weak position of the Board effectively left the Regional Minister in a powerful position as the Chief Political Coordinator of all government establishments in the region. As the second Program Manager informed me, the Regional Minister in question, in 1993 attempted to annex NORRIP as part of the Regional Administration and tried to give direct instructions on aspects of the day-to-day operations of NORRIP instead of playing his role as Chairman of the Board of the Directors.

The Regional Minister was made aware by the second Program Manager that the interference was not welcomed and that NORRIP "was not an annex of the Regional Administration." By making the Regional Minister aware of his line of authority regarding the day-to-day operation of NORRIP, the Program Manager was apparently trying to give himself and NORRIP more autonomy and power vis-à-vis the Regional Minister. As one of the former NORRIP senior administrator I interviewed pointed out to me, the second Program Manager seems to have failed to realize or understand that "NORRIP was to be based on the local landscape, managed and controlled at the local level."[11] As such it was not wise on his part to contest the people's representative who reported directly to the President and was accountable to Parliament. Underlying this problem for ultimate directional control of NORRIP was the overriding question of the resources made available by NORRIP and who was to get what and when.

These are questions of politics and power which the "development" apparatus for NORRIP was not designed to handle. NORRIP's second Program Manager may not have visualized or understood well enough that "development" projects are not simply a matter of rendering services and administering a project to the best of one's ability, but also involve questions of politics and power. The fight for directional control and autonomy of NORRIP may have created some unbearable tensions for him and, in view of the other unsubstantiated allegations, he may have had no choice other than to resign. What we see here is a case in which the "developmental" elite located within the NORRIP bureaucracy was challenged in its attempt to secure some degree of relative autonomy from the interests of some sections of the political elite. In the process, the chief executive of NORRIP lost a political fight and had to step down. While it is difficult to speculate on the degree of autonomy that the developmental elite within the NORRIP bureaucracy might have secured (after all, they still had to relate to central government), nevertheless, the struggle for autonomy and power on the local landscape points to the degree to which the developmental elite had to negotiate for room to maneuver in the promotion of "development" in the region.

Dismantling NORRIP?

In 1993 there were attempts by the Northern Regional Minister that were interpreted by most officials within NORRIP as a ploy by the Regional Administration to dismantle NORRIP by making it redundant. The Regional Minister submitted a proposal to CIDA for the establishment of a "Development" Policy Analysis and Coordination Facility under the control of the Regional Minister. The proposal called for the establishment of a capacity for "development" policy analysis and donor coordination at the level of the regional administration. The purpose of this facility was among others "to document existing 'development' projects and programs in the region . . . [and to] facilitate the provision of direct professional support . . . from accomplished Ghanaian professionals in the field of regional economic policy analysis, process and institutions for decentralization . . . ."[12]

The creation of the facility, the Regional Minister indicated, would also assist the regional administration in its effort to assemble information on the status of various regional initiatives, and build a capacity for information management in the region. The rationale for the establishment of this facility was to enable the Regional Minister's "office . . . [to] understand and articulate the development priorities of the country from a regional perspective".[13] In a response from CIDA, the Head of Development Assistance at the Canadian High Commission in Accra, Ghana, noted "elements of complementarity" between the Regional Minister's proposal and aspects of NORRIP's proposal for a District Assemble support package. He therefore suggested that a common proposal be submitted by the Regional Minister in his capacity as both Chairman of the NORRIP Board of Directors and Regional Minister.[14]

Institutionally, NORRIP had the personnel, resources and capacity to fulfill most of the basic requirements that the Regional Minister's proposal called for. And in any case his role as Chairman of the NORRIP Board made it easier for him to have access to all the information and sectoral reports pertaining to the development potentials of the entire region generated by the NORRIP Technical Unit. An obvious question is why the Regional Minister did not think that NORRIP, the premier "development" institution for Northern Ghana, was capable of performing the task he had envisaged for his new facility. The answer perhaps may be found in the inability of the Regional Minister's office to directly influence the direction and purpose of how NORRIP's resources were to be used. This then precipitated the call for the establishment of a new regional wide "development" institution with all its personnel and resources directly responsible to the Regional Minister. This in turn sent strong signals to the NORRIP bureaucracy about moves within the Regional Administration to dismantle NORRIP by making the organization redundant. NORRIP officials may have felt vindicated when a report later suggested that the future of such an institution under the direction of the Regional Administration was uncertain, "because its continuous existence will invariably depend on the interests and commitment of the politicians of the day. In the event of disinterest, scarce resources would have been wasted."[15]

The conceptual framework establishing the design for the "development" of Northern Ghana implicitly assumed that since the purpose of government was to provide services, there was bound to be a harmony of purpose between the developmental elites within NORRIP and the political administrators of the region in the delivery of developmental services. But as my narrative illustrates NORRIP's task was not only to secure the best administrative machinery to provide services to the rural poor. Rather, the project became an arena of contestation between the political and "development" elites for the ultimate control of the project and regional politicians trying to secure more "services" for their constituents. Unfortunately, the perspective on the apolitical nature of "development" has been reinforced by the approach of most bilateral and multilateral agencies "that development projects and development strategies are politically unproblematic and...bringing political considerations to bear on them is an undesirable complication" (Ake 1991: 325).

The apolitical and ahistorical development discourse outlining the conceptual apparatus of NORRIP might have assumed that a harmonious relationship was inevitable given the fact the functions of government were ultimately to bring about "development." But as I have noted citing Ferguson (1994: 253), government services cannot be seen as merely rendering a service. Instead it may be at least as appropriate to think of government "services" as a political means to an end. In the section of the report providing reasons for the Canadian withdrawal, there was no mention of the alleged mismanagement by the second Program Manager. Rather the motives of the Regional Administration were implicitly questioned and used as one of the reasons for the termination of funding.

problems of sustainability and ownership of the project emerged since the organization reported to a distant Accra, and as an umbrella organization, relied on resources from line organizations ill-equipped to free up resources for NORRIP. NORRIP therefore created an extra level of bureaucracy and resulted in two regional institutions operating in parallel. CIDA has since shifted its focus from this type of institutional building to initiatives which promote or re-enforce democratization and decentralization…and in the context of a new CIDA financed community governance project ($25 Canadian million), it was decided to

> close NORRIP II prematurely, effective 31 December 1994. In addition to the problems outlined...Canadian Executing Agency performance and continued ambiguity surrounding the role and nature of the Ghanaian region administration argued for disengagement from the project.[16]

The problems with the regional administration, as the Reports indicate were seen as that of ambiguity and not understood as a political exercise of power. This only reinforces the idea that "government" as far the "development" industry is concerned is just machinery for the delivery of services and never a device through which certain classes or interests control people's choices.

Conclusion

This study suggests that "development," broadly conceived as concerned with social change and transformation, also involves the exercise of power with significant outcomes. The political confrontations over the day-to-day directions, use or perceived misuse of resources between the NORRIP bureaucracy and some elements of the Northern Ghanaian political establishment and attempts to make NORRIP redundant should not be seen as isolated incidents. Rather, it suggests that the projects of NORRIP were not simply an effort to secure the most conducive administrative environment for providing potable water, formal training, and vehicles to poverty-stricken villages and neglected government bureaucracies. Instead, NORRIP as an institution was itself grabbed, pulled and confronted by forces it did not understand and did not have the means to deal with. In other words, the NORRIP "development" intervention was not just finding the "right managerial and administrative mix" for the effective delivery of services. NORRIP at a certain time, found itself in a confrontation with the very "Government" representative with whom it was supposed to be in partnership in the fight against poverty.

The political attacks on NORRIP were seen or understood by the "development" bureaucracy as lack of good public relations on the part of NORRIP. Thus a feasibility report on the restructuring of NORRIP noted that the lack of self-promotion and the publicization of NORRIP's functions, activities and its achievements appear to have worked against the Programme in general and management in particular. To some schools of thought, NORRIP is a waste pipe and has achieved only marginal success (if any) since its inception. This is evidenced by unsubstantiated adverse press coverage on NORRIP. As a result, NORRIP was encouraged to publicize more of its achievements, particularly in the provision of water.

The refusal to view the confrontations about the purpose and goals of NORRIP in the press, the meeting between the Northern Region Parliamentarians and the eventual clash for autonomy between the Regional Minister and the second Program Manager as political issues might have been due to the way the conceptual framework for "development" understood the principle of governmentality as the mere provision of a service. As Ferguson (1994: 225) has observed in a different but relevant context, the Regional Administration representing the authority of central government "was never understood as a political fact, as the mode of exercise of a form of power. Government was seen as a machine for deliver[ing] services; but never as a [means]...of 'governing' people, a device through which certain classes and interests control the behavior and choices of others". Institutionally, CIDA's neglect of the political nature of the problem is reflected in the fact it saw the role of the Regional Administration as that of ambiguity when almost everyone I interviewed knew that there was an overt political contest over the autonomy and ultimate control of NORRIP. But as Ferguson (1994) suggests, the explanation may lie in another social fact. "Development" projects, by their very nature, are not equipped to engage in the politics which confronts them.

This study illustrates what most academics writing on "development" see as a basic form of contention over the role that "development agencies" are intended to play. Most "development agencies" are designed to engineer some form of social change, something that has tremendous political implications. But at the same time, the agencies are not supposed to be involved in politics. As this study illustrates, even though the "development" discourse saw the purpose of government as the provision of services in the form of an effective administrative environment, it was clear that politics and power were central to the activities of NORRIP. By reducing the promotion of "development" to a technical issue requiring the best and most efficient administrative environment, the "development" industry de-politicizes questions of poverty and "development" and in the process ignores some of the political pre-conditions which might make for the effective promotion of "developmental" efforts.

Notes

* The author acknowledges with gratitude commentary on this paper by Professor Kwamina Panford. For commentaries on earlier versions, I will like to thank, Professor Kate Crehan, Professor W. Ofuatey-Kodjoe, Professor Tony Pereira and Professor Aristide Zolberg.

1 Interview with Dr. Awudu Tinorgah, Ministry of Health, Accra, October 10, 1996. Dr. Tinorgah also served as the head of Health Unit of NORRIP.

2 Tape recorded interview with Donald Amuah, Bolgatangah, September 5, 1996.

3 Tape recorded interview with Atta Nantogma, Acting Program Manager, NORRIP, Tamale, September 18, 1996.

4 Marie, National Patriotic Party (NPP) Regional Youth Organizer, Tamale, "What's Wrong at NORRIP" The Statesman June 27 1993 Weekending Issue. In a tape-recorded interview with Marie when I probed him about the sources of his information he indicated to me that: "You know what? I got these facts from . . . senior officers [of NORRIP]." Tape recorded Interview, Tamale, September 7, 1996.

5 Tape recorded interview, September, 1996.

6 See NORRIP II, Quarterly Progress Report for January to March, 1993, Hull and Tamale, May 14, 1993: 22.

7 Debrah Fynn and Joe Okyere, "House Invites Minister," People's Daily Graphic, March 26, 1993, 1993.

8 Interview, September 30, 1996.

9 CIDA, Plan of Operation, Hull and Accra, 1987: 143. Also see, Ghana Gazette, Ghana Publishing Corporation, Accra, 1st August, 1980: 245.

10 NORRIP 11, Plan of Operations: 30.
11 Office of the Regional Minister, Northern Regional Administration, Proposal For Development Policy Analysis and Coordination Facility, Tamale, March 1993.
12 Office of the Regional Minister, Northern Regional Administration, Ibid: 1, 3–4.
13 Office of the Regional Minister, Northern Regional Administration, Ibid: 3–4.
14 See Correspondence between Peter Mousley, First Secretary (Development) Head of Development Assistance, Canadian High Commission and Lt. Col (Rtd) Abdullai Ibrahim, Subject: NORRIP II Proposals for District Assembly Support Package and Coordination Facility at the Regional Administration, dated June 9, 1993.
15 CIDA, Feasibility Report: Restructuring of NORRIP II (Final Draft Report), Hull and Tamale, March 1994: 33.
16 CIDA, NORRIP Feasibility Report: Restructuring of NORRIP (Final Draft Report), Hull and Tamale, March 1994: 38.

References

Adedeji, Adebayo (ed.) (1991). *The Challenge of African Economic Recovery and Development.* London: Frank Cass.

Ake, Claude (1991). "How Politics Underdeveloped Africa" in Adebayo Adedeji (ed) *The Challenge of African Economic Recovery and Development.* London: Frank Cass.

Amanor, K., Denkabe, A. and Wellard, K. (1993). "Ghana: Country Overview." In Wellard, Kate and Copestake, James G. (ed.) *Non-governmental Organizations and the State in Africa: Rethinking Roles in Sustainable Agricultural Development.* London and New York: Routledge.

Botchway, K. (2001). "Paradox of Empowerment: Reflections on a Case Study from Northern Ghana." *World Development.* Vol. 29, No.1.

CIDA, NORRIP. *Feasibility Report: Restructuring of NORRIP* (Final Draft Report). Hull and Tamale. March 1994.

Crush, Jonathan. (ed.) (1995). *Power of Development.* London and New York: Routledge, London and New York.

Ferguson, James (1994). *The Anti-Politics Machine.* Minneapolis: University of Minnesota Press.

Ghana Gazette (August 1, 1980). No. 38. Accra, Ghana: Ghana Publishing Corporation, Barnes Road.

Jackson, E.T and Associates Ltd. and G.A.S Development Associates Ltd (1993) NORRIP II Baseline Study: Draft Issue Papers (Prepared for the Canadian International Development Agency, Hull and the Ministry of Finance and Economic Planning, Accra) February

Kassim, Abdallah "Trouble Brews at NORRIP." *Chronicle*, August 15, 1993.

Leftwich, Adrian (1990). "Politics and Development Studies." In Leftwich, Adrian (ed.). *New Developments in Political Science.* Hants, England: Edward Elgar Publishing Limited.

Leftwich, Adrian (1994). "Governance, the State and the Politics of Development." *Development and Change.* Volume 25, No. 2. April

Leftwich, Adrian (2000). *States of Development.* Cambridge, UK: Polity Press.

Martin, Guy (1995). "Francophone Africa in the Context of Franco-American Relations." In John W. Harbeson and Donald Rothchild (ed.) *African in World Politics.* Boulder, CO: Westview Press.

Nelson, Paul (1995). *The World Bank and Non-Governmental Organizations: The limits of Apolitical Development.* London: Macmillan Press Ltd.

NORRIP II (1987). *Plan of Operation—CIDA PROJECT 400/11449.* Tamale and Hull.

Panford, Kwamina (1998). "Elections and Democratic Transition in Ghana: 1991–1996." In Jean-Germain Gros (ed.). *Democratization in Late Twentieth-Century Africa*. Westport, CT: Greenwood Press.

Samatar, Abdi. (1999). An African Miracle. Portsmouth, NH: Heinemann.

World Bank (1992). *Governance and Development*. Washington, DC: World Bank.

Chapter 19

Currency Devaluation and Poverty in Mauritania*

Mohameden Ould-Mey

Introduction

Mauritania occupies a vast land area (1.03 million square km) of the Sahara and Sahel regions along the northwest African coast, and had a sparsely distributed population of 3 million in 2004. Straddling the Arab World and Sub-Saharan Africa, Mauritania is a member of the League of Arab States, the Arab Maghreb Union, the African Union, the Organization of the Islamic Conference, and the Economic Community of West African States. With an exchange-rate-converted GNI per capita of $430 in 2003, an external debt of $2.5 billion (over 200 percent of GDP), a population growth of 2.7 percent, an average life expectancy of 53 years, an infant mortality of 10.6 percent, and with nearly 50 percent of the population living below the national poverty line, Mauritania is classified by the IMF and the World Bank as one of the 64 lowest-income economies, and one of the 40 Heavily Indebted Poor Countries (HIPC). Mauritania's agro-pastoral sector is highly vulnerable to frequent drought, while its export earnings depend almost exclusively on two commodities: iron ore and fish. From 1984–1985 Mauritania embarked on a Structural Adjustment Program (SAP) sponsored by the IMF and the World Bank and supported by the Paris Club, the Consultative Group (of lenders) for Mauritania, and a number of international NGOs. Since then the country has implemented many World Bank and IMF-supported reforms aimed at liberalizing trade and the exchange rate, and moving the country toward a market-oriented economy. By July 2000, IMF and World Bank cumulative lending to Mauritania had reached $1,078 million ($771 million from the Bank and $307 million the Fund). Two-thirds of IMF cumulative lending to Mauritania has been provided since 1984 (see Table 19.1). Mauritania has so far repaid a total of $216 million to the IMF (including charges and interest paid).

IMF/World Bank Loans in Exchange for the Liberalization of the Exchange Rate

IMF and World Bank loans to Mauritania are provided in exchange for changes in economic policy. Loans consist of investment and restructuring expenditures that are not recorded in the treasury accounts. Such operations take place either abroad, with lenders and donors paying suppliers and Mauritania receiving imported goods, or

Table 19.1 IMF Loand and Mauritania Repayments from January 1, 1984 to March 31, 2002

Year	IMF Loan Disbursements (SDRs)	Mauritania's Loan Repayment (SDRs)
2002	0	3,967,500
2001	18,210,000	10,737,363
2000	6,070,000	8,718,834
1999	6,070,000	7,166,497
1998	0	5,491,289
1997	14,250,000	5,800,977
1996	14,250,000	7,296,006
1995	14,250,000	6,240,141
1994	16,950,000	4,367,716
1993	8,475,000	8,475,000
1992	8,475,000	6,393,738
1991	0	10,900,046
1990	8,475,000	14,000,255
1989	8,475,000	11,593,399
1988	4,000,000	7,941,147
1987	18,870,000	9,684,712
1986	18,480,000	14,410,650
1985	9,600,000	17,337,928
1984	0	13,641,541
Cumulative in US$	$222,827,840	$216,989,656

(SDRs) (SDR1=US$1.27403, as of May 10, 2002)

Source: Compiled from IMF (2002). Mauritania: Transactions with the Fund from January 01, 1984 To March 31, 2002. IMF Treasurer's Department, Accounts and Financial Reports Division, available at: http://www.imf.org/external/np/tre/tad/extrans1.cfm?memberKey1=660&endDate=2002%2D03%2D31&finposition_flag=YES

domestically through an account at the Central Bank of Mauritania (IMF 1999b: 18). In exchange for loans, policy measures are detailed in a series of policy framework papers (PFPs) prepared by the government in close collaboration with the IMF and the World Bank, and reviewed by the IMF's Executive Board and by the Committee of the Whole of the Executive Board of the World Bank. Among a sample of 13 sub-Saharan African countries, PFP agreements in 1999–2000 had an average of 114 policy reform conditions, each (Roodman 2001: 48). The PFP represents a rigid system of economic planning, with a very detailed matrix of policy measures and deadlines for implementation. Table 19.2 lists the detailed measures necessary to implement just one out of 124 policy measures the Mauritanian Government must implement under the PFP for the 1999–2002 period. In this case, the IMF literally instructs the government to implement 13 policy measures designed to "further liberalize the exchange system to promote external competitiveness and ensure a viable balance of payments position in the medium term." Moreover, the Mauritanian Government must provide to Division D of the IMF Middle Eastern Department data on every foreign exchange market session held at the Central Bank of Mauritania at the end of each week as well as data on the Central Bank of Mauritania's gross foreign exchange reserves, within two weeks of the reference period (IMF 2001b). This type of IMF micromanagement of members' exchange rate policy is more intrusive and more carefully planned than perhaps in the case of what was called the planned or command economies, especially in terms of its macroeconomic scope, its top down approach, and its political and economic incentives.

The declared objective of the 13 policy measures is to liberalize the exchange rate system in order to promote external competitiveness, i.e. make exports cheaper. The first measure consists of "improving" the methodology used to calculate the weekly official exchange rate of the *ouguiya*, which was determined on the basis of a basket of currencies comprising the Belgian franc, the Deutsche mark, the French franc, the Italian *lira*, the Spanish peseta, and the US dollar. In 1995 the government implemented a series of IMF foreign exchange reforms including: (i) the elimination of the requirement of prior approval by the central bank for most current account transactions, (ii) the creation of an inter-bank foreign exchange market, and (iii) the licensing of more than 40 foreign exchange bureaus. As a result of these reforms, market segmentation increased and the central bank ceased to set the official exchange rate, which became a reference rate calculated daily as the weighted average of the rates applied to bank, foreign exchange bureau, and inter-bank transactions that had taken place.

In 1998 the government enacted more reforms, including the elimination of foreign exchange surrender requirements for fish export proceeds, the lowering of the surrender requirement for SNIM (the iron ore mining company) export proceeds, and the commitment by the central bank to sell all foreign exchange demanded at the selling official rate (IDA and IMF 2000). In 1999 Mauritania accepted Article VIII of the IMF Articles of Agreement, according to which an IMF members may not impose restrictions on payments and transfers for current international transactions, or engage in discriminatory currency arrangements or multiple currency practices without IMF approval. In 2000, the central bank established the expanded exchange market integrating banks and exchange bureaus into a single market, and establishing a daily fixing of the exchange rate (IMF 2000a). Beginning in September 2000, Mauritanian residents were to be authorized to maintain foreign exchange deposits, remunerated at market rates. The percentage of export receipts (other than those from mineral products) that exporters were to be able to keep available was to be raised to 100 percent in December 2000 (with unlimited maximum duration). The obligation to surrender to the central bank the foreign exchange repatriated by SNIM was to be reduced to 20 percent in December 2000, while the authorities were to send the IMF a copy of the annual agreement between the government and SNIM regarding the amount of foreign exchange that this enterprise is supposed to repatriate. According to Mauritania's exchange regime (known as Managed Floating with No Predetermined Path for the Exchange Rate), "the mon-

Table 19.2 IMF Required Foreign Exchange Policy Measures Under Mauritania's PFP, 1991-2002

	Policy Measure: Further liberalize the exhcnage system to promote external competitiveness and ensure a viable balance of payments position in the medium term	**Deadline**
1	**Improve** the methodology used to calculate the weekly official exchange rate.	1999
2	**Increase** the percentages of proceeds from non-mineral exports remaining at the disposal of exporters to: 60% in 6/1999, 70% in 12/1999, 80% in 6/2000, 100% in 12/2000.	1999-2000
3	**Increase** the periods during which exporters may retain the proceeds from non-mineral exports to: 6 months in 6/1999, 9 months in 12/1999, 1 year in 6/2000, unlimited in 12/2000.	1999-2000
4	**Reduce** the surrender requirement (to the central bank) on SNIM's repatriated export proceeds as follows: from 80% to 50% (6/1999) from 50% to 40% (12/1999), from 40% to 30% (6/1999), from 30% to 20% (12/1999), to 0% (6/1999).	June 1999 - December 1999
5	**Adjust** the limits on commercial banks' net open forward positions on foreign exchange in three stages: To a maximum of 5% (6/1999), from 7.5% (12/19999), and 10% (6/2000) of net capital per currenty. To a maximum of 13% (6/1999), 16% (12/1999), and 20% (6/2000) of net capital for all currencies. Apply these limits to both short and long positions.	1999-2000
6	**Allow** residents to open foreign currency deposit accounts with commercial banks and enforce a corresponding prudential regulatory framework.	June 2000
7	**Review** agreement on the interbank exchange market taking into account recommendations of the March 1999 MAE technical assistance mission concerning: operations, quotations, obligations to complete transactions organizational issues.	June 1999
8	**Utilize** the provisions of the revised convention to initiate central bank purchase of foreign exchange in the interbank market.	June 1999
9	**Elminiate** the restrictions on foreign exchange sales for travel abroad.	June 1999
10	**Reduce** the spread between the central bank's buying and selling rates to +/- 0.75%	May 1999
11	**Review** legislation and procedures governing capital transactions of non-residents, including repatriation of dividends and payment of interest.	June 1999
12	**Improve** the payment system by lining the central bank to SWIFT.	2000
13	**Establish** the appropriate organizational arrangements for exchange transations within the central bank.	December 1999

Source: Compiled from IMF (2000b),"Mauritania Enhanced Structural Adjustment Facility: Medium-Term Economic and Financial Policy Framework Paper 1999-2000, "Prepared by the Mauritanian Autorities in Collaboration with the Staffs of the Fund and the World Bank, Annex 1: Mauritania: Foreign Exchange Market and Monetary Instruments, 1999-2000, available at: http:///www.imf.org/external/np/pfp/1999/mauritan/index.htm.

etary authority influences the movements of the exchange rate through active intervention in the foreign exchange market" (IMF 1999a). This is how the Mauritanian currency lost *vis-à-vis* the US dollar through large one-shot devaluations, a series of mini-devaluations, a policy of gradual exchange rate depreciations, and above all a firm government commitment not to allow a sustained appreciation of the *ouguiya*.

The IMF and the World Bank continue to claim that under their sponsored economic reforms, Mauritania "has made considerable progress in restoring positive rates of growth, reducing macroeconomic imbalances and inflation, and moving toward a market-oriented economy." They emphasize that the economic reforms have been accompanied by "an improvement in social indicators and poverty reduction," as well as by "a democratization process, with parliamentary, presidential and local elections regularly held" (IMF 2000b). Meeting in March 1998, a consultative group of 12 donor/lender countries and 14 international organizations declared that Mauritania has made "excellent progress in reforming the economy and improving macroeconomic performance in recent years" (World Bank 1998). Along the same line of satisfaction, the Mauritanian president proudly announced that in recent years Mauritania's economy has grown at the steady rate of four percent (Ould Sid'Ahmed Taya 1998). In June 2000, the International Monetary Fund concluded the 2000 Article IV consultation with Mauritania and commended the government for implementing the first phase of the program supported by the Poverty Reduction and Growth Facility (PRGF).

In May 2000 I was on a visit to Mauritania. While conducting some fieldwork research on currency devaluation, I met a dozen state officials mostly working for the Ministry of Economic Affairs and Development, the Ministry of Finance, and the Central Bank of Mauritania. Most of these state officials were working in one way or another on the implementation of IMF and World Bank programs. At the Ministry of Economic Affairs and Development, much effort is concentrated on reducing the role of the public sector in the economy and promoting a private sector-led economic growth. This restructuring of the public sector reform involves reducing the size of the whole apparatus of government, creating a legal and regulatory environment conducive to private sector development, and privatizing or restructuring some 80 public enterprises, including 22 non-commercial enterprises (such as schools and the only university) and 58 commercial enterprises. Of the latter, the government owns 20, is majority shareholder in another 20, and minority shareholder in the remaining 18 enterprises. These enterprises employ more than 25 percent of the modern workforce. During the period of 1990–1997, 11 public enterprises were liquidated, seven totally privatized, and four partially privatized. Under the PFP of 1999–2002, four more public enterprises were to be privatized, while private sector participation in the capital and management of seven others were to be opened up for the first time.

At the Ministry of Finance, the main concerns include remaining current on external debt-service obligations and preventing the emergence of new arrears. The Mauritanian government must first consult closely with IMF staff on any new external borrowing, even if on concessional terms, to ensure the sustainability of external debt indicators. Under the PFP 1999–2002, the government was to acquire and use new debt management software, prepare quarterly reports on the work of the debt monitoring committee, and strengthen staff training to improve debt recording and analysis. I visited the Service of International Debt and found a team of young people working hard on the implementation of these policies. They were assisted in their mission by the proceedings (including text, tables, and graphs) of the National Workshop on the Debt Strategy of Mauritania held in February 2000 in Nouakchott and financed by various government agencies in Austria, United Kingdom, Denmark, Sweden, and Switzerland. Indeed the entire Mauritanian government has become a big implementing agency for IMF and World Bank-supported macroeconomic reforms and development projects. During the 1980s and 1990s the focus of these reforms was on the liberalization of trade and currency exchange. With liberalization reforms almost completed, the new focus is on what I think is their single most important consequence: poverty, whose reduction has now become the first objective of development in Africa (Economic Commission of Africa, 2001).

But while the IMF, the World Bank, and the Mauritanian government are shifting away from the discourse of "development" to a new discourse of "poverty reduction," they continue to ignore the role played by the liberalization of trade and currency exchange in the process of impoverishing the country. In their report to the 2000 G8 Summit, the IMF and the Multilateral Development Banks listed the following causes of widespread poverty in Africa: (1) low levels of productivity and production technology, (2) high illiteracy and population growth rates, (3) frequent natural disasters, (4) inadequate infrastructure, (5) excessive dependence on a narrow range of commodities for export earnings, (6) counterproductive economic policies in the 1970s and the early 1980s, (7) political instability and conflict, and (8) gender inequality (IMF and MDBs 2000). The blame for poverty was put solely on the internal structure of production rather than on external exchange with the world market, a new intellectual reiteration and revival of the old environmental and cultural explanations of the geography of underdevelopment in the South. There was no mention of North-South resource transfer through debt service, terms of trade, and currency devaluation. Any explanation of poverty in Mauritania cannot and should not ignore the chronic depreciation of the *ouguiya* (see Table 19.3) and its contribution to the decline of Mauritania's GDP and export earnings and to the worsening of external debt.

Currency Devaluation and the Global Market Value of National Production

Regardless of the rationales, assumptions, or declared objectives for currency devaluation, its immediate as well as long-term consequence is that exports become cheaper and imports more expensive. Within the framework of the typical North-South exchange of manufactured goods for raw materials, currency devaluation changes the price system by raising the price of the former while reducing the price of the latter. This contributes to a devaluation of national production as measured by the value (in US dollars) of GDP/GNP/GNI and exports. Since we are measuring the US dollar value of national production in the global market, the estimates of GDP/GNI, exports, imports, and external debt in Mauritania are based on the so-called World Bank Atlas method, which converts national currency units to dollars at prevailing exchange rates, adjusted for inflation and averaged over three years (World Bank 1999: 15). This method of conversion provides a more accurate measure (of how much can Mauritania actually buy from the US market) when compared to the purchasing power parity (PPP) calculations. The latter constitute rough estimations based on extrapolations published by the UN International Comparison Program and by Robert Summers and Alan Heston of the University of Pennsylvania (Central Intelligence Agency 2000; Heston and Summers 1997).

Table 19.4 illustrates the decline of Mauritania's leading economic indicators during the heyday of IMF-supported SAPs. It indicates a decline in the value of Mauritania's exports despite sustained production of iron ore and fish, the two major sources of export earnings. This has a lot to do with the 531 percent depreciation of the *ouguiya*

Table 19.3 Devaluation of the Mauritanian Ouguiya, 1980-2002

Year	1980	1986	1988	1990	1992	1994	1996	1998	2002
Ouguiyas per US dollar	45.91	74	75	80.6	87	123.6	137.2	189	289.28

Source: Compiled from: IMF's International Financial Statistics Yearbooks, 1990-2000. For the year 2002, the exchange rate between the ouguiya and the dollar is based on the inter-bank exchange rate, and calculated by "Currency Converter," of The Currency Site, available on May 9, 2002, at: http://www.oanda.com/convert/classic

vis-à-vis the US dollar between 1980 and May 2002. A decline in the value of exports often leads to a decline in imports, which in itself represents a decline in overall welfare for a country that imports almost everything. Because the *ouguiya* cannot be used directly to pay for imports (it must be converted into dollars or other hard currencies), its depreciation *vis-à-vis* the US dollar means that more units of it (i.e., more units of iron ore or fish) in a given year are needed to import the equivalent of the previous year's imports. Since increasing the volume of exports is not always an option, reducing the volume of imports or contracting more debt would be the logical consequence of currency depreciation in this case. Between 1980 and 2000, the 1980 dollar value of Mauritania's GDP declined from $810 million to $454 million, its exports of goods and services declined from $253 million to $183 million, and its imports of goods and services declined from $449 million to $242 million. However, Mauritania's external debt (measured in 1980 dollars) increased from $843 million in 1980 to $1,207 million in 2000. The decline of the value of Mauritania's exports in the 1990s was taking place amidst a global increase in iron ore demand and a global increase in supply from major exporting countries such as Australia, Brazil, India, Venezuela, Mexico, and Mauritania (Labson 1997: 247).

If we take into consideration both population growth and inflation, the decline of Mauritania's GDP per capita (from $497 in 1980 to $168 in 2000) would be 66 percent between 1980 and 2000 because what cost $497 in 1980 would cost $1028 in 2000. Mauritania's export earnings declined from $253 million in 1980 to $183 in 2000, a 28 percent decline because what cost $253 in 1980 would cost $524 in 2000. During the same period (1980–2000) the 1980-dollar value of United States' merchandise exports increased 16 times while its direct investment abroad (as opposed to debt) increased 70 times (Ould-Mey 2003). The systematic depreciation of the dollar value of Mauritania's GDP and export earnings seems to explain why after nearly two decades of systematic currency devaluation, Mauritania's GNI per capita ($370) "remains somewhat lower than the average for sub-Saharan African countries [$480 in 2000]" and "the statuary minimum wage has remained unchanged at UM 42.83/hour [less than $.25] since 1993," while Mauritania's external debt reached 247 percent of GDP at end-1997 (IMF 1999b: 7, 39). Moreover, the restructuring of budget revenues was apparently made so that the burden of taxes would progressively shift from international trade to domestic trade. The proportion of taxes on international trade declined from 37.7 percent in 1993 to 12.1 percent in 1997, while the proportion of taxes on domestically-traded goods and ser-

Table 19.4 Mauritania Leading Economic Indicators, 1980-2000

Socioeconomic Indicators/Year	1980	1990	2000
GDP at current prices (millions of US$)	810	1,000	940
GDP at 1980 prices (millions of US$)	810	633	454
Population (millions)	1.63	2	2.7
GDP per capita at current price US$)	497	500	348
GPD per capita at 1980 prices (US$)	497	316	168
Exports of goods and serves at current prices (millions of US$)	253	465	378
Exports of goods at 1980 prices (millions of US$)	253	294	183
Imports of goods and services at current rices (millions of US$)	449	619	500
Imports of goods and services at 1980 prices (millions of US$)	449	392	242
Total external debt outstanding at current prices (millions of US$)	843	2,096	2,500
Total external debt outstanding at 1980 prices (millions of US$)	843	1,326	1,207
Total debt/GDP	104	206	265.3
Total debt service/exports	17.3	28.1	22.6
Average annual exchange rate (ouguiyas per US$)	45.9	80.623	238.9
Inflation (the purchasing power of $100 in US CPI 1998)	100	158	207

Source: World Bank (2001). World Development Indicators Database, Washington DC: World Bank. http://www.worldbank.org/data/databytopic/keyrefs.html, http://www.worldbank.org/data/wdi2001/pdfs/tab4_16/pdf; IMF. 1980-2001. International Financial Statistics, Washington, DC: IMF. United States Bureau of Labor Statistics. 2001. Consumer Price Indexes: Inflation Calculator. http://www.bls.gov/cpi

vices increased from 12.5 percent to 26.4 percent (IMF, 1999b: 90). This represents a major shift of the burden of taxes from global producers (who pay less and less in terms of tariffs) to national retailers (who made local consumers pay more and more taxes), with some serious implications for the purchasing power of wage earners and consumers as well as the overall tax-dependent infrastructure and public services.

Currency Devaluation and the Purchasing Power of Wage Earners and Consumers

Prior to SAPs, the government of Mauritania used to stabilize consumer prices through subsidies and price controls. Under successive structural adjustment programs, domestic prices were liberalized and made to respond quickly to changes in the exchange rate, with the exception of utility prices (water, electricity, and telecommunications), airline prices, and petroleum prices. Regarding the last, the government introduced a new pricing policy in September 1998, in which the government-set pricing schedule would be updated on a monthly basis (IMF 1999b: 16) to reflect the depreciation of the *ouguiya*. In May 2000 I witnessed one episode of the updating of the government-set pricing schedule for petroleum prices. The government uses a simple "political technique" to justify the price increase and to contain any potential popular anger. For a week or so, the government made people believe that petroleum products (especially gas) were running out of supply. In the middle of the artificially created shortage of supply, the government announced a new increase for petroleum price. The official consumer price index (CPI) is calculated only for low-income households in the capital city (Nouakchott). Even the IMF points out that the current CPI underestimates the inflation rate because of various technical and methodological difficulties. These include: (i) limited breadth of coverage, both geographically and in the range of commodity prices; (ii) lack of some data for certain commodities; and (iii) the use of an ad hoc weighting scheme (IMF 1999b:16). Nevertheless the index (see Table 19.5) indicates a sharp increase in consumer prices in Nouakchott between 1987 and 1997, especially foodstuff prices whose index reached 231 percent.

With the exception of meat, which is still largely supplied by domestic producers, Mauritania imports almost everything else, including food products, machinery, construction materials, petroleum, and consumer goods. Such increases in consumer prices were never offset by commensurate salary and wage raises.

Despite occasional salary and wage raises, devaluation has severely weakened the purchasing power of civil servants and wage earners in general. The Government determines civil service salaries and the minimum wage for industry and agriculture, while wage rates in public enterprises and the formal private sector are set through collective bargaining. Minimum wages were not raised during 1982–1991, whereas wages in the public sector were increased under the 1992 budget for the first time since 1985. The minimum wage was raised by 37 percent in 1992 and by 28 percent in 1993. Civil servant salaries were raised between 11 percent and 31 percent in 1992, and between 10 percent and 24 percent in 1993 (IMF 1995: 8). In 1999, the statuary minimum wage has remained unchanged at UM 42.83/hour since 1993. However, the government increased the lowest salaries by up to 15 percent within the context of the 1998 budget law (effectively increasing the overall wage bill by about four percent for the year 1998), the first such increase since 1992. Given the leading role played by government salaries, public enterprises and the formal private sector and trade unions agreed in August 1998 to an increase of up to 15 percent for low salaries (IMF 1999b: 16).

Currency Devaluation and Indebtedness

Between 1980 and 2000, Mauritania's external debt increased from $843 million (101 percent of GDP) to $2500 million (266 percent of GDP), while its debt service ratio to exports increased from 19.3 percent to 22.6 percent. Most of Mauritania's external debts are labeled in the few "hard" currencies against which the *ouguiya* has been systematically devalued for over two decades. Even when we measure Mauritania's foreign debt in 1980 constant dollars, the external debt would still increase from $843 million in 1980 to $1,200 million in 2000. The external debt crisis and the desperate search for foreign aid from the United States had led the Mauritanian government to go as far as dispatching its foreign minister to the State Department's ballroom in Washington, DC in October 1999 in order to sign an agreement establishing full diplomatic relations with the State of Israel, despite strong criticism from Arab and Muslim countries. US Secretary of State Madeleine Albright noted at the signing ceremony that this opening "will bring real benefits to the Mauritanian people" (Albright, 1999). It needs to be noted that Mauritania fearlessly broke diplomatic relations with the United States in 1967 in response to US massive aid to Israel during the 1967 Arab-Israeli war, an unthinkable diplomatic move today. Moreover, debt and resource transfer from Mauritania and the South in general seem to be accelerating through the rise of an information sector within the world economy and the emergence of information goods whose comparative advantage resides in the low cost of duplication. When exchanged with Southern agricultural and even industrial goods, Northern information goods seem to be in a position to generate huge margins of profits and extract huge amounts of wealth from the South. For example, the cost for duplicating software is nearly zero for companies like Microsoft. Because of this unique comparative advantage, information goods create a highly unequal exchange when traded for industrial or agricultural goods. As Roberto Verzola put it "an information economy like the United States can come to the Philippines, and trade one copy of its WordPerfect for our [sic] 2,000 pounds of sugar, or for one of Taiwan's color television sets. Yet, how long does it take to produce 2,000 pounds of sugar, compared to another copy of WordPerfect? How many Filipinos have to work, how many days, to produce value that is equated to a product which can be copied by one person in a few minutes?" (Verzola 1995).

Conclusion

As explained elsewhere (Ould-Mey 2003), the analysis of the North-South income gap in light of the politics of currency devaluation and resource transfer shows that the gap is still geographic (notwithstanding the significance of its class dimension within indi-

Table 19.5 Consumer Price Index for Nouakchott, 1987-1997

Year	Foodstuff	Clothing	Lodging	Other	Overall Index
1987	122.08	113.35	111	100.2	116.22
1988	125.03	109.2	113.27	100.58	117.77
1989	147.4	112.3	125.2	103.8	133.1
1990	152.9	115.4	142.7	114.7	141.8
1991	157	119.1	158.7	129.7	149.7
1992	168.8	153.1	172.9	134.8	164.9
1993	185	160.2	193.6	143.9	180.2
1994	191.4	169.4	204	144.9	187.6
1995	206.7	183.4	213.3	143.4	199.8
1996	122.2	179.2	222	140.8	209.3
1997	231.6	195.4	230.5	141.9	218.8

Source: Office National de la Statistique. (1997.) Annuaire Statistique.
Ministere des Affaires Economiques et du Developpement, Nouakchott, Mauritania.

vidual countries) in essence and development geography is still at the core of development theory and policy. After two decades of economic reforms and development projects, the International Monetary Fund, the Multilateral Development Banks, other Multilateral Financial Institutions, and borrower governments among developing countries are increasingly focusing on poverty in their development discourse and policy. The World Bank has redefined its central mission as "fighting poverty," and has titled its World Development Report 2000/2001: "Attacking Poverty." The International Monetary Fund has transformed its Enhanced Structural Adjustment Facility into "Poverty Reduction and Growth Facility." At the United Nations Millennium Summit of 2000, concerned world leaders pledged to cut poverty in half by 2015. While these changes in development discourse and policy seem to acknowledge the serious problem of poverty, they fail to link poverty to the whole array of liberalization reforms that have scanned the macro as well as micro economic policies of those poor countries for over 20 years. They rather explain poverty as a result of low productivity and widespread corruption in developing countries. By doing so they divert attention away from critical issues such as currency devaluation and its impact on the devaluation of national economies. International organizations such as the World Trade Organization, various United Nations agencies, the Organization for Economic Co-operation and Development (OECD), the Organization of American States, the European Union, and the Council of Europe are now addressing corruption as an important policy concern without pointing out that resource transfer from the South to the North is increasing poverty which in turn is driving corruption as a terrible consequence of fierce competition for increasingly scarce resources. The major finding here is that poverty has increased because of the nature of unequal exchange between lenders and borrowers, especially through currency devaluation. Lenders give openly with one hand (loans, grants, and technical assistance) what they retake stealthily from borrowers by the other hand (through devaluation, capital flight, debt service, and deteriorating terms of trade). A reversal of the current flow of resource transfer from the South to the North will require a rethinking of the neo-liberal "Washington Consensus" and its "market fundamentalism" (Srinivasan 2000: 265) as well as some creative reworking of a Keynesian or post Keynesian model for national economies (Marangos 2001). I think this must include the re-establishment of some level of protectionism involving the restoration of exchange controls and import restrictions as well as the temporary suspension of debt servicing. Since such policies amount to a serious questioning of the current neoliberal policies, their conception, formulation and implementation will require a drastic popular and democratic regulation of, and government intervention into, the so-called market, as indicated by the December 2001 "populist" decision by Argentina to suspend payments on its $132 billion foreign debt and print money (to circulate alongside Argentine *pesos* and US dollars) to help cut the poverty and unemployment behind bloody riots and a succession of five Argentinean presidents in two weeks.

Notes

*An earlier version of this chapter was published under the title "Currency Devaluation and Resource Transfer from the South to the North" in the *Annals of the Association of American Geographers* 93(2):463-484

References

Albright, M. (1999). Transcript: *Albright Hosts Signing Ceremony Between Israel and Mauritania.* http://www.usis.it/file9910/alia/99102809.htm

Central Intelligence Agency (CIA). (2000). *The World Factbook: Notes and Definitions.* http://www.odci.gov/cia/publications/factbook/docs/notes.html

Economic Commission for Africa. (2001). *Review and Appraisal of the Implementation of Agenda 21 in Africa. Second Meeting of the Committee on Sustainable Development.* Addis Ababa, Ethiopia, 26–29 November 2001.

http://www.uneca.org/eca_resources/Major_ECA_Websites/csd/CSD2_Agenda21.htm

Heston, A. and Summers, R. (1997). *PPPs and Price Parities in Benchmark Studies and the Penn World Table: Uses.* CICUP 97–1. http://pwt.econ.upenn.edu/papers/BRUSSELS.PDF

IDA and IMF (2000). *Mauritania: Decision Point Document under the Enhanced Heavily Indebted Poor Countries (HIPC).* Initiative Prepared by the Staffs of the International Development Association and the International Monetary Fund, January 14.

http://www.imf.org/external/np/hipc/pdf/mauritad.pdf.

IMF (1995). "Mauritania: Recent Economic Developments." *IMF Staff Country Report.* No. 95/20. Washington, DC: International Monetary Fund.

IMF (1980–2001). *International Financial Statistics.* Washington, DC: International Monetary Fund.

IMF (1980–2001).. *International Financial Statistics Yearbooks.* Washington, DC: International Monetary Fund.

IMF (1999a). *International Financial Statistics Yearbook 1999*. Washington, DC: International Monetary Fund.

IMF (1999b). "Mauritania: Recent Economic Developments." *IMF Staff Country Report*. No. 99/21. Washington, DC: International Monetary Fund.

IMF (2000a). "IMF Concludes Article IV Consultation with Mauritania." *Public Information Notice (PIN)* No. 00/45. Washington, DC: International Monetary Fund. http://www.imf.org/external/np/sec/pn/2000/pn0045.htm

IMF (2000b). Enhanced Structural Adjustment Facility, Medium-Term Economic and Financial Policy Framework Paper 1999–2002. Prepared by the Mauritanian Authorities in Collaboration with the Staffs of the Fund and the World Bank http://www.imf.org/external/NP/PFP/1999/Mauritan/index.htm

IMF (2001a). *Articles of Agreement of the International Monetary Fund*. Washington, DC: International Monetary Fund. http://www.imf.org/external/pubs/ft/aa/index.htm

IMF. (2001b). *IMF Survey Supplement 30*. http://www.imf.org/external/pubs/ft/survey/2001/090101.pdf

IMF (2002). *Mauritania: Transactions with the Fund from January 01, 1984 To March 31, 2002*. IMF Treasurer's Department, Accounts and Financial Reports Division, available at: http://www.imf.org/external/np/tre/tad/extrans1.cfm?memberKey1=660&endDate=2002%2D03%2D31&finposition_flag=YES

IMF and MDBs (2000). *Global Poverty Report*. Presented to the G8 Okinawa Summit, July. http://www.worldbank.org/html/extdr/extme/G8_poverty2000.pdf.

Labson, S.B. (1997). "Changing Patterns of Trade in the World Iron Ore and Steel Market: An Econometric Analysis." *Journal of Policy Modeling*. 19(3):237–251.

Marangos, J. (2001). International Trade Policies for Transition Economies: The post-Keynesian Alternative. *Journal of Post Keynesian Economics* 23 (4): 689-704.

Office National de la Statistique (1997). Annuaire *Statistique*. Nouakchott, Mauritania: Ministere des Affaires Economiques et du Developpement.

Ould Sid'Ahmed Taya, M. (1998). *Horizons 2223*. November 27–29.

Ould-Mey, M. (2003). "Currency Devaluation and Resource Transfer from the South to the North." *Annals of the Association of American Geographers*. 93(2).

Roodman, D.M. (2001). "Still Waiting for the Jubilee: Pragmatic Solutions for the Third World Debt Crisis." *Worldwatch Paper* 155. Washington, DC: Worldwatch Institute.

Srinivasan,T.N. (2000). TheWashington consensus a decade later: Ideologyand the art and science of policy advice. *TheWorld Bank Research Observer* 15 (2): 265-70.

The Currency Site (2001). *OANDA Currency Conversion*, available on December 10, at: http://www.oanda.com/convert/classic.

United States Bureau of Labor Statistics (2001). *Consumer Price Indexes: Inflation Calculator*. http://www.bls.gov/cpi/

Verzola, R. (1995). *Towards A Political Economy of Information*. Available online: May 18, 1999, at http://www.solinet.org/THIRDWORLD/obet1.htm

World Bank (1998). *World Bank Press Release*. March 26. http://www.worldbank.org/html/extdr/extme/afrpr98.htm.

World Bank. (1999). *World Bank Atlas*. Washington, DC: World Bank.

World Bank (2001). *World Development Indicators Database*. Washington, DC: World Bank. http://www.worldbank.org/data/databytopic/keyrefs.html http://www.worldbank.org/data/wdi2001/pdfs/tab4_16.pdf

Chapter 20

Changing Urban Development: Africa's Opportunities and Challenges in a Global Economy at the Dawn of the 21st Century*

Richard Grant

Introduction

Africa is increasingly becoming characterized as urban. One-third of the African population now resides in urban areas, and this will increase to more than one-half by 2025 (HABITAT 2001: 268). Some cities in Africa (e.g., Cairo, Accra, and Lagos) have achieved their present size in one-fifth to one-tenth the time it took European cities to reach the same size. Accra, the capital of Ghana, for example, grew from 190,000 at independence in 1957, to one million in 1984 and to 1.7 million in 2000 (Grant and Yankson 2003:1). Population projections envision a city of four million by 2020. The scale of urban development is posing acute challenges for planners and especially for inhabitants who live in cities with limited opportunities and resources.

The portrayal of Africa as a region devoid of urban development until the coming of colonialism is inaccurate. Significant evidence identifies indigenous urban development throughout the continent, particularly intense in North and West Africa (Stewart 1997: 251). Colonialism did, however, radically alter the urban hierarchy in Africa, from one aligned along historical trade patterns, mainly in the interior, to a system designed to extract resources for European economies based on ports linked to the colonizing countries (Simon 1989). The early independence period was characterized by efforts to transform unbalanced, fragmented and dependent colonial economies into diversified, integrated and sustainable national economies. Urban growth poles were part of this strategy, but the overall emphasis in the nationalist phase of development was to curtail the free market and to reduce disparities among cities in national economies. Clear change came in the mid-1980s through redirection of the policy environment in Africa as countries implemented liberalization policies and opened up their economies to foreign direct investment (FDI) and foreign participation.

In this chapter I situate urban development in terms of the cities' roles in the wider global political economy. I contend that the city can be understood by how it is linked to the external economy, which is as much a function of the idiosyncratic features of the city as a place and location, as it is a function of developments in the global economy. I employ a political economy conceptualization of the city and its spatial organization because (sub)national policies determine to a large degree the exposure of the urban arena to global economic forces. I outline the four historical phases in urbanism that led to the emergence of the contemporary city: pre-colonial, colonial, national and global. I argue that, during each phase, urban geographies have changed in relation to the role of the city in the global political economy.

I use Accra, Ghana, as a case study to illustrate the changing nature of urban development. Within the historical context of African cities, Accra is a relatively new city, originating in the late nineteenth century when the British decided to build up the site. Since it is not possible to examine the entire city and all that it encompasses in one chapter, I focus on the corporate sector. Examining the corporate sector in terms of the mode of integration in the world economy and the effects on the spatial organization allows us to assess one important layer of urban development. The contemporary layering of the corporate geography of Accra provides both opportunities as well as constraints on future development.

This chapter is organized into five sections. After the introduction, I outline the main features of Accra's urban development in historical phases. Second, I review the data and methods used to discern the spatial organization of the city in the global phase. Third, I highlight the key urban economic changes in the global phase. Fourth, I analyze the continuity and/or change in the urban landscape and the effects of increased corporate activity on the city's economic geographies in terms of functional specialization and concentration. This research is based on fieldwork that I conducted in Accra between 1998 and 2000, which resulted in datasets on foreign and domestic corporations. In the conclusion, I deal with the opportunities and challenges for Accra and other similar cities in Africa in the twenty-first century.

Historicizing the Integration of Accra into the Global Economy

The distinction between pre-colonial, colonial, national and global phases is based on the organization of the global political economy. It is a distinction that highlights a city's external connections (facilitated or constrained by domestic factors) to the global economy as key to its internal spatial development. In this section, I first detail the development of Accra and its mode of integration into the global economy in each of the historical phases. I then draw connections between the intensity of integration into the wider global political economy and the most salient effects on the city's economic geography.

The Mode of Integration

Pre-colonial: Most local experts link the establishment of Accra with the development of a coastal fishing village in the late sixteenth century (Gough and Yankson 1997: 9). The earliest known settlers on the stretch of coastline now named Accra were the Kpesi people. Ga-speaking migrants from "Niger country" reached this area in the sixteenth century, and made their homes among the Kpesi and absorbed them into their communities (Acquah 1957: 16). During the pre-colonial period, the main urban settlements were largely inland, where they functioned as desert ports along the southern termini of the trans-Saharan trade in gold, slaves, salt and forest products (Gugler and Flanagan 1978: 6). European accounts of this period refer to the numerous ports on the littoral and to the "great towns" in the interior of the country that contained "multitudes of people" and were "richer in goods and gold than the coastal towns" (Kea 1982: 23).

Colonial: The colonial period is best characterized by two episodes. First, from the fifteenth to mid-seventeenth centuries, most contact between European traders and West Africans occurred in coastal settlements. The slave trade reinforced the development of coastal trade centers, where warehouses and permanent installations were needed to accommodate commodities and people from the interior. During this time a number of forts were built in what is known as present-day Accra (Fort Ussher by the Dutch in 1605, Christiansborg Castle by the Swedes in 1657 and Fort James by the British in 1673). However, a Portuguese map of the seventeenth century indicates that Accra was not connected to any of the major trade routes along the Gold Coast (Kea 1982: 31). Moreover, Accra was largely outside the wider urban spatial system, which was centered on Kumasi in the interior of the country (Campbell 1994).

The second episode during the colonial period involved the British consolidating power in the Gold Coast in 1874, when they defeated the Ashantis. The rise of Accra as an urban center dates to 1877, when the colonial headquarters were relocated there from Cape Coast (Acquah 1957). Accra was chosen as the site of the colonial administration for a number of reasons. Prominent among them were health issues (specifically securing the health of the European residents) as well as geographical and strategic concerns (Accra was the geographical center of gravity for the UK colony and located near the prime meridian, which runs through present-day Tema). Moreover, the earthquake of 1862, which severely destroyed large portions of Accra, presented colonial rulers with an important opportunity to rebuild and reorganize the space. Its selection as the seat of government, though, ran contrary to the pattern in most other West Africa countries. For instance, Abidjan and Dakar were chosen as capitals because of preexisting economic advantages, but Accra was selected based on initial noncommercial advantages.

With the arrival of the colonial administrative machinery came a large number of merchants, and in the process political and economic power became focused on Accra for the first time. It became linked to the UK as a gateway city and expanded in size and population. The integration of Accra into the external economy reversed the traditional urban and economic patterns in Ghana by anchoring the economy to a coastal location. The major terminal point of the colonial system was Accra, and transport links pushed directly inland by the early 1920s to sources of exportable commodities. The cocoa boom in that decade deepened the interdependence of Accra with the external economy, and at the same time most external investment became concentrated on a single resource and sector. Once cocoa grew to preeminence among Accra's exports, commerce replaced government as the primary element in the urban economic base. Over one-half of all firms in Accra were engaged in cocoa trade by 1930 (Brand 1972a: 105). Accra continued to develop as a warehouse rather than a factory city throughout the rest of the colonial period.

National: From 1957 to 1982 Accra was shaped by nationalist economic policies. The Nkrumah government promoted the capital city as a growth pole for the national economy, and successive administrations prioritized building up the infrastructure of Accra in national development planning (AMA, 1999). Specific policy measures aimed for a Ghanaization of industries. For instance, the Ghanaian Business (Promotion) Act of 1970 permitted Ghanaian monopolies for small firms engaging in import-export trade, for some manufacturing, such as cement production, and for a variety of service industries, such as taxis, printing and advertising (Killick 1978). Moreover, the government starved the foreign sector of imported raw materials, spare parts and equipment by tariffs and import licensing arrangements. The combination of these policy measures limited xposure to the international economy. Indeed many foreign companies curtailed their activities in Ghana by the early 1980s. For example, the American Firestone pulled out of Ghana in 1984 (Dzorgbo 1998: 223). Instead, the government dominated the economy, functioning as the major shareholder in over 400 different enterprises in the financial, manufacturing, extractive and agricultural sectors (Grayson 1979; World Bank 1994).

Global: The global phase was initiated with the introduction of liberalization policies in 1983. Market reform involved full adoption of the World Bank's and the International Monetary Fund's (IMF) structural adjustment policies to halt the economic decline that had begun in the 1970s. Policy measures were implemented to attract foreign companies by eliminating barriers to foreign direct investment, upgrading the physical infrastructure, privatizing state-owned enterprises, establishing export-processing zones and reducing barriers to trade. The net impact of liberalization policies was to increase exposure to the global economy. The government of Ghana continued its promotion of Accra as a gateway city serving to connect West Africa with the global economy. The World Bank also contributed $50 million to support further development of Accra's gateway projects (World Bank 2000). The dominance of Accra as a command center and gateway city, however, had been firmly established.

Internal Spatial Organization of Accra

The mode of integration into the global economy has implications for Accra's internal economic geography. I sketch the main features of the city's economic geography in each of the phases.

Pre-colonial: The first coastal settlement was located to the east of Korle Lagoon, called the "fish village" (Acquah 1957: 16). It appeared that this original settlement expanded to encompass the oldest adjoining parts of present-day Accra; namely, Jamestown and Ussher Town. There is not much information about the spatial organization of Accra of that time. Archeological evidence suggests that the village was spatially organized around the sheltered harbors (Kea 1982) with "low density shelters adjoining the coastline in an unplanned fashion" (Hubbard 1925: 21).

Colonial: Three European forts situated within three miles of each other formed a nucleus for foreign commercial enterprise in the early colonial period. In the shadows of the forts were walled Ga villages partially oriented to trading with European merchants. Scattered settlements connected by footpaths rather than an urban clustered center characterized the emerging organization of Accra. Europeans lived in the forts, which additionally served as places for holding both slaves and commodities (Kea 1982).

During the nineteenth century, the role of the forts changed, as they became centers of administration, housing government officials, troops and later police. When this occurred, European traders began to locate outside the forts, and the township of Accra was established. With the arrival of the seat of government in 1877, the British attempted to explicitly improve sanitation and living conditions in the area. As they had been for a long time, foreign and domestic sector distinctions were paramount. However, in the colonial phase, the spatial organization of the urban economy was formalized. There developed a sharp contrast between the large foreign companies dominating the extractive industries and the relatively small manufacturing sector on the one hand, and the small-scale enterprises of indigenous groups or recent immigrants (e.g., Lebanese in Accra) on the other (Brand 1972a). European commercial and residential areas were clearly separated from indigenous commercial and residential areas. A schematic representation of the spatial organization of Accra (similar to other colonial port cities) during the colonial period is shown in Figure 20: 1.

There were four main features of colonial Accra. First, the city was spatially organized around the port that functioned as a central node in the trade between its hinterland and England. The city became the strategic center linking rail lines and shipping routes. The docks, warehouses and railway terminals supported the storage and distribution of trade items. The port area was particularly important in terms of command-and-control and functioned as a strategic bridgehead for the British government. Most of the buildings of the colonial administration and military bases were located in the immediate vicinity. Slum clearing took place, and the British attempted to superimpose rectangular-style patterns as a morphological variation on the existing unplanned city (Brand 1972a). Second, adjacent to the port area was a well-defined European central business district (CBD) that functioned as the designated location for foreign companies. Most economic activities in this European commercial area involved trade, distribution, transport, banking and insurance. Zoning and building codes were strictly enforced to maintain an orderly European character and atmosphere.

Third, traditional markets or bazaars were located in a business district in "Native Town." This area comprised a mix of commercial and residential land uses. Much of its commercial activity involved trade in agricultural produce and crafts, small-scale industry and retailing. The colonial government paid relatively little attention to urban planning in Native Town, which tended to exhibit congestion, poor structures and unsanitary health conditions. The area was inhabited by indigenous people as well as recent rural immigrants. Importantly, the European town and Native Town were physically separated with a barrier: an open green area.

Fourth, a rigid policy of segregation ensured clearly demarcated zones for European residences near Accra's commercial center (e.g., Victoriaborg) or retreats further away on higher elevations (e.g., Cantonments). With its luxurious homes, race and golf

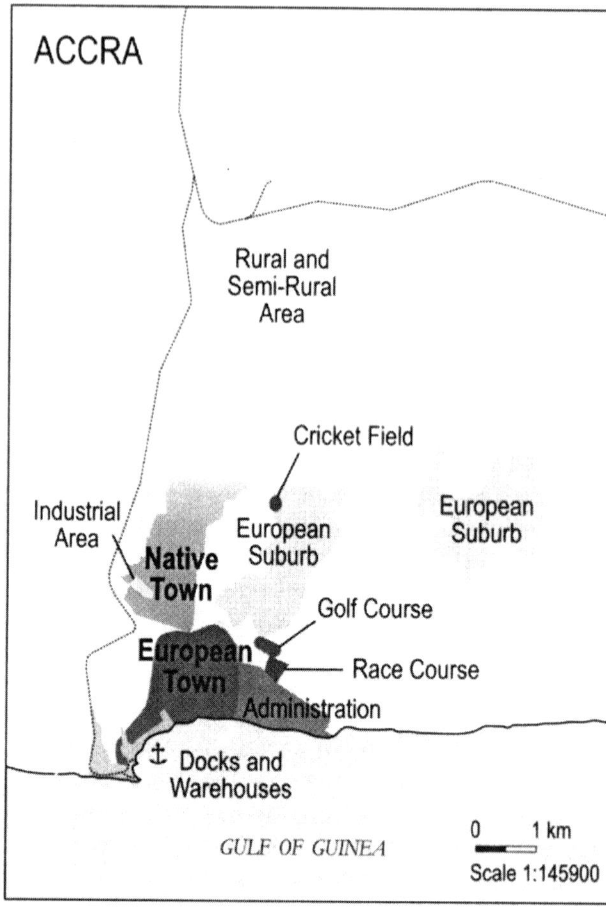

A schematic representation of the economic geographies of Accra during the colonial phase.

Figure 20.1 Accra Economic Geographies during the Colonial Phase

courses, polo and cricket field, tennis courts and racially segregated hospital, "Victoriaborg was like a piece of England grafted into the townscape of Accra" (MacDonald 1898: 199–200). In sum, the colonial landscape of Accra exhibited a high level of segregation of foreign and indigenous commercial and residential activities, with its economic geography displaying a significant degree of functional specialization and concentration (Brand 1972b). As participation in the international economy increased in the early twentieth century and as population pressure built up, the boundaries between the different areas gradually blurred.

National: Transformations in the spatial organization of Accra occurred in the wake of independence (Acquah 1957; Brand 1972a). Apart from rapid population in Accra, which resulted in significant geographical expansion, the spatial configuration was altered in four main ways. First, the foreign corporate and residential presence declined. Elimination of legislation that had formerly discouraged native enterprises led to a rapid growth in the number of domestic companies, which were now free to locate around the city.

Second, the former European CBD was at once de-Europeanized and nationalized, politically and economically. Administrative and military functions in the area were taken over by the national government. New and large domestic companies favored a location in this area, leading to growing corporate density. In addition, the area was nationalized in a symbolic sense with the location of a new central bank and state-controlled companies.

Third, the former native CBD (Native Town) became even more characterized by small-scale businesses, as larger companies moved to the emerging national CBD (the former European CBD). As a result of massive rural-urban migration in the post-independence years, the density and congestion in Native Town increased. The removal of the strict zoning policies that characterized the colonial era facilitated excessive growth, and unregulated growth meant the boundary with the former European CBD became increasingly blurred. Moreover, the rise of a national middle class meant that an explicit foreign urban space was diluted, as income became the criterion for determining commercial and residential location. By the early 1980s, there was only a modest foreign presence in the economy of Accra.

Data, Survey Methods and the Mapping of Corporate Activities in the Global Period

Data on foreign corporate activity in African cities are generally scarce and incomplete. Internationally monitored datasets (e.g., Dun and Bradstreet 1997; United Nations Center on Transnational Corporations 1988) provide directories on foreign companies and their affiliates abroad, but they contain information only on the largest multinational corporations in the world. In addition, these data are biased toward companies from the Organization for Cooperation and Development (OECD), are often out of date and underestimate the extent of foreign corporate activity in Africa.

Locally generated datasets also inadequately represent information on foreign companies. Prior to this research, there were no directories of foreign companies in Accra that were accurate or even remotely complete. Government agencies that monitor foreign investment can provide information on foreign companies, but their information relates to approved investments or collaborations, not to currently active companies. The Ghana Investment Promotion Centre (GIPC) provided me with a listing of 630 companies that had newly registered at its office between 1994 and 1998. The GIPC notes that 26 percent of all companies that have registered are not functionally operating and that some foreign companies choose not to register with the GIPC (even though they are required to by law) (Grant 2001). Therefore, the GIPC listing is only an estimate and cannot be taken to represent accurately the population of foreign companies in Accra.

Collecting primary data in African cities is very time-consuming in a number of ways because of the lack of business directories and data bases. A foreign company is defined here as a company with FDI of over $10,000. The very liberal investment climate in Ghana since the early 1980s permits foreign investors to own up to 100 percent equity in companies. The data collection on foreign corporations consisted of three steps, implemented over two years: 1) the identification and use of listings of foreign companies and their addresses from local sources; 2) the combination of these listings and checking for duplications to create a single master-list of foreign companies and addresses; and 3) the conducting of a survey among these companies using the "total design method" (Dillman 1978). The datasets pertain to the headquarters of each company, but the "location" of a company may not be confined to the address of the headquarters. Many of the larger companies have their headquarters and managerial staff in a prime business area, while administrative support work and factories are located elsewhere in the city or beyond.

I contacted all government organizations working closely with foreign companies for information. Organizations besides the GIPC that provided detailed information include the Divestiture Implementation Committee, the Minerals Commission, the Ghana Free Zone Board, the Ghana Stock Exchange, and the embassies or consulates of the UK, the Netherlands, Italy, the United States, Japan, Denmark, Switzerland, Germany, France, China and Lebanon. The lists were crosschecked for accuracy with existing business directories in Accra, including the Ghana Telephone Directory (1998) and the FIT Business Directory (1999).

The resulting master-list formed the basis for the survey. Eventually, a database of 655 foreign companies was constructed. The foreign company surveys focused on company names, addresses, year of establishment, type of activity, economic sector, country of origin, and company size. To increase the rate of response, the surveys were returned to a mailbox that was established in Accra. The initial mail surveys were followed up by a second round of mail surveys and then by phone calls to increase response rates. The final response rate was around 51 percent. N-values are provided for all the maps and statistics in the analysis of this chapter.

Existing data on domestic companies were extensive, relatively reliable and more easily obtainable. As a result it was not necessary to survey those companies. Domestic company listings used in the empirical analysis were obtained from the Ghana National Chamber of Commerce, which produces an annual listing of domestic companies by location and type of activity. The domestic company list for Accra contained over 1,800 entries. Both the foreign and domestic datasets permitted me to analyze, over time, the relative importance of foreign corporate presence in the city, the nature of foreign investment and, particularly, the geography of foreign corporate activity in comparison with domestic corporate activity.

The General Economic Geography of Accra in the Global Phase

The liberalization era in Ghana has gone hand-in-hand with rapid rates of urbanization. The metropolitan area itself has expanded, and the city of Accra presently comprises an area bound by the Gulf of Guinea in the south, Achimota Forest in the north, Tema port in the east and Korle Lagoon in the west. The area's dimensions are about fifty-kilometers east to west and about ten-kilometers north to south. The average population density in built-up areas is 7,000 people per square kilometer. The highest densities, 25,000 per square kilometer, are found in Jamestown and Ussher Town. Outside of the built-up areas there is considerable open space between Teshie and Tema, where large tracts of land are reserved for military use.

The traditional landholding system has historically influenced land values and land use in the city. Much of the land is either vested in various stools and families with customary tenure or is owned by the government. There is a shortage of land for commercial use, and the real estate market began responding to this trend in the late 1990s. Tema is an exception in terms of available commercial land; an exclave of sorts, it is geographically separated from the city of Accra by a zone of open space that has gradually been developed for residential purposes. The port of Tema has been developed in 1962, when Accra harbor was abandoned in favor of Tema's deeper and more sheltered harbor. Since then, an industrial area, warehouse and storage facilities, and extensive housing for workers have been built in the Tema area.

Accra's economic geography has become more dispersed over the years, and in the 1980s and 1990s, high population concentrations occurred in western parts of the city bordering the Ring Road (Nima, Korle Gonno, and Kaneshie). The suburbanization of economic activity, especially manufacturing, at that same period has centered on Tema and the Light Industrial Area. Small concentrations of export-oriented industries have emerged in Export Processing Zones (EPZs), the most built up of which is the Light Industrial Area.

Liberalization and Foreign Corporate Activity

In Accra, the single most important impact on foreign corporate activity in the twentieth century was the implementation of liberalization policies (Yeboah 2001). The establishment of new foreign companies was accelerated to unprecedented levels in the liberalization period: over 80 percent of all foreign companies currently active have been established since 1983. A surge in the establishment of new foreign companies also coincided with the transition to democratic government in the 1990s.

The geographical origins of foreign companies in Accra reveal that liberalization policies have entailed opportunities for investors from across the world. By 1999, foreign companies from 56 countries participated in businesses in Accra. Historically, most FDI in Ghana has originated from the UK, because of ties dating back to the colonial period. Firms such as Unilever, Cadbury, British Petroleum (BP), Standard and Charter and Barclay's Bank have operated in Ghana since the colonial era. The development of Ghana's major hydroelectric power project in the 1960s marked the beginning of a gradual shift away from the near-monopoly of British firms to a more diversified base of foreign companies (Table 20.1).

UK companies are still the most active investment partners in Ghana. In the 1990s many companies from the developing world (particularly from China, South Korea, and

South Africa) have also become active. Companies from India and Lebanon have been returning to Ghana, reviving early twentieth-century links when many Indian and Lebanese firms forged a major presence in the wholesale and retail trade sector largely ceding the manufacturing sector to European firms (Garlick 1960). Within the process of liberalization, the government has become an active participant in the private sector and is forming new private sector partnerships, establishing itself as a minor partner. For instance, the Ghanaian government, international development agencies and a Malaysian company are developing an area in Tema as the first private free zone in Africa.

Geographies of Foreign and Domestic Corporate Activities

The general geography of foreign and domestic corporate activities in Accra is illustrated in Figure 20.2.

First, Ussher Town is the traditional CBD and corresponds closely to the old European town in colonial times. It is the most densely concentrated area in terms of corporate activities, containing many high-rise buildings in close proximity to the government ministries. It contains the second highest concentration of Ghanaian-controlled companies in Accra and a small number of foreign companies, many of which were among the first foreign companies to be established in Ghana.

Table 20.1 Origins of Top Ten Most Active Foreign Countries in Corporate Activites in Accra, Ghana (2002)

Country	Total number of companies	Rank
UK	139	1
India	117	2
China	112	3
USA	97	4
Lebanon	89	5
German	83	6
South Korea	54	7
Italy	50	8
Switzerland	48	9
Netherlands	43	10

Source: GIPC (2003).

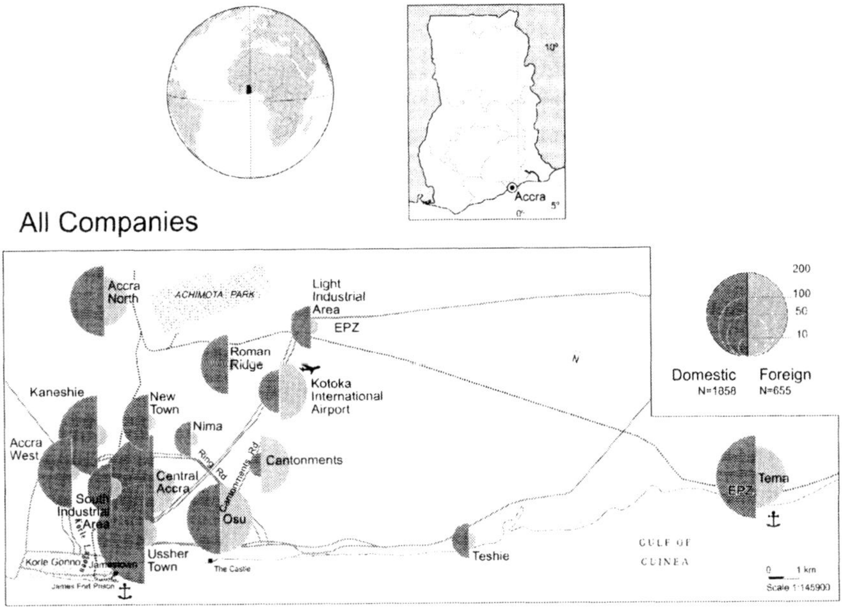

Figure 20.2 All Companies in Accra, Ghana

Market, the largest market in the city, the most crowded commercial area in the city and the focus of most trips within the city. The bustling market spills over onto the walkways and roadways and leads to acute traffic and pedestrian congestion. The area has a mix of corporate and residential functions, a visible presence of firms of Lebanese and Syrian descent, and a maze of side streets and back alleys. This business district has the largest share of Accra's domestic companies, though generally of small size. The number of foreign companies in this district is also small except for a cluster of foreign airline offices in its center.

The newest, and arguably most prominent, business district in Accra in the early 21st century is an area that stretches from Osu along Cantonments Road to the airport. It also covers the Ringway Estate and Ridge Area. The entire area is not commercial but foreign corporate activities are concentrated in a ribbon fashion along the main thoroughfares. Much of this area was initially used for residential purposes, but since the introduction of liberalization policies, properties along the main roadways have been redeveloped for commercial purposes. The area has modern low-rise buildings with off-street parking and stands in sharp contrast with the colonial architecture of Ussher Town and the bazaar atmosphere of Central Accra.

Foreign Companies in Mining, and Finance and Producer Services

The fastest growing sectors of the economy for foreign company involvement are in services (management consulting, internet providers, mobile phone providers; and financial services, banks and investment brokers) and mining. In 1999, 16 percent of foreign companies were in the services sector. Mining is still the largest sector in terms of the numbers of foreign companies (19 percent of total). The privatization of mining after 1996 has aided this trend. However, many mining companies are small and seldom move beyond the initial stages of exploration, thus inflating the real number of active mining companies. Falling gold prices have been taking their toll on the number of foreign companies engaging in mining (*Financial Times* 1999: 3). Foreign mining companies tend to locate their headquarters and concentrate near the area of the airport, often operating out of residential houses that have been converted into office space. Cantonments and the airport residential area operate as command centers for mining operations that are located beyond the city.

A similar geographical concentration of foreign companies in finance and other services is found in the districts of Osu, Cantonments and the airport. The heavily trafficked area along Cantonments Road in Osu (locally known as "Oxford Street") is the focal point for most foreign producer services companies. Newly paved roads, hotels, shops and restaurants have increased the attractiveness of the area for engaging in face-to-face business, an important aspect of producer services businesses. In the airport area, a large number of these firms cater to mining companies concentrated there (Grant 2001) and provide the kinds of services that rely heavily on airport facilities (e.g., courier firms).

The producer services functions are in a formative stage in Accra. The vast majority of producer service companies are small operations, and many of the business and communication centers that specifically target businesses also have to take on consumer clients in order to turn a profit. Moreover, the location choices available to newly arriving foreign companies within Accra are limited. For national security reasons, property developers have been prevented from developing the only nearby vacant area, adjacent to the Castle, and recently arrived foreign companies have located further away from the existing business districts. Still, they are less than a half an hour away from the old center (except during rush hours).

A Contrast: The Geography of Domestic Corporate Activity

To better appreciate the distinct spatial patterns of foreign corporate activity in mining and finance and producer services, it is useful to provide a contrast. This kind of economic activity is internationally oriented, but it is small scale, controlled locally and of older vintage. There is a long tradition of relatively small trading companies in Accra, dating back to the colonial period. The nucleus of import-export firms has been in the Native Town since the 1920s, when petty traders started to offer narrow lines of locally, nationally, and internationally traded goods. Europeans were disinterested in participating in these activities that produced little income beyond subsistence living. Many firms were originally owned by immigrants, particularly Lebanese and Syrian. During the national phase, legislation was introduced to reserve businesses for Ghanaians, inducing these one-time immigrants to become naturalized Ghanaian citizens. Thus, their firms have since been classified as domestic companies.

The Emergence of Specialized Business Districts

The most significant change in the organization of corporate activities in Accra is the emergence of different CBDs. The lack of any planning in terms of land use and functions for the commercial heart of Accra (particularly manifest in the shortage of corporate office space and the city-wide growth of micro-enterprises) has meant that market forces have become more salient in determining land use. Presently, three CBDs are discernable and represent the main clusters of corporate headquarter activities in Accra. A response to the geographical agglomeration of many of Ghana's economic activities in Accra, these CBDs—Osu/Cantonments and Airport, Ussher Town and Central Accra—are all different in terms of historical origin, economic activity and, most importantly, relevance for foreign and domestic companies.

Central Accra overlaps in large part with the old Native Town from colonial times (Figure 20.3). It has residential functions and a mix of small domestic trade, craft and retailing businesses; there is a noticeable absence of foreign companies. Central Accra also contains the Makola Market, the largest market in Accra for petty trade, in spite of the government's efforts to decentralize market functions by its promotion of Kaneshi Market. Most businesses are locally oriented within the metropolitan area, and the area functions as a local CBD. Ussher Town corresponds fairly closely with the European CBD from colonial times. The district's residential function is limited, and it contains many large domestic companies and a substantial number of foreign companies, many of which are older established companies in Accra (e.g. Cadbury and Barclays). Most businesses have a pronounced orientation to the economy of the country as a whole, so the area functions as a national CBD. Finally, Osu/Cantonments and Airport are relatively newly developed business areas. As already mentioned, this district has a large concentration of foreign mining and finance and producer services, and functions as a global CBD. Osu along Cantonments Road is quite distinctive within the district, as a prominent up-market commercial strip has emerged along this major thoroughfare. The rising urban middle class and the cosmopolitan elite can be found shopping and dining in this area. In contrast, the vast majority of Cantonments and Airport areas are residential with commercial clusters of new buildings along the major roads and converted residential office space within the neighborhoods. Businesses in this area, more so than in any other district, are articulated with the global economy. The overall success of these new CBDs and their abilities to develop complementarities will be vital to the success and future development of the Accra metropolis.

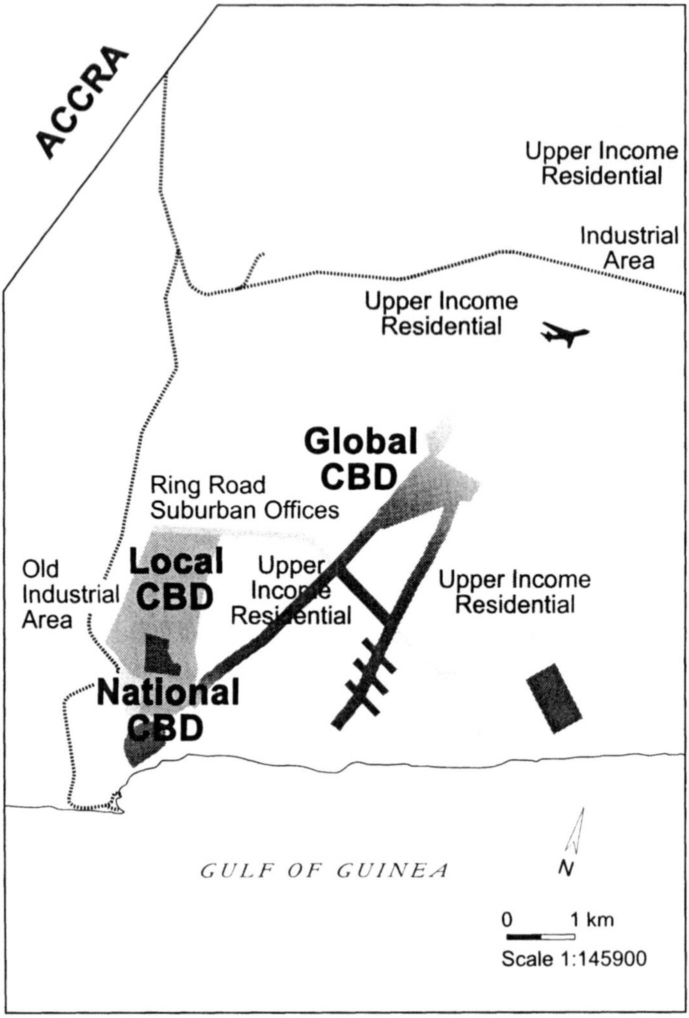

A schematic representation of the economic geographies of Accra during the global |

Figure 20.3 Accra Economic Geographies during the Global Phase

Conclusion: Opportunities and Challenges for Accra and in the 21st Century

Globalization has resulted in powerful new imprints on the urban corporate landscape. The global phase of urbanism is comparable to the colonial phase in terms of the clearly visible spatial articulation of external linkages in the urban economy (cf. Figure 20.3 with Figure 20.1). The main difference in the contemporary period is that market forces rather than colonial spatial planning are driving spatial formations (Grant and Short 2002).

The most significant recent development in the corporate geography of Accra is the formation of three distinctive CBDs. The further development of these may help promote synergies among businesses in each specific district. It may also alleviate some pressures on the traditional CBD, which suffers from acute traffic congestion. The development and promotion of three distinct corporate identities for the three CBDs may bring some order to the currently fragmented economic geography of the city (Konadu-Agyemang 2001).

However, the development of corporate sectors only represents a small portion of Accra's business activities. Much more prominent today (outside of the CBDs) are home-based micro-enterprises. Low-level services and production activities, such as chop bars (local fast-food operations), kiosks (corner stores), cement block manufactures and building material retailers, are the norm along major roads. Often these informal sector eonomic activities fuel the further expansion of Accra's frontiers. The further development of micro-enterprises development, unless it is held in check, could hinder existing as well as future FDI. Clearly investors are interested in a city that both functions efficiently and has good aesthetics. Planning seems to be the best way to enhance the attractiveness of the city.

One of the most pressing challenges for Accra policymakers is to embark on comprehensive land-use planning. To date, most planning has been based on the outdated Town and Country Ordinance of 1945, which does not provide for connections between land-use planning and policies for social and economic development. Comprehensive land-use plans have not been implemented in the liberalization era. Planning since 1983 has centered on initiatives to attract FDI and has been more infrastructure-oriented and sector-based to the detriment of spatial planning (Ofori 2002). The Strategic Plan for the Greater Accra Area, developed in the early 1990s (UNDP and HABITAT 1992) with assistance from the World Bank, has not been implemented (except for the Ring Road and industrial development components). Because planning has only focused on the formal economic sector, the problems of physically accommodating informal economic units within the built environment and of providing the necessary supporting infrastructure and services have not been addressed. The problems of the central city (crowding, congestion, inadequate infrastructure, environmental and other hazards) are a driving force in Accra's spatial development outwards from the center. The lack of planning has led to very weak coordination among Accra's economic activities.

There are also broader policy opportunities as well as challenges raised by the contemporary economic geography of Accra. In the current liberalization climate, the government has put its hopes on *laissez-faire* development strategies that strengthen regional clusters of economic activity. The notion of "regional push" connotes the role of regional engines of growth in the wider economy (Scott 2002). In Ghana and many other African countries, the geographic agglomeration of economic activities is now primarily based in large urban centers that serve as drivers of the national economy. This unbalanced economic development raises important challenges. First, can the Accra economy and its specialized CBDs drive the entire national economy? Second, can unbalanced and unplanned urban development in Accra be sustained in the long run?

If the population projections for Accra for the future are correct, it appears that more and more Ghanaians and foreigners will make a living in the city. If investors continue to view Accra as a stable environment with good returns on investment then Accra's exposure to the global economy will grow, and there will be opportunities for policymakers to seed more development. However, if investors withdraw—and there is evidence to suggest that the post-9/11 FDI environment is a more uncertain environment—then FDI-led development may be too risky. Overall, flows of FDI have enormous implications for the sustainability of the urban environment. In economic good times, Accra may be able to support reasonable livelihoods for many residents, but in bad times it may not. A deep economic recession could plunge the city into chaos, upheaval and social unrest. There are already signs that Accra's exposure to the global economy and regional immigration are putting a strain on it. Immigrants have flocked to Accra from other states in disarray. One negative impact of this is the current rise in violent property crime. Companies and individuals now spend more resources on protecting their properties and persons. There is the possibility that increasing crime could encourage investors to move FDI to other locations perceived to be safer. However, even in the face of a crime wave, Accra is still one of the safest and most profitable urban corporate environments in Africa.

Finally, it is highly likely that the experiences of Accra are shared by other cities in the less-developed world (especially gateway cities). In other words, cities in Africa with a high exposure to the global economy are likely to experience a similar layering of urban development. Cities that come to mind are Lagos, Mombasa and Dar es Salaam. Thus, how Accra policymakers deal with the current challenges as well as opportunities in the early 21st century may have significant relevance beyond their immediate vicinity.

Notes

*The National Science Foundation funded this research, grant BCS 0213648.

Special thanks to Chris Hanson, who provided cartographic expertise.

References

Accra Metropolitan Assembly (AMA) (1999). *Five-year medium term development plan.* Unpublished report. Accra, Ghana: AMA.

Acquah, I. (1957). *Accra survey.* London: University of London Press.

Brand, R. (1972a). *A geographical interpretation of the European influence on Accra, Ghana since 1877.* Ph.D. dissertation. New York: Columbia University.

Brand, R. (1972b). "The spatial organization of residential areas in Accra, Ghana, with particular reference to aspects of modernization." *Economic Geography*, 48, 284–298.

Campbell, J. (1994). "Urbanization, culture and the politics of urban development in Ghana, 1875–1980." *Urban Anthropology* 23, 409–450.

Dillman, D. (1978). *Mail and telephone surveys: The total design method.* New York: Wiley.

Dun and Bradstreet. (1997). *Principal international businesses: The world marketing directory.* New York: Dun and Bradstreet.

Dzorgbo, D. (1998). *Ghana in search of development.* Uppsala: Uppsala University.

Financial Times (1999). *Ghana survey.* November 4, 3.

FIT (1999). *FIT business directory.* Accra, Ghana.

Garlick, P. (1960). "Levantine trading firms in Ghana." *Economic Bulletin of Ghana.* 4, 1–12.

Ghana Telecom (1998). *Ghana phone directory.* Accra: Ghana Telecom.

Ghana Investment Promotion Centre (GIPC) (2003). *Statistics on Registered Projects.* Accra: GIPC.

Gough, K. and Yankson, P. (1997). *Continuity and change in peri-urban Accra.* Copenhagen: Danish Council for Development Research.

Grant, R. (2001). "Liberalization and foreign companies in Accra, Ghana." *Environment and Planning,* A 33: 997–1014.

Grant, R. and Short, J.R. (eds.) (2002). *Globalization and the margins.* London: Macmillan/ Palgrave.

Grant, R. and Yankson, P. (2003). "Accra: City Profile." *Cities,* 20, 65–74.

Grayson, L. (1979). *Managing the economic development of Ghana.* Charlottesville: University of Virginia.

Gugler, J. and Flanagan, W. (1978). *Urbanization and social change in West Africa.* New York: Cambridge University Press.

HABITAT (United Nations Center for Human Settlements) (2001). "Cities in a Globalizing World." *Global Report on Human Settlements 2001.* Sterling: Earthscan.

Hubbard, J. (1925). *Accra: A geographical study of the historical background to development up to 1920.* Accra: Gold Coast Government Printer.

Kea, R. (1982). *Settlements, trade, and politics in the seventeenth-century Gold Coast.* Baltimore: Johns Hopkins University Press.

Killick, T. (1978). *Development economics in action: A study of economic policies in Ghana.* New York: St. Martin's Press.

Konadu-Agyemang, K. (2001). "A survey of housing conditions and characteristics in Accra, an African city." *Habitat International,* 25:15–33.

MacDonald, G. (1898). *The Gold Coast, past and present: A short description of the country and its people.* London: Longmans.

Ofori, S. (2002). *Regional policy and regional planning in Ghana.* Burlington: Ashgate.

Scott, A. (2002). "Regional push: Towards geography of development and growth in low- and middle- income countries." *Third World Quarterly,* 23:137–161.

Simon, D. (1989). "Colonial cities, postcolonial Africa and the world-economy: A reinterpretation." *International Journal for Urban and Regional Research,* 13: 68–91.

Stewart, D. (1997). "African urbanization: Dependent linkages in a global economy." *Journal for Economic and Social Geography* (TESG) 88: 251–261.

United Nations Center on Transnational Corporations. (1988). *Transnational corporations in world development: Trends and prospects.* New York: United Nations.

United Nations Development Program and HABITAT. (1992). *Strategic Plan for Greater Accra Metropolitan Area (GAMA).* 3 vols. Accra: UNDP and HABITAT.

World Bank (1994). *Adjustment in Africa: Reforms, results and the road ahead.* New York: Oxford University Press.

World Bank (2000). World Bank's support Ghana's gateway project. http://www.worldbank.org/html/extdr/extme/1874.htm

Yeboah, I. (2001). "Structural adjustment and emerging urban form in Accra, Ghana." *Africa Today,* 7:61–89.

Chapter 21

Africa's Participation in the Revolution in Information and Communications Technology: Opportunity for Economic Development or Deprivation?

Peter A. Kwaku Kyem and Olivia Kyem

Introduction

Information and Communications Technology (ICT) has become a dominant economic and political force sweeping across the globe and inducing revolutionary changes in human society (ITU 1999; UNDP 1999). As the most potent instrument of globalization, ICT has stimulated unprecedented redistribution and spread of wealth and knowledge in several countries. The technology has also exacerbated perhaps the most pernicious aspect of modern global deprivation, bringing alienation to countries that have not been able to take advantage of it (UNDP 1999). The importance of understanding the interdependence between ICT and economic development, and the influence, which such a connection can exert on the socio-economic lives of people in Africa, is clear. However, such a realization has yet to evolve on the continent. In the mean time, public discourse about the adoption of ICT in Africa has been dominated by two competing viewpoints.

On one hand, technological optimists including Friedman (1998) and International Telecommunications Union (2002), proclaim a better world awash with information for everyone. The authors explain that ICT will enhance the economic capacities of African countries and become an important mechanism for poverty alleviation, democratic governance, and social justice. On the other hand, authors who are less enthusiastic about the benefits of the ICT revolution raise issues about availability, access, and the cost. (Castells 1989; Sah and Stiglitz 1993; Boafo1991). These proponents argue that progress in ICT development and adoption will broaden the digital divide between rich and poor nations and facilitate further exploitation of poor nations while destroying traditional cultures and restricting economic development (Boafo 1991; Wresch 1996; Moisy 1997; Tong 2001). The ensuing debates, which emphasize only the negative and positive impact of ICT, mask the real problem and prevent a true discussion of the role ICT can play in economic development in Africa. The ICT debates provide little guidance for policy making and often offer leaders of African countries with no clear cut answers to how long their people must wait to reap concrete benefits from the ICT revolution. Meanwhile, as the debates rage on, many Africans, including their leaders have, without any policy guidance on ICT adoption, joined the global demand for ICT products.

Disparity in the use of information technology between citizens of poor African countries and those from the rich nations is not surprising. After all, inequality in the use of information technology, much like gaps in economic development between African countries and the rich nations, stems from poverty and only by reducing destitution can African countries close the technology gap. An important question is: can African countries break the poverty cycle with the new tools derived from ICT? We believe ICT is a tool with which African countries can revitalize.

Empirical evidence of the growing gap in ICT usage between rich and poor countries is well known but so too is the gap between the haves and have-nots within both the rich and the relatively poor African countries, implying the processes of uneven accumulation are unfolding in accordance with a social order and not a national logic (Robinson 2002). According to Robinson (2002), the ICT revolution has led to social polarization and selective integration of social groups from different countries into transnational networks. This process suggests we may need to rethink development under ICT not as a national event in which what develops is a nation but in terms of developed, underdeveloped and intermediate population groups occupying contradictory locations in a transnational development (Robinson 2000). The information divide between rich and poor nations therefore remains important for its theoretical and practical implications for development in less developed countries such as those in Africa. The main issue however, is whether the divide is something innate, or represents a particular spatial configuration of uneven development during a particular phase of economic development, or that the self-reproduction of this rich-poor divide can be offset by counter tendencies emanating from the development and use of ICT. We may point out that recent development experience of some Asian countries (South Korea, Malaysia, and Singapore) reveal that the rich-poor divide is not static. Given the speed with which ICT is invading every sphere of activity on the African continent, and the breadth of socio-economic impact that has already begun to flow from ICT usage, it is imperative to ensure that African countries are not excluded from ICT development and usage.

However, as the information revolution has accelerated, African countries seem to have taken a back seat. Even though people all over the continent crave for mobile phones, radios, computers and other contraptions of information technology, few African countries have laid the foundations for rationalized and clearly formulated policies to guide their participation in the ICT revolution. The questions we need to ask are: does the ICT revolution herald a new dawn of re-colonization or does it provide an opportunity to improve the welfare of Africans? What will be the implications for Africa's participation or non-involvement in the revolution? These questions form the basis of discussion in this chapter. We review the discourse about the ICT revolution and economic development in Africa. We argue that a more productive discussion of ICT's role in Africa's economic development must involve a critical appraisal of the link between the ICT revolution and structural changes that are currently occurring in the creation of wealth, in industries, capital markets and labor movements within ICT adopting countries. The chapter focuses on ways by which ICT could influence conditions in Africa to induce changes that promote economic and social development and concludes with suggestions for strengthening the adoption of ICT in Africa.

ICT and Socio-economic Development

The term "information and communication technology" (ICT) is used in this chapter to refer to an array of electronic-based products (including computers, line and mobile phones, radio, e-mails, worldwide web, and the internet), and related services generated out of innovations within the computer and telecommunication industries. Other information communication technologies such as film, audio recordings and print media have implications for organizations and communities in Africa, but we do not include them in this analysis. The economic advantage of the information technologies ensue from a succession of what Beninger (1986) calls "control innovations" that play crucial enabling roles in capitalist economic development through timely delivery of the information required for industrial expansion. The widespread adoption of these technologies has ushered a new phase of global economic development. The production of information goods and services dominate wealth and job creation, with computers and telecommunications providing the technological potential for products and process innovations (Jonscher 1983; Hepworth 1990; Jeffrey 2001).

The ICT revolution has accelerated the flow of information and technology across national borders and offered citizens of both rich and poor countries the opportunity to become more interconnected than before. ICT has therefore become essential for emerging industries and an indispensable tool in transactions in international trade among nations. There is currently a global recognition that information technology is the key to future vitality in society and the means by which the future of nations would be determined. In fact, the technology has become a critical factor in the creation and redistribution of wealth within nations and in the world. Yet, in Africa, ICT development and usage has barely taken a foothold. By the end of 2002, only two out of 100 people in developing countries had access to telephone lines and those lines were located in affluent urban areas (ITU 2002). Of the current twenty most wired countries based on networks per millions of the population, none is in Africa. TeleGeography, a US company that specializes in ICT development, revealed that in 2001, international Internet bandwidth grew slowest in Africa at 89.6 percent (Table 21: 1).

This is compared to a world average growth rate of 174 percent during the same period, with Latin America recording an increase of as much as 479 percent. This left Africa with 13 times less international bandwidth than the second least-connected, Latin America, and nearly 223 times less than the connectivity of North America (*TeleGeography* 2001). Combining this data with Population Reference Bureau's records of 2001 reveals that the average North American resident had access to about 570 times more international bandwidth than the average African in 2001. The International Communication Union estimates that 96 percent of Internet hosting computers are found in high-income countries and that by 2002, there were more internet hosts in New York than all of Africa (ITU 2002). With nearly ten percent of the world's population in 2002,

Table 21.1 Rate of Growth in International Internet Bandwidth 2000-2001

Region	2000Mbps	2001 Mbps	Percentage of Change
Africa	649.2	1,230.8	89.6%
Asia	22,965.1	52,662.9	129.3%
Europe	232,316.7	675,637.3	109.8%
Latin America	2,785.2	16,132.5	479.2%
US & Canada	112,222.0	274,184.9	144.3%
The World			174%

Source: Telegeography Inc. (2001). * Note: Data as of mid-year.

only about 28 percent of Africans had fixed phone lines, 14 percent used mobile phones and an estimated 7.6 percent had Internet connections (ITU 2002). The critics therefore contend that regardless of the excitement, which heralded the advent of ICT on the global scene, access to the technology is available mostly to rich countries with the basic infrastructure (phones, computers and electricity). The question we must ask ourselves is: Can ICT be adopted and used for the benefit of Africans? While some authors agree, others disagree, so in the section that follows, we review some of the main arguments.

The Discourse about ICT Adoption in Africa

The implications of the disparity in the global distribution of ICT revealed in the preceding section becomes obvious if we consider the connection between telephone line density and economic growth. In this regard, the critics contend that what appears to be emerging as ICT has evolved and gained global acceptance is a pattern of wealth distribution that follows the established pattern of global inequality initiated by European colonization and the spread of western/industrial capitalism (Boafo 1991; Wresch 1996; Tong 2001). The argument is that the rich countries would use their wealth and power to strengthen their hold in the ICT industry (Moisy 1997) and then use it to exploit poor African countries. Developed nations will control the means of production through the licensing of hardware and software used for translating raw data into usable forms. Microsoft Company for example, owns both the operating system for computers and the explorer for internet communications (two key components of ICT). For some authors, the diminishment of global spatial barriers under ICT gives transnational capital new-found power to exploit African countries (Castells 1989; Schiller 1996; Rusciano 2001). The critics therefore predict that the world may be witnessing another era of colonization, this time led by western media conglomerates that are poised to take full control of social and economic activities in poor countries (Wresch 1996; Rusciano 2001; Tong 2001).

Africa's participation in the ICT revolution is also opposed on grounds of lack of financial resources and the infrastructure to support African entrepreneurs attempting to cash in on sales from ICT subscription and development. In reference to this point, Internet Service Providers (ISPs) in Kenya recently complained that giant western internet companies such as America Online (AOL) and British Telecom (BT) exploit young ISP businesses in Africa as they refuse to pay their share of the cost of sending and receiving e-mails by African Internet users (BBC News Online 2002). The critics therefore argue that African countries that dabble in ICT development would become pawns of multinational ICT companies (Moisy 1997; Castells 1989). Besides, the critics point to the fact that getting online requires a computer and necessary peripherals (electricity, software and phones) that are beyond the reach of many Africans (Boafo 1991; Tong 2002). With commercial interests focused on the Web, the information that is valuable is often not free. For example, online academic and e-libraries require hefty subscription fees that many African scholars cannot afford (Hamelink 1996). Thus, there is the realization that the information superhighway is not a super freeway. Consequently, the critics maintain that for African countries that are struggling to meet the requirements for even simple analog phone lines, the global village constructed under ICT will remain a gated community (Boafo 1991; Tong 2001). That is, Africans face severe restrictions.

One cannot deny that the adoption of ICT in African countries will produce unintended consequences. In fact, ICT's diffusion tends to follow the already established global patterns of the distribution of wealth, education and power (Moisy 1997; Wilson, 2000). Even in Africa, the largest concentrations of Internet users are found mainly in Tunisia and Egypt in the north and South Africa in the south. These are countries that already enjoy relatively higher levels of economic development and also possess relatively good infrastructure. Additionally, the spread of ICT and the consequent deepening of the globalization process could generate a new capital-labor relationship that the rich countries might use to poach skilled labor from Africa. It is therefore important to acknowledge the disadvantaged position of Africa in the development and use of ICT. It must, however, be noted that Africa's participation in the ICT revolution is inevitable and that African countries are seeking the path to economic progress and have made commitments to modernization. In the streets of the capitals of African countries, shops replete with the latest information technology stick out as islands of wealth characteristic of European or American cities. Demand for ICT products by Africans grows in leaps and bounds and it seems there is little that African leaders can do to stop the insatiable demand for mobile phones and other ICT products. As shown in Table 21.2, Africa recorded the highest percentage increase (48 percent) in the global penetration of mobile phone systems in 2001. Europe recorded 40 percent while the Americas together registered 43 percent in the same year. Even with the penetration of the Internet, Africa's 15 percent increase in 2001 compares favorably with the 21 percent increase for the Americas and Europe. In addition, Internet use in Africa is growing at a very fast rate. As at year-end 2000, there was one Internet user per 150 people on the continent. This is low compared to the world average (one user per 15 people) and extremely low in comparison with North America's record (one user per two people) but more than South Asia (one user per 250 people) (UNDP, 2000). The neglected aspect of the emerging high demand for mobile phones and other ICT products on the continent is that the demand is occurring with little governmental support or directive that could have linked ICT usage with business applications and general economic development.

The insatiable demand for ICT products is a clear indication that Africans are not averse to new technology. It is therefore inappropriate, in the midst of mass demand for ICT in African countries, to advocate against adoption. With thousands of citizens already hooked on ICT products, African leaders seem to have run out of time to decide whether to be passive or active participants in the ICT revolution. What people are missing is the ability and the determination by their policy makers to adapt the technology to produce ICT products they demand from the West. Besides, it is necessary to examine the options that would be available to African countries should they elect not to adopt ICT. We may point out that Africa's need for the adoption of ICT is not only driven by internal factors but also bolstered by international requirements and the social and economic realities of modern times. External trade and international commitments, and the obligations that African countries have as members of the international community make it necessary and at times even obligatory for them to participate in the ICT revolution. Moreover, adoption of such new technologies by African countries is often tied to financial assistance (e.g. loans and grants) provided for economic development (Hanna and Boyson, 1993). It seems rather prudent for the countries to plan for the adoption and use of ICT in ways that suit their needs and resources. It is possible that if they delay their citizens would import and use the technology (thereby increase external debts), or the technology would be imposed on them through some bilateral donor assistance and international trade.

Table 21:2 Percentage Increase in Global ICT Network Penetraton 2000-2001

Region	Mobile Phone Users	Fixed Phone Line Users	Internet Users
Africa	48%	37%	15%
Americas	43%	36%	21%
Europe	40%	39%	21%
Asia/Pacific	40%	34%	26%

Source: International Telecommuncations Union (2002).

Maintaining Cultural Identity in Africa under Widespread Adoption of ICT

Besides technological inequality, critics are also concerned about homogenization of cultures as ICT spreads to connect fragile African communities with global networks. The concern revolves around two main issues:

1. The predominance of English language on the internet and the fear that Africans would lose their identities under Western popular culture (Roach 1997) and
2. The imposition of a singular worldview underpinned by capitalist values of liberalization, privatization and market supremacy (Hamelink 1996; Slaughter 1997)

The opponents explain that English is the mother tongue of computer data and encodes 80 percent of all messages and data content even though only about a tenth's of the world population speak English. The English language is encoded in digital networks through the binary system, the most common of which is the American Standard Code for Information Interchange (ASCII). Computer software, including the all-important Operating Systems, is written in the English language. Applied cross-culturally therefore, the authors believe ICT would intensify the assimilation of Africans into Western culture. We would like to point out that extended versions of ASCII make exceptions for special characters in Spanish, French German, Korean and Japanese. The Asian market currently has a large number of non-Anglophone software products and translations. The rise of machine translation has also made possible Chinese, Korean and other versions of the English language to natives of East Asian countries. It therefore becomes clear that competing economic forces, rather than communication needs, dictate the direction of ICT software development.

It is also not clear whether local audiences accept cultural images in a passive fashion. According to Fejes (1981), several factors intervene in the interpretation of cultural images from foreign countries. In support of this claim, Katz and Liebes (1984, 1986) have demonstrated that individuals rely on social networks to decode and interpret imported images. Roach (1997) has accordingly argued that cultural images are difficult to deconstruct and that there is no one grand totalizing interpretation of media messages. He therefore discounted the notion that there is a passive audience that indiscriminately absorbs messages. Instead, he explained that audiences everywhere remain active and consciously attach meanings to the messages they hear (Roach 1997). It is true that the English language currently dominates the Internet but it is doubtful if Africa will be turned into Anglo-Saxon communities (more than what most already are) by the adoption of ICT. What is real is that every culture will develop its own analogies in cyber space (Gardels 1997). In Africa, ICT could provide an opportunity to have a greater control over their images unencumbered by the vast western media. Slaughter 1997). In fact, when the Internet takes hold in Africa, the people would be able to tell their own stories to the world (Friedman 1998). Currently over 120 magazines and newspapers in Africa are online presenting daily accounts of events from the continent.

Besides, it is doubtful whether a solution to the problem of national identity lies with steadfast adherence to outmoded African traditions that can no longer respond to contemporary needs of society. Wiredu (1980, 1993) has explained that every human culture has two constitutive elements. There are some elements of a culture such as procedures, customs, language, music, dance, and recreation that have no objective bearing on human well-being, truth, or falsehood. Such elements of a group's culture, according to Wiredu (1980), are contingent and their adoption makes no difference to one's beliefs about the world. Consequently, there can be no compelling reason to change such elements of a group's culture for foreign substitutes. There are, however, other elements of a group's culture, including religion, science, technology, and philosophy that occurs in the domain of thought and as such truth is continuously sought and verified. Such knowledge domains of a society's culture, he explains, are anchored in truth, and therefore have a bearing on human well-being. As an illustration, we wish to point out that there may be no compelling reason for an African chief to substitute his ceremonial dress for an European suit but it would be unthinkable for a medical officer in Africa to ignore a scientific discovery about a cure for some disease or for an African businessman to decline an offer to use a mobile phone to conduct his business. Consequently, Wiredu concludes that it is not desirable, even when possible, to ignore developments in such knowledge domains as technology that occur in cultures other than ones' own (Wiredu 1993).

ICT Unique Qualities as an Engine for Economic Development

ICT is not just another western technology but a tool with an exceptional power to affect the lives of people everywhere. It is the most rapidly diffused, most widely adopted and the fastest growing technology on record. According to the International Telecommunications Union (ITU 1999), it took only four years for the Internet to be subscribed by 50 million people distributed throughout the world. In the same manner, the telephone took 74 years and radio 38 years to attain a similar subscription. None of the earlier popular technologies (i.e., printing press, vehicles, etc) spread throughout the world in such a rapid manner.

Added to the attractiveness is the transformative power of the information technology. ICT has the unique ability to transform the processes, people, and the phenomena it encounters. The impacts range from enhanced financial transactions, wealth generation and its distribution, improved education, and expansion in democratic practice. Unlike previous engines of economic development (i.e. industry) whose influences were limited to urban enclaves in Africa, the beneficial impacts of ICT products (i.e., mobile phones, computers etc) can reach anywhere without an expensive landline infrastructure and with little capital outlay. As a result, information technology provides special access to many Africans who have been excluded from other means of economic advancement. While market solutions have generally not proven useful for redistributing economic rewards to communities in hinterlands of African countries, the unique openness of information technology could reverse this trend and spread benefits around (Attali 1997).

With ICT, African countries can leapfrog by skipping generations of intermediate technologies to adopt more recent and advanced technological products. This is particularly important for the quest for development in Africa where efforts to put advanced technologies to work for the people are often thwarted by the failings of an older infrastructure (e.g. ancient electric grids, poor roads, and old phone lines). Technological innovations have a tendency to spread and take root faster in non-industrialized countries (*Tele-Haves and Have-Nots* 1996). African countries with very low investments in telecommunication infrastructure can adopt new and cheaper information technologies faster because they have little investments in traditional technologies. Their urban spaces are also not clogged with infrastructure that is increasingly becoming obsolete. The high demand for mobile phones compared with fixed phone lines in African countries is a case in point. By year-end 2001, more Africans subscribed to mobile phone than fixed phone lines (ITU 2002). The lack of unreliable telephone networks compels citizens in African countries to adopt mobile phones that come with no geographic barriers and local controls. This mass adoption of mobile phones is helping to narrow the information divide between rich and poor nations (Worldwatch Institute 2003).

Similarly, leapfrogging makes the expansion of the Internet into developing African countries a great possibility. The countries can avoid investments in fixed phone lines and move on to wireless technology for Internet and e-mail delivery. In fact, the Internet currently grows at a faster rate in developing countries than it does in industrialized countries. In its annual global ICT report for 2002, TeleGeography revealed that while an overwhelming percentage of global bandwidth flows to and from North America, reliance on the United States as a switching centre is slowly decreasing as regions establish their own switching centers. For example, new connections in North Africa led to ten percent of the international bandwidth there shifting from North America to Europe in 2001. The report revealed that there were 152 local Internet exchange (IX) points worldwide including South Africa's JINX and CINX points in Johannesburg and Cape Town respectively.

In many ways, ICT, and computer programming in particular, creates a degree of scientific autonomy that releases human creativity in new forms (Attali 1997). The technology can provide an excellent opportunity for African countries to be self reliant in their development if the necessary investments in education are made. The technology offers tools that skilful African workers can utilize to create home-made goods (CDs, music, etc) to promote indigenous culture and possibly put a dent on Africa's technological dependency. In addition, the decentralized, small private enterprises promoted by ICT are not only more efficient but also better able to respond to the subtle rapid changes that characterize today's international markets and technologies. In the post industrial world with a global shift to services and away from mass manufacturing and raw material production, ICT offer the best opportunity to reverse the deteriorating economies of African countries. It is ICT's micro-enterprise (i.e., diffuse, small scale ventures) rather than raw materials production that can empower individuals to create their own sustainable futures in the 21st century.

Furthermore, ICT offers a great avenue for Sub-Saharan African countries to join and actively participate in the global information economy because it is cheaper than other forms of capital input required for development. Small investors could tap into economic resources to develop global commercial ventures. In so far as the same satellites circle the space above cities in the West and the capitals of African countries, setting up an internet in Africa for example, would not be difficult and that would be vastly easier than building something like a factory. ICT offers opportunities for business groups from different African countries to be electronically linked thereby making possible vast transnational cooperatives and coalitions that can share resources, information and ideas for a more effective organization, expansion and production. Rural communities currently separated by distance and time from state capitals can develop new virtual relationships uninhibited by conventional notions of distance and transportation links. The implications of these cross-community and national contacts for the development of the hinterlands of Africa can be tremendous.

Potential Benefits from ICT Adoption in African Countries

Given that increased agricultural output is vital for Africa's rapidly growing population, a tool like a mobile phone or the internet which effectively links farmers, scientists and policy makers could contribute to development. Small and medium sized agribusinesses would become more efficient and productive by using electronic networking to gain access to critical market and weather information. Also, since most remote villages in Africa lack easy access to hospitals and medical centers, telemedicine and digitized health information could play a crucial role in helping to save millions of lives. ICT products including Internet, CD-ROMs, digital cameras, and electronic databases could provide doctors and patients with the resources and information to increase the reliability of diagnosis for cure to be administered. Perhaps the most popular way disconnected communities are getting connected in rural Africa is through public access points (PAPs). These PAPs include multipurpose community telecenters (MCTs), telecottages and traditional cybercafes that are often located in low-income and underserved areas of the continent. The PAPs employ a variety of ICT (e.g. computers, phone lines, Internet access) to bring the digital age to marginalized communities. Many PAPs also provide users with a variety of business services, including computer training, Web hosting and even distance education. Although they can take many forms, multipurpose community telecenters in India for example, have proven to be a crucial factor in helping the underprivileged to overcome poverty, illiteracy, inequality, and isolation. African countries could also benefit from job creation. Although many of the continent's first technology jobs have been simple outsourcing tasks for foreign countries, the jobs can open the door to more complicated and better-paid work as programmers improve their skills and move from data entry, for example, to software programming. The Internet would enhance the capabilities of law enforcement agencies on the continent and enable them to exchange information and coordinate efforts with police and justice officials within and outside the continent. The Internet can also make possible classrooms online to facilitate distant tertiary education as a way of providing cheap educational facilities to many African children who would normally not be able to afford even a secondary school education.

ICT and Gender Empowerment in Africa

Although gender parity has been a focus of development in many African countries, women still represent the largest social segment of the digital divide. By helping to spread information to remote parts of Africa, ICT could offer African women unprecedented opportunities to actively participate in controlling their own futures. ICT has proven an effective tool for empowering marginalized societies and, for women in Africa, the technology could prove to be an important means for ending their oppression, exclusion and isolation. Not only does access to modern information technologies help level the playing field between the genders, but such access also significantly enhances the freedoms of women. If properly employed, ICT has the potential to empower African women to help themselves. However, in order for the empowerment to be effective, African governments need to make a deliberate effort to incorporate the gender dimension into ICT policy design and implementation.

E-Democracy and Political Development in Africa

The Internet has the potential to move much of current public discourse and agenda setting in African countries from community to national and even international levels. ICT has the potential to link Africans in the diaspora with political discourses that are taking place in their respective native countries. Already websites created by Africans in diaspora for particular countries (i.e. Ghanaweb and NigeriaWeb) are one-point shopping for local news and new developments. Accompanying discussion boards provide opportunities for Africans in diaspora to comment and participate in local political discourses. Information flow is the basis of democracy and therefore the links provided by the Internet can have a significant impact on governance and democratic practice in the African countries.

E-Government

The increased flow of information between the public and the private sectors can help establish an environment of trust and reliability between African citizens and their elected officials. Governments around the world embrace ICT, specifically the Internet, to streamline public sector processes and make their operations more efficient and transparent while also providing citizens with easy access to government services. The digitization of public service information in African countries can also make government agencies and public officials more accountable. While African governments have only recently begun to modernize institutional structures, successful implementation of ICT could prove to be an effective instrument for connecting disparate government communication networks at every level.

Why ICT Adoption has not Progressed in Africa

In Africa, ICT is variously embraced, resisted and subverted even as it makes contacts with hundreds of people every day. This is partly because the information technology, which connects people with little regard to cultural differences and boundary restrictions, is being implemented in Africa by politicians with very strong beliefs about national sovereignty and protection of state boundaries. In many African countries, telecommunication companies are state-owned and monopolistic, often unreliable and inefficient (NRC 1996). Their services are often less innovative, although more expensive than private telecommunication companies, but they their clouts as state companies to stifle competition and prevent penetration into the local telecommunication market. ICT poses a great threat to many African leaders because it has the capability to bypass the gaze of official structures to redefine local and national politics. The Internet for example, affects internal and interstate communication and therefore allows local journalists to interact directly with global media and international audiences bypassing local restrictions and censorship. ICT therefore threatens security operations of unpopular African governments. It is therefore no wonder that unpopular leaders would openly resist ICT adoption in order to hold on to power.

Besides, the technology influences public policy-making by allowing citizens to express their opinions about public policy and to also demand accountability from public officials. By giving the people a voice, albeit electronic, ICT can significantly increase citizen participation in public decision-making. It can therefore be argued that ICT development is not high on the agenda of African leaders partly because many are not bold enough to allow their citizens to access information about their governments. Whether it is streamlining the provision of government services or speaking out for a marginalized population, ICT products have become the convenient medium for expressing dissenting viewpoints. Consequently, the products have become targets for executive control in many African countries. In other cases, African leaders have treated computers and related information technologies as luxuries and imposed heavy taxes that make such imported products very expensive and therefore unobtainable by the majority of their people. The half-hearted approach to ICT adoption in Africa could partly be due to the undemocratic practices of many African governments. Until the leaders embrace ICT and make bold efforts to plan for their adoption, African countries will only serve as markets for ICT products.

Suggestions for Strengthening ICT Development in Africa

A fundamental requirement for the development and effective applications of ICT in Africa is for the countries to undertake parallel efforts to join the ICT revolution both as generators of ideas in ICT development and consumers of ICT products. To do this, the African countries will have to give priority to the education of the masses. The information economy places increasing value on personalized professional services. The greatest economic productivity results when frontline workers are vested with the tools, knowledge and responsibility to direct their own work. In an obsolete industrial or raw materials-based economy, workers who pull levers and follow orders need not be educated. However, in the decentralized service economy brought about by ICT, workers are vital resources. They are repositories of skills, knowledge and expertise that must be nurtured and retrained. African countries need to also develop telecommunication infrastructure to provide universal and affordable access to people in all geographic regions. This will bring the benefit from ICT adoption to all parts of the continent and help break the chain of uneven development promoted under industrialization and raw material production.

In addition, the countries need to design comprehensive ICT policies that would allow them to cash in on the magnanimity and good will of their citizens abroad to supply relatives, distant neighbors, former schools and colleges with computers, computer skills and ICT products. The global dispersal of native Africans has created a pool of skilled people in diaspora that can become valuable networks of finance, business contacts and skills transfer for their home countries. According to a report by the United Nations Development Program (UNDP 2001), many Africans in the United States and other developed countries have important skills and wealth in terms of human and material resources that could effectively address Africa's development challenge. Unfortunately, there are currently not many avenues to apply these resources for the benefit of Africa. Tapping the vast breadth of human and other resources from those in diaspora would require careful planning and public policy support which many African leaders currently do not have in place.

It is also important for African countries to make long-term plans for prosperity that fully integrate ICT development and usage. The countries should gradually introduce digital technology into local, regional and national organizations, administrative institutions, commerce and banking, sports and other spheres of life. There should be plans to introduce computers into schools, universities and research institutions in Africa to enhance computer literacy and facilitate the development of local expertise in ICT usage. Universities and Research Institutions must be encouraged and assisted to take the leading role in research, development of software and training of ICT personnel. Some standardization in ICT hardware, software, data structures, and metadata must also be adopted in each country and if possible among regional groups (e.g. countries in the Economic Community of West African States) to facilitate easy and widespread ICT applications. Such standards must be chosen in recognition of developments in information technology elsewhere.

Furthermore, it is necessary to create legal and regulatory frameworks that foster ICT development, adoption and applications. One difficulty that arises with ICT applications is ambiguity about whether data that has been created and stored in electronic form has evidentiary value in a court of law. Another legal issue is that of intellectual property law in general, and copyright in digital materials in particular. Digital technologies are complex and their impacts are profound. When data storage, information, and funds flow freely across national borders, the ability to enforce the law or collect the taxes on which government agencies depend, could be greatly reduced. Currently, copyright statements accompany many on-line databases, but it is not entirely clear how enforceable these statements are, and what steps governments need to take to protect the rights of the authors. There are also ways in which national sovereignty could be threatened by the global information infrastructure. It is important for African leaders to deliberate on these issues in tandem with the development and use of ICT products.

Conclusion

ICT networks are transforming the traditional model of development, expanding people's horizons and creating the potential for people to realize economic prosperity that has eluded several generations of Africans. In spite of this potential, African countries seem not to be ready to fully participate in the ICT revolution. We find the technological optimists' expectations about benefits from ICT adoption in Africa to be unrealistic but neither do the technological pessimists' predictions of doom adequately explain the role ICT can play in the economic development of African countries. We have explained that the acceptance of ICT products by African's must be evaluated on the basis of the technology's overall contribution to socio-economic development of the people. More importantly, we need to consider the options that would be available to African countries should they fail to adopt ICT and related computer systems. On the other hand, an early involvement of the people with ICT would help the countries develop skills that are necessary for efficient uses of the technology. Familiarization with the technology would help in the development of local capacity for effective uses of the products. It would then be possible for the countries to adapt the technology, anticipate its problems, and then develop the capability to deal with the problems locally. In this regard, Winner (1993) has advised that, if less privileged people are to be empowered in the world to come, then they should learn to be skillful in areas that affect them but which they are profoundly ignorant. It is through such measures that the countries can avoid merely drifting to wherever the constraints and facilities of global technologies take them and then begin to realize their full potentials.

It must however be noted that persistent efforts by Africans to import and use ICT products, coupled with the rapid innovations being experienced in information technology might enable Africa to bridge the digital divide. However, such efforts will hardly generate the much-needed economic gains African countries need. It is the full integration of the African countries into the ICT revolution (as both developers and consumers) that will bring mutually beneficial e-commerce, enhanced education and economic development to the people. African states should therefore provide favorable environments for innovation to take place. They must also ensure equal access to ICT by all citizens.

References

Attali, Jacques (1997). "Cultural Imperialism on the Net." In *The Internet and Society*. Jim O'Reilly and Associates (ed.) Cambridge: Harvard University Press.

Barber, B.R. (1988). "Pangloss, Pandora or Jefferson? Three scenarios for the future of Technology and Democracy." *In Information Technology: the Public Issues*. P. Raymond, G. Frank, and B. Alan (eds.) Manchester: Manchester University Press.

BBC News online (2002). *The great African Internet Robbery*. Available at http://news.bbc.co.uk/1/hi/world/africa/1931120.stm (Accessed from the web on May 2002).

Beninger, J. (1986). *The Control Revolution: Technological and Economic Origins of the Information Society.* Cambridge, MA: Harvard University Press.

Boafo, S.T.K. (1991). "Communication Technology and Dependent Development in Sub-Saharan Africa." In *Trans-National Communications: Wiring the Third World*. G. Sussman and J. A. Lent. (eds.) Newbury Park, CA: Sage.

Bolter J. D. (1984). *Turing's Man*. London, England: Duckworth.

Castells, M. (1989). "The Rise of the Network Society." In *The Informal Economy: Study in Advanced and Less Developed Countries*. Manuel Castellas and Alejandro Portes. (ed.) Baltimore MD: John Hopkins University Press.

Frejes, F. (1981). "Media Imperialism: An assessment." *Media, Culture and Society* 3: 281–289.

Friedman, Thomas (1998). Booting Up Africa. *New York Times*. May 5, 1998 A. 31.

Gardels, N. (1997). "Cultural Imperialism on the Net." In *The Internet and Society*. Jim O'Reilly and Associates. (ed.) Cambridge: Harvard University Press.

Giddens, A. (1990). *The Consequences of Modernity*. Cambridge, MA: Polity Press.

Hamelink, C. (1996). *The World Communication Disempowerment and Self-Empowerment*. London: Zed Books.

Hanna, N. and Boyson, S. (1993). *Information Technology in World Bank Lending: Increasing the Development Impact*, Asia Technical Department, Washington, DC: World Bank.

Hepworth, Mark. E. (1990). *Geography of the Information Economy*. New York: Guilford Press.

ITU (1999). *Challenges to the Network: Internet for Development*. Geneva: International Communications Union.

——— (2002). *Internet Reports 2002: Internet for a Mobile Generation*. Report available at http://www.itu.int/osg/spu/publications/sales/mobileinternet/exec_summary.html (Accessed from the web on June 2003).

Jeffrey, J. (2001). "Information Technology, cumulative causation and patterns of Globalization in the Third World." *Review of International Political Economy* 8 (1) 147–162.

Jensen, M. (2001). *Africa Internet Status*. Online available at www3.sn.apc.org/Africa/afrmain.htm (Accessed from the web on February 3, 2003).

Johnson, Robert C. (1993). Science, Technology and Black Community Development. In *Technology and the Future*, Albert H. Teich (Ed.), New York: St. Martin Press, 265–349.

Jonscher, C. (1983). "Information Resources and Economic Productivity." In *Information Economics and Policy* 2(1) 13–35.

Katz, E. and Liebes, T. (1984). "Once Upon a Time in Dallas." *Intermedia*, 3 (12) 28–32.

——— (1986). "Mutual Aid in the Reading of the Dallas: Preliminary Notes from a Cross-Cultural Study." In *Television in Transition*. P. Drummond and R. Peterson. (eds.) London: British Film Institute.

Moisy, Claude (1997). "Myths of the Global Information Village." *Foreign Policy*, 107: 78–87.

National Research Council (1996). *The bridge builders: Africa's experiences with Information Telecommunication Technology.* New York: National Academy Press.

Polikanov, D. and Abramova, I. (2003). "Africa and ICT: a chance for breakthrough?" *Information Communications and Society*. 6(1) 42–56.

Roach, C. (1997). "Cultural Imperialism and Resistance in the Media Theory." *Media, Culture and Society*. (19) 47–66.

Robinson, W. (2002). "Remapping development in the light of globalization: from a territorial to a social cartography." In *Third World Quaterly* 23(6) 1047–1071.

Rusciano, F. K. (2001). The Three faces of Cyberimperialism. In *Cyberimperialism? Global Relations in the New Electronic Frontier*. Bosah, Ebo (ed.) Praeger Westport, Connecticut, USA. 9–25.

Sah, R. K. and Striglitz, J.E. (1993). "Sources of Technological Divergence between Developed and Less Developed Economies." In G. Calvo, R. Findlay, P. Kouri, and J. Braga de Macedo, eds. *Debt, Stabilization, and Development*. Baltimore, MD: Johns Hopkins University Press.

Schiller, H. (1996). *Information Inequality*. London and New York:. Institute for Media Analysis.

Slaughter, Ann-Marie (1997). "Cultural Imperialism on the Net." In *The Internet and Society*. Jim O'Reilly and Associates (ed.) Cambridge: Harvard University Press.

Telegeography (2002). "Packet Geography: Global Internet Bandwidth 2001." Report available at; http://www.telegeography.com/press/releases/2002/19-nov-2002.html (Accessed from the web on October 2002).

——— (2003). *All in One International Telecom Almanac*. Summary report available at http://www.telegeography.com/pubs/voice/reports/tog.html. (Accessed from the web on June 2003).

Tele-Have and Have-Nots (1996). *The Economist*. May18, 19–20.

Tong, D. (2001). "Cybercolonialism: Speeding Along the Superhighway or Stalling on a Beaten Track?" In *Cyberimperialism? Global Relations in the New Electronic Frontier* (Bosah Ebo, ed.) Praeger Westport, CT: USA. p. 65–79.

UNDP (1999). *World Development Report 1999*. New York: Oxford University Press.

UNDP (2000). *World Development Report 2000*. online available at www.undp.org/hdro/index2.html (Accessed from the web on August 15, 2002).

——— (2001). *Human Development Report 2001: Making new technologies work for human development*. Available at http://hdr.undp.org/reports/global/2001/en/pdf/completenew.pdf (Accessed from the web on January 2004).

Wilson, E. J. (2000). *Closing the digital divide: an initial review*. Internet Policy Institute. Online available at: http://www.internetpolicy.org (Accessed from the web on July 2002).

Winner, L. (1993). *Artifacts, Ideas and Political Culture, in Technology and the future*. Albert H. Teich. (ed.) New York: St. Martin Press.

Wiredu, K. (1980). A Philosophical Perspective on the Concept of Human Communication" in *International Social Science Journal*, Vol. 32, (2). 199–202.

——— (1993). "African Philosophical Tradition: A case Study of the Akan." In *The Philosophical Forum*. 24, (1–3) 33–62.

Worldwatch Institute (2003). "Communication networks expands." *Vital Signs*, 60–61. Available at: http://www.worldwatch.org/topics/vsow/2003/12/22/ (January 2004).

Wresch, William. (1996). *Disconnected: haves and have-nots in the information age*. New Brunswick, NJ: Rutgers University Press.

Chapter 22

Making Change: Reinventing Africa for the 21st Century

Kwamina Panford and Kwadwo Konadu-Agyemang

Introduction

The preceding chapters in this book have attempted to grasp some of the complexities of Africa's development conundrum and related challenges of the 21st century. The authors have sought to delve into specific aspects of the African development dilemma that range from the weak or collapsed African state, governance, corruption and democracy; the challenges of military intervention, political and economic integration, food self-sufficiency, transportation and the Internet and related communications technology (ICT as it is called in Africa), human capital/education and training to the problems linked to excessive urbanization in contemporary Africa. While we would have liked to be more exhaustive in our coverage of topics, issues and countries selected, due to spatial limitations we are only able to offer mostly snapshots and overviews of issues and countries that may be of interest to the analyst of modern Africa.

Our main concern has been pooling together chapters that deal with issues that impinge on the survival and thriving of Africans in the current century. The lesson we have learned and the theme we seek to convey through this book is that it is clear that both the problems and the solutions that will work are especially daunting. The African development paradox itself, it still ongoing and hence its resolution goes beyond what a single book, even if it is authored by several experts, can offer. Our goal was thus to bring to bear on Africa's problems the experiences and insights of authors from different academic disciplines who reside both in and out of Africa.

The African Development Conundrum

Twenty-first century Africa presents a wide array of paradoxes and still more contradictions. One of the most revealing is that although it is one of the most naturally endowed continents, Africans are some of the poorest in the world today. Africa has a little over 13 percent of the world's population and almost 20 percent of the world's land area. Nigeria and the Democratic Republic of Congo (DRC), to cite only two countries, have vast arable land that if cultivated properly, could feed the bulk of sub-Saharan African populations to avoid periodic bouts of hunger.

Africa's abundance goes beyond agricultural potentials because, for virtually every mineral or ore used for military or commercial purposes, Africa is a leading producer. For some minerals, it has more than its ample share of both deposits and actual output. Fifty percent of the world's gold and manganese; 5.7 percent of coal; 13 percent of copper; 15 percent of iron ore; 30 percent of uranium; 7.4 percent of natural gas and seven percent of petroleum; the bulk of both industrial and commercial diamonds and 40 percent of hydro-electric power potential lie within the borders of Africa (BP 2001; UNDP 2000). We might add the enormous forest resources, which Africa has even after years of non-stop exploitation since colonial days.

Two cases can illustrate the commercial and military/strategic value of Africa's natural resources. The uranium that was used to make the atomic bombs the US dropped on Japan was mined in South Africa. It was in Sierra Leone that the single most important and expensive piece of diamond was found. This diamond is now in the jewelry of the British royals. The US and the other western powers' unflinching support for both Mobutu Sese Seko's tenacious hold on power from 1965 to 1997 and the white racist minority rulers in South Africa from 1948 to 1986 can be attributed to those two countries' wealth in minerals and ores used for military and commercial purposes. The former in particular included but were not limited to platinum, uranium and cobalt. Both the commercial and military uses of cobalt are highly instructive in explaining why the former Zaire (now DRC) has always found itself in the grip of wars and schemes to assassinate its first democratically elected leader, Prime Minister Patrice Lumumba. At the start of the 1998 civil war in the DRC, coltan, the dirty black crude material that yields cobalt, sold for between \$300 and \$400 per pound. Cobalt, the refined product, fetches astronomical prices on the world market; as much as \$200,000 per pound, a 500 percent rise in value after extraction (CBS News, "Spoils of War," December 17, 2002). Cobalt has several uses including as an industrial lubricant and computer, cell phone, computer games, and airplane engine components. The availability of such important resources is at the root of the support both Mobutu and the racist regimes of South Africa received from the US, Britain, Germany, France and Belgium while the bulk of the African population was politically suppressed and materially deprived. This explains why both apartheid and the kleptocracy headed by Mobutu lasted many decades.

The material poverty of Africa today is captured by the following data. Africa produces the bulk of most of the world's raw materials and yet due to declining terms of trade, unequal and unfair trade, Africans earn only a paltry three percent of the revenues from international trade. One result is that whereas the *per capita* spending in the US is as high as \$21,233, in super-poor Ethiopia, the country with the lowest spending, it is only \$83 per year per person (*National Geographic*, November 2001).

There is additional evidence of Africa's poverty, which contrasts widely with its natural endowment, including *per capita* income as low as \$2,100 for all of Africa and a mere \$1,670 for sub-Saharan Africa (World Bank 2002). Other developing nations had much higher *per capita* incomes: \$3,860 for all developing nations; Latin-America and the Caribbean combined, \$6,820 and Asia, \$4,680 (World Bank 2002, PRB 2004). It is not thus surprising that Africa has been described as the continent with the proverbial one or two dollars per day *per capita* income or expenditure (UNDP 2002). Such low incomes are bound to doom any society to abject poverty.

The material poverty of Africa, which stems largely from low-value exports and hence meager financial resources and the benign or total neglect of human capital and other physical and social infrastructure, should be at the heart of discussions and explanations of why Africa has produced so many poor nations. Forty-four of the world's poorest nations and 33 of the least developed 48 nations are in Africa. Besides, 30 of 34 countries with the least human development are located in Africa (United Nations Development Program 2000).

As we have stated, Africa's level of poverty contrasts dramatically with the material abundance of the developed nations of the west and the new Asian Tigers, which have emerged in the last three decades, led by Japan.[1] The colonization of the continent engendered the initial marginalization which made Africa more vulnerable to modern-day globalization's disparate impact.

The Prospects for Africa: Is there Still Hope for Africans?

Questions that may flow directly or indirectly from the chapters in this book may be summed up as: can there be hope for Africans who today face Herculean odds in terms of challenges? A related question that arises is: what happened to past African-initiated and international (both bi- and multi-lateral) plans to develop Africa some three to four decades ago? In light of efforts by the newly-founded African Union (AU) we might add: What are the prognosis for the AU's plans, activities and programs aimed at turning the 21st century into a century for African peace, development and democracy? Lastly, under what circumstances can Africa be reborn for the benefit of the majority of its over 700 million citizens? We attempt to address these and other closely linked matters in our conclusion of this book.

While some of our colleagues have presented data and other information that could lead to concluding that the future for Africa is severely grim, we observe that Africans would improve their well being by overcoming some past tendencies and by avoiding erroneous policy practices based on inherently faulty policy assumptions. Some of our policy prescriptions could enhance the capacity of the AU and African leaders to achieve the laudable aims of the new AU: "peace, security and prosperity in Africa."

As some of the authors in our book have demonstrated, some of the measures taken by the AU in the last two-and-a-half years, although they may not be deemed to be extraordinary, are steadily confirming that at least some African leaders are not conducting intra-African relations in "a business as usual" manner. There seems to be a clarion call for a new thinking at the political leadership and continental levels (Panford, chapter 5 in this volume). Two examples will be provided. Because of the position taken by the Economic Community of West African States (ECOWAS) and the AU, the son of President Eyadema of Togo was pressed into stepping down as the successor to his father as president.[2] This was unprecedented in Africa where in the past, life-long civilian presidents and military personnel ruled with impunity. Second, against all odds, the AU is standing firm and insisting that because "an African solution should be found," the international community should funnel all assistance for resolving the

Darfur war situation through the AU and its peacekeeping endeavors. The AU is also urging its "international partners," that is, the US, the EU., UN., Britain, Germany, France, Japan, and Canada not to undercut Africans' own peace initiatives. We, however, need to emphasize that the AU and other African regional groups have not as yet resolved all or even most of Africa's raging conflicts. But close observation should point to these efforts leading to a long and arduous road to establishing peace and ameliorating the deplorable living and working conditions on the continent.

Our mild and what we term guarded optimism about the future of Africa is premised on other factors. Africans have proven their resilience in previously perilous conditions. They outlived over 300 years of the European slave trade plus another 150 years of political brutality and economic exploitation of the worst kind through colonialism (Rodney 1982). The end of colonial rule did not stop the dehumanization of Africans. First, colonial rule did not cease until 1994 when South Africa had multi-party/racial elections. In Angola and Mozambique, independence was not a guarantee of peace as these nations were plunged into war after 1975 (Keller and Rothchild 1996). Even where independence led to the assumption of the nominal reigns of power, neo-colonialism combined with cold war exigencies to continue the rape of Africa's natural and human resources by the west with the assistance of African collaborators (Nzongola Ntalaja 2002).

Despite the attention-grabbing headlines (especially in the western media) from conflict and war zones (Darfur, Western Sudan, Côte d'Ivoire, DRC, and Somalia) a closer scrutiny of trends in Africa may indicate that the continent is experiencing more stability than was the case in the last two decades. This is especially the case if we compare the cold war era to the post-cold war period. We might take for granted the miracle wrought in South Africa through a smooth and harmonious transition from racist and economically exploitative apartheid to multi-racial and multi-party political system. First Mozambique and then Angola ended decades of some of the deadliest civil wars. The former is having one of the fastest economic growth rates in Africa and the rest of the developing world due to peace established after over 25 years of unending warfare.

In the political arena, even if we cannot take the position that genuine multi-party systems and other highly desirable features of long-lasting democracies have been firmly implanted, recent developments might point to the right initial steps being taken by several African nations. The initial resolution of the presidential succession crisis in Togo in 2005 that led to Eyadema's son stepping down as president is one additional basis of our tempered optimism about the political future of Africa. Another is the case of Madagascar. Due to controversies surrounding elections in Madagascar in 2001, the AU suspended this country from participation in its activities for two years. The AU's decision was based on the principle that the government failed to allow the nation's electoral laws to operate fully. As it were, by suspending Madagascar and pressing Eyadema's son to step down, the AU was sending a message that Africa had entered a new era of constitutional rule. The AU and Africa seem to be at the brink of using meaningful clout to discourage or even stop disruptive and undemocratic changes in government. If such trends continue, we might see the end of military coups and life-long presidencies that were the norm in the past.

Corruption: The Boogeyman/woman of Failed Development Policies in Africa?

First, we wish to preface our treatment of corruption in Africa by stating that it is not unique to and inherent in Africa. That is, there is nothing unique about corruption, which has often been treated as the prime cause of all of Africa's problems. Second, as much as we wish to stress that corruption in all its forms is wasteful, inappropriate and also morally reprehensible, as Nzongola-Ntalaja (2002) aptly demonstrated, the most corrupt African leaders were the ones ardently supported and propped up financially and militarily by the west. Examples include Mobuto Sese Seko of Zaire and Sgt. K. Doe of Liberia. In spite of the corrupt financial practices of Sgt. Doe and the reprehensible nature of the political repression he unleashed on Liberians, US military aid to Doe's government was half a billion dollars. Mobutu could not have reigned for 32 years without active intervention by the US, Belgium and France with the tacit support of the UK. These nations literally propped up Mobuto under the guise of he being the "glue" that held that vast African country together (Schatzberg 1991).

In reality, the US and their allies were solely motivated in their unflinching support for Mobutu by their Cold War military/strategic and financial interests that lasted from the time of the brutal murder of Prime Minister Patrice Lumumba to the fall of Mobutu in the Spring of 1997. The parochial western interests were protected and sustained at a heavy and ruinous cost for not only the Congolese but also the entire Great Lakes area of Africa. We will cite a few such devastating consequences.

The assassination of Patrice Lumumba had a chilling effect on the emergence of genuine African and Pan-African leaders. As it were, the message sent by especially the US and Belgium to newly independent African nations was that leaders who fought for the interests of Africans would face the wrath of the west, including death. Second, with the chaos that followed the killing of Lumumba, the Congo was never able to recover. That continued to the unabated chaos which since 1998 had turned into an all-out civil, and Africa's first international, war. Another means by which the west propped up Mobutu was that both multi-lateral international financial institutions such as the World Bank and bi-lateral organizations such as US Agency for International Development (USAID) pumped massive doses of finances into Zaire under Mobutu completely neglecting the regime's blatant corruption. Due to the west's selfish interests, the fact that Mobutu headed a kleptocracy (that is a government of thieves) was conveniently ignored. One result: while Mobutu oversaw the collapse of the country and the looting of its resources, his personal fortunes climbed to $6 billion while the national debt rose to $13 billion toward the end of his rule (*Economist Intelligence Unit*, "Zaire" Country Profile 1996). With the support of the west, for 32 years, Mobutu failed to utilize the wealth of the nation for physical and human capital development.

The DRC is a classic example of a country that has failed to appropriate its resources to benefit its citizens. One glaring legacy is the eight-year war that has caused massive deaths, famine, the spread of diseases and the displacement of millions of people. Even the deployment of the largest contingent of UN peacekeeping forces has not been able to contain the profound havoc, a key consequence of the inept and corrupt Mobutu government, which was favored by the west, especially France, Belgium and the US.

We might therefore be correct to assert that internationally supported political and economic corruption was, until less than ten years ago, one of the banes of post-independence Africa. It was responsible and still accounts for much of the underdevelopment, wide socio-economic disparities and, since 1989–1990, the chaos and, in cases such as Liberia and Sierra Leone, the civil wars that have gripped these countries. This is one humongous challenge that Africans have to overcome to ensure long-term safety and security and prosperity in the 21st century.

Building up Africa's Human Capital/Human Resources: The Key to 21st Century Success

Classic economic theorists posited the view that there are only two basic sources of production. These are nature and human beings. This maxim is highly relevant to 21st century Africa. Africa today is materially poor for two main reasons. One, Africa produces and exports low value raw materials/commodities and then imports expensive items including even food (see the "Commodities" Section in Africa South of the Sahara, 2003, 2004). Two, Africa is least developed because of its poor quality and quantity of human capital and other physical and social infrastructure. The latter constitutes the foundation on which development is based. Hence these two bottlenecks have combined to make Africans poor by not allowing them to utilize for their benefit their tremendous natural assets.

In light of the fundamental roles of human capital, we may be correct in stressing that an important avenue to overcoming poverty in Africa is building up the available human resources, especially with regard to skill levels and scientific knowledge. Adopting policies and practices that place high premium on basic human needs such as health, education, sanitation and improved nutrition could initiate this. These have been the major engines of growth in especially China and India that are fast becoming global economic rivals to the US and Japan (Friedman 2005).

Africa needs to reverse quickly the deeply flawed structural adjustment programs that the World Bank, International Monetary Fund (IMF) and international donor community have thrust upon Africa in the last two and a half decades. Instead, more emphasis should be shifted toward human capital formation through educational and training programs geared to the real needs of Africa. Similarly, with the disastrous effects of IMF/World Bank policies in the health sector, African nations have to adopt health and nutritional policies and standards that will guarantee the well-being of most Africans and not only a minority that is affluent. Advocates of policies implemented under the tutelage of Bretton Woods' institutions seem to conveniently neglect the fact that all nations' economic success hinges largely on massive investments in education, training, health, agriculture/food and communications. These are necessary for successful exploitation of natural resources and the capacity to accumulate domestic savings and/or foreign direct finances.

Africa on the other hand, under structural adjustment policies, has been misled into adopting policies that grossly and erroneously assume that offering only cheap, unskilled or uneducated labor will be the solution to its lack of capital for development or industrialization (Panford 2001). Because of these false assumptions, Africans have been lulled into abandoning policies which, from the late 1950s through the 1970s, aided them to acquire meager amounts of social and physical infrastructure. Africa needs to fast track the development of socially and technologically relevant educational systems to avert being the continent that is most adversely impacted by globalization. 20 years experiencing structural adjustment has taught Ghana a hard lesson about globalization: having massive numbers of hungry, unskilled or uneducated and unhealthy workers cannot guarantee economic growth in the 21st century (Panford 2001).

There is in Africa an acute need for a healthcare system that works and is not priced beyond the means of most citizens. Good healthcare is the solution to some of the shortest life spans, higher infant and child mortality and adult morbidity rates in the world today. Poor health in Africa seriously undercuts labor productivity in all sectors, especially in the agriculture/food and rural sectors. Poor health and poor nutrition exacerbate the debilitating effects of old diseases such as TB and malaria and new ones like AIDS, with profoundly adverse consequences all over Africa (McNulty 1995: 37–38).

Closely aligned with the spread of diseases and poor nutrition is one paradox Africa needs to eliminate soon. Africans have access to more than adequate supplies of fertile land and yet some Africans are hungry or not fed properly in terms of nutrients and calorific intake. This is due to two main factors: Africans devote too much energy and commit excessive sources to produce so-called cash crops — raw cane sugar, cotton, coffee, tea and cocoa beans — for export, meanwhile billions of hard-earned foreign exchange is spent on food imports, like rice and other processed grains/food. Hence while the Government of Ghana spent at least $100 million on rice imports in 1996, a whole quarter of the food produced by local farmers was lost to wastage due to poor processing, storage and marketing and transport facilities (Panford 2001). Ghana is not alone in paying lip service to "the strategic role of food production" in Africa's development. During and since colonial rule, food production for local consumption has been largely neglected.

The Strategic Importance of the Internet and Communications Technology

Africa lags the rest of the world in additional substantive ways. One of these is Internet and Communications Technology (ICT) which is so crucial in this era of globalization. Due to the low quality and amount of communications infrastructure developed in the colonial era and the failure to accelerate a build-up, Africa ranks low in all types of communications. It has the least Internet connectivity, the availability of telephones and telephone lines, faxes and other means of modern communications ("The Global Technology Gap," *African Link*, Vol. 9, Nos 3 and 4: 13; J.D. Bierdorfer, "High Tech Center to Open in Sub-Saharan Ghana, *New York Times*, August 23, 2001). Even countries like South Africa, Ghana, and Kenya, which are modestly endowed, face severe challenges compared to the rest of the world. This could be a major reason for the low rates of intra-African trade and the extreme difficulties African businesses have to contend with in acquiring overseas capital. Africa's success in harnessing its own internal savings for business purposes and capacity to attract foreign investments may hinge on how fast it grows technologically and overcomes its information inadequacies.

In marshalling capital for businesses, Africans need to focus first on growth in local incomes, which will lead to substantial domestic savings. The latter will contribute to the availability of local investments in business and ensure greater financial self-sufficiency, which is currently lacking. In addition to savings from increased local incomes (paid to workers and farmers), the savings from the stoppage of expensive food imports, military expenditures and the huge costs of expatriate personnel (of over $4 billion dollars at the end of the 1990s) could be used to bolster appreciably the investments needed in human resources, irrigation and improvements in food production, ICT, and other physical infrastructure and directly productive activities such as manufacturing to add value to Africa's current cheap exports. Cutting down expenses on expatriates, for example, will help to eliminate an anomaly in contemporary Africa: while billions of dollars go to foreign personnel, thousands of African college/university graduates cannot find employment. This constitutes a huge waste of societal resources expended through free or subsidized education.

Lastly, to turn the "brain-drain into a brain gain" (Orjiako 2005), Africans need to create opportunities for qualified Africans to return to be productive and contribute to the revitalization of the continent. The AU has taken a crucial first step by declaring the Diaspora as the sixth African Region. A remaining challenge is converting more of the financial remittances of the Diaspora into economically productive ventures that will generate jobs and better incomes for the benefit of more Africans. Currently, substantial remittances go to funerals and other activities which do not directly affect the material conditions of poverty on a sustainable basis. This calls for better organized relationships between African governments and businesses and their nationals abroad and the creation of channels which will be effective in mobilizing such potentially important sources of capital.

We may conclude by observing that, with a full realization that Africa's problems are of human origins and historical causes, these impediments could be overcome if certain conditions are met. Africa requires careful and creative planning and policies that are sensitive to African needs and unusual circumstances. For such policies to work, they must genuinely unite Africans and harmonize their policies *vis-à-vis* especially the IMF-World Bank and WTO trio and other international bodies not excepting the UN. These policies should be geared at reinforcing Africa's position in all international negotiations including trade agreements.

Last, but not least, such policies should be firmly and practically grounded in finding solutions to the lack of peace, safety and security and then real social progress. Real social progress refers to Africans experiencing better working and living conditions and being able to fulfill the promise and excitement unleashed by the liberation struggles throughout Africa. Recent developments in Togo and Darfur (Western Sudan) and the conclusion of a peace deal between the Government of Sudan and the rebels of Southern Sudan could be indicative of new positive phenomena that may occur if Africans persist in defining on their own terms what their real and long-term interests are. Against all odds and in the face of gloom and doom from nay sayers, peace may be found at last in the Sudan. This, like other problems confronting Africa, requires more perseverance to overcome.

Notes

1 For a history of the origins and continued poverty in Africa, see Rodney (1982) and Thabo Mbeki, "Africa, the Truth and the Asian Miracle," *New African*, March 2005: 30–34.

2 For details on the Togo Presidential succession situation and steps taken by the AU and ECOWAS, see AU, "Communiqué," Peace and Security Council, 25th Meeting, Addis Ababa, Ehtiopia, Frebruary 25, 2005; Graphic (Accra, Ghana) "ECOWAS to meet over Togolese Crisis," February 8, 2005, BBC, "West Africans Lift Togo Sanctions," February 26, 2005, and Desmond Orjiako, "The African Union—Our Common Home" address at Northeastern University, Boston, MA, March 24, 2005.

References

BP. (2001). *BP Statistical Review of World Energy*. June. London: BP.

Chinweizu. (1975). *The West and the Rest of Us*. New York: Random House.

Edoho, F.M. (2001). "Management Challenges for Africa in the 21st Century." In Edoho, F.M., ed., *Management Challenges for Africa in the 21st Century: Theoretical and Applies Perspectives*. Westport CT: Praeger.

Europa Publications (1999). *Africa South of the Sahara 2000*. London: Europa Publications.

Europa Publications (2004). *Africa South of the Sahara 2003*. London: Europa Publications.

Friedman, Thomas (2005) *The World is Flat*. Giroux NY: Farrar Straus.

Heidenheimer, A.J., Victory, M and Levine, V.T (1989). *Political Corruption: A Handbook* New Brunswick NJ: Transactions Books.

Hope, R.K. (2000). "Corruption and Development in Africa." In R.K. Hope and B.C. Chikulo, eds. *Corruption and Development in Africa*. Houndmills, Hampshire UK: Palgrave.

Keller, E. and Rothchild, D. (1996). *African in the New World Order*. Boulder CO: Reinner.

Mbaku, John M., ed. (1998). *Corruption and the Crisis of Institutional Reforms in Africa*. Lewiston NY: Mellen Press.

McNulty, Michael L. (1995). "The Contemporary Map of Africa." In *Africa* (Third Edition), 10–48. Bloomington IN: Indiana University Press.

Njoku, T.N. (1998). *Corruption in Africa: Finance and Development*. 35 (2): 8–12.

Nye, Joseph S. (1989). "Corruption and Development: A Cost Benefit Analysis." In Heidenheimer, A.J., M. Johnston, J., Victory M and Levine, V.T. (eds.) *Political Corruption: A Handbook*. New Brunswick NJ: Transactions Books. 963–984.

Nyoni, J., Katerere, Y. and Moyo, S. (1997). "Zimbabwe: The Inner Situation." Lead International Leadership for Environment and Development. April 21 – May 3.

Nzongola Ntalaja, Georges (2002). *The Congo from Leopold to Kabilla*. London: Zed Books.

Obadina, T. (2004). "Vicious trap for poor nations." *Africa Today*. February.

Panford, K. (2001) *IMF-World Bank and Labor's Burdens in Africa*. Westport CT and London: Praeger.

PRB (2004). *World Population Data Sheet*. Washington DC: PRB.

Rodney, W. (1982). *How Europe Underdeveloped Africa*. Washington DC: Howard University.

Schatzberg, Michael G. (1991). *Mobutu or Chaos?: The United States and Zaire*, 1960–1990. Lanham MD: University Press of America.

Szeftel, Morris (2000). "Between Governance and Underdevelopment: Accumulation and Africa's Catastrophic Corruption." *Review of African Politcal Economy*. 27 (84): 287–306.

Theobald, R. (1990). *Corruption, Development and Underdevelopment.* London: Macmillan.

Theobald, R. (1997). "Can Debt Be Used to Combat Political Corruption in Africa? *Crime, Law and Social Change*. 27 (3/4): 299–314.

UNDP (2000). *World Energy Assessment: Energy and the Challenge of Sustainability*. Geneva: UNDP.

UNDP. (2002). *Human Development Report*. New York: Oxford University Press.

World Bank. (2002). *World Development Report*. New York: Oxford University Press.

Index

G

H

I

N

T

U